GLOBAL HOUSING MARKETS

The *Robert W. Kolb Series in Finance* provides a comprehensive view of the field of finance in all of its variety and complexity. The series is projected to include approximately 65 volumes covering all major topics and specializations in finance, ranging from investments, to corporate finance, to financial institutions. Each volume in the *Kolb Series in Finance* consists of new articles especially written for the volume.

Each volume is edited by a specialist in a particular area of finance, who develops the volume outline and commissions articles by the world's experts in that particular field of finance. Each volume includes an editor's introduction and approximately thirty articles to fully describe the current state of financial research and practice in a particular area of finance.

The essays in each volume are intended for practicing finance professionals, graduate students, and advanced undergraduate students. The goal of each volume is to encapsulate the current state of knowledge in a particular area of finance so that the reader can quickly achieve a mastery of that special area of finance.

Please visit www.wiley.com/go/kolbseries to learn about recent and forthcoming titles in the Kolb Series.

GLOBAL HOUSING MARKETS

Crises, Policies, and Institutions

Ashok Bardhan
Robert H. Edelstein
Cynthia A. Kroll

The Robert W. Kolb Series in Finance

WILEY

John Wiley & Sons, Inc.

Published by John Wiley & Sons, Inc., Hoboken, New Jersey.
Published simultaneously in Canada.

For general information on our other products and services or for technical support, please contact our Customer Care Department within the United States at (800) 762-2974, outside the United States at (317) 572-3993 or fax (317) 572-4002.

Wiley also publishes its books in a variety of electronic formats. Some content that appears in print may not be available in electronic books. For more information about Wiley products, visit our web site at www.wiley.com.

Library of Congress Cataloging-in-Publication Data:

Global housing markets: crises, policies, and institutions / Ashok Bardhan, Robert Edelstein, Cynthia Kroll, editors.
    p. cm. – (Robert W. Kolb series)
    Includes index.
    ISBN 978-0-470-64714-1 (hardback); ISBN 978-1-118-14421-3
(ebk); ISBN 978-1-118-14422-0 (ebk); ISBN 978-1-118-14423-7 (ebk)
    1. Housing policy–Case studies.   2. Global Financial Crisis, 2008–2009.
3. Globalization.   I. Bardhan, Ashok Deo, 1957-   II. Edelstein, Robert H.   III. Kroll, Cynthia A.
    HD7287.3.G57 2011
333.33′8–dc23

2011021443

Printed in the United States of America.

10 9 8 7 6 5 4 3 2 1

Contents

Acknowledgments

We would like to thank the Fisher Center for Real Estate and Urban Economics, the Center's Policy Advisory Board, and the Center chair and co-chairs, Ken Rosen, Robert Helsley, Dwight Jaffee, Atif Mian, and Nancy Wallace, for the resources that made the preparation of this book possible. Several graduate and undergraduate students over the past few years contributed efforts to the underlying research and to manuscript preparation, including Jackie Begley, Tyler Fach, Sean Wilkoff, Sandra Winkler and Tiffany Yu. The Homer Hoyt Institute provided funding for the chapter on the United States. In addition to those already mentioned, we received helpful comments and advice from many different individuals, some of whom include Shaun Bond, John Duca, Samir Dutt, Robert Kolb, Lu Ming, Maury Seldin, Felix Schindler, Branko Urosevic, Richard Walker, and Peter Westerheide. The staff of Wiley's editorial department, ably led by Emilie Herman, has been both helpful and patient in shepherding the manuscript through the final preparations for publication.

Editor's Note

The financial crisis of 2008–2009 originated within the U.S. housing markets and the U.S. financial system. This volume presents articles containing detailed analysis of national housing markets around the globe, and was conceived for the purpose of examining if and how the contagion spread to housing markets throughout the world; what were the transmission paths and mechanisms by which it spread; and what was the institutional and regulatory context in which policy measures were adopted in response to the spreading financial crisis. The timeline in most of the papers starts with the period prior to the crisis, proceeds through the unfolding months of the crisis, and concludes with the post crisis recovery period up to the present time (summer 2011). The widely divergent experiences of both the housing and mortgage markets across various countries provide evidence of the complex interplay between and among economic conditions, the institutional settings, international linkages, regulatory frameworks, and policy responses in directing and responding to the flow of the crisis. Indeed, the interaction of the global linkages of the crisis, the economic fundamentals underlying the housing market at the local and national level, and the remedial policy measures being played out on the national stage constitute the recurring theme of this book.

CHAPTER 1

The Financial Crisis and Housing Markets Worldwide

Similarities, Differences, and Comparisons

ASHOK BARDHAN
Fisher Center for Real Estate and Urban Economics,
University of California–Berkeley

ROBERT H. EDELSTEIN
Haas School of Business, University of California–Berkeley

CYNTHIA A KROLL
Fisher Center for Real Estate and Urban Economics,
University of California–Berkeley

INTRODUCTION

The subprime crisis that began in the United States in 2007 sent the world into a financial crisis of unprecedented proportions. In the United States, this was manifested in a boom-bust cycle in residential real estate markets, the near shutdown of the country's financial sector in 2008, and a prolonged Great Recession of a magnitude not seen in the country in any cycle since the 1930s. The contagion in financial markets became clear very quickly, affecting countries around the world, including Singapore, New Zealand, Iceland, the United Kingdom, Germany, France, and Ireland, to name a few, as well as a some fast-growing emerging economies to a lesser extent. Both residential and commercial real estate markets as well as stock, bond and asset markets appeared vulnerable worldwide.

As the dust settles, it has become clear that some countries were more vulnerable than others. In particular, impacts on residential real estate ranged from unnoticeable in countries as far apart as Australia, Germany, and Israel to sharp downturns in Ireland, Spain, and the United Kingdom; the latter group at a level that at a cursory glance appears to closely mirror the U.S. experience. This book was conceived for the purpose of examining if and how the contagion spread to housing markets throughout the world, what were the paths and transmission mechanisms by which it spread (through financial markets, directly through global real estate markets), and what was the institutional and regulatory context in which policy measures were adopted in response to the spreading financial crisis. The timeline in most of the papers in this volume covers the period starting with the run-up prior to the crisis, the unfolding months of the crisis itself, and the post-crisis recovery period up to the present time (summer 2011). The widely varying experiences of both the housing and mortgage markets in the countries described here provide evidence of the complex interplay of the roles of economic conditions, the institutional setting, regulatory framework and policy responses in directing and responding to the flow of the catastrophe.

The financial crisis was global; housing markets are local; and the primary geographic unit of analysis in the chapters in this book is national, albeit with numerous examples of subregional and urban housing markets in those countries. The institutional structure of housing markets and the policy domain in most countries is national, as was the political and economic response to the crisis. It is the interaction of the global linkages of the crisis, the economic fundamentals at the local and national level, and the policy issues being played out on the national stage that is the recurring theme of this book.

The book is organized in five sections, and each primarily groups together nations along geographic lines, although there are also other shared characteristics among the national market settings in each section. Part I is devoted to the housing market experience of the United States, as the epicenter of the global financial crisis (hereafter referred to as GFC). Part II includes chapters on six different European countries that experienced widely varying effects from the financial crisis, ranging from Germany, which continued its long-term but gradual downward trend in home sales and prices; to Denmark and the Netherlands, which, although affected, were able to contain the impact and did not need banking bailouts; to Ireland, Spain, and the United Kingdom, each of which experienced different combinations of financial and housing market woes.

Part III includes three chapters on Eastern European transition economies. Two of the chapters examine various aspects of the housing market and mortgage finance system in Russia, while the third describes the transformation of the Serbian housing market since the political situation stabilized at the beginning of the twenty-first century.

Part IV is divided into two sections. The first consists of papers on the largest Asian economies. Two chapters look at two critical urban housing markets—Beijing and Shanghai—and the financial system in the People's Republic of China. Two other chapters analyze the housing market and financial system in India, one focusing on the transformation of the mortgage finance system and its implications for housing India's population with all of its diverse needs, and the other focusing in more detail on the evolution of its housing market and its experience during the GFC. This subsection of Part IV is rounded out by a paper describing the Japanese experience over a series of real estate cycles and economic challenges that began long before the GFC and continue through to the present day.

The remainder of Part IV includes chapters on other, smaller Asian markets. In terms of institutional setting, Hong Kong, Taiwan, Singapore, and Korea are even more diverse than the European markets described in Part II. However, these countries all came into the GFC after enduring the common and painful experience of the Asian Financial Crisis (hereafter referred to as AFC) more than a decade earlier. Each chapter describes not only the GFC from the country's perspective but also the manifestations of the current crisis in comparison to the AFC.

Part V is the only section of the book that is not based on a common geographic region. Instead, this section covers four countries from around the globe—Australia, Brazil, Canada, and Israel—whose housing markets showed various levels of immunity to the consequences and contagion effects of the GFC.

In this chapter, we take the liberty of briefly summarizing some of the key points of each paper by the contributors in this volume and draw on their research, as well as on some other key studies that have provided a comparative context for examining housing markets and housing finance across countries, in order to describe the commonalities and differences in the behavior of these markets in the context of the GFC. We conclude the chapter with our observations on some common knowledge gleaned and lessons learned regarding the factors that made housing markets and financial systems in different countries more or less vulnerable to the consequences of the GFC, with particular attention to economic structure and institutions, role of the public sector, global financial and economic linkages, housing market specifics, and regulatory stance as key elements.

A COMPARATIVE LOOK AT HOUSING AND FINANCIAL SYSTEMS

Earlier research has compared housing finance systems across different parts of the globe and housing price trends before and during the GFC. Green and Wachter (2005), Ben-Shahar, Leung, and Ong (2009), Kim and Renaud (2009), Duca, Muellbauer, and Murphy (2010), and Lea (2010 and 2011) deal with a selective, comparative analysis of mortgage and housing markets worldwide. To our knowledge, our book stands out in two respects: (1) It is set against the backdrop of the financial crisis, which helps to bring out the differences and commonalities of markets and institutions across the world in a vivid fashion; and (2) it is very broadly representative, with examples from every major continent and most significant markets, particularly those with important distinguishing characteristics and structural attributes in their housing systems.

The countries examined in this volume vary along several important dimensions, including size of the economy, role of government in economic and housing affairs, structure of financial institutions, the role of the private sector in housing production and finance, and the history of the housing market. Several of these dimensions are summarized in Exhibit 1.1. The group of countries includes two city states with a housing base on the order of a million units, small countries with approximately 2 to 8 million housing units, mid-sized countries with housing stock in the range of 12 to 30 million units, and larger countries, with stock ranging from close to 60 million to over 200 million. Owner occupancy ranges from only 42 percent in Germany to close to 100 percent in Serbia, with many countries averaging between 60 and 70 percent.

The institutional setting also varies widely, with some governments heavily involved in either the ownership, control, and distribution of land (as in China), the construction of housing (Singapore), or the privatization of previously public

Exhibit 1.1 Comparative Data on Housing Market and Housing Finance Systems

	Housing Stock 2009 (millions of units)	Percent Home-owners	Loan to Value Ratio	Variable or Fixed Rate (majority)	Government Role in Housing	Mortgage Deducti-bility	Fee-Free Prepay-ment?	Government Guarantee or Mortgage Insurance	Mortgage Securitization	Recourse or Nonrecourse
Australia	8.3	70%	70%	Variable	Low	No	Partial; full after mid 2011	For lenders	Moderate	Recourse
Brazil	58.6	81%	62%	Variable	Low	No*		Mortgage subsidies	Moderate, gov't presence	Recourse
Canada	12.4	65.9%	90%	Short-term fixed	Low	No		CMHC	Moderate, gov't presence	Recourse
China	[11.2B m²]	~80% in urban areas	60%	Variable	Moderate/ High	No	Yes	Insurance required for HPF loans	None	Loans linked to compulsorary savings
Denmark	2.7	54%	65%	Variable	Low	Yes	Yes	No	Covered Bonds	Recourse
Germany	39.4	43.2%	74%	Variable with fixed limits	Moderate (for rental)	No	No	Covered bonds	Bonds	Recourse
Hong Kong	2.5	52.5%	70%	Variable	Moderate/ High	Yes (10 years)	Yes after 3 years	Mortgage Insurance may increase LTV	Yes	Recourse
India	211.9	74.5%	65%		Moderate	Yes	No	On the table	Partial	Recourse
Ireland	2.0	90%+		Variable		Yes (5 years)				
Israel	2.2	65.8%	NA	Both	Moderate	No*	Partial	Small share with private mortgage insurance	None	Recourse

Japan	58.0	61.1%	80%	Variable 44%, Hybrid 31%, Fixed 25%	Low/Moderate	No	For some lenders; most no	JHF (GHLC until 4/2007) 35% of loans	REITS, JHF (GHLC until 4/2007)	Recourse
Korea	13.8	60.3%	50–70%	Variable	High	No	No	Yes	Yes	Recourse
Netherlands	7.1	57.2%	80%	Fixed	Moderate	Yes	Limited	Government loan guarantees	Small OTC	Recourse
Russia	59.0	64% to 82%	60–70%	Mostly fixed	High historic	Yes	Limited	Being established	New since 2000	Recourse
Serbia	2.7	98%	95%	Variable	High historic	No	No	Yes	Under-developed	Mostly recourse
Singapore	1.1	80%+	80% private, 90% public	Variable	High	No	Yes, after teaser period	Insurance mandatory for public housing purchase	None	Both; non-R requires co-borrower
Spain	25.6	85%	70-80%	Variable	Moderate	Only for low income as of 2011	No	No	64% Covered Bonds, 36% ARM	Recourse
Taiwan	7.8	87%	70%	Variable	Low	Yes for 1st home.	No	Not yet	<5%	Recourse
United Kingdom	27.1	67.4%	74%	Short-term fixed, then turn variable	Moderate	No*	Yes if rate not discounted	Insurance available for mortgagor	Grew 2000–2007. now negligible	Recourse
United States	130.2	67.2%	80–90%	Both, currently mainly fixed	Low, local limits	Yes*	Varies by state	Multiple agencies involved	Highly Developed	Non-Recourse

*Capital gains tax limited.

Sources: Country statistical data centers; European Mortgage Federation; Housing Finance Information Network; Van den Noord 2005.

housing stock (Serbia and Russia), while others rely primarily on market mechanisms and the private sector to take the lead in housing construction and sales. In some countries the government role involves encouraging homeownership through everything from subsidized transfer of government property to individual households, to tax relief from interest payments, down-payment support, or capital gains relief. Other countries focus instead on "social housing," with an emphasis on using government subsidies for the rental sector. Similarly, in some countries the mortgage financing system for housing is largely government-operated or heavily regulated, whereas others provide extensive leeway to the private sector, and even opportunities for foreign lenders. The capital market for securitized mortgages is another dimension along which there is a great deal of variation. These institutional differences set the stage for the degree of vulnerability of individual housing and mortgage markets, the degree and direction of a country's policy response, and the extent of intervention in financial and real estate markets once the GFC began.

THE FINANCIAL CRISIS AND GLOBAL HOUSING MARKETS

It is not surprising, given the local and national attributes of housing markets, that the GFC had different degrees of impact around the world. Exhibits 1.2 and 1.3 provide a rough comparison of housing market reaction globally, by focusing on price gains during the run-up to the peak in a country's housing market, price declines in the period just following the GFC, and any subsequent price gains,

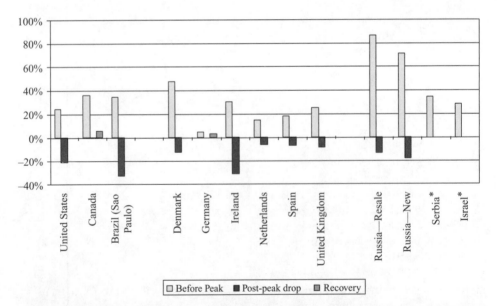

Exhibit 1.2 Annual Average Housing Price Changes, American and European Countries (three years up to peak, losses following peak, and recovery, if any).

*Housing market has not seen a price drop; three years to peak is the most recent three-year period.

Sources: European Mortgage Federation; World Economic Outlook; Australian Bureau of Statistics; chapter authors.

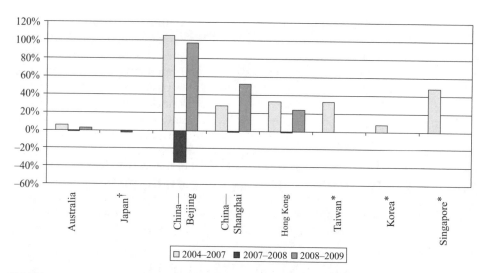

Exhibit 1.3   Annual Average Housing Price Changes, Asia-Pacific Countries (three years up to peak, losses following peak, and recovery, if any).
*Housing market has not seen a price drop; three years to peak is the most recent three-year period.
†Housing market saw price declines even during the boom. Drop is for the 2007–2009 period.
Sources: European Mortgage Federation; World Economic Outlook; Australian Bureau of Statistics; chapter authors.

through 2009. The comparison is tentative because housing market statistics are not directly comparable across countries, with measures varying from indices drawn from repeat home sales, to time series of average or median prices. What is most relevant here is the direction of change, rather than small differences among trends. The United States did not have the highest rate of growth in housing prices in the period leading up to the crisis, nor the highest rate of decline in prices in 2008 and 2009, but the pattern of price build-up and decline is apparent. Most European markets also had price increases in the mid-2000s, followed by a price decline, but only in Ireland did the magnitude of the decline come close to that of the United States. Canada had a much milder drop, and was already seeing price recovery in 2009. Sao Paulo, in Brazil, had large gains and losses, although these were explained as much by a change in mix of homes sold as by the GFC, as described later. Two other markets on the periphery of the European sphere, Serbia and Israel, have not as yet shown any price downturn.

The Asian and Pacific markets had a very different profile from that of the United States and most of Europe. With the exception of Japan, which did not participate in the upswing at all, all Asia/Pacific markets that had a downturn during the GFC have had recovery upturns by now. In general, the urban or city state markets (Beijing, Shanghai, Hong Kong, and Singapore) showed much larger percentage upswings. Beijing and Shanghai had relatively large downturns as well, but these were smaller than the previous price gains and were quickly counterbalanced by price recovery in 2009. The greater volatility of these concentrated urban markets is consistent with the experience in the United States, where the largest gains and losses were concentrated in a few metropolitan areas, and much of the rest of the country experienced much milder price changes. Australia had much smaller gains and dips, and as with many parts of Asia was also experiencing housing market recovery by 2009. The booming cities of India, such as Mumbai, Delhi, Bangalore, and others, saw significant price rises in the 1990s, continuing through in the twenty-first century, as well, as a result of economic growth, pent-up demand, and supply-side restraints, and, for most, the GFC proved to be a minor hiccup.

ONE WORLD, ONE CRISIS? DIFFERENCES AND SIMILARITIES BY REGION AND COUNTRY

Each of these chapters highlights the institutional and economic setting of the country and the interaction of these factors with the housing market and the global financial conditions.

United States

Bardhan, Edelstein, and Kroll highlight the factors that led the country into a situation where the financial sector and housing sector interacted to produce two bubbles that fed on each other. They describe the genesis and evolution of the crisis, including the role of federal policy in keeping rates low, the investor response leading to exotic and risky financial instruments, predatory lending, rampant speculation, the rise of household debt, leverage and other factors. They also present a cross-state analysis revealing the role of regulatory laxness in the growth of subprime mortgages and foreclosures. They point out that U.S. policy was reactive rather than proactive, and took many months to address the housing side of the problem. The crisis has led to a reworking of the mortgage finance system, with some stricter controls, but other troubling features, such as the "too big to fail" financial institutions, remain. The authors evaluate and analyze the policy initiatives proposed, and suggest some essential elements of a fair, effective, and viable plan to fix the residential finance system and the housing market.

Western Europe

Denmark
Despite having a funding model that fully matches the cash flow for loans and the bonds used to finance the loans, the Danish housing market was a full-fledged participant in the frenzy of the price-rise preceding 2007–2008. Gyntelberg, Kjeldsen, Nielsen, and Persson point out that house prices dropped 20 percent during the crisis, and Danish policy makers were forced to introduce measures to stabilize the financial sector. Despite the turmoil, the mortgage system, including the mortgage bond market, continued to function throughout the crisis period. Furthermore, the authors argue, there were very few defaults, which was perhaps attributable to a combination of the recourse nature of Danish mortgages and the underlying social safety net that helped preserve household income even during financial stress.

Germany

Lindenthal and Eichholtz point out that the German market is unique in Europe. Home ownership is low and German real home prices have been in a steady decline for 15 years. The housing market continues to show the aftereffects of the merger of East and West German economies, as the authors illustrate with the Berlin housing market, and there is no evidence of the economy being influenced by the most recent boom/bust cycle associated with the GFC. Prices neither surged any time during the 2001–2007 period, nor experienced an accelerated collapse any time during or after the GFC. In addition, Germany's housing policy is more heavily directed to rental housing than in many other parts of the world, with lower emphasis on encouraging home ownership. The secondary market is based on covered bonds tied directly to mortgages.

Ireland

Although at first glance Ireland's housing market boom appears to be a close sibling of the U.S. bubble, Simon Stevenson argues that, in fact, the origins are of a different nature. The boom in home prices spurred by the economic transformation of the Irish economy that began in the 1990s spanned more than a decade; average house prices in Dublin rose by 580 percent from 1994 to 2006. Only in the latter half of this boom, which ended in 2006, did a credit bubble, rather than economic and demographic factors, push prices into the speculative range. This credit bubble was built on a range of factors, including negative real interest rates, the increasing participation of banks (as opposed to more specialized building societies) in mortgage lending, and expanding mortgage products that required less stringent lending criteria. The unraveling of this bubble since 2006 was intertwined with the effects of the GFC, and the impacts were particularly severe for Ireland, destroying the stock value of three of the country's largest banks and ultimately leading the government into deep indebtedness.

Netherlands

Home prices in the Netherlands have been on a trajectory of price growth since 1985, well before the most recent boom in the United States. Brounen and Eichholtz describe the history of these price increases as "stimulating demand; controlling supply." The government stimulates housing demand both by subsidizing rents for low and moderate income households, while at the same time offering tax deductibility for mortgage interest rates for households at all income levels. Banks are said to provide financing of home purchases through mortgages with very high loan-to-value ratios, which further stimulates demand. In contrast, the growth of supply, especially for owner-occupied units, has been tightly controlled and micromanaged, with the result that both rents and prices are at their all-time high, and the GFC has had little effect on rents and prices in the Dutch housing market. Much of the country's rental housing stock was built through the social rental sector in the period from 1945 through 1975. These units continue to comprise a large share of the housing stock, but growth of both social and market rate units have been greatly curtailed in recent years by local government controls.

Spain

The housing market in Spain was a poster child for the manic boom and bust characterized by the period preceding the GFC and the crisis itself. Like the other

European examples described above, price increases began well before the 2000 to 2007 period (in this case in the mid-1990s), stimulated at first by an expanding economy that benefited from EU membership. Antoni Sureda-Gomila argues that expansion post 2000 was based not only on the expectation of growing demand, both domestic and pan-European, but also on the activities of lenders. Mortgagors who traditionally focused on local customers took part in this expansion, providing financing for much riskier (but potentially higher paying) loans for apartments and second homes. From 2000 to 2009, 5 million new housing units were added to an existing stock of 20 million, while the population grew by only 6.25 million to about 46 million. As the boom began to slow, new units were added at about twice the rate of absorption. The most problematic loans have not been those for individual mortgage holders but for real estate development and construction. As in the United States, real-estate development was a significant part of the economic boom, and as prices began to turn, the effects were felt in national employment figures, as well as in real estate, asset markets and the financial sector. The government has stepped in with loan modification measures, deferred payments for the unemployed, and a temporary fiscal stimulus. Longer-term measures include abolishing tax deductibility of mortgages and some restructuring of the banking system. As part of a single European currency, Spain, like Ireland, has had limited monetary response options.

United Kingdom

The United Kingdom has had a volatile housing market for four decades. Whitehead and Scanlon show that financial deregulation gradually led to widening access to mortgages, while supply constraints limited how quickly supply could adjust to demand, leaving demand growth to be met by price increases. After a stagnant period in the 1990s, price growth took off from 2000 through 2007. While at first this growth appeared to be based on fundamentals, by the middle of the first decade of the twenty-first century, investors expecting continued value gains and a small but increasing share of subprime borrowers were also contributing to the growth. Growth in borrowing came less from expanding owner-occupant home purchases and more from investors and refinancing. During this period, the authors argue, U.K. lenders became increasingly dependent on the securitized mortgage market for funding home mortgages. It was the freezing of access to short-term credit, rather than direct links to any risky U.S. investments, that sent the U.K. financial system into disarray. Nevertheless, the larger economic outcome for the United Kingdom, to date, has been less extreme than for either the United States or Ireland. Unemployment rates have been lower than predicted, as have mortgage defaults. Homeowners with troubled loans have been given the possibility of giving the unit back to the bank while renting back.

Overall, the European markets in this book that were most integrated with global markets, either through capital flows, as in the case of Ireland and the United Kingdom, or in terms of housing demand, as in the case of Spain, were particularly vulnerable to the crisis. While in most cases one could argue that the roots of the problem were planted well before the U.S. housing bubble grew, these economies were sensitive to the effects of the bubble because of their integration with the larger European and global economies. Germany is an interesting counterexample, one that is also heavily integrated into both goods and financial markets worldwide, but where a combination of institutional, political, and historic factors did not foster a boom and kept the "double bubble" effect in check.

Eastern Europe

At the time when many of the European markets were starting off on a 15- or 20-year housing price growth cycle, many of the economies of Eastern Europe were just beginning their transition from planned to free-market economies. Countries where property ownership for decades had been in the hands of the state were looking to transfer this ownership into the hands of the housing occupants. These countries also began with no private development sector—the great majority of modern housing stock as of 1990 was built by the public sector. Overall, the experiences described in these chapters are set in the context of an economic and institutional system in the throes of deep structural change.

Russia's Housing and Mortgage Market

Unlike most European countries, Russia still has significant pent-up demand, arising out of the turbulent 1980s and 1990s. Kosareva and Tumanov highlight the fact that a mix of household savings and funds, and loans from a variety of other sources, including government support, rather than just bank loans have historically been the primary source of funding home purchases. Mortgages are more likely to be used in the purchase of new homes rather than in re-sales. In 2008, mortgage loans accounted for only 2.8 percent of GDP, which, nevertheless, was 28 times the level of 2004. There was no secondary market for loans until 2000, and through 2008 less than one fifth of all mortgages were securitized. The share of foreign currency loans declined, from over one third of all securitized loans in 2008 to less than one sixth in 2009. Public policy in this period adjusted how loans could be used (allowing mortgage-type loans to be made to the purchaser at the time construction began) and the type of funding available to lenders, with an expanded role for government-housing finance agencies and quasi-public banks. Kosareva and Tumanov argue that although prices have risen substantially in Russia in the last decade, the underlying factors do not indicate a bubble.

Russia's Financial Markets and Regional Manifestations

The second chapter on Russia (by Sprenger and Urošević) explores the differential impacts of local and global capital in the period preceding and during the crisis, as well as some of the factors leading to regional variation in the housing market and GFC consequences. Russia's natural-resources-based economy led to sustained economic growth for much of the past decade, but also made it vulnerable to a global crisis. It was the downturn in exports, the drop in commodities prices, and the global financial consequences of the U.S. meltdown that slowed Russia's economy and housing market, rather than a housing and financial bubble within Russia. Although the majority of mortgages came from large, state-controlled banks, the smaller share of euro-denominated loans proved to have much more volatile payment rates (because of varying exchange rates), leaving borrowers more vulnerable to default. Home prices, which dipped in 2009, had already begun recovering by 2010 in the re-sale market (which is less dependent on loans), while defaults have been much higher in the foreign currency denominated loans.

Serbia

Like Russia, Serbia went through a period of transition from state to private home ownership. Because of civil war, the transition only began in 2000, but has been more complete than in Russia. Šoškić, Urošević, Živković, and Božović point out that even under the previous socialist system, there was private, or rather individual, property, and many families obtained ownership rights to housing through their companies; homes that transferred from public ownership often transferred at nominal rates. The country now has a home ownership rate of 98 percent, the highest of all of the countries in this book. However, for many existing homes, the registration of home ownership has been informal, making ownership title transfer difficult. Thus, much of the home sale activity, especially as financed by mortgages, has been in the relatively small new home market. The country's financial institutions were totally dismantled during the period of political strife; and mortgage lending, while growing, still applies to a relatively small share of the market. The country does not have a secondary mortgage market, but the Serbian government has actively promoted and subsidized mortgage lending, and is helping develop a mortgage insurance system. The authors observe that while prices did not dip with the GFC, this may in part be due to postponed sales, and a price adjustment could take place in the future. Further risks, including legal, liquidity, and currency risks, will also affect the continuing development of the Serbian housing market.

The Large Asian Markets

Three of the largest housing markets in the world are located in Asia: China, India, and Japan. All three economies are integrated with the world financial markets to varying degrees. Indeed, heavy Chinese investments in U.S. treasuries and agency bonds have been singled out as one factor in the complex mix of forces contributing to the boom, through the lowering of interest rates. In the case of India and China, rapid economic growth and demographic factors formed the fundamentals of housing demand. However, financial integration and the importance of trade in these economies still left them vulnerable to fallout from the financial crisis.

China—Beijing

As Ping, Zhen, and Xu point out, the Chinese housing market presents an unusual mix of public sector and private sector participation. With full, statutory public ownership of land and public regulation of investment activity, the authorities have an unusual array of resources and tools to control the pace and direction of the market. Beijing home prices grew rapidly in the period just preceding the GFC, dropped sharply for a brief period in the last quarter of 2008, but by late 2009 had fully recovered and were continuing to rise rapidly, leading to global concerns of a fresh bubble. The authors point to several factors to explain the resiliency of the Beijing housing market. The nature of the real estate finance market, with relatively little securitization, as well as strict due diligence of borrowers, limited the number of problem loans. International funds continued to flow into China during the GFC, while problems in the economy actually led investors to look to real estate as a safer direction for investment than into export-oriented businesses. The Chinese government was aggressive in its fiscal response to the GFC, moving to stabilize the economy through social, administrative, and economic measures. Authors argue that speculation and local government actions may be bringing Beijing prices to levels beyond what would be supported by the fundamentals.

China—Shanghai

Jie Chen's chapter on Shanghai uses recent data to examine the relationship between the expansion of the mortgage market in China and the boom in home prices. The Shanghai housing market has experienced several large swings in the past three decades, the most recent of which occurred in the wake of the GFC. Access to mortgage credit has been one factor in these cycles. Most recently, mortgage availability has been used as a tool to stimulate the housing market during periods of slowdown and to rein in price increases during periods of too-rapid price gains, but with limited success. Fiscal stimulus and loose monetary policy also contributed to surging property prices since 2009, providing further evidence that China could still face a possible housing bubble.

Indian Housing Finance

The development of the Indian housing market must be viewed in the broader context of the country's urbanization and robust urban economic growth, which is creating strong demand for urban housing. India was not directly exposed to the subprime mortgage crisis. Verma argues that the India banking system, in some ways modeled on the U.S. and British systems, has been well capitalized and well regulated, and did not face some of the issues of the more liberalized models on which they were based. Even so, some effects of the GFC filtered through to the Indian economy. The real-estate market experienced slowdowns in both supply and demand, in response to the global economic downturn. Fiscal stimulus and liquidity infusions from the Indian government and the Reserve Bank of India have helped to support the real-estate sector. In the longer term, India faces issues of affordable housing policy as well as the need to expand access to credit.

Indian Housing Market and the Indian Economy

Housing prices in India continued rising, after a short lull during the worst part of the GFC. High-income growth concentrated in urban areas contributed to the strength of the market. Chandrasekhar highlights the role of India's demographic profile in giving long-term stimulus to housing demand, along with an expanding middle class. Government interest rate and tax policy have also supported housing demand, and the author argues for strong controls and regulatory oversight over the banking and housing sector. Chandrasekhar also expresses concern that more recent price increases could reflect speculative demand, at the same time that loosened lending standards were beginning to allow loans to a wider range of borrowers. The Reserve Bank of India, however, is reported to have taken a series of prudential measures and has tightened lending policies to head off this risk.

Japan

The collapse of Japan's real-estate and asset bubble in the early 1990s has had long-term consequences for the country's economy, leading to prolonged stagnation. The financial sector, badly damaged by overextended lending, had to be restructured through government bailouts and mergers. As Seko, Sumita, and Naoi point out, restructuring has affected not just the private banks. The Government Housing Loan Corporation, which historically accounted for up to one third of housing loans in Japan, was affected by government privatization policies after 2000, and began to lose share and revenue. Currently private banks hold a much larger share of mortgages than the restructured public provider. Japan's vulnerability in the GFC was not triggered by a real-estate bubble or bad loans, but by vulnerability to global markets and a significant decline in exports. The consequent GDP contraction was worse than the one following Japan's earlier bubble. Despite current economic issues in Japan and the country's experience with real-estate bubbles in the past, the authors see some lessons for long-term housing policy in some features of American mortgages. For example, non-recourse loans could improve home turnover and mobility, and securitization of mortgages could expand the lending pool.

Overall, the experience of these large Asian markets demonstrates several points. Any major financial upheaval will be felt by the economy in some way, in spite of the relative robustness and size of the large domestic sector and partial immunity to global events. Even if the banking and financial sectors are heavily regulated and controlled, the goods market linkages might be the transmission channel. The countries are large enough that trends in the housing markets are likely to be driven first by local factors, although to the degree that broader global conditions affect financial health and employment, these factors can then affect the housing market.

Smaller Asian Markets

The AFC was felt in the real-estate markets of three of the four countries highlighted in this section, and became the gauge against which the effects of the GFC are measured. In general, controls put in place after the AFC kept these markets from expanding at the rate observed during the housing boom in the United States and parts of Europe. The fourth, Taiwan, also experienced several real-estate cycles in earlier decades, and developed policy measures to dampen booms. To the extent that the economies are linked globally to the United States and European countries through financial flows and global trade, they could not but experience some of the impacts of the GFC, yet these appear to have been less severe and less long-lasting than those experienced in the Western Hemisphere.

Hong Kong

Leung and Tang describe the evolution of the Hong Kong housing market during the GFC in the context of the events during the AFC. During the AFC, the Hong Kong housing price index dropped by more than 50 percent in a year. Hong Kong's experience in the AFC was complicated by the "handover" of Hong Kong from the United Kingdom to the People's Republic of China. Even following the AFC, government control of land sales combined with a small number of land developers kept prices high and gave the government leverage over building activity. Efforts to set up a mortgage guarantee and mortgage-backed securities system were not very successful. In the GFC, real-estate prices dropped less and recovered more quickly than in the AFC, while GDP dropped a similar amount but also recovered more quickly. In addition to institutional changes since the AFC, the close linkages with mainland China's economy helped to bolster Hong Kong through the most recent crisis.

Korea

Kyung-Hwan Kim emphasizes that in both the AFC and the GFC, the housing market became the victim of the economic crisis rather than the cause. In the AFC, prices were already declining, but turned down more sharply as other economic problems unfolded. The GFC occurred at a time of growing home prices, but the effect on prices was less severe. The aggregate output shock was also less in the GFC. Following the AFC, attention focused on policies to help the real-estate sector recovery, and Korea went from experiencing a housing shortfall at the time of the AFC to having a housing surplus by 2007. The government's initial reaction in the GFC was to try to support the housing market through changes in transfer and capital gains taxes, and easing mortgage credit availability. As prices began to recover, mortgage tightening and higher loan to value ratios were introduced. Having suffered less severe impact, the GFC failed to serve as important a platform for policy reform in Korea as had the AFC.

Singapore

The Singapore housing sector is very directly managed and controlled by the public sector. As Lum Sau Kim describes, strong economic expansion and liberalization of the public housing market before the AFC led to strong demand growth for housing. Demand dropped following the AFC, and the state curtailed public housing production and also reduced the supply of state-owned land for private housing. Over the next decade, Singapore's economic strength, growing global stature, and maturing financial sector led consumption and asset demand for housing to expand rapidly, with high appreciation both before and after the GFC, with a swift yet temporary downturn during the crisis. Since September 2009, the state has instituted several rounds of market cooling measures and has boosted the supply of both land and public housing to control the pace of price appreciation.

Taiwan

In the past four decades, Taiwan's housing market went through four boom periods, from 1972 to 1974, from 1978 to 1980, from 1987 to 1989, and from 2004 to the present. The government attempted to dampen the first three booms by controlling credit availability, land supply, and development activity. In the most recent boom, the government did not try to dampen the rate of housing price increases because of broader concerns regarding the global economic slowdown. As Chang and Chen argue, Taiwanese house prices continued to grow throughout the GFC, raising housing affordability concerns for low and moderate-income households, particularly in Taipei.

Other Markets

Australia, Brazil, Canada, and Israel represent four distinct markets that interacted with places closely impacted by the GFC but which in various ways seemed insulated from the worst impacts. The specific institutional settings, as well as the nature of their economic linkages, help to explain the success of these markets to date.

Australia

The Australian economy has a significant natural resource base and is closely integrated with the major Asia-Pacific economies. These factors have formed the context within which to view the impact of the GFC. Housing price trends have varied across the different regions in the country, with the highest levels of appreciation occurring in the resource-based regions that have seen substantial economic growth due to exports to China. As Tirtiroglu points out, the Australian banking and mortgage system is unusual in that it leaves most of the risk in the hands of borrowers and depositors rather than with the banks. Until September 2008, the country had no deposit insurance. Moreover, the great majority of mortgages have been adjustable rate, with very short adjustment terms. One of the first government acts in response to the GFC was to stabilize the banking system by offering 100 percent deposit insurance. Australia entered the GFC with a budget surplus, which was quickly directed into stimulating the economy, keeping unemployment below 6 percent, and maintaining the gains that had been achieved in home prices. A concern going forward is whether the home price gains are sustainable and whether the banking portfolio remains too heavily invested in these loans.

Brazil

Wide income and wealth disparity in Brazil have led to a housing deficit of close to eight million units in a country of almost 60 million households, mostly for very low-income families. Haddad and Meyer point to the history of the Brazilian Housing Financing System, which was created in 1964. It provided a base for mortgage lending for two decades, but various crises of both an economic and political nature made it unsustainable, resulting in a long period of mortgage loan stagnation, from 1983 to 2005. Later structural changes in the economy, with inflation stabilization, lowered interest rates, growth in family incomes, effective redistribution policies, and implementation of a new regulatory system, led to increased mortgage and housing activity by 2006. The advent of the GFC reduced new starts and home sales overall, but most of the decline came at the higher end and for larger units, while the mix of smaller units continued to grow.

Canada

Like Australia, the Canadian housing market experience has varied widely across the country, with some of the highest price gains occurring in natural resource exporting regions. Carter highlights the fact that despite price gains in some regions and metropolitan centers, Canadians escaped the most extreme consequences of the housing bubble and subsequent meltdown experienced by housing consumers in the United States. There has been no freefall in prices and no significant escalation in mortgage defaults and bank foreclosures. The author argues that Canada has had a more conservatively managed and regulated financial system, and mandatory mortgage insurance and the small levels of subprime lending helped to prevent many of the problems experienced in the United States. Nevertheless risks remain, primarily from economic spillovers from the GFC in the form of impacts on the economy and unemployment.

Israel

Ben Shahar and Warszawski conclude that the GFC had only a minor and short-term effect on the Israeli economy and its housing market. In the period preceding the GFC, housing prices were stable and flat. The country had entered a period of growth, following recovery from a prolonged recession brought on by a combination of the bursting of the dot-com bubble and the political environment. Housing market response in this period of economic growth was affected by the institutional structure underlying the market. The Israeli government owns 93 percent of the land, which it leases to private developers; there is relatively little public housing, and only limited support on the demand side for home ownership. At the time of the crisis the number of households was growing more rapidly than new supply coming into the market. Despite the importance of trade to the country and the slowdown of trade flows, the impact of the GFC was short-lived; the flow of mortgages slowed briefly, interest rates ultimately dropped, and housing prices rose sharply—by 21 percent in 2009. The authors' analysis of factors underlying housing prices and housing affordability lead them to the conclusion that this increase went beyond fundamentals, indicating that although Israel seemed immune to the worst effects of the GFC, its housing market may not be immune to the price bubble phenomenon.

LESSONS FROM THE GLOBAL EXPERIENCE

Given the wide range of national housing markets analyzed in this book, are there any far-reaching lessons that can be drawn from their experiences in the course of the global financial crisis and in its aftermath? Different institutional structures, regulatory settings, economic conditions, global linkages, demographics, and political factors all combine to determine both the level of vulnerability of local housing markets to domestic and international shocks and the nature, direction, and robustness of the policy response. The following are some tentative conclusions that can be drawn:

- Regulatory structure and the will to enforce regulations made a difference. Countries experiencing the most serious negative outcomes tended to have more deregulated financial systems and often had lax regulatory oversight. However, it was possible to have a severe effect even without participating in the types of lending experiments that infused the U.S. subprime market.
- Global linkages played a role. Extensive foreign financial institutional participation in a country's mortgage market, significant foreign capital flows, and even heavy trade linkages, albeit to a lesser degree, made both the financial system more vulnerable when the global credit system froze up, as well as adversely impacted employment and other "real" economic variables because of a trade downturn.
- Quick, decisive public sector response was able to divert the worst of the impact in some settings. Australia's quick acceptance of deposit insurance, for example, diverted a potential banking disaster.
- Small interventions may keep a market from going off the cliff. Countries with strong control over the land market that used this to influence the

supply side were able to moderate booms and busts, although the temptation for frequent and arbitrary meddling remains.

- There was no "right" answer in responding to the impacts of the GFC. The chapters that follow provide many different examples of policy responses, from interventions in the national banking systems to providing programs aimed at individual homeowners, such as the rent-back alternative offered to defaulting homeowners in the United Kingdom.
- No country is immune from these bubbles, whatever the nature of the economic-institutional structure in place, but some managed this episode better than others. Many of the countries that managed well in this period were operating with safeguards that were established following previous bubbles.
- The combination of full recourse, prepayment penalties, and absence of mortgage rate deductibility may help reduce the chances of a bubble by imposing a risk burden on households, but at the cost of reducing ownership and mobility; in any case, more research is needed before a global conclusion is drawn.

The evidence from these diverse countries emphasizes the fact that, despite globalization, housing markets are ultimately local. They are influenced not only by market forces such as interest rates, mortgage availability, employment, and demographics, but also by the regulatory and institutional framework in which housing supply (e.g., zoning and land use controls) and housing demand (financial subsidies, social policies, etc.) interact. At the same time, as national economies and financial systems become more globally integrated, no country is fully immune from major economic disruptions originating in a distant part of the world. Housing markets will be impacted through the medium of international financial flows; through the effect transmitted by goods or services traded; or through a combination of global social psychology, expectations, and "animal spirits" that seem to link investors everywhere. The case for coordinated global financial policy in times of crisis seems strong, even if the process of achieving it may be cumbersome. Furthermore, the repercussions of the global financial crisis have not necessarily ended in many economies described in this book, as some countries cope with national debt crises that arose out of efforts to stem the local impacts of the GFC, others struggle with sputtering economies and feeble employment growth, and yet others appear at risk of being on the brink of their own delayed housing downturn. A common and comprehensive lesson arising out of the experiences of this wide range of markets and institutional arrangements seems to point to a greater role for state structures and government institutions in the future, not merely due to the structural likelihood of a recurrence of financial crises, but also because of the dramatic increase in financial complexity and its regulatory requirements, the increasing range of conflicting interests, and issues of equity and fairness.

REFERENCES

Ben-Shahar, Danny, Charles Leung, and Seow-Eng Ong. 2009. *Mortgage Markets Worldwide*. Hoboken, NJ: Wiley-Blackwell.

Duca, John V., John Muellbauer, and Anthony Murphy. 2010. "Housing Crisis and the Financial Markets of 2007–2009: Lessons for the Future." *Journal of Financial Stability* 6:4, 203–217.

Green, Richard K., and Wachter, Susan M. 2005 (Fall). "The American Mortgage in Historical and International Context." *Journal of Economic Perspectives* 19:4, 93–114.

Kim, Kyung-Huan, and Bertrand Renaud. 2009. "The Global House Price Boom and Its Unwinding." *Housing Studies* 24:1, 7–24.

Lea, Michael. 2010. *International Comparison of Mortgage Product Offerings*. Research Institute for Housing America. Washington, D.C.

Lea, Michael. 2011 (January). "Alternative Forms of Mortgage Finance: What Can We Learn from Other Countries?" Paper presented at the AREUEA Annual Conference, Denver, Colorado.

ABOUT THE AUTHORS

ASHOK BARDHAN is Senior Research Associate in the Fisher Center for Urban Economics at the Haas School of Business, University of California–Berkeley. He has an MS in Physics and Mathematics from Moscow, Russia, an MPhil in International Relations from New Delhi, India, and a PhD in Economics from UC–Berkeley. His research includes papers on global financial integration and real estate; on the impact of the offshoring of jobs; on firm organization and innovative activity; on the responsiveness of the U.S. higher education sector; and on trade and technology linkages between the United States, China, and India. He is coauthor of *Globalization and a High-Tech Economy: California, the United States and Beyond* (2004), and coeditor of the forthcoming *Oxford Handbook on Global Employment and Offshoring*. His current research projects include the study of determinants of sustainable urban development, land and housing market failures in emerging economies, and the carbon footprint of urban commercial real estate in the United States.

ROBERT EDELSTEIN joined the faculty of the University of California–Berkeley in 1985 after being a Professor of Finance at the Wharton School, University of Pennsylvania, and is active in the fields of real estate economics, finance, and property taxation; energy and environmental economics; public finance; and urban financial problems. He has been published widely in prestigious economic and business journals on topics related to commercial and residential analysis and real estate markets. He has testified before the United States Congress on many real estate finance issues. Edelstein has been President and has served on the Board of Directors of the American Real Estate and Urban Economics Association. He is the President and a member of the Board of the Asian Real Estate Society. In addition, he has served as member of the boards of directors of several prestigious corporations, such as AMB (NYSE) and CapitaLand (Singapore). Dr. Edelstein received an AB, AM, and PhD in Economics from Harvard University.

CYNTHIA KROLL is Executive Director for Staff Research and Senior Regional Economist at the Fisher Center for Real Estate and Urban Economics, Haas School of Business, University of California–Berkeley. She is a prominent author and advisor on real estate, development, and housing policy in California. Her research spans a broad range of topics and disciplines, including industrial structure, innovation, and financing building in the green economy; the globalization of high tech and services sectors, including globalization of the real estate industry; the transforming housing market and California's future; affordable housing policy in California; the effects of the credit crisis on local public sector revenues; state and national responses to the housing and credit crisis; and patterns of firm births, deaths, and relocations at times of economic upheaval.

PART I

The United States Leads the Housing Bubble's Rise and Collapse

CHAPTER 2

The U.S. Housing Market and the Financial Crisis

Causes, Policy Prescriptions, and Future Stability

ASHOK BARDHAN
Fisher Center for Real Estate and Urban Economics,
University of California–Berkeley

ROBERT H. EDELSTEIN
Haas School of Business, University of California–Berkeley

CYNTHIA A. KROLL
Fisher Center for Real Estate and Urban Economics,
University of California–Berkeley

INTRODUCTION

In 2007, the United States and much of the world entered a financial and economic crisis of unprecedented proportions. Housing values started declining in the United States at a rate not seen since the Great Depression, credit markets seized up, balance sheets of financial and non-financial corporations were in dire straits, widespread contagion spread across global markets, and there emerged a heightened perception of risk and uncertainty regarding all counterparties.

The so-called subprime crisis is likely to be a major historical milestone for the United States and the world economy. The forces unleashed by the subprime crisis in the United States could take many years to dissipate. The federal government (and thus U.S. taxpayers) committed hundreds of billions of dollars to rescue packages, primarily for bailing out insolvent banks and other financial institutions, and further billions for stimulating the stalled U.S. economy. The first line of defense concentrated on resurrecting the world financial system, while the approach for rescuing the U.S. housing market appeared to be an afterthought; even three years later, policies are still under discussion for dealing with residuals of the problem—underwater mortgages, homeowners defaulting on mortgage payments, and title issues muddying the foreclosure process. Nevertheless, the substantive nature of the housing crisis is a core fundamental problem that has to be solved in order to resolve the issues of the financial system at large.

This chapter describes the housing crisis as it emerged and its interconnections with the U.S. financial system and financial crisis; analyzes the U.S. policy framework and its contributions and responses to the crisis, and discusses the degree of success and issues that remain from the crisis. We begin with a brief review of the U.S. housing market and financial system prior to 2000. A description follows of the interplay between and among the housing bubble, financial bubbles, and economic impact of the burst bubbles. We then examine the differences in housing markets and the housing bubble across states to highlight some of the unique features of the U.S. experience. Later portions of the paper address the policy arena, including the major financial and economic interventions and more restricted direct responses in the housing market. We conclude with lessons learned from the crisis and its aftermath, issues remaining to be resolved, and an assessment of what still needs to be done.

THE U.S. HOUSING MARKET AND FINANCIAL SYSTEM BEFORE THE MELTDOWN

The U.S. housing market and the financial system interacted to generate the build-up to a bubble (or two bubbles) from 2005 to 2007, and ultimately to a housing market and financial collapse in 2008. However, the housing market and financial system have a much longer history of fairly steady growth, with occasional crises followed by waves of financial deregulation or reregulation. Before describing the elements of the meltdown, we provide an overview of housing market growth and policy, and the changing financial structure prior to 2000.

The U.S. Housing and Urban Policy before the Bubble

For decades following the Great Depression, the United States experienced a healthy housing market that seemed to create wealth for middle-class households. While affordable housing provides challenges for lower-income households, and homelessness remains a pervasive problem for a small segment of the population, the overall quality of housing, even for the poorest households, improved during the first few decades following World War II. In the period between the end of the Great Depression and the beginning of the Great Recession, the U.S. housing stock more than tripled (to 128 million units in 2007), the median price of a home rose by more than four times in real terms, the number of people per dwelling unit declined from 3.8 to 2.6, and the percent of units lacking full plumbing facilities dropped from 45 percent to 1 percent. (U.S. Department of Commerce, Bureau of the Census, Statistical Abstract, 1950, 1951, and 2010).

Most of these changes happened not through direct government investment in the housing market, but through significant public investments in infrastructure, on the supply side, and broad economic growth, as well as extensive tinkering with financial resources and tax incentives, on the demand side. Direct government housing expenditures have been largely oriented towards the housing needs of low-income or special groups (e.g., the military), but account for only a small share of growth. After World War II, and leading up to the Great Recession, about 20 to 25 percent of total construction in the United States was with public funds. However, the great majority of public funds went to infrastructure (from about one third to more than half for highways alone) or non-residential buildings. The private market has dominated housing construction: since 1947, less than 3 percent of direct expenditures on housing have been from the public sector. The bulk of public housing in the United States was built between 1949 and 1990, but by the mid-1990s, amounted to less than 1.5 million units (compared to a net increase in total units of about 35 million during that period). By 2008, the bulk of the 7 million subsidized rental units (out of a total of 129 million units) were provided through vouchers, project-based subsidies, tax credits, or tax-exempt bond financing (Schwartz 2010; U.S. Department of Commerce, Bureau of the Census 2008).

Greater indirect expenditure has gone to support goals of home ownership, largely for middle and upper income households. Homeownership rates increased from 44 percent in 1940 to 55 percent in 1950 and 66 percent by 2000, in part supported by the tax deductibility of local property taxes and mortgage interest payments, and in part due to financial programs. Federal policy also influenced the type and location of housing built. A robust national highway program in the 1950s and 1960s, combined with tax incentives for home ownership, encouraged the construction and sale of single family homes in suburban communities. Schwartz 2010 emphasizes that this subsidy for homeownership continues, with "mortgage interest deductions and other tax benefits exceeding $121 billion" in 2008, compared to approximately $40 billion for direct housing assistance.

U.S. Financial Policy Prior to 2000

Much of the success of U.S. home-ownership policy has depended on support from the financial system. Financial reforms following the Great Depression and World War II provided resources for expanded housing production and home purchases. The Federal Home Loan Bank System was established to provide a "stable source of funds" to thrift institutions, whose major charge was to provide home loans. The Home Owner's Loan Corporation helped to clear the inventory of distressed homes during the depression by purchasing and refinancing distressed mortgages on one- to four-family homes. Government insurance programs provided new stability, through the Federal Housing Administration, insuring qualifying mortgages on one- to four-family homes, and the Federal Savings and Loan Insurance Corporation (FSLIC, folded into the Federal Deposit Insurance Corporation in 1989) provided deposit insurance for thrifts. Mortgage funding was expanded through the Federal National Mortgage Association (FNMA, known as Fannie Mae), which provided a secondary market for the purchase of FHA-insured loans (Wheelock 2008). The 1933 Glass-Steagall Act created the Federal Deposit Insurance Corporation (FDIC) and provided additional stability to the financial system by separating commercial banking from investment banking.

The federal role in the secondary market for mortgages became more complex in the period from 1960 to 1980, with the addition of the Government National Mortgage Association (GNMA) in HUD, providing guarantees for FHA and Veterans Administration loans on the secondary mortgage market, the quasi-privatization of FNMA in 1968, and the creation of a second government-sponsored enterprise (GSE), the Federal Home Loan Mortgage Corporation (FHLMC, known as Freddie Mac) in 1970.

In the late 1970s, high inflation generated pressure to deregulate a broad set of banking activities and to modify banking structure. By 1980, the Depository Institutions Deregulatory and Monetary Control Act phased out interest rate caps, expanded lending authority, and established new reserve requirements for depository institutions (see www.fdic.gov/regulations/laws/important/index.html).

The less stringent regulatory environment allowed savings and loans (S&Ls) to enter new areas of lending—and ultimately some of them overextended and collapsed. The policy response to the S&L debacle in the 1980s was much less wide-sweeping than that of the depression era. With a less severe national economic downturn during the 1980s crisis, policy focused narrowly on maintaining confidence in depository institutions through reorganizing the insurance system and minimizing costs by disposing of problem assets that had become the property of the U.S. government. The Financial Institutions Reform, Recovery, and Enforcement Act of 1989 (FIRREA) abolished FSLIC, expanded FDIC powers and access to funding, and established the Resolution Trust Corporation (RTC) to dispose of problem assets. Despite the savings and loan crisis, various measures in the 1990s continued to broaden banking opportunities, including expanded interstate banking and repeal of the final vestiges of the Glass-Steagall that had continued to separate banking from other financial services such as investment banking and insurance.

In the decade preceding the peak of the housing bubble, attention was also focused on identifying means of enhancing home-ownership opportunities for lower-income households. In the private sector, a number of new institutional financial participants entered the housing finance arena, greatly broadening what had been the traditional lending infrastructure for home loans, while capital market innovations provided a seemingly endless stream of resources for supporting new loan products.

ELEMENTS OF THE MELTDOWN

The institutional changes mentioned above set the stage for the housing market bubble. Several additional factors contributed to the housing market bubble, some of which were also intertwined with credit market developments.

The Housing Bubble

The inflating of the housing bubble is reflected in data on home sales and home prices (Exhibit 2.1). Housing sales and prices had been growing at a rapid pace, particularly since the early- to mid-1990s, until the downturn began in 2006–2007. The downturn, which initially appeared modest, then accelerated, with median prices declining below 2003 levels; by 2010 the rate of housing value decline apparently had started to moderate in most, but not all, of the largest metropolitan statistical areas.[1] Some home-sales indexes have declined 10 to 30 percent nationwide from their peak, and by 40 to 50 percent or more in certain regional markets. Even some of the more modest losses in housing value become more significant when one considers how home purchases are financed. Since housing ownership is

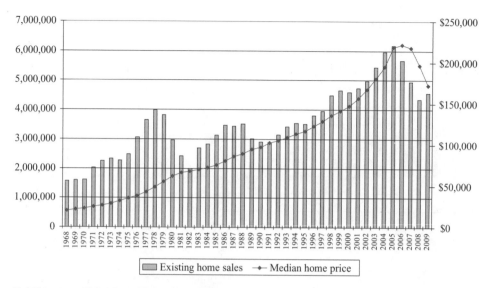

Exhibit 2.1   U.S. Home Sales, 1968–2009
Sources: California Association of Realtors; National Association of Realtors.

frequently highly leveraged, an initial 20 percent equity stake in a home purchased near the price peak has been, in all likelihood, wiped out. The assumption that home ownership is a good means of wealth accumulation has come into question.

Home-ownership rates were affected by the bubble and its aftermath. Home-ownership rates surged in the United States from about 65 percent to almost 70 percent at the height of the bubble. The increase in home-ownership rates was skewed to the western part of the United States, toward a younger population, and toward Hispanics and other minorities. A decomposition of the growth in the number of homeowners between 2000 and 2007 reveals that over half of the home-ownership rate growth is attributable to households under 29 years of age (see Exhibit 2.2). New homes were created based upon optimistic economic scenarios. U.S. Census data shows new housing starts peaked at over 2 million units in 2005 (later dropping by almost three fourths to slightly more than 500 thousand by 2009).

The Housing Finance-Securitization Bubble

Factors in the rise of subprime lending included a monetary policy leading to low interest rates after the 2001 recession, regulatory laxity promoted by relevant institutions (Demyanyk and Van Hemert 2008), investor desire for higher returns, a transactions-based incentive structure for mortgages and securitization, predatory lending to vulnerable segments of the population (Gramlich 2007), expanded mortgage products and complex securitization vehicles (Ashcroft and Schuerman 2008; Keys et al. 2010), and foreign-financed trade deficits leading to large inflows into U.S. Treasury and Agency securities, and consequently, lower mortgage rates (Bardhan and Jaffee 2007).

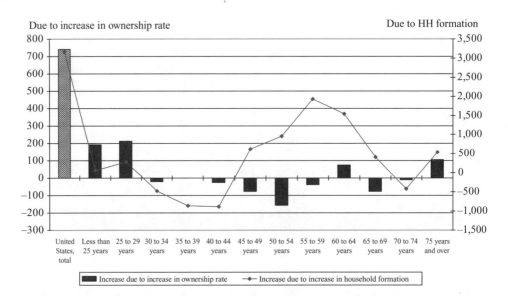

Exhibit 2.2 Decomposition of Change in Number of Home Owners: (a) Natural Growth of Households versus (b) Pure Growth of Ownership Rate: 2000–2007
Source: Author analysis from American Community Survey and U.S. Department of Commerce, Census of Population and Housing.

Successful experience with early subprime lending and the insatiable demand of investors for higher returns created a market for a wider range of mortgage-backed securities, beyond those with implicit and explicit U.S. government backing through the government-sponsored enterprises—Fannie Mae, Freddie Mac, and Ginnie Mae (hereafter, the first two are referred to as the GSEs). As shown in Exhibit 2.3, all types of mortgage-backed securities grew rapidly between 1998 and 2007 with the exception of tightly controlled Ginnie Mae securities. However, the

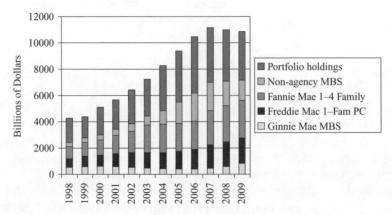

Exhibit 2.3 Trends in One- to Four-Family Home Mortgage Servicing Outstanding
Source: Inside Mortgage Finance, July 2008 and October 2010.

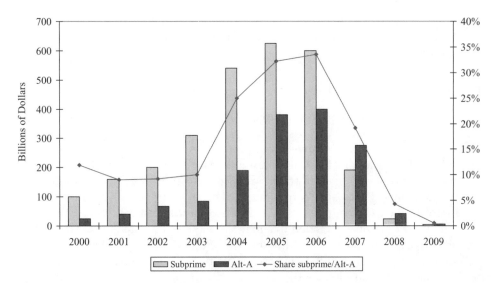

Exhibit 2.4 Subprime and Alt-A Mortgage Originations—Value and Share of Total Originations
Source: Inside Mortgage Finance, May 2010.

most rapid increase was in non–agency serviced private label mortgage-backed securities. Much of this growth was in the subprime and the alt-A mortgage sectors, whose share grew to more than one third of all mortgages issued by 2006 (Exhibit 2.4).

As the volume of subprime and alt-A loans expanded, the loan "quality" diminished, as illustrated in Exhibit 2.5. Based on First American CoreLogic Loan

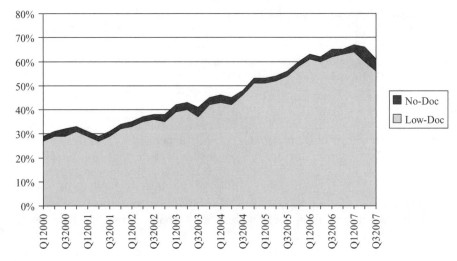

Exhibit 2.5 Percent of Loan Value, Low-Doc or No-Doc (all except agency prime loans, 2000 Q1 to 2007 Q2)
Source: Authors using First American CoreLogic Marketing Reports, LoanPerformance data, May 2008.

Performance data, which tracks the majority of non-agency securitized loans, the share of non-agency loans issued with low or no documentation rose from 30 percent in 2000 to over 60 percent in 2007.

The Two Bubbles Collide

The two bubbles had an almost symbiotic relationship until approximately late 2006 through early 2007. With overall strength in the economy, interest rates began to rise, demand growth slowed, and payments on adjustable rate loans began to increase. The number of defaults jumped sharply by mid-2006, but the early increases were reported by data-tracking agencies with reassuring words. For example, DataQuick's president commented: "This is an important trend to watch but doesn't strike us as ominous. . . . The increase was a statistical certainty because the number of defaults had fallen to such extreme lows" (DataQuick 2006a). The default rate tripled within a few months. Early signs of collapse continued with the bankruptcy of New Century Financial, the nation's largest independent subprime lender, in March 2007. By the time Bear Stearns suffered its collapse in early 2008, both bubbles were well on their way to deflating. The section that follows tracks the effects of the bust among different players.

The subprime crisis affected multiple segments of the population and economy in a variety of ways. On the housing side, most homeowners lost unrealized capital gains, but it is those with underwater mortgages (where price declines left the home worth less than the mortgage) who were most vulnerable to losing their homes (and to defaulting on their loans). We estimate that of the approximately 50 million households with mortgage debt in 2008, between 10 and 12 million homes had mortgages with outstanding loan balances greater than the house value (based on the number of annual sales, home price declines, and down payment amounts).

Issues with rental property affected both property owners and tenants. Renters became most vulnerable when the property owner/landlord carried high levels of debt on the property. In parts of the country most heavily affected by declining property values and foreclosures, the carrying cost on a rental property purchased near the peak (mortgage plus associated housing expenses and costs) is no longer covered by market rents.

The degree of vulnerability of borrowers has depended on the type of loan, as well as income and employment status. By May 2010, 6 percent of all mortgages outstanding were subprime, down from 14 percent in June 2007 and 11 percent in June 2008; 7 percent of prime loans and 40 percent of subprime loans were delinquent 60 days or more, up from 3 percent and 28 percent in June 2008. The incidence of delinquency and foreclosures has been heavily concentrated in a set of "sunshine" and/or economically troubled states. In June 2008, California and Florida together accounted for one fifth of prime loans, one fourth of subprime loans, almost one third of loans delinquent more than 60 days, and almost two fifths of all loans in foreclosure.[2]

Culpability varies widely among borrowers; there are owner occupants who borrowed an affordable amount, had unexpected financial problems (such as a job loss, a medical emergency, inability to sell because home prices declined); there is a middle ground (inexperienced borrower acting on the advice of a lender and contracting for unaffordable payments); and then there are the risky borrowers, who used subprime refinancing to cope with existing cash-flow problems, as well as dishonest borrowers and speculators who took out loans based on falsified income and employment information, planning to "flip" the home for a gain.

Builders were quickly hit by the collapse of housing demand and of credit markets. Close to 200,000 establishments, with almost 1 million employees, were involved in homebuilding in 2006. By 2008, even before the credit crisis peaked, the number of establishments had dropped by 6 percent and employment by 16 percent. Unlike homeowners, many of whom can have more flexibility to choose whether to sell in a down market, homebuilders were pressed to reduce inventory.

Mortgage originators, including large subsidiaries of banks and thrifts and independent mortgage lenders, underwent substantial changes in the early part of the crisis. Of the top 15 mortgage originators in 2005, shown in Exhibit 2.6, at least 7 had failed, been acquired by other lenders to avoid failure, and/or ceased all retail lending by 2008. More than half of the 15 top mortgage originators were also among the 25 top subprime lenders in 2005. Some still hold a portion of these loans in their asset portfolio, but many played a role mainly as "pass-through" agents, with loans eventually becoming securitized, thus allowing a much larger volume of mortgages to be originated and relaxing the incentives for due diligence. Retained recourse on securitized loans eventually contributed to the collapse of some of these institutions.

Private companies, GSEs, and public agencies (FHA, Ginnie Mae) were involved in converting the loans into financial instruments, either directly as securitizers, or by providing insurance and guarantees that enhanced credit ratings for mortgage-backed securities. The role of the private securitization market expanded rapidly in the first decade of the twenty-first century. Non-agency MBS share of mortgage servicing grew from under 8 percent in 2000 to 20 percent in 2006 (over a 400 percent increase in value serviced, compared to a doubling of overall loan value in the market, as estimated from data reported by Inside Mortgage Finance). Analysis by Mian and Sufi (2009) suggests that the expansion of mortgage credit to "subprime zip codes" was closely correlated both with declining relative income growth, and with the increase in securitization of subprime mortgages. The growth of securitization was also supported by activities of investment banks and private sector insurers in the credit default swap market.

Insurance played a critical role, both in primary and secondary markets. Several federal agencies are involved in mortgage insurance, and there is a private mortgage insurance industry as well. Regulated mortgage insurers were subject to capital standards held against losses. A number of other financial products were developed (e.g., credit default swaps) that essentially were utilized to hedge against investor losses from the secondary market in bonds and mortgage-backed securities. Many of these financial products and insurers did not fall within the definition of (or under regulatory statutes for) insurance. For these and other reasons, such as lack of "insurable interest" of parties to the transaction, these derivatives have proved to be extraordinarily risky. AIG, a large insurer, had both traditional insurance products and a small group in London generating credit default obligations that were sold not only to the holders of securitized mortgage instruments, but also to other investors "betting" on a downturn in the mortgage

Exhibit 2.6   Trends in Top Mortgage Originators

Top Mortgage Originators 2005	Volume 2005 ($Bil)	Status 2000	Status 2008 ($Bil; through 6/08)
Countrywide Financial*	$490.95	#3; $61.69	#2; ($132.03); acquired by Bank of America, January 2008
Wells Fargo Home Mortgage*	$392.33	#1; $76.46	#1; $133.69
Washington Mutual*	$248.83	#5; $50.73	#8; $30.50; Chapter 11 Bankruptcy 9/08; bank assets sold to JP Morgan Chase
Chase Home Finance*	$183.49	#2; $76.01	#3; $116.40
Bank of America Mtg. & Affil.	$158.82	#4; $51.82	#4; $74.80; acquired Countrywide
CitiMortgage, Inc.	$124.29	#14; 19.65	#5; $72.73
GMAC Residential Holding Corp.	$91.54	#15; 17.82	Now Residential Capital LLC; #7; $35.73
Ameriquest Mortgage Co.	$79.68	Not in top 30	Retail lending shut down and wholesale servicing acquired by Citicorp, 2007
GMAC-RFC*	$64.27	Not in top 30	Acquired by Mortgage Express Ltd. in 2005
IndyMac*	$60.77	#21; $9.26	#14; $15.42; failed July 2008
National City Mortgage Co.	$59.03	#11; $21.49	#17; $12.66
Wachovia Corporation	$57.71	Not in top 30	$6; $37.94; purchased by Wells Fargo, October 2008, following large losses.
New Century Financial Corp.*	$56.10	Not in top 30	Filed for bankruptcy March 2007
ABN AMRO Mortgage Group	$53.34	#6; $23.84	Not on top 50 list
Aurora Loan Services	$51.93	Not in top 30	Not on top 50 list; subsidiary of Lehman; stopped originating loans in early 2008

*Among top 25 subprime lenders in 2005.
Sources: Inside Mortgage Finance, 2006 Mortgage Market Statistical Annual and September 26, 2008 newsletter; http://newsroom.bankofamerica.com/index.php?s=press_releases&item=7956; http://money.cnn.com/2007/04/02/news/companies/new_century_bankruptcy/index.htm; www.rockymountainnews.com/news/2008/sep/18/aurora-loan-contributed-to-downfall-of-lehman/

securities and housing markets. These instruments were sold against insufficient underlying collateral and lay at the core of AIG's 2008 collapse (Dash and Sorkin 2008).

Investors from around the world, including individuals, institutional investors, hedge funds, corporations, financial firms of various kinds, and a multitude of governments, became tied to the bubble. Investment banks, such as Lehman Brothers and Bear Stearns, speculated on their own account as well. These two investment banks failed because of liquidity, as well as solvency issues caused by their highly leveraged portfolios of mortgage-backed assets. Many other investors suffered massive losses, although actions undertaken by the federal government through Troubled Asset Relief Program (TARP) and the Federal Reserve through a variety of programs tended to limit them. Indirect impacts were felt by investors and corporations as stock values dropped (although for the surviving entities, there has been significant recovery in the markets, as well as a return to pre-crisis levels of profitability). In the immediate term, investor reluctance in the face of heightened risk perceptions, counterparty uncertainty, and general risks of unreliability slowed new investments.

Unquestionably, the size of the bailout of financial institutions and of the stimulus package, as well as the indirect costs of various Federal Reserve initiatives will place a large (not fully defined) bill in the hands of current and future taxpayers. The long-term costs and duration remain uncertain. Over time, economic recovery may help recoup costs at the federal level and thus spell some relief for the taxpayers. The Congressional Budget Office (2008a) estimates of the costs of Housing and Economic Recovery Act (HERA), for example, has immediate costs of $42 billion, but net costs of $25 billion after a variety of related revenues are taken into account. The remaining costs may become an intergenerational issue, as the large deficits contracted in 2008, 2009, and beyond, to address the credit crisis and related problems become a tax on subsequent generations. Whoever pays off the new deficits, today's taxpayers are likely to suffer other long-term losses in their retirement accounts, in addition to the drop in housing wealth.

Vulnerability versus Culpability

A number of experts have analyzed aspects of vulnerability versus culpability in examining the role of different players in this set of bubbles. Several authors have identified minorities as among the most vulnerable households in the build-up of subprime lending activity and the subsequent foreclosure activity, as summarized in Barwick (2010) and Rugh and Massey (2010). African American households were particularly likely to receive subprime mortgages, compared to non-minority or Asian households, controlling for other neighborhood, household, borrower and timing characteristics (Rugh and Massey 2010, citing not only their own empirical research but also a 10-year history of a range of research on subprime lending that in part preceded the housing bubble).

Other factors, apart from racial discrimination, have also been identified as making borrowers vulnerable to delinquency and foreclosure. Earlier research by Calem and Wachter (1999) showed a link between delinquency and poor credit history. Foote, Gerardi, Goette, and Willen et al. (2008) found evidence that many subprime borrowers took on loans they could not afford even before interest resets; in addition, these borrowers often used high-interest-rate second loans to cover down payments.

Subprime lending played a role, but by no means an exclusive one, in the creation of the housing bubble. Analysis by Coleman, Major, LaCour-Little, and Vandell (2008) shows little impact of subprime lending on house price inflation. Other factors—such as the role of non-owner investors and the decreasing GSE market share—played a larger role in the decoupling of the market from fundamental economic factors.

Gerardi, Shapiro, and Willen (2008) conclude that the expectation that housing price appreciation would continue supported risky investments, based on the historic belief that a downturn in housing prices was unlikely. In reviewing market analyst literature prior to the bust, they found many who were aware of the potential downside of declining house values, but discounted the possibility. Case (2008, p. 12) notes that "the housing market is quite susceptible to the formation of bubbles" for exactly the reason that sales are driven by consumer expectations of continued price increases. Risk was compounded by weak underwriting (Das and Stein 2009).

Calomiris (2008, p. 6) argues that "the most severe financial crises typically arise when rapid growth in untested financial innovations coincides with very loose financial market conditions." Ready availability of credit is also the theme of Mian and Sufi (2009). Jaffee (2009) dwells on the investment side as a critical element in turning a problem in a small segment of the mortgage market into a national financial crisis. The role of the financial sector for engendering a crisis of this magnitude is a major reason that initial responses focused on the credit markets.

A CROSS-STATE ANALYSIS OF SUBPRIME TRENDS

Public policy and regulations controlling and overseeing the issuance, origination, and servicing of residential mortgages, as well as the entire institutional structure that is involved in the process, are governed by both federal and state authorities. This is true for both the mortgage industry, per se, and the banking and financial industry at large. There has been considerable academic research on mortgage markets using grassroots, individual mortgage data across zip codes (Mian and Sufi 2009), counties (Gerardi, Shapiro, and Willen 2008), and other jurisdictions. We use a state-level analysis to generate additional insights on yet another hierarchical level of government institutions.

Differences in States' Economic, Demographic, and Housing Conditions

The need to analyze the subprime crisis at the state level is underscored by two factors. First, the economic boom years and the run-up in housing market activity and housing prices, as well as the subsequent housing downturn have had varying impacts on states. Second, even prior to the crisis, there existed a wide range and variation in the structure and performance of the housing market across states in terms of housing values; exposure to subprime loans; foreclosure rates; and demographic, social, and economic factors, such as household size, home ownership rates, and other variables. For example, median 2007 home values ranged from $88,000 in Mississippi to $536,000 in California. Home ownership rates at their peak ranged from a high of 80 percent for West Virginia to a low of 45 percent for the District of Columbia.

Exhibit 2.7 shows shares of subprime in total mortgages outstanding, shares of all mortgages in foreclosure, and median homeowner age in 2000, by state. Exposure to subprime loans varies widely, ranging from a low of under 10 percent in North Dakota to a high of almost 28 percent in Rhode Island. Foreclosure rates also vary, both within subprime loans and spilling over into prime loans as well. Florida and Nevada, both of which had very high rates of construction in the middle of the first decade of the twenty-first century, are experiencing the highest rates of foreclosure both among subprime loans, as well as other types of loans, but five other states (Arizona, California, Illinois, New Jersey, and Rhode Island) also had more than one fifth of all subprime mortgages in foreclosure, and at least 4 percent of all loans in foreclosure by mid-2010.

Social and Institutional Factors Underlying State Differences

An ordinary least-squares analysis of state subprime exposure and foreclosure activity identifies the role of underlying social, economic, and institutional characteristics in different U.S. states. Data sources for the fifty states and the District of Columbia include First American CoreLogic LoanPerformance, the U.S. Census Bureau, Bureau of Economic Analysis, and Bureau of Labor Statistics, the American Community Survey, the American Housing Survey, and a set of state survey results from CFED (Corporation for Economic Development).

Using these datasets, we estimated cross-sectional OLS regressions for the determinants of subprime share and for each state's share of mortgage loans in foreclosure. The results are shown in Exhibits 2.8 and 2.9. Exhibit 2.8 shows that states with younger populations and higher shares of minorities were likely to have more subprime activity, while states with protections against predatory lending had lower shares of subprime mortgage loans. Economic factors, such as per capita income and income growth did not appear as significant, although the signs were as expected. (Alternative model specifications led at times to changes in the level of significance of estimated coefficients, but the size and signs of the coefficients were extremely robust with regard to alternative model specifications.)

Exhibit 2.9 shows the factors found significant for determining the share of mortgages in foreclosure in 2007, just as the economic issues began to emerge. Not surprisingly, states with high shares of subprime mortgages experienced high shares of foreclosures. In addition, changing home values and changing economic conditions (proxied by unemployment shifts) had the expected effects. States providing protections prior to foreclosure saw lower shares overall. Judicial review states, where foreclosures can be considered as part of the bankruptcy process, were more likely to have higher shares of foreclosures, perhaps because of the perceived convenient resolution of the mortgage process.

Our data is aggregated at the state level, and for many variables (e.g., age, income, race) the correct level of analysis should be the individual mortgage holder. However, a state-level analysis, with the inclusion of state-level regulatory institutions and practices highlights the role of state-level oversight and regulatory environment (or lack thereof) in the generation of problem mortgages. The U.S. case is complicated by the diversity and the multiplicity of institutional levels at which lending and foreclosure policies are set.

Exhibit 2.7 U.S. State Housing Market Characteristics

State	Population 2005 (Thousands)	Median Age 2005	Median Home Price 2006	Home Ownership Rate 2005	Price Change, Peak to Q4 2009	Percent of All 2005 Loans Subprime	Percent All/Subprime Mortgages in Foreclosure May 2010
Alabama	4558	35.8	$ 107,000	76.6%	−2.8%	16.5%	1.7/8.6%
Alaska	664	32.4	$ 213,200	66.0%	−0.7%	12.1%	1.1/10.9%
Arizona	**5939**	**34.2**	**$ 236,500**	**71.1%**	**−31.2%**	**20.5%**	**6.2/23.6%**
Arkansas	2779	36.0	$ 93,900	69.2%	−2.1%	16.2%	1.6/7.6%
California	**36132**	**33.3**	**$ 535,700**	**59.7%**	**−31.7%**	**25.7%**	**5.9/24.7%**
Colorado	4665	34.3	$ 232,900	71.0%	−3.6%	17.0%	2.3/12.5%
Connecticut	3510	37.4	$ 298,900	70.5%	−10.6%	16.1%	3.1/18.4%
Delaware	844	36.0	$ 227,100	75.8%	−9.8%	12.4%	2.6/17.1%
District of Columbia	551	34.6	$ 437,700	45.8%	−8.9%	11.6%	2.9/20.0%
Florida	**17790**	**38.7**	**$ 230,600**	**72.4%**	**−32.9%**	**21.4%**	**11.7/34.9%**
Georgia	9073	33.4	$ 156,800	67.9%	−8.1%	20.5%	3.0/13.0%
Hawaii	1275	36.2	$ 529,700	59.8%	−14.3%	17.3%	3.5/17.9%
Idaho	1429	33.2	$ 163,900	74.2%	−11.4%	15.2%	2.9/15.3%
Illinois	**12763**	**34.7**	**$ 200,200**	**70.9%**	**−10.2%**	**22.1%**	**3.9/23.4%**
Indiana	6272	35.2	$ 120,700	75.0%	−2.8%	18.4%	3.4/15.1%
Iowa	2966	36.6	$ 112,600	73.9%	−0.8%	12.6%	1.9/14.9%
Kansas	2745	35.2	$ 114,400	69.5%	−1.7%	13.9%	1.6/11.2%
Kentucky	4173	35.9	$ 111,000	71.6%	−1.5%	17.1%	2.4/14.2%
Louisiana	4524	34.0	$ 114,700	72.5%	−1.6%	19.5%	2.2/10.1%
Maine	1322	38.6	$ 170,500	73.9%	−7.8%	15.8%	3.5/20.9%
Maryland	5600	36.0	$ 334,700	71.2%	−17.1%	21.0%	3.7/19.7%
Massachusetts	6399	36.5	$ 370,400	63.4%	−12.2%	18.2%	2.8/18.1%
Michigan	10121	35.5	$ 153,300	76.4%	−19.6%	22.7%	3.7/16.9%
Minnesota	5133	35.4	$ 208,200	76.5%	−12.6%	18.1%	3.1/23.1%

State							
Mississippi	2921	33.8	$ 88,600	78.8%	−3.1%	23.6%	2.2/8.3%
Missouri	5800	36.1	$ 131,900	72.3%	−4.4%	18.7%	1.7/9.1%
Montana	936	37.5	$ 155,500	70.4%	−3.8%	11.1%	1.4/12.1%
Nebraska	1759	35.3	$ 119,200	70.2%	−1.3%	13.1%	1.3/9.5%
Nevada	**2415**	**35.0**	**$ 315,200**	**63.4%**	**−40.7%**	**23.9%**	**9.8/28.1%**
New Hampshire	1310	37.1	$ 253,200	74.0%	−12.2%	16.9%	2.0/12.2%
New Jersey	**8718**	**36.7**	**$ 366,600**	**70.1%**	**−13.1%**	**16.4%**	**4.5/26.2%**
New Mexico	1928	34.6	$ 141,200	71.4%	−7.3%	13.7%	2.2/13.0%
New York	19255	35.9	$ 303,400	55.9%	−8.4%	18.9%	3.1/19.4%
North Carolina	8683	35.3	$ 137,200	70.9%	−4.3%	13.4%	1.5/8.3%
North Dakota	637	36.2	$ 99,700	68.5%	*	9.4%	0.8/10.4%
Ohio	11464	36.2	$ 135,200	73.3%	−4.5%	17.3%	3.6/17.6%
Oklahoma	3548	35.5	$ 94,500	72.9%	−0.4%	17.9%	2.0/11.3%
Oregon	3641	36.3	$ 236,600	68.2%	−14.0%	17.2%	2.3/15.3%
Pennsylvania	12430	38.0	$ 145,200	73.3%	−4.6%	13.0%	2.2/11.5%
Rhode Island	**1076**	**36.7**	**$ 295,700**	**63.1%**	**−17.0%**	**27.6%**	**4.1/20.6%**
South Carolina	4255	35.4	$ 122,400	73.9%	−4.1%	13.4%	2.6/12.9%
South Dakota	776	35.6	$ 112,600	68.4%	−1.5%	10.1%	1.3/15.8%
Tennessee	5963	35.9	$ 123,100	72.4%	−3.6%	18.9%	1.8/7.8%
Texas	22860	32.3	$ 114,000	65.9%	−1.3%	21.5%	1.5/6.7%
Utah	2470	27.1	$ 188,500	73.9%	−12.7%	20.5%	2.4/13.0%
Vermont	623	37.7	$ 193,000	74.2%	−3.5%	10.3%	1.7/18.1%
Virginia	7567	35.7	$ 244,200	71.2%	−10.0%	15.0%	2.2/12.1%
Washington	6288	35.3	$ 267,600	67.6%	−13.1%	16.6%	2.1/14.2%
West Virginia	1817	38.9	$ 89,700	81.3%	−3.0%	14.3%	1.9/9.8%
Wisconsin	5536	36.0	$ 163,500	71.1%	−4.7%	13.5%	2.6/21.9%
Wyoming	509	36.2	$ 148,900	72.8%	−3.7%	14.8%	0.9/8.5%

*North Dakota home prices peaked in first quarter 2010.

Source: Authors from U.S. Department of Commerce, Bureau of the Census; FHFA Housing Price Index; and First American CoreLogic LoanPerformance Reports.

Exhibit 2.8 OLSQ Results: Dependent Variable, Share of Subprime in all Mortgages, November 2005

Explanatory Variables	Coefficient	t-statistic	Significance Level
Median age	−0.0063	−2.24	5%
Home price change 1995–2005	0.0311	2.58	5%
Per capita income 2005	8.23 E-07	0.68	Not significant
Per capita income change 2000–2005	−0.1368	−1.20	Not significant
Percent minority	0.1228	2.27	5%
State predatory lending protections (Dummy Variable)	−0.0079	−1.87	10%
Constant	0.4965	3.55	1%

Adjusted R-squared = 0.4373; Prob > F = 0.0000

Exhibit 2.9 OLSQ Results: Dependent Variable, Share of Mortgages in Foreclosure, November 2007

Explanatory Variables	Coefficient	t-statistic	Significance Level
Share of mortgages subprime 2005	0.1040	5.34	1%
Home price change from 2006 peak to Q3 2007	−0.0533	−2.18	5%
Unemployment change 2006 to 2007	0.0159	1.75	10%
Judicial review state (dummy)	0.0074	5.53	1%
State pre-foreclosure protections (dummy)	−0.0042	−3.12	1%
Constant	0.0194	−2.25	5%

Adjusted R-squared = 0.6868; Prob > F = 0.0000

PUBLIC POLICY RESPONSES TO THE TWO BUBBLES

At the federal level, initial policy responses were directed primarily at the financial sector, although a few housing related programs were included in the hopes of dampening the impact of the housing bubble collapse on the economy. At the state level, in contrast, public policy responses were largely directed at the housing aftermath, assisting those facing foreclosure and developing new protections for future homebuyers.

The federal governmental responses began as fire-fighting measures—enhancing available credit to the largest banks, injecting liquidity, shoring up large financial market participants whose unregulated activities had become so extensive and so deeply enmeshed with credit flows that their failure could conceivably lead to systemic failures and freezing of financial markets. Other measures included the placing under conservatorship of government-sponsored enterprises (Fannie Mae and Freddie Mac only) in order to prop up their mortgage activities as well as the value of agency bonds (many of which were held by foreign governments). At the same time, the Federal Reserve, the Treasury, Congress, and regulatory bodies such as the FDIC began crafting measures to deal with the large-scale collapse of the credit system, with local and individual issues directly related to mortgage default and foreclosure, and with preventing the recurrence of these problems in the future.

The State Approach

At the state level, measures focused primarily on two aspects—limiting predatory lending and providing relief for troubled borrowers. Thirty-six states passed at least 115 "responsive" measures between 1999 and 2008. North Carolina responded early to predatory lending activity, passing the North Carolina Predatory Lending Law in 1999 (Smith 2002). The District of Columbia and South Carolina followed in 2000, with measures that were later strengthened in 2002 or 2003. About half of all legislation had been passed by 2003, but a dozen states continued to modify or pass new measures through 2007 and 2008. Few of the policy prescriptions directly addressed borrowers currently confronting foreclosure or growing negative equity, although some related concerns are widely covered, such as limiting prepayment penalties on high-cost mortgages.

Apart from legislation, states have worked in concert with major lenders to encourage workouts that avoid foreclosure, such as actions by the State Foreclosure Prevention Working Group. In addition, the Conference of State Bank Supervisors and the American Association of Residential Mortgage Regulators have developed a universal licensing system that states may adopt.

An Overview of Federal Responses

Exhibit 2.10 summarizes the U.S. federal government responses to the unfolding crises. The early stages of policy were implemented through infusions of cash and loans to maintain or restore the viability of the credit markets. As problems continued to evolve in the housing market and the wider economy, additional funding was allocated to housing relief and for economic stimulus. Only much later were policies developed that addressed the underlying issues going forward.

The response options for troubled borrowers are complicated because several different types of organizations or businesses have responsibilities for different segments of the troubled loans, and the loans may in fact serve as collateral for several different types of investors, with varying interests in the possible workout options. Many of the policy "solutions" addressed only small segments of the problem (e.g., only borrowers currently in default, with no negative equity).

Policy efforts have been divided among programs to address existing troubled loans, programs to stimulate home ownership and thus stabilize home prices, and programs to improve the mortgage system in the future. The initial programs established in 2008 and 2009 were primarily oriented to mortgage modification and home purchase stimulus.

Refinancing and Mortgage Modification

Several mortgage modification programs were established in 2008, including one implemented quickly by the FDIC (Bair 2008), and others established by Congress (Streamlined Mortgage Modification Plan, Hope for Homeowners). These programs in general applied to subgroups of distressed owner-occupant mortgage

Exhibit 2.10 Major Responses at the Federal Level

Date	Event or Response	Description
December 2007	Mortgage Forgiveness Debt Relief Act of 2007	From 2007 to 2012, eliminates taxes on canceled debt related to a principal residence. (U.S. IRS 2009)
March 2008	Term Securities Lending Facility program	Extended access (up to 28 days) to treasury security borrowing for financial institutions (including investment banks), using troubled assets as security.
March 2008	Bear Stearns failure	Buy-out/bail-out by JP Morgan, with federal loan/guarantee.
July 2008	IndyMac failure	FDIC takeover of bank, mortgage workouts.
July 2008	Housing and Economic Recovery Act	Purchase of GSE Debt; Housing Trust Fund; Hope for Homeowners; first-time homebuyer tax credit; redevelopment assistance; other.
September 2008	Fannie and Freddie takeover	The two GSEs placed in conservatorship.
September 2008	AIG infusions	Immediate $85B infusion in September 2009; additional purchase of toxic assets.
October 2008	Emergency Economic Stabilization Act	Troubled Assets Relief Program (TARP); $700B authorized for release: half in October 2008, half in January 2009.
February 2009	American Recovery and Reinvestment Act	Fiscal stimulus of $800B through tax cuts; education, health, and welfare; and investment in projects for future growth.
March 2009	Treasury Department Making Home Affordable Plan	HAMP and related programs to support workouts of housing loans.
Q3 2010 to Q2 2011	Quantitative Easing Round 2	$600 billion allocated to purchasing long-term treasuries.
July 2010	Dodd-Frank Wall Street Reform and Consumer Protection Act	Consumer Financial Protection Bureau; Financial Stability Oversight Council; programs to address systemic risk.

borrowers, determined by degree of delinquency, income, and other financial conditions, and loan-to-value ratios. Various loan modifications (reduced payments through lower interest rates, longer duration, or forbearance on some of the principal) emanated from these programs, with costs at least in part borne by the current owner of the loan (which ultimately could be the investors in a mortgage-backed security). Lender and borrower motivation for participating in the programs hinged on circumstances where foreclosure is imminent, and where the costs of modification would be less than those of foreclosure.

These early-response programs had limited applicability, each with different standards for assessing how financially troubled the loan and borrower were, who currently held the loan, and whether the loan was held in multiple liens or not. The workout process was arduous and time-consuming, with adjustments made on a loan-by-loan basis. Participation by the lender was voluntary unless the lender was in receivership with FDIC and the loan still in the lender's portfolio. The Congressional Budget Office in 2008 (2008a) estimated that the requirement that all lienholders should be on board could limit the number of eligible loans to 400,000 (about 5 percent of all subprime and alt-A loans on owner-occupied housing).

Coming into office in 2009, the Obama administration broadened the housing market policy responses of the previous year, and the types of borrowers to whom assistance was offered. The new plan was designed to address both at-risk borrowers current in their payments, and those who had begun to fall behind, to encourage workouts rather than foreclosures, to make available lower-interest rates, and to provide resources for other groups affected by the credit crisis, such as renters and neighborhoods.

The Home Affordable Refinancing Program (HARP) assists borrowers current with loans that were once conforming, but because of a decrease in home value have an LTV ratio above 80 percent and below 125 percent, to achieve lower interest rates. Home Affordable Modification (HAMP) targets borrowers whose ability to pay is at risk or are already in default because of changed economic circumstances. With HARP, the borrower receives a new fully amortized fixed-payment mortgage, and, with HAMP, new interest rates apply for a five-year time horizon, after which the payments may gradually increase to the prevailing market rate for conforming loans.

HAMP has incentives for homeowners to remain current, in the form of a subsidy of up to $1,000 per year for five years, to be directly applied for reducing the remaining principal balance. The program also offers incentives to servicers and mortgage holders to modify early, before default occurs. Servicers of loans held by or guaranteed by the GSEs must participate in the programs, while other servicers are also able, but not obligated, to sign up for HAMP. Separate programs exist to help unemployed homeowners and to find foreclosure alternatives, such as short-sales or deeds-in-lieu for distressed borrowers not qualifying for other programs. There is also a program for second liens if the holders agree to participate.

Under these and the earlier voluntary programs, over 4 million borrowers had received counseling by December 2010, about 2.4 million loans had been permanently modified in HAMP and Hope Now, and an additional 1.4 million were in trial modification under HAMP. As a benchmark, underwater borrowers were estimated at 11.3 million in mid-2010, and at 10.8 million in December 2010 (U.S. Housing and Urban Development and Department of the Treasury, 2010).

Many issues surfaced and remain under the auspices of this set of programs. First, the programs still require time-consuming case-by-case workouts. Second, servicer flexibility to modify securitized loans remains limited. Third, since many homeowners carry multiple mortgages, there may be a need for a more explicit role and responsibility for holders of second mortgages, to allow the plan to function smoothly. Fourth, there may be many homeowners in locales such as coastal California who are not assisted by this plan because nominal loans exceed the conforming limits, and are not eligible for refinancing. Finally, significant segments of the market remain unassisted.

Additional issues emerged in 2010 as foreclosures proceeded, related to the complexities of the securitization process. Delays and legal challenges have revolved around adequate documentation of loan ownership transfers during securitization. Individual foreclosure actions have been stopped by the court when documentation was deemed inadequate, and several large servicers placed a moratorium on foreclosure activity to review documentation issues.

Demand-Side Programs

Delaying foreclosure through refinancing and modification was a major measure for stabilizing home prices. In addition, homebuyer tax credits were used to stimulate the housing market. First time home-buyer credits of up to $8,000 were introduced as part of HERA in 2008, extended in 2009 and ended in April 2010. The credit was initially limited to households with incomes ranging to $75,000 for a single earner and $150,000 for married couples, rising to $125,000/$225,000 after November 2009. For a narrow window of time (November 2009 to April 2010), repeat home buyers were eligible for a $6,500 tax credit. Credits applied only to homes of $800,000 purchase price or less. A variety of other stimulus housing programs were enacted, including additional funding for rental vouchers and homelessness programs, and rehab funding for public housing.

Other Housing Market Policy Alternatives

Many other proposals have emerged to address some of the shortcomings of the early official responses (see Bardhan, Edelstein, and Kroll 2009), and as long-term solutions to the housing market problems. Suggestions range from modification of loans with negative equity to across-the-board strategies for addressing problem loans in a swift, systematic way, rather than case by case, and for dealing with securitized loans.

Several proposals address negative equity issues. The Shared Appreciation Mortgage (SAM1) proposed by Caplin, Cunningham, Engler, and Pollock (2008) would replace an "underwater" mortgage with two loans, one interest-paying with a loan to value ratio of less than 100 percent of the current price, and a second non-interest paying loan for the remainder, to be repaid upon home or loan disposition, with the lender sharing any upside gains. Replacing 20 percent of the outstanding mortgage balance with a low-interest rate recourse loan, according to Feldstein (2008), would reduce monthly payments, while making default less attractive. Standardized strategies for principal reduction, combined with future shared equity gains would enable large numbers of loans to be modified more quickly (Zingales 2008). Various strategies for keeping borrowers in their homes as renters after defaulting on the loan have been suggested (e.g., Alpert 2008). Internal Revenue Service taxation policy, where loan forgiveness may generate phantom income, is one roadblock to implementing many of the negative equity strategies.

Another set of proposals address the issue of dealing with securitized mortgages. Geanakoplos and Koniak (2008) offered a community-based trustees proposal, where the decision on the fate of a mortgage—whether no modification, modification, or foreclosure—would be made by a government-appointed, community-based trustee, who would be knowledgeable regarding local market conditions but "blind" to the investment status of the mortgage. Many economists have recommended a vehicle similar to the Homeowners Loan Corporation (HOLC) of the depression era. There are many variations on this theme, but generally the government entity would purchase troubled mortgages and would issue new, affordable mortgages to distressed homeowners. One variation, for example, combines automatic refinancing to low interest rates of eligible mortgages with an HOLC type vehicle for purchasing underwater mortgages, with a workout involving future shared equity (Mayer and Hubbard 2008). While portions of some of these proposals were worked into the current relief strategies, others that challenge fundamental underwriting standards have not been adopted.

A Further Public Policy Step—The Dodd-Frank 2010 Bill

Federal legislation passed mid-year 2010, entitled the "Dodd-Frank Wall Street Reform and Consumer Protection Act," focused on the aftermath of the subprime crisis, as well as on the creation of a less-vulnerable banking system. The parts of the legislation that most directly impact the housing market provide new housing related funding, as well as services to borrowers or further regulation of the home mortgage industry. Key provisions are as follows.

- Neighborhood Assistance: The Act allocates funding to the U.S. Department of Housing and Urban Development (HUD) Emergency Homeowner's Relief Fund to provide emergency loans and payments for borrowers suffering financial stress due to temporary economic problems, and to HUD's Neighborhood Stabilization Program for state and local government revitalization of neighborhoods with abandoned and foreclosed homes. The act funds the establishment of a grants program for state and local foreclosure-related legal assistance and a Multifamily Mortgage Resolution.
- Relating to Mortgage Origination & Securitization: Designed to avoid similar problems in the future, the act adds several layers of new controls for the mortgage industry. At every stage, the act attempts to add "skin in the game" to mortgage issuance and securitization. The new legislation requires mortgage-backed securities issuers to retain at least 5 percent of the credit risk. It also requires issuers to disclose more information and analysis about the nature and quality of the underlying housing assets. For high-cost loans, requirements include pre-loan counseling, prohibition for a number of "predatory lending" practices, limits for mortgage features, and caps for fees. More broadly, the act defines minimum underwriting standards for mortgage originators, including determination that the borrower has an ability to repay the loan, and steering borrowers to eligible "qualified" mortgages.
- Regulation and Oversight: The act also addresses larger issues of financial risk. A Financial Stability Oversight Council has the responsibility for evaluating systemic risks. Oversight responsibilities over credit institutions are redefined and clarified, and new areas of regulation are introduced, including oversight of investment advisors for hedge funds, and regulation

of credit rating agencies and derivatives markets. The bill seeks to eliminate technical and legal loopholes that allow abusive, cost-free, risk-transfer
practices in over-the-counter derivatives and asset-backed securities. It also
regulates OTC derivatives transactions by creating central clearing houses,
and by requiring margins for uncleared swap trades. Furthermore, a new
Consumer Financial Protection Board is granted authority and responsibility
for monitoring consumer finance.
- Credit Rating Agencies: The bill establishes a new office to regulate CRAs,
  with new requirements for transparency, specifically on methodological issues, and third-party due-diligence disclosures. The law creates new liability
  provisions, permitting investors to bring lawsuits against agencies for failure
  to conduct proper investigation on relevant new, independent information.

While broad and sweeping, these reforms do not confront several remaining
lynchpin issues. Credit default swaps can continue to be issued without "insurable
interest" (i.e., insurance issued for underlying bonds or mortgage-backed securities
not in the portfolio of the purchaser). Credit-rating agencies may still be paid
by issuers, thus retaining potentially perverse misalignments of incentives and
conflicts of interest. Initial restrictions on bank proprietary trading at the discount
window were watered down, leaving opportunities for banks either unchanged or
expanded. Finally, the legislation does nothing to reduce the likelihood of moral
hazard arising out of the necessity to bail out, in future, financial institutions that
are too important systemically, and "too big to fail."

Further Proposals for Housing Finance Reform

Housing market recovery and financial system reform will be an incremental process. The appetite for large sweeping measures seems limited. Yet a number of other
actions are under consideration. Proposals in the recent U.S. Treasury report[3] by
the Obama administration recommend phasing out GSEs from financing of mortgages by increasing guarantee fees to attract private capital, reducing conforming
loan limits, and winding down their investment portfolio. The report also calls
for FHA to focus upon the affordable end of the housing market, and providing
support for small and medium-sized financial firms. It also emphasizes the importance of consumer-protection measures, curbing abusive practices, and promoting
choice and clarity at the mortgage issuance stage; access to information and transparency in the securitization process; capital standards; and regulatory oversight,
all measures described in the Dodd-Frank bill but awaiting further clarification
through implementation. Finally, the report introduces a commitment to maintain or improve access to affordable rental and ownership housing, while raising
questions about the long-term viability of keeping the mortgage interest deduction
program.

CONCLUSION

A confluence of international, macroeconomic, social and financial forces generated the preconditions for the U.S. housing and subprime bubbles to grow into a
perfect financial, economic, and housing market storm. U.S. consumer debt fueled

the trade deficit, which was financed substantially with savings by U.S. trading partners. These global imbalances and capital inflows combined with official Fed interest-rate policy (in response to the dot-com bust and the recession of 2001) to generate cheap and plentiful debt. There was copious, cheap mortgage money for homebuyers at one end, and a willing pool of global investors for securitized mortgages, at the other, all lubricated by lax oversight and weak regulation.

New borrowers emerged to meet the expanding supply of mortgage money. Home-ownership rates rose among younger and lower-income households. The financial sector frenetically expanded products to serve the demand from home-owners and satisfy yield-starved investors. Through what might be characterized as financial alchemy, security issuers created derivatives with higher ratings than what the underlying securities could support. Fee structures rewarded lenders, mortgage brokers, rating agencies, and securitizers for originations rather than financial product viability, thereby creating incentives for increased transactions. Regulatory laxness and ineptitude passively permitted diluted underwriting standards and predatory lending practices, supporting the growth of subprime and alt-A mortgages, which were then securitized and sold to investors around the world.

Subsequently, with lower growth in demand for homes, prices began to flatten or dip, and the boom in home construction collapsed. Simultaneously, the many subprime mortgages with interest reset provisions started to come due. Combined with lower sales activity and prices, a self-perpetuating loop was created, causing marginal borrowers to default, further worsening housing market conditions. As home prices sank and mortgage default rates rose, the value of mortgage securities began to decline and the derivatives market started unraveling. The failure of major U.S. financial institutions, heavily invested in dodgy assets, and the repeated need for tens and then hundreds of billions of dollars from government-provided funds to keep them afloat, led to a much broader financial crisis across all asset markets, not only within the United States but globally.

Important lessons emerge from this experience. First, although a dynamic financial system can help growth and innovation, it has inherent risks. Regulations played a role in the past in restraining risky practices, and deregulation has often been followed by costly excesses. Second, the troubles of the housing market have been on an individual, neighborhood, micro-economic level, and thus have not received infusions of money on the same scale as the major financial institutions. Yet the housing sector, heavily dependent on employment and wage growth, may be a drag on economic recovery for much longer than the financial businesses that failed so spectacularly. Third, measures enacted to deal with the housing markets are perhaps no more than band-aids, and further stimulus may be required to assist the housing market and employment recovery. Fourth, it is difficult to visualize an economic and financial recovery without a substantive rejuvenation of the housing market and employment growth, and vice versa.

Going forward, several factors will be important for fostering stability in the housing and housing finance markets:

- A sustainable, viable plan is likely to require elements of a standardized approach (e.g., for interest-rate reduction), as well as triage for case-by-case loan modifications in case of future crises.

- Losses and gains may have to be shared among three parties: lenders, borrowers, and government.
- Legal reform may be necessary in order to delink servicers from security investors and clear the way for security restructuring and refinancing.
- An overhaul, restructuring, and redistribution of federal and state regulatory responsibilities might combine the best institutional features of both.
- Recognition of Fannie-Freddie, in their present form, as a potential weak link in the housing finance supply chain.

The Dodd-Frank bill and the Treasury report "Reforming America's Housing Finance Market," lay the groundwork for several necessary reforms. They offer a blueprint for changing the incentive structure within the mortgage-lending industry and tackle aspects of regulatory shortfalls in the shadow banking sector. Rebuilding U.S. housing policy, however, may require more than the stop-gap responses and consumer protections already enacted. A reevaluation is needed of how homeownership can or should be fostered, and how to promulgate an equally vibrant rental sector satisfying the needs of those who will not become homeowners. Perhaps, at a deeper level, the overreliance on and overinvestment in housing, arising out of a range of policies, need to be reexamined, thus reducing the exposure and vulnerability of the macroeconomy to the housing sector. As this review process goes forward, the lessons posed by the most severe financial and economic crisis since the Great Depression need to be remembered.

NOTES

1. The median home price is not the only measure of home price changes, nor is it the best, but it is the one for which we have the longest time series. The median price is as much a measure of the change in mix of homes sold as of the change in value. Indexes more closely reflecting the change in value include the FHFA index, which is based on "conforming" loans—essentially the middle of the market—nationwide, and the Case-Shiller index, which is computed utilizing a repeat sales econometric model for the 20 largest U.S. metropolitan markets. The FHFA index shows a drop of around 11 percent in value nationwide as of second quarter 2010 from its peak in April 2007. The Case-Shiller index was down by approximately 30 percent from its peak in the first half of 2007.
2. Statistics in this paragraph are calculated by authors from data reported by First American CoreLogic LoanPerformance.
3. Reforming America's Housing Finance Market: A Report to Congress, February 2011, www.treasury.gov/initiatives/Documents/Reforming%20America's%20Housing%20Finance%20Market.pdf.

REFERENCES

Alpert, Daniel. 2008 (October). "The Freedom Recovery Plan for Distressed Borrowers and Impaired Lenders." Westwood Capital, LLC. New York.

American Association of Residential Mortgage Regulators. 2010 (July 17). "American Association of Residential Mortgage Regulators." Available at www.aarmr.org/.

Ashcraft, Adam and Til Schuermann, 2008 (July) "Understanding the Securitization of Subprime Mortgage Credit." *Foundations and Trends in Finance 2*, no. 3: 191–309.

Bair, Sheila. 2008 (November 18). "Federal Deposit Insurance Corporation on Oversight of Implementation of the Emergency Economic Stabilization Act of 2008 and of Government Lending and Insurance Facilities." Federal Deposit Insurance Corporation. U.S. House of Representatives; Room 2128, Rayburn House Office Building, Washington, D.C. Speech.

Bank of America. 2008 (January 11). "Bank of America Agrees to Purchase Country-wide Financial Corp." Bank of America. Available at http://newsroom.bankofamerica.com/index.php?s=43&item=7956.

Bardhan, Ashok D., and Jaffee, Dwight M. 2007. "Global Capital Flows, Foreign Financing, and U.S. Interest Rates." Fisher Center Working Paper 303. Fisher Center for Real Estate and Urban Economics, University of California–Berkeley.

Bardhan, Ashok D., Robert H. Edelstein, and Cynthia A. Kroll. 2009. "The Housing Problem and the Economic Crisis: A Review and Evaluation of Policy Prescriptions." Fisher Center Working Paper. Fisher Center for Real Estate and Urban Economics, University of California, Berkeley. Available at http://escholarship.org/uc/item/2c77x7r2.

Barwick, Christine. 2010. "Patterns of Discrimination against Blacks and Hispanics in the U.S. Mortgage Market." *Journal of Housing and the Built Environment* 25:1, 117–124.

Calem, Paul S., and Wachter, Susan M. 1999 (March). "Community Reinvestment and Credit Risk: Evidence from an Affordable Home Loan Program." *Real Estate Economics* 27:1, 105–134.

Calomiris, Charles. 2008 (August 21–22). "The Subprime Turmoil: What's Old, What's New, and What's Next." Paper presented at the Federal Reserve Bank of Kansas City's Symposium, "Maintaining Stability in a Changing Financial System." Jackson Hole, WY. Caplin, Andrew, Noël B. Cunningham, Mitchell Engler, and Frederick Pollock. 2008 (September). "Facilitating Shared Appreciation Mortgages to Prevent Housing Crashes and Affordability Crises." The Hamilton Project Working Paper 2008-12. The Brookings Institution.

Case, Karl. 2008 (September). "The Central Role of House Prices in the Financial Crisis: How Will the Market Clear?" Paper prepared for the *Brookings Papers on Economic Activity*.

Coleman IV, Major D., Michael LaCour-Little, and Kerry D. Vandell, 2008. "Subprime Lending and the Housing Bubble: Tail Wags Dog?" *Journal of Housing Economics* 17:4, 272–290.

Conference of State Bank Supervisors. 2009. "Conference of State Bank Supervisors Website." Available at www.csbs.org/AM/Template.cfm?Section=Home.

Conference of State Bank Supervisors. 2008 (February, April, September). "State Foreclosure Prevention Working Group Reports." Conference of State Bank Supervisors, Data Reports 1–3. Available at www.csbs.org/Content/NavigationMenu/Home/StForeclosureMain.htm.

Congressional Budget Office. 2008a (July 23). "H.R. 3221 Housing and Economic Recovery Act of 2008." *Congressional Budget Office Cost Estimate*. Washington, DC.

Congressional Budget Office. 2008b (April). "Policy Options for the Housing and Financial Markets." *A CBO Paper*. Washington, DC.

Corporation for Economic Development (CFED). 2011 (January). "2009–2010 Assets and Opportunities Scorecard." Available at http://scorecard.cfed.org/.

Dash, Eric, and Andrew Ross Sorkin. 2008 (September 17). "Throwing a Lifeline to a Troubled Giant." *New York Times*. Business Section.

Das, Ashish and Roger Stein. 2009 (Summer). "Underwriting versus Economy: A New Approach to Decomposing Mortgage Losses." *The Journal of Credit Risk* (19–41) Volume 5/Number 2.

DataQuick Information Systems. (2006a). Available at www.dataquick.com/.

Demyanyk, Yuliya S., and Van Hemert, Otto. 2008 (December 5). "Understanding the Subprime Mortgage Crisis." Working Paper. Available at http://ssrn.com/abstract=1020396.

Federal Deposit Insurance Corporation. 2009. "Loan Modification Program for Distressed Indymac Mortgage Loans." Available at www.fdic.gov/consumers/loans/modification/indymac.html.

The Federal Housing Administration. 2008. "FHA Secure Fact Sheet—Refinance Option."
    Federal Housing Administration web site. www.hud.gov/buying/loans.cfm.
Feldstein, Martin. 2008 (March 7). "How to Stop the Mortgage Crisis." *Wall Street Journal*.
    Available at www.nber.org/feldstein/wsj03072008.html.
FHA Housing Stabilization Home Ownership Retention Act of 2008, H.R.5830, 110th Cong.
First American CoreLogic, Inc. LoanPerformance HPI data, various issues.
Foote, Christopher L., Kristopher Gerardi, Lorenz Goette, and Paul S. Willen. 2008. "Just the
    Facts: An Initial Analysis of Subprime's Role in the Housing Crisis." *Journal of Housing
    Economics* 17:4, 291–305.
Freddie Mac. 2007 (October). "Freddie Mac Responds to the Subprime Crisis." *Freddie Mac
    Public Policy Perspectives*.
Geanakoplos, John D., and Koniak, Susan P. 2008 (October 29). "Mortgage Justice Is Blind."
    New York Times. Available at www.nytimes.com/2008/10/30/opinion/30geanakoplos
    .html.
Gerardi, Kristopher, Adam Hale Shapiro, and Paul S. Willen. "Subprime Outcomes: Risky
    Mortgages, Homeownership Experiences, and Foreclosures," *Federal Reserve Bank of
    Boston* Working Paper 07-15. 2008 (May).
Gramlich, Edward M. 2007. "Subprime Mortgages: America's Latest Boom and Bust." Urban
    Institute Press. Washington, D.C.
Hope Now. "Hope Now." 2009. Available at www.hopenow.com/index.html.
Hope Now. 2008 (November). "Hope Now Joins with Government to Create
    Streamlined Mortgage Modification Plan." Available at www.hopenow.com/upload/
    press_release/files/SMP%20Release%20Final.pdf.
Housing and Economic Recovery Act of 2008, H.R.3221, 110th Cong. Enacted.
Housing Assistance Tax Act of 2008, H.R. 5720, 110th Cong.
Inside Mortgage Finance Publications, Inc. *Inside Mortgage Finance*. Various issues.
Inside Mortgage Finance Publications, Inc. 2006. *The Mortgage Market Statistical Annual*.
    Inside Mortgage Finance, Inc. New York.
Keys, Benjamin J., Tanmoy Mukherjee, Amit Seru, and Vikrant Vig. 2010. "Did Securitization
    Lead to Lax Screening? Evidence from Subprime Loans." *Quarterly Journal of Economics*
    125:1, 307–362.
Jaffee, Dwight M. 2009. "The U.S. Subprime Mortgage Crisis: Issues Raised and Lessons
    Learned." In Michael Spence, Patricia Clarke Annex, and Robert M. Buckley, eds., *Ur-
    banization and Growth*, chap. 7. World Bank. Available at www.growthcommission.org/
    storage/cgdev/documents/ebookurbanization.pdf.
Mayer, Christopher, and R. Glenn Hubbard. 2008 (October 31). "House Prices, Interest Rates,
    and the Mortgage Meltdown." Paper presented at the University of California–Berkeley
    and University of California–Los Angeles Mortgage Meltdown Symposium, Berkeley,
    CA.
Mian, Atif R., and Sufi, Amir. 2009. "The Consequences of Mortgage Credit Expansion:
    Evidence from the U.S. Mortgage Default Crisis." *Quarterly Journal of Economics* 124:4,
    1449–1496.
National Association of Home Builders. 2009 (June 2). *Housing Statistics*. Available at
    www.nahb.org/category.aspx?sectionID=819&channelID=311.
National Association of Realtors. 1968–2008. *Trends*. National Association of Realtors,
    various reports. Washington, D.C.
Neighborhood Stabilization Act, H.R. 5818, 110th Cong.
The Pew Research Center. 2008 (April). "Defaulting on the Dream: States Respond to
    America's Foreclosure Crisis." The Pew Research Center. Washington, D.C.
Rugh, Jacob S., and Douglas S. Massey. 2010. "Racial Segregation and the American Fore-
    closure Crisis." *American Sociological Review* 75:5, 629–651.
Schwartz, Alex F. 2010. *Housing Policy in the United States*, 2nd ed. New York: Routledge.

Smith, Jr., Joseph A. 2002 (July 26). "North Carolina's Predatory Lending Law: Its Adoption and Implementation." Paper presented to the National Conference of State Legislatures Annual Meeting, Denver, CO.

Statistical Abstracts from various states.

U.S. Congress. 2008 (July 30). Housing and Economic Recovery Act. Public Law 110–289.

U.S. Department of Commerce, Census Bureau. 2008 (October 16). *American Community Survey 2007.* Available at www.census.gov/acs/www/.

U.S. Department of Commerce, Census Bureau. 2008 (December 19). *American Housing Survey.* Available at www.census.gov/hhes/www/housing/ahs/ahs.html.

U.S. Department of Commerce, Census Bureau. 2009 (June 2). *Comparing New Home Sales and New Residential Construction.* Available at www.census.gov/const/www/salesvsstarts.html.

U.S. Department of Housing and Urban Development. 2009 (April 9). "Hope for Home-owners." Available at www.hud.gov/hopeforhomeowners/index.cfm.

U.S. Department of Housing and Urban Development and U.S. Department of the Treasury. 2010 (December). "Obama Administration's Efforts to Stabilize the Housing Market and Help American Homeowners."

U.S. Department of Treasury and Housing and Urban Development. 2011 (February), "Reforming America's Housing Finance Market: A Report to Congress." Available at www.treasury.gov/initiatives/Documents/Reforming%20America%27s%20Housing%20Finance%20Market.pdf.

U.S. Federal Deposit Insurance Corporation. 2007 (May 15). "Important Banking Legislation," Federal Deposit Insurance Corporation. Available at www.fdic.gov/regulations/laws/important/index.html.

Wheelock, David C. 2008 (May). "The Federal Response to Home Mortgage Distress: Lessons from the Great Depression," *Federal Reserve of St. Louis Review* 90:3 (Part 1), 133–148.

Zingales, Luigi. 2008 (October 10). "Plan B." *Economists' Voice.* Vol. 5: Iss. 6, Article 4.

ABOUT THE AUTHORS

ASHOK BARDHAN is Senior Research Associate in the Fisher Center for Urban Economics at the Haas School of Business, University of California–Berkeley. He has an MS in Physics and Mathematics from Moscow, Russia, an MPhil in International Relations from New Delhi, India, and a PhD in Economics from UC–Berkeley. His research includes papers on global financial integration and real estate; on the impact of the offshoring of jobs; on firm organization and innovative activity; on the responsiveness of the U.S. higher education sector; and on trade and technology linkages between the United States, China, and India. He is coauthor of *Globalization and a High-Tech Economy: California, the United States and Beyond* (2004), and coeditor of the forthcoming *Oxford Handbook on Global Employment and Offshoring.* His current research projects include the study of determinants of sustainable urban development, land and housing market failures in emerging economies, and the carbon footprint of urban commercial real estate in the United States.

ROBERT EDELSTEIN joined the faculty of the University of California–Berkeley in 1985 after being a Professor of Finance at the Wharton School, University of Pennsylvania, and is active in the fields of real estate economics, finance, and property taxation; energy and environmental economics; public finance; and urban financial problems. He has been published widely in prestigious economic and business journals on topics related to commercial and residential analysis and real estate markets. He has testified before the United States Congress on many real estate finance issues. Edelstein has been President and has served on the Board of Directors of the American Real Estate and Urban Economics Association. He is the President and a member of the Board of the Asian Real Estate Society. In addition, he has served as member of the boards of directors of several prestigious corporations, such as AMB (NYSE) and CapitaLand (Singapore). Dr. Edelstein received an AB, AM, and PhD in Economics from Harvard University.

CYNTHIA KROLL is Executive Director for Staff Research and Senior Regional Economist at the Fisher Center for Real Estate and Urban Economics, Haas School of Business, University of California–Berkeley. She is a prominent author and advisor on real estate, development, and housing policy in California. Her research spans a broad range of topics and disciplines, including industrial structure, innovation, and financing building in the green economy; the globalization of high tech and services sectors, including globalization of the real estate industry; the transforming housing market and California's future; affordable housing policy in California; the effects of the credit crisis on local public sector revenues; state and national responses to the housing and credit crisis; and patterns of firm births, deaths, and relocations at times of economic upheaval.

PART II

The European Union—One Continent, Many Markets: A Gauge of Government Institutions and Interventions

CHAPTER 3

The 2008 Financial Crisis and the Danish Mortgage Market*

JACOB GYNTELBERG
Bank for International Settlements

KRISTIAN KJELDSEN
Danmarks Nationalbank

MORTEN BAEKMAND NIELSEN
Nykredit

MATTIAS PERSSON
Sveriges Riksbank

INTRODUCTION

This chapter is a case study of how one of the most sophisticated housing finance markets in the world, the Danish mortgage market, performed during the recent financial crisis.

The Danish mortgage market has undergone a significant transformation over the past five to ten years. First, there has been a shift from fixed rate to adjustable rate mortgages as households have increasingly been taking one-year adjustable rate loans. This has been facilitated partly by low and stable short-term interest rates and partly by regulatory changes. Until five years ago, the Danish mortgage market was dominated by one standard contract: long-term (up to 30 years) loans at a fixed rate with an option to make penalty-free prepayments (Frankel et al. 2004).

The dramatic increase in the use of adjustable-rate mortgages (ARMs) as the dominant loan type has however, not changed the funding strategy used to fund the vast majority of mortgages. The mortgage banks have continued to operate according to a model that historically has been perhaps the key defining characteristic of the Danish mortgage system—namely cash-flow-based matching of loans and

*The views expressed in this article are those of the authors and do not necessarily reflect those of the Bank for International Settlements, Danmarks Nationalbank, Sveriges Riksbank, or Nykredit. We would like to thank Søren Korsgaard, Danmarks Nationalbank, for helpful comments, and Kathe Ørtoft Iversen, Danmarks Nationalbank, for editorial assistance.

the bonds used to fund the loans. This practice no doubt reflects that regulation for many years allowed mortgage banks to hold only limited amounts of credit risk. They were effectively prevented from retaining interest and prepayment risk.

This regulatory restriction, the so-called balance-principle, essentially required mortgage banks to fund their lending activities by issuing mortgage bonds with cash flows that fully matched those of the underlying mortgage loans until maturity. While the funding model used by the mortgage banks has not changed fundamentally, the Danish covered bond legislation was amended to incorporate recent changes in the European Union's Capital Requirement Directive (CRD), effective from January 2008. The amendments introduced a new covered-bond definition. A key change was a requirement for covered bond issuers to perform regular validation of loan-to-value (LTV) ratios, which are limited to 80 percent for residential mortgages and 60 percent for commercial mortgages.

In contrast to several other mortgage and securitization bond markets, trading continued in the Danish covered-bond market during the 2008 financial crisis. Both the government and the covered bond markets, however, did experience substantial declines in liquidity and increases in yield levels. The outstanding volume of mortgage bonds is around 140 percent of gross domestic product (GDP). In comparison, the outstanding volume of government bonds corresponds to around 35 percent of GDP.

Similar to policy makers in many other countries (Fender and Gyntelberg 2008), the Danish government at short notice in October 2008 had to introduce measures to stabilize the banking sector as well as restore confidence among market participants. To ensure continued access to funding for Danish banks and mortgage banks, two bank-rescue packages providing government guarantees (in return for a fee) on banks' liabilities were introduced. To avoid a significant drop in investor demand for mortgage bonds, pension funds—who have historically been among the largest investors in mortgage bonds—were given permission to use a higher discount rate for their liabilities during the crisis period. The government also initiated limited direct mortgage bond purchases to shore up investor confidence at the peak of the crisis. Finally, the Danish central bank, in line with other central banks, established temporary lending facilities. The large mortgage market, however, meant that most of banks had sufficient amounts of eligible collateral for central bank repo funding during the crisis.

This chapter is structured as follows. We first briefly describe how the Danish mortgage system has evolved over the past five years. This groundwork is a primer that is necessary to understand the following section, which discusses the developments seen in the Danish mortgage bond market during the recent financial crisis. In the section that follows we provide a brief overview of developments in the housing market before, during, and after the financial crisis. In the final section we provide concluding remarks.

THE MORTGAGE SYSTEM

The Danish mortgage market has undergone a rapid transformation over the past five years. First, retail mortgages have to a large extent become floating-rate as households have increasingly been taking one-year ARMS. This has been facilitated partly by low, stable, short-term interest rates and regulatory changes. Until five years ago, the Danish mortgage market was dominated by one standard contract: long-term (up to 30 years) loans at a fixed rate, with an option to make penalty-free prepayments (Frankel et al. 2004). The most popular new loan type is 30-year loans with an interest rate that changes once a year based on the funding conditions at the time of refinancing of the underlying bonds. By June 2010 nearly two-thirds of all outstanding residential mortgages and almost 90 percent of all new mortgages were of this type.

The dramatic change towards one-year ARMs as the dominant loan type has however not changed the funding strategy used by the mortgage banks, which account for around 90 percent of all outstanding mortgages. The mortgage banks have continued to operate according to a model that historically has been the, perhaps, defining characteristic of the Danish mortgage system—namely cash-flow-based matching of loans and the bonds used to fund the loans. Historically mortgage banks have not been allowed to retain any market or prepayment risk and have therefore only held credit risk. This regulatory restriction, the so-called "balance-principle," essentially required mortgage banks to fund their lending activities by issuing mortgage bonds with cash flows that fully match those of the underlying mortgage loans until maturity on a loan-by-loan basis.

In line with the balance-principle, the one-year ARMs are funded by issuance of one-year noncallable bullet bonds. The interest period on these bonds exactly matches the interest period of one year for the homeowner and thereby creating a natural interest-rate hedge for the mortgage bank. For each interest period of one year, the cash flow of the loans and the bonds issued to fund them match, and the mortgage bank is therefore fully hedged regarding interest rate, currency, and prepayment risk. In addition, as the borrower pays the mortgage bank's cost-of-funds plus a margin, the mortgage bank is also hedged against rising funding spreads. However, the mortgage bank is exposed to the risk of a complete freeze in the funding markets when the issuance of new bonds to roll over the funding of maturing bonds is impossible at any price.

In addition, the mortgage banks have continued to issue identical callable (covered) bonds to fund their longer-term mortgage lending. Thus, a 30-year fixed-rate callable mortgage loan is funded by a cash-flow matching 30-year fixed-rate callable bond. For example, 30-year fixed rate mortgages with a coupon of 4 percent are funded by each bank's current issue of the 4 percent fixed-rate callable covered bond maturing October 2041. The bonds of the three largest issuers all trade at the same price in the bond market on a cheapest-to-deliver basis. This is referred to as the unity market for Danish covered bonds. See Frankel et al. (2004) for an in-depth description of the Danish market for callable fixed-rate mortgage bonds.

A Danish mortgagor can—in addition to making penalty-free prepayment—buy back her loan by purchasing corresponding bonds in the secondary market and delivering them to the mortgage bank. Thus, borrowers may decide to buy back loans and refinance at a higher coupon, thereby reducing the size of the loan, when interest rates rise. The 30-year mortgage loan contract also does not have a due-on-sale clause, which would require the mortgage to be repaid in the event of a house sale. Thus, demographic events that involve house sales do not necessarily generate prepayments as a mortgagor has the right to buy back the loan or assign the existing loan to the new owner. This means that borrowers are never obliged to prepay when the current mortgage interest rate is above the mortgage contracted rate. The presence of this buyback option means that forecasters of prepayment rates for Danish mortgages need not concern themselves with demographic sources of prepayment. Second, the buyback possibility is likely to smooth out prepayments over time. Buyback opportunities have occurred only very infrequently in recent years as interest rates have mainly moved downwards. Borrowers have, however, displayed a keen awareness of this possibility, and have used it when rates have increased. This buyback option should be a stabilizing factor in the Danish callable bond market. Normally there are very few buyers of fixed-income product in a market environment with rising interest rates.

Although the funding model used by the mortgage banks has not changed fundamentally, there have been some interesting new developments in response to regulatory changes that allowed mortgages to be funded using covered bonds. In 2007 the Danish covered bond legislation was amended to incorporate the latest changes in the European Union's Capital Requirement Directive (CRD). The amendments introduced a new definition of covered bonds, effective from January 1, 2008. The most important change was a requirement for covered-bond issuers to perform regular validation of LTV ratios for the mortgage loans backing the issued covered bonds. If the statutory maximum LTV ratios of 80 percent for residential mortgage loans and 60 percent for commercial mortgage loans are breached, the issuers are obliged to either add extra eligible collateral to the cover pool or substitute the mortgage loan in breach of the LTV requirement with another mortgage.

Danish mortgage banks are not allowed to remove mortgages from the cover pool as long as the loans are still performing according to the loan contract. Hence the issuers of covered bonds must add extra collateral to comply with the regulation. The collateral will typically take the form of either own capital (equity), government, or covered bonds. The amount of own capital is unlikely to be sufficient to withstand a substantial fall in house prices. In such a scenario the issuer will therefore fund the required extra collateral via borrowing. Reflecting this, the 2007 legislation introduced a new type of bond called a Junior Covered Bond. This bond is a secured claim on the cover pool. It ranks second to the covered bonds in case of the issuer's insolvency, but senior to any other claims including unsecured debt. In early 2010 the Danish central bank (Danmarks Nationalbank) decided to accept the mortgage banks' junior covered bonds as eligible collateral, as these bonds are considered an integral part of the new covered bond environment.[1]

Issuance of Junior Covered Bonds should ensure that covered bond investors will not be exposed to the risk that LTVs exceed their statutory 80 percent (and 60 percent) limits if house prices decline. A potential downside of the requirement to add extra collateral is that this may introduce liquidity risk for lenders who are now required to fund extra collateral and hence issue more debt when housing markets, balance sheets, and profits are weak. Ultimately, an issuer may find it difficult to pay the higher interest on new issues of Junior Covered Bonds, as interest payments are likely to be high exactly when the issuer is in financial difficulties.

THE FINANCIAL CRISIS AND DANISH MORTGAGE BOND MARKETS

The Danish mortgage bond market was visibly affected by the financial crisis, with yields on both short- and long-term bonds increasing considerably in September

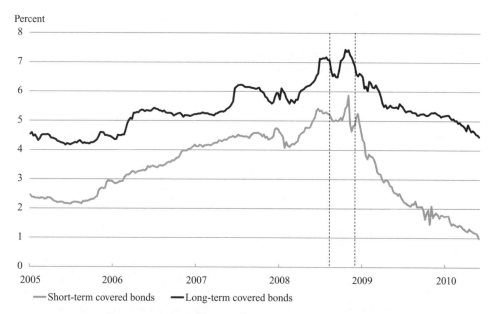

Exhibit 3.1 Yields on Danish Covered Bonds

Notes: Weekly observations. The yields on covered bonds are average yields to maturity, the short-term yield being based on one- to two-year noncallable covered bonds, the long-term yield on 30-year callable covered bonds, cf. the Association of Danish Mortgage Banks.
Source: Association of Danish Mortgage Banks.

and October 2008 (Exhibit 3.1). At the same time, the spread to swap rates widened (Exhibit 3.2). These price developments clearly suggest a reduction in liquidity in the covered bond market during the crisis.

The Danish covered bond market's resilience to refinancing risk of short-dated bonds funding ARMs was tested after the collapse of Lehman Brothers in September 2008. The Danish mortgage banks had to execute the annual refinancing of one-year bullet bonds, funding the stock of ARMs with a one-year interest period during two weeks in early December. The aggregated amount was DKK 600 billion or approximately €80 billion. Spreads widened but the refinancing was done at a rate of 5.25 percent in a period when the majority of covered bond markets in Europe were effectively closed for new issuance.

Similar to policy makers in other countries, the Danish government had to introduce measures to stabilize the banking sector as well as restore confidence among market participants at very short notice in October 2008. The combination of these measures was immediately reflected in the sharp yield (Exhibit 3.1) and spread (Exhibit 3.2) declines for covered bonds.

The first policy measure adopted by the Danish parliament in October 2008, the Act on Financial Stability, offered government guarantees of all liabilities of Danish banks in return for a fee or insurance premium. While the majority of the banks decided to be covered by the act, the mortgage banks opted not to be included in the guarantee scheme, as they were able to continue funding new loans by issuing long-term mortgage bonds. The government guarantee under the Act on Financial Stability expired on September 30, 2010. To ensure continued longer-term funding

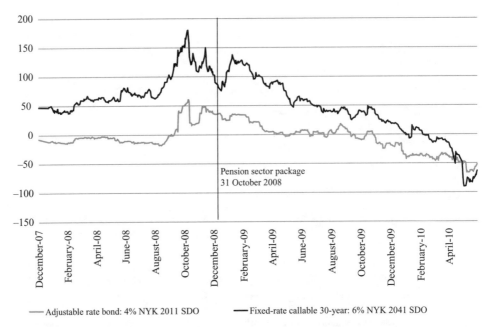

——Adjustable rate bond: 4% NYK 2011 SDO   ——Fixed-rate callable 30-year: 6% NYK 2041 SDO

Exhibit 3.2 Spread between Bond Yields and Swap Rates, Percentage Points

Notes: For the fixed-rate callable bond, the spread is the option-adjusted spread. That is, the yield spread between the bond and the swap rate minus the estimated spread value of the prepayment option embedded in the callable bond. This spread can be used to compare the yield a buy-and-hold investor would receive in addition to the swap rate with the same maturity, net of the cost of insuring against the embedded option.

Source: Nykredit.

for the banks, a second policy measure (Bank Rescue Package II) was introduced in January 2009. The package allows banks and mortgage banks to issue longer-term funding in the form of senior debt or junior covered bonds with a government guarantee—for a fee.

Third, similar to other countries the Danish FSA, from October 2008 temporarily allowed pension funds to use the mortgage bond term structure to calculate the market value of the liabilities, bringing the valuation of the liabilities more in line with the valuation of the assets. Prior to this change, the present value (market value) of the pension funds liabilities was priced using the government bond term structure. Danish pension funds are important investors in Danish mortgage bonds. This measure reflected that a crucial funding source for the mortgage banks was threatened by the substantial widening of the yield spreads between government and mortgage bonds during the crisis period.

Finally, at the beginning of November 2008, it was announced that the Social Pension Fund (SPF), which is managed by the Danish central bank on behalf of the government, would invest around €3 billion in short-term covered bonds in the December 2008 auctions with the aim of covering the central-government interest-rate risk related to the financing of subsidized housing.

This relatively small measure was officially attributed to the government's interest-rate risk management. It was, however, widely interpreted by the market participants as a signal that the government was ready to support the market in case of further turmoil. Ultimately, the SPF invested around €3.6 billion in short-term covered bonds at the auctions in December 2008 and around €6 billion the following year (Danmarks Nationalbank 2009, 2010).

Bond Market Liquidity

Recent work on the liquidity of mortgage and government bond markets in Denmark before, during and after the 2008 financial crisis suggests that even though trading continued during the crisis, both markets experienced substantial declines in liquidity and significantly increased liquidity risk (Buchholst et al. 2010). The study uses a variety of liquidity measures including the price impact of trade measure suggested in Amihud (2002) which measures the percentage change in price per traded unit, to adjust for the possibility that large trades may have a higher price impact than small trades.

In Exhibits 3.3 and 3.4, which are taken from Buchholst et al. (2010), one can clearly see that liquidity declined significantly during the crisis period in the mortgage bond markets—both for short- and long-term bonds. For short-term covered bonds the price impact of trade approximately doubled during the crisis compared to the period before. For long-term covered bonds the price impact of trade more than tripled during the crisis. However, the impact was of similar size as in the case of government bonds. Thus, the analysis seems to confirm that Danish

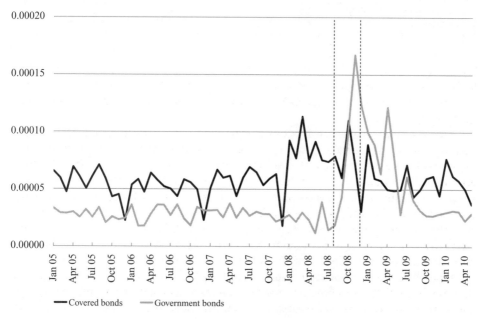

Exhibit 3.3 Price Impact of Trade in Percent, Short-Term Bonds

Notes: Only bonds with an outstanding nominal amount of at least €1 billion and trades of at least DKK 10 million have been included.

Sources: Nasdaq OMX, Danish FSA and Danmarks Nationalbank.

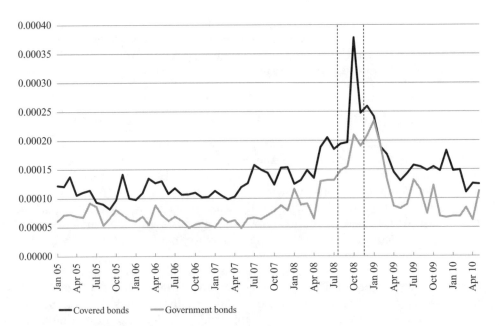

Exhibit 3.4   Price Impact of Trade in Percent, Long-Term Bonds

Note: Only bonds with an outstanding nominal amount of at least €1 billion and trades of at least DKK 10 million have been included.

Sources: Nasdaq OMX, Danish FSA, and Danmarks Nationalbank.

benchmark mortgage bonds are almost as liquid as government bonds even in times of severe stress.

Mortgage Bonds as Repo Collateral

In Denmark the bulk of assets used as collateral for central bank repo-funding are mortgage bonds. This is in line with the European Central Bank and other EU central banks, which accept certain types of covered bonds as eligible collateral. Due to the relative size of the mortgage-bond market, banks held large amounts of mortgage bonds prior to the crisis as part of their trading portfolio (Exhibit 3.5). Thus, although the Danish central bank, like other central banks, established temporary lending facilities during the crisis, most banks had sufficient eligible collateral to use for central bank funding.

The significant use of mortgage bonds as collateral for central bank funding illustrates the importance of the mortgage market in Denmark and the importance of the central bank's collateral rules for the market (Exhibit 3.6). As in most other countries hit by the crisis, the Danish money market moved to the balance sheet of the central bank, which acted as a de facto central counterparty for the money market from the fall of 2008 through early 2009.

The central bank's collateral rules moderated the impact of the financial crisis on the bond prices and hence the borrowing costs for households. The importance of the banks' ability to fund their mortgage lending during market stress periods with the central bank is illustrated by the significant increase in the amounts of

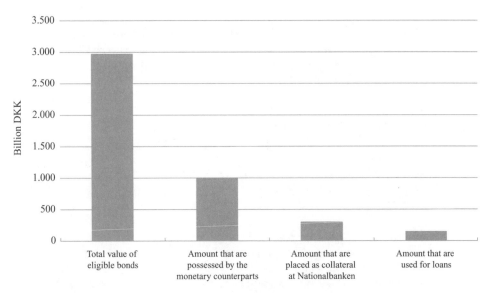

Exhibit 3.5 Collateral Eligible for Central-Bank Repo Funding
Source: Danmarks Nationalbank.

covered bonds used as collateral. Furthermore, the Danish central bank accepts that issuers pose their own issued mortgage bonds as collateral. This is also the case in other central banks, including the European Central Bank. The reason is that these bonds are UCITS $(22.4)^2$ bonds, where the owner of the bonds has a privileged status. This was a stabilizing factor during the large annual end-of-year refinancing auctions for the ARMs.

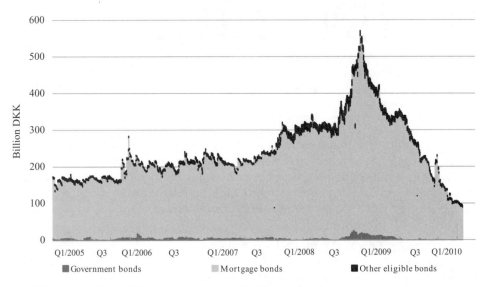

Exhibit 3.6 Collateral Held by the Danmarks Nationalbank
Source: Danmarks Nationalbank.

The Danish population of some 5.5 million people inhabit 2.53 million dwellings. The average household has declined from 2.5 persons in 1981 to 2.1 persons in 2009, and the average size of a dwelling has increased from 106.4 sqm to 111.7 sqm. The number of square metres per resident averaged 52.1 in 2009. The reason for the increase in space per resident is twofold: Households have become smaller and dwellings have become larger.

Number of dwellings at end-2009

Type of dwelling	Number (1,000)	Distribution
Owner-occupied	1,308	52%
Housing cooperatives	194	8%
Non-profit housing	507	20%
Other rental property	520	20%
Total	2,529	

Housing construction peaked in 2006

Economic growth and house price inflation pushed up the number of housing starts significantly from 2001 to 2006 when they peaked at 34,000. Detached houses accounted for the main part of the upturn. Housing construction has tumbled since the crisis in the housing market started in 2006.

New Housing Starts

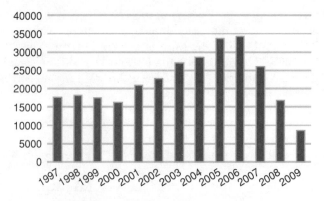

Exhibit 3.7   The Danish Housing Market
Source: Statistics Denmark.

The significant increase in the use of covered bonds as collateral with the central bank might also reflect adverse selection for collateral whereby high-quality collateral (government bonds) is used in the private repo market whereas mortgage bonds are posted as collateral for central bank funding. However, at the peak of the crisis the private repo market was not functioning.

HOUSING MARKET

Exhibit 3.7 describes the main characteristics of the Danish housing stock.

Similar to most developed economies, Denmark experienced significant house-price inflation from 2004 to 2007 (Exhibit 3.7). With the benefit of hindsight it seems

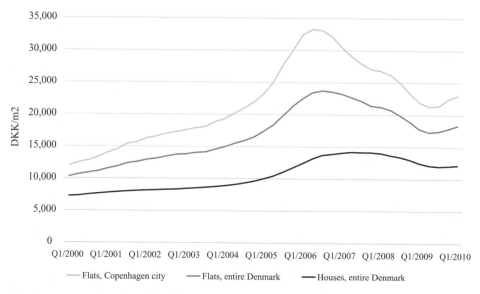

Exhibit 3.8   House and Flat Prices
Note: DKK per square meter.
Source: Association of Danish Mortgage Banks.

clear that prices for flats in particular and houses to a lesser degree experienced a bubble, with the largest metropolitan areas being most clearly affected. From mid-2007 until mid-2009, however, house and flat prices dropped by around 20 percent on a national level and by 30 percent in the most affected areas. The advent of house price depreciation was accompanied by a significant slowdown in turnover of real estate as homeowners were slow to adjust ask prices to a new and more negative sentiment of potential home buyers. This led to a rise in the stock of properties for sale and reinforced the shift from a "seller's market" to a (reluctant) "buyer's market."

Not surprisingly, the significant house price inflation from 2004–2007 over-shadowed increases in households' disposal income. This led the affordability index to rise as households used a significantly higher portion of disposable in-come to pay for housing (Exhibit 3.8). At the peak in 2007, the affordability index was around 40 percent higher than in the late 1990s and almost 20 percent higher than at the beginning of 2004. After the crisis, it has returned to the level seen in the late 1990s.

The Housing Affordability Index in Exhibit 3.9 measures total housing costs including housing finance relative to income after tax. The calculation is based on an average family consisting of two adults and two children living in an average house that is 144 square meters. It is assumed that the house is acquired on the calculation day at the national average house price per square meter and that 80 percent of the purchase price is financed by a 30-year fixed-rate mortgage loan and the remaining 20 percent by a bank loan.

There has been a limited increase in arrears in the housing market (Exhibit 3.7). This is somewhat surprising as Danish house prices have fallen significantly,

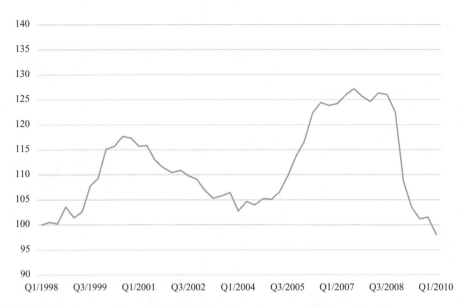

Exhibit 3.9 Average House Affordability Index, January 1, 1998 = 100
Source: Association of Danish Mortgage Banks.

resulting in a much higher number of borrowers with a loan-to-value ratio of
above 100 percent. In addition, there has been a significant and rapid increase in
unemployment.

The limited increase in the number of arrears, despite the very difficult economic environment, clearly suggests that there are several stabilizing factors that
provide important support for Danish housing and mortgage markets. No doubt,

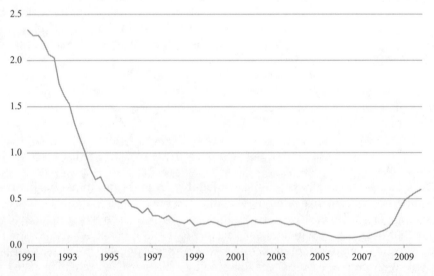

Exhibit 3.10 Owner-Occupied Dwelling in Arrears for More Than 75 Days, Percent of
Total Stock
Source: Association of Danish Mortgage Banks.

the emergency policy measures taken by both the central bank and the government helped ensure that market rates stayed low in December 2008/January 2009. These initiatives, the high fraction of ARMs and the market based funding allowed borrowers to benefit quickly from lower interest rates. Second, the mortgage system does not provide room for "strategic defaults" by borrowers with a LTV above 100 percent. Third, Denmark has a well-developed unemployment benefit system as well as a comprehensive welfare state system that likely helps lower the impact of higher unemployment on mortgage default rates. Finally, the strict and easy way to enforce foreclosure rules in the Danish mortgage market provides strong ex-ante initiatives for borrowers to avoid taking out loans they cannot service.

The special-purpose vehicle nature of the mortgage banks with matching cash flows from assets and liabilities has continued to facilitate a kind of co-op system where the mortgagors in the different mortgage banks are offered the same basic products at more or less the same terms. Thus, any price differences on loans between mortgage banks will lead to a stop of business for the mortgage bank with a higher price (interest) on loans. This further underlines the importance of the market. If a mortgage bank, during the pre-crisis housing boom took a higher credit risk compared to the other mortgage banks, for example, this could result in a lower rating than its competitors. The lower rating will lead to lower prices/higher interest rates on the bonds issued by the lower-rated mortgage bank. Due to the strict balance principle, this would make the borrowers' loans more expensive than those of borrowers in the other mortgage banks. The result could be a "slow-motion run" on the mortgage bank where the "good" customers easily could obtain a similar loan at a lower price at the competitors. The "bad" (high credit risk) customers would be forced to stay in the mortgage bank, as no other mortgage banks would be willing to accept them as customers. This could start a vicious circle where the credit risk of the mortgage bank would continue to increase as more and more of the low-credit-risk customers leave the bank.

It is too early to draw any firm conclusions on whether any of the Danish mortgage banks is in such a situation. However, the Danish mortgage banks lowered their credit standards during the housing boom before the crisis and took large write-downs in the aftermath of the crisis, especially on loans to commercial properties.

CONCLUSION

Denmark has a highly sophisticated housing finance market. The Danish market has two main types of mortgage contracts. The Danish mortgage market has undergone a significant transformation over the past 5 to 10 years. First, retail mortgages have increasingly become floating-rate as households have increasingly been taking one-year floating rate loans. This has been facilitated partly by low stable short-term interest rates and regulatory changes. Until five years ago, the Danish mortgage market was dominated by one standard contract – long-term (up to 30 years) loans at a fixed rate with an option to make penalty-free prepayments (Frankel et al. 2004).

As discussed above, during the recent financial crisis, the Danish mortgage system, despite significant changes, still has a structure that, with a little help from its friends, was able to continue to function. Thus, the institutional characteristics of the system should be of interest to other policy makers, borrowers, and investors outside Denmark.

Finally, there is no subprime market in Denmark. This reflects a combination of strong mortgage legislation, a relatively equal income distribution and the provision of good-quality housing for the poorest part of the population by the welfare state. In addition, the funding approach used by the mortgage banks mean that they cannot price discriminate based on the credit risk of the borrowers. Thus, the co-op nature of the Danish mortgage banking system means that "subprime" borrowers cannot obtain a mortgage loan, but to a large extent would instead be living in public-owned apartments.

NOTES

1. Junior Covered Bonds denominated in euro are also eligible as collateral with the ECB classified as senior unsecured debt.
2. Directive on Undertakings for Collective Investments in Transferable Securities (UCITS). Article 22(4) of this Directive defines the minimum requirements that provide the basis for privileged treatment of covered bonds in different areas of European financial market regulation.

REFERENCES

Amihud, Y. (2002). "Illiquidity and Stock Returns: Cross-Section and Time-Series Effects." *Journal of Financial Markets* 5:1, pp. 31–56.

Buchholst, Birgitte V., J. Gyntelberg, and T. Sangill. 2010. "Liquidity of Danish Government and Covered Bonds—Before, during, and after the Financial Crisis—Preliminary Findings." Danmarks Nationalbank, Working paper 2010-70.

Danmarks Nationalbank. 2008. "Recent Economic and Monetary Trends." *Monetary Review,* 4th Quarter.

Danmarks Nationalbank. 2009. *Danish Government Borrowing and Debt 2008.*

Danmarks Nationalbank. 2010. *Danish Government Borrowing and Debt 2009.*

Fender, I., and J. Gyntelberg. 2008 (December). "Overview: Global Financial Crisis Spurs Unprecedented Policy Actions." *Bank for International Settlements Quarterly Review,* pp. 21–24.

Frankel, A., J. Gyntelberg, K. Kjeldsen, and M. Persson. 2004 (March). "The Danish Mortgage Market." *Bank for International Settlements Quarterly Review,* pp. 95–109.

ABOUT THE AUTHORS

JACOB GYNTELBERG holds a PhD in Economics and is currently working as a Senior Economist at the Bank for International Settlements (BIS) in the Monetary and Economic Department. He has been working for many years on financial market issues, including the Danish housing finance system. Before joining the BIS he worked for the Danish Central Bank and for Nykredit, one of the largest mortgage banks in Denmark.

KRISTIAN KJELDSEN holds a PhD in Finance and is head of Payments Systems at Danmarks Nationalbank. He has written several articles on the Danish as well as other mortgage systems and has been an advisor on the implementation of a Danish-style mortgage system in Mexico. Before joining Danmarks Nationalbank he worked for the European Investment Bank, the long-term financing institution of the European Union.

MORTEN NIELSEN is First Vice President in Nykredit's Group Treasury responsible for investor relations, funding research and development. He holds a Master's degree in Economics from the University of Copenhagen. Morten worked with the Danish Association of Mortgage Banks and other parties on the new Danish Covered Bond legislation that came into force in July 2007. In his previous work Morten has been involved in developing new mortgage products, analyzing covered bond markets and creating the framework for Nykredit's structured covered bonds. Nykredit is Denmark's largest mortgage bank and the largest issuer of mortgage covered bonds in Europe.

MATTIAS PERSSON is Director and Head of the Financial Stability Department at Sveriges Riksbank. He has been with the central bank for nine years and he holds a PhD in Economics. Mattias is a member of the Committee of the Global Financial System and the Committee of Payment and Settlement Systems at the Bank for International Settlements (BIS).

CHAPTER 4

Prolonged Crisis

Housing in Germany and Berlin

THIES LINDENTHAL
Maastricht University

PIET EICHHOLTZ
Maastricht University

Germany's housing market is an outlier in two aspects. Home ownership is low, while Germany is among the wealthiest countries in Europe and the world; and real house prices have fallen for most of the past 15 years, especially in the East. The current global crisis seems not to have affected the German market much, as the fall in German real house prices has not accelerated, but merely continues. This chapter provides an overview of the institutions and fundamentals underlying Germany's housing market, and provides new information on price behavior. The chapter gives a special focus on one of Germany's most interesting regional housing markets: Berlin. German unification and the fall of the Berlin Wall did not lead to a sustained rise in house prices, but rather to a long-extended bust that seems to have bottomed out only in recent years.

INTRODUCTION

The global housing market crisis that started in 2007 largely left Germany untouched, and that also holds for the housing market boom that preceded it. Germany's housing market follows its own path: House prices in Europe's largest economy seem to move countercyclical to those of its neighbors. They have been stalling and gradually falling for most of the last decade and a half. In this respect, Germany's role of European outlier seems to match closely with that of Japan's role as the Asian outlier.

Germany's distinct dynamic is caused by a set of institutional issues and by Germany's specific housing market fundamentals. In addition, the unique historic event of Germany's unification in 1990 induced a property boom in the early 1990s followed by a long wane of home values ever since. This cycle is probably one of the least documented housing booms and busts in the literature, partly for lack of accurate data concerning housing transaction prices that would be needed for an accurate picture of market developments.

Germany's position as a housing market outsider is underlined by another aspect: a very low homeownership rate. The average home ownership rate among the 17 richest European countries is approximately 64 percent, while Germany's is only 43.2 percent (EMF 2009a). Only Switzerland has lower home owner-occupation. Again, this is quite surprising given Germany's economic success. So in two of the main outcomes of housing policy, prices and home ownership, Germany stands out.

This research sheds light on the long-run implications of housing crises—what will happen to markets and economies if the recent global price falls turn out to be long-lasting, and housing markets do not revert back to growth? The main lessons are threefold.

First, housing markets can remain insular relative to global developments, even in economies with open borders and free movement of capital. Germany's house prices were rising in the early nineties, when many other European countries experienced housing market crises; they were stalling and falling in the late nineties and in the years after 2000; and they held steady in the recent global crisis. This chapter suggests that house prices are far less driven by the global forces of finance, or even by inflation, than by a combination of (local) economic fundamentals, the institutional framework surrounding the housing market, and government policy.

Second, long-lasting, but gradual, falls in real house prices can go together with an otherwise healthy economy. While the German economy has had its problems, it has by no means fallen into an extended recession that could be blamed on a fall in housing asset values. The German experience may take away some of the generally held fear that falling house prices are necessarily bad (Claessens, Kose, and Terrones 2008).

Third, the chapter provides some evidence for the positive association between loss of human capital and falling house prices, as predicted by Glaeser and Gyourko (2005). In Berlin, where house prices have halved in real terms since 1994 after 12 consecutive years of nominal and real price decline, well-educated residents have been partially replaced by low-educated immigrants (Destatis 2010a).

The remainder of this chapter first describes and discusses the characteristics of the market for residential real estate that (in their combination) make the German case special. The focus is on market transparency and structure, regulation, taxation and subsidies, and the mortgage system. This part is descriptive and draws from existing research and sources.

The second part of the chapter puts more perspective on the two market outcomes in which Germany stand out: private home ownership and recent price behavior. The paper provides some insights regarding the low home-ownership levels seen in Germany, and discusses how previous policy changes may have prevented Germany from entering in the leverage–house price spiral that has characterized many other housing markets.

The third part of the paper investigates the dynamics of this prolonged and substantial decline for the one German city for which housing transaction data is available: Berlin. We have access to a dataset covering all residential real estate transactions in Berlin, spanning the period from 1978 through 2007. This is the same dataset as the one used by Clapp, Lindenthal, and Eichholtz (2011), who test a hedonic regression model with real option components. The level of detail of the data allows not only for the estimation of a hedonic price index but also enables us to focus on the dynamics of market segments and neighborhoods within an MSA in decline.

MARKET INSTITUTIONS AND FUNDAMENTALS

Market Transparency

Despite the sheer size and the economic importance of the market, German residential real estate prices are still relatively unchartered territory. In the last few years, several competing home prices indexes have emerged, but none reaches the quality and reputation of foreign equivalents like the Case-Shiller index in the United States, and they cover relatively short time periods.

Creating a home price index for Germany is a delicate matter as data on individual transactions is difficult to obtain. The law considers all details related to a transaction as private information, so these are not published. Representative samples that allow for the estimation of any kind of transaction-based index are therefore simply not available for academic research on a national level.

On the local level, however, transaction data do exist: Every transaction of land or buildings needs to be certified by a notary, who sends the title deed to the local land register. A copy of each contract is forwarded to local "committees for land price valuation" (*Gutachterausschuss für Grundstückswerte*). These independent expert panels maintain transaction databases and disseminate aggregated information on price trends for land and buildings for individual cities or counties. In addition, they offer plot-specific appraisals for the government, the mortgage industry, and private parties. Third parties are not granted access to these databases. The committees are ruled by state laws, which vary slightly regarding the degree of privacy protection across Germany.

So these privacy rules, rather than a lack of data, hamper the development of good, constant, quality house-price indexes. Nevertheless, a variety of indexes exist, but they suffer from a number of problems: The constant quality indexes that do exist have a very short history, and the indexes that have longer histories are just based on average transaction prices, and are therefore not constant quality. We discuss each of these indexes below. Exhibit 4.1 provides background information regarding these indexes.

The Federal Statistical Office of Germany (Destatis) started to compile a national sample based on this local transaction data and estimated a hedonic home price index starting in 2000 (Behrmann and Kathe 2004). Destatis distinguishes between three market segments: newly built homes, existing homes, and turnkey homes. The index is based on a representative sample, but the index numbers are published with a substantial time lag. At the time of writing of this study, the most recent numbers were for 2008, so this index does not really provide timely market information. Regional sub-indexes are not provided (Destatis 2010b).

The association of German Pfandbrief Banks (VDP) aggregates transaction information collected by 20 of its member banks to a national sample and provides hedonic indexes for apartments and for single-family homes. The VDP indexes are updated on a quarterly basis and reach back to the year 2003. The core hedonics are comparable to Destatis, while information on the year of construction, and amenities are added. VDP does not differentiate between new housing stock and

Exhibit 4.1 Hedonic House Price Indexes for Germany

Index Provider	Data Source	Weaknesses	Start Year/ Frequency	Market Segments Covered
Federal Statistical Office of Germany (www.destatis.de)	Gutachteraus schüsse für Grundstückswerte	Index numbers published infrequently (up to two years lag) No regional sub-indexes	2000 quarterly	Turnkey buildings New (semi-) detached Existing (semi-) detached
Association of German Pfandbrief Banks (www.hypverband.de)	Transaction information of member banks	Representativeness not clear No regional sub-indexes No distinction new and existing homes	2003 quarterly	New and existing (semi-) detached homes Apartments
Hypoport (www.hypoport.de)	Transaction information from mortgage financing transaction database Europace.	Representativeness not clear No regional sub-indexes	2005 monthly	New (semi-) detached Existing (semi-) detached Apartments

Sources: Behrmann and Kathe (2004); VDP (2010a); Hypoport (2010).

existing homes, which have very different price behavior. Moreover, it is not exactly clear how representative the index sample is, and regional sub-indexes are not available.

Hypoport AG, a private company, offers a third hedonic house price index based on transaction information processed in its Europace platform. Europace is an independent marketplace for mortgage financing transactions, which has a market share of 10 percent in Germany. Hypoport offers an overall market index and information about new homes, existing homes, and apartments. The indexes are updated every month and start in 2005. The core hedonic characteristics used in the index estimation are similar to the competitors (Hypoport 2010). The representativeness of this index is doubtful, given Europace's market share. Moreover, regional sub-indexes are not available.

While these three hedonic indexes do control for quality characteristics of sold properties, they lack regional sub-indexes. Additionally, they do not allow for long-run price comparisons since they cover only 5 to 10 years. Traditional indexes based on averages or median values fill this gap. The DEIX German home price index (average values), for instance, reaches back to 1989 for West Germany and to 1995 for East Germany (Gewos 2008). The commercial data provider BulwienGesa offers regional price information for German cities and counties, which are also based on average transaction values (BulwienGesa 2010).

In short, accurate and timely housing market price information is currently not available in Germany, despite the fact that adequate data on all transactions are recorded. The available indexes show marked differences in their movements in time, so it is not very clear where German house prices are going at any moment in time.

This lack of transparency in housing markets may partially be explained by the fact that two of the major stakeholders in the housing market do not demand that more detailed information be published: Both property taxes and mortgage risks are not as tightly linked to home values as they are in other countries, like the United States.

Property Taxes and Transaction Costs

German municipalities levy a property tax of 0.26 to 0.35 percent of a building's assessed value (or *Einheitswert* in German) multiplied with a municipality-specific factor (Federal Ministry of Justice 2010a). In 2009, the total collected property tax added up to €10.6 billion, which constituted 24 percent of all local authorities' tax revenues (before any financial transfers from the federal government or the states). The economically weaker communities in the East and North particularly depend on this source of income. For all eastern states (Mecklenburg-Vorpommern, Brandenburg, Saxony-Anhalt, Thuringia, Saxony, and Berlin) the ratio is above the national index, while in the prosperous southern states of Hesse, Bavaria, and Baden-Württemberg, municipalities fund themselves to a greater extent through trade taxes. Exhibit 4.2 shows the property tax revenues for German municipalities from 1999 through 2009 compared to other tax income. Every year, property taxes exceeded the volume of the previous years (Destatis 2010c). Rising property values, however, do not drive this increase. In the original tax design, the underlying property values should be reassessed every six years to reflect changes in the buildings' values. However, the last time that all buildings' values were assessed

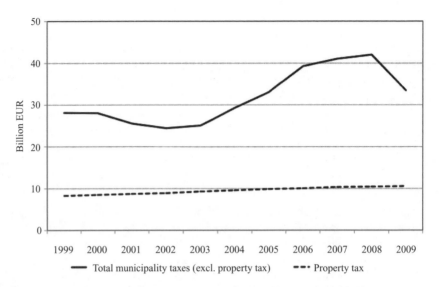

Exhibit 4.2   Tax Revenue Sources for German Municipalities, 1999–2009
Source: Destatis (2010c).

was in 1964 in West Germany and 1935 in East Germany. As a result, base values are now as low as 10 percent of current market values.

Municipalities can adjust their multiplier and increase property taxes independently. Theoretically, this gives them the possibility to cash in on value changes at least on an aggregate level, disregarding changes in the value of individual buildings or neighborhoods. In reality, however, seizing part of the home equity for financing communal budgets is financing of the last resort. Munich, for instance, experienced a robust increase in housing wealth, but can afford to forgo property tax income. Poorer Berlin cannot tap other sources of income and taxes housing wealth more aggressively.[1]

The German states charge a transaction tax on all sales, which is 3.5 percent of the sales price in the majority of states (Federal Ministry of Justice 2010b), and 4.5 percent in Berlin, Hamburg, and Saxony-Anhalt. These percentages put Germany in the midfield of European tax regimes. Total revenues from this tax are volatile, as they depend on both market prices and the liquidity of the market. In 2009, only €4.87 billion was collected, compared to €6.95 billion in 2007 (Destatis 2010c).

Imputed rent is not taxed as personal income since 1986, when it was abolished together with the mortgage interest rate deductibility. Capital gains for residential property are tax-exempt in cases where the dwelling had been lived in by the seller for at least 10 years. Inheritance tax on estates is smaller than on financial assets, making it more tax-efficient to pass on housing wealth instead of financial wealth.

The European Mortgage Federation estimated the costs of buying a typical German home to be to be 4.5 percent of the home's value in 2004 (assuming a value of €277,000, a loan to value ratio of 71 percent, and a mortgage maturity of 26 years). The costs for notaries and solicitors are below 1 percent, while mortgage-related fees for solicitors and notaries, and mortgage registration costs are about 0.25 percent, both relatively low compared to other European countries (EMF 2006).

Primary Mortgage Markets

Low, Sebag-Monteflore, and Dübel (2003) assess a mortgage market's complete-ness based on four main criteria. First, the range of products is described along both interest rate structures and repayment structures. A high index number corresponds with a large variety of products offered to consumers. Second, the types of borrowers eligible for a mortgage and the kind of purposes allowed for a mortgage are summarized. A low number refers to very strict loan requirements, while high numbers represent more loose credit policies. The third and fourth dimension concern the ease of distribution and the availability of information and advice (Low, Sebag-Monteflore, and Dübel 2003). Exhibit 4.3 presents the components of the mortgage-market completeness measures for Germany and selected European countries.

Along these dimensions, Germany is ranging in a conservative midfield with regard to the number of mortgage products offered, lagging Denmark, The Nether-lands, the United Kingdom, and France. German borrowers can choose from both adjustable rate (ARM) and fixed rate (FRM) mortgages. Referenced ARMs and discounted rates in the first years are not readily offered. Capped ARMs are quite common (Low, Sebag-Monteflore, and Dübel 2003).

The interest rate can be fixed for periods below a year (15 percent of all FRMs) up to more than ten years (30 percent of FRMs), while 5 to 10 years is the most popular fixation period (38 percent). Seventeen percent of FRMs are open for renegotiation after one to five years (Bundesbank 2009).

For repayment, borrowers can choose from amortizing or interest-only mort-gages. More flexible repayment structures are not common. Prepayment involves a penalty when rates have fallen, so prepaying to refinance is not beneficial.

Exhibit 4.3 Mercer Oliver Wyman Index on Completeness of Mortgage Markets, 2003

Country	Product	Borrower Type and Purpose	Distribution	Information and Advice	Completeness Index
Denmark	85%	62%	71%	80%	75%
France	81%	67%	42%	70%	72%
Germany	62%	48%	54%	100%	58%
Italy	65%	51%	42%	50%	57%
Netherlands	81%	73%	88%	80%	79%
Portugal	35%	58%	71%	40%	47%
Spain	58%	67%	88%	90%	66%
United Kingdom	77%	92%	100%	100%	86%
Weighting	50%	35%	10%	5%	100%

Note: Low, Sebag-Monteflore, and Dübel (2003) assess market completeness based on four main criteria. First, the range of products is described along both interest rate structures and repayment structures. A high index number corresponds with a large variety of products that a consumer can choose from. Second, the types of borrowers eligible for a mortgage and the kind of purposes allowed for a mortgage are summarized. A low number refers to very strict markets; high numbers represent more accessible markets. The third and fourth dimension concern the ease of distribution (how easy is it to access the mortgage product) and the availability of information and advice.

German mortgage originators are the most conservative lenders in the set of countries ranked by Low, Sebag-Monteflore, and Dübel. While credit is readily available to young households, households aged 50 and older have only limited access to mortgages. Previous bankruptcy of the applicant or other credit impairments will lead to rejection by lenders, not to a mortgage with a higher default risk premium. The applicant must prove sufficient income to serve the debt. Being self-employed is generally not a reason for rejection, on condition that income is sufficient. Second mortgages are readily available, however, mortgage supply for the purpose of overseas vacation homes, equity release, or shared ownership is limited (Low, Sebag-Monteflore, and Dübel 2003).

More than 80 percent of all new mortgages are sold in branches of retail banks, leaving only marginal roles for independent advisors or direct marketing through phone or mail. Information on mortgage products and rates is available and of high accuracy, comparable to, for example, the U.K. market. Mortgage rates are actively published and advertized by lenders. The general media and specialized news providers and web sites offer mortgage comparisons and independent advice (Low, Sebag-Monteflore, and Dübel 2003).

Mortgage owners cannot simply walk away from their mortgages, as mortgages are full-recourse private debt collateralized by the home. Even when home equity turns negative, owners have to continue honoring the debt.[2] The main default risk a lender is facing is, therefore, not house price risk but the risk of the individual not being able to make her debt payments. Foreclosures occur only in the rare event of personal bankruptcies. Nevertheless, home values still determine the recovery rate in case of foreclosures, so lenders mitigate this risk by lending cautiously: the loan-to-value ratio for new mortgages is only 72 percent (EMF 2009b).

Exhibit 4.4 provides historic information of Germany's mortgage rate. This rate has gradually been falling from the mid-1990s onward and has now reached levels of about 3.5 percent (Bundesbank 2010a). A further remarkable issue is the level of the mortgage rate spread over German government bonds. This spread has varied between 1 and 2 percent, and now stands just under 2 percent. Given the fact that German consumers cannot prepay, and the mortgages are full recourse, this spread seems rather high. It is, for example, comparable to spreads in the United States, where consumers do have valuable prepayment and default options, and much higher than in the Netherlands, where these options are as worthless as in Germany, and where loan-to-value ratios are much higher, implying more risk for the lender.

On the aggregate, €1.15 trillion of residential mortgage debt was outstanding in 2008, which is the second-largest amount in Europe. Despite Germany's bigger economy, U.K. households borrowed even more: mortgage debt totaled €1.46 trillion in 2008. The mortgage debt to GDP ratio for Germany is 0.46, which is among the lowest levels in Europe. In 1998, this ratio stood at 0.52 (EMF 2009a). It is likely that the abolishment of tax deductibility for mortgage interest payments has played a role in this falling ratio, as it has taken away a strong incentive for high household mortgage debt. Sweden, another example of a country where mortgage tax deductibility was abolished, also did not see a rise in the mortgage debt to GDP ratio (International Monetary Fund 2008). In the Netherlands and Denmark, where tax deductibility is still present, this ratio has been rising fast over the decade

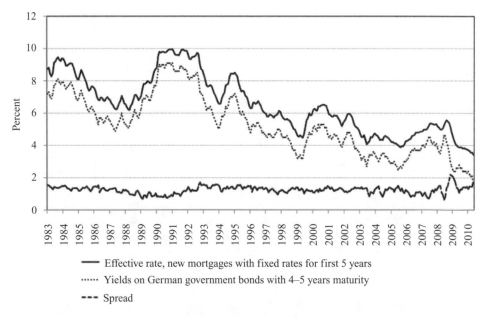

— Effective rate, new mortgages with fixed rates for first 5 years

······ Yields on German government bonds with 4–5 years maturity

--- Spread

Exhibit 4.4 Effective Mortgage Rate and Spread over Government Debt

Source: Bundesbank (2010a). For January 1983 to December 2002, we use the effective rate on newly issued mortgages with five-year fixed rates. This time series is not continued after 2002. From 2003 onwards, we therefore use the effective rate on new mortgages with a shorter maturity of one to five years. For the years 1983–1990, the rate is for West Germany only; from 1991 onward, East Germany is included as well.

preceding the financial crisis, and is now the highest in the world (International Monetary Fund 2008).

Secondary Mortgage Market

Mortgage originators mainly fund themselves by issuing so-called Pfandbriefe. A Pfandbrief is a covered bond, backed by a pool of assets containing mortgages, public debt, ships, or aircraft. The Pfandbrief legislation has its roots in eighteenth-century Prussia when credit for agricultural production was made more accessible by introducing the use of land as collateral, enhanced with government guarantees against default risk. Throughout the centuries, a combination of over-collateralization and government backing ensured liquidity and stability in the secondary mortgage market.

Pfandbrief banks are subject to strict regulation and supervision. They need a general banking license, core capital of at least €25 million, and a suitable risk management system in place. Pfandbrief banks can originate mortgages up to 90 percent of the independently estimated value of a building. Over-collateralization is accomplished through the requirement that, at most, 60 percent of the mortgage can be included into the asset pool securing the Pfandbrief. Only mortgages from EU/EEA countries, Switzerland, United States, Canada, and Japan, can be included in the asset pool (VDP 2010b).

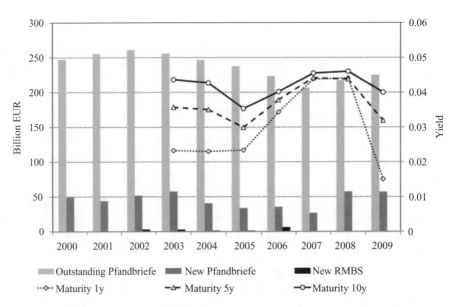

Exhibit 4.5 Volume of Outstanding Pfandbriefe, New Pfandbriefe and RMBS Issuance, and the Yield Curve for New Pfandbriefe Emissions
Sources: VDP (2010b); Deutsche Bundesbank (2010a).

All mortgages in this pool remain on the bank's balance sheet but are listed in an asset register that ensures seniority to the Pfandbrief holders in case of bankruptcy. Still, Pfandbrief investors ultimately hold a claim against the bank, not the underlying mortgages. When a bank issues several Pfandbriefe, one big pool will cover all claims. The value of the assets in the pool has to exceed the nominal value of all Pfandbriefe at any time. In addition, the net present value of the Pfandbriefe needs to be covered even in the event of extreme currency or interest rate fluctuations, with stress tests conducted in intervals of a week at most. This leads to even more safety buffers, as banks pledge more assets to their pools. In the first quarter of 2010, for instance, German Pfandbriefe had a combined face value of €217.7 billion, but were covered by pools of mortgages with a face value of €272.1 billion (VDP 2010b).

As a result of this relative safety, banks have kept on issuing Pfandbriefe, and the amount outstanding has actually increased during and since the financial crisis, as Exhibit 4.5 shows.

Given this overcollateralization, it does not come as a surprise that the government guarantee against a default of a mortgage bank has not been used for over 100 years before the European Union's competition laws ended this form of indirect state support for German mortgage banks in 2005. Even without government backing, the investors did not require an increased risk premium for Pfandbriefe. In January 2006, the asset swap spread on Pfandbriefe was merely two basis points, while the spread for unsecured bonds issued by AAA-rated European financial institutions was ten basis points for maturities of three to five years. Triple-A-rated German RMBS tranches with comparable maturities traded in the same period at about 21 basis points. The negligible spread for Pfandbriefe displays the solid track record of these instruments (Bundesbank 2006).

Housing Subsidies

Home ownership is not exactly the German dream. In surveys regarding their home ownership preferences, Germans generally express some desire to own their own home, mainly for reasons of long-term tenure security[3], but they also express anxiety concerning the financial risks involved. German government policy concerning the housing market shows a similar ambiguity.

In the East, a wide mismatch existed between the preferences of the households and the existing housing stock, where socialist central planning created too many multi-unit dwellings in precast concrete slab structures and too few detached homes. One of the challenges of German reunification was to close this gap.

Mortgage interest deductibility had been replaced by tax refunds for first time buyers in 1986. To support German citizens from the eastern states on their way towards home ownership, these first-time buyer subsidies were intensified in 1996, to help households finance the purchase of a home through tax refunds (or "tax credits"), not deductions from taxable income. The tax breaks were limited to low- to moderate-income households buying as owner occupants. The tax refunds amounted to €2,500 per year for a maximum of eight years for new construction and €1,300 per year for existing structures, with an additional €800 for each child in the household. In 2004, the total magnitude of this subsidy was €11.4 billion, which is about 3 percent of the federal government budget or 0.5 percent of total GDP. The massive first-time buyer credit was eliminated on January 1, 2006 after much political discussion: A purchase made on December 31, 2005, was eligible for the full eight years of subsidy whereas a purchase one day later was not.

Compared to many Western nations, housing subsidies in Germany have remained relatively moderate, even in the early part of the first decade of the twenty-first century. The interest rate deductability in countries like Denmark and the Netherlands is more generous than the German tax refund. The effective interest rate for a household living in the Netherlands in the last decade was lowered through the favorable tax treatment by 1.6–2.0 percent, while German households received support comparable to a 0.7–0.8 percent interest reduction (Cologne Institute of Economic Research 2009).

Demographic Challenges

Demographic change is one of the key challenges many industrialized countries will face in the future. To give a brief example, the United Nations Population Division (2007) estimates that Russia will lose 24 percent of its current population by the year 2050. For Bulgaria, the expected decline in total population is 35 percent in the same period, while neighboring Turkey will experience an impressive population growth of 29 percent.

Germany has already entered the phase of population decline. Since 2002, the number of residents has been falling year by year. On the national level, the rate of decline is still relatively small: for 2009 it is estimated to be –0.3 percent (Destatis 2010d) When focusing on the regions, however, huge regional differences can be observed. The German federal state of Thuringia, for example, is already losing 1 percent of its population annually (Thüringer Landesamt für Statistik 2008)—in demographic terms, this rate of change is breathtakingly fast.

Exhibit 4.6　Change in Total Population in German States, 1991–2008
Note: The population for Germany increased by 2.2 percent from 1991 to 2008.
Source: Destatis (2010d).

Exhibit 4.6 shows that all Eastern states but Brandenburg experienced double-digit population decline rates since Germany's re-unification. Since birth rates are below replacement value in all of Germany, population dynamics constitute a negative-sum game: The modest growth in the West's population can be attributed to the migration of East Germans taking up jobs in the West.

In a cynical sense, Eastern Germany is the avant garde for the West of Germany and many industrialized areas in Europe. All German states are expected to lose population on a large scale within the next 50 years. Exhibit 4.7 presents the long-term population change for Germany and for each of her states as forecasted by the Federal Statistical Office of Germany. Under the positive scenario, Germany will lose 14 percent population, while the lower scenario estimates a 20.7 percent negative growth. All Eastern states will lose at least another 25 percent of their population (30.9 percent under the lower variant), while the Western states will follow the East and experience shrinkage of up to 25 percent. Only the city-state of Hamburg has a more robust population outlook and is predicted to keep a more or less constant population (Destatis 2010e).

In the long run, the falling population numbers will cap the demand for housing services. A reduction in household size could offset the falling numbers,

Exhibit 4.7   Predicted Population Decline for German States (2010–2060)

Region	Predicted Population Change, 2010–2060 (in %)	
	Lower Variant	Higher Variant
Germany total	−20.7	−14.0
Saxony-Anhalt	−42.1	−37.4
Thuringia	−40.4	−36.1
Mecklenburg-Vorpommern	−35.5	−29.8
Brandenburg	−34.9	−30.9
Saarland	−32.4	−26.0
Saxony	−30.9	−25.2
Lower Saxony	−21.8	−14.9
Schleswig-Holstein	−20.9	−14.6
North Rhine-Westphalia	−20.1	−13.9
Rhineland-Palatinate	−19.0	−10.9
Hesse	−18.6	−11.8
Baden-Württemberg	−15.8	−9.5
Berlin	−15.3	−5.0
Bavaria	−14.5	−7.2
Bremen	−13.7	−2.7
Hamburg	−5.9	3.6

Source: Destatis (2010e).

but household sizes are falling at slower rates than population numbers.[4] Thus, Germany will ultimately need fewer units than there are in place today. Regional differences will become more pronounced, with most of the decline concentrating in the East. Vacancy rates of more than 20 percent already distort the housing markets in many Eastern cities. Taking down the excess units is the last option to save at least part of the value of the housing stock. Germany is the only country we know of that currently subsidizes the demolition of housing stock on a large scale. Saxony, for instance, plans to have demolished 250,000 of about 410,000 vacant units by 2013 (SAB 2007). In that sense, Germany is a testing ground for housing policy choices dealing with demographic decline.

MARKET OUTCOMES

Homeownership Rates

Home ownership rates in Germany are low. They have been increasing in the past decades, from as low as 35.8 percent in 1972 to 43.2 percent in 2008 (EMF 2009a), but this level is still only the second lowest in Europe, undercut solely by Switzerland. On the household level, the tenure choice literature consistently shows a positive relation between household wealth and income and the likelihood of home ownership. Intuitively, one would expect this micro relationship to hold also at the macro level, implying higher home ownership in rich countries than in poor ones. The situation in Switzerland and Germany runs counter to this intuition.

The literature does not provide an explanation for this, and it is beyond the scope of this study to fill the gap, but we will propose some explanations that may be tested in subsequent work.

Due to the incompleteness of the housing market, and the lumpiness of a house, home ownership produces specific risk that is not rewarded, yet cannot be diversified away. So from a pure asset management point of view, it may be more efficient if larger investors hold a diversified portfolio of homes, to be rented out to individual households. According to that reasoning, the Germans and the Swiss do the right thing, and the high-home-ownership countries require explanation.

One way to explain international differences in home ownership may lie in inflation hedging. Most countries lack instruments like index-linked government bonds, which would allow their citizens to hedge inflation risk. In these circumstances, home ownership provides an inflation hedge that is by no means perfect, but may be the best possible choice. If that would indeed be a motivation for owning a home instead of renting it, then we would expect a positive association between historic inflation and current home ownership, since overall home ownership at any time is the cumulative result of individual household decisions over many years. In order to investigate this notion, we have taken the average annual inflation for the period between 1975 and 1990, and have compared that to home ownership rates in 17 countries in Western Europe. This comparison is provided in Exhibit 4.8, which shows indeed a positive relationship, with a correlation of 0.7, so Germany's low home-ownership rate may be related to its low historic

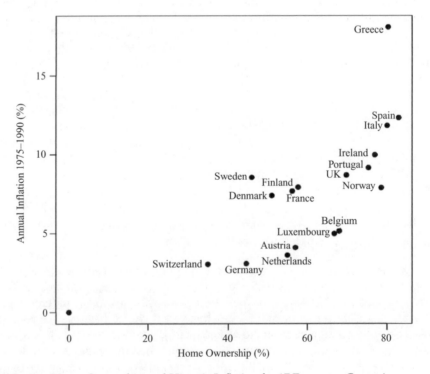

Exhibit 4.8 Home Ownership and Historic Inflation for 17 European Countries

inflation. Of course, this issue needs more formal research attention before any firm conclusions can be drawn.

Another explanation for the low homeownership rate lies in the housing market policies adopted by Germany after World War II. The areal bombings of the war left much of the housing stock in the majority of German cities destroyed. In addition, millions of Germans expelled from formerly German territories, today Poland and Czech Republic, needed new housing in the West. In total, more than 6 million housing units were lacking in 1949. To cope with that, Germany started massive residential rebuilding programs in the 1950s and 1960s, mostly geared towards the rental sector. Private developers or co-operatives could obtain financial support from the social housing programs as well, which led to a diverse and complete rental supply, also appealing to middle-class households. This is different from the United Kingdom, for example, where social housing quarters built after the war were oftentimes so low quality that only tenants unable to live somewhere else would move in (Cologne Institute for Economic Research 2009).

From the 1960s onwards, rents in this huge amount of new housing stock were gradually liberalized. Since then, landlords can set competitive rents, so they have no incentive to sell their assets, as they do, for example, in the Netherlands, where rents are still controlled. Social housing institutions and private landlords continued to provide attractive rental units (Cologne Institute for Economic Research 2009). The diverse rental housing supply gives households a true tenure choice: the decision to rent or buy is separated from housing type and quality preferences. It is not uncommon to rent a good quality detached house or an upscale apartment.

Differences in income and land prices on the state level do not sufficiently explain the differences in the ownership rates. Exhibit 4.9 shows that households in the economic powerhouses of Bavaria, Hesse, or Baden-Württemberg are not more likely to own their home than in less prosperous states. The price of building land alone does not drive homeownership rates either. Hesse and Bavaria, for instance, have similar GDP per capita values, but land in Bavaria (251 € per square meter) is twice as expensive as in Hesse (127 €/m²). Still, the home-ownership rate in both states is almost the same.

The fact that home ownership was very low in the former GDR also plays a role in the current low national average home ownership rate. Yet, the East is catching up, as Exhibit 4.10 shows. Within 10 years, home-ownership rates in the states of Thuringia (43 percent) and Brandenburg (41 percent) have reached levels comparable to the West. It is interesting to note that the cumulative home-ownership growth rate in the East has been 56 percent in 10 years while vacancy rates were above 20 percent. This indicates a mismatch between the existing rental housing stock and the preferences of households.

First-time home buyers are relatively old in Germany. In 2007, only 10.9 percent of households in the age cohort younger than 30 years owned their home. For the cohort aged 31 through 40, Exhibit 4.10 triples to 30.8 percent, growing further for ages 41 to 50 (44.8 percent), peaking at 55.4 percent for the cohort aged 51 to 65, and slowly falling again for older cohorts. In 1991, the distribution was similar for households younger than 50 years, suggesting that the baby boom generation entering the housing market in 1991 and the following and younger cohorts have similar tenure preferences. The older cohorts that entered the housing market after World War II, however, are characterized by a weaker desire to own. For instance,

Exhibit 4.9 Home Ownership Rates in German States

	Ownership Rate (%)		Change 1998–2008	GDP/Cap. 2008 (000 €)	Vacancy Rate 2006 (%)	Price Land, 2007 (€/m2)	Urbanization, Share of Dev. Area (%)*
	1998	2008					
Germany total	40.3	43.2	7.2	30.4	8.0	134	6.8
West							
Saarland	59.9	59.5	−0.7	30.1	8.3	74	12.3
Rhineland-Palatine	55.1	57.2	3.8	26.4	8.0	102	5.9
Baden-Württemberg	49.6	53.3	7.5	34.0	6.9	182	7.5
Schleswig-Holstein	45.3	51.6	13.9	26.1	5.3	109	6.9
Lower Saxony	45.7	50.4	10.3	26.8	5.3	73	7.2
Bavaria	49.4	49.2	−0.4	35.5	6.6	251	5.7
Hesse	45.7	47.5	3.9	36.5	6.0	127	7.5
North Rhine-Westph.	37.8	43.1	14.0	30.5	7.8	144	12.7
East							
Thuringia	33.1	43	29.9	22.2	10.5	35	4.4
Brandenburg	26.5	41.4	56.2	21.6	11.4	–	4.6
Saxony-Anhalt	29.1	38.2	31.3	22.6	16.6	34	4.4
Mecklenburg-Vorp.	22.5	34.4	52.9	21.4	11.3	46	3.5
Saxony	27.2	32.1	18.0	22.6	14.5	55	6.8
City-States							
Bremen	41.6	42.6	2.4	41.4	4.3	134	34.5
Hamburg	20	23.9	19.5	49.4	4.3	659	37.2
Berlin	12.1	16.2	33.9	25.8	8.7	238	41.3

*Share of developed area (residential and commercial use) divided by total area, 2008.
Source: Statistical office Saxony-Anhalt (2010); Voigtländer et al. (2009); Destatis.

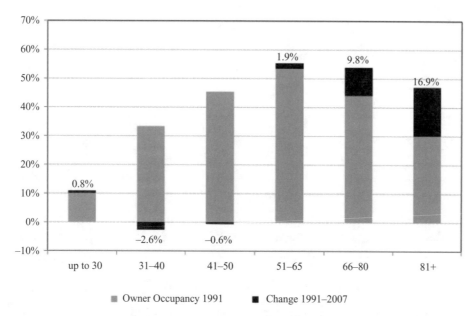

Exhibit 4.10   Home Ownership Rates across Age Groups, 2007
Source: Vogtländer et al. (2009).

the ownership rate of the cohort aged 66 to 80 rose by 9.8 percent in the period 1991 to 2007 (Voigtländer et al. 2009, p. 164). Thus, the increase in German ownership rate in the last decades can (at least partially) be explained by baby boomers replacing the generations that have experienced the war. Since the cohorts that are young now do not have different preferences from their direct predecessors, it is doubtful whether the ownership rate in Germany will continue its upward trend, especially after the Eastern states have fully caught up with the Western part of the country.

Home Values

Given the developments in German mortgage rates in the past two decades, one would expect that Germany's house price trajectory would have been close to that of other countries. After all, the mortgage rate steadily decreased from the early 1990s onwards, just as it did in most of the other industrialized nations. However, house prices in Germany followed their own path.

Exhibit 4.11 displays the price path of the total residential real estate market, apartments, existing homes, and newly built homes in real terms. As we discussed before, the longest time series based on a hedonic estimation technique starts in the year 2000. For a more long-run view, we therefore have to rely on a combination of data sources, which can only give us an indication of true developments.

For the years 1989–2005, we chose the DEIX index, which is based on the mean values reported by the committees for land-price valuation (in German, *Gutachterausschüsse*). From all German indexes, the DEIX reaches back the furthest in time. From August 2005 onward, we rely on the Hypoport hedonic price indexes. We select the Hypoport index because of two reasons: first, it is updated on a

Exhibit 4.11 Real House Price Index of Germany
Notes: The real index exhibits are calculated by dividing the nominal index values (Gewos 2008; Hypoport 2010) by the corresponding CPI values (Destatis 2010f).

monthly basis, while the hedonic index provided by the Federal Statistical Office of Germany (Destatis) is updated on a quarterly basis only and ends in 2008. The third hedonic index for Germany, the VDP index, is estimated on a quarterly basis and does not distinguish between existing and newly built homes.

In the first half of the 1990s, home values experienced an enormous price build-up. Home values rose by 36.5 percent in the four years from January 1990 through December 1994, which by far outpaced the increase in consumer prices of 15 percent. Apartments and detached homes both grew at a similar pace. This growth was "out of sync" with many other economies, who suffered from the housing slump of the early 1990s. The Case-Shiller 10 city composite index lost 6 percent (Case and Shiller 2010) in the same period while U.K. homes lost 4 percent in nominal terms (BIS 2006).

By 1995, the market had reached its peak, and from 1995 onwards the average real price level started falling: for 1995 through 2000, the index for the entire markets grew by 5 percent, which is below the inflation rate of cumulatively 6.7 percent. Since 2000, the overall market index has fallen by 2.5 percent in nominal terms, while the CPI increased by 16 percent (Destatis 2010f). Existing homes prices experienced even stronger losses in value. In the five years since August 2005, the Hypoport index showed a decline of 9.8 percent. Apartments lost 2.1 percent and only prices for new homes increased by 6.5 percent (Hypoport 2010).

Observing such a long period of stagnation and losses is even more fascinating against the background of the bullish market trends in economies close by. Germany is the big outlier in Europe, again. For the period 1995 to 2000, for instance, prices of homes in the Netherlands increased by 82.2 percent, in Denmark by 53.7 percent, and in the United Kingdom by 59.2 percent (BIS). Looking at the price performance since 1995, therefore, the German housing performance becomes even more pronounced.

German Housing during the Global Credit Crunch Crisis

In the past 20 years, the German housing markets moved anticyclically to other national housing markets, like those in Britain or the United States. Did this detachedness persist during the global credit cruch and the meltdown in home values around the globe? Exhibit 4.12 displays the Hypoport total market index for Germany, the Halifax house price index for the United Kingdom, and the Case-Shiller 20 cities composite index. The exhibit suggests that the United Kingdom follows the U.S. market trends while the German index is uncorrelated. The correlation coefficient for housing returns between Germany and the United States is 0.20, for Germany versus the United Kingdom it is a mere 0.05, while the United Kingdom and the United States are more closely correlated (0.56). We read this as first evidence that German house prices are not integrated into the global housing cycles.

One avenue for contagion of the housing crisis would be the financing channel. Pressure from international financial markets could lead to higher mortgage rates in Germany and/or reduced housing finance availability in Germany. We do not observe either of these developments. Liquidity for Pfandbriefe remained high during the dry-up of financial markets in 2007–2008. The effective mortgage rate is currently at historically low levels. In May 2010, the rate on newly issued mortgages with a maturity of one to five years was on average 3.42 percent. The

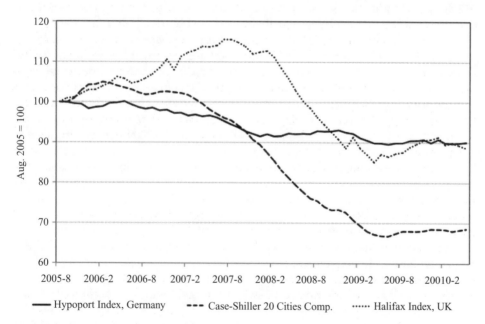

Exhibit 4.12 Real House Price Indexes: Germany, United States, and United Kingdom
Sources: Hypostat (2010); Case and Shiller (2010); Halifax index (2010). CPI data was obtained from national statistical offices.

Exhibit 4.13   Summary Statistics Housing Transactions, Berlin, 1978–2007

Variable	Mean	SD	25th	50th	75th	Min	Max
Sales prices	345	211	225	302	404	30	4,318
Ln (lot size)	6.12	0.50	5.75	6.15	6.48	3.99	8.27
Ln (interior floor space)	4.92	0.33	4.71	4.89	5.13	3.04	6.21
Replacement value building	153	121	75	135	203	0	2,726
Ln (distance to public transport)	6.93	0.80	6.41	6.94	7.40	2.64	8.84
Ln (distance primary school)	6.32	0.63	6.02	6.42	6.73	0.69	8.04
Ln (distance to green space)	6.95	1.22	6.26	7.16	7.88	−2.49	8.75
Ln (distance to water)	7.72	0.87	7.32	7.93	8.38	−0.22	9.01
Ln (distance to kindergarten)	6.15	0.72	5.78	6.21	6.61	0.69	8.04
Distance to railway tracks < 200 m	0.10	0.31	0.00	0.00	0.00	0.00	1.00
Distance to border < 200 m	0.07	0.25	0.00	0.00	0.00	0.00	1.00
Ln (minutes to center)	3.21	0.35	2.94	3.26	3.53	1.79	3.81

Notes: Full sample, N = 19825. Sales prices and the estimated replacement values denoted in thousands, inflated to 2007 euros. Lot size and interior floor space are measured in square meters. All distances are in meters. *Distance to public transport* measures the distances to light rail, subway, and railway stations (bus stops are not considered). *Minutes to center* describes the commuting time in minutes from the closest public transport hub to the city center proxied by the new central station.

spread over German government debt of comparable maturity is now above the long-run average of 125 basis points, but mortgage credit is still readily available for households wanting to buy a home.

During the credit crunch, €26.8 billion worth of Pfandbriefe were newly issued in 2007, which is about 13 percent of the volume of all outstanding Pfandbriefe, or two thirds of the 2004 volume (see Exhibit 4.13). The yields on Pfandbriefe with 10 year maturities increased by 55 basis points in 2007, which mirrors the increase in the risk-free rate. Spreads on both short and longer maturities remained narrow all through 2007 and 2008. As an example, three weeks before the collapse of Lehman Brothers depressed the markets, the Münchener Hypothekenbank was able to place a Pfandbrief with even a negative re-offer spread versus the swap curve (VDP 2010b). After the Lehman crash, spreads in swaps increased to as much as 86 basis points for five-year Jumbo Pfandbriefe in April 2009. Spreads to German government bonds were even more pronounced and reached 135 basis points in March 2009. Since then, spreads have been falling, almost reaching pre-crisis levels again (VDP 2010b).

German residential mortgage-backed securities (RMBS), in contrast, did not survive the crisis. Introduced only in 2002, RMBS had gained market shares relatively quickly since they offered. In 2006, new RMBS issuances had grown to 17.5 percent of the size of newly issued Pfandbriefe. Since the credit crunch unfolded, no new RMBS have been issued in Germany.

The credit crunch did leave its footprints on the German financial industry, nevertheless. Many German banks held sizable portfolios of RMBS (or related) products from the United States. The IKB bank, for instance, had been invested in the U.S. subprime mortgage market to such a large extent that it was the first German institution that had to be bailed out in 2007. Other prominent victims are the industry leader HypoReal, which needed to be saved by enormous credit lines in 2008, or the partially state-controlled Landesbanken,[5] which had lost fortunes overseas as well. The troubled industry, however, still served the home market and provided funds for private homeowners.

In sum, the fundamentals of the German housing finance market remained stable during the credit crunch. Real rents did not decline and fresh housing financing was available to households. During the crisis year of 2008, for instance, mortgages worth €174.5 billion were originated by German financial institutions, which is only marginally below the 2003–2010 annual average of €177.2 billion (Bundesbank 2010). Banks could continue providing mortgages since the market for Pfandbriefe remained liquid. Again, the German housing market seems to have proved itself to be insulated from housing market developments elsewhere.

BERLIN'S HOUSING MARKET: 15 YEARS OF DECLINE

That Germany did not participate in the current crisis that depressed housing markets around the world looks like good news. Politicians and bank managers are quick to claim credit for the seemingly stable German housing markets. We take a different stance on this point. We think that the "robustness" is a sign of long-run weakness, not strength. If a market has been losing value for more than a decade, it simply cannot fall much deeper very fast. For homeowners trying to accumulate housing wealth, these "lost decades" are painful; for housing economists, however, they provide a fascinating research environment. What other market offers years of losses in real home values in combination with otherwise robust economic growth?

To understand the remarkable development of German house prices in recent decades, it is important to realize that German housing consists of two very different markets: the market in the western states, and the market in the states that formerly constituted the GDR. The performance shown in the previous sections is the average of these two markets, where prices in the former have been holding steady in recent years, while those in the latter have fallen. The unique performance of the German housing market is to a large extent caused by the development in the East. So it would be nice to have an aggregate index for the Eastern states. Unfortunately, that index does not exist, nor can we construct it, for reasons described earlier. However, there is one German state for which transaction data does allow us to estimate a good constant-quality index: the state of Berlin, Germany's capital and largest city.

That is why we now turn to the performance of the Berlin housing market. We first create a price index for homes in Berlin, then look at the performance of this index, and finally discuss implications of the Berlin experience for Germany as a whole. We will see that Berlin experienced a housing bubble in the early 1990s, followed by an extended bust period that only recently seems to have come to an end.

The story of post-war Berlin has been told mostly for its political and historical significance. Still, it is just as fascinating for an urban economist. Ironically, before the collapse of communist rule in Eastern and Central Europe, West Berlin experienced a period of tranquility and relative prosperity. Sealed off from its direct surroundings by the iron curtain, protected by NATO against external threats, and financed by generous transfer payments from West Germany, the lucky western part of the divided city lived a quiet but comfortable life. As a result, home prices rose throughout the 1970s and 1980s (Clapp, Eichholtz, and Lindenthal 2011).

Between 1990 and the mid-1990s, Berlin was a city of great expectations, with matching property developments to boot. For example, more than 130,000 housing units were developed between 1992 and 1999. In a very close vote in June 1991, the unified German parliament decided to make Berlin the political capital of Germany again.[6] Moving the government, parliament, and about half of the federal administration, including approximately 9,000 civil servants, took several years and was finalized by 1999.

But many of these expectations did not pan out and Berlin became a city in decline. Soon after the events of the early 1990s, Berlin's economy started stagnating. From 1991 through 2005 the number of jobs declined by 14 percent (Destatis 2009). Berlin's population has declined along with its economy, as did those of the surrounding areas of Brandenburg.

To make things worse, Berlin lost a major part of its income. While being a "front city," West Berlin received disproportionate transfers from the West German federal government, ultimately aimed at sustaining the city's population levels. Through 1995, these subsidies were gradually phased out. Berlin became a "normal" city that has to fend for itself. An important counterforce to emigration was thereby removed, and this was strengthened by a wave of residents of Eastern Germany who moved to the West. Since the opening of the border in 1989, the eastern parts of Berlin and all the German federal states that used to lie in the former GDR have seen their populations decline year by year.

Contrary to popular belief, and to widely held expectations at the time, the fall of the Berlin Wall in 1989 left homeowners worse off. Housing markets started an extended collapse briefly after the dust stirred up by the re-unification of Germany had settled. During the past 15 years home prices have halved—even in nominal terms. Such a deep and continuous decline of a major metropolitan market is unparalleled in Europe's recent history.

Data

Access to housing transactions data in Germany is state specific. For the state of Berlin, universities are allowed to analyze the data as long as no information can be traced back to single transactions. Clapp, Eichholtz, and Lindenthal (2011) got access to a database including all transactions of single-family homes for West Berlin from 1978 through 1990, and for both single-family homes and condos for the united Berlin from 1990 through 2007.[7] All records include the sales price and date, the address, and key hedonics.

The single-family dwellings data set comprises 37,276 transactions between 1978 and 2007. The database contains measures of the building's interior floor space and the size and dimensions of the lot.[8] Furthermore, the data contains information on the administrative entity the dwelling is located in.

The database contains a variety of additional hedonic variables describing the characteristics of each building, the replacement value of the structures, and the maximum development size possible under current zoning. Unfortunately, these variables are not strictly required to be filled in by the notaries and appraisers when recording a transaction. Some variables are simply missing in selected years, while others are sketchy throughout the entire observation period. The missing observations create a trade-off between the level of detail per observation and the number of observations. Only two of the unbalanced variables are included as the information gained outweighs the cost of thinning out the sample.

First, we include the structure's replacement value as estimated by a professional appraiser during an external inspection before the sale is entered into the database. This inspection was not conducted in some cases. Obviously, the replacement value is not only missing for incomplete records but for all sales of naked land that is zoned for residential use, but not developed yet. These transactions even include temporarily deviating uses like ad-hoc parking lots and so forth. Unfortunately we cannot identify these very interesting cases of land-only transactions from the information given in the records. We have to exclude 3,369 observations that do not have information on this umbrella variable for all structures in place.

We translate the street-address into longitude and latitude coordinates through the Google Maps web service.[9] Distances to railway tracks, parks, lakes, rivers, and to other open green space are calculated based on free GIS maps created by the OpenStreetmap project (2010). Locations of the subway, railway, and lightrail stations are obtained from the Berlin transportation authorities. We calculate the fastest route to the center, which is a combination of the walking time to these public transport hubs and the subsequent commuting time to the center. We look up the commuting time on a Monday morning to Berlin central-station[10] for each of the public transport stations in the 2009 transportation schedules. The school administration's official address list reveals the location of all of primary schools and kindergartens. In addition, we define dummy variables for the distances to the fortified East-West border (Berlin Wall and Brandenburg border). Exhibit 4.13 presents the summary statistics for the core hedonics and derived location information for the final sample of 19,825 observations.

Methodology and Results

Transaction prices are explained by a basic linear model, in which the logarithm of the transaction price is explained by a linear combination of the dwelling's characteristics. Formally, the following equation is estimated in an ordinary least squares regression (OLS):

$$\ln(P_{it}) = \beta_0 + \sum Y_{yi}\beta_y + \sum L_{li}\gamma_l + \sum \ln(X_{it})\delta_x + \varepsilon_{it} \qquad (4.1)$$

In this equation $\ln(P_{it})$ is the logarithm of the transaction price for housing sale i in year t. Y_y is a dummy variable defined 1 if house i was sold in year y (and 0 otherwise). L_l is defined 1 for all houses in neighborhood l (and 0 otherwise), X_i is a vector describing the characteristics of dwelling i. β, γ, and δ are vectors of regression coefficients, while ε_i is the independently and normally distributed error term.

The straightforward regression model of Equation (4.1) explains 85.6 percent of the variation in the transaction prices. All regression coefficients have the expected signs or are statistically not significant (with robust standard errors). A 10 percent increase in the lot size is found to increase the transaction price by 4.2 percent, for a similar increase in the interior floor space or the replacement value of the building, the price elasticity is 2.6 percent or 2.4 percent, respectively.

Berlin households value proximity to open water. The bigger the distance of a dwelling to major water bodies, the lower is the sales price. A 10 percent increase in the distance leads to a 0.3 percent reduction in value. Similarly, buildings that are close to parks or forests are more valuable (elasticity of 0.006). The regression coefficients for the distance to primary schools and kindergarten are not significantly different from zero. Locations closer than 200 meters to railway tracks carry on average a discount of 0.9 percent. The noise from Berlin's rattling trains can be a reason for this observed effect. Similarly, the overall price effect of being very close (< 200 m) to the border is –1.7 percent.[11] The coefficients for being close to a public transportation hub or to a primary school are positive, which is against our expectations. However, they are statistically not significant, when estimating the regression using robust error terms. All coefficients for the location and year dummies are statistically different from zero at the 5 percent confidence level.

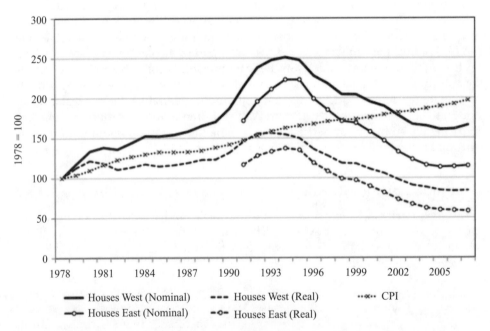

Exhibit 4.14 Hedonic Price Index for Houses in West Berlin, 1978–2007

Note: The indexes for West and East Berlin are independently estimated by the equation:

$$\ln(P_i) = \beta_0 + \sum_{1979}^{2007} Y_{y,i}\beta_y + \sum L_{l,i}\gamma_l + \sum \ln(X_{x,i})\delta_x + \sum D_{i,d}\eta_d + \varepsilon_i,$$

with Y being year dummy variables, L dummy variables for each of Berlin's official neighborhoods. The hedonic variables X contain the lot size, replacement value of the structure, the interior floor space, and the distances to kindergarten, primary schools, major parks or other green spaces, and large water bodies. The hedonic dummy variables D indicate if a house is located within a distance of 200 meters to railway tracks or the east-west border, respectively. The East index is scaled to the ratio in 2006 median sales prices in West and East Berlin.

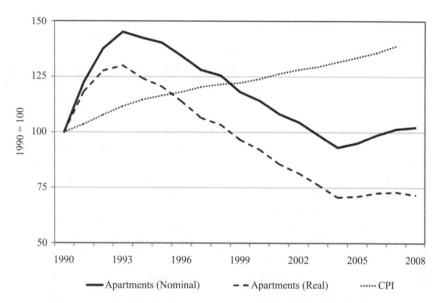

Exhibit 4.15 Hedonic Price Index for Apartments in West Berlin, 1990–2008

Exhibit 4.14 shows the price index for West Berlin houses based on the year dummy coefficients, while Exhibit 4.15 presents the index for apartments. In the first 10 years of the sample period, the increase in house prices is modestly exceeding the general increase in consumer price index (CPI). After the fall of the Berlin Wall, however, home values went through the roof: From 1989 through 1994, nominal prices increased by 47.5 percent, while the CPI increased by 17.7 percent only. Market participants believed in a new era for Berlin, which not only became the capital of the reunified Germany again, but held a key position at the gates of Central and Eastern Europe.

Unfortunately, the high expectations did not last long. From 1994 through 2005, the house price index has been losing value every year—even in nominal terms. In 11 years, home values fell by 36 percent in nominal terms (45 percent in real). In real terms, home prices in 2007 stabilized at 87 percent of their 1978 values. For apartments, the losses are comparable. From 1994 through 2007 the real index for apartments decreased by 44.8 percent.[12]

We test a variety of model specifications in order to check for the robustness of the results. Omitted variable bias is a major concern due to the limited hedonic characteristics available in our dataset. A repeated sales index directly controls for quality differences by comparing sales of the same building in different points in time and therefore does not rely on any hedonic information. We estimate a repeated sales index for West Berlin and find support for our hedonic index. Both indexes show the same magnitudes of boom and bust. Still, we prefer the hedonic regression model, since it allows us to analyze neighborhood dynamics in a next step.

The unification of the city provided for a massive shock to housing supply. The city had been divided and sealed off from its hinterland. After the opening up of the East, households could live in East Berlin or in surrounding Brandenburg instead of just West Berlin. This increased competition is hypothesized to lower prices in peripheral locations of West Berlin. In the same time, the central quarters became "more central," since they are now in the middle of an overall larger metropolitan area. Before 1990, the Kreuzberg neighborhood, for instance, was a dead-end corner of West Berlin. Since reunification, however, it has been in direct proximity to the historic center of Berlin again, ending its cul-de-sac status.

We investigate potential shifts in the geographic distribution of prices by estimating a modified version of (1). Instead of using year dummies, this model just distinguishes between observations in the years 1978–1989 (variable T defined as 0), and the post-Wall period (T defined as 1). Interacting T with the location dummies estimates the aggregated change in house prices for each neighborhood before and after the reunification.

$$\frac{\ln(P_{it})}{CPI_t} = \beta_0 + \sum L_{li} T_i \beta_l + \sum L_{li} \gamma_l + \sum \ln(X_{it}) \delta_x + \varepsilon_{it} \qquad (4.2)$$

The vector of interaction coefficients β is mapped in Exhibit 4.16. Each of the circles represents one neighborhood. The circles' size visualizes the magnitude of the price change, with larger circles indicating larger price falls. The losses are concentrated in the periphery in the north and the southeast of the city, where the average value in the years 1990–2007 is up to 32 percent below the average prices in the period 1978–1989. The more central neighborhoods of West Berlin and the historically rich Western areas of Dahlem, Grunewald, Charlottenburg, and

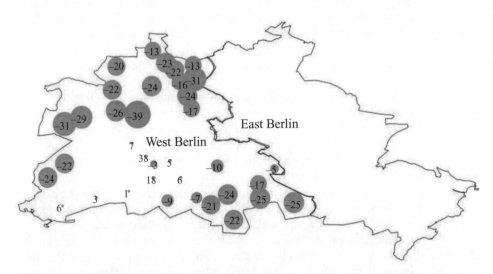

Exhibit 4.16 Geographical Distribution of Real Prices Changes for Single-Family Homes in West Berlin Neighborhoods after Unification (in%)
Notes: The map displays the change in house prices for 36 neighborhoods in West Berlin after the Wall came down. We regress the natural logarithms of the inflation-adjusted house sales prices against a set of hedonic variables describing the quality and size of the home. The numbers in the map represent the change in the coefficients for the location dummy variables L comparing the time periods 1978–1989 to 1990–2007, converted to percentages. All changes are in real terms.

Zehlendorf, in contrast, experienced stable prices or even capital gains. The map suggests a tilt in the price gradient with a strong core of housing wealth remaining in the center and eroding prices in the periphery. Berlin is still a polycentric city – but one with a recovering heart.

Berlin and Germany

The lessons for the rest of Germany are threefold. First, although a constant quality index does not exist for the other eastern states, their demographic situation is in many ways comparable to Berlin, and they, too, have experienced severe economic hardship in recent years. It is therefore likely that the performance of the housing markets in the other Eastern states is comparable to that of Berlin, especially after 1995. In other words, these parts of Germany have all lost significant amounts of house value in the past two decades.

Second, the adverse performance of the housing markets in the East has likely amplified migration effects. For example, more highly educated citizens from the Eastern states have consistently moved to Germany's Western states, only partly to be replaced by immigrants with lower levels of human capital,[13] and, in selected cities, by students. As a result, prices in the housing markets in the East are falling even more, while those in the West have been more or less steady.

Third, neighborhood price trends are not uniform within the same city. Some areas can keep their value, even against the background of massive losses in housing wealth at the city level. Identifying these strong cores is essential for both investors and urban planners, who have to rely on gut feelings and insider information as spatially detailed indexes are missing for Germany.

CONCLUSION

Germany's housing market is an outlier. It has been out of sync with housing markets in other industrialized nations for as far as we can observe, experiencing rising house prices in the early nineties, and steadily falling real prices since the mid-1990s, when many other housing markets experienced unprecedented housing market booms.

The current global housing market crisis has left Germany largely unaffected. That may partly be attributable to the fact that real house prices have not much room to fall any further, but there are more solid reasons why the global credit crisis has passed by Germany's housing market without inflicting much harm.

First, Germany already abolished the income tax deductibility of mortgage interest payments in 1986, thereby removing an important incentive for the accumulation of household debt. It is difficult to establish causality, but it is likely that this has played a role in keeping Germany's cumulative mortgage debt low. Germany has not been affected by the high mortgage debt/high house-price spiral that has destabilized other housing markets.

Second, loan-to-value ratios in Germany's mortgage market are low, and all loans are full recourse. Both aspects diminish the likelihood of mortgage default by households, and the default rate has remained low, even with falling nominal house prices in many parts of the country.

Third, mortgage credit is still readily available, and has hardly fallen since the beginning of the global crisis. Germany's homemade secondary mortgage market, the market for Pfandbriefe, is still functioning much as before, while the residential mortgage-backed securities market, which also started to gain some importance in Germany before the crisis, has completely dried up.

The other aspect of Germany's uniqueness is in its very low home owner-ship rate. While that rate has steadily been rising in the last four decades, it still stands only at 43 percent, the second lowest in Europe. This may be due to Germany's low historic inflation rate, but it is also likely that that the historic housing policies enacted by the German government play a role: The massive rebuilding programs after the war focused on delivering rental housing, both by local governments and by the private sector, and the absence of rent control has not diminished the incentive to supply rental housing, as it has in other coun-tries. From a consumer standpoint, Germany's rental market is competitive to the owner-occupied market in terms of location and object quality.

The German experience shows that an open economy, with free movement of capital and goods, can have a housing market that remains only weakly integrated with foreign housing markets. The evidence presented in this study suggests that local and national factors like demographics and government policy may be af-fecting house price dynamics more strongly than the global forces of finance. It also suggests that a healthy economy is not necessarily associated with a thriving housing market and rising prices. Germany's housing market suggests that falling real house prices may not be the grave economic problem that the nation fears it to be.

NOTES

1. The leverage in Berlin in 2010 is 8.1 (Berlin Senatsverwaltung für Finanzen. 2010), while Munich claims only 4.9 (Landeshauptstadt München, 2010).

2. When selling the property, the seller can prepay the mortgage, but has to compensate the bank for losses from prepayment. Mortgages are not assumable.

3. A survey by Postbank AG, for instance, finds that owning a home is the most trusted form of non-governmental pension provisions for German households.

4. In Berlin, more than 50 percent of the households already consist of only one person (Destatis, press release No. 518).

5. The Landesbanks are a group of state-owned/state-controlled banks unique to Germany. Their core business is predominantly wholesale banking. Landesbanks have a regional focus and are the head banking institution of the local savings banks (Sparkassen). Landesbanks are supervized by local politicians—a fact that did not serve them well, as the disastrous performance during the financial crisis has shown.

6. Three hundred and thirty-seven members of parliament voted for Berlin to host gov-ernment and parliament again, while 320 voted for staying in Bonn, which had served as the temporary capital of West Germany. The closeness of the votes makes it unlikely that this was fully anticipated by the housing market.

7. Schulz et al. (2003) and Schulz and Werwatz (2004) are the only papers we know of that use (subsets of) these data.

8. We could link several exceptionally large buildings to new embassies, organizational buildings, or other non-residential uses being established in residential areas, while

other extremely small or large outliers are probably recording errors: 39 observations with plots larger than 4,000 square meters are excluded from the sample, as they are very special cases clustering around a single street in the outskirts of Berlin. Four hundred and three observations with interior sizes below 20 square meters or above 500 square meters are excluded from the sample

9. Detailed information on how to use the Google Maps API for geocoding can be obtained from the authors on request. They can be reached by e-mail at thies@lindenthal.eu.

10. The new central station is located in what can be considered the center of united Berlin, close to government quarters and parliament. It is Berlin's central transportation hub. During the cold war, Berlin Zoo station served as interim main station. It is about four train-minutes west of the new center.

11. Interestingly, the disamenity of being close to the border is smaller before 1990. Apparently, being direct neighbors with the Berlin Wall was less of a disamenity than being in the periphery of the united city.

12. When testing for potential breakpoints in the real index, 1989/1990 and 1994/1995 are indeed suggested breakpoints. The F-statistics from Chow tests for these breakpoints are 14.4 and 20.8, respectively.

13. The socio-economic panel for Germany shows drastic differences in educational attainment, wage levels, and employment rates for migrants from non–European Union countries like Turkey, Serbia, or Croatia (Destatis 2008), which constitute a large share of all non-EU inflows.

REFERENCES

Bank for International Settlements. 2006. "Housing Finance in the Global Financial Market." Available at www.bis.org/publ/cgfs26.htm.

Behrmann, Timm, and Alfons Kathe. 2004. "Zur Anwendung hedonischer Methoden beim Häuserpreisindex." Wiesbaden: Federal Statistical Office of Germany.

Berlin Senatsverwaltung für Finanzen. 2010. "Grundsteuer." Available at www.berlin.de/sen/finanzen/steuern/themen/grundsteuer.html.

BulwienGesa. 2010. "Datenquellen." Available at www.bulwiengesa.de/index.php?id=135.

Bundesbank. 2006. "Monthly Report 2006: New Legal and Regulatory Framework for the German Securitization and Pfandbrief Market." Available at www.bundesbank.de/download/volkswirtschaft/mba/2006/200603mba_en_german_securisation_pfandbrief_market.pdf.

Bundesbank. 2009. "Bankenstatistik January 2009." Frankfurt am Main.

Bundesbank. 2010a. "MFI Interest Rate Statistics." Time series available for download at www.bundesbank.de/statistik.

Cardarelli, R., D. Igan, and A. Rebucci. 2008. "The Changing Housing Cycle and Its Implications for Monetary Policy." World Economic Outlook, International Monetary Fund.

Case, K., and R. Shiller. 2010. "S&P/Case-Shiller Home Price Indexes." Available at www.standardandpoors.com.

Claessens, S., M. A. Kose, and M. E. Terrones. 2008 (December). "What Happens during Recessions, Crunches, and Busts?", IMF Working Paper, International Monetary Fund.

Clapp, J., T. Lindenthal, and P. Eichholtz. 2011. "Real Option Value and the Long-Term Dynamics of House Prices in Berlin, 1978–2007." Maastricht University Working Paper, 2011.

Cologne Institute for Economic Research. 2009. "Mieternation Deutschland." Available at http://entw.iwkoeln.de.

Destatis. 2008. "Datenreport 2008." *Federal Statistical Office of Germany.* Available at www .destatis.de/jetspeed/portal/cms/Sites/destatis/Internet/DE/Content/Publikationen/ Querschnittsveroeffentlichungen/Datenreport/Downloads/Datenreport2008,property =file.pdf.

————. 2010a. "Ausländerstatistik." *Federal Statistical Office of Germany*, Destatis database available at www.destatis.de.

————. 2010b. "Preisindizes für Häuser."

————. 2010c. "Steuereinnahmen: Bundesländer, Quartale, Steuerarten vor der Steuerverteilung."

————. 2010d. "Fortschreibung des Bevölkerungsstandes."

————. 2010e. "Bevölkerungsvorausberechnungen."

————. 2010f. "Verbraucherpreisindex für Deutschland."

European Mortgage Federation (EMF). 2006. "Study on the Cost of Housing in the EU." Available at http://62.102.106.72/docs/1/AJIFHFLBOOAGPGJDFJMC JMBLPDBN9DBD2DTE4Q/EMF/Docs/DLS/2006-00050.pdf.

European Mortgage Federation (EMF). 2009a. "Hypostat 2008: A Review of Europe's Mortgage and Housing Markets." Available at www.hypo.org.

————. 2009b. "EMF Factsheet Germany." Available at www.hypo.org.

Federal Ministry of Justice. 2010a. "Grundsteuergesetz." Available at www.gesetze-im -internet.de/grstg_1973/index.html.

————. 2010b. "Grunderwerbsteuergesetz." Available at www.gesetze-im-internet.de/ grestg_1983/index.html.

Gewos. 2008. "Preisentwicklung für Wohneigentum in Deutschland." Hamburg: *GEWOS Institut für Stadt-, Regional- und Wohnforschung GmbH.*

Glaeser, E., and Gyourko, J. 2005. "Urban Decline and Durable Housing." *Journal of Political Economy* 113:2.

Hypoport A. G. 2010. "HPX Hedonic." Available at at www.hypoport.com/hpx_hedonic_ en.html.

International Monetary Fund. 2008. "World Economic Outlook 2008: Housing and the Business Cycle." Washington DC: IMF Publication Services.

Landeshauptstadt München Stadtkämmerei. 2010. "Hebesatz." Available at www .muenchen.de/Rathaus/ska/fachinfos/grdabgaben/334975/Hebesatz.html.

Low, S., Sebag-Montefiore, M., and A. Dübel. 2003. "Study on the Financial Integration of European Mortgage Markets." Mercer Oliver Wymann and European Mortgage Federation. Available at http://hypo.org.

OpenStreetmap. 2010. Available at www.openstreetmap.org.

SAB Sächsische Aufbaubank. 2007. "Wohnungsbaumonitoring 2006/2007." Available at www.sab.sachsen.de.

Statistical Office Saxony Anhalt. 2010. Available at www.statistik.sachsen-anhalt.de/ apps/StrukturKompass/indikator/tableByTime/37?zma=1998.

Schulz, R., and A. Werwatz. 2004. "A State Space Model for Berlin House Prices: Estimation and Economic Interpretation." *Journal of Real Estate Finance and Economics* 28:1, 37–57.

Schulz, R., Sofyan, H., Werwatz, A., and R. Witzel. 2003. "Online Prediction of Berlin Single-Family House Prices." *Computational Statistics* 18, 449–462.

Thüringer Landesamt für Statistik. 2008. "Entwicklung der Bevölkerung ab 1950." Time series available at www.tls.thueringen.de.

United Nations Population Division. 2007. "World Population Prospects: The 2006 Revision Population Database." Available at http://esa.un.org/unpp/.

Verband deutscher Pfandbriefbanken. 2010a. "VDP Immobilienpreisindex." Available at www.pfandbrief.de.

Verband deutscher Pfandbriefbanken. 2010b. "The Pfandbrief 2009/2010—Facts and Exhibits about Europe's Covered Bond Benchmark." Available at www.pfandbrief.de.

Voigtländer, M., et al. 2009. "Die Immobilienmärkte aus gesamtwirtschaftlicher Perspektive." *Journal of Interdisciplinary Property Research*.

ABOUT THE AUTHORS

THIES LINDENTHAL received his PhD in Real Estate Finance from Maastricht University. His main research interests are price dynamics in residential real estate markets, concentrating on declining cities. In particular, he investigates the interplay of demographics and housing demand, long-run price deviations, spatial dispersion home price shocks, and endogeneities in home prices. He is a frequent speaker at academic conferences, and his advice on housing markets in shrinking cities is sought after by policymakers. Thies teaches courses in corporate finance and real estate finance at the undergraduate, graduate, and executive level. He has been a visiting scholar at Harvard University and at the University of California–Berkeley.

PIET EICHHOLTZ is Professor of Real Estate and Finance and chair of the Finance Department at Maastricht University in the Netherlands. Most of his work involves real estate markets, with a focus on international investment, housing markets, and sustainable real estate. Eichholtz's academic work has resulted in a great number of publications, both internationally and in the Netherlands. He has provided extensive services to public society, mainly through board memberships of industry organizations in the property sector, but also as an advisor to various government agencies. Besides his academic career, Eichholtz has been active as an entrepreneur. After having gained practical experience at the ABP and NIB Capital, Eichholtz started Global Property Research, an international consultancy firm specializing in property companies. In 2004, he was a co-founder of Finance Ideas, a financial consultancy company. He is currently a non-executive board member at IPD Holding.

CHAPTER 5

The Dynamics of the Irish Housing Market

SIMON STEVENSON
Henley Business School, University of Reading

In the summer of 2006 the Irish housing market was looking back on a decade of remarkable growth. From the end of 1994 to the third quarter of 2006, house prices in
Dublin increased by 580 percent, from an average of €80,000 to just shy of €550,000.
On a national level prices had followed the trends in Dublin, with even the "worst"
performing city, Limerick, seeing nominal house price appreciation of over 370 percent during this period. The Irish economy had seen real GDP growth averaging
7.8 percent per annum since 1992, over 10 percent in nominal terms, and total employment had grown by 67 percent. However, the economic phenomenon that was
called the Celtic Tiger was soon to see a dramatic reversal of fortunes. By the end of
2009 house prices had fallen, according to conservative estimates, by 46 percent in
Dublin; housing construction had collapsed from 90,000 new units in 2006 to less
than a quarter of that figure; government revenues, for so long dependent on the
property and construction sectors, had fallen by 27 percent and the banking sector
that helped to finance the real estate and construction sectors was in turmoil, with
a new government agency established to manage €80 billion of bad debt.

Explaining the events of the past 15 years in Ireland is, as is the case in many
markets, not as simple as one may think or as some commentators would like us
to believe. It is all too easy to blame the housing boom on speculative behavior in
the housing market and to lay responsibility for the downturn on the aftermath
of the global credit crisis of 2007–2008. Without doubt, these two elements did
play an important role in the Irish case; however, there is a "but." It is important
to appreciate the specifics of the Irish case and to look beyond these two issues.
The recent cycle can be separated out into three distinct phases. The first centers
on the house price appreciation that occurred during the mid to late 1990s. The
increases in house price observed in this period can largely be explained through
reference to the economic growth that characterized the Celtic Tiger. Furthermore,
key social and demographic factors also played an important role in the events of
the 1990s. The second period was following 2001 through to the peak of the market
in 2006. While this period saw strong economic growth, it was not to the levels
previously observed. The key element during this five-year period was what Kelly
(2009) refers to as Ireland's Credit Bubble. Not only were lending criteria relaxed
but both the banking sector and the Irish Government became heavily dependent
on the property and construction sectors in delivering increased revenue. The third

and final period is concerned with the past four years. While inevitably the credit crisis and global events had an impact, structural issues in the domestic real estate and banking sectors together with government finances contributed to subsequent events. This chapter details some of the key factors that played a role both in the boom in the Irish housing market and the subsequent crash.

BOOMTOWN: THE CELTIC TIGER

The Economic Turnaround

In the early 1990s the Irish economy appeared to the outside observer to have changed little since the 1970s, looking like an economy that the 1980s boom had bypassed. Unemployment had remained stubbornly over 10 percent since the early eighties; inflation had averaged 8.95 percent during the decade while net emigration totaled more than 200,000 from the 1981 to 1991 census.[1] The government's deficits had continued to deteriorate through the first half of the 1980s, with the annual deficit reaching over 15 percent of GNP, while total government debt peaked at 120 percent of GNP. The impact of that was that secondhand house prices fell by 4.72 percent in real terms. However, the incoming government in 1987 made a number of steps that contributed to the subsequent economic and housing boom. These included addressing the twin budget deficits, increased EU structural grants, the introduction of a 10 percent corporate tax rate for manufacturing firms,[2] moderation in wage demands linked to a social partnership, and a number of incentive-based regeneration schemes. These factors were also aided by a reduction in interest rates during the lead-up to monetary union, as can be seen in Exhibit 5.1. While many of the building blocks had been set in place, it wasn't until the mid-1990s that the Irish economy started to accelerate. As one can see from Exhibit 5.2, economic growth started to accelerate from the early 1990s. From

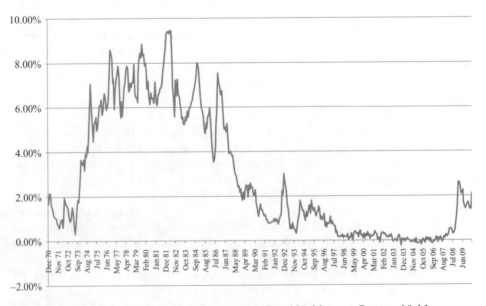

Exhibit 5.1 Spread of Irish 10-Year Government Bond Yields over German Yields
Source: Datastream.

Exhibit 5.2 Annual Growth Rates in Key Housing and Economic Variables

	1990	1991	1992	1993	1994	1995	1996	1997	1998	1999	2000
Average House Prices (National)	6.11%	5.21%	−0.27%	4.07%	−0.29%	13.05%	16.69%	28.82%	27.74%	17.89%	13.96%
Average New House Prices (National)	4.76%	5.57%	0.43%	0.55%	7.52%	7.08%	14.50%	21.79%	21.30%	16.43%	13.83%
Average House Prices (Dublin)	7.68%	5.72%	−0.27%	−2.00%	4.60%	14.80%	20.50%	34.72%	25.31%	22.49%	10.82%
Average New House Prices (Dublin)	9.73%	1.84%	−1.84%	−4.55%	12.54%	5.53%	15.10%	36.48%	21.74%	22.58%	12.46%
Disposable Income per Capita	9.27%	4.44%	3.80%	7.65%	6.99%	11.30%	9.99%	13.05%	12.98%	10.43%	13.43%
GDP	4.49%	4.30%	8.25%	6.67%	9.82%	12.20%	11.59%	18.83%	8.74%	21.61%	14.46%
Employment	3.67%	−0.86%	1.00%	2.02%	4.02%	4.90%	3.37%	6.60%	5.41%	6.49%	3.97%
Industrial Production	3.03%	4.62%	7.63%	5.22%	16.67%	22.49%	4.71%	18.48%	18.40%	18.24%	19.00%
Retail Sales	2.96%	3.86%	3.01%	5.61%	5.82%	6.05%	8.23%	10.78%	7.51%	12.52%	10.19%
Mortgage Interest Rate	11.20%	10.95%	13.99%	7.99%	7.00%	7.10%	6.75%	7.40%	5.85%	4.19%	5.99%
CPI	2.65%	3.67%	2.36%	1.41%	2.40%	2.34%	1.93%	1.54%	2.33%	2.28%	6.56%
Spread of Irish Gov't Bond Yields over German Yields	1.20%	0.99%	2.78%	0.41%	1.30%	1.27%	0.79%	0.15%	0.04%	0.45%	0.18%

Notes: Exhibit 5.2 displays annual nominal growth rates plus inflation and mortgage interest rates for the end of each year in question. The housing and mortgage interest rate data is sourced from the DoEHLG while the remaining data was obtained from the CSO.

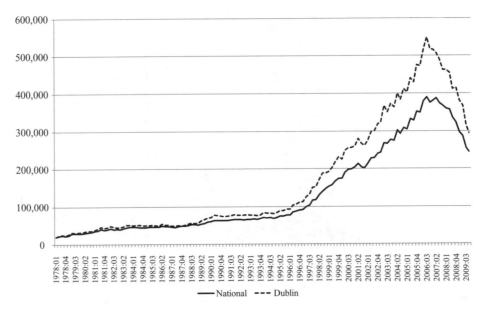

Exhibit 5.3   Average Secondhand House Prices
Source: DoEHLG.

1992 to 2000 GDP growth averaged 12.46 percent, while industrial production and retail sales grew by an average of 14.54 percent and 7.75 percent respectively. In real terms, Irish GDP grew by over 80 percent in eight years.

    This strong economic growth would alone have a positive impact upon house prices. Indeed, house prices did rise substantially from 1995 onward. Exhibits 5.3 and 5.4 display the growth in house prices nationally and in the capital, while

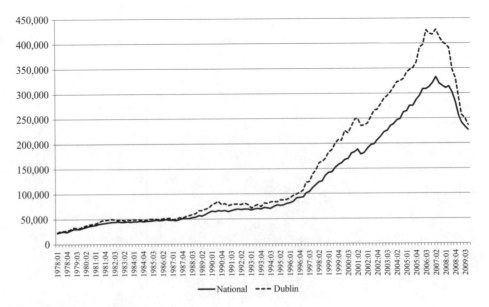

Exhibit 5.4   Average New House Prices
Source: DoEHLG.

Exhibit 5.5   House Price Appreciation, Q4 1994 to Q4 2000

	Existing Homes		New Homes	
	Nominal	Real	Nominal	Real
National	191.7%	90.4%	140.0%	70.9%
Dublin	217.0%	98.7%	178.2%	85.7%
Cork	173.8%	84.1%	125.4%	64.6%
Galway	156.6%	77.6%	118.5%	61.5%
Limerick	162.5%	79.9%	111.2%	58.1%
Waterford	201.4%	93.7%	106.4%	55.8%
Other Areas	170.9%	83.0%	141.5%	71.5%

Notes: Exhibit 5.5 displays nominal and real house price appreciation over the six-year period from Q4 1994 to Q4 2000. The housing data is sourced from the DoEHLG.

Exhibit 5.5 shows that average house price appreciation was above 10 percent for each year from 1995 to 2000 both in Dublin and across the state. Exhibit 5.5 reports the overall house price appreciation across all areas in the late 1990s. The extent of the house price appreciation is very clear, with average house prices rising by at least 150 percent nominally and 75 percent in real terms. While the economic growth was more pronounced in the Greater Dublin Region, house price grew substantially in all areas of the country.[3] However, while a large proportion of the house price appreciation observed could be attributed to the economic growth present, the Irish case was also influenced by a number of other key factors, none more so than demographic changes.

Demographic Factors

Ireland had, for much of the previous two centuries, been the subject of significant net emigration. Exhibit 5.6 shows net migration from census to census from 1881 and the large-scale net emigration that took place over the course of much of the past century can be clearly observed. This trend continued into the 1980s, with net emigration totaling over 200,000 from the 1981 to 1991 census, due to poor economic performance and the lack of employment opportunities available domestically. The economic recovery in the 1990s, however, altered this trend, and during the decade Ireland changed from a position of net emigration to one of net immigration, with the role of the two migration directions shown in Exhibit 5.7. The effect of this on the housing market became apparent in a number of respects. First, there is the overall impact upon the size of the population. The population of the country increased by 7.68 percent during the 1990s to 3.77 million, a total population increase of over 200,000, offsetting the impact of the net emigration witnessed in the 1980s. Indeed, net immigration accounted for 16 percent of that increase in population.

However, more importantly in a property context, the population growth was concentrated in key age groups and in particular in the prime first–buyer range of age 25–44. During the 1990s this age group increased in size by over 15 percent, indeed the increase in population in this age range, 142,000, accounted for over 60 percent of total population growth. In the following decade this trend continued. While the overall population grew by 18.42 percent to just short of

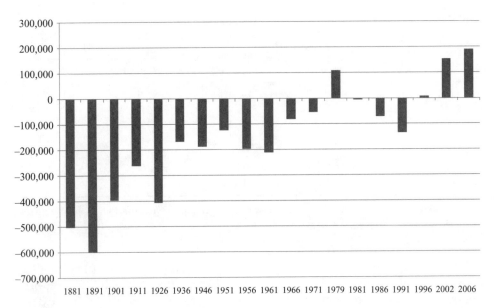

Exhibit 5.6   Net Migration from Past Census
Source: CSO.

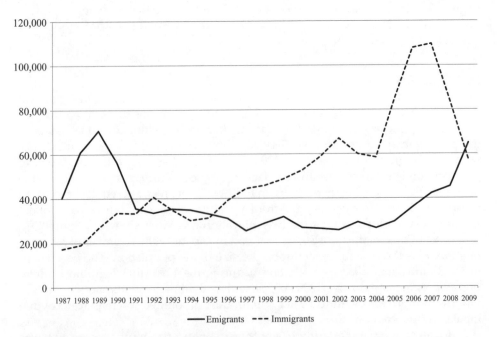

Exhibit 5.7   Annual Migration, 1987–2009
Source: CSO.

4.5 million, the 25–44 age group increased in size by 358,000 or 32.88 percent and accounted for 49 percent of total population growth and, as can be seen in Exhibit 5.9, this led to this age cohort, accounting for over 30 percent of the total population. While some of this growth was due to a natural bulge in the population and a fall in emigration, a substantial proportion was due to immigration. Of the net increase of 142,000, 51 percent was due to net immigration in that age range. As Exhibit 5.8 shows, from 1991 onward, over 40 percent of immigrants in any given year were in the first-time buyer group.

Housing Supply

The economic and demographic factors obviously increased the demand for housing stock in the state, especially so given that such a high proportion of population growth was immigration based. As Exhibit 5.10 illustrates, supply had been fairly constant from the mid-1970s onward, in the region of 15,000 to 20,000 new private homes each year. The increased housing demand due to the demographic mentioned previously, together with appreciating new house prices did lead to new supply expanding considerably in the late 1990s, doubling to over 30,000 new private homes by 1996 and 40,000 by 1999. While this appears to be a large increase in supply, it does need to be placed in context. New construction as a proportion of total housing stock did increase from less than 2 percent, as it had stood from 1987 to 1993, to over 3 percent from 1997. However, this was merely in line with figures seen in the 1970s and 1980s. Indeed, annual new construction averaged 2.42 percent of housing stock in the 1990s in comparison to 2.44 percent in the 1980s. Furthermore, the construction figures alone do not adequately reflect the change in housing stock. While during the period 1995–1999, 218,866 new housing units were constructed, the total housing stock actually increased by only 145,000. One has to remember that the 1990s were continuing to see a major effort with respect to urban renewal and regeneration. If one then considers that the population in the 25–44 age range alone rose by 93,500, the increase in construction is perhaps seen in a different light. In addition to these effects a considerable number of social changes in Ireland during the 1990s also led to increased demand for housing. The legalization of divorce in 1995 and other social changes led to a reduction in household size far later than in many other industrialized countries. In the mid-1970s the average household consisted of 3.78 people, far in excess of many other Western economies, falling to below 3 only in 2000 (Stevenson 2008).

The location of much of the new development in the 1990s also needs to be taken into account. As Exhibit 5.11 shows, from 1997 onward fewer than a quarter of new residential units were in Dublin city and county, despite the capital accounting for a large proportion of the population and being the focus of much of the increase in economic activity. Even if one includes those neighboring counties (Meath, Westmeath, Kildare, and Wicklow) that increasingly became viewed as commuter territory, the total for the Greater Dublin area is consistently less than 40 percent. The impact of the social and demographic changes previously noted also impacted upon housing in terms of supply. While official data does not particularly capture this affect, anecdotal evidence would suggest that the supply constraints were more pronounced in those properties aimed at first-time buyers.

Exhibit 5.8 Population and Migration Statistics, 1987–2009

	Total Population Change	Natural Population Increase	Immigrants	Emigrants	Net Migration	Net Migration as % of Population Change	Net Migration 25–44	Percentage of Immigrants 25–44	Net Migration 25–44 as % of Population Change
1987	6,000	29,000	17,200	40,200	−23,000	−383.33%	−5,700	35.47%	−95.00%
1988	−15,700	26,200	19,200	61,100	−41,900	266.88%	−11,100	37.50%	70.70%
1989	−21,300	22,600	26,700	70,600	−43,900	206.10%	−11,300	39.70%	53.05%
1990	−3,900	19,100	33,300	56,300	−23,000	589.74%	−2,900	41.92%	74.36%
1991	20,000	22,000	33,300	35,300	−2,000	−10.00%	4,100	43.84%	20.50%
1992	28,700	21,400	40,700	33,400	7,300	25.44%	7,700	40.54%	26.83%
1993	19,600	20,000	34,700	35,100	−400	−2.04%	5,400	41.67%	27.55%
1994	11,900	16,600	30,100	34,800	−4,700	−39.50%	3,900	40.07%	32.77%
1995	15,300	17,200	31,200	33,100	−1,900	−12.42%	6,100	46.79%	39.87%
1996	24,700	16,700	39,200	31,200	8,000	32.39%	8,800	43.11%	35.63%
1997	38,200	19,000	44,500	25,300	19,200	50.26%	12,600	40.81%	32.98%
1998	38,900	21,500	46,000	28,600	17,400	44.73%	14,100	43.36%	36.25%
1999	38,600	21,200	48,900	31,500	17,400	45.08%	13,900	44.06%	36.01%
2000	47,800	21,800	52,600	26,600	26,000	54.39%	18,800	44.57%	39.33%
2001	57,600	24,800	59,000	26,200	32,800	56.94%	25,100	50.08%	43.58%
2002	70,100	28,800	66,900	25,600	41,300	58.92%	32,100	52.54%	45.79%
2003	62,600	31,900	60,000	29,300	30,700	49.04%	20,000	48.00%	31.95%
2004	65,300	33,300	58,500	26,500	32,000	49.00%	19,600	49.23%	30.02%
2005	88,700	33,500	84,600	29,400	55,200	62.23%	34,200	53.02%	38.56%
2006	106,000	34,200	107,800	36,000	71,800	67.74%	43,000	53.06%	40.57%
2007	106,100	38,800	109,500	42,200	67,300	63.43%	40,500	54.56%	38.17%
2008	83,100	44,600	83,800	45,300	38,500	46.33%	18,900	46.78%	22.74%
2009	37,300	45,100	57,300	65,100	−7,800	−20.91%	−600	52.01%	−1.61%

Source: CSO.

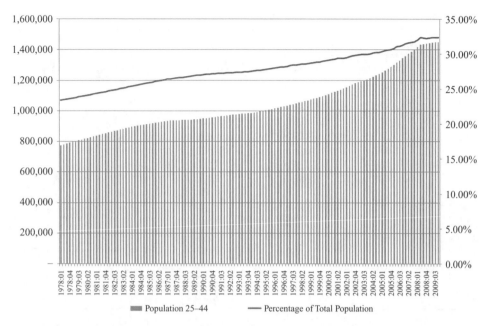

Exhibit 5.9 Population in 25–44 Age Range
Source: CSO.

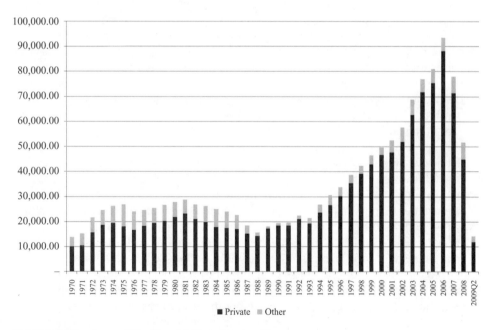

Exhibit 5.10 Annual Residential Construction Figures
Source: DoEHLG.

Exhibit 5.11 New Construction, 1994–2008

	Dublin		Greater Dublin		
	Number	Percent	Number	Percent	Ireland
1994	7,891	29.37%	3,169	11.80%	26,863
1995	8,823	28.86%	3,988	13.04%	30,575
1996	9,446	28.01%	4,924	14.60%	33,725
1997	9,325	24.01%	5,489	14.13%	38,842
1998	8,957	21.15%	6,371	15.04%	42,349
1999	10,035	21.58%	6,333	13.62%	46,512
2000	9,405	18.88%	7,731	15.52%	49,812
2001	9,605	18.26%	8,410	15.99%	52,602
2002	12,623	21.88%	9,239	16.01%	57,695
2003	14,394	20.92%	10,043	14.59%	68,819
2004	16,810	21.84%	11,230	14.59%	76,954
2005	18,019	22.31%	11,445	14.17%	80,757
2006	19,470	20.84%	12,221	13.08%	93,419
2007	17,725	22.72%	8,957	11.48%	78,027
2008	11,342	21.93%	6,122	11.84%	51,724

Source: DoEHLG.

Empirical studies of housing supply are relatively short in number in comparison to those considering price dynamics. However, those papers that have examined the issue do point to supply constraints being present in the late 1990s, despite the increase in new construction. Kenny (2003) finds evidence of asymmetric adjustment costs, with the cost of adjustment greater during an expansion in output in comparison to a contraction. Using an asymmetric error-correction model, Kenny's (2003) findings would be supportive of the hypothesis that supply constraints were a key factor in the house price behavior observed in the Irish market in the late 1990s. Stevenson and Young (2007) in a comparative analysis of house supply forecasts, find evidence that in the mid to late 1990s supply did not keep pace with the forecasts. They argue that a possible reason behind this can be linked to the arguments forwarded in Spiegel's (2001) paper of developer behavior. Spiegel argues that in situations where house prices are rising faster than the rate of interest, developers may delay projects due to the enhanced return potentially available from waiting for house prices to continue to rise. Furthermore, given the relationship between land costs and the value of housing, it is also possible that the developer will profit from seeing the value of the site increase. This potential enhanced profit can therefore offset the gain to be obtained from developing immediately. This can therefore lead to supply constraints being observed, particularly during the early stages of a house price boom. An alternative argument in this regard that can be advanced in order to explain the behavior of developers is that the delay in the response is due to risk aversion. A desire to control business risk and to have a greater degree of evidence with respect to both demand and the economic viability of projects, may also lead to delays in supply responding in the early stages of a housing boom.

There are further implications of this behavior by developers, in that supply constraints may aid in the explanation of high levels of house price appreciation in response to shocks in demand side variables, such as income. It is generally accepted that participants in the housing market display extrapolative (Poterba 1991) and myopic expectations (Malpezzi and Wachter 2005). This can mean that the resulting impact on supply though the actions of developers will encourage further price increases due to supply constraints. A number of recent papers (McQuinn 2004; Addison-Smyth, McQuinn, and O'Reilly 2008; and Stevenson and Young 2010) model Irish housing supply in an error-correction context. All three papers find the error-correction term with respect to supply negative and significant, implying that developers do respond to disequilibrium. However, the findings also illustrate the slow rate of adjustment back to equilibrium, with coefficients of −0.172, −0.194 and −0.3920, respectively.[4]

Did a Speculative Bubble Develop in the 1990s?
A number of studies have considered whether house prices in Ireland in the 1990s were displaying signs of speculative behavior and whether they could be justified in terms of economic, financial, and demographic fundamentals. The results from the various studies are relatively consistent in finding that while prices did perhaps move ahead of fundamentals in the late 1990s; the vast majority of the price increases witnessed could be justified with reference to fundamentals. Roche (1999) estimated that the probability of a crash in the market increased to 2 percent in 1998 and that the estimated non-fundamental price was approximately 10 percent. Stevenson (2008), using a variety of methodological approaches, broadly concurs with these findings. While some of the specifications did result in prices being substantially above estimated values, in the majority of cases prices were broadly in line with fundamentals by 2001 and 2002. Indeed Stevenson (2008) shows that from the fourth quarter of 1995 to the end of 2003, while secondhand house prices across Ireland rose by 260 percent, fundamentally based models showed an increase in prices of at least 162 percent. Similar findings are also observed in papers such as Kenny (1999) and McQuinn (2004). The findings do support the view that given the strong economic growth observed in the 1990s, the demographic impact of net immigration and the failure of supply to fully adequately respond, the majority of the house price appreciation could be justified with reference to fundamentals. However, if the appreciation in house prices in the late 1990s was broadly justifiable with respect to fundamentals, what changed in the subsequent years?

THE YEARS OF EASY MONEY

Most economic and real estate commentators take the view that the nature of both the economic performance of Ireland and that of the housing market changed after the turn of the past decade. By 2000 the Irish economy had effectively reached full employment. As Exhibit 5.12 illustrates, unemployment had fallen from over 12 percent in the mid 1990s to 4 percent by 2000. While net immigration continued into the first decade of the new millennium, contributing over half of the growth in population, economic growth did slow. In part this is not unexpected. Much of the growth in the Irish economy in the 1990s was a consequence of the structural shift

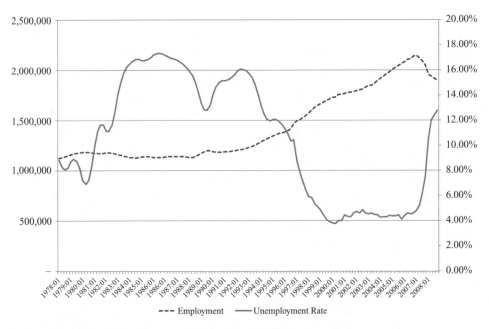

Exhibit 5.12   Total Employment and the Rate of Unemployment
Sources: CSO.

away from agriculture and traditional manufacturing toward the service and high-tech sectors. The technology crash of 2000 was inevitably going to have an impact on output, and indeed GDP growth slowed to less than 4 percent in 2000. However, this trend was to continue. While real GDP growth had averaged 8.97 percent in the 1990s, it averaged 4.23 percent from 2000 to 2006. The growth figures for real disposable income per capita slowed even more dramatically, from 6.72 percent per annum in the 1990s to 2.76 percent in the 2000–2006 period. Given that economic growth was not as pronounced, how then did house prices, with the exception of a brief respite in 2001, continue to advance with average secondhand homes averaging nominal increases of 9.3 percent, both in Dublin and across the country? The answer to a large degree rests with what Kelly (2009) refers to as Ireland's "Credit Bubble." Furthermore, the economic turnaround in Ireland during the 1990s is a key element not only in understanding the initial phase of the housing boom, but also placing into context subsequent events. It created an environment whereby the population, business and government believed the good times would continue indefinitely. Effectively, they displayed the classical symptoms of extrapolative and myopic expectations frequently observed in housing markets.[5]

The Irish Credit Bubble

While the fall in interest rates during the 1990s had played a role in the housing boom of that period, it had not been the dominant factor. That was, however, to change. While the lending policies of the financial institutions will be discussed shortly, it is important to initially discuss the impact of Ireland's membership in the euro. Membership of the single currency provided enormous benefits to Ireland. Not only did Ireland's commitment to the ERM and subsequently to the euro enable interest rates to fall during the 1990s but it also provided other stabilising benefits. As Honohan and Leddin (2006) argue, it meant that expectations with respect to foreign exchange movements and to medium-term inflation were no longer sensitive to domestic issues. However, the primary disadvantage for any country, particularly a small and open economy such as Ireland, is the loss of an independent monetary policy. Regling and Watson (2010) argue that the European Central Bank (ECB) can perhaps be criticized, together with other central banks, for pursuing a monetary policy predominantly concerned with the targeting of inflation, without placing sufficient attention on other elements and in particular growth in credit and asset prices. They argue that the period of low interest rates, and in Ireland's case negative real rates, reduced risk aversion on the part of investors and encouraged increased availability of credit and the extensive use of leverage.[6]

Exhibit 5.13 shows real interest rates in Ireland from 1996 onward. It can be seen that bar brief periods, real three-month interbank rates have been consistently negative over the past decade. Furthermore, for much of the past ten years, real mortgage rates have also been negative. As many papers have argued (e.g., Honohan and Leddin 2006; Kelly 2009; Honohan 2010; Regling and Watson 2010) the negative real rates played a major role in the credit boom that developed. The impact was not, however, concerned only with the cheapness of borrowing. This period was also characterized by a further liberalization of the mortgage market.

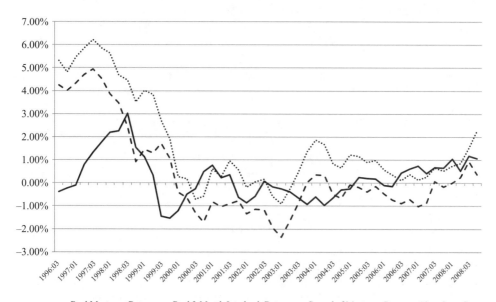

Exhibit 5.13 Irish Interest Rates, 1996–2009
Sources: DoEHLG and Datastream.

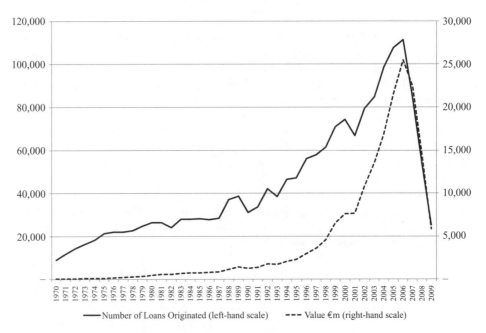

Exhibit 5.14　Mortgage Loan Originations
Source: DoEHLG.

Doyle (2009) notes that there was an increase in the number of mortgage products from 181 in 1997 to 254 by 2009. The increased variation of products included extensive use of loans with discounted teaser rates: interest-only loans and tracker products. Furthermore, there was a move toward longer terms, in part due to the increased pressure on affordability.

The greater choice of mortgage products can in part be viewed in conjunction with increased competition in the mortgage market. As with the United Kingdom, up until the 1990s the primary players in the mortgage market were the building societies. In the 1990s the banks entered the market. Furthermore, foreign entrants to the market also increased competition. However, increased competition was not just limited to this arena. The Irish financial institutions were generating increasing revenues from the property market. Exhibit 5.14 shows the growth in mortgage lending over the period. As can be seen, the number of loans originated increased throughout the housing boom from less than 50,000 in 1995 to over 70,000 by 1999 and over 100,000 by 2005. Naturally this increase in the number of loans originated largely reflects increased volume in the market. However, if one considers the amount of the loans then the picture begins to look slightly different. In 1996, even as the housing boom was beginning to accelerate, less than €3 billion in new loans were originated. By 2000 this figure had increased to over €7.5 billion and in 2005, 2006 and 2007 over €20 billion of new mortgage loans were originated.[7]

The growth in mortgage lending played a significant role in the increasing profitability of the Irish financial institutions. For example, Ireland's two largest banks, Bank of Ireland and Allied Irish Banks (AIB), saw annual pre-tax earnings increase by an average of 29 percent and 24 percent from 1993 to 2006. The impact upon banks balance sheets can be seen that between 2003 and 2006 the com-pounded annual average growth in loans for each Irish bank was over 20 percent and in the case of Anglo Irish Bank's case over 40 percent (Regling and Watson 2010). However, there was a further issue in that not only was lending increasing substantially to residential property, but the banks were also lending extensively to the development/construction and commercial real-estate sectors. We will return to this issue shortly, but to provide some indication of the level of concentration of lending, Regling and Watson (2010) report that in 2006 Anglo Irish had over 70 percent of their loan book in property and construction-related loans. The corre-sponding figures for AIB and Bank of Ireland were over 30 percent and 15 percent. They also report that if one estimates these loans as a multiple of their capital case, both AIB and Bank of Ireland had multiples of over three and for Anglo Irish the figure was 12.5. Finally, the Central Banks 2007 Stability Report states that by 2005 nearly 60 percent of all loans were in some way property related.

Another area of liberalization in mortgage lending relates to the loan-to-value ratios and the amounts lent. As in the United Kingdom, there was a shift in lending criteria away from a multiple of gross annual earnings, to a monthly criteria based on ability to pay, contributing to lending at higher LTVs. Naturally other factors came into play in this regard. The high level of house prices and affordability issues meant that many buyers, and in particular first-time buyers, required higher loans. The low and stable interest-rate environment also meant that not only were insti-tutions prepared to lend higher amounts, but that borrowers were prepared to take the additional burden on board. Up until 2001 the Central Bank had maintained a fairly tight grip on mortgage lending in terms of LTVs and it was relatively rare for a buyer to obtain a loan in excess of 92 percent LTV. As Exhibit 5.15 shows, this changed quite substantially. From 2004 on, the majority of first-time buyers had

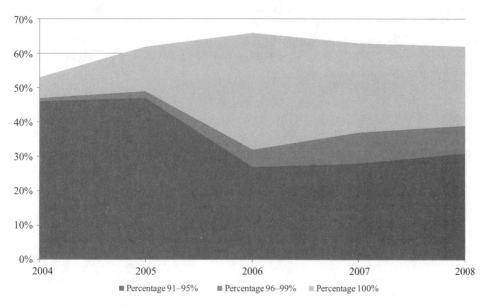

Exhibit 5.15   First-Time Buyer LTVs
Source: DoEHLG.

Exhibit 5.16   Percentage Growth in Average Loan Amounts and House Prices

	1994–2000	2000–2006
Average House Price	172.69%	94.93%
Average Mortgage Loan	137.91%	147.62%
Average New House Price	132.62%	80.65%
Average Mortgage Loan on New House	116.40%	101.19%

Notes: Exhibit 5.16 reports the percentage growth rates in both the average mortgage loan and the average house price. The figures are reported for both new and existing houses. The average loan amount data is based on the total value and total number of mortgage loans originated each year. All data is sourced from the DoEHLG.

LTVs, at origination, in excess of 90 percent, and in 2006 34 percent had taken out 100 percent loans. The figures are naturally lower for existing owner-occupiers due to the equity they would be re-investing. Up until 2007 less than 20 percent took out loans with LTVs greater than 90 percent.[8] In Dublin though, due to the higher house prices, the figures for first-time buyers were even higher. In 2004, 59 percent of first-time buyers in Dublin had origination LTVs above 90 percent, rising to 68 percent, 71 percent, 67 percent, and 66 percent in the subsequent four years.

Based on the total value of loans and the number originated, it is possible to obtain a rough estimate of the average loan amount. While, it would be crude to use this to construct long-term average LTVs, it is possible, in a more reasonable way, to look at the growth rate in both average house prices and average loan sizes. Exhibit 5.16 shows that between 1994 and 2000, while the average loan did increase for both new and secondhand homes by over 100 percent, the growth rate was less than the amount that average house prices appreciated. In contrast, however, from 2000 to 2006, the average loan increased by more than the average house price. Indeed, in the case of secondhand homes, while average house prices increased by less than 100 percent, in comparison to over 170 percent in the 1990s, the rate of growth in the average loan was higher than in the 1990s, 148 percent versus 138 percent. McCarthy and McQuinn (2010) analyzed mortgage payments based on the EU survey on income and living conditions. They found that the top decile had a repayment burden of just short of 30 percent (29.87 percent). This decile was concentrated not only in later originations, but also in single people (50.5 percent), they had the lowest average income of all deciles (€45,500) and had also taken loans out for longer terms on average than other the deciles. While the evidence of loan quality is not as comprehensive as in other markets, Honohan (2010) does argue that during this period there was a "distinct decline in loan appraisal quality for residential mortgages" (p. 25).

The easier availability of credit did play an important role in contributing to the continued rise in house prices during the 2002–2006 period. Addison-Smyth, McQuinn, and O'Reilly (2009) model the average level of mortgage credit as a function of disposable income and interest rates. They find that from 2004 onward mortgage credit increased beyond its equilibrium level. The authors estimate that it contributed to an 18 percent increase in house prices. A further element that came to the fore during this period was the growth in buy-to-let investment in the residential sector. The Central Banks 2007 Stability Report estimates that in the

Exhibit 5.17 Household Assets and Liabilities (€ million)

	Total Net Wealth	Housing Assets	Financial Assets	Total Liabilities	% of Assets in Housing
2001	355,560	237,903	180,422	62,765	56.87%
2002	401,998	291,891	185,477	75,370	61.15%
2003	472,167	346,930	214,929	89,692	61.75%
2004	522,056	394,198	240,129	112,271	62.14%
2005	577,088	446,102	276,958	145,972	61.70%
2006	648,220	516,349	308,182	176,311	62.62%
2007	598,976	484,479	311,815	197,318	60.84%

Notes: Figures sourced from Cussen et al. (2007).

2005–2007 period buy-to-let mortgages averaged just less than 20 percent of all new mortgages, peaking at 26 percent. In comparison, in the United Kingdom the figure averaged 12 percent during the same period. The role of extrapolative and myopic expectations in the housing market played a key role in the continuing rise in prices and the growth in buy-to-let investment. In addition, it led to a concentration of household wealth in housing. Cussen et al. (2007) examined household wealth, finding that not only did overall wealth increase, but that it was highly concentrated in real estate. The authors report that net worth as a percentage of net disposable income peaked in 2006 just short of 800 percent, while from 2001–2006, net wealth increased by over 80 percent. Exhibit 5.17 reports some of the key figures from Cussen et al. (2007). It can be seen that not only did overall wealth rise, but that it was concentrated in housing and that the debt burden was also increasing. In the 2001–2006 period total household liabilities increased by over 180 percent to €197 billion. While financial assets did increase, they did by only 70 percent. However, housing assets rose 117 percent to over €500 billion. Housing consistently constituted over 55 percent of gross household wealth and from 2002 onward over 60 percent. The level of concentration, not only in terms of assets but also in debt, given that a large proportion of the liabilities would be mortgage debt, made the Irish populace highly vulnerable to a fall in the market.

An Error-Correction Model of House Price Dynamics

In order to consider the dynamics of the market during the 2001–2006 period, we update the analysis undertaken in Stevenson (2008), who examined the Irish market up until 2003. We model the house prices in an error-correction framework. The long-run demand model is an inverted demand model, which has been used extensively in the European housing economics literature (e.g., Muellbauer and Murphy, 1997), and in particular in recent papers of the Irish market (McQuinn, 2004; Stevenson 2008). The empirical version of the inverted demand model to represent the long-run equilibrium house price is defined as:

$$\ln HP_t = \alpha_1 + \beta_1 \ln POP_t + \gamma_1 \ln RDI_t + \lambda_1 \ln HS_t + \chi_1 r_t + \varepsilon_t \qquad (5.1)$$

Where HP is real house prices, POP is population (25–44 age range), RDI is real disposable income per capita, HS is the per capita housing stock, and r is the real after-tax interest rate. The population and income figures were obtained from the Irish Central Statistics Office (CSO) and per capita housing stock figures were based on data from both the CSO and the Department of Environment, Heritage, and Local Government (DoEHLG). The real after-tax interest rate series was defined in a similar manner to Abrahams and Hendershott (1996) and therefore takes into account the increasing LTV ratios in the Irish context. The lagged residuals from the long-run model acts as the measure of the divergence from long-term equilibrium. Therefore, the error-correction specification can be displayed as follows.[9]

$$\Delta \ln HP_t = \alpha_1 + \beta_1 \Delta \ln POP_t + \gamma_1 \Delta \ln RDI_t + \lambda_1 \Delta \ln HS_t + \chi_1 \Delta r_t$$

$$+ \delta_1 \varepsilon_{t-1} + \omega_t \tag{5.2}$$

The nature of the housing data used in this paper does however necessitate adjustments to these models given that quarterly data is used throughout the analysis. The housing price data used in this study is the DoEHLG average house price indices. These are based on simple averages of prices on mortgaged properties. The data is not weighted in any form and is therefore also subject to seasonalities. For this reason in both the long run and ECM models seasonal dummy variables are included in the models. Given that all four quarterly dummy variables cannot be included, as it would lead to perfect multicollinearity, one has to be excluded. For the purposes of this paper the fourth quarter is selected as the omitted dummy. The results in Exhibit 5.18 highlight that broadly the models do provide a good representation of the data and the market. Both the demographic and income series are positive and significant in both the equilibrium and short-run specifications. The housing stock variable is just significant in the long-run model; however, it is perhaps surprising that the interest rate series, although of the anticipated sign, is not significant in either case.[10] The error-correction term is of the anticipated negative sign and is significant, implying that the market does respond to disequilibrium. Based on these findings we estimate the fundamentally modeled house price.[11] To do this, we assume that Quarter 4 1996 is a period that the market was approximately in equilibrium. We then estimate a house price series from this base. Exhibit 5.19 shows the percentage actual house prices deviated from the fundamentally modeled series. It also shows, on an annual basis, the modeled and actual annual change in prices in each year. The results are broadly in line with previous work on the Irish market. They show that during the late 1990s, house price appreciation ran ahead of fundamentals, peaking at a premium to fundamentals of nearly 16 percent in 1999. As with other previous research (e.g., Stevenson, 2008), the market had broadly returned to equilibrium in 2001, in large part due to the fact that actual percentage increases in house prices were below those that could be fundamentally justified. The later period sees a similar pattern. Prices do run ahead of fundamentals and rise faster than the modeled estimates, with the market returning to a premium of close to 14 percent in 2005.

THE FALL FROM GRACE AND NAMA

As noted at the start of this chapter, in 2006 Ireland stood at the peak of its housing and economic cycle. What was to follow has been extreme even in the context of

Exhibit 5.18 Long-Run and ECM Models

	Coefficient	Standard Error	t-Statistic
Panel A: Long-Run Equilibrium Model			
Constant	−2.7343	2.5512	−1.0717
Population 25–44	1.0070	0.2580	3.9035‡
Real Disposable Income per Capita	1.7729	0.1172	15.1306‡
Per Capita Housing Stock	−2.2593	0.3149	−7.1745‡
Real After-Tax Interest Rates	−0.0228	0.0548	−0.4166
Quarter 2 Dummy	0.0245	0.0329	0.7438
Quarter 3 Dummy	0.0065	0.0329	0.1981
Quarter 4 Dummy	0.0158	0.0329	0.4791
Adjusted R^2	0.9418		
Panel B: Error-Correction Model			
Constant	−0.0236	0.0069	−3.4350‡
Population 25–44	4.2799	1.5930	2.6866‡
Real Disposable Income per Capita	1.2753	0.2375	5.3692‡
Per Capita Housing Stock	0.0350	0.1504	0.2324
Real After-Tax Interest Rates	−0.0144	0.0289	−0.4993
Quarter 2 Dummy	0.0442	0.0084	5.2764‡
Quarter 3 Dummy	−0.0014	0.0084	−0.1664
Quarter 4 Dummy	0.0034	0.0085	0.4036
Error-Correction Term	−0.0754	0.0281	−2.6886‡
Adjusted R^2	0.4354		

Notes: Exhibit 5.18 reports the results from the long-run demand and error-correction models as displayed in Equations 5.1 and 5.2. * indicates significance at 90 percent, † at 95 percent and ‡ at 99 percent.

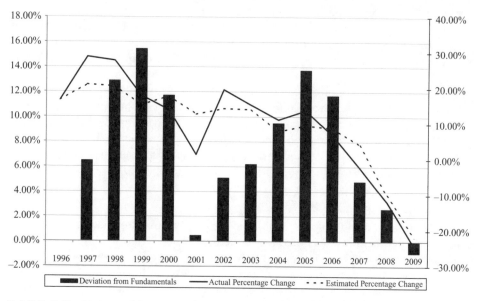

Exhibit 5.19 Estimated Deviation from Fundamentally Modeled Price
Notes: Exhibit 5.19 displays the percentage deviation of actual house prices from those modeled using the error-correction model reported in Exhibit 5.18. It also reports the estimated nominal percentage changes in both actual house prices and in those estimated from the Error-Correction Model.

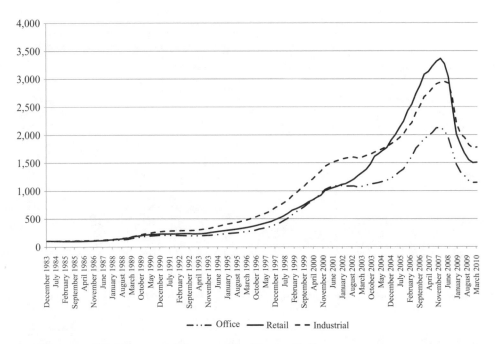

Exhibit 5.20 IPD Commercial Property Total Return Indices

the global economic climate of the past four years. While this book is primarily concerned with the residential market, it is important to note the performance of the Irish commercial market, which had out-performed all major global real estate markets. According to the IPD/SCS Indices, the office and retail sectors had seen capital values increase by over 250 percent in the ten years to December 2006. The total return indices for the two sectors had risen by 512 percent and 681 percent, respectively. Exhibit 5.20 displays the IPD/SCS total return indices for the three primary commercial sectors. The similarities in terms of the timing of the performance with the residential market can be clearly seen. As with many commercial markets globally, yield compression in the 2002–2006 period had increased capital values, and in an Irish context, the scarcity of quality investment grade stock had led to this effect being more pronounced than in other markets.[12] This strong performance led to increased economic and financial exposure to the commercial as well as residential sector.

The Construction Boom
The performance of both commercial and residential markets had resulted in a major construction boom. As noted earlier in the chapter, while housing supply had increased in the late 1990s, it was not sufficient to satisfy the increase in demand. This however changed. In 2000 less than 50,000 new units were constructed. As Exhibit 5.14 shows, by 2003 this figure had increased to 68,000, by 2004 to over 70,000 and at its peak in 2006 over 90,000 new units. To put this into context, between 2003 and 2007 over 4 percent of the existing housing stock was added to each year, and in 2006 this figure exceeded 5 percent. It would appear that if

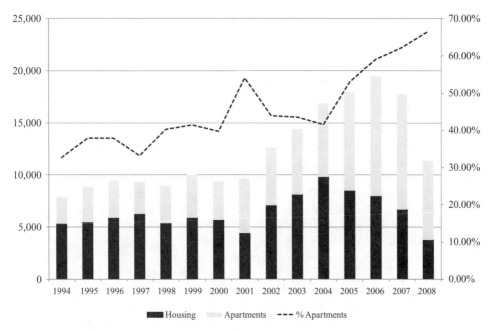

Exhibit 5.21   Annual Construction in Dublin
Source: DoEHLG.

developers had held back supply in the initial stages of the boom, as discussed earlier in the chapter, then this would have changed dramatically. Even in Dublin, which had seen the most severe supply constraints, new construction began to take off. In 2001 only 9,605 new units were completed; by 2006 this figure had increased to over 19,000. However, of interest is the nature of the construction, as Exhibit 5.21 illustrates. The proportion of units that were apartments was consistently above 40 percent from 2002 onward and from 2005 on above 50 percent.

The construction boom led to employment in the sector increasing by over 50 percent from 2002 to 2007, accounting for 13.4 percent of total employment, the highest of any EU member state. The value of output from construction increased by double figures for four consecutive years from 2002, leading to a cumulative increase of over 75 percent.[13] Furthermore, national income related to construction peaked at 21 percent in 2006, 15 percent coming from residential development (Kelly 2009). Just as with the residential sector, the banks had accumulated a large exposure to the commercial sector and to developers, meaning that an extremely large proportion of their loan books was property-related in some shape or form. As Kelly (2009) notes, the performance of property and bank lending was reinforcing. The availability of financing enabled continued construction, investment, and house purchases, while price appreciation meant that the banks were willing to continue to lend property-related loans. The Central Bank estimated that by 2006 over 60 percent of bank assets were in property-related loans, while development lending alone is currently standing at over €100 billion (Kelly 2009). As Regling and Watson (2010) state, the banking crisis that followed wasn't one related to the use of complex financial securities or to exposure in the capital markets. In many respects it was a traditional banking crisis, created by excessive lending and over-reliance on a single sector of the economy, in this case real estate.

The housing market started to slow in 2006; in most sectors the third quarter was retrospectively the peak of the market. Over the following three years, average house prices fell by 27 percent nationally and by 46 percent in Dublin. In fact, given that the official government house price data is based on pure and simple average house prices and that volume in the market has been very thin, it is felt in some quarters that these figures actually underestimate the decline in values. The major rise in construction in the 2003–2007 period also led, to some degree unusually in a residential context, to oversupply in some specific markets. The commercial market also began to weaken, and in line with the United Kingdom values began to fall in the fourth quarter of 2007. Some of the issues were common with the general turnaround in commercial real estate, and as with the United Kingdom there was a major reversal in yield movement. From September 2007 to March 2010 capital values in the office and retail sectors fell by 54 percent and 60 percent respectively, while the industrial sector has not faired much better seeing a fall of 49 percent. The fall in the value of properties, both residential and commercial, obviously had an impact upon the vulnerability of the banking sector. However, the related fall in trading volume also impacted upon the banks, particularly so given their reliance on the mortgage market for growth over the previous decade. As the market at first flattened and then start to fall, mortgage lending also fell. In 2007 the number of loans originated fell by 24 percent and that rate of decline quickened to −36 percent in 2008 and −53 percent in 2009.

Yet while the housing market was already observing falling values in 2007, many commentators at the time were arguing for a "soft landing." These commentators did not, however, solely consist of those with vested interests. The Central Bank's 2007 Financial Stability Report also concluded that a soft landing would be the most likely outcome. Honohan (2010) criticizes this conclusion on the basis that it was not underpinned by any quantitative analysis. Indeed, he shows that had the Central Banks own model, a variation of the McQuinn (2004) model, been updated to 2007, it would have suggested that prices were currently standing at 35 percent above fundamental value.[14] The subsequent banking crisis and the associated negative impact it had upon property was a combination of both domestic structural problems concerned with the level of lending to property and also to the global events of 2007 and 2008. As Honohan (2010) argues, even if the global crisis had not occurred it is highly likely that institutions such as Anglo Irish Bank and Irish Nationwide would have encountered severe difficulties due to the size of the exposure to real estate and the quality of their loan books.

The Credit Crisis and the Banking Sector

The problems encountered in the interbank market in the late summer and autumn of 2007 created major problems for the Irish banks. In common with many banks globally, Irish institutions had over the previous decade come to rely extensively on the wholesale market for their funding. Exhibit 5.22 shows the proportion of net loans to deposits for Bank of Ireland, AIB, and Anglo Irish Bank. The increase in wholesale funding facilitated the increase in the availability of credit (Addison-Smyth, McQuinn, and O'Reilly 2009). The turmoil in the interbank market did not have the same effect on the Irish mortgage as in the United States. Unlike

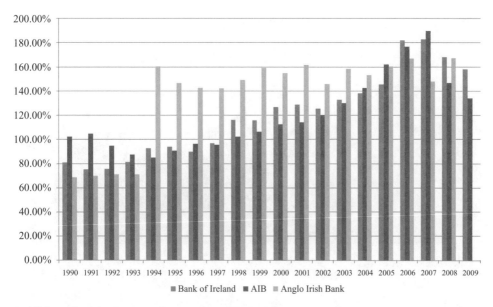

Exhibit 5.22 Net Loans as Percentage of Deposits
Source: Datastream.

the United States, where adjustable rate mortgages were generally linked to the interbank market, tracker mortgages in Ireland were in most cases tied to ECB rates. Therefore, Ireland has avoided the problems associated with the resetting of loan rates that has been a major and ongoing issue in the United States. However, the Irish institutions faced another form of problem in that the interest payments on tracker products were falling as the ECB reduced rates. In addition to this exposure, the economy overall was highly vulnerable to the global economic shock that occurred in 2007–2008. As Kanda (2008) argues, a small and open economy, such as Ireland's, is subject to increased exposure to shocks that can be transmitted through factors such as migration and FDI. As he notes, Ireland has a very high trade-GDP ratio and capital flows. The combined export/import-GDP ratio reached a peak of over 180 percent in 2000, while both gross capital inflows and outflows have exceeded 100 percent of GDP since 1999, and in 2005 were both in excess of 170 percent.[15]

The effect on the financial institutions from the combined impact of worsening conditions in the property market and the credit crisis can be seen from Exhibit 5.23, which shows the market capitalization of three of the main listed banks: Bank of Ireland, AIB, and Anglo Irish. From a peak of over €50 billion in 2007 the combined market cap of the three firms plummeted during 2008, as the extent of their exposure to property and construction and the severity of the downturn in the markets became apparent. Indeed, during 2008 Bank of Ireland's share price fell by 92 percent, AIB's by 89 percent, and Anglo Irish's by 98 percent. Exhibit 5.24 illustrates the impact on the pre-tax earnings of the banks as they began to write down losses; indeed, in 2009 alone both Bank of Ireland and AIB made provisions for over €5 billion of loans. The relatively small degree of mortgage securitization that took place in the Irish market also contributed to the ongoing exposure of the

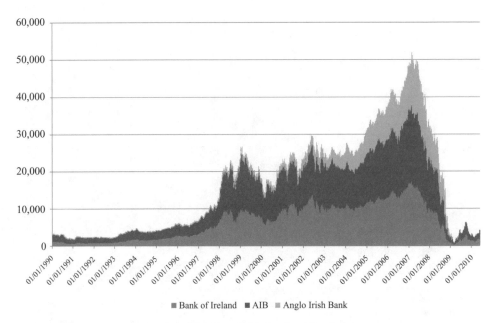

Bank of Ireland ■ AIB ■ Anglo Irish Bank

Exhibit 5.23 Market Capitalization of Irish Banks (€ million)
Source: Datastream.

financial institutions. However, the most dramatic events were concerned with the collapse of Anglo Irish Bank. Anglo Irish had expanded considerably over the previous decade and had become extremely dependent on the commercial real estate market for the majority of its loan book. As late as May 2008 Anglo was reporting a 15 percent rise in earnings, yet eight months later it had been nationalized and in the corresponding interim statement in May 2009 the bank reported a loss of €3.5 billion.[16] On a broader level, in September 2008 the government guaranteed all of the liabilities of the six main financial institutions and over the course of the next few months injected capital into a number of the firms. The most dramatic steps taken with respect to the financial institutions came in April 2009 when the government announced the creation of The National Asset Management Agency (NAMA). It is designed to provide an outlet for the financial institutions in terms of their poor performing loan books and to aid them in repairing their capital base and their balance sheets. The creation of NAMA has not been without controversy, with many commentators opposing the terms of its creation. The structure established is that NAMA will purchase loans from all but one of the main financial institutions.[17] It is currently estimated that the following proportions of loan books will be purchased by NAMA: Allied Irish Banks (18.7 percent), Anglo Irish Bank (39.2 percent), Bank of Ireland (11.4 percent), EBS (4.74 percent) and Irish Nationwide (79 percent). It is estimated that the loans in question are based on properties and development land initially valued at €88 billion. The loans have a book value of €80 billion and are to be purchased for over €50 billion.[18]

The Collapse in Government Tax Revenue
Not withstanding the problems outlined thus far, the crisis was not just limited to housing, commercial real estate or the banking sector. One of the other major

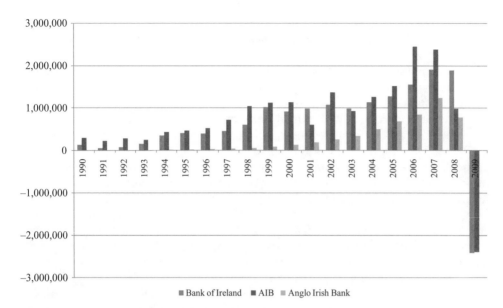

Exhibit 5.24   Irish Banks Pre-Tax Earnings
Source: Datastream. Note that given the nationalization of Anglo Irish Bank in January 2009 the reported earnings for the bank are not included for 2009.

elements in the case of Ireland is that not only were households, investors and banks over-reliant on property, but so too was the government. In 2006 Ireland had reported a budget surplus of 3 percent of GDP, while the overall debt-to-GDP ratio was 25 percent, both figures were the second best within the Eurozone (Addison-Smyth and McQuinn, 2009). Indeed, tax revenues had increased by 10 percent per annum since 2002. However, the budget situation masked structural failings, and an over-reliance on cyclical sources of revenue, many of which were real-estate related. Regling and Watson (2010) note that while prior to 2000 public sector expenditure had lagged behind GDP growth, from 2001 growth in current expenditure outpaced GDP. Furthermore, there was a shift in the tax base toward more cyclical sources of revenue.

Both Kanda (2010) and Regling and Watson (2010) highlight that the reliance on cyclical asset-based sources of revenue allowed reforms to be made with respect to income tax. Regling and Watson (2010) also note that the shift in the tax base was partly a result of government policy aimed at reducing wage demands in order to maintain wage restraint. However, it meant that the percentage of government revenue arriving from more stable sources, such as income tax, fell. As Kanda (2010) argues, this made government revenue more exposed to cyclical effects. Furthermore, he states that the reason why so little attention was placed on the nature of the tax revenue and the dangers inherent in being reliant on cyclical based sources was that the traditional OCED approach doesn't fully capture asset-based imbalances. However, it should be noted that the European Commission highlighted the issue of the cyclicallity of tax revenues as far back as 2001 (Regling and Watson, 2010). The net effect was that the percentage share of cyclical tax increased post-2001, reaching 30 percent in 2006. The IMF estimate that in 2007, while the budget was approximately in balance, the structural deficit was actually 8.75 percent of GDP. In 2009 the government deficit had deteriorated to 11.3 percent of GDP.[19]

The main sources of revenue related to property are Stamp Duty, Capital Gains Tax and VAT. Addison-Smyth and McQuinn (2009) not only note that the average annual growth rates for these three sources were 19.4 percent, 32.3 percent and 10.6 percent respectively, but in addition, after 2003 they accounted for in excess of 40 percent of all revenue. Given the level of volume in the housing market and the high stamp duty rates it is not surprising that property, and in particularly the residential market accounts for the majority of proceeds. In fact from 2003–2009 residential property on average made up 69 percent of stamp duty revenue. According to Addison-Smyth and McQuinn (2009) at the peak of the market in 2006 stamp duty in total accounted for 8.2 percent of government revenue and the residential market in turn accounted for over 80 percent of that figure. What is perhaps surprising is the broader impact of property. While capital gains tax is not payable by owner-occupiers, the strong state of the commercial market, together with revenue on development land and from investors in the residential market, also made this highly dependent on the real estate sector. However, it is actually VAT that accounts for the largest proportion of property related tax revenue. VAT is payable on new housing and, given the construction boom, became a major source of government revenue, accounting for over 20 percent of VAT receipts in each year from 2005–2008 (Addison-Smyth and McQuinn, 2009). This translates into over 6 percent of total government revenue for those years.[20] Goodbody Stockbrokers estimated in 2006 that property-related tax revenue accounted for up to 17 percent of all government revenue and had accounted for approximately a third of the increase in tax revenue in the 2004–2006 period. In contrast, in 1996, Goodbody's estimated that property-related taxes accounted for 4 percent of revenue.[21]

Regling and Watson (2010) argue that while the Irish government may no longer have had control of monetary policy, they failed to utilize other forms of policy to control both the housing and credit booms. Indeed, Regling and Watson (2010) argue that with respect to tax policies the government actually aided in fueling the boom. The use of tax relief, allowances, and exemptions all further reduced the role of income tax in government revenues. The OECD estimated in 2005 that these "tax expenditures" were three times the EU average. Furthermore, many of the allowances were related to the property sector. Ireland is one of the few developed countries that not only has maintained interest relief on mortgage payments but also has no actual property tax. It is estimated that in 2007 mortgage interest relief cost the exchequer €543 million.

Problems ahead for the Housing Market

The impact of the past four years on the Irish housing market is not only severe in terms of falling prices. As will be discussed, vacant properties, particularly concentrated in developments completed either toward the end of the boom or subsequently, are a major concern. However, the fall in prices and the worsening economic conditions have obviously had an impact upon the potential for default due to falling LTVs. While detailed default information is not readily available, nor is data on current LTVs, Duffy (2010) has provided the most comprehensive analysis thus far on the impact of falling house prices in terms of negative equity.

The analysis is based on a number of assumptions, necessary due to the lack of data. The 2006 census finds that 40 percent of households have a mortgage while the total housing stock is 1.5 million. Based on these figures, and after adjustments to the housing stock, Duffy estimates that in 2009 18 percent of mortgaged households were in negative equity, with this figure rising to just short of 30 percent by the end of 2010.

The impact of negative equity is naturally concentrated upon borrowers who took out loans toward the peak of the market and therefore did not have the protection of any upward swing in prices prior to the downturn. Furthermore, given that the LTVs at origination for first-time buyers are generally higher, the impact will be most clearly felt within that group. Duffy estimates that of the 116,083 households in negative equity in 2009 over 75 percent are first-time buyers, due to a combination of their higher LTVs and the timing of the purchases. The impact is currently affecting those who borrowed as far back as 2004 with high original LTVs. The 2010 estimates make very gloomy reading. Duffy estimates 196,015 households in negative equity, equating to 12 percent of all households and 29.6 percent of mortgaged households. Furthermore, the extent of the negative equity, not just the presence of it, is concentrated in first-time buyers. Based on the assumptions used, Duffy finds that of those in negative equity in 2010, 30 percent of households are in a negative position to the region of 10–20 percent of the house price and 29 percent in excess of 20 percent of the house price. This again is concentrated amongst first-time buyers, with the majority of those in less than 10 percent of negative equity being existing owner-occupiers. As noted previously, the lack of transactions does mean that it may be possible that prices have actually fallen further than the available statistics state. Therefore, Duffy (2010) re-estimates the number in negative equity with an assumed 50 percent fall in prices from the peak of the market to the end of 2010. The result is an estimate of 349,715 households.

Negative equity obviously has an impact upon the mobility of homeowners, as well as increasing the risk of default. The mobility issue is possibly more important in Ireland than in other markets due to the history of migration. To some degree, Ireland has historically had a correction mechanism with respect to economic conditions and employment opportunities. As noted at the start of the chapter, Ireland has long witnessed net emigration during periods of poor economic conditions. This had helped to keep unemployment to a manageable level. While Ireland has already returned to a position of net emigration, the constraint that negative equity imposes is likely to hinder the ability of homeowners to move, both within Ireland and internationally. This could lead to higher unemployment figures than would have been the case if that outlet had not been closed off. Furthermore, while Duffy (2010) highlights that negative equity is concentrated in first-time buyers, to some extent his analysis actually understates the problems facing many young households in Ireland. The construction boom of 2004–2006 had led to a major issue in some locations of over-supply and vacant space. Even in the 2006 census it was reported that over 120,000 homes were vacant, which equates to one in six homes or over 15 percent of the housing stock. The situation today will be worse given the housing that has subsequently been completed. This vacant space is however concentrated in a number of ways. First, it is primarily in new developments. Indeed, the problems developers had in selling units from 2006 onward was what led to many of the issues with development-based loans.

Second, it is further concentrated in apartment developments in Dublin and in the greater Dublin commuter belt in housing aimed at first-time buyers. This is why, if anything, Duffy understates the issues facing first-time buyers. The final issue is that due to this concentration Ireland is observing what have been dubbed "ghost estates." A number of housing developments, particularly in the counties surrounding Dublin, have been completed but with virtually none of the properties sold. Likewise, in Dublin itself, a number of apartment developments have seen similar problems while a few developments that were not completed prior to the crash have been mothballed. With such over-supply in some areas, and in properties specifically aimed at first-time buyers, a problem arises of how to value a house on an estate where only two out of approximately 50 properties are occupied. Valuation in particular is going to be an issue for the new agency NAMA, as many of the ghost estates are now effectively owned by the government, due to defaults on development loans.

CONCLUSION

The past 15 years have seen an extreme cycle in the Irish housing market. The cycle has, however, had three quite distinct phases and it is important when considering the Irish market to fully appreciate the different dynamics in each phase. The initial period of house price appreciation in the 1990s can largely be justified in terms of the strong economic fundamentals concerned with the Celtic Tiger economy. Furthermore, demographic forces also added to the increased demand, while supply constraints added to the rises in house prices observed. However, while the behavior of the housing market can be largely justified in this period the second phase, from 2001 to 2006, displayed quite different dynamics. While the housing market continued to boom it was in quite different circumstances. The price increases were no longer supported by the extent of the economic growth observed in the 1990s. Rather, the primary driving force during this period was liberalization in the mortgage market.

Many of the elements that have contributed to the extent of the crash of the past four years also date back to this second phase. Not only were households becoming increasingly indebted with respect to housing, but in a diversification sense, they were extremely reliant on the market with respect to their wealth. In addition, both the banks and the Irish government became remarkably reliant on the property sector in terms of revenue. This not only related to the housing market but also with respect to developers and commercial real estate. This lack of diversification meant that once the market started to weaken, the consequences for both the financial institutions and the state were going to be potentially severe. While the Credit Crisis of 2007–2008 did add to the problems, the core structural failings were already present. The Credit Crisis indeed merely exaggerated the effect. However, the combination of the drop in tax revenue and the financial consequences of supporting the banking sector have led to continuing major problems for the Irish Exchequer. The joint EU/IMF bailout of €67.5 billion that came into effect in November 2010 does illustrate the problems, not only from a domestic economic viewpoint, but from the broader perspective in relation to the single currency.

In part, Ireland's small size, in terms of both its population and its economy, have made the country more exposed to the dynamics that influenced the economic upswing and also those that contributed to the crash. However, Ireland currently looks forward to a potentially long road back to a sustainable housing market. Recent first-time buyers have been particularly caught out by the crash. They not only purchased later in the cycle, they generally bought at higher LTVs, and are therefore more exposured with respect to negative equity. The so-called ghost estates were also the most common places where first-time buyers did invest, further adding to their problems and potentially leading to long-term issues regarding mobility.

NOTES

1. The inner city of Dublin had lost 39 percent of its population from 1961 to 1981 (Berry et al., 2001).

2. The reduced 10 percent rate also extended to some international traded services and played an important role in the development of the International Financial Services Centre in Dublin's Docklands.

3. Stevenson (2004) examines in greater depth the issue of house price diffusion in the Irish market. The results indicate that a large degree of diffusion takes place, particularly from Dublin to the other regions, in a manner that is similar and consistent with the United Kingdom ripple effect. Evidence of the importance of contiguous and non-contiguous areas is also evident beyond Dublin and the interrelationship between provincial markets.

4. The Irish government commissioned three reports (Bacon et al., 1998, 1999 and Bacon and MacCabe, 2000) to consider not only the price appreciation present in the market but also supply issues. The first Bacon report (Bacon et al., 1998) recommended that planning authorities increase the residential densities allowed in order to increase supply. It also recommended changes that would have speeded up the development process.

5. Issues also arose in the auction market. Auctions were frequently used in the Irish market, particularly in the middle to upper end of the market. Concerns were raised about the apparent premium of sale prices in comparison to the advertised guide prices (see Stevenson et al., 2010).

6. The adoption of the euro also had an impact upon wage competitiveness for Ireland. Regling and Watson (2010) note that in the period 1997 to 2008 compensation per employee increased by over twice the average within the Eurozone, leading to a situation that by 2007 annual gross wages in Ireland were the second-highest in the euro area. Due to the lack of an independent currency that could adapt to such changes wage competitiveness internally was unduly affected. The net result was that Ireland's real effective exchange rate increased by more than any other member of the Eurozone. Honohan and Leddin (2006) show that wage competitiveness declined substantially following monetary union, falling by an average of 3.3 percent per annum with respect to the United States and 2.1 percent per annum against Germany. Indeed, Ireland saw a fall in export market share in every industry, although the impact was to some extent masked by the fact that the Irish economy was concentrated in those sectors whose world markets were growing.

7. In addition to the increase in mortgage loans, consumer credit increased from €15 billion to over €25 billion between 2003 and 2006.

8. In addition to the use of equity, the reported LTV figures for existing owner-occupiers may also be reduced as the government data does not separate loans for purchase and for refinancing. As the majority of Irish mortgage loans are to some degree variable rate,

refinancing is smaller than it would be in markets such as the United States. However, a possible bias remains in this data.

9. In addition to the primary long-term model, more tests for co-integration were undertaken on the variables used. For both the Trace and Maximum Eigenvalue tests, evidence was found of one co-integrating relationship. The Trace Statistic under a null hypothesis of 1 co-integrating equation was 46.76 (p value of 0.0631). The equivalent Maximum Eigenvalue test produced a statistic of 45.9941 (p value of 0.0011). Simple Granger Causality tests were also undertaken on the primary variables used in the analysis. In relation to house prices, significant results were found with respect to income on a bilateral basis. No significant results were found with respect to Housing Supply. In relation to Population, house prices were found to Granger Cause population. The full causality results are available from the author.

10. The models were also estimated using a User Cost of Capital variable instead of the real interest rate. The results did not differ substantially. The variable was insignificant in all specifications tested and generally of a positive sign.

11. In order to test the stability of the model, Chow Tests were used with break points as of the end of 1992 and 2001. In both cases the Chow test provided an insignificant test result.

12. The performance of the Irish market also led to a large-scale increase in overseas investment in the commercial sector. Jones Lang LaSalle in their European Capital Markets Bulletin 2007 reported that across Europe, Irish investors were second only to those from the United Kingdom in terms of their investments, with gross purchases of €13.9 billion. Irish investors were the largest single net purchasers, with a figure of just less than €10 billion.

13. CSO: Construction and Housing in Ireland, 2008 Edition.

14. The Honohan (2010) report was written by the incoming governor of the Central Bank and Financial Services Authority at the request of the minister for finance.

15. On a related note Duggar and Mitra (2007) illustrate the exposure of the Irish banks to external shocks in terms of their share price reaction.

16. Three major scandals came to light with respect to Anglo Irish during 2008 and early 2009. The first concerned what became known as the "Golden Circle." During 2007 businessman Sean Quinn had built up a 25 percent stake in Anglo stock. These were held in contracts for difference (CFD's) in order to avoid having to declare the stake once it went above 3 percent. As Anglo's stock started to fall during 2008, Quinn converted 15 percent into actual stock. He had planned to sell the remaining 10 percent in the market. However, given Anglo's share price performance the offloading of such a large position would inevitably have led to a major fall in the share price. Therefore, during the summer of 2008 Anglo arranged for 10 investors to purchase the shares. However, the funds used to purchase the holding were lent to the investors by Anglo itself and furthermore, 75 percent of the €451 million required was itself secured against Anglo stock. This led to accusations of Anglo establishing a share support scheme. The second scandal occurred toward the end of September and Anglo Irish's year-end when the bank faced a run on deposits. Given that most of the depositors were corporations the run actually went largely unnoticed. Anglo was therefore able to cover its position by arranging for one of the other major Irish financial institutions, Irish Life and Permanent, to make a €7.5 billion deposit in Anglo in order to shore up its position. However, the money deposited by Irish Life was lent to the firm by Anglo Irish in the interbank market. The final scandal was the first to become public knowledge and led to the resignation of both the Chairman and CEO of Anglo. In December 2008 it was revealed that the Chairman of Anglo, Sean Fitzpatrick had borrowed up to €120 million from the bank.

The loans had however not been revealed as loans to a director in Anglo's accounts. The reason for this was that toward the end of each of the previous eight financial years the loans had been temporarily transferred to the building society Irish Nationwide prior to the end of Anglo's financial year and then transferred back to Anglo following the year-end.

17. Irish Life and Permanent is excluded due to the low level of loans assessed as being impaired.

18. Two recent commissioned reports, Honohan (2010) and Regling and Watson (2010) highlight a number of areas that contributed to the banking crisis. Honohan (2010) argues that there was a systematic failure of supervision to realize that the institutions were facing underlying problems. Furthermore, supervision concentrated upon verifying governance and risk management procedures rather than attempting to provide an independent assessment. Regling and Watson (2010) note four key areas where there were failures in the banking crisis: (1) A concentration of bank assets in property and construction; (2) liberalization of lending criteria; (3) increased remuneration and incentives, not only at a senior level but also for middle bank management and loan officers, and (4) serious breaches of governance principles, particularly with respect to Anglo Irish Bank.

19. The Irish government was one of the first, when faced with this rapidly worsening budgetary situation, to instigate an austerity program (Lane 2009).

20. The Construction Industry Federation in 2006 estimated that on average €100,000 was paid in tax for each new home constructed. This figure was based upon not only VAT receipts but also stamp duty, capital gains tax on the land, and also income tax with respect to the construction workers.

21. Addison-Smyth and McQuinn (2009) estimate the impact of the housing boom on tax revenues. Based on a fundamental model of house prices they estimate the tax revenue that would have been received, with any excess defined as a windfall. This estimated windfall was €1 billion in 2004, €1.5 billion in 2005, €2.4 billion in 2006 and €2 billion in 2007. At its peak in 2006 this windfall equated to 1.1 percent of GDP.

REFERENCES

Abrahams, J., and Hendershott, P. 1996. "Bubbles in Metropolitan Housing Markets." *Journal of Housing Research* 7, 191–208.

Adair, A. S., J. N. Berry, and W. S. McGreal. 1995. "Fiscal Policy, Taxation Incentives and Inner City Housing Development." *Housing Studies* 10, 105–115.

Addison-Smyth, D., and K. McQuinn. 2009. "Quantifying Revenue Windfalls from the Irish Housing Market." Research Technical Paper, 10/RT/09, Central Bank and Financial Services Authority of Ireland.

Addison-Smyth, D., K. McQuinn, and G. O'Reilly. 2008. "Estimating the Structural Demand for Irish Housing." Research Technical Paper, 1/RT/08, Central Bank and Financial Services Authority of Ireland.

Addison-Smyth, D., K. McQuinn, and G. O'Reilly. 2009. "Modeling Credit in the Irish Mortgage Market." *The Economic and Social Review* 40, 371–392.

Bacon, P., and F. MacCabe. 2000. *The Housing Market in Ireland: An Economic Evaluation of Trends and Prospects*. Dublin: The Stationery Office.

Bacon, P., F. MacCabe, and A. Murphy. 1999. *The Housing Market: An Economic Review and Assessment*. Dublin: The Stationery Office.

Bacon, P., F. MacCabe, and A. Murphy. 1998. *An Economic Assessment of Recent House Price Developments*. Dublin: The Stationery Office.

Berry, J., S. McGreal, S. Stevenson, and J. Young. 2001. "Government Intervention and Its Impact on the Housing Market in Greater Dublin." *Housing Studies* 16, 755–769.

Cussen, M., J. Kelly, and G. Phelan. 2007 (July 3). "The Impact of Asset Price Trends on Irish Households, Quarterly Bulletin." Central Bank and Financial Services Authority of Ireland.

D'Agostino, A., K. McQuinn, and G. O'Reilly. 2008. "Identifying and Forecasting House Price Dynamics in Ireland." Research Technical Paper 3/RT/08, Central Bank and Financial Services Authority of Ireland.

Doyle, N. 2009 (October). "Housing Finance Developments in Ireland." Central Bank and Financial Service Authority of Ireland Quarterly Bulletin 04.

Duffy, D. 2010. "Negative Equity in the Irish Housing Market." *The Economic and Social Review* 41, 109–132.

Honohan, P. 2010. "The Irish Banking Crisis: Regulatory and Financial Stability Policy, 2003–2008." Report for the Minister of Finance, Government Publications.

Honohan, P., and A. J. Leddin. 2006. "Ireland in EMU: More Shocks, Less Insulation?" *The Economic and Social Review* 37, 263–294.

Honohan, P., and B. Walsh. 2002. "Catching Up with the Leaders: The Irish Hare." *Brookings Papers on Economic Activity*, 1–57.

Kanda, D. 2008. "Spillovers to Ireland." IMF Working Paper, European Department, WP/08/2.

Kanda, D. 2010. "Asset Booms and Structural Fiscal Positions: The Case of Ireland." IMF Working Paper, European Department, WP/10/57.

Kelly, M. 2009. "The Irish Credit Bubble." Department of Economics, University College Dublin, Working Paper 09/32.

Kenny, G. 1999. "Modelling the Demand and Supply Sides of the Housing Market: Evidence from Ireland." *Economic Modelling*, 16, 389-409.

Kenny, G. 2003. "Asymmetric Adjustment Costs and the Dynamics of Housing Supply." *Economic Modelling* 20, 1097–1111.

Lane, P. 2009. "A New Fiscal Strategy for Ireland." *The Economic and Social Review* 40, 233–253.

McCarthy, Y., and K. McQuinn,. 2010. "How Are Irish Households Coping with their Mortgage Repayments? Information from the SILC Survey." Research Technical Paper, 2/RT/10, Central Bank and Financial Services Authority of Ireland.

McQuinn, K. 2004. "A Model of the Irish Housing Sector." Research Technical Paper 1/RT/04, Central Bank and Financial Services Authority of Ireland.

Malpezzi, S., and S. M. Wachter. 2005. " The Role of Speculation in Real Estate Cycles." *Journal of Real Estate Literature* 13, 143–166.

Miles, D., and V. Pillonica. 2007. "Financial Innovation and European Housing and Mortgage Markets." Working Paper, Morgan Stanley.

Muellbauer, J. and Murphy, A. 1997. "Booms and Busts in the United Kingdom Housing Market." *The Economic Journal* 107, 1701–1727.

Poterba, J. 1991. "House Price Dynamics: The Role of Tax Policy and Demography." *Brookings Papers on Economic Activity* 2, 143–203.

Regling, K., and M. Watson. 2010. "A Preliminary Report on the Sources of Ireland's Banking Crisis." Report for the Minister of Finance, Government Publications.

Roche, M. 1999. "Irish House Prices: Will the Roof Cave In?" *The Economic and Social Review* 30, 343–362.

Roche, M. 2001. "The Rise in House Prices in Dublin: Bubble, Fad, or Just Fundamentals." *Economic Modelling* 18, 281–295.

Spiegel, M. 2001. "Housing Returns and Construction Cycles." *Real Estate Economics* 29, 521–551.

Stevenson, S. 2004. "House Price Diffusion and Inter-Regional and Cross-Border House Price Dynamics." *Journal of Property Research* 21, 301–320.

Stevenson, S. 2008. "Modelling Housing Market Fundamentals: Empirical Evidence of Extreme Market Conditions." *Real Estate Economics* 36, 1–29.

Stevenson, S., and J. Young. 2005. "Pricing Policy in the Irish Mortgage Market." Report for EBS Building Society.

Stevenson, S., and J. Young. 2007. "Forecasting Housing Supply: Empirical Evidence from the Irish Market." *European Journal of Housing Policy* 7, 1–17.

Stevenson, S., and J. Young. 2010. "A Multiple Error Correction Model of Housing Supply,." Working Paper, Real Estate Finance and Investment Group, Cass Business School, City University.

Stevenson, S., J. Young, and C. Gurdiev. 2010. "A Comparison of the Appraisal Process for Auction and Private Treaty Residential Sales." *Journal of Housing Economics*. 19, 157–166.

Van Norden, S. 1996. "Regime Switching as a Test for Exchange Rate Bubbles." *Journal of Applied Econometrics* 11, 219–251.

ABOUT THE AUTHOR

SIMON STEVENSON is Professor of Real Estate Finance and Investment in the School of Real Estate and Planning at the Henley Business School, University of Reading. He joined Reading in 2010 from Cass Business School, City University, London. Prior to Cass he worked from 1994 to 2005 at the Smurfit School of Business, University College, Dublin, where he remains a Research Associate. During 2010 he held a visting position at the University of Adelaide Business School. Simon's primary research interests are in the fields of housing economics, REITs, real estate investment, and international finance, and he has published over 60 papers in these fields.

CHAPTER 6

House Prices and Market Institutions

The Dutch Experience

DIRK BROUNEN
Professor of Real Estate Economics, Tilburg University, The Netherlands

PIET EICHHOLTZ
Professor of Real Estate Finance, Chair of the Finance Department, School of Business and Economics, Maastricht University, The Netherlands

In this chapter we begin by providing a perspective on the Dutch housing market. This market allows us to study house prices and rents not only for the past decades, but also for much longer periods, extending to the sixteenth and seventeenth centuries, to put current dynamics in these variables in a unique perspective. Looking at prices and rents at long horizons is all the more important because of the long holding periods many citizens have for their housing. The historic analysis shows that recent housing market performance is exceptional.

The remainder of the chapter is devoted to analyzing and discussing the fundamental characteristics of the Dutch housing market. We discuss the government's housing policies that underlie the market's dynamics, both on the demand and on the supply side of the housing market. After discussing the influence of government policy, we review the prevailing mortgage configurations and discuss how the recent credit crisis has impacted the Dutch homeowner market. With all this in mind, we finally look ahead to the major challenges shaping the future dynamics and risks of the housing market, and suggest policy changes to improve the Dutch housing market. These amount to more flexibility and efficiency, more freedom for citizens, and less interference in the tenure decision of households.

LONG-TERM DEVELOPMENTS OF RENTS AND PRICES

The last time the Dutch housing market experienced a crisis was around 1980, and prices had hit their low points by 1985. Since then, average Dutch house prices have risen 313 percent in nominal terms, while rents have gone up 111 percent since then. In real terms, these numbers were 153 percent and 35 percent, respectively. In that respect, the Netherlands resembles many of the other countries discussed in this book. However, as we show in this section, the boom in Dutch house prices was not caused by the same forces that shaped the housing market booms in many other countries. For the Netherlands, the boom was a historic exception, and to show the extent of this exception, we compare the performance of the Dutch housing market, both in terms of rents and of prices, to its own long-run history.

Fortunately, it is possible to put recent Dutch experiences regarding house prices in a long-term perspective also. We combine data from housing transactions at the Herengracht, a canal in Amsterdam (previously used in Eichholtz, 1998) with data from the NVM, the Dutch realtors association, to create an annual index of house prices that has also been used in Ambrose, Eichholtz, and Lindenthal (2010). Until 1965, this index was based on repeat sales regression, and from 1965 onward it was based on median house prices for the country as a whole, as collected by the Central Bureau of Statistics and the NVM. The index has to be interpreted with some caution, due to the changing index estimation technology used for different time periods, and due to its changing regional coverage, going from one canal in Amsterdam to the country as a whole.[1] The resulting index runs from 1649 through the end of 2009, and is provided in Exhibit 6.1.

The graph clearly shows that the post-1985 period has been unique. Historically, the price index did not show a long-run upward trend. Volatility in the short and medium run was high, but real prices in 1900, 1960, and 1985 were about as high as they had been in 1649. This casts some doubt on the generally held belief that house prices eventually always go up: They do go up, but only by as much as the long-run inflation rate, leaving real prices stationary. This is also one of the key lessons of Shiller's (2005) house price index for the United States that starts in 1890. Given the trajectory of the rent index in Exhibit 6.1, the absence of a historic upward trend before the twentieth century no longer comes as a big surprise.

Like the rent index, the house price index reflects changes in the economic fabric of Amsterdam and the Netherlands. For example, the deepest and longest housing

Exhibit 6.1 Dutch House Prices in the Very Long Run, Real Terms

market crisis that the city has experienced took place in the last decade of the eighteenth century and the first 15 years of the nineteenth century. The beginning of this crisis coincided with the Fourth Anglo-Dutch war, which substantially weakened the Netherlands' role as a trading nation, as much of the Dutch trading fleet was either sunk or captured by the British Royal Navy. The subsequent French occupation killed the remaining trading activity through the continental system and the British reaction to it, and also ended Amsterdam's role as a financial center. As a result, the positive wage gap that had existed between Amsterdam and the surrounding country, and that had been the engine of a consistent net migration towards the city, came to an abrupt end. Since the birth rate in the city was lower than the death rate, this meant that the population went into decline. On average, Amsterdam lost nearly 1 percent of its population per year for 20 years, leading to a structural decline in housing demand. House prices fell approximately 80 percent in real terms between 1780 and 1814. House prices stayed depressed until well into the second half of the nineteenth century.

For the 1930s, we see the same outlier as we did for rents in that time period. Real rents declined for a number of years after that, continuing until the period directly after World War II. From then onward, real prices did show a long-term upward trend, with the house price index rising from 30.9 in 1954 to 235.6 in 2009. However, this trend was associated with a lot of volatility, and in that respect, house prices have behaved very differently than rents in the post-war period. The crisis of 1979–1983 stands out in particular, during which Dutch prices lost approximately half their value in real terms.

This crisis was mostly caused by a combination of developments on the financial markets, monetary policy, and tax deductibility of mortgage interest payments. Throughout most of the 1970s, the interest rates on Dutch mortgages had been comparable to Dutch inflation, implying a very low real interest rate. However, since nominal mortgage interest payments were fully tax-deductible (at the highest marginal tax rate), this low before-tax real interest rate translated into a mortgage rate that was substantially negative after taxes. Under these circumstances, borrowing to buy a house became very attractive, leading to strong increases in the demand for houses.

By the late 1970s, monetary policy thinking all over the world had changed, and reduction of inflation became a key policy target. The monetary contraction that was a result of this policy change was indeed successful, and inflation rates in the industrialized world went down, including in the Netherlands. In 1979, annual inflation was 4 percent. The flip side was that government bond rates had become much higher than they had been before, and the mortgage rates followed suit. The Dutch mortgage rate stood at 14 percent by the end of 1979, so the real mortgage rate jumped up, also at an after-tax basis. In just one year, borrowing to buy a home, which had been possible at negative cost before, suddenly became expensive again, and this reversal lead to a severe turnaround in the housing market, setting in motion a free-fall of house prices that took until 1985 to stabilize.

House prices resumed their upward trajectory only after 1985, and have currently almost reached the highest level recorded by the index. In that sense, the message told by the graph seems to resemble the one told by Shiller's (2005) long-term housing index for the United States, just before the U.S. housing crisis started, namely that house prices have risen far beyond historic valuations, and that this is bound to come to an end in the near future. However, Shiller based these conclusions not only on the historic performance of his housing index, but also on the extraordinarily low level of the rent/price ratio. For the Netherlands, Ambrose, Eichholtz, and Lindenthal (2010) investigate the relationship between the rent developments and the price developments, and conclude that prices have diverged from their equilibrium levels for long periods of time, but that current house prices in the Netherlands are in line with fundamentals.

In other words, the boom in the Dutch housing market does not seem to have been driven by the same forces as the booms in other markets: house prices boomed, but so did rents, which suggests that the availability of capital for households did not drive prices above their fundamentals. Moreover, as can be seen from Exhibit 6.1, house prices had lost most of their upward momentum already in 2001, and the market seemed to be making a soft landing just as the booms in other housing markets reverted to deep busts. But if the developments in Dutch house prices are indeed isolated from those abroad, then the question arises of what *does* drive them. The Dutch housing market is characterized by a large degree of government involvement, and price movements may be partly due to that. Therefore, we now turn to housing policy matters.

DUTCH HOUSING POLICY

Stimulating Demand

On the demand side, the three cornerstones of Dutch housing policy are rent control, individual rent subsidies, and mortgage interest deductibility. We discuss each of these next.

Rent control, as currently practiced by the Dutch government, nearly provides blanket coverage, as 70 percent of all rental housing falls under the regulation. This makes the Dutch rent-control system among the most pervasive in the world. In the Dutch system, rents in new contracts can be set to a government-prescribed quasi-market rent level based on the physical characteristics of the house or apartment. However, once the landlord and tenant have entered into the contract, rents can at most be increased by a national percentage that is annually set by the Dutch parliament. The percentage chosen depends on the political wind of the season. In some years the national annual rent increase is quite high, whereas in other years, it does not even match inflation. This creates a perverse incentive for landlords: they do not like loyal tenants, as these generally pay—much—lower rents than new ones. Needless to say, this hardly leads to optimal customer service. The literature also shows that rent control leads to less labor mobility (Ault, Jackson, and Saba 1994; Nagy 1995, 1997), higher prices in the remainder of the housing market (Early and Phelps 1999), and misallocation of housing (Glaeser and Luttmer 2003). Apart from that, it supports those who already have a home (insiders) against those who do not (outsiders), and therefore does not protect the truly weak in society.

The second key housing policy instrument used by the Dutch authorities consists of individual rent subsidies. These subsidies are means tested, and are only given to households living in houses with a monthly rent below €680. Subsidies can amount to 40 percent of the gross rent. In principle, over three million households (out of a total of 7.3 million) are entitled to this subsidy, making it mostly an item of income policy for the low and low-middle income groups. Households have to apply to get it, and it turns out that 400,000 households entitled to the subsidy do not do so—mostly households with income below the minimum wage (about 275,000), and retired households (about 150,000). So substantial numbers of the very weakest households do not get the subsidy (VROM 2004a).

The rent subsidy gives an incentive for low and low-middle income households to rent, which contradicts the stated aim of Dutch housing policy, which is to increase private home ownership. Partly to compensate this, the government has created an individual buying subsidy as well, but the amounts involved are so small that they do not compete with the rent subsidy, so they do not really help in increasing home ownership among low-income groups (VROM 2004b).

Besides supporting the housing market by facilitating the social rented sector, the Dutch government also offers a big tax incentive to homeowners by allowing deductibility of mortgage interest expenses at the highest marginal tax rate paid by the household. That implies that the advantage increases with income levels due to the progressive tax system, with a current highest bracket of 52 percent for gross annual incomes in excess of €48,000. Currently, the average deduction is around 37 percent. This favorable tax rule for home owners was initiated with the introduction of income taxes in the early twentieth century, and was designed to compensate the imputed rent taxes that are charged to homeowners, since owning a home was labeled as a source of income.

The government also sees tax deductibility of mortgage interest payments as a tool to stimulate homeownership. Whether it really does is doubtful, however. An international comparison of housing tenure suggests that mortgage interest deductibility hardly supports private home ownership. For example, the Netherlands and Sweden, where tax deductibility had historically been most generous (although Sweden has recently abolished deductibility) are below the European average when it comes to owner-occupation. Even for the highest income deciles, for which the deductibility is worth most, there is no positive relationship between deductibility and home ownership (Eichholtz 2002).

Nevertheless, home ownership has gradually increased over the years to 55 percent in 2008.[2] Given that the Dutch housing market comprises around 7.3 million homes, the owner occupied housing market represents close to 3.8 million households. During the nineties, the favorable economic circumstances and the structural fall in interest rates fueled Dutch house price from an average of €75,000 in 1990 to over €230,000 by the end of 2009.

To illustrate the Dutch institutional setting, we first present some descriptive statistics that position the Dutch market in the context of a selected number of neighbouring countries in Exhibit 6.2. This table shows that the Dutch housing market is different from other European markets in that the typical loan-to-value ratio of Dutch homeowners is very high. The average loan-to-value ratio of 112 percent is not due to a recent fall in house prices, but rather to the fact that banks are willing to grant mortgages that exceed the value of the house. The tax deductibility gives borrowers an incentive to make their tax shield as big as possible, and the willingness for mortgage lenders to extend themselves so far has probably to do with the fact that residential mortgages are full recourse, and with the default history of Dutch mortgage borrowers, which is very good. As a result of these liberal lending practices, the Dutch mortgage market is in relative terms the second

Exhibit 6.2 Market Statistics of European Housing and Mortgage Markets, Year-End 2008

	Average House Price	Owner-Occupancy Rate	Loan-to-Value Ratio	Mortgage Debt to GDP Ratio
Belgium	130.000	67%	83%	31.7%
France	214.000	58%	66%	28.8%
Germany	200.000	45%	70%	42.9%
Netherlands	230.000	55%	112%	72.9%
Denmark	264.000	49%	80%	92.1%
United Kingdom	300.000	69%	80%	78.2%

largest after Denmark, with a mortgage-to-GDP ratio of almost 73 percent. This is very high, especially considering the relatively low owner-occupancy rate of only 55 percent.

Besides focusing on explicit government instruments like mortgage tax incentives and housing subsidies, we also briefly review the prevailing mortgage structures that are in place in the Netherlands. The existing literature has identified mortgage markets as being among the key drivers of house price dynamics. In Exhibit 6.3 some characteristics of mortgage take-up are presented. The information available shows characteristics for a "typical" mortgage in a country. Note that

Exhibit 6.3 Characteristics of Mortgage Take-Up, 2008, by Country

	Mortgage Characteristics			
	Type (%)	Duration (years)	Fixed Interest Period	Share Floating Rate*
Belgium	Repay (90%)	20	Ren, Fix (20 y)	24%
France	Repay (100%)	15–20	Fix, Ref (12 y)	20%
Germany	Repay (100%)	20–30	Ren, Ref (> 5 y)	29%
Netherlands	Endow/repay (76/24)	30	Rev, Fix (11 y)	25%
United Kingdom	Endow/repay (40/60)	25	Rev, Ren (< 1 y)	95%

Note:

Repay(ment): annuity/serial mortgage.

Endow(ment): savings or investment mortgage.

Rev(iewable): the interest rate is changed at the end of the agreed period, the level being fixed by the lender.

Ren(egotiable): the interest rate is changed at the end of the agreed period, with the borrower re-negotiating the level of the interest rate for the next period.

Ref(erenced): the interest rate changes on the basis of an index pre-agreed by the parties; for example, the interest on a given government bond.

Fix(ed): the interest rate is fixed for the full term of the mortgage.

*American households can prepay their mortgage without any penalties; so when interest rates decrease, many of them take on a new mortgage.

**Adjustable rate loans are defined as those where the interest rate is floating for the whole duration of the mortgage or fixed for at least the first three years.

Source: ECB (2003), mortgage characteristics based on studies of Calton (2002), EMF, Maclennan et al., and Mercer Wyman Oliver (2003).

within a country the variety of mortgage products offered can be great, creating room for homeowners to satisfy their individual preferences.

In other countries the supply of mortgages is more limited; in the latter cases the outcome—in terms of, for instance, the fixed interest rate period—gives fewer insights into choice behavior by homeowners, but instead reflects a lack of variety within mortgage markets. Nonetheless, remarkable differences occur.

In most countries "traditional" mortgages like the well-known serial and annuity mortgages are common, while in some northwestern European countries endowment mortgages are more popular. Note that these mortgages are not only popular in the Netherlands, where a favorable tax system exists, but also in the United Kingdom. The average duration of a typical mortgage loan typically decreases from North to South, topping in Sweden at 30 to 40 years, while in Southern countries 15 to 20 years is more common. In terms of the average period that interest rates are fixed, the choices are rather divergent. In the United Kingdom, short-term/variable mortgages dominate, while the average fixed term in Belgium is 20 years. In Denmark and the Netherlands, households opt for mortgages with long durations and fixed interest rate periods. One should note, however, that in Denmark—unlike the other countries in Europe—no penalty is raised for early prepayment. Hence, households opt for fixed interest rates, while refinancing when interest rates have decreased.

Controlling Supply

The current Dutch housing system has strong roots in the period just after World War II. As in many countries in the continent, the war had led to a large housing shortage, which was aggravated by rapid growth of the number of households in the decades after the war. The government intervened, and as policy makers were contending with increasing costs of living and construction, a program was designed that contained substantial subsidies and which emphasized volume. The need to build cheaply and quickly led to an emphasis on the social rented sector, which rapidly expanded from 12 percent of the housing stock in 1945 to 41 percent in 1975, and which represents around 38 percent of the Dutch housing market to the present time. From the 1970s onward, the era of massive building came to an end, to be replaced by increasingly restrictive house-building polices.

An enduring myth in the Netherlands is that house prices are inevitably high, due to the fact that the Netherlands is a small and densely populated country. While there is no doubt that the country is indeed very densely populated, it is not at all certain whether this causes high house prices. If that were the case, there should be a positive relationship between population density and tightness of the housing market, but this correlation is not found.

Exhibit 6.4 provides for the European Union member states the population density and the household housing expenses as a percentage of income, which is an indicator of the tightness of the housing market. The table shows that the Netherlands has by far the highest population density, but is somewhere in the middle when it comes to housing expenditure. Overall, the correlation between the two variables is only 0.06.

The crucial feature setting the Dutch housing market apart is not its population density, but the fact that the supply of new housing does not react accurately to

Exhibit 6.4   Population Density and Housing Expenditure, European Union Member Nations, 2008

	Population Density: Persons per Square Kilometer	Housing Expenditure as Percent of Net Income
Sweden	22	28.10%
Denmark	124	28.00%
Finland	17	25.20%
Estonia	32	24.40%
Germany	230	24.20%
France	96	23.50%
Belgium	338	23.00%
Slovakia	110	22.90%
Poland	122	22.40%
Luxemburg	169	22.30%
Latvia	38	21.00%
Czech Republic	133	21.00%
Netherlands	470	20.70%
Slovenia	99	20.00%
Ireland	55	19.40%
Italy	193	19.40%
Hungary	110	19.00%
Austria	97	19.00%
United Kingdom	241	17.70%
Greece	84	15.90%
Spain	80	14.20%
Lithuania	56	14.10%
Portugal	111	10.70%
Cyprus	75	7.90%

demand. Vermeulen and Rouwendal (2007) have recently made an investigation into the price elasticity of Dutch housing supply. They conclude that this elasticity is very close to zero.[3] In other words, housing supply does not react to price signals, and that holds both for quantity and for quality. This is illustrated by a lack of growth in Dutch housing construction, even when house prices broke record after record between 1990 and 2008.

Dutch housing supply is curtailed in three ways: spatial planning policy, municipal interference in the quality of the new housing stock, and ever lengthening procedures. We discuss each of these causes of low supply elasticity next.

The first and foremost supply restriction for housing is spatial planning. The Netherlands is a small country, and there is broad popular support for the idea that the availability of land for new construction should be limited. To maintain a good living climate in the country, open space is important, and that is the reason that the government has been regulating the supply of new housing locations since the 1950s, and increasingly tightly from the 1970s onwards (Rouwendal and Vermeulen 2008).

This policy has been successful, and the Netherlands has lots of open space, mainly in the form of agricultural land. Compared to other European countries of similar size, the ratio between residential land and agricultural land is very low in the Netherlands. The most recent numbers from Eurostat—for 2000—give a ratio of 9.5 percent for the Netherlands, against 11.9 percent for Denmark and 12.8 percent for Belgium. One could wonder if it is beneficial for such a small country to have such a lot of agricultural land: It can be seen, but not accessed by the public. If the Netherlands would bring its ratio of residential to agricultural land to the Belgium level, this would imply that 58.000 hectares of agricultural land would be converted into housing land, which would amount to an increase in the supply of housing land of 31 percent.

The comparison with Belgium is interesting, as that is the only country that comes close to the Netherlands in terms of population density (see again Exhibit 6.4). The big difference with Belgium is that the latter country has let the supply of housing land go up quickly, compared to the Netherlands. Between 1981 and 2003, the most recent period for which comparable data is available, the increase was 39 percent in Belgium, against 12 percent in the Netherlands (Nationaal Instituut voor de Statistiek België 2008; CBS 2008b).

It is to be expected that this difference in housing land supply is reflected in the prices of housing land. Exhibit 6.5 provides more information, and gives average prices per square meter for housing land in the two countries.

For the Netherlands, that price is slightly more than four times as high as it is in Belgium. When the comparison is made between the Dutch provinces of Noord Holland, Zuid Holland, and Utrecht and the Belgian province of Antwerp—which are even more comparable in terms of population density and economic success—we find again that housing land prices in the Netherlands have more than four times the level of Belgium. These differences are so big that they cannot be explained by the fact that the Dutch prices reflect bigger investments in infrastructure than prices in Belgium. The comparison between the two countries suggests that the difference in land costs for housing are at least partly caused by

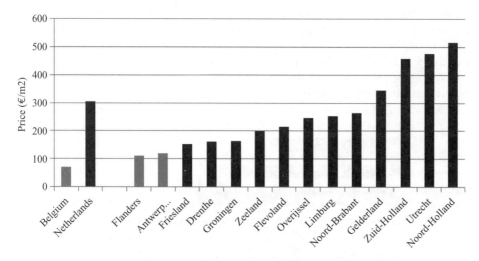

Exhibit 6.5 Prices per Square Meter for Housing Land in Belgium and the Netherlands, 2005

differences in the supply of land, which are direct results of government policies in the two countries.

The second direct restriction the Dutch government puts on the housing market is of a more qualitative nature. Municipalities rather than housing developers determine the mix of houses offered in new housing construction. For example, they may stipulate that X percent of new homes in a development are aimed at higher income groups, and Y percent at low-income groups. Municipalities have been qualitatively micro-managing supply with a vengeance, and almost always have a disproportionate preference for social housing. This market distortion could be defended if the country needed such low-priced and low-quality housing, but it does not. According to a study by the Dutch Central Planning Bureau (Romijn and Besseling 2008) the country has 2.3 million housing units with a low or affordable rent, while there are only 1.3 million households with a low income. This suggests the Netherlands already has an oversupply of approximately 1 million social houses.[4]

Why then do municipalities still want to have more of them? That is because in these 2.3 million houses live 1.7 million middle- and high-income households, so there seems to be an immediate shortage of social housing of about 700,000 units. The law does not give social landlords the power to remove middle- and high-income households from their properties, so these 1.7 million households can stay in subsidized houses that are not meant for them for as long as they want. Under these circumstances, municipalities will keep prescribing more social housing development, even as the Netherlands has far too many of these already.[5] This market distortion will likely be very costly, since it forces a misallocation of capital into a housing market segment that Dutch citizens do not need.

A third limitation of housing supply can be found in the ever-lengthening procedures for new development. Building a house in the Netherlands involves a host of procedures that give citizens living nearby many opportunities to protest and thereby stall the new development. Of course, nothing is wrong with a careful weighing of private and public interests, or with opportunities for the local population to participate in the decision making in this area. The question is, however, how far one should go in this, and why these procedures take so long. Exhibit 6.6 gives some information on the average time it takes for a housing project to get to the building stage. In 1970 it took an average of 33 months to go from first plan to building, but that period has lengthened substantially. In 2000, the time was 73 months, and that has increased to 90 months in 2010.

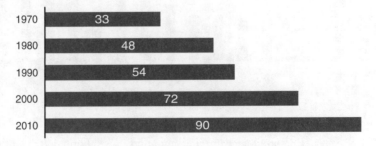

Exhibit 6.6　Average Time to Construction for a Housing Project, 1970–2010, Months

These increasing time periods can be blamed on ever-lengthening procedures and more and more use of local citizens' possibilities to block building plans. Building houses in the Netherlands involves changing the zoning for the land, and also requires permits for construction and the cutting of any trees on the land. Also, studies of the environmental impact of the development and of the potential pollution of the land are required. All these changes, permits, and studies have maximum terms, and increasingly, they take the maximum allotted time. On top of that, citizens have opportunities to appeal planning decisions at numerous levels, which is also very time-consuming.

Policy Results

So to sum up, overall Dutch housing policy can be characterized as "stimulating demand; curtailing supply." This combination leads to structurally increasing rents and prices. In a well-functioning market, these higher prices would sooner or later lead to a signal to developers to increase supply, thereby stabilizing the market, and bringing it back to equilibrium. However, Dutch housing policies prevent this from happening, so prices and rents keep on rising. Probably because of that, the current global crisis has hardly affected pricing in the Dutch housing market. Rents have not fallen at all, and prices have fallen by a cumulative 7 percent since their high at year-end of 2007. These price falls can hardly be characterized as a crisis.

DUTCH DEFAULT DYNAMICS

Despite the fact that Dutch house prices have not fallen much, the economic consequences of the recent credit crisis have been felt in other ways, and have left traces in the Netherlands. From 2008 onwards, consumer confidence plunged and GDP growth weakened and eventually reversed into a decline of 4 percent in 2009. These circumstances have weakened consumers' willingness to spend, especially regarding large expenses, such as homes. The Dutch housing market came to a standstill in 2008, with the number of sales falling by half during the course of 12 months. The restrictive supply policy has prevented large price declines. The government enhanced some demand incentives, and the construction industry swiftly reduced the new supply of housing, which resulted in mild price decreases. Nevertheless, central bankers and policy makers voiced their concern regarding a rise in mortgage foreclosures as the economic outlook worsened and unemployment levels rose.

The question, however, is whether these concerns are warranted. Cosemans and Eichholtz (2009) analyzed mortgage defaults during the last major crisis in the Dutch housing market. They looked at the experiences of mortgages guaranteed under the national mortgage guarantee system (currently called NHG). House prices fell almost 50 percent in real terms between 1980 and 1985, so by 1985, many homeowners had negative home equity, especially those who had bought their home in 1980 or just before. However, even for that worst-case cohort, the mortgages issued in 1980, the guarantor had to pay out only 1.36 percent of the total issued mortgage amount to creditors. The cumulative amount paid out for all guaranteed mortgages combined was 0.33 percent. Given the severity of the crisis of that time, which coincided with very high unemployment, these default rates are very low. One explanation for this could be that Dutch residential mortgages are full recourse, implying that the negative-equity-default-option approach is not a valid way to model mortgage default in the Netherlands. Mortgage default seems more related to the credit quality of the borrowers than to the collateral value of the house. On top of that, in case of default, the foreclosure process is very much tilted against the interests of the borrower, giving households a very strong incentive to avoid default, as we will see in the analysis below.

In the Dutch mortgage market, residential mortgage contracts clearly state the process of foreclosure. In case the mortgagee fails to meet his or her monthly mortgage duties, the bank automatically obtains the right to repossess the home. After notifying the mortgagee, the bank can evict the client from the home within two months and organize a public sale of the property to redeem the loan balance. The fastest sales method is the foreclosure auction, where the home will be sold on the spot, assuming that a predetermined minimum sale proceed is met. Alternatively, the house can also be sold at an over-the-counter fire sale. In this case, a local real-estate broker is hired by the bank to facilitate the sale in the open market. Here the home will be advertised in the traditional manner, without signaling the distressed state of the mortgagee. Prospective buyers are offered the opportunity to visit the property and the home is sold after bilateral negotiations between the brokers of buyers and sellers. Also in this sale process the bank is in charge of the sale and will collect the proceeds up until the outstanding loan balance. Given that the average sale period of these OTC fire sales exceeded well over 120 days in 2010, banks often opt for the foreclosure auction to swiftly salvage their loan.

Buying a home at foreclosure auction, however, is costly. This became more apparent when the global credit crisis started to influence the sentiment on the Dutch homeowner market. The auction sale is managed by a notary on behalf of the bank. In these events notaries charge higher fees than the standard, given the additional work that is involved in filing the distressed background of the mortgagee. The auction itself will also induce additional costs, for instance renting the auction house and hiring an auctioneer. On average these fees amount to around 4 percent of the sale proceeds, whereas a regular sale requires only around 1 percent of notary fee. This cost difference, of course, will depress the sale proceed at auctions.

For an empirical analysis of the price dynamics of mortgage recovery dynamics, we turn to a sample of 690 forced sales that occurred in the period 2004–2009. In this sample we distinguish two sale platforms through which the sales have been executed: in 403 cases the house was sold over the counter (OTC) in a fire sale by the bank that issued the mortgage, and in 287 cases, the house was sold during a foreclosure auction. Before we turn to an analysis of the price discounts for the two sales methods, we first test whether the choice of the sales mechanism can be related to some key characteristics of the dwelling, or some other contextual variables. If that would be the case, then discounts that we have found earlier might not be related to the sales mechanism, but instead to other variables. We have therefore estimated a probit model where the choice for an auction (1) or OTC fire sale (0) is the dependent binary variable. Exhibit 6.7 summarizes the findings of these regressions.

Exhibit 6.7 Potential Factors Driving the Choice for the Sales Mechanism

Model Specification	S1	S2	S3	S4	S5
Intercept	111.281	71.084	108.241	53.637	82.592
	(22.596)	(25.012)	(29.962)	(25.156)	(19.167)
Hedonic value [€,000]	−0.861	−0.805	−0.844		
	(0.145)	(0.147)	(0.148)		
Density of homes in region		0.106	0.166	0.082	
[# of homes/km^2]		(0.003)	(0.004)	(0.042)	
Av. value of homes in			−225.924	−37.528	
region [€,000]			(98.309)	(100.020)	
Dwelling size [m^2]				−0.676	−0.779
				(0.272)	(0.269)
No. of rooms				−6.702	−7.440
				(5.870)	(5.845)
Garage [0/1]				−21.373	−26.253
				(21.319)	(21.023)
Parking or carport [0/1]				−78.753	−82.326
				(28.466)	(28.562)
Well-kept garden [0/1]				−12.981	−17.708
				(18.8)	(18.736)
McFadden R^2	0.041	0.057	0.062	0.063	0.056
Percent correctly predicted	58.84	62.90	63.33	63.33	62.90
N	690	690	690	690	690

Note: This Table presents probit estimates (MLE estimation with Newton-Raphson algorithm) for the choice between an auction ($\Pr(y=1 \mid xi,\beta)$) and an OTC fire sales ($\Pr(y=0 \mid xi,\beta)$) for different specifications with increasing number of variables. Entry shows attribute coefficients with t-stats beneath in parentheses, both reported in percentage points (i.e., multiplied by 100 due to small coefficients).

We test the following model specifications. In the first specification (*S1*) we expect that the hedonic value of the property is negatively related to the probability of being auctioned once in distress. Since more expensive homes may have more idiosyncratic features that drive the value, one may reason that these homes are better sold through a broker. Though the sign of the slope estimator confirms this reasoning, the overall model fit is very weak.

Next, we have added two context variables, being the number of homes per square kilometer in the region, and the average value of a home in the region (for both variables we took the annualized averages in the year of the forced sale). We expect that in areas with a high population density, it is likely that demand for homes is higher, and the auction may be more successful. When the average value of homes is high in some region, we expect auctions to be less suitable because of the aforementioned idiosyncratic value drivers. Again the sign of the slope estimators is confirmed, but the overall model fit is still very poor.

In the fourth specification, we took out the estimated hedonic value of the dwelling and replaced it with some key characteristics of the home, without much improvement. Lastly, we have taken out the contextual regional data, and focused solely on the characteristics of the dwelling. None of our model specifications is able to explain more than a 6 percent of all variation in the choice between auctioning a distressed property or selling it through a broker. It thus seems plausible that any price discounts are indeed driven by the respective sales mechanism, and not by some key characteristics of the dwelling itself.[6]

The main difference between the two sales methods is the speed of the sale. In the auction the house is sold on the spot to the highest bidder present in the audience. In the OTC fire sale the bank engages a real-estate broker who attracts potential buyers and negotiates the prices bilaterally after visiting the property. To illustrate this, we included a comparison of dwelling characteristics for both sale mechanisms in panel A of Exhibit 6.8. These statistics show that distressed homes sold at an auction are more likely to be relatively small, old, and typically apartments, when compared to homes sold at OTC fire sales. But as already shown in the probit analysis of Exhibit 6.8, these differences are mild at best. Obviously, the time pressure and aforementioned limitations in information that characterize the foreclosure auctions will have a depressing effect on the sale price. We measure the effects of the sale platform by comparing the realized transaction prices of both sales methods with the fair-market value that is estimated by applying the hedonic

Exhibit 6.8 Price Discounts at Forced Sales

	Foreclosure Auctions	**OTC Fire Sale**
Panel A: Dwelling Characteristics		
Proportion apartments	41.3%	26.3%
Proportion post-1970s (age)	20.1%	37.0%
Proportion with garage	6.0%	17.6%
Proportion well-kept garden	6.0%	12.0%
Mean floorspace (m^2)	82.7	95.7
Mean number of rooms	3.5	4.0
%2005 transactions	21.8%	22.2%
%2006 transactions	20.5%	21.7%
%2007 transactions	20.9%	19.8%
%2008 transactions	18.5%	23.1%
Panel B: Price Formation		
Mean sales price	€92,603	€138,494
Mean fitted market value	€145,431	€163,226
Mean price discount	−36.5%	−14.6%
t-stat	1.97**	0.67
Median price discount	−38.9%	−12.8%
Minimum price discount	−69.9%	−67.1%
Maximum price discount	16.8%	50.4%
# negatives	274 (95%)	301 (75%)
# positives	13 (5%)	102 (25%)
Total	287	403

Note: This table presents the differences between dwelling characteristics and prices for homes sold on foreclosure auctions and in OTC fire sales market for the period 2004–2008. In panel A, we report statistics on the most relevant dwelling characteristics, which indicates that homes sold in foreclosure auctions are typically of lower quality than homes sold in OTC fires sales. The difference in quality is also imbedded in the fitted market value that results from the hedonic price model, which is lower for the sample of foreclosure auctions. We derive the price discount by comparing the realized sale price with the fitted market value for every observation in our subsamples. The reported t-statistics measures the significance of the differences in means of the sales price and market value.

price model on the dwelling characteristics. In panel B of Exhibit 6.8, we show that in 95 percent of all observed transactions at foreclosure auctions, the realized sale price fell short of the free market value.

On average, this price difference exceeds 36 percent, which equals an amount of €52,000. In the case of the OTC fire sales, this oscillation is milder. Here we find a negative price difference of less than €28,000, which equals around 15 percent of the fair market value. All in all, these results are in line with previous studies on U.S. foreclosure sales that documented price discounts of 22–25 percent.[7]

Given that the average forced sale in our sample occurs four years after the house was acquired and typically financed at an LTV of 115 percent, the bank needs a price appreciation of more than 8 percent per year to compensate the recovery loss that is realized in the foreclosure auction. In the 403 OTC fire sales, the bank still recovers its outstanding mortgage as long as house price has risen 3.5 percent each year during the four years of living that precede the default. Since 1970 the average nominal price appreciation in the Dutch housing market equaled 6 percent. However, over the ten most recent years, this average price appreciation faltered and amounted to less than 4 percent a year, and during 2009 Dutch house prices fell by 5 percent. Since the beginning of the global financial crisis, Dutch banks have become much more reluctant to provide loans that exceed the value of the underlying value, a development that has partly been forced by the regulator.

Mortgage foreclosure is one of the key issues in the Dutch housing market. It is not so much the increased frequency of foreclosure—since the start of the credit crisis the number of forced sales increased only 15 percent—but rather the level of organization. The fact that auctions perform poorly with respect to setting an adequate price is a concern that is now addressed in Parliament. Homeowners ought to have a fair chance of obtaining a foreclosure price that is close to the fair market value. In the Netherlands, mortgage loans are full recourse, so the financial consequences of a depressed foreclosure price may be profound for the households involved. Results of the empirical analysis in this section are assisting to adjust legislation and stimulate the surge of professionally managed auction houses to compete in the market for mortgage foreclosure in recent years. In that sense, the credit crisis has had a positive effect on the Dutch housing market, since the importance of a well-functioning foreclosure auction system has become more apparent.

FUTURE CHALLENGES AHEAD

The developments described above provide arguments for a substantial overhaul of the Dutch housing market, aimed at flexibility, individual choice, and the reintroduction of prices as an information mechanism. Demand-side policies should be restructured, diminished, and streamlined, and should stop incentivizing certain income groups to own, and other groups to rent. At the same time supply should become much more flexible, both quantitatively and qualitatively. Besides that, supply needs to be based on consumers' wishes, not on the preferences of policy makers.

Rent subsidies should be abolished; income policies should be implemented through the tax system. This could be done through an increase of the tax exemption threshold. For the bottom income groups, who already have an income below that level, the rental subsidy can be replaced by a negative income tax. This would both be more efficient and more fair than the current subsidy system, as it would make the current labor-intensive subsidy distribution system redundant, and it would be automatic, so that all those who are entitled would benefit, including those with very low education, who currently have trouble applying for the subsidy they are entitled to. It would also stop the current incentive for low-income groups to rent instead of own, and would give citizens a neutral tenure choice.

The second key policy change is in rent control. Since rent control without means testing harms mobility in the housing market, there seems to be a shortage in low-rent housing, causing a permanent pressure to build more of it. But given that industrialized countries tend to get richer as time progresses and labor productivity increases, the Netherlands will probably need a more expensive, higher-quality housing stock in the future rather than a low-rent, low-quality one. In other words, the social houses built now will likely be obsolete in the near future, amounting to a big waste of capital. That means rent control should ideally be abolished, thereby reintroducing the price mechanism in the rental market. That would end the incentive for middle-income households to stay where they are, and would free up social housing to those who really need it. Unfortunately, this may be politically unpalatable, as rents could end up much higher than they are right now: Romijn and Besseling (2008) estimate that rents would double.

A potentially less painful way to increase mobility in the rental housing market is rigorous income testing. Current regulation regarding rents and privacy stands in the way of an effective means testing by social landlords. They do not have access to their tenants' salary information, and even if they would, they could not act upon it: The current housing rent regulation prevents them from expelling tenants with a high income from their properties, and from asking a market-level rent from those who can afford it. This should change.

Regarding the owner-occupied market, mortgage tax deductibility should be gradually abolished. Given Dutch supply rigidities, this tax break only leads to higher prices, and gives households an incentive for high leverage. It may well have played a role in the high-leverage, high-prices feedback loop that has characterized the Dutch housing market in the past two decades. It is probably not a good idea, especially not now, to abolish this measure all at once, as this could create a severe drop in prices. The example of Sweden, the most recent European country to abolish tax-deductibility, suggests that the cold-turkey approach can cause severe price drops in the housing market. But there are several ways to cancel the measure gradually, possibly avoiding or diminishing a drop in house prices. For example, one could now maximize the measure at a certain high nominal house-price level, which would gradually diminish the real value of the deductibility through the long-term inflationary house price growth. Another possibility is to gradually lower the deductibility over, for example, 20 years, or one could announce now that deductibility will be abolished all at once in, say, 15 years. This would lead to higher after-tax house expenses by then, but the present value effect of that would initially be small, and would go up with the years, partly or wholly compensated by normal nominal house price growth. Whatever method is chosen, the abolishment of the measure should be accompanied with a lower tax rate, making it budget-neutral for the treasury.

Regarding housing financing policy, the Netherlands has a reasonably efficient system, but it could be improved in a number of ways. First, banks are still allowed to provide loans above the market value of the home, which, combined with the tax incentive for high leverage, leads to a very high mortgage-to-GDP ratio, so jeopardizing the financial stability of the country. Abolishing tax deductibility of mortgage payments would take away the incentive, but forbidding mortgage loans above the market value would also decrease leverage and societal risk.

Second, the foreclosure process of mortgage loans can be improved. The empirical results in Section III show that home owners in a mortgage default situation are very badly served in the current system: They lose their house in a forced sale in which their house is sold at an average discount of 36 percent to market value. The problem is that the bank, which organizes the foreclosure sale, has a very weak incentive to get the maximum amount possible for the house, since the loans are full recourse. The discount is fully at the expense of the household, which does not have a say in the foreclosure process. To mend this, it is probably good to give households in a default situation a certain time period, say six to nine months, to try to sell the house themselves on the open market, initially avoiding the forced sale auction. If the house would not be sold in that period, the bank would get the right to repossess and sell the house in auction after all.

On the supply side, our analysis suggests that high prices are not necessary in a densely populated country. International comparison shows that high land prices are predominantly a function of political choices regarding the availability of building land for housing. So an affordable housing market can be accomplished by increasing the supply. This is also important with respect to the type of homes that can be built. Market research consistently shows that Dutch households prefer houses with a garden, and that apartments are generally far less popular. This goes against the wishes of policy makers, who prefer high-density housing within city limits. Citizens should be the ones making the choices, implying the need for a more generous housing land policy. Here, the national government should lead the way: As we argued earlier, municipalities do not have a strong incentive to liberalize the supply of housing and land. The government can shorten the maximum terms for legal procedures regarding zoning and building, and can curtail the possibilities for appeal. To go toward more lenient urban planning, and to introduce normal market circumstances in Dutch housing, the national government holds the key.

CONCLUSION

For the Dutch housing market, reform is badly needed. The current system, in which housing demand is systematically supported—while supply is as systematically curtailed—leads to high prices, inflexibility, and a housing stock the country does not want in the long run.

The central pillars of reform should be freedom to choose for consumers and producers alike, a flexible supply of housing, both quantitatively and qualitatively, and financial support for those who really need it. The government should stop its current micro-management of the market

A balanced housing policy starts with a housing supply that can adjust to demand in a flexible manner. That requires simplification of procedures. At the same time, the structural support of housing demand, in the form of tax deductibility of mortgage interest payments, purchase subsidies, rent subsidies, and rent protection, should be abolished, while lowering taxes at the same time, and to the same amount. This will result in a more balanced housing market, a broader tax rate with lower taxes, and more freedom to choose.

These measures, and especially the flexibility in supply, would probably lead to a more modest development of rents and house prices, making our children and grandchildren relatively less wealthy in terms of asset value, but better off in terms of the annual costs needed to sustain their quality of life. It is not clear whether that would make the housing market less or more susceptible to the international financial forces that have caused the global housing market boom and bust. However, Dutch home developers tend to follow demand if the government allows them to, and largely avoid speculative developments. The reforms suggested here would allow them to follow demand even more closely, leading to a balanced future for the Dutch housing market.

NOTES

1. Ambrose, Eichholtz, and Lindenthal (2010) have done extensive analysis of the statistical properties of the different parts of the rent and price indices. That analysis suggests that the changing statistical moments around index breakpoints can largely be attributed to real underlying changes in the economy rather than in measurement of the index. However, the post–World War II standard deviation for house prices is much higher until 1965 than after that year, which can possibly be attributed to measurement error of the index before 1965, and/or the fact that the level of aggregation changes from the level of one canal to that of the country as a whole.

2. The institutional settings of the Dutch housing market are elegantly discussed in more detail by Boelhouwer (2002) and Charlier and Van Bussel (2003).

3. Topel and Rosen (1988) estimate a short-term elasticity of supply of 1 and a long-term elasticity of 3 for the United States. The estimates of Poterba (1984) and Blackley (1999) are of a similar magnitude.

4. The Netherlands stock of social housing is highest of all European countries. The Netherlands has 162 social houses per 1,000 inhabitants, which is four times the European average.

5. The VROM Raad (2007), the advisory council for the Dutch Government on housing and urban planning, distinguishes between middle- and high-income groups (high income groups earn more than twice the national average). Even if one would regard middle-income groups as a target group of social housing, the current stock would be sufficient, since the low- and middle-income groups together comprise 2.2 million households.

6. In addition to reporting the likelihood ratio, we have analyzed the predictive ability of our various model specifications. The predictive ability of each of our probit model specifications is close to a model with an intercept only. The constant probability model has an overall predictive ability of 58.41 percent. In the case of models S4 and S5 the independent variables help to improve the predictive ability by 11.85 percent relative to the constant probability model. In all other models the percent gain is less, which is another indicator that the dwelling characteristics hardly help to improve the prediction whether an auction or OTC fire sales will be used.

7. See Shiling et al. (1990), Forgey et al. (1994), and Hardin and Wolverton (1996) for U.S. evidence on price discounts realized at foreclosure auction sales.

REFERENCES

Ambrose, B., P. Eichholtz, and T. Lindenthal. 2010. *House Prices and Fundamentals: 355 Years of Evidence*. Maastricht University Working Paper.

Ault, R., J. Jackson, and R. Saba. 1994. "The Effect of Long-Term Rent Control on Tenant Mobility." *Journal of Urban Economics* 35, 140–58.

Blackley, D. M. 1999. "The Long-Run Elasticity of New Housing Supply in the United States: Empirical Evidence for 1950 to 1994." *Journal of Real Estate Finance and Economics* 18:1, 25–42.

CBS Central Bureau of Statistics. 1939. "De Nederlandse volkshuishouding, 1914–1918. Nederlandse conjuctuur speciale onderzoekingen, 3." *Een economisch-statistische schets*. Voorburg, The Netherlands: CBS.

———. 1948. "Het nationale inkomen van Nederland, 1921–1939." *Monografieën van de Nederlandse conjunctuur*, 7. Voorburg, The Netherlands: CBS.

———. 1999. "De raming van diensten uit eigenwoningbezit." *Sector Nationale Rekeningen*. Voorburg, The Netherlands: CBS.

———. 2008. "De gemiddelde verhoging woninghuur in Nederland 1978–2005." Available at www.cbs.nl/en-GB/menu/cijfers/statline/default.htm.

Cosemans, M., and P. Eichholtz. 2009. "De NHG in crisistijd." *Tijdschrift voor de Volkshuisvesting*.

Dol, K. and H. van der Heijden. 2005. *Knelpuntenmonitor Woningproductie*. OTB, TU Delft.

Early, D. W., and J. T. Phelps. 1999. "Rent Regulation's Pricing Effect in the Uncontrolled Sector: An Empirical Investigation." *Journal of Housing Research* 10: 2.

Easterlin, R. A. 1966. "Economic-Demographic Interactions and Long Swings in Economic Growth." *American Economic Review* 56:5, 1063–1103.

Eichholtz, P. M. A. 1997. "A Long-Run House Price Index: The Herengracht Index, 1628–1973." *Real Estate Economics* 25:2, 175–92.

———. 2002. "Iedereen een eigen huis." In H. van Dalen and F. Kalshoven, *Meesters van de Welvaart*. Uitgeverij Balans.

———, and M. Theebe. 2006. *Housing Market Rents in the Long Run: Amsterdam 1550–1850*. Maastricht University Working Paper.

Forgey, F., R. Rutherford, and M. Van Buskirk. 1994. "The Effect of Foreclosure Status on Residential Selling Price." *The Journal of Real Estate Research* 9:3, 313–318.

Glaeser, E. L., and E. F. P. Luttmer. 2003. "The Misallocation of Housing under Rent Control." *The American Economic Review* 93:4, 1027–1046.

Green, R. K., and P. H. Hendershott. 1996. "Age, Demographics, and Real House Prices." *Regional Science and Urban Economics* 26:5, 465–80.

Hardin, W.G. and M.L. Wolverton. 1995. "The Relationship between Foreclosure Status and Apartment Price." *The Journal of Real Estate Research* 12:1, 101–109.

Hendershott, P. H. 1991. "Are Real House Prices Likely to Decline by 47 percent?" *Regional Science and Urban Economics* 21:3, 553–563.

Holland, S. 1991. "The Baby Boom and the Housing Market: Another Look at the Evidence." *Regional Science and Urban Economics* 21:3, 565–571.

Israel, J. 1995. *The Dutch Republic: Its Rise, Greatness, and Fall, 1477–1806*. Oxford, UK: Clarendon Press.

Kaiser, R. W. 1997. "The Long Cycle in Real Estate." *Journal of Real Estate Research* 14:3, 233–257.

Kling, J. L., and T. E. McCue. 1987. "Office Building Investment and the Macroeconomy: Empirical Evidence, 1973–1985." *AREUEA Journal* 15:3, 234–255.

Mankiw, G. N., and D. N. Weil. 1989. "The Baby Boom, the Baby Bust, and the Housing Market." *Regional Science and Urban Economics* 19:2, 235–258.

————. 1991. "The Baby Boom, the Baby Bust, and the Housing Market: A Reply to Our Critics." *Regional Science and Urban Economics* 21:3, 573–557.

Nagy, J. 1995. "Increased Duration and Sample Attrition in New York City's Rent-Controlled Sector." *Journal of Urban Economics* 38, 127–137.

————. 1997. "Do Vacancy Decontrol Provisions Undo Rent Control?" *Journal of Urban Economics* 42, 64–78.

Poterba, J. M. 1984. "Tax Subsidies to Owner-Occupied Housing: An Asset Market Approach." *Quarterly Journal of Economics* 99:4, 729–752.

Riel, Arthur van. 2006. *Prices and Economic Development in the Netherlands, 1800—1913: Markets, Institutions, and Policy Restraints.* Universiteit Utrecht.

Romijn, G., and P. Besseling. 2008. *Economische effecten van regulering en subsidiëring van de huurwoningmarkt.* Centraal Planbureau, CPB Document 165.

Rouwendal, J., and W. Vermeulen. 2008. *Struggling for Rents: The Adjustment of Land Use Constraints in an Expanding Housing Market.* VU working paper.

Shiller, R. 2005. *Irrational Exuberance.* Princeton, NJ: Princeton University Press.

Shilling, J.D., J.D. Benjamin, and C.F. Sirmans. 1990. "Estimating Net Realizable Value for Distressed Real Estate." *The Journal of Real Estate Research* 5:1, 129–140.

Topel, R. H., and S. Rosen. 1988. "Housing Investments in the United States." *Journal of Political Economy* 96:4, 718–740.

Vermeulen, W., and J. Rouwendal. 2007. *Housing Supply in the Netherlands, Centraal Planbureau.* CPB Discussion Paper 87.

VROM. 2004a. *Betaalbaarheid van het wonen.*

————. 2004b. *Evaluatie Wet Bevordering Eigen Woningbezit.*

VROM Raad. 2007. *Tijd voor keuzes: Perspectief op een woningmarkt in balans.* VROM-Raad advies 064.

ABOUT THE AUTHORS

DIRK BROUNEN is Professor of Real Estate Economics at Tilburg University, and initiator of the Real Estate LAB, where relevant real estate knowledge is created, gathered, and communicated (www.realestatelab.nl). In his academic research, Dirk focuses on international investment strategies, sustainability, and risk and return of publicly listed real estate vehicles. His research has been published in leading academic journals such as *Financial Management, Journal of Banking and Finance, Journal of Environmental Economics and Management, Financial Analyst Journal, Real Estate Economics,* and *Journal of Real Estate Finance and Economics.* Besides his research, Dirk Brounen is also very active as a teacher in several real estate and finance courses at TiasNimbas Business School and in workshops for professionals. Besides his academic work, Dirk has also been active as advisor for various firms and organizations, including the ABP, Achmea, Amvest, Bouwfonds, McKinsey, Vesteda, VendexKBB, and the Dutch Ministries of Housing, Internal Affairs, and Justice.

PIET EICHHOLTZ is Professor of Real Estate and Finance and Chair of the Finance Department at Maastricht University in the Netherlands. Most of his work regards real estate markets, with a focus on international investment, housing markets, and sustainable real estate. Eichholtz' academic work has resulted in a great number of publications, both internationally and in the Netherlands. He has provided extensive services to public society, mainly through board memberships of industry organizations in the property sector, but also as an advisor to various government agencies. Besides his academic career, Eichholtz has been active as an entrepreneur. After having gained practical experience at the ABP and NIB Capital, Eichholtz started Global Property Research, an international consultancy firm specialized in property companies. In 2004, he was a co-founder of Finance Ideas, a financial consultancy company. He is currently a non-executive board member at IPD Holding.

CHAPTER 7

Real Estate Boom and Crisis in Spain

ANTONI SUREDA-GOMILA
"La Caixa"*

Spain was one of the countries in the European Union that more fervently embraced the real estate mania and has also been one of the countries most badly hit by the housing meltdown. At the peak of the cycle, which in Spain took place between 2006 and 2007, residential investment accounted for 9.3 percent of GDP and 13.5 percent of employed Spaniards were building houses. In comparison, residential investment as a share of GDP peaked at 6.1 percent in the United States in 2005.

From 1995 to 2008 Spain experienced a long property cycle. During the most dynamic part of the cycle, the first eight years of this century, property prices multiplied by 2.5, and 5 million homes were built (almost 25 percent of the existing homes at 2000). As can be seen in Exhibit 7.1, the increase in home prices was even larger than in the United States, the cycle lasted longer, and the price correction has been, as yet, smaller. Indeed, Spanish housing prices peaked at the beginning of 2008, while in the United States the apex was reached between the second and third quarters of 2006; from prices in 2000 to the highest level recorded, prices multiplied by 2.5 in Spain and by less than 2 in the United States; and, as in March 2010, prices had fallen 30 percent in the United States, but only 11 percent in Spain.[1] Prospects are grim for the Spanish real estate sector and the price correction will continue because, as we discuss later, there is a large stock of unsold homes that accumulated during the boom years. The economic outlook in Spain, where the unemployment rate has reached 20 percent, is still dire and recovery might take longer than in other developed economies. Furthermore, factors other than prices that might increase home affordability have been exhausted.

During the boom years, the increase in prices translated into rises in housing market indicators as the price-to-rent ratio and the affordability index shows in Exhibit 7.2.[2] Starting from a price-to-rent ratio of 16.5 at 1998, it climbed to almost 32 at December 2007 and it has fallen to slightly more than 26 in the first quarter of 2010. This fall in the ratio during 2008, 2009, and the first quarter of 2010 is due in

---

*The opinions expressed in this chapter are those of the author only and do not necessarily reflect views of "la Caixa."

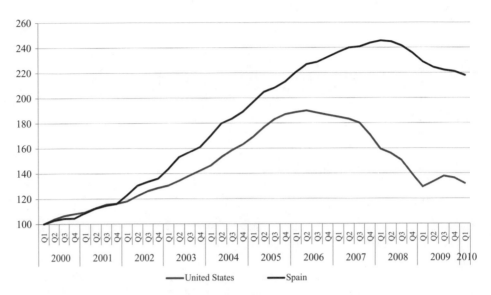

Exhibit 7.1 Comparison of the Evolution of Home Prices between the United States and Spain
Note: Index 2000 Q1 = 100.
Sources: Based on data from S&P/Case-Schiller U.S. National Home Price Index and Spanish Ministry of Housing.

part to the 11 percent fall in prices but also to a 7 percent increase in rental prices. According to a report by Standard & Poor's, this ratio is still 13 percent above its long-term average. In my opinion, given the increase in the supply of houses in the rental market, the current low inflation level, and the weak economy, further decreases of this ratio in the short-term will come from lower prices for properties rather than increases in rents.

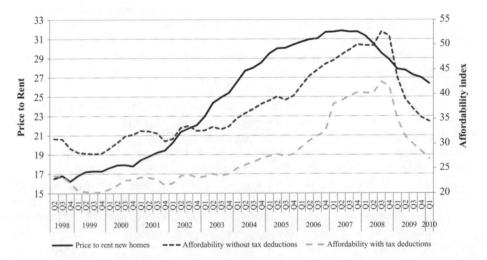

Exhibit 7.2 Price-to-Rent Ratio and Affordability Index
Source: Based on data from the Spanish Ministry of Housing, National Statistics Institute, Sociedad de Tasación, and Spanish Mortgage Association.

Exhibit 7.3 Evolution of Mortgage Interest Rates
Source: Spanish Mortgage Association.

The second housing market indicator in Exhibit 7.2, the affordability index, increased from a level of 31 in 1998 (23.5, when taking into account tax deductions[3]) to 52.6 (40,3) in the third quarter of 2008; this means that in the third quarter of 2008, an average household would had to spend more than 50 percent of its income in mortgage installments for buying an average house; and, even taking into account tax deductions, this household would need more that 40 percent of its income. It is not strange then, as shown in Exhibit 7.4, that in September of 2007, housing was Spain's main problem, according to the opinion barometer that the Sociological Research Centre[4] updates monthly by means of an opinion poll addressed to Spaniards aged 18 or older. From that peak, the affordability index has fallen to 34.5 (27) in March 2010, but one of the main drives of this drop in the index has been the fall in interest rates (Exhibit 7.3): In September 2008, a one-year Euribor rate was 6.34 percent, but one year later, it had plunged to 1.26 percent. However, given that it is reasonable to think that interest rates will not be kept in the mid-term at current levels—they will rise—and that average household income will stagnate, without a further decline in housing prices the affordability index will increase. Moreover, it has been approved that the current tax deduction will disappear in 2011 for incomes larger than €24,000; therefore, keeping current household income, interest rates, and average mortgage maturity constant, a further decrease of 13 percent in home prices (from its March 2010 level) will be needed to reach a ratio of affordability of 30 percent. To sum up, both market indicators seem to indicate that the Spanish housing market is still overpriced and prices are expected to fall by, at least, 13 percent on average from its March 2010 level; therefore the total price correction from the peak to trough would be around 23 percent or more, although there are large regional differences in previous price increases and in the size of the correction.[5]

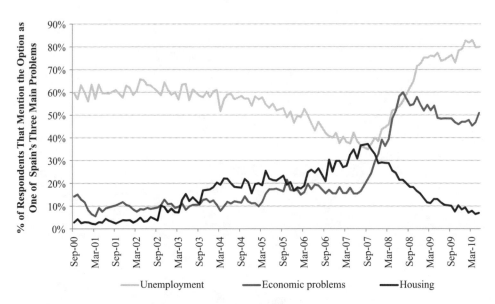

Exhibit 7.4 Perception of Housing as a Main Problem
Source: Sociological Research Centre (perception of Spain's main problems).

The surge in real estate prices led to a large increase in building activity and in the supply of homes. If during the 1990s, 276,000 homes were initiated per year, during the first 10 years of this century, an average of 582,000 homes were initiated every year; therefore more than 5 million homes were built from 2000 to 2009, in a country that increased its population by 6.25 million people, and that in 2000 had 40 million inhabitants and 20 million houses. During 2006 and 2007 almost 800,000 homes were initiated every year, while sales accounted for around 400,000 homes. Exhibit 7.5 shows the evolution of the supply of housing and the number of transactions of new homes.

We estimate that about 12 percent of these 5 million houses remained unsold, 25 percent were vacation homes or were empty (60 percent bought by Spaniards and 40 percent by foreigners), and the remaining 63 percent were main residences. The stock of unsold homes reached 688,000 at the end of 2009,[6] and there were 440,000 homes under construction. Assuming that no new homes were initiated, and that demand will account for around 350,000 houses per year (an optimistic projection, taking into account that during 2009 fewer than 250,000 new homes were sold), it would take more than three years to absorb the stock available in 2010. However, there are areas where this stock will be very difficult to sell because there is no demand for homes—instead, there is a glut of undesirable properties, such as the 5,000 homes built in Seseña (Toledo), where 13,000 apartments were projected, or the thousands of half-built villas and vacation apartments along the southeastern coastline, and areas where the stock could be rapidly eliminated if prices adjust.

The accumulation of this large stock has produced a drastic halt in the initiation of new buildings. Indeed, as can be seen in Exhibit 7.5, during the second semester

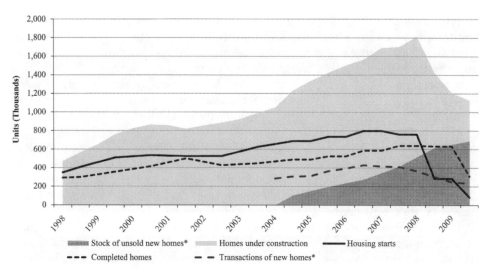

Exhibit 7.5   Supply: Activity and Housing Stock
*The series begins in 2004.
Source: Based on data from Sociedad de tasación, Spanish Ministry of Housing, and National Statistics Institute.

of 2009 the annualized number of initiated homes fell to 84,000 units, slightly more than 10 percent of the initiated homes three years earlier or almost a 90 percent drop in housing starts. While during 2006 and 2007, residential investment accounted for 9.3 percent of GDP and it contributed in 0.5 percent per year of the GDP growth from 1998 to 2007; the contraction in residential construction will reduce GDP by 5.4 percent from 2007 levels. The contraction in building activity will continue until mid-2011, given that current activity focuses on finishing buildings that were initiated in 2009 and are yet under construction. Before the sector starts growing again, its weight in the Spanish economy will be at around 4 percent, below the lowest level observed in 1994. Considering the moderate fall in prices compared with the dramatic stop in construction activity, one can conclude that, during the crisis, the Spanish real estate sector has been very flexible in quantities but sticky in prices.

Several social, economical, and financial factors fueled this expansive real estate cycle; some of them are commonly cited in the literature on this subject and apply to many markets, while others are particular to Spain.[7] For instance, the high rate of home ownership in Spain, around 85 percent, has been explained by a cultural inclination toward owning a home, as compared to being a tenant, which is associated with low social status. Other causes are the strong demographic growth due to the five million immigrants that entered Spain in the first decades of this century; an increase of women in the labor market, which increased household income; and baby boomers reaching household formation age (the baby boom in Spain took place 10 years later than elsewhere in Europe). There is also a large stock of lower quality and older housing in Spain and, as a consequence, a potential demand for new homes.

Other causes are related to the legal environment. Cumbersome and slow administrative procedures have also been blamed for the rises in home prices. Indeed, there are many regulations in Spain that restrict building and, furthermore, building permit processing is lengthy: Depending on the municipality, it can take more than two years to obtain a building permit. This causes housing supply to react slowly to rising prices and unmet demand, although, as we have previously seen, building activity at the end soared. Other factors include a weaker shareholder protection than in other economies and the burst of the Internet bubble, which shifted investment toward real estate assets. Other relevant causes are generous tax deductions for the purchase of the main residence and an undeveloped rental market, in which only 12 percent of residential properties were in the renting market in 2005 and half of them were social housing, due, in part, to weak landlord protection that reduced the supply of rentable homes.

Finally, other factors were the vigorous economic growth and a significant decrease in unemployment; the decrease in interest rates as shown in Exhibit 7.3, which in real terms dropped to around zero; the macroeconomic stability gained as consequence of Spain's entry in the Eurozone; and the expansion of securitization and innovations in the mortgage markets—particularly the lengthening of the amortization period.

To sum up, many factors have been proposed as fundamental causes of home price increases, and many stories have been spun to sustain the boom, although the actual relevance of some of these factors has been disputed. Note that some of these are both causes for and consequences of the growth in prices and quantities. Indeed, the growth of the real estate sector was an important component of GDP growth (0.5 percent per year), immigrants were attracted by a strong demand for workers to build homes (a quarter of construction workers are foreigners), and increases in housing prices produced the illusion that collaterals would be more valuable in the future, which led banks to reduce concession standards and accept higher loan-to-values[8] ratios; all this gave birth to the chimera that the Spanish economy had found a perpetual motion machine.

Non-fundamental factors have also been blamed for the increases in house prices, especially the role of expectations: Buyers and future buyers thought that prices would continue growing and, simultaneously, that homes were overvalued.[9] These expectations became self-fulfilling prophecies: Some people thought that it was their last chance to buy a property because prices would climb further, and others saw the leveraged purchase of a property as a highly profitable and riskless investment opportunity.[10] Furthermore, although vacation home purchases by foreigners might be around 10 percent of housing completions, there was the belief that demand for vacation homes by North Europeans seeking a place in the sun for their retirement would absorb any supply, even if these vacation homes were not built at prime locations on the coast, provided that there was a golf course. The reality is that many of these foreign buyers were investors and were more interested in capital gains than in tanning—consequently, foreign investment in real estate started to decline in 2005.

The boom in the Spanish housing market translated into unsustainable levels of activity, debt, and prices that would inevitably revert. The trigger of the correction was the implosion of the subprime crisis in the United States that drained most of

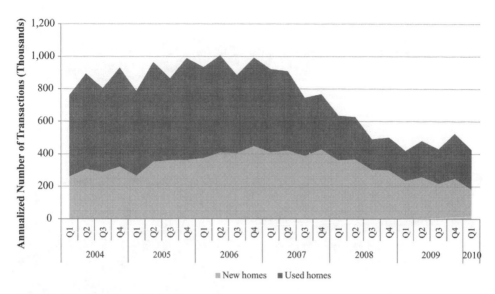

Exhibit 7.6 Number of Sales Transactions
Source: Spanish Ministry of Housing.

the liquidity in financial markets and increased interest rates. The combined effect of the tightening of credit conditions and the increase in interest rates caused a contraction in the number of transactions in 2007, as shown in Exhibit 7.6. Note that the contraction was initially larger for used homes, because deals for new homes were usually closed during construction (or even before) and the buyer could often *subrogate*[11] the developer's loan.

The Spanish cycle has been characterized by large increases in quantities and prices during the growth period and, as yet, a large correction in quantities but a mild fall in prices. This cycle has had an impact on the whole economy. As I've mentioned, the growth in the real estate sector was an important component of GDP growth; therefore the adjustment in activity will have a huge impact on GDP and unemployment.[12] It has also contributed to the current fiscal deficit because the central, regional, and municipal governments regarded the temporary inflows from the housing market boom as permanent, but now the number of unemployed workers and the proliferation of almost uninhabited neighborhoods are a liability instead of a source of taxes and fees. Another consequence of the cycle is that Spanish households are highly indebted by historical standards, reaching 125 percent of the households' gross income, and have cut their consumption levels in order to deleverage. But the worst consequences of this expansive cycle will be lasting. In fact, the construction boom attracted unskilled foreign workers but also disincentivized students from pursuing their educations, given that there were plenty of relatively well-paid job openings in the construction sector; this, combined with the current high level of long-term unemployment, might constrain an already anemic productivity growth, and it will be a handicap to improve the weak international competitiveness of the Spanish economy in the future. Last but not least, the construction fever has had an irreversible and harmful environmental

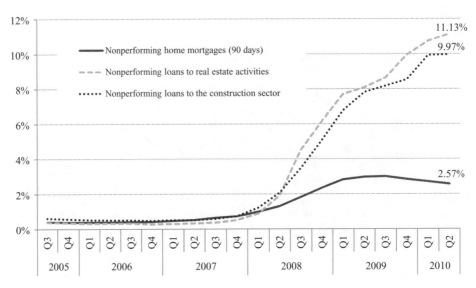

Exhibit 7.7   Percentage of Nonperforming Loans
Source: Spanish Mortgage Association.

impact and has encroached upon large areas of previously unspoiled coastline, damaging one of the assets of the largest Spanish industry, tourism, and furthermore has left an oversized and unoccupied stock of real property that will be expensive to maintain in the future.

There are significant differences between the Spanish and the U.S. primary mortgage markets and in the characteristics of a typical mortgage loan; therefore, delinquency rates (in mortgages given to households) and foreclosures are far lower in Spain that in the United States. Indeed, Exhibit 7.7 shows that the delinquency rate (90+ days) of mortgages given to households was 2.57 percent in July 2010 (in the United States, it was above 9 percent, according to the Mortgage Bankers Association). There were 93,319 foreclosure starts during 2009 in Spain, which is high by historical standards but far less than the 2.8 million foreclosures in the United States during the same period. Exhibit 7.7 also shows that, as discussed in the next section, the real trouble for the Spanish banking system are the loans given to the real estate and construction sectors, and not the mortgages given to households. Households that cannot meet their obligations are typically led by investors who borrowed to buy properties in the expectation of earning capital gains, but who now cannot sell their properties, in addition to households headed by people who have lost their jobs. However, those households that are now unemployed are mainly those who were employed in temporary jobs—the Spanish labor market is "dual," in that permanent employees who are expensive to dismiss work alongside a large fraction of workers on temporary contracts—and households on temporary jobs seldom are extended a mortgage in Spain. There has been some laxity underwriting mortgages, but not to the extent seen in subprime and alternative-A (Alt-A) mortgages in the United States.

THE SPANISH FINANCIAL SYSTEM, ITS CHARACTERISTICS, AND THE IMPACT OF THE MELTDOWN

The Spanish financial system and real estate market are interconnected. The availability of cheap credit fueled the housing boom, and the banking system has been hit by the burst. The characteristics of the Spanish banking system, the way in which real estate developments are financed, the way that loans to real estate developers were seen as a catalyst of growth, and the types of mortgage loans that are more common in Spain are all having a significant impact on the evolution of the crisis and need to be taken into account to understand the future of the sector and the effectiveness of policy responses.

In contrast with the United States, where subprime mortgages were the trigger of the first wave of the global financial crisis, the Spanish version of *subprime loans* are those loans given to real estate developers. For instance, the largest bankruptcy in the Spanish history is the one of Mantinsa-Fadesa in July 2008; Mantinsa-Fadesa is a large real estate developer whose debt was €5.2 million. Exhibit 7.7 shows how delinquency rates (90+ days) on loans given to real estate and construction activities have climbed to more than 11 percent and almost 10 percent respectively, far above those of mortgages given to households. Moreover, not all bad construction loans are actually delinquent—it is common to accept buildings in lieu of payment, refinance until the developer has finished the construction, or even, in some cases, swap debt for equity. Overall, the Spanish banking system as a whole has enough muscle to withstand these processes: Only two relatively small savings banks (*cajas* in Spain) had to be rescued, although many other weak *cajas* have merged and have been aided by the state.

At the end of 2009, the total exposure of the Spanish financial system to the real estate and construction sectors was €453 billion[13] (€323 billion in real estate activities and €130 billion in construction): This is around 12 percent of the system total assets and 25 percent of all outstanding credit to households and firms. Of this €453 billion, €44 billion (or close to 10 percent) were nonperforming loans. However, this large exposure of the financial system to the real estate sector is already highly provisioned. The Bank of Spain established, in year 2000, an accounting requirement called *dynamic provisioning*,[14] by virtue of which banking institutions must reflect the losses of their portfolio before an event actually uncovers them. In other words, it takes the view that the event that causes a future loss is the origination of the loan. In periods when specific loses are revealed, the dynamic provision fund can be drawn down in order to cover those specific losses for individual assets. Thanks to this dynamic provisioning, financial statements better reflect the true financial situation of the bank, and this provides the right incentives for bank managers. According to the Bank of Spain, the Spanish financial system has accumulated provisions that cover 35 percent of all the troubled exposure[15] in the real estate and construction sectors; in other words, banks might recover only 65 percent of the collateral book value of this exposure and they still would not record any loss on their income statement. Nevertheless, the fraction of loans to real estate developers, the fraction of nonperforming loans, and the thickness of the provisions buffer differ across institutions.

We have previously mentioned that there are significant differences between the Spanish and the U.S. primary mortgage markets and in the characteristics of a typical mortgage loan. The more common type of mortgage loans in Spain differs from what is standard in the United States. First, in Spain, mortgages usually have adjustable rates (ARM mortgages) and the rate is revised once a year.[16] Second, they are recourse loans, therefore, in case of foreclosure, the borrower remains responsible for any residual debt after the sale of the property by the lender. These characteristics of the mortgage market in Spain have consequences in the number of foreclosures and the velocity of the price correction. Indeed, the fact that houses are financed through ARMs makes the rate of foreclosures and metrics of effort for purchasing a property a function of interest rates, in particular a function of the Euribor which, as shown in Exhibit 7.3, increased at the beginning of the crisis but has been kept below 1.5 percent from mid-2009 to mid-2010. Furthermore, the fact that loans are recourse makes borrowers with negative equity less likely to default for strategic reasons. There are also differences in the primary mortgage markets: Underwriting standards are tougher in Spain and banks rarely lend to subprime and alt-A borrowers. For all this, delinquency rates (Exhibit 7.7) have not risen as much as in the United States. Securitization of mortgages is done mainly through covered bonds (*cédulas hipotecarias*) and also, but to a lesser extent, through asset-backed securities.

The exposure of the banking system to real estate developer comes, mainly, from the financing of mergers and acquisitions between them (usually through syndicated loans) and development loans. The latter usually consist of a large mortgage with maturity around 30 years, in which during the first two years (the construction period) there is no amortization of capital and the borrower pays only interests; once the construction is finished, this large original loan is divided into smaller mortgages, keeping the conditions of the original loan (interest rate, maturity), and to which the buyers of the homes in the development can subrogate. Therefore, by financing one development the bank can sell, very efficiently, many mortgages that might have been costly to sell one by one directly to customers. This procedure allowed a bank to increase its portfolios of mortgages, which, when given to individuals in order to finance their home, were seen as almost riskless loans that increased customer's loyalty and opened the door to a large range of cross-selling opportunities; therefore, many banks were eager to finance developments in order to expand their portfolios. The weak link in this reasoning is that the developer might not be able to sell the homes and, as a consequence, be unable to repay his debt, and these development loans were not priced according to this risk factor. This is precisely the current situation in Spain, and why we say that the Spanish version of a subprime loan is the kind of loan given to real estate developers; although, in contrast with U.S. subprime loans, these were kept on the bank's balance sheet and weren't marked to market. Banks will refinance the developer until the construction has finished and then, if the developer has not been able to sell the units, the bank initiates the repossession process. Once the bank has taken the property, it puts it on the market, offering mortgages with favorable conditions, lower interest rates, or without the requirement of a down payment. This, jointly with the usual rationing of credit during recessions increases the stress faced by other developers or sellers of used homes that might still be honoring their loans.

The present crisis has triggered a restructuring process of the Spanish banking system. Currently, the Spanish banking system consists of three types on institutions: banks, saving banks or *cajas*, and credit unions. According to the Bank of Spain, banks' total assets are €1.7 trillion ("trillion" meaning millions of millions), saving bank's €1.3 trillion and credit unions €0.12 trillion[17]; therefore banks represent 54 percent of the system, saving banks 42 percent, and credit unions the remaining 4 percent. The Spanish banking system, and especially savings banks, has experienced an unsustainable growth fueled by the housing boom, low interest rates, and easy access to international credit markets.[18] Although at the peak of the cycle the size of the sector was coherent with the volume of financial transactions, the slowdown has revealed an excess capacity that, jointly with an increase in delinquency rates and tougher conditions in debt markets, has eroded the efficiency of some institutions. The sector—particularly the *cajas*—is in a process of concentration supervised by the Bank of Spain and financed by the Fondo de Reestructuración Ordenada Bancaria (FROB, Fund for Orderly Bank Restructuring) to make the system leaner. Furthermore, a new regulation facilitates the conversion of saving banks into banks for those institutions that will need to increase their core capital beyond what can be obtained by the capitalization of profits. It is likely that many of the intuitions that have received funds from the FROB will have trouble returning the funds without issuing equity and converting into banks.

POLICY RESPONSES

Spanish policy responses focus on five fronts: helping households that temporarily cannot meet their mortgage payments, mitigating the effects of the contraction of the real estate sector, facilitating the absorption of the current stock, correcting distortions that have favored the housing boom, and restructuring the banking system.[19] The policies adopted to aid households that temporarily cannot meet their mortgage payments, and to avoid foreclosures, were approved in 2008, when interest rates and therefore affordability index were the largest (see Exhibits 7.2 and 7.3) and follow a strategy similar to the *foreclosure avoidance initiative* in the United States. As we have mentioned, most mortgages in Spain are ARM and in order to mitigate the effect of the increase in interest rates, the government promoted the reduction of the expenses associated to the expansion of the mortgage loan period. The plan consisted in promoting agreements between the borrower and the lender and the exemption of transfer tax, stamp duty, and notary and registration fees. Interest rates declined shortly after the approval of this measure. The second plan was aimed to aid the unemployed, and consisted of the temporary deferral, for them, in the obligation to pay 50 percent of mortgage installments for the period from March 2009 to February 2011. The deferred payments will have to be paid off starting on March 2012 and during the following 15 years. Given that the agreement of the corresponding lender was needed, the deferred amounts will be guaranteed by the state in order to facilitate the consent. Jointly with these measures, the government approved extensions of the periods in which homes must be purchased in order to enjoy tax deductions for savings, and also to enjoy tax exemptions for the sale of the current home and the purchase of a new one.

The policy responses aimed to mitigate the contraction of the construction sector and its effects on unemployment are the Fondo Estatal de Inversión Local (Local Investment Fund) and other increases in public spending on infrastructures; and, more recently, measures to boost the rehabilitation of homes. The Fondo Estatal de Inversión Local, endowed with €8 billion in 2009 and €5 billion in 2010, was designed to finance labor intensive public works by municipal governments that could be executed immediately to boost the economy in the short term. Municipal governments proposed the public works projects (such as to change curbs) and the funds were distributed proportionally to the number of inhabitants of the municipality. There are two sets of measures to boost the rehabilitation of homes. The first is the Plan Estatal de Vivienda y Rehabilitación 2009–2012 (State Housing and Rehabilitation Plan) that, among others, provides loans and subventions to promote social housing and the rehabilitation of homes and neighborhoods. The second set of measures includes tax deductions and a reduced VAT for the rehabilitation of homes. Note that these measures complement the automatic stabilizers in the Spanish economy; for example, the relatively generous unemployment benefits that also have been temporarily expanded. Some of these fiscal expansion measures, specially the Local Investment Fund, have been criticized as a waste of valuable resources in unproductive projects and, following the sovereign risk crisis in Europe, future public spending on infrastructures has been heavily reduced. Therefore, the only measures that will continue in 2011 are the ones that favor housing rehabilitation and energy efficiency. Further cuts in infrastructure investment will put further stress on the construction sector.

To facilitate the absorption of the existing stock, the creation of the Spanish equivalent to U.S. REITs (Sociedades de Inversión en el Mercado Inmobiliario [SOCIMI]) has been approved, and it has facilitated the transformation of unsold free housing into social housing, especially if the units are intended for the rental market. Furthermore, the elimination in 2011 of home purchase tax deductions has been announced, which might stimulate the purchase of homes during 2010 but reduce them during 2011.

Among the measures adopted to correct the distortions that have favored the housing boom are the suppression of the tax deductions for the purchase of homes and the promotion of the rental market. The latter is done through a €3 billion credit line for bringing unsold homes into the rental market, and through other measures, such as providing funding for social housing in the rental market, transfers to young tenants and tax deductions for tenants, subsidizing house owners who put homes on the rental market, granting tax deductions to landlords, and a simplification of the judicial procedures in case of default by the tenant.

CONCLUSION

Real estate development will continue contracting in the near future. During 2010, the completion of initiated buildings showed some activity but new starts plunged. According to the Bank of Spain, the stabilization will not arrive until 2011. I think that the combination of a large stock of unsold homes and the contraction of the demand will put further downside pressure on prices.

The Spanish banking system has been hurt by the real estate crisis. Although the largest banks and saving banks have resisted well, some financial institutions, especially some medium-size and small savings banks, have been badly hit. These weaker institutions are currently under restructuring and will either merge among themselves or with more solvent institutions in order to become more efficient and better capitalized. Given that during the next years home prices will likely continue falling and that economic growth will be, at best, anemic, it is natural to think that most banking institutions will have to make an extra effort at improving efficiency and retaining earnings; moreover, further write-downs are likely, and in some cases additional capitalization will be needed.

Finally, the current sovereign risk crisis in Europe and the commitments to cut the fiscal deficit leave little room for measures to sustain the construction sector by the state; therefore, policy responses are limited to measures to promote the rental market and housing rehabilitation.

NOTES

1. There is no consensus on the actual decline in house prices from its maximum. An estimate by the Spanish Ministry of Housing suggests an 11 percent drop, based on assessed prices; another estimate also based on assessed prices by the appraisal company TINSA shows a 15 percent fall. The National Statistics Institute, using transaction prices, also estimates a decline of 11 percent. Finally, using asking prices, the real estate web site Fotocasa, jointly with IESE business school, has estimated a decline of 21 percent.

2. Price-to-rent ratio is the quotient between price of a property and the estimated yearly rent that would be paid if renting. The affordability index measures the fraction of gross income that an average household would need to meet its monthly mortgage payments.

3. Spanish households receive generous tax deductions for the purchase of their home; however, these deductions will disappear beginning in 2011 for incomes larger than €24,000.

4. The Sociological Research Centre (Centro de Investigaciones Sociologicas [CIS]) is a government agency established to study Spanish society and whose public opinion polls are widely followed by the media.

5. There is no consensus on the level of overvaluation in the Spanish housing market. Studies by BBVA (the second-largest Spanish Bank) and the IMF forecast a correction of 30 percent from peak to trough. A recent article in *The Economist* quantifies the current overvaluation at 50.4 percent.

6. This is an estimate by the Spanish Ministry of Housing; other institutions have estimated that the stock is even larger; for instance, BBVA has estimated a stock of more than one million homes.

7. See, for instance, OECD (2005) and IMF Country Report 09/129.

8. Especially when financing developments and the purchase of land.

9. See García-Montalvo (2006).

10. It was common, for instance, to close a deal to buy a house while in construction or even before the construction started, paying a portion of the final price in advance (usually between 10 and 20 percent), expecting to resell the house, or the right to buy the house, before the actual purchase would take place.

11. The most common type of construction loan in Spain can be seen as a pool of regular mortgages (one for each unit being built) with an interest-only initial period (usually two years, to allow for the construction). Once the unit is sold, the buyer can take over the developer's loan instead of applying for a new mortgage. To take over the developer's loan is know in Spain as a subrogation and has the advantage for the buyer that set-up costs are lower. From the point of view of the lender, the subrogation is the desired outcome, and a bank will seldom oppose it if the buyer is fairly creditworthy.

12. Spain has a large share of workers on temporary contracts and, under these circumstances, unemployment is highly responsive to changes in output.

13. Thousands of millions.

14. Sometimes it is called generic or statistical provisioning.

15. Here, the term *troubled exposures* includes delinquent loans, foreclosures, collaterals accepted in lieu of payment, acquisitions, and also performing loans that are likely to degenerate and become delinquent; see Roldan (2010) for more details.

16. According to the Spanish statistics bureau, Instututo Nacional de Estadística (INE), 95.8 percent of mortgages constituted in May 2010 were ARM and 88.8 percent of all new mortgages were referenced to the Euribor.

17. Information extracted from financial statements built to reflect the activities of these institutions within Spain.

18. For instance, the number of bank branches increased from 14,072 in 2002 to 15,580 in 2008 (a growth of 10.7 percent) but the number of branches of *cajas* increased from 20,326 to 24,985 (a growth of 22.9 percent). As of March 2010 there were 14,774 branches of banks and 24,004 branches of *cajas*.

19. The last-mentioned area has been commented on in the previous section.

REFERENCES

Bank of Spain. 2009. "Informe anual."

Bank of Spain. 2010 (June). "Boletín estadístico."

Bank of Spain. 2010 (June). "La reestructuración de las cajas de ahorro en España: Situación a 29 de junio de 2010." In *Nota informativa*.

BBVA Servicio de Estudios Económicos. 2009 (December). "Situación inmobiliaria."

Callau, Jorge Biesla, and Rosa Duarte Pac. 2008. "Sobre el peso del sector de la construcción en la economía española." In *Boletín Económico del ICE*, (2944): 39–45.

The Economist. 2010 (July 8th). "Froth and Stagnation." Available at www.economist.com/node/16542826.

Fotocasa—IESE. 2009. "La vivienda en el año 2009." Available at www.fotocasa.es.

Fotocasa—IESE. 2010. "La vivienda en el segundo trimestre de 2010." Available at www.fotocasa.es.

García-Montalvo, José. 2006. "Deconstruyendo la burbuja: Expectativas de revalorización y precio de la vivienda en España." In *Papeles de Economía Española*, (109): 44–75.

García-Montalvo, José. 2007. "Algunas consideraciones sobre el problema de la vivienda en España." In *Papeles de Economía Española*, 113: 138–155.

García-Vaquero, Víctor, and Jorge Martínez. 2005. "Fiscalidad de la vivienda en España." Documentos Ocasionales 0506, Bank of Spain.

Henn, Christian, Keiko Honjo, Marialuz Moreno-Badia, and Alessandro Giustinian. 2009 (April). Spain: Selected Issues. IMF Country Report 09/129. International Monetary Fund.

idealista.com. 2010. "Evolution of Resale Housing Prices: Second Quarter 2010." Available at www.idealista.com.

Marqués, José Manuel, Luis Ángel Maza, and Margarita Rubio. 2010 (January). "Una comparación de los ciclos inmobiliarios recientes en España, estados unidos y reino unido." *Boletín Económico*, 108–119.

Martin-Oliver, Alfredo, and Jesús Saurina. 2007. "Why Do Banks Securitize Assets?" Bank of Spain.

Ministry of Housing. 2009 (December). "Stock de viviendas nuevas a 31 de diciembre de 2009." Available at www.mviv.es.

Ministry of Housing. 2010 (April). "Informe sobre la situación del sector de la vivienda en España." Consejo de Ministros.

Pérez, José Manuel Naredo. 2004. "Perspectivas de la vivienda." *Información Comercial Española*, 815, 143–154.

National Statistics Institute. 2010 (May). "Estadística de hipotecas." Press release.

OECD. 2005. "Recent House Price Developments: The Role of Fundamentals." *OECD Economic Outlook* 78.

Roldán, José María. 2010 (March). "Exposure of the Spanish Financial System to the Construction and Property Development Sector: Myths and Realities." Address to the Board of the Spanish Mortgage Association (Madrid).

Roldán, José María, and Jesús Saurina. 2009. "Dynamic Provisioning in Spain." In *IASB Meeting*. Bank of Spain.

Spanish Mortgage Association. 2010. "Estadística de dudosidad (segundo trimestre 2010)." Available at www.ahe.es/bocms/images/bfilecontent/2006/04/26/90.pdf.

Standard & Poor's. 2010 (May). "Advance Signals from Europe's Housing Markets Point to Steadying Prices—for Now." Ratings Direct on the Global Credit Portal, Standard & Poor's.

TINSA. 2010 (May). "Índice de mercados inmobiliarios españoles." Available at www.tinsa.es.

ABOUT THE AUTHOR

ANTONI SUREDA-GOMILA is a credit risk modeler at "la Caixa" where he is responsible for credit rating models. Prior to joining "la Caixa", Sureda-Gomila worked at Banco Sabadell and has taught finance courses at Universitat Pompeu Fabra and others universities. He holds a PhD in Finance from Universitat Pompeu Fabra, and a BS in mathematics from the Polytechnic University of Catalonia. Sureda-Gomila has authored several scientific articles and presentations at international conferences.

CHAPTER 8

The UK and Europe's Selective Housing Bubble

CHRISTINE WHITEHEAD AND KATHLEEN SCANLON
LSE London, London School of Economics

During the past decade the UK housing market experienced a very significant house price boom followed by a sharp decline in prices and housing market activity from mid-2007. It is easy in the light of the apparent similarities between the finance markets of the United Kingdom and the United States, notably the existence of subprime lending and the use of mortgage-backed securities, to argue that the United Kingdom's pattern of boom and bust both mirrors and has, to a significant degree, been led by U.S. experience. It is equally easy to argue that because prices rose rapidly, what was observed was a bubble. Yet there are reasons to suggest that these are over-simplistic interpretations of both the causes and outcomes. The market fundamentals and regulatory structures in the United Kingdom differ greatly from those in the United States. The differences between the countries are just as important as the similarities, and may well lead to very different longer-term trajectories.

In this chapter we aim to examine the determinants of the UK housing and mortgage-market crisis that started in 2007, and to clarify whether the outcomes reflect economic fundamentals or have aspects of "irrational exuberance." To do this, we first provide some background about the operation of the UK housing and mortgage markets from the 1970s, when the first steps were taken toward dismantling the special circuit of housing finance, to the middle of the first decade of this century, when the current crisis started to emerge. We then turn to examine the two-stage mortgage-market crisis. The first stage covered the period from 2005 to 2007 and culminated in September 2007 in the failure of Northern Rock. The perception up to this point was of a well-signaled market correction followed, it was hoped, by a soft landing. The second stage started a year later with the collapse of Lehman Brothers when mortgage market concerns were overtaken by the much broader global financial crisis, which was followed in turn by economic recession. The third section of this chapter aims to clarify the immediate outcomes of the crisis, not only for the mortgage market and industry but also for the UK housing market more generally, and to make some predictions about the trajectory into the medium term. Finally we make a very preliminary assessment of similarities and differences with the U.S. market and the importance of the contagion factor.

In examining this period of crisis and its aftermath, it is not possible to use formal techniques because of lack of data and the evidence of structural change. Instead, this chapter looks at evidence from earlier econometric analyses on fundamental relationships and adopts a jigsaw approach to available quantitative and qualitative evidence covering the period, to clarify the main trends and turning points in the crisis in the United Kingdom—and to a limited extent to compare the pattern of events with those found in other parts of Europe and the United States.

THE FUNDAMENTALS OF THE UK HOUSING MARKET

There are four main fundamentals of the UK housing market that are of immediate relevance to the experience of the first decade of the new century. First, the UK housing market has been consistently more volatile than most markets in the rest of Europe throughout the post-war period in terms of prices, transactions, and investment in new housing. Second, the supply of housing, measured by new construction, is relatively price-inelastic compared to much of the rest of Europe and particularly the United States. Third, the mortgage market over the past three decades moved from a period of strong regulatory constraint to one of the most open markets in the world. Deregulation and liberalization of the mortgage market led to the large-scale entry of foreign providers; massive restructuring of the local industry, including the near-demise of specialist housing finance institutions; and the diversification of funding sources, including the development of mortgage-backed securities. Finally, the government maintains a strong interest in housing, both with respect to the relationship between housing and the macroeconomy and in terms of policy, including supporting owner-occupation as the tenure of choice.

Looking at these fundamentals in more detail, starting with house prices: In the post-war period the UK experienced two extreme periods of volatility prior to the current crisis, and many other smaller but significant cycles. The first major period of volatility occurred in the 1970s before deregulation had really begun. It arose as a result of rapid growth in real incomes, significant reductions in income tax, monetary expansion, and underlying demographic change—all of which increased effective demand and resulted in rapidly increasing inflation and even stronger house-price increases. The boom came to an abrupt end with the oil crisis and the housing market took many years to recover. This period of boom and bust could be ascribed mainly to economic fundamentals and government mismanagement. A particular aspect of this cycle was that prospective homeowners were attracted by the possibility of using housing as a hedge against the very rapid inflation that defined that period.

The second period of extreme volatility started in the late 1980s, when a buoyant economy together with a change in the way mortgage interest was treated for tax purposes, led to rapid increases in demand. The mortgage market was by then very open; borrowing was extremely easy; and large numbers of loans were made at loan-to-value ratios of 100 percent or more. The introduction of mortgage-backed securities also brought U.S. institutions into markets where they had little local knowledge. Again the turnaround came as a result of changes in economic expectations, increasing unemployment and initially rapid inflation, followed by stagnation. House prices fell in both real and money terms, and there were very large numbers of arrears followed by possessions. From the peak of the boom in 1989, the market took some seven years to recover to normal levels of transactions and to exhibit consistent increases in prices. Again, one could argue that fundamentals generated the boom and that changes in these fundamentals led to the decline. Even if these fundamentals provide a reasonable explanation of the volatility, there must also be concern that both consumers and institutions lacked the capacity—or perhaps the motivation—accurately to assess risks, particularly in an environment where even people in marginal employment had become owner-occupiers and there was little past experience of house-price falls. The mortgage market undoubtedly became more risky, and that risk was disproportionately borne by mortgagors. As a result large numbers of households experienced arrears and foreclosure.

While many households suffered, the mortgage industry itself proved robust and suffered no significant losses (Megbolugbe and Whitehead 1994). In retrospect it is clear that lending was often over-generous, and the industry learned slowly in the early years of the 1990s how to mediate problems of arrears for those borrowers who would ultimately be able to pay off their loans. As a result possessions fell well before arrears and the worst problems of supply overhang were overcome (Whitehead with Gaus 2007).

After 1994, house prices rose—first slowly and then, after the turn of the century, much more rapidly. Exhibit 8.1 shows house prices in both money and real terms. Prices flattened around 2004 but then took off again, at least in money terms. At the height of the boom, house prices were roughly double the level they had been at the beginning of the twenty-first century.

In this context it may be worth noting that the housing market has remained somewhat separate from the markets for stocks and other types of property.

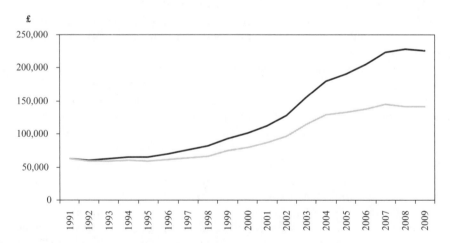

Exhibit 8.1   The Rise in UK House Prices since the Last Crisis (Simple Average House Prices)

Note: Dark line: unadjusted for inflation; gray line: adjusted for inflation, based on the annual all-items Retail Price Index.

Source: Department of Communities and Local Government Live Table 571.

Compared with indices such as Investment Property Databank's commercial property index and the FT100 stock-market index, house prices were generally less buoyant and sometimes more volatile. The commercial property market saw fourteen years of continuous growth to 2007, including total returns of just under 20 percent in the final three years of that period. The stock market on the other hand was far more volatile year on year. It fell significantly in the early part of the century from a high of around 6,000, and only recovered to this level in 2006. It fell again to under 4,400 in late 2008 and now (end 2010) is running at around 5,900.

The second fundamental of the UK housing market, which has long been recognized, is that the country's restrictive planning framework, the limited supply of available land, and the structure of the development industry (whose firms operate more like traders) make housing supply in the UK relatively unresponsive to price changes (Barker 2003). In fact, econometric analysis of long-run supply adjustment suggests that UK housing supply has one of the lowest price elasticities in the Western world. Simple estimates always produce a figure of below one, while the figure for the United States is generally reckoned to be around three. More sophisticated techniques for estimation suggest that the difference is even larger (Meen 2005). Moreover, the price elasticity of supply has fallen since the early 1990s. The result has been that over the long run, UK house prices have risen in real terms by between 1 and 1.5 percent per annum more than those of our European comparators (Barker 2003).

While in the main house prices were rising, particularly after 1996, housing completions in England fell from around 165,000 in 1990 to under 130,000 in 2001 (Department of Communities and Local Government [DCLG] 2009). This was a matter of grave concern to the government because of its impact on competitiveness, especially as, in the new century, output levels continued to fall to levels below projections of household formation, tightening the market still further. Following the Barker Review (2004) the government therefore made a concerted effort to increase investment. However, even at the peak of the market in 2007, only 175,000 dwellings were being completed in England, which left the net increase in dwellings still well below projected household growth. This persistent lack of responsiveness means that, unless incomes decline or demographic patterns change very significantly, real house prices will probably continue to rise in the longer term—a rather different prognosis from that in the United States.

The third fundamental is that the UK has had an increasingly liberalized housing finance market since the 1980s. The tax-favored treatment of the building society sector,[1] which provided a special circuit of housing finance, was discontinued during the 1970s and 1980s, at the same time as the general finance market was opened up to enable foreign banks to operate in the UK (Boleat and Coles 1987; Whitehead 1994). Building societies were given the right to demutualize in 1988, enabling them to either become or join with banks. Initially only one major lender did so, but in the late 1990s after further legislation most of the larger ones followed. In the year 2000, 6 of the top 10 UK mortgage lenders ranked by mortgage assets were former building societies and therefore still quite specialized. Building societies that had retained their status accounted for only 21 percent of new lending in that year (Council of Mortgage Lenders [CML] Statistics Table MM8). Over the same period, the government finally did away with the favorable tax treatment of mortgage interest payments.[2]

Exhibit 8.2 Aspects of Housing Affordability in the Twenty-First Century

	First-Time Buyers				
	Year-on-Year House Price Increases	Interest Payments as a Proportion of Income	Deposit as % of Purchase Price	Average Household Incomes (£000s)	House-Price-to-Earnings Ratio
2000	10.4	14.3	16.4	21.1	5.82
2001	4.3	13.4	16.7	22.0	5.97
2002	15.1	12.2	19.0	23.7	6.73
2003	11.2	11.8	23.0	26.6	7.40
2004	7.9	15.0	21.1	27.1	7.88
2005	3.5	16.3	19.3	29.3	8.05
2006	1.5	16.8	16.4	32.0	8.11
2007	6.5	19.4	17.2	33.8	8.69
2008	−4.9	19.6	21.8	35.0	8.32
2009	−7.6	15.0	27.7	34.5	7.56

Sources: DCLG Live Table 539; affordability tables.

This liberalization went further than it did in much of the rest of Europe, where special circuits were maintained, notably in France, Germany, and Austria (European Mortgage Federation [EMF] 2010). The UK market was extremely competitive, and the major institutions, many of which were still heavily concentrated in residential mortgage lending, looked to expand their market share. Regulation by the Bank of England and the Financial Services Authority imposed relatively few constraints on the behavior of either institutions or consumers. This arguably provided the necessary conditions for the rapid growth in house prices—a growth that was out of line with incomes, and that is not confined to the UK but seen across many industrialized countries (Girouard et al. 2006). There were increasing concerns from early in the first decade of the twenty-first century that the growth in house prices were becoming unsustainable—and indeed in 2004–2005 there was a slowdown (Exhibit 8.2). Even so analyses showed that there was little sign of a bubble (Cameron, Muellbauer, and Murphy 2006). It was only after 2005 as the market picked up rapidly, with very high levels of transactions and rapid rises in house prices, that there was some limited evidence of over-valuation (Meen 2008).

The final fundamental factor is government policy. During the boom period ministers argued that concerns about house prices should be addressed by the regulators within the context of the broader financial environment rather than be a matter of direct government concern. Indeed, the government's main policy emphasis was on increasing effective demand for owner-occupation among marginal buyers, as they were concerned that the falling proportion of first-time buyer mortgagors and increasing problems of access and affordability were jeopardizing their goal of expanding owner-occupation to at least 70 percent (Labour Party 2005). This aspect of policy bears comparison with the United States—with two distinct differences: Unlike in the United States, tax relief on mortgage interest was finally completely removed in 2000 and the policy of expanding owner-occupation was unsuccessful. More fundamentally, despite the removal of mortgage tax relief, the tax system continued to favor owner-occupation through the removal of imputed income tax in the 1960s and the fact that capital gains on the principal home remain exempt from tax (without even a cap as in the United States) (Stephens, Munroe, and Whitehead 2005).

These four elements—volatility, inelastic supply, mortgage-market deregulation, and government policy—came together by around 2005 to produce a long-term imbalance between the demand and supply of housing, which would cause particularly acute problems if the economy continued to expand. Demand increased because of long-term demographic trends and income growth, as well as lower costs of borrowing and expectations of continued capital gains in the short term. Supply remained constrained and prices rose.

Whether there was a bubble in house prices in 2004–2005 is unclear. As we have noted, most commentators argued that the system was not far out of line with fundamentals at least until 2005—although some, particularly *The Economist*, warned of major downward adjustment (*Economist* 2005). But even the more negative forecasts generally envisaged at worst a soft landing, with demand reined in as individual borrowers faced increasing costs. The data gave some support to this view (Exhibit 8.2). House-price increases slowed from 2004 and mortgage payments increased as a proportion of first-time buyer incomes—although only to levels that had been normal in the 1990s.

THE INITIAL CRISIS: UK-SPECIFIC OR CONTAGION FROM ABROAD?

Lending Patterns

The most important concern in the middle of the first decade of this century was the very rapid growth in mortgage lending, particularly in 2006 and 2007 (Exhibit 8.3). Gross advances in 2007 were 25 percent above the 2005 level, and more than 200 percent up from the beginning of the century. Just as important was the composition of this lending. According to estimates for the Turner Review, loans for home purchases made up a relatively small proportion of advances. These grew by less than 40 percent between 2001 and 2007, at which point they accounted for only 35 percent of total residential mortgage lending (Turner 2009). Instead lending was going increasingly to the "buy to let" market (individual investment in private rented housing). This reflected the widespread view among consumers that capital gains in housing would continue, and that easy access to credit would enable them to earn large, geared returns. The other type of borrowing that saw an increase was remortgaging and equity withdrawal, which more than doubled over the period and accounted for 39 percent of borrowing at the end of 2007. A significant proportion of this borrowing went back into the housing market to fund buy-to-let purchases and improve existing homes, or as equity-rich parents provided house-purchase deposits for their children.

Subprime lending was an important but not overwhelming element of this growth. Some 20 percent of adults were refused credit in 2005 by mainstream lenders, generating a large potential market (Pannell and Anderson 2006). Subprime lenders provided a full range of mortgage products for these borrowers, including interest-only and short-term fixed-rate mortgages. In 2004, loans to

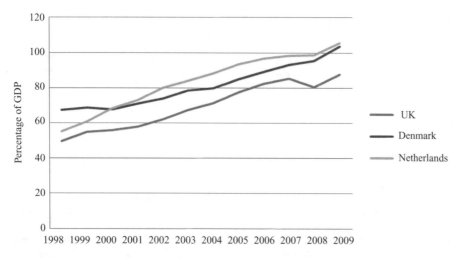

Exhibit 8.3 Residential Mortgage Debt to GDP Ratio: UK, Denmark, and the Netherlands, 1998–2009

Source: Hypostat 2009, European Mortgage Federation.

borrowers with impaired credit, as the subprime market is known in the UK, made up about 5 percent of overall lending, with some 30 lenders active in this submarket (Burton et al. 2004). After 2004 it grew in importance but remained a relatively small, if high-risk, market sector (Munro et al. 2005). Evidence in 2006 suggested that arrears were four times and possessions 10 times as high as in the prime market. The higher possession rate arose partly because lenders took borrowers in arrears to court far more quickly than did the prime lenders. In part this was because loan-to-value ratios for subprime loans were relatively low, which made possession worthwhile (Stephens and Quilgars 2007).

With this expansion of lending, housing indebtedness grew to over 80 percent of GDP in 2007 as compared to around 55 percent in 2001 (Turner 2009). This put the UK among the more indebted nations—above the United States although still behind Iceland, the Netherlands, Denmark and Switzerland in Europe and Australia globally (Girouard et al. 2006a; EMF 2010).

The owner-occupation rate did not rise after 2000 in spite of the enormous increase in lending that took place. Indeed from 2004 to 2007, in the period when advances were increasing most rapidly, it actually fell from around 70 percent in England to 68 percent (DCLG 2009). Potential problems were therefore more associated with "credit hungry" households than with traditional first-time buyers.

In the third quarter of 2007, total gross residential lending to individuals hit a peak of £102 billion. Buy-to-let lending, often used as an indicator of speculative activity in the housing market, also reached a peak (Exhibit 8.4). Some of the characteristics of that lending were of considerable concern. About 46 percent of the £102 billion went to borrowers whose income had not been verified by the lender—so-called "self-certification" mortgages. The Financial Services Authority (FSA), the industry regulator, suggested that the largest part of this self-cert market was for remortgaging, where the mortgagor was restructuring their overall debt against the higher value of their home (FSA 2005). A similar proportion went on

Exhibit 8.4   The UK Mortgage Market in the Twenty-First Century

	Mortgage Lending Gross Advances (£m)	% Buy to Let	Other Specialist Mortgage Lenders % Balances Outstanding	Number of Mortgages (Million)
2000	119,794	3%	7.6%	11.1
2001	160,123	4%	9.6%	11.3
2002	220,737	6%	12.1%	11.4
2003	277,342	7%	15.3%	11.5
2004	291,258	8%	19.6%	11.5
2005	288,280	8%	22.3%	11.6
2006	345,355	11%	26.0%	11.7
2007	362,632	12%	29.8%	11.9
2008	254,022	11%	34.7%	11.7
2009	143,639	6%	24.8%	11.4

Source: CML Statistics Tables MM4, MM8, MM17.

loans worth more than three times the borrower's (sole or joint) income (CML Table MM21). Over 14 percent of new lending for home purchase was at loan-to-value ratios of 90 percent or over, and nearly 9 percent combined two higher-risk characteristics: both a high LTV (over 90 percent) and a high income multiple (over 3.5 times single income or 2.75 times joint income). Although comparable data are not available for previous years, all these measures were probably at near-peak levels at least for this cycle, although probably not in comparison to the late 1980s (Whitehead with Gaus 2007).[3] Equally worrying was the extent to which new mortgage instruments were being used to improve affordability in the short run. Interest-only mortgages became increasingly dominant, especially in the remortgaging market, as borrowers (and lenders) assumed that they could be rolled over into new interest-only loans at the end of the interest-only period. First mortgages tended to be short-term fixed-rate loans that required re-negotiation every couple of years. These trends could be seen across much of Europe as house prices rose faster than incomes and access to home ownership became increasingly difficult (Scanlon, Lunde, and Whitehead 2008).

Even so, it should be remembered that the loan-to-income ratios appropriate to the period of high inflation and interest rates of the 1970s and 1980s were not necessarily appropriate in the low-inflation environment of the early part of the first decade of the twenty-first century. As can be seen in Exhibit 8.2, interest payments as a proportion of income, while rising, remained below 20 percent, and it could be argued that borrowing was not out of line with households' actual and expected outgoings. In addition, borrowing as a proportion of individual wealth was declining because capital values were rising faster than additional debt. As a result the Bank of England's assessment was that most households had a reasonable safety net to cope with any increase in interest rates (Waldron and Young 2006).

Industry Structure and Funding Sources

During the first few years of the twenty-first century the general structure of the UK mortgage market remained fairly stable, with two main exceptions. One was the merger of Halifax and Bank of Scotland (numbers one and 10 among UK banks in 2000), which created an organization whose assets were more than twice those of its nearest competitor. Even so, taken together the group lost share within the top 10 over the period to 2007. The second was the explosive growth of Northern Rock, which increased its assets by more than 300 percent over the period and moved from the number eight to the number five position.

Since deregulation mortgage lenders in general had come to rely less on retail deposits for funding and more on a range of wholesale sources, including the use of mortgage-backed securities. In 2000, the category of "other specialist mortgage lenders" (which included the subprime subsidiaries of the main lenders, other centralized lenders, and special-purpose vehicles—that is, mortgage-backed securities) accounted for £41 billion of lending secured against property. This was less than 8 percent of the total. By 2007 this segment of the market had grown to £355 billion, accounting for almost 30 percent of balances outstanding (CML table MM4). According to the industry body the Council of Mortgage Lenders (CML), mortgage-backed securities accounted for some 20 percent of mortgage debt finance in 2007 as compared to well below 10 percent in the early years of the century (CML 2009).

One reason why Northern Rock was able to grow so rapidly was that they took this approach to extremes as part of a business plan based on growth far above that which could have been supported by on-balance-sheet lending. As of June 2007, only 23 percent of the bank's liabilities consisted of retail deposits. Most were securitized notes and funds from wholesale money markets (44 percent and 25 percent respectively), with a small proportion of covered bonds (Northern Rock 2008). Much of this funding was short-term and needed to be rolled over on a regular basis. In 2005 and 2006, about half of the bank's wholesale borrowing was at a maturity of less than one year (Applegarth, quoted in Milne and Wood 2009). This was clearly an extremely risky approach given that wholesale markets had shut in the past—for example, in 1997–1998—although not for long periods (CML, 2009).

Northern Rock and Its Immediate Aftermath

The problems in the markets for U.S. mortgage-backed securities, first evident in early 2007, spread rapidly to other countries. The rise in default rates on U.S. subprime mortgages triggered an examination of the assets of financial institutions across the globe, and it turned out that an hitherto unrecognized number of non–U.S. institutions held these securities on their balance sheets.

In mid-2007 Northern Rock, which had little or no involvement with the U.S. market, found it could no longer sell its own securitized loans, and turned instead to the wholesale money markets. But events in the United States had made banks increasingly reluctant to lend to other banks. On 9 August, the London Inter-Bank Offer Rate (LIBOR), the rate governing loans between banks, rose dramatically to 6.7975 percent. Inter-bank markets froze as many banks were unwilling to lend at any price, and Northern Rock found it could not re-finance its short-term debt.

Northern Rock's problems in securing ongoing funding stemmed not from investor concerns about its mortgage assets, as the bank had a high-quality, relatively low-risk portfolio with little exposure to subprime loans. As of end-2007, some 0.57 percent of the bank's residential accounts were three months or more in arrears, significantly below the CML average of 1.10 percent (Northern Rock 2008).[4] Rather, the problems were the result of a systemic seizure of money markets that affected institutions whether or not they had exposure to U.S.-based risks.

Northern Rock reported its problems to the Financial Services Authority, and in September arranged for a liquidity facility from the Bank of England. The day before the formal announcement was due the news leaked, and depositors panicked. Customers queued by the thousands to withdraw their savings from the bank's 56 branches, taking out more than £1 billion over a few days.

The government's immediate response was to try to reassure retail savers rattled by the widely-publicized images of the run on Northern Rock. The government moved to guarantee all deposits in Northern Rock. A few weeks later it extended the existing Financial Services Compensation Scheme to other banks. It also speeded up the procedure for paying compensation, so that savers could be reimbursed at least in part within seven days, rather than a month. These measures were successful and there were no more bank runs, even though several major UK banks faced huge shocks in 2008. However, the government could not broker the acquisition of Northern Rock by another bank, and nationalized the company in February 2008. Existing shareholders received no compensation for the loss of their shares.

From Northern Rock to Lehman

Mid-2007 represented the high point of the UK housing market, although housing starts had actually slowed some time before and mix-adjusted price indices suggested that the market was beginning to stall (DCLG live table 590). Market experts generally saw this as a long-awaited market "correction" rather than the start of a full-scale crash.

The market plummeted on all measures between late 2007 and the end of 2008. The most watched and commented-on indicator was house prices, which on the simple average index, fell by over 11 percent between January 2008 and January 2009. But this decline was small compared to the movement in financial variables, transactions, and new building (Exhibit 8.5).

Exhibit 8.5 Major Housing Market Indicators

Indicator	2008	2009	% Change
Average house price (January)	£221,130	£195,114	−11.8
	2007	*2008*	
Gross new mortgage lending (annual)	£362.8 bn	£254.0 bn	−30.0
Net new mortgage lending (annual)	£9.4 bn	£547 mn	−94.2
Number residential property transactions (August)	146,000	63,000	−56.8
Housing starts	178,080	99,290	−44.2
Proportion of which are private	154,600	75,950	−50.9
Number of new buy-to-let loans (3rd quarter)	93,100	42,400	−54.5
Amount of new buy-to-let loans (3rd quarter)	£12.4 bn	£4.8 bn	−61.3

Sources: CML Tables MM8, MM13, PT2, HP3, HB5, MM17.

Gross new mortgage lending, which had reached a peak of £362.6 billion in 2007, fell by nearly 30 percent in 2008. Net lending was even more dramatically affected, falling from £9.4 billion in August 2007 to just £547 million in August 2007, as borrowers repaid debt but took out fewer loans. The number of residential property transactions also declined dramatically, falling 45 percent on an annual basis and by over 56 percent from August 2007 to August 2008. Purchases by buy-to-let investors mirrored the fall in overall transactions, as the number of new buy-to-let loans fell by 54 percent between the third quarter of 2007 and the same quarter in 2008. The amount of new buy-to-let lending fell by even more.

As demand fell and funding grew harder to secure, developers withdrew from the market. Housing starts fell 44 percent between 2007 and 2008. This decline in investment was wholly in the private sector. Social-sector housing starts held steady at about 23,500 in each year. Initially, the reasons for these declines in activity were associated with the collapse of the wholesale and inter-bank financial markets and the resultant credit rationing. However concerns spread rapidly to demand as the possibility of declining house prices and perhaps rising unemployment became more real.

Lehman Brothers declared bankruptcy in September 2008. The failure of this major U.S. investment bank—and more important, the fact that the U.S. government did not act to rescue it—initiated a global financial crisis and triggered a further tightening of credit conditions and falls in asset prices (OECD 2009).

Late 2008 and early 2009 saw extraordinary changes in the UK mortgage market, as banks and building societies merged (often as a result of government intervention) and those institutions in the worst difficulties were part-nationalized (Exhibit 8.6). The first crisis saw the shares in Halifax Bank of Scotland (HBOS)

Exhibit 8.6 The Fate of the UK's Top 10 Mortgage Lenders in the 2008 Crisis (Largest UK Mortgage Lenders Ranked by Mortgage Assets as of December 2006)

	Name	What Happened in Crisis
1	HBOS	Taken over by Lloyds Banking group with government help in September 2008.
2	Abbey	Owned since 2004 by Santander, which bought assets of nationalized Bradford & Bingley in September 2008.
3	Lloyds TSB	Acquired HBOS (see above); government now owns about 40% of shares.
4	Nationwide	Acquired Cheshire & Derbyshire Building Societies (September 2008) and Dunfermline Building Society (March 2009).
5	Northern Rock	Taken into government control, February 2008.
6	Royal Bank of Scotland	Government takes stake in October 2008; subsequently rises to 84% ownership.
7	Barclays	
8	HSBC	
9	Alliance & Leicester	Acquired by Santander in October 2008.
10	Bradford & Bingley	Nationalized in September 2008; savings business sold to Santander.

Source: CML; authors' additions.

plunge by 37 percent over three days amid fears it was on the brink of collapse. Lloyds TSB took the bank over with the help of the government, which took 43 percent of the shares in the combined institution. The merged group became the country's single largest mortgage lender, with over 30 percent of the market in 2008. In October 2008 the government announced that it would take a stake in the Royal Bank of Scotland in order to recapitalize the group; its original holding of 57 percent has now grown to 84 percent. RBS was the fifth-largest mortgage lender in 2008.

Only two of the top 10 lenders in 2006 remained relatively unaffected by the turmoil in the markets: Barclays and HSBC. Of the others, three disappeared as separate entities (HBOS, Alliance & Leicester, and Bradford & Bingley) and two remain under government control (Northern Rock and Royal Bank of Scotland).

Not surprisingly, the market for funds for the centralized lenders which supported the subprime market almost completely closed. Most such lenders basically left the new lending market; buy-to-let mortgage providers also withdrew as funding became almost impossible to obtain. The remaining mainstream lenders had to depend on retail funding, including the repayment of existing mortgages, to maintain some level of activity. Gross lending remained relatively buoyant, as over a million households had to refinance their short-term discounted fixed-rate mortgages (Croft 2007). However, net lending almost completely collapsed in the face of funding and valuation difficulties.

THE IMPACT OF THE CRISIS

The Evidence on Revival

As the 2008 financial crisis developed, its most important impacts were not on the UK's housing market but on the real economy and on expectations about the future. The country entered recession in the second quarter of 2008, before the collapse of Lehman Brothers. This downturn lasted six quarters, longer than any other post-war recession. At its nadir in the third quarter 2009, GDP was 6.4 percent below its peak, a much larger decline than in earlier post-war recessions. Since then GDP has increased and as of mid-2010 stands at 4.5 percent below peak levels—also a relatively slow improvement compared to earlier cycles (ONS, 2010).

Although the recession has been deeper and slightly longer than earlier periods of decline, unemployment has not increased to anything like the expected extent. At 7.8 percent in mid-2010, the unemployment rate is 2.6 percent lower than at the equivalent stage in the recession of the early 1980s and 2.1 percent below that of the early 1990s (ONS 2010a). This is argued to be, in part, because employers are trying to keep their experienced labor force available for the expected upturn, given the costs of redundancy, employment, and training. Indeed, the employment rate grew more quickly in the second quarter of 2010 than at any period since 1989, reflecting increased confidence. Moreover, although the rate of growth in average earnings fell from 4 percent in mid-2008 to not much more than 1 percent in 2009, implying a considerable fall in real terms, earnings are now picking up again.

The biggest benefit to consumers in general and mortgagors in particular came from the reduction in interest rates. In June 2008 a mortgagor with a tracker[5] mortgage might have been paying around 6.3 percent. This rose to over 7 percent in

October in the immediate aftermath of Lehman but fell fairly consistently thereafter, reaching 3.55 percent in August 2010. Those who purchased tracker mortgages well before the crisis have done even better as the spreads over base rate were lower in previous years. The Bank of England's bank rate, the most widely used benchmark in the UK, first fell to 2 percent by the end of 2008 and since March 2009 has been held at 0.5 percent. Large numbers of existing mortgagors have benefited from these interest-rate falls, which have enabled them to continue to make mortgage payments despite declining incomes from shorter hours and other cutbacks.

UK house prices undoubtedly declined significantly—although the measurement of the extent of decline is made difficult by the enormous reduction in transactions. Using the mix-adjusted measure, house prices in the UK started to stabilize and then decline in the third quarter of 2007 and continued to decline for nine months. On this measure the decline was 14 percent, although headline simple average measures suggested a fall of as much as 19 percent. Since early 2009 prices have risen again—in July 2010 they were within 2 percent of the original peak, although there were also signs of the market beginning to stumble. This pattern is similar to that observed across most of Europe, but in all cases the figures are based on much lower transaction levels than obtained during the boom. Only Ireland, and perhaps Greece, have seen price falls comparable to the United States (Scanlon et al. 2011.).

There have been major declines in transaction levels, new investment, and access to funds, while the terms and conditions under which mortgages are now available have worsened significantly. Residential property transactions reached their peak, based on seasonally adjusted data, in the first quarter of 2007; the lowest quarter was the first in 2009—that is, the downturn in transactions lasted eight quarters from peak to trough, and numbers declined by over 60 percent. By the final quarter in 2009 the number of transactions had risen from 170,000 to 260,000, still 40 percent below the peak; moreover, this included those transactions brought forward by borrowers in order to qualify for a tax incentive[6] that ran out at the end of the year (DCLG Live Table 530). It is too early to say what the level of sales will be once the impact of that stimulus has worn off, but it seems likely that transactions will remain well below 50 percent of the peak—which was itself far below the high observed in the late 1980s (DCLG Live Table 532).

Housing starts fell, as we noted in Exhibit 8.5, by almost 50 percent between 2007 and 2008. In England the trough, at well under 20,000 units, was reached in the fourth quarter of 2008. Starts nearly doubled to over 30,000 by the second quarter 2010, reflecting a significant increase in private sector activity—but also an upward blip in social sector activity because of a government stimulus package (DCLG Live Table 213). Commentators are not expecting significant further increases, in part because of the end of the stimulus package and developers' difficulties in obtaining credit, but also because of lack of confidence in both the mortgage and housing markets.

The most immediate issue has been the difficulty of obtaining a mortgage—for both owner-occupation and buy-to-let. The year-on-year increase in the number of house-purchase loans in July 2010 was only 6 percent, although the increase in the value of loans was 15 percent. First-time buyers have not been able to benefit from lower interest rates because lenders have greatly increased the deposit required—the average deposit for first time buyers in July 2010 was 26 percent of the purchase price and rising. Fewer than 20,000 first-time buyers were able to obtain a mortgage in that month, accounting for just 34 percent of the market—the lowest proportion since the credit crunch began. Thus even though monthly mortgage costs have declined, only those with large savings or with parents or others prepared to support their purchases are able to enter home ownership (CML 2010). The buy-to-let market also almost closed, as Paragon and other specialist lenders stopped lending. However there are signs of improvement in 2010, as well as evidence that funding can be raised from abroad, using simple securitized products (CML 2010a; Paragon 2010).

Finally, how have existing mortgagors fared in the financial crisis? Early predictions were that the problems might be as bad as in the early 1990s when possessions reached 0.8 percent of mortgages and 1.5 percent of all mortgages were over a year in arrears. In actuality, the situation has turned out to be very different, in part because lenders employed well-organized forbearance strategies to deal with some one-third of arrears cases (CML, Table AP9); in part because unemployment has remained lower than expected; and in part because interest rates for many mortgagors have fallen considerably because they hold variable or tracker-rate mortgages. Lenders developed structured forbearance measures partly voluntarily and, partly as a result of government pressure, and have used these measures heavily (Ford and Wallace 2009). Possessions reached a maximum of 0.11 percent in the third quarter of 2009 and have now declined to 0.08 percent. The percentage of mortgages in arrears of over one year reached a maximum of 0.59 percent a little later, in quarter four of 2009, and is continuing to fall. Buy-to-let mortgage arrears and possession, which were anyway rather lower, are also beginning to fall (CML Tables AP1, AP4, AP5). The main problem into the future, unless the economy worsens again, is with respect to a proportion of those in long-term arrears who are not able to improve their position, and who may slip over into foreclosure, especially if interest rates rise. However, even this problem is nothing like as bad as in the early 1990s (CML 2010b).

Overall therefore there are signs of improvement. Yet these are relatively fragile and there are still concerns that there might be a double-dip recession. Perhaps most importantly house prices have not, at least yet, adjusted downwards, as many commentators had predicted. Economic fundamentals still remain too unclear to be sure what the medium-term equilibrium price trajectory might be.

Policy and Regulatory Responses
There have been a number of short-term government policy responses to maintain the market and to support existing mortgagors who fall behind with their payments. These were similar to those in other European countries. On the supply side they concentrated on increasing investment in social housing. On the demand side the government introduced a short-term holiday for lower rates of stamp duty (the tax on house-purchase) as well as a mortgage rescue scheme to help troubled borrowers. Under this scheme, a social housing provider would buy the mortgaged dwelling and rent it back to the previous owner, who would thus not be forced to move home. The mortgage-related schemes have been quite marginal, in the main because arrears and possessions have not risen as expected (Scanlon et al. 2011.). Of far more importance are the longer-term changes in regulation that are beginning to be put in place.

After 2008 there was a wide-ranging examination of how weaknesses in the supervision of financial institutions might have contributed to the crisis (see for example Turner 2009; Crosby 2009; CML 2010c). This led to a series of proposals to strengthen the regulation of lenders, from the general (increasing the quantity and quality of bank capital) to the specific (prohibiting certain types of mortgage product). The cumulative effect of these measures, if they are enacted as expected, will be to reduce the availability of mortgage loans even when finance markets become more normal, which will have a long-lasting effect on the UK housing market.

Although the housing and financial market problems in the UK did not stem as directly from mortgage market developments as those in the United States, the Financial Services Authority (soon to be replaced by a new prudential regulator that will operate as a subsidiary of the Bank of England) has made clear that mortgage markets will in future be subject to much closer and more detailed supervision than in the past. Some commentators, including representatives of the mortgage industry, argue that further regulation is unnecessary because lenders have already taken measures to reduce risk. UK mortgage providers have indeed become dramatically more conservative in their lending since 2007, and the availability of higher-risk products such as interest-only mortgages, high-LTV loans (90 percent or above) and self-certification mortgages has been reduced or eliminated entirely. But the regulators want to ensure that the next period of economic growth cannot lead to a repetition of risky lending behavior.

In the past, the regulatory emphasis was on supporting liberalization by ensuring that mortgage lenders provided comprehensive and accurate information to consumers, on the assumption that borrowers were rational and could make reasonable assessments of risk. The new approach, heavily influenced by the findings of behavioral economists, is explicitly paternalistic. According to the FSA, "Our policy approach to date has been underpinned by a view that mortgage consumers will act rationally to protect their own interests. We believe that we need to change that approach, recognize the behavioral biases of consumers and be more interventionist to help protect consumers from themselves" (FSA 2009b).

For the first time the FSA intends to intervene directly to affect both the types of products lenders can offer and the way in which they assess how much borrowers can afford to pay. The FSA's analysis of the relationship of mortgage characteristics to defaults and possessions showed that the most important single predictor of default was if the borrower had impaired credit—in other words, was a subprime borrower. Defaults were more likely if the loan had a combination of several high-risk characteristics, such as impaired credit, high LTV, and interest-only. This is hardly surprising. A rather more important question is what the alternative might be and why these risks were inadequately priced.

In July 2010 the FSA announced it would require lenders to seek independent verification of income for all loans—effectively banning self-certification mortgages (FSA 2010). Interest-only and long-term mortgages will not be banned, but the proposed regulations will have the effect of making them much less attractive to borrowers. In particular, lenders will have to ensure that borrowers who apply for interest-only mortgages, or loans with a term of more than 25 years, could afford to make payments on 25-year annuity mortgages for the same amount.

Modeling exercises undertaken by the FSA indicate that in the short term, house prices could fall sharply as a result of the reduction in mortgage lending caused by these changes, "and would regress to their baseline value in the long run. As a result the costs of the policy emerge in the short term while benefits accrue over the longer term" (FSA 2010, p. A1:33). Research by CML suggests that anything up to 50 percent of loans granted between 2005 and 2009 would not have been granted under the proposed changes (CML 2010d). The FSA's approach does not recognize that such regulations potentially generate perverse incentives for consumers to move to less-regulated types of borrowing, as occurred before deregulation; nor does it address the alternatives available to households excluded from owning. So far the FSA's main comment on this has been to argue that adverse perceptions of private renting should be addressed by initiatives aimed at "re-educating consumers away from the idea that renting is bad and home ownership good" (FSA 2009, p. 15).

CONCLUSIONS

The question of whether there was, strictly speaking, a bubble in house prices in the UK in the first decade of the twentieth century depends mainly on how a bubble is defined—and in any case will not be resolved until better data are available. It is clear that there were large-scale reductions in the cost of borrowing as inflation came under control in the 1990s. The costs of house purchases therefore declined, and increased competition in the finance market enabled the resultant demand to be more readily met. Given these factors, the econometric evidence suggests that prices were not far out of line with fundamentals—particularly demographics, income growth, and the costs of purchase—at least until 2004–2005. At that point there was a reduction in demand, reflecting concerns that expectations of continued house-price growth were becoming unrealistic. Thereafter, as prices rose again, the evidence on the expansion of lending and the growth of buy-to-let borrowing after 2005 suggests that demand from both established owner-occupiers and buy-to-let mortgagors increased again, in part as a result of unrealistic expectations of long-term capital gains.

The slowdown in the housing market resulted in part from concern that the market was overheating, but also from a growing awareness of problems with subprime borrowing in the United States. But the UK subprime market was rather different and a great deal smaller than that in the United States—so developments there were not, of themselves, enough to cause a sharp decline (CML 2007; Whitehead with Gaus 2007). The decline was instead mainly an outcome of the near-closure of markets for mortgage-backed securities and inter-bank lending, and this was clearly the result of contagion from the United States. No country avoided this funding crisis, but the UK was more dependent on these markets than most other European countries and was therefore more deeply affected.

Up to at least 2010 the increases in mortgage arrears and possessions, while worrying, have been far less disastrous than expected and less severe than in the crisis of the early 1990s. This is largely because of the decline in interest rates, which reduced outgoings for a large proportion of existing mortgagors, and to the unexpectedly small increase in unemployment. House-price reductions have also been relatively short-lived in many parts of the country. Although some borrowers are in negative equity, the fact that UK mortgages are full-recourse means that relatively few mortgagors walk away from their housing debt.

It could be argued that the outcomes of the crisis have been less traumatic than had been predicted because of actions taken to resolve earlier problems in the UK market. The crisis of the early 1990s led to forbearance procedures that have reduced possessions; the Northern Rock crisis meant that the government was more aware of the likely problems when Lehman occurred; the macro-economic response to the global crisis was to reduce interest rates, which helped those on variable-rate mortgages; and the underlying inelasticity of supply meant both that the overhang of unsold units was quite small and that expectations about longer-term house-price rises remained strong. Moreover, the private rental market had grown by over a third during the previous decade, partly because legal changes in 1988 made it easier to evict tenants, and because lenders in the mid-1990s introduced mortgages targeted specifically at individuals investing in residential rental property (known in the United Kingdom as "buy-to-let" investors). This growth meant that potential first-time buyers excluded from the mortgage market by the lack of funds had other housing options in the private rental sector.

The continued near-stagnation of the market is however very damaging to the housing system. This stagnation has massive negative impacts on housing investment and on the capacity of households to adjust as circumstances change. There is very little reason to think that these problems will be solved in the near future, as funding for mortgage lenders remains in very short supply and expectations about the future are generally negative. Yet there are some signs of improvement in finance markets, as "vanilla" wholesale products return. The current situation is by no means stabilized and any signs of a double dip could generate problems comparable to those initially predicted. There is at least the possibility of a downward "bubble" as activity and prices decline in the face of these continuing uncertainties.

The fundamentals of the UK housing market remain. Demand is far more volatile than supply and there will be upward pressure on prices if the economy returns to more normal growth rates. Regional differences have been exacerbated both in terms of the housing market and the overall economy. Downward structural pressure on prices can come only from changes in these fundamentals, including modifications in the user cost of purchase arising from regulatory changes, reductions in fiscal benefits, unexpected rises in interest rates, and quantity constraints on lending. The new government's austerity measures could have widespread implications if job creation is not as buoyant as predicted. No one can be sure what the outcome of the continuing financial crisis will be—but future developments will come more from economic fundamentals than from the housing market itself.

NOTES

1. The composite tax rate paid by building societies meant that higher-rate taxpayers received a significant subsidy if they saved through the sector.

2. Mortgage interest payments are no longer tax-deductible in the UK, unlike the United States. Beginning in the late 1960s, restrictions on deductibility started to be put in place and were further limited during the 1970s. From 1989 these limits were gradually tightened and in 2000 tax relief was abolished completely.

3. Data are originally from the Financial Services Authority's Mortgage Lending and Administration Return, which was first compiled in the first quarter of 2007.

4. Although Milne and Wood (2009) say that the quality of Northern Rock's book was not in fact great, in part because it included a high proportion of lending to first-time buyers and borrowers in the South of England.

5. A mortgage whose interest rate "tracks" movements in a benchmark rate; the interest rate on the mortgage is generally 2 to 4 percent above the benchmark rate.

6. The government temporarily raised the threshold for the sales tax on dwellings from £125,000 to £175,000. A tax of 1 percent of the purchase price would normally have applied at this level. They also formalized what had been a voluntary forbearance regime among lenders introduced after the last crisis.

REFERENCES

Barker, K. 2003. *Delivering Stability: Securing Our Future Housing Needs*. Barker Review of Housing Supply, Interim report. HM Treasury.

Barker, K. 2004. "Review of Housing Supply: Delivering Stability: Securing Our Future Housing Needs," Final report. HM Treasury.

Boleat, M., and A. Coles. 1987. *The Mortgage Market*. London: Building Societies Association.

Burton, D., D. Knights, A, Leyshon, C. Alferoff, and P. Signoretti. 2004. "Making a Market: The UK Retail Financial Services Industry and the Rise of the Complex Subprime Credit Market." *Competition and Change* 8: 1, 3–25.

Cameron, G., J. Muellbauer, and A. Murphy. 2006. "Was There a British House Price Bubble?" Working Paper No 276, Department of Economics, University of Oxford.

Council of Mortgage Lenders. 2007. "No Special Relationship: Sub-Prime in the UK and the U.S." *News and Views* 6, 1–4.

Council of Mortgage Lenders. 2009. *The Outlook for Mortgage Funding Markets in the UK 2010–2015*. London: CML.

Council of Mortgage Lenders. 2010 (September 13). "July Sees Continued Subdued Mortgage Market." Press release. London: CML.

Council of Mortgage Lenders. 2010a (August 10). "CML Reports Second Quarter Buy-to-Let Results." Press release. London: CML.

Council of Mortgage Lenders. 2010b (August 12). "CML Reports Decline in Arrears and Repossessions." Press release. London: CML.

Council of Mortgage Lenders. 2010c. *The Outlook for Funding Markets in the UK in 2010–2015*. London: CML.

Council of Mortgage Lenders. 2010d. *An Evidence-Based Review of MMR Proposals on Responsible Lending*. London: CML.

Croft, J. 2007 (June 2). "Time Bomb for 1 Million Mortgagors." *Financial Times*.

Crosby, J. 2009. "Mortgage Finance: Interim Report." London: HM Treasury.

Department of Communities and Local Government (DCLG). 2009. *Housing and Planning Statistics Annual Review*. London: DCLG.

DCLG. 2009. *Fifteen Years of the Survey of English Housing 1993–1994 to 2007–2008*. London: DCLG.

Economist. 2005 (June 16). "The Global Housing Boom." *The Economist*.

European Mortgage Federation. 2010. *Hypostat 2009*. Brussels: EMF.

Financial Services Authority. 2005. Press release, FSA/PN/095/205. London: FSA.

Financial Services Authority. 2009b. "Mortgage Market Review." Discussion Paper 09/3. London: FSA.

Financial Services Authority. 2010. "Mortgage Market Review: Responsible Lending." Consultation Paper 10/16. London: FSA.

Girouard, N., M. Kennedy, P. van den Noord, and C. Andre. 2006. "Recent House Price Developments: The Role of Fundamentals." OECD Economics Department Working Paper No 475. Paris: OECD.

Girouard, N., M. Kennedy, and C. Andre. 2006a. "Has the Rise in Debt Made Households More Vulnerable?" OECD Economics Department Working Paper No. 535. Paris: OECD.

Labour Party. 2005. *Labour Party Manifesto: Looking Forward, Not Back*. London: Labour Party.

Meen, G. 2005. "On the Economics of the Barker Review of Housing Supply." *Housing Studies* 20: 6, 949–972.

Meen, G. 2008. "Ten New Propositions in the UK Housing Macroeconomy: An Overview of the First Year of the Century." *Urban Studie* 45: 13, 2759–2781.

Megbolugbe, I., and C. Whitehead, eds. 1994. "Understanding Structural Adjustment of the Mortgage Market in the U.S.: Lessons from the Protracted Real Estate Recession in the UK," *Housing Policy Debate Special Issue* 5: 3, 219–230.

Milne, A., and G. Wood. 2009. "Shattered on the Rock? British Financial Stability from 1866 to 2007." *Journal of Banking Regulation* 10: 2, 89–127.

Munro, M., C. Leishman, N. K. Karley, and J. Ford. 2005. *Lending to Higher Risk Borrowers: Sub-Prime Credit and Sustainable Home Ownership*. York, UK: JRF Foundation.

Northern Rock. 2008. *Annual Report and Accounts 2007*. Available at http://companyinfo .northernrock.co.uk/downloads/2007_annual_report.pdf.

Northern Rock. 2009. *Annual Report and Accounts 2008*. Available at http://companyinfo .northernrockassetmanagement.co.uk/downloads/2008_annual_report.pdf.

OECD. 2009. *OECD Economic Surveys: United Kingdom*. Paris: OECD.

ONS. 2010. *Quarterly National Accounts, Second Quarter 2010*. London: ONS.

ONS. 2010a (September). *Labour Market Statistical Bulletin*. London: ONS.

Pannell, R., and S. Anderson. 2006. "Adverse Credit Mortgages." *Housing Finance* 10. London: CML.

Paragon. 2010 (September 28). "Paragon Returns to New Lending." Press Release. London and Solihull: Paragon.

Scanlon, K., J. Lunde, and C. M. E. Whitehead. 2008. "Mortgage Product Innovation in Advanced Economies: More Choice, More Risk." *European Journal of Housing Policy* 8:3, 109–131.

Scanlon, K., J. Lunde, and C. M. E. Whitehead. 2011. "Responding to the Housing and Financial Crises: Mortgage Lending, Mortgage Products, and Government Policies." *International Journal of Housing Policy*, 11: 1, 23–49.

Stephens, M., M. Munroe, and C. Whitehead. 2005. "Lessons from the Past, Challenges for the Future, the Evaluation of English Housing Policy, 1975–1999." London: Office of the Deputy Prime Minister.

Stephens, M., and D. Quilgars. 2007. "Managing Arrears and Possessions." *Housing Finance* 5: 2007, 1–14.

Turner, J. A. 2009 (March). *The Turner Review: A Regulatory Response to the Global Banking Crisis*. Financial Services Authority, UK. Available at www.fsa.gov.uk/pubs/other/turner_review.pdf.

Waldron, M., and G. Young. 2006. *The State of British Household Finances: Results from the 2006 NMG Research Survey*. London: Bank of England.

Whitehead, C. 1994. "The Opening Up of UK Housing Finance." In *European Housing Finance: Single Market or Mosaic*. Bristol: SAUS Publications, University of Bristol.

Whitehead, C., with K. Gaus. 2007. "At Any Cost? Access to Housing in a Changing Financial Marketplace." Shelter Policy Discussion Paper. London: Shelter.

ABOUT THE AUTHORS

CHRISTINE WHITEHEAD, OBE, PhD, BSc Econ (University of London), is an internationally respected housing economist. She has been working in the fields of housing economics, finance, and policy for many years covering both UK and international issues. She is currently Professor in Housing in the Department of

Economics, London School of Economics. Until the end of 2010 she was also Director of the Cambridge Centre of Housing and Planning Research, which celebrated its twentieth anniversary in September 2010. Her latest book, coauthored with Sarah Monk and titled *Making Housing More Affordable* (Wiley Blackwell), was launched at the celebratory conference.

KATHLEEN SCANLON is a research fellow at LSE London, a research group within the London School of Economics. She specializes in urban and housing issues, particularly housing finance and social housing, and is one of the coordinators of an international group of experts looking at the effects of the global financial crisis on mortgage and housing markets in developed countries. She recently returned to London after three years in Copenhagen, where she was a guest researcher at the Danish State Building Research Institute. She has contributed to and edited several books, including two volumes of *Social Housing in Europe*.

PART III

Eastern Europe: European Emerging Markets Ride the Waves

CHAPTER 9

The Housing Market in Russia

Lessons of the Mortgage Crisis

NADEZHDA KOSAREVA
The Institute for Urban Economics, Russia, Moscow

ANDREY TUMANOV
The Institute for Urban Economics, Russia, Moscow

This chapter is devoted to the analysis of the impact of the global financial crisis on the nascent housing market in Russia, which started developing less than 10 years ago. At the same time we make an attempt to estimate whether there were "bubbles" in this market. This chapter has the following structure.

It starts with an overview of the housing sector in Russia before the meltdown and analysis of the evolution of housing property rights. Next we look at both the supply side (housing stock and new construction) and the demand side of the housing market before 2009. The section ends with a summary description of the situation in housing mortgage finance and affordability of housing, which is a big challenge for a developing housing market.

The second section analyzes the impact of the global financial crisis on the mortgage sector in Russia and highlights new trends in the housing sector. We focus on government anti-crisis measures in the housing market and the role of government-sponsored organizations. Two main areas of government intervention in the housing and mortgage markets are analyzed: state support of mortgage borrowers and the housing construction industry.

Next we raise the issue of the presence of a housing bubble in Russia and analyze main determinants of housing price trends and their impact on housing price dynamics. We argue that there was no bubble in the Russian housing market.

The chapter concludes with an outline of the prospects for the housing and housing mortgage markets in Russia.

OVERVIEW OF THE HOUSING SECTOR IN RUSSIA BEFORE THE MELTDOWN

Housing Property Rights

During the USSR days, the Soviet government carried out a highly centralized housing policy and most of the national housing stock was owned by the state

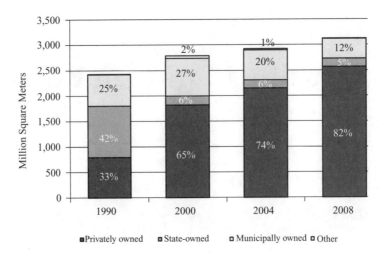

Exhibit 9.1   Housing Total Floor Space Distribution in Russia by Types of Ownership
Note: Back in 1990, "municipally owned" housing was the state housing transferred to local Soviets to
be managed by the latter.
Source: The Federal Service of State Statistics (Rosstat).

and managed by state enterprises or by local Soviets. Only single-family homes in
small towns and rural settlements were privately owned, and a minor portion of
apartment buildings in cities were owned by housing cooperatives (see the data
for 1990 in Exhibit 9.1).

Almost immediately after the declaration of Russia's independence in 1990,
we witnessed activity in Russia's housing market establishment.[1] Already in 1991
both the privatization of the state and municipal housing stock reform, and the
transfer of the state housing stock into real municipal ownership were initiated.
All citizens were entitled to a free-of-charge privatization of apartments occupied
by them in apartment buildings belonging to the state or municipalities. A tenant
who privatizes his unit receives full rights to dispose of it: The unit can be sold
or rented in the open market without restriction. Although initially the housing
privatization time line has not been fixed, at present there are legislative plans to
end the housing privatization by March 2013.

However, while the ownership right to apartments was assigned to new owners, the apartment buildings management and maintenance were still the responsibility of municipalities. Only in recent years has the pace of the reform, which
implies transfer of responsibility for apartment building management to owners
of apartments and associations of apartment owners (homeowners associations),
intensified in Russia.

Housing Stock and Housing Consumption

At present the housing stock in Russia consists of 59.5 million housing units with
the total floor space of 3.2 billion square meters.[2] There are 419 dwelling units per
1,000 people. Over the past 20 years the average housing floor space consumption
in Russia increased by 35 percent and reached the level of 22.4 square meters

per capita in early 2010. Nevertheless, the gap between Russia and European countries is still wide. Some people still reside in so-called "communal apartments" shared by several households that are not connected by family ties, and rooms in such apartments can be privatized.[3] There is yet another problem—that of multi-generation families residing in the same dwelling unit.

Forty-two percent of the total housing floor space in Russia was built before 1970, 53 percent during 1971–1995, and only 5 percent after 1995. Only 61 percent of the housing stock is equipped with major amenities.[4] In urban settlements this figure reaches 75 percent, and in rural areas only 22 percent. In 2008, 77 percent of the housing stock had water pipes, 73 percent had proper sanitation, 82 percent were heated, 66 percent had a bathtub or shower unit, and 64 percent had a hot water supply. The category of housing without proper amenities consists mainly of owner-occupied houses built in small urban settlements and rural areas during the Soviet rule. For example, there is no water piping in 4 percent of small urban settlements and in 70 percent of rural settlements, and no sanitation in 20 percent of small urban settlements and in 95 percent of rural settlements.

The practices of underfinancing the rehabilitation of housing buildings and refurbishment of utility networks in the 1990s resulted in the dilapidation of build-ings, deterioration of the quality of housing and utility services, and the increase in the number of accidents. Over the past two decades the volume of dilapidated and unsafe housing increased 3.1-fold to reach 99.5 million square meters (or 3.2 percent of the total housing stock) in 2008.

Regional differentiation in terms of the average housing floor space consump-tion by population was great: from 6.2 square meters in the Chechen Republic up to 30.8 square meters in Chukotka Autonomous District. In 2008, one resident of Moscow had, on the average, 20.1 square meters of housing floor space, and a resident of St. Petersburg had 23.5 square meters. Large cities with a high con-centration of economically active population have, on the average, less housing floor space per one resident than far-away small villages populated mainly with senior single persons or aged couples. For example, in 2008 housing consumption in Moscow was 50 percent lower than in rural areas of central and northwestern parts of Russia (30.1 square meters per capita).[5]

Housing Construction

In the 1990s to early in the first decade of this century, Russia saw a decline in the volume of housing construction. In the early 1990s, approximately 0.28 square meters of housing per capita were commissioned every year, and by 2000 approximately 0.21 square meters. Starting in 2001, a favorable macroeconomic situation in the country, growth of household incomes and enhancement of the legislative framework contributed to a constant growth of housing completion volumes, which reached the level of 0.45 square meters per capita in 2008 (for data on housing completion in Russia, see Exhibit 9.2).

Volumes of housing floor space completion per capita vary considerably from region to region, so that the minimum is sometimes 10 times lower than the highest amount: 0.03 square meters in Murmansk Oblast and 1.24 square meters in Moscow Oblast (region). Housing construction in Russia is characterized by excessively complicated procedures of obtaining required construction permits: Developers

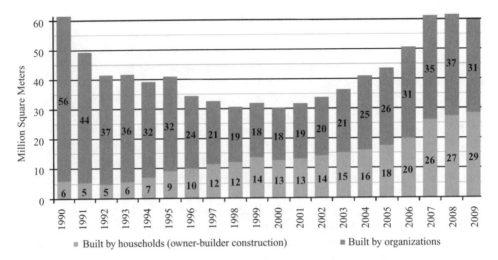

Exhibit 9.2   Volumes of Housing Total Floor Space Completion in Russia
Source: Data from Rosstat.

depend on the actions of state or municipal authorities when they want to obtain
a plot of land (due to the fact that the land market is still poorly developed) and
on local monopolists/utility organizations when it is necessary to be connected to
the physical infrastructure (due to low investment attractiveness of this sector for
private investors). According to the "Doing Business in 2011," research conducted
every year by the World Bank, Russia occupied the 182nd place among 183 ranked
economies in terms of the "Dealing with Construction Permits" indicator.[6]

The key source of housing construction finance in Russia is household savings
or loans extended in limited volumes to households for housing construction or
participation in construction projects, and people either build single-family homes
on their own (individual housing construction), or participate in a multifamily
apartment building construction finance (as a rule, via direct investment in construction through various types of contracts with developers). Although lending
to developers for the purposes of housing construction project finance is being
developed, its share in the housing construction finance is insignificant. Unfortunately, there is no available information on the sources of housing construction
finance in Russia. Nevertheless, we estimated that in 2009 76 percent of the total
housing floor space and 67 percent of all housing units were built with the help of
household savings and their debt finance.

Housing Needs, Demand for Housing, and the Housing Market

Based on sociological surveys, housing needs were, and still are, the most acute
social problems facing Russian citizens: 61 percent of households are dissatisfied,
to a greater or smaller degree, with their housing conditions, and every fourth
family resides in dwellings that are in bad or extremely bad condition.[7] In 2008,
based on a random survey of household budgets conducted by Rosstat, housing
consumption of 22.8 percent households was less than 13 square meters per capita,
and 40.2 percent of households considered that the number or the size of rooms in

their apartments did not meet a normal dwelling requirement. It is estimated that it will be necessary to increase the housing stock by 46.1 percent (1,569.8 million square meters) to satisfy the overall needs of the Russian population in housing.[8]

Municipal authorities should provide free-of-charge municipal residential premises (social housing), in accordance with the existing waiting lists, to families that live in unsafe housing, have no housing at all, or occupy overcrowded dwellings. Since 2005, only low-income households have been entitled to join such waiting lists and obtain such social housing. However, today a considerable portion of families on the current waiting lists for social housing are the ones that were registered before 2005. Their right to obtain social housing is preserved and does not hinge on their income. At the end of 2008 there were nearly 2.9 million households (6 percent of all households in Russia) on the waiting list for municipal social housing. However, due to limited budget funds allocated for this purpose, the process of social housing acquisition is too slow, and the average time of queuing on the waiting list is 15 to 20 years.

Certain categories of citizens (nearly 430 thousand households, including military servicemen, those leaving the far northern regions of Russia, unwilling migrants, and some other categories) are entitled to obtain housing with the federal budget funds under State Housing Programs. Nevertheless, the rate of providing housing to these categories of people is too slow as well. Some other federal, regional, and local programs aimed at supporting the purchase of housing by citizens in the market are also implemented. For example, there is a federal program co-financed from the federal budget, the budgets of the constituent entities of the Russian Federation, and/or municipalities aimed at granting subsidies to young families to assist them with making a partial payment toward the purchase of housing.

The housing market, which was created in Russia when the process of housing stock privatization started, began to play a pivotal role in addressing the housing problem. However, even today only a minor portion of the Russian population can afford to purchase housing in the market (the issue of housing affordability is covered further on in this chapter). On the average, in 2005–2009, only 4 to 4.5 percent of the housing stock were annually involved in the sales-purchase market transactions.

Effective housing demand was supported by a stable growth of real household incomes (which increased by 1.9 times during 2004–2008), as well as by intensive development of mortgage lending over the same period, which provided an access for citizens to credit resources required for housing purchase in exchange for their future incomes (more details are given below). Moreover, housing sector reforms implemented during this period of time turned out to be more efficient in terms of encouraging housing demand, rather than increasing housing supply.

Constant growth of both nominal and real housing prices after the appearance of the housing market in Russia nurtured household expectations of further growth and was a strong incentive to buy (Exhibit 9.3).

Such growth of prices was caused not only by the growing effective housing demand, but also by an insufficient rate of housing completions. The latter could be explained by lack of competition in the housing construction market and numerous barriers facing those who intended to enter this market.

The prevailing market conditions, and extremely low price elasticity of newly built housing supply, resulted in a situation in which the main volume of growing

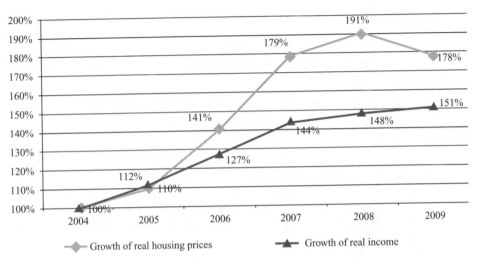

Exhibit 9.3 Changes in the Market Average Real Price of Housing and Average Real Household Incomes, per Annum (2004 = 100%)
Source: Data from Rosstat.

effective demand for housing was satisfied in the secondary housing market, while the share of transactions in the primary housing market[9] was on the average at 25–30 percent of all housing purchases.

The total number of households that purchased housing in the market in 2008 was 2.5 million, which accounted for:

- 4.8 percent of the total number of households.
- 26.7 percent of households that had income enabling them to purchase housing (nearly 18 percent of all households had such income).
- 8 percent of households that experienced a need to improve their housing conditions (almost 60 percent of households experienced a need to improve their housing conditions).

An additional factor that contributed to the growth of the effective demand and housing prices was the absence of alternative ways of investing surplus household funds in order to make savings and extra earnings. Traditionally, bank deposits and foreign currency were considered to be the most reliable and convenient way of investing surplus funds by the Russian citizens. However, in 2006–2008, bank deposits in rubles could not ensure that those who had them could earn any profits, because interest rates on ruble deposits were lower than the inflation rate. Dollar deposits and investments in foreign currency yielded no profits either (excluding 2008), since interest payments on them were smaller than the losses caused by high inflation rate and because of the fact that foreign currency became cheaper against the ruble (Exhibit 9.4).

Other financial instruments, such as equity, bonds, and mutual investment funds have not so far become attractive to Russian people, because they are associated with higher risks and frequently are less liquid instruments not yet thoroughly

Exhibit 9.4 Trends in 2004–2009 of Consumer Prices Index, One-Year Deposit Rate, Ruble Exchange Rate

	2004	2005	2006	2007	2008	2009
Consumer prices index, % against last December	11.7	10.9	9.0	11.9	13.3	8.8
One-year deposit rate (without on-demand deposits), annual interest rate, %	11.4	8.7	7.9	7.2	7.6	10.4
Changes in the ruble—U.S. dollar exchange rate, y-o-y, %*	−5.8	3.7	−8.5	−7.2	19.7	2.9
Changes in the ruble—euro exchange rate, y-o-y, %	1.9	−9.7	1.1	4.2	15.2	4.7

*Is calculated as a ratio of the exchange rate (rubles for one US$) at the end of the year to the exchange rate at the beginning of the year.
Source: Data from Rosstat, Bank of Russia.

studied in this country. Nevertheless, given a competent investment strategy, they could yield high profits to an investor. In addition, until 2009 the real estate market in Russia, as opposed to the bank deposits and the stock market, had not experienced stress that resulted in the loss of all or most of the invested funds.

As a result, by the end of 2008, investments in residential real estate guaranteed much higher returns. Unfortunately, there are no reliable estimates of the share of investment transactions in the housing market, but the impact of the foregoing factor on the dynamics of prices in the housing market cannot be ruled out—at least with regard to individual local housing markets, for example, those in Moscow and St. Petersburg, where high-income households are highly concentrated.

Housing Affordability

Housing affordability ratio (HAR), which is usually measured in Russia as the ratio of the price of a standard apartment to the annual income of an average household,[10] during 1998–2003 had been increasing due to the accelerated rate of household income growth (HAR dropped from 7.4 years in 1998 to 4.1 years in 2003). Starting in 2004, due to the fact that the rate of housing price growth was higher than that of household income growth, this trend reversed, and by 2007 this ratio increased up to 5.3 years (see the analysis of housing price dynamics given above).

Meanwhile, if housing affordability is estimated with due account for the rapid development of mortgage lending since 2005 and the enhanced opportunities for obtaining a mortgage loan, we get a more positive picture. In this case the housing affordability index (HAI) is the ratio of an average three-person household income to the income that is required for purchasing a standard 54 square-meter apartment with the help of a mortgage originated on standard terms.[11]

The affordability of housing purchase based on HAI in 2005 surged against the level of 2004, whereas in 2006–2009 it remained virtually unchanged at the level of 66–70 percent. This is the result of income growth and improved terms of lending, on the one hand, and, housing price growth, on the other hand.

According to the third method to measure housing affordability in 2004 the percentage of households capable of purchasing housing, which met the housing space standards, using household savings and bank loans,[12] was 9 percent, and by 2006 it increased to 18.6 percent. In 2007–2008, due to the fact that the rate of price growth was higher than that of household income growth, and in spite of improved lending terms, the percentage of families that could afford to purchase housing dropped to the level of 17.7–17.8 percent.

Housing Mortgage Lending[13]

Intensive mortgage lending development started in Russia only in 2005, although a government institution for mortgage loan refinancing—the Agency for Housing Mortgage Lending (hereinafter, the AHML)—had already been created in 1997 to make long-term credit resources affordable to banks for the purposes of financing the origination of mortgage loans.[14] Moreover, the task of the AHML is to design and disseminate mortgage lending standards that should be met by the AHML partners and can be used by other creditors as well.[15]

Stable macroeconomic situation, growth of real household incomes, favorable legislation[16] and state support of the mortgage market establishment process through the AHML contributed to the rapid development of mortgage lending. The volume of mortgages originated in 2008 was 6.7 times higher than in 2005 (Exhibit 9.5), and in 2008 outstanding mortgage debt accounted for 2.8 percent of the GDP, which was 28 times more than in 2004 (Exhibit 9.6).

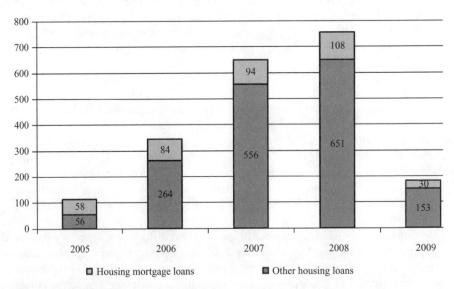

Exhibit 9.5 Volumes of Housing Mortgage Lending, Billion Rubles
Note: Housing mortgage loans are housing loans secured by pledge of real estate extended in accordance with the procedure specified in the Federal law "On Mortgage (Pledge of Real Estate)."
Other housing loans are loans extended to natural persons for purchasing a land plot and making all necessary improvements on it for future housing construction, for housing construction (renovations), and for housing acquisition (including the cases when a surety is issued by a third party).
Source: Data from the Bank of Russia.

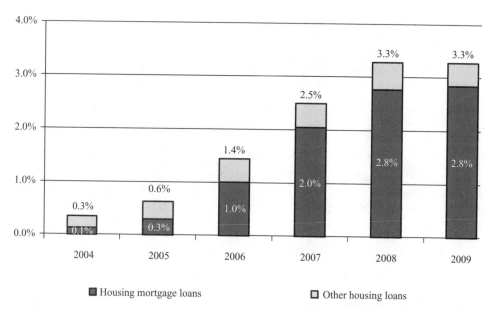

Exhibit 9.6 Outstanding Debt under Housing Mortgage Loans and Other Housing Loans as a Share of GDP, %
Source: Data from the Bank of Russia.

Until mid-2008, volumes of originated mortgages had been dynamically growing, competition in the lending market had increased, and terms of mortgage lending had been constantly improving. Nevertheless, the level of concentration of mortgage lending was still extremely high in 2008: Two quasi-state banks (Sberbank of Russia and VTB-24), which are the largest Russian banks in terms of volumes of mortgage lending, controlled over 40 percent, and the 15 largest banks (in terms of mortgage lending) controlled almost 80 percent of this market (Exhibit 9.7).

From 2006 almost through mid-2008 we witnessed the trend of increasing terms of mortgage loans and decreasing interest rates on both ruble-denominated and foreign currency denominated loans[17] (see Exhibits 9.8 and 9.9).

The prevailing type of mortgages was a standard annuity loan for a finished housing purchase. Initially, banks relied on conservative underwriting standards: maximum loan-to-value ratio (LTV ratio), as a rule, was never higher than 70 percent; a borrower had to prove with documents the sources and the stable nature of his income; there were no automatic scoring systems for evaluating the probability of default. In such circumstances, the number of default loans was negligible (constantly growing housing prices and household incomes contributed to this), which enabled banks to fall into the state of euphoria about their bright and problem-free future. As of January 1, 2008, the share of delinquent (at least one day overdue) payments under mortgage loans was 0.1 percent of the total volume of mortgage outstanding debt.

It is noteworthy that the Russian System of Accounting (RSA) envisages that only payments towards repayment of loan principal, which the creditor did not receive upon the expiration of the term fixed in the loan agreement, are accounted for in the total volume of delinquent debt.

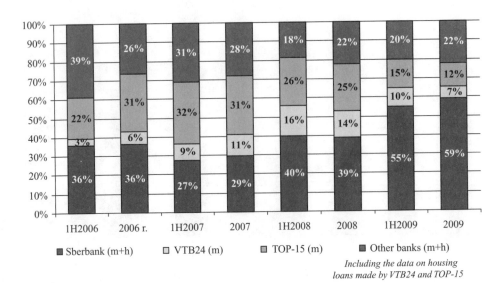

Exhibit 9.7 Structure of Housing Loans Origination by Banks in 2006–2009
Note: (m) = data only on mortgage loans; (m+h) = data on housing loans and mortgage loans; TOP-15 = 15 largest banks in terms of mortgage loans' origination (without the data about Sberbank and VTB-24).
Source: Authors' calculations based on the data of the Bank of Russia and RosBusiness Consulting.

Along with the improving macroeconomic situation, growing housing prices, and expectations of their future growth, the market saw an increase in the supply of high-risk mortgages: loans with high LTV ratio, loans made without formal confirmation of income, loans with a variable interest rate, and loans made in exotic currencies (for example, in Swiss francs or Japanese yen). On the one hand,

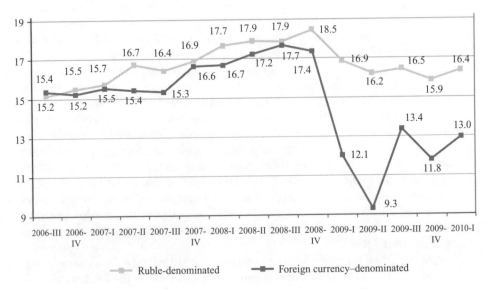

Exhibit 9.8 Weighted Average Term of Housing Mortgage Loans, Years
Source: Authors' calculations based on the data of the Bank of Russia.

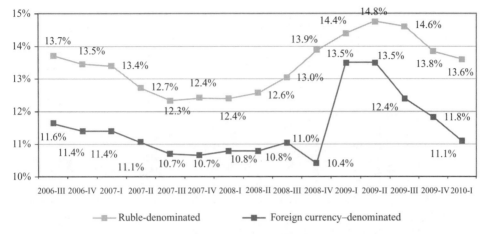

Exhibit 9.9   Weighted Average Interest Rates on Housing Mortgage Loans
Source: Authors' calculations based on the data of the Bank of Russia.

this resulted in the enhancement of mortgage loans' affordability, and, on the other hand, it enabled banks to actively build up volumes of mortgage lending and profits. Based on our evaluations (there are no official statistical data), by the beginning of the global financial meltdown, high-risk mortgage had not yet become a prevailing product in the market, although the proportion of such loans increased significantly.

Initially, the financing of mortgage loans was implemented with banks' own resources, primarily with their deposits. It created high liquidity risks, since deposits were raised for a term that rarely exceeded 1.5–2 years.[18] As mortgage lending volumes increased and lending experience accumulated, banks started to gradually master new procedures of funding, including the refinancing of loans (direct sales-purchase of mortgage loans) and issuing mortgage-backed securities (MBS).[19] Therefore, mortgage loans refinanced or securitized during 2006–2008 accounted for almost 18 percent of the total volume of mortgage loans originated over the same period (Exhibit 9.10).

Over 2006–2008, banks implemented mainly off-shore securitization,[20] which created currency risks for banks due to the fact that the currency of loans and that of MBS was different. The total volume of MBS issued by Russian issuers abroad in 2006–2008 amounted to almost $2.2 billion.[21] Domestic securitization was implemented in compliance with the Federal law "On Mortgage-Backed Securities" adopted in 2003,[22] and amounted in 2006–2008 to 30.3 billion rubles.[23]

One of the main actors in the domestic refinancing market is the AHML, which purchases loans from banks in accordance with AHML standards and issues corporate bonds backed by the guarantees of the Russian Government, and in limited volumes—MBS in the form of CMO. During 2006–2008, the AHML refinanced bank mortgages to the tune of 93 billion rubles, or 35 percent of the total volume of refinanced and securitized mortgage loans over the same period. The remaining mortgage volumes in the domestic refinancing market were purchased by banks with further issuing MBS or by keeping mortgages on their balance sheet as an

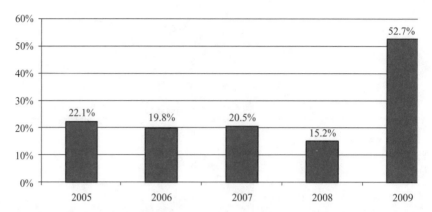

Exhibit 9.10 The Ratio of Refinanced or Securitized Mortgage Loans to the Total Volume of Mortgage Loans Originated during the Same Year, %

Note: 2005–2007 bars reflect the data only on refinancing of mortgage loans. Refinanced or securitized mortgage loans could include mortgage loans originated both in the current year and during previous years.

Source: Authors' calculations based on the data of the Bank of Russia.

asset. Mutual funds and common bank management funds, as well as other non-banking institutional investors, rarely participated in secondary mortgage market.

The ratio of mortgages refinanced by the AHML in 2005 to the total volume of mortgage loans originated by banks in the same year accounted for almost 14 percent. As Russian banks gained more experience and enhanced their ability to raise resources using refinancing or securitization instruments, as volumes of originated mortgage loans increased, the percentage of mortgages refinanced by the AHML was gradually falling down to 4.1 percent in 2008.

MORTGAGE CRISIS: IMPACT OF THE GLOBAL FINANCIAL CRISIS ON THE MORTGAGE SECTOR IN RUSSIA

Housing Mortgage Lending is the institute of the housing sector in Russia that has been most badly hit by the global financial crisis started with a chain of delinquencies on subprime mortgages in the United States. Volumes of mortgage lending drastically declined to the level of early 2006, and interest rates grew up to the maximum level for the period from the third quarter of 2006.

Deepening recession in international markets brought about deterioration of the economic situation in the Russian financial market in 2008. Three- and six-month MosPrime rates were about 5 to 6 percent per annum at the start of the year, and by the end of the year they reached 22 to 23 percent. The maximum growth of interest rates in the money market was registered during the period from the end of October through the end of December 2008, when three- and six-month MosPrime rates more than doubled.

In 2008 the refinancing rate of the Bank of Russia, which is an official indicator of the cost of money in the Russian economy, reflected the general trend and

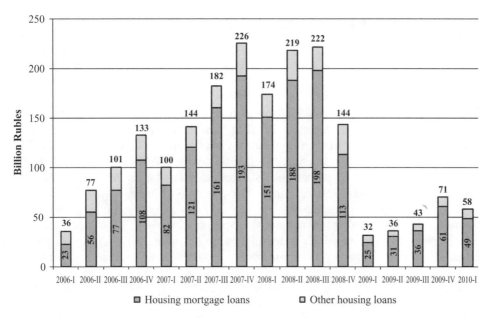

Exhibit 9.11 Volumes of Mortgage Loans and Housing Loans Originated Quarterly during 2006–2010

Source: Data from the Bank of Russia.

changed four times within one year, from 11.5 percent to 13 percent per annum. The refinancing rate increased for the first time in 10 years.

Therefore, in 2008, especially in the fourth quarter, Russian banks had to operate in a situation when liquidity was very limited and there was a constant growth of the cost of raised resources. Most banks were completely deprived of any access to foreign market borrowings, which used to be the major base for lending to the real estate sector of Russia's economy and its population. Spreads on long-term yields increased most markedly, and even the first-class borrowers could not avoid it.

The market of housing mortgage lending felt the full impact of liquidity shortages already in the second half of 2008 (see Exhibit 9.11). While in 2007 volumes of originated housing mortgage loans increased by 87 percent (y-o-y) to the level of 556 billion rubles, the rate of growth in 2008 dropped: Loans worth 633.8 billion rubles were closed, which was only 14 percent more than in 2007 (and in comparable prices of 2007, the volume of housing mortgage loans made in 2008 amounted only to 559 billion rubles, which was just 0.5 percent more than in 2007). The growth registered in the third quarter of 2008 was only 5 percent against the previous quarter (the growth registered in 3Q2007 was 33 percent against 2Q2007). There was a sharp reduction of the volume of originated mortgages in the fourth quarter of 2008: It halved against the level of the third quarter of 2008 (in 2007, a 20 percent growth was registered in the respective period). 2009 saw a further decline: The number of mortgage loans closed in the first quarter of 2009 was six times smaller y-o-y, and the figure for the whole of 2009 accounted for only 23 percent of the level of 2008.

Unpredictable situations in the financial market increased the cost of borrowing for Russian banks. At first, this resulted in the stabilization of mortgage interest rates in 3Q2007–1Q2008, and later, in their growth during 2008. Mortgage interest rates reached their maximum level in the second quarter of 2009 (14.8 percent on ruble-denominated loans, and 13.5 percent on foreign currency-denominated loans), but afterward they started to gradually drop (see Exhibit 9.9). In addition mortgage loan terms were considerably reduced (see Exhibit 9.8).

Investor trust in the mortgage lending market was undermined, which not only detrimentally affected mortgage interest rates, but also undermined the banks' ability to raise resources in the higher-risk environment. As of January 1, 2010, 584 credit organizations (49.5 percent of the total number of operating credit organizations) were engaged in operations in the housing mortgage market. Meanwhile in 2009, only 400 credit organizations extended housing mortgage loans, whereas the rest were engaged in servicing loans originated earlier. Ruble-denominated mortgage loans were regularly extended by approximately 130 credit organizations, and foreign currency-denominated mortgages by 17 such organizations.[24] Over the two-year period (2007–2009), the number of organizations engaged in refinancing and securitizing mortgage loans shrank from 233 to 167, which mainly sold their loans to the AHML.

As a result, in 2009 new mortgage loans continued to be originated mainly by the largest banks with an impressive deposit base (however, even such banks made loans in volumes that did not surpass volumes of repayment of earlier originated loans) and other banks that mainly sold loans to the AHML.

During 2009, the structure of originated mortgage loans also changed: The percentage of foreign currency-denominated loans reduced due to a considerable currency risk faced by a borrower, especially, in the light of ruble devaluation in the end of 2008 (U.S. dollar gained 40 percent from 26, up to 36 rubles per one dollar) and the high inflation rate (13.3 percent in 2008 and 8.8 percent in 2009).[25] For example, in 2009 foreign currency-denominated mortgage loans accounted for only 6.3 percent of the total volume of originated mortgages.

As the overall financial and economic situation in Russia deteriorated, we witnessed the growth of the delinquency rate on all loans extended to the population, including mortgage loans. Overall, the delinquency rate on all loans to the population (according to RSA) increased from 4.7 percent, as of April 1, 2009, up to 6.8 percent, as of January 1, 2010. The average level of delinquencies on mortgage loans increased (according to the RSA) from 0.1 percent in 2006–2007 to 3.1 percent in January 2010 (see Exhibit 9.12).

The main reason behind such growth of the delinquency rate was job cuts entailing a considerable income drop for many a borrower, and a substantial increase of payments on foreign currency-denominated mortgages (as of January 1, 2009, delinquencies on foreign currency-denominated mortgages reached almost 20 percent) and on mortgages with a variable interest rate. Accordingly, the maximum growth of delinquencies (according to the RSA) was registered in foreign currency-denominated mortgage loans—a 28.8 times increase over 2008–2009, whereas ruble-denominated loans saw a 23.4 times increase of delinquencies over the same period.

According to the Bank of Russia, estimates based on IFRS, 30-plus days delinquent mortgage loans' share in the market was 9.3 percent, as of February 1, 2010.

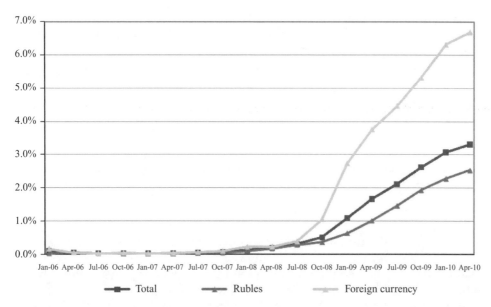

Exhibit 9.12 Mortgage Delinquency Rate for Loans in Rubles and Foreign Currency (according to RSA)
Source: Data from Bank of Russia.

Unfortunately, there is pretty scanty data to analyze the dynamics of the foregoing loans' share in the market, but it is possible to analyze the dynamics with regard to the AHML mortgage portfolio. However, the latter represents less than a quarter of the total market. The share of the 30-plus days delinquent loans in the mortgage loans portfolio supervised by the AHML[26] increased, from 5.3 percent in March 2008 to 8 percent in January 2010.[27]

Based on the latest AHML data (finalized in accordance with the IFRS), on May 1, 2010, the 30-plus days delinquent mortgage loans accounted for 10.76 percent, and the 90-plus days delinquent mortgages (which according to Russian legislation can be placed in the category of "default loans," since it is possible to foreclose on the collateral that secures such mortgages) accounted for 9.43 percent of all mortgage loans serviced by the AHML (see Exhibit 9.13).

Exhibit 9.13 Initial LTV Ratio-Driven Share of Delinquent Mortgage Loans in the Mortgage Loans Portfolio Supervised by the AHML, as of May 1, 2010, %

Initial LTV Ratio	30-Plus Days Delinquency	90-Plus Days Delinquency
Up to 50%	3.29%	2.60%
51–70%	5.57%	4.46%
71–80%	18.76%	16.61%
81–90%	24.01%	21.99%
As a proportion of the whole portfolio	**10.76%**	**9.43%**

Source: Data from AHML.

Exhibit 9.14 Share of Delinquent Mortgage Loans in the Mortgage Loans Portfolio
Supervised by the AHML, as of May 1, 2010, % (Depending on the Original Loan Value)

Original Loan Value, Million Rubles	30-Plus Days Delinquency	90-Plus Days Delinquency
Up to 0.7	3.67%	2.99%
0.7–1.5	7.03%	5.98%
1.5–2.5	18.31%	16.20%
2.5–4.0	29.03%	26.17%
More than 4.0	47.19%	44.79%
Total for the portfolio	**10.76%**	**9.43%**

Source: Data from AHML.

The analysis of the AHML data revealed the fact that risks of default are 8.5 times higher for mortgage loans with initial LTV ratio in excess of 80 percent than for mortgages with LTV less than 50 percent (90-plus days delinquencies accounted for 21.99 percent and 2.6 percent accordingly) (see Exhibit 9.13).

The analysis of the AHML data also pointed to the fact that as the original mortgage loan value grew, the probability of default also increased: the 90-plus days delinquent mortgage loans accounted for 2.997 percent of the mortgages worth less than 0.7 million rubles (at the moment of mortgage origination), and for 44.79 percent of the mortgage loans worth more than 4 million rubles (see Exhibit 9.14).

It is worth noting that the reduction of housing prices during the crisis period had no considerable impact on defaults of borrowers with high LTV ratio. This is explained by the fact that, according to Russian laws, after a foreclosure on the pledged housing the outstanding debt under a mortgage loan remains a personal liability of a borrower. Moreover, according to the AHML, as of April 1, 2010, as a result of reappraisal of the value of collaterals against the backcloth of dropping housing prices,[28] the LTV ratio of 49.4 percent of the mortgages supervised by the AHML increased, although only 4.78 percent of the AHML-supervised mortgages had the LTV ratio in excess of 100 percent.

The increase in the number of default mortgage loans forced banks to step up their work with "bad" borrowers, which included initiating a procedure of foreclosure on the pledged property[29] and mortgage loans' restructuring programs.

Meanwhile, court deliberations and the process of handing down court rulings on such lawsuits are rather time-consuming, although during the crisis the time spent on them has slightly decreased: in 2008, according to the AHML, this process took from four to eight months, whereas in 2009–2010 it took from two to three months (in the cases when the ruling is not disputed in a higher court). Once a court ruling is made, enforcement proceedings begin, within the framework of which the collateral is sold at an auction. This process is even slower: According to the AHML, during 2008–2010 only 12 percent of all enforcement proceedings launched over the same period pursuant to lawsuits filed by the AHML were brought to fruition, and the average time spent on them was 18–24 months in 2007–2008, and 8–12 months in 2009–2010. At the same time, eviction of a borrower can be implemented only via court proceedings pursuant to a lawsuit filed by a new owner of a dwelling once he had purchased the pledged dwelling, which resulted in the reduction of the sale price of such collateral.

The implementation of foreclosure on the pledged property, including court proceedings and execution against property, faces the following major problems in Russia:

- Excessively prolonged foreclosure procedures.
- High risk of reduction of the housing prices in the market during the period of foreclosure and of substantial increase of the debt amount due to piling interests, penalties, and so forth, which rules out the possibility of full enforcement of the creditor's claims through the sale of the pledged property and leaves the borrower indebted to his creditor even after the sale of the collateral.
- Complications associated with eviction of borrowers from the pledged premises, which can be explained, among other things, by the above-mentioned legislative intricacies of such procedure, as well as by the absence of municipal maneuverable housing stock for temporary occupancy by former housing owners, which leads to reduction of the sale price of the collateral;
- Inadequate awareness of potential buyers about auctions for the pledged residential premises, which results in the disruption of auctions.
- Unfair appraisal of the collateral value made at the mortgage loan origination time, which fact has been detected in the process of foreclosure.

To mitigate the negative trends and to avoid book losses after foreclose process, banks started to offer mortgage loans' restructuring programs to their borrowers, including conversion of foreign-currency loans into ruble-loans, albeit at the current interest rates (which considerably increased compared to the beginning of 2008), as well as loan prolongation, and so forth. In 2009, a state program for mortgage loans' rescheduling was launched, and it is implemented by the AHML subsidiary: the Agency for Housing Mortgage Loans Restructuring (more details are given further on).

Now the remaining mortgage creditors generally take a more conservative approach to evaluating a borrower's ability to pay. They announced that an officially confirmed income is a mandatory condition for receiving a mortgage loan, and increased the down-payment benchmark requirement to the level of a minimum of 30 percent.[30]

The market of mortgage loans' refinancing (which actively evolved during several years before the crisis) and the nascent market of mortgage loans securitization have been virtually left without investors, who were scared off by the rapid growth of uncertainty and credibility crisis. This contributed to the increase in the cost of funds raised for mortgage lending both in the domestic and in foreign financial markets.

In such a situation, the market witnessed a rapid depreciation of long-term assets with a fixed interest rate, and the earlier originated mortgage loans were exactly such an asset. As a result, while in the first quarter of 2008 major market participants were actively engaged in loans' purchasing operations in the secondary mortgage market,[31] in the third quarter of 2008 they suspended such operations.

The banks that managed to create a substantial pool of mortgages for securitization by early 2008 were forced to suspend or postpone the issue of MBS for an indefinite period of time. While in 2008 the number of credit organizations operating in the secondary mortgage market shrank by 12.5 percent (from 233 to 204), in 2009 it decreased by yet another 18 percent (to 167).

In 2008, the volume of the secondary mortgage market dropped by 14.6 percent against the level of 2007 (from 115.9 billion rubles to 99 billion rubles), and in 2009 it decreased by yet another 18 percent, down to 80.4 billion rubles. While in 2008 funds obtained by credit organizations through refinancing or securitization accounted for only 15.2 percent of the total volume of originated mortgage loans, in 2009 the volume of the secondary mortgage market accounted for 52.7 percent of the mortgage loans originated in the year. The raising of funds through refinancing or securitization of mortgage loans, including the earlier originated loans, became one of the obligatory components of housing mortgage lending, first of all, for small and medium-sized banks.

The structure of secondary mortgage markets changed as well (Exhibit 9.15). Direct sale of pools of mortgage loans continue to be used as the main instrument but its portion was reduced from 67.6 percent of the total volume of the secondary

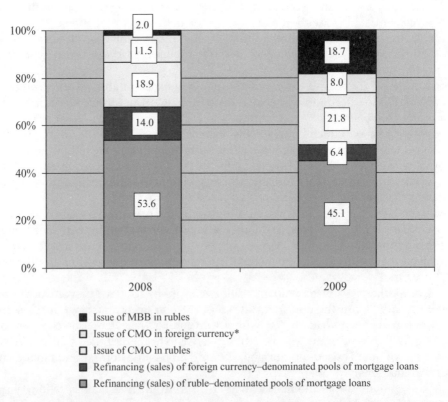

Exhibit 9.15 The Structure of Mortgage Loans' Refinancing and Securitization in 2008 and 2009, %
Note: The issues of CMO in foreign currency were made based on off-shore securitization.
Source: Authors' calculations based on the data of the Bank of Russia.

market in 2008 to 51.5 percent in 2009. The portion of CMO issues remained at the same level (30.4 percent in 2008, and 29.8 percent in 2009). In 2008, banks virtually avoided the practice of issuing MBB: The volume of such securities was worth only 2.0 percent of the total volume of secondary mortgage market, and in 2009 it increased to 18.7 percent. The portion of off-shore securitization decreased in favor of domestic securities.

During the crisis, the Russian government allocated additional resources for the AHML to repurchase mortgage loans from banks. This measure, along with the shrinking volume of the mortgage market, has increased the share of mortgages refinanced by the AHML in the total volume of mortgages originated in 2009 up to 19 percent.[32]

Banks faced yet another problem, that of growing conditional prepayment rate (CPR) of mortgage loans. In 2005–2007, the CPR for mortgages was 6–8 percent, in 2008–2009 it grew to 11 percent. It means that the actual life of a 15-year loan made at 14 percent shrank from 8.8 years in 2006 to 6.9 years in 2009.

The current situation in the housing mortgage market is characterized by a considerable increase of the cost of borrowing for banks, reduction of competition and tighter requirements to borrowers. All of the aforesaid makes mortgage loans less affordable to people, especially in the regions where mortgage lending was mostly supported by the AHML through its regional operators and small and medium-sized banks.

Lack of long-term sources for financing mortgage lending in the current situation necessitated a considerable government support for mortgage loans refinancing and MBS repurchasing vehicles, including support through the AHML and other state government-sponsored organizations, the Bank of Russia, and the National Welfare Fund. It also made it necessary to attract long-term resources to this sector from the State Pension Fund (see further on).

By mid-2010, commercial banks, assisted by the Bank of Russia and the AHML, managed to overcome, in general, the problem of tight liquidity, although there is still a shortage of long-term funds in the banking system. Since December 2008, the refinancing rate of the Bank of Russia was reduced 14 times (the most recent reduction was that of June 2010) and came down from 13 percent to 7.75 percent. Mortgage lending is still fraught with high risks, which are associated, first and foremost, with the growing delinquency rate and uncertainty about price trends in housing markets.

There are the first tentative signs of recovery: In the first quarter of 2010, the volume of loans originated doubled y-o-y (see Exhibit 9.11); the interest rate on ruble-denominated mortgage loans dropped by 0.7 percentage points in the first quarter of 2010 (against the fourth quarter of 2009) to 13.6 percent, and on foreign currency-denominated mortgage loans by 1.6 percentage points to 11.1 percent (see Exhibit 9.9). The average term of originated mortgage loans slightly increased, by 0.2 months on ruble-denominated and by 1.4 months on foreign-currency de-nominated loans (see Exhibit 9.8).

The delinquency rate (according to the RSA) in the first quarter of 2010 continued to grow and reached 2.5 percent on ruble-denominated and 6.7 percent on foreign-currency-denominated mortgage loans (see Exhibit 9.12). Relevant indicators for the loan portfolio supervised by the AHML calculated in accordance with the IFRS remained unchanged (against the end of 2009).

THE LATEST TRENDS IN THE HOUSING MARKET

In 2009, the number of transactions in the housing market declined by 340 thousand to 2.24 million transactions (13.3 percent y-o-y).[33] This is the most vivid proof of severe repercussions of the crisis for the housing market in Russia. The effective housing demand satisfied in the market considerably decreased due to appearance of pent-up demand geared to the housing price reduction dynamics and buyers' expectations of further reduction of housing prices. Housing price trends underwent changes: Not only did real prices of housing started to drop in 2009, but nominal prices dropped as well (see Exhibit 9.16). Average real housing prices dropped by 18 percent against the third quarter of 2008, when "peak" prices were recorded.

At the same time, real household incomes in 2009 increased by 1.9 percent. As a result, housing affordability measured by HAR was enhanced: The ratio decreased from 5.3 years to 4.6 years. However, due to worsening terms of mortgage lending, in 2009 the value of HAI (66 percent in 2008 and 68 percent in 2009), as well as the percentage of people who could afford to purchase housing with their own savings or bank loans (17.8 percent in 2008 and 17.5 percent in 2009), remained virtually unchanged.

According to the latest data, in the first quarter of 2010, housing price reduction slowed down. Average nominal housing prices started to gradually gain the lost ground (they increased by 1 percent in the primary market and by 12 percent in the secondary housing market against the level registered in the fourth quarter of 2009). At the same time, average real prices in the primary housing market, after

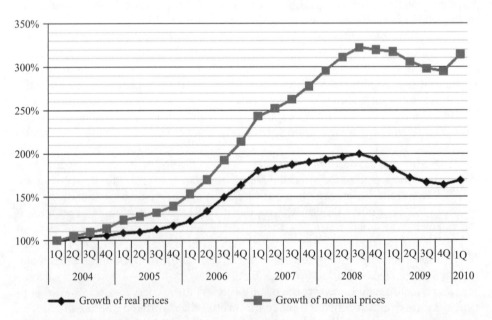

Exhibit 9.16 Changes in Average Nominal and Real Prices in the Housing Market in Russia (1Q2004 = 100%)

Source: Authors' calculations based on the data of Rosstat.

all, dropped by 2 percent against the fourth quarter of 2009, whereas average real prices in the secondary market even increased by 8 percent.

HAR calculated on the basis of the average figures for 2Q2009–1Q2010 decreased by only 0.1 years to 4.5 years in the first quarter of 2010. However, due to a certain improvement of terms of mortgage lending, the HAI increased by four percentage points to 73 percent. Such a high level of HAI was last time registered at the end of 2005 to the beginning of 2006.

The financial crisis at the end of 2008 had a considerable impact on housing construction by professional developers. In spite of the fact that the share of housing construction financed with bank loans extended to developers was, on the average, rather small, already in autumn 2008, some especially large-scale developers experienced a shortage of working capital, which they used to supplement earlier with bank loans.

In 2009, total housing completion volumes in Russia amounted to 702 thousand housing units, or 59.8 million square meters, which was 8.6 percent (6.3 percent, in terms of floor space) less than in 2008. The overall drop in housing completion by professional developers in 2009 was 16 percent in terms of constructed housing units (492 thousand in 2009 versus 568 thousand in 2008) and 16.2 percent in terms of total floor space (31 versus 37 million square meters).

According to our evaluations, in 2009 professional developers practically did not launch any new housing construction projects, and the main reasons behind this were as follows: decreased demand for housing due to buyer's expectations of future price reduction; and sharp decline in volumes of housing finance, including mortgage lending, lending to citizens who wanted to participate in housing construction projects, and lending to professional developers due to the increased risk for such investments.

At the same time, in 2009, housing completion by owner-builders increased (in terms of number of housing units by 5 percent, and in terms of total floor space by 7.4 percent, y-o-y) and owner-builders completed 210 thousand single-family homes (with a total floor space of 28.5 million square meters), which accounted for 30 percent of the total number of completed housing units (47.7 percent of the totally completed housing floor space).

In light of the foregoing, we can forecast the reduction of housing completion by professional developers in 2010–2011, and in the event that no efficient incentives are created (primarily, to encourage household demand for housing), an even further reduction of housing completion in 2012–2013.

Government Support to the Housing Sector in Crises and the Role of Government-Sponsored Organizations

Anti-crisis housing policy became an integral part of the overall anti-crisis government package of measures in the banking and housing construction sectors. Housing mortgage lending and housing construction, including construction of supporting infrastructure, would have to go through dire straits in the next couple of years, if they had been left without government support during the economic meltdown. The necessary measures were taken both within the implementation of the anti-crisis package of the Government of the Russian Federation during 2009–2010, and within the framework of activities carried out by government-sponsored organizations, including those in the housing sector (the Agency for Housing Mortgage Lending, Fund for the Promotion of the Housing and Utility Sector Reform, Russian Housing Development Foundation, and Vnesheconombank).[34]

The main common idea behind the anti-crisis package in the housing sector was to achieve a synergistic effect from maximum possible concentration of the state demand and household demand supported by the government in the primary housing market and housing construction market, with the purpose to support economy-class housing construction that meets the modern standards of energy performance, environment protection and the requirement of affordability to the middle class. Such an approach is based on the idea of using housing construction as a lever for stabilizing the overall economic situation. Due to the high multiplication effect of this particular sector, it would contribute to the support of other sectors of economy, enhancement of employment opportunities, and accumulation of household savings.

We offer a summary description of the main measures that have been taken.

First, at the end of 2008 changes to the government housing provision program were made. It became possible to purchase apartments using government funds at the stage of construction to provide housing to certain categories of Russian citizens. This measure was intended to contribute to the completion of construction of apartment buildings that was started during previous years and to prevent financial losses by citizens who invested their savings in apartment buildings' construction before the onset of the crisis.

Second, to support housing mortgage lending, the state provided for an access of creditors to new sources of funding mortgage loans. In the beginning of 2009, an additional contribution was made by the government to the authorized capital of the AHML in the amount of 60 billion rubles for the purposes of refinancing mortgage loans and rescheduling mortgage loans for those borrowers who found themselves in a dire situation as a result of the crisis.

Moreover, in November 2008, the Bank of Russia changed its regulations so as to be able to finance mortgages (in form of origination of lombard loans and closing REPO transactions using prime MBS as the collateral). The AHML expanded the range of its operations via offering sureties for MBS of other issuers. Such MBS backed by the AHML surety can be used by banks to obtain loans from the Bank of Russia.

In 2010, a decision was made to allocate 250 million rubles to support household demand for newly built housing (the funds of Vnesheconombank or funds managed by it, including State Pension Fund and the National Welfare Fund money).[35] These allocations can be used by banks within a three-year period to sell MBS backed by mortgages originated to borrowers at a maximum of 11 percent for purchasing newly built housing. The AHML as well will use the loan of the National Welfare Fund for the implementation of a program of lending to banks for the purposes of financing loans to developers and citizens who participate in construction of apartment buildings. Once the construction is completed and borrowers obtain mortgage loans, a bank can use these loans to repay its debt under the AHML loan.

Thirdly, in 2009, the AHML created a subsidiary (Agency for Housing Mortgage Loans Restructuring [AHMLR]),[36] through which it implements the rescheduling of mortgage loans for those borrowers who either became unemployed or whose wages were cut down. Such rescheduling pursues the goal of giving a one-year grace period on mortgage loans. The loans rescheduling program of the AHMLR targets economically active middle class borrowers who pledged their only housing. This makes it possible to avoid foreclosure on the pledged housing when prices are dropping, and enables borrowers to improve their financial standing.

In 2010, the AHMLR moved to a new phase of its program to assist those borrowers who failed to restore their ability to pay. The upgraded program targets borrowers from the company towns[37] or borrowers who fall into other most socially vulnerable categories of population for whom the pledged housing is their only housing.

Fourthly, at the end of 2008, as a response to the crisis, a law was adopted that envisaged, starting in 2009, the possibility of using the money from so-called "maternal capital"[38] towards improvement of housing conditions (including debt repayment under mortgage loans) immediately after childbirth and receipt of a relevant certificate. This measure provided substantial support to many a borrower.

To strengthen the demand for mortgage loans and increase the affordability of mortgage loans during the period of shrinking volumes of mortgage lending, the legislation on mortgage securities was changed to increase the maximum LTV on mortgage loans, which may be used to secure MBS, from 70 percent to 80 percent. We think that such a decision is erroneous because it may entail a considerable buildup of risks and undermine the sustainability of the overall mortgage lending system and the market of MBS in Russia.

We believe that a much more effective tool to reduce the down payment for mortgages is mortgage insurance. Therefore, in 2010, the AHML established a subsidiary insurance company, OAO or "Insurance Company of the Agency for Housing Mortgage Lending," to support the development of mortgage insurance in Russia through the mechanism of re-insurance of mortgages that are already privately insured.[39] It has just started its operations.

Finally, the Russian Housing Development Foundation was set up to promote housing construction: first of all, economy-class housing affordable to middle income households.[40] The foundation pursues the objective of involving federal land that is either idle or inefficiently used in business transactions, equipping it with physical infrastructure and allocating it on auctions for housing construction purposes. In addition, the government of the Russian Federation developed the plan of actions and regulations to reduce administrative barriers for the purposes of implementation of investment-construction projects, including projects on housing construction.

Housing Prices in Russia: "To Bubble or Not to Bubble"?

Rapid and sustainable growth of housing prices in Russia over 10 years before the crisis generated, just as in most other countries, discussions about the nature of this situation: whether it was a "bubble" or not. Sure enough, over 2001–2008, real housing prices in Russia increased 2.5 times. Moreover, they were on the rise both during periods of economic decline and during economic growth periods. Only in 2009 did they start to come down against the background of the global economic meltdown.

As a definition of the term *bubble*, we shall use the one offered by J. Stiglitz in 1990: "If the reason the price is high today is only because investors believe that the selling price will be high tomorrow—when 'fundamental' factors do not seem to justify such a price—then a bubble exists."[41] According to this definition, the growth of housing prices is not a direct indicator of a bubble. So far, academic papers have not created a well-defined set of fundamental factors that influence housing prices. As a rule, experts refer to factors ensuing from the investment model devised by Poterba in 1984[42] and its later modifications, or from the model of asset pricing adapted to housing[43] (such housing demand factors as real disposable income, growth of real GDP, inflation rate, real interest rates, unemployment rate, the size of the housing stock, population growth rate, and housing supply factors, such as cost of housing construction, availability of land plots and town planning legislation).

Meanwhile, most research papers on the housing market focused on developed countries of Asia, North America, and West European states, whereas the housing market of transition economies, such as Russia and countries of the former Soviet Union, have been studied less thoroughly. Egert and Mihaljek[44] found out that housing prices in eight countries of Central and Eastern Europe changed mostly because of such factors as per capita GDP, real interest rates, affordability of housing loans, and demographic situations. Moreover, they came to the conclusion that the development of the housing market and housing finance institutions produces a considerable impact on the level of housing prices. Stepanyan, Poghosyan, and Bibilov[45] conducted a similar investigation in the former Soviet states and confirmed that this conclusion was correct. They also noted that in a number of countries covered by their research such factors as remittances and foreign inflows (other than foreign direct investments), mostly in the form of bank borrowings from abroad, play a very important role.

Investigations of Russian researches of the pre-crisis housing market in Russia in general confirmed the findings of foreign experts who concluded that key factors influencing the price were the factors of demand.[46] For example, Trade Marketing Research Company conducted an investigation based on the method of a panel analysis of the regional data for 2000–2007 and found out that household income growth accounted for 70 percent of the housing price growth.[47]

To answer the question about existence of bubbles in the housing market in Russia we shall focus on the outputs of the analysis of the following factors (a detailed analysis is given in the first section of the chapter): housing needs, housing supply (housing construction), household incomes, an ability to purchase housing with the help of bank loans (mortgage lending).

Due to the fact that Russian households experienced a pressing need in housing, before the crisis, the main portion of housing was purchased to satisfy basic needs, rather than to make an investment, although investment demand also existed, especially in the largest Russian cities.

Volumes of housing construction in Russia are poorly correlated with housing demand. Low housing supply elasticity ensues from high administrative barriers impeding the process of implementation of investment-construction projects and difficulties facing those who want to have an access to land plots for housing construction purposes.[48] Moreover, the growth of volumes of total floor space of newly built housing in Russia was ensured mainly by the growth of volumes of owner-builder construction.

In such circumstances, the growth of purchasing power due to the growth of income level, as well as due to the enhancement of the mortgage debt finance system, inevitably results in the increase of housing prices. And this is exactly what happened in Russia in the first decade of the twenty-first century.

The financial crisis has virtually halted the growth of household incomes (real disposable incomes grew by 2.9 percent in 2008 and by only 1.9 percent in 2009 y-o-y) and cut down mortgage loans supply by banks (in 2009 banks made four times fewer mortgage loans than in 2008). The immediate consequence was a housing demand contraction (number of transactions in the housing market in 2009 decreased by 13.3 percent against the level of 2008), and, accordingly, a price drop.

We should also take into account the impact of psychological factors, i.e. creation of a pent-up housing demand resulting from anticipations of further reduction of prices. As K. Styrin and O. Zamulin[49] pointed out, the factor of price expectations in the Russian housing market can play a significant role. They used the model of rigid prices to describe the dynamics of housing prices from 1997–2001 and demonstrated that pricing in the Russian market can be better explained by adaptive expectations than rational ones.

Stepanyan, Poghosyan, and Bibilov[50] found out that before the crisis (1Q2005) housing prices in Russia were 25 percent lower, during the global crisis (2007–2008) 20 percent higher, and after the crisis (3Q2009) 55 percent higher than basic values. The situation in other countries of the former Soviet Union was more or less the same. It means that before the crisis, housing prices calculated in accordance with fundamental factors should have been higher and during the crisis the drop in prices should have been much deeper but for the existing rigidity of prices.

In a word, the analysis of fundamental factors influencing price changes in the housing market in Russia, contained in this article, enabled us to conclude that a bubble in the housing market does not exist. Summarizing the outputs of the analysis, we can identify the following key factors that influenced the growth of housing prices in Russia before the crisis:

Demand factors:

- Pressing household needs in improving housing conditions.
- Stable growth of real household incomes.
- Enhanced affordability of mortgage loans.
- Lack of alternative investment options that could guarantee stable positive yield.

Supply factors:

- Low price elasticity of housing supply resulting from high administrative barriers in the construction sector, limited access to land plots for construction purposes, including low supply of land plots equipped with necessary physical infrastructure and, as a result, an absence of real competition between developers.

PROSPECTS FOR THE HOUSING AND HOUSING MORTGAGE MARKETS IN RUSSIA

Currently, the market of mortgage lending is at crossroads. The economic meltdown has taught us a number of very useful lessons and created an opportunity for amending both the strategies of the market participants, and the government policy.

In July 2010, the Government of the Russian Federation approved a rather ambitious long-term strategy for the development of housing mortgage lending up to 2030.[51] The strategy sets a target of enhancing the affordability of mortgage lending to Russian people: By 2030, 60 percent of households should be able to afford to purchase housing with their own savings and bank loans.

The strategy defines the conditions that will enable the mortgage lending market to develop at a sustainable rate in the next twenty years. Toward this end it is necessary to meet the following key objectives:

- To overcome the current crisis in the Russian Federation and create conditions for preventing and alleviating possible future crisis situations.
- To establish an efficient primary market of housing mortgage lending that will ensure the balance of interests of creditors and borrowers.
- To develop a sustainable system of attracting long-term resources from the capital market to the mortgage market.
- To create a reliable and efficient infrastructure for the housing mortgage market.
- To develop not only classic housing mortgage lending, but also other forms of housing lending backed by the pledge of residential real estate, including housing construction finance.
- To take into account regional and local specificities of development of the housing and mortgage markets.

As planned, the strategy implementation will go through three stages. At the first stage—up to 2012—mortgage lending should become affordable for 23 percent of families, and the number of originated mortgages should at least double to 230 thousand loans per year. During the second stage (2013–2020) the rate of growth of mortgage lending in Russia must further increase. By 2020 mortgage loans should become affordable to 50 percent of households, and the average weighted interest rate will come down to 6 percent annual (in rubles), with inflation at 4 percent. The number of originated loans should increase to 868 thousand loans per year, and, as a result, the ratio of outstanding mortgages to the GDP should reach almost 11 percent (in 2009 it was 2.8 percent). As expected, by then, there will be a large-scale demand for MBS not only on the part of professional investors, but of retailer-investors as well. This will also encourage the growth of the mortgage market. Later on, during the third stage (2021–2030), volumes of mortgage lending should be growing just as rapidly. By 2030 the number of originated loans should reach the level of 873 thousand loans per year and the ratio of outstanding mortgages to the GDP should be at least 15.5 percent.

MAIN LESSONS TO BE LEARNED FROM THE CRISIS IN THE HOUSING AND HOUSING MORTGAGE LENDING MARKETS IN RUSSIA

The global crisis has given new impetus to the analysis of housing mortgage lending, housing market, and housing construction market development, including their development during the crisis, both in Russia and beyond. This analysis is conducted not only for the purposes of implementing more reasonable policies by the participants of these markets, but also with the goal of conducting more efficient public policy to support the housing sector. The economic meltdown made it possible to identify major problems in the way of these markets' development that should be taken into account when defining activity strategies. In this chapter we summarize the main lessons, which, in our opinion, must be taken into account at the next stages of development in Russia.

Housing mortgage lending, like any other type of lending, may face exposure to considerable risks, especially during periods of crises. It can become an efficient instrument for addressing housing problems of households only if major requirements that keep in check creditors' "appetite for risk," especially when the market is growing, are met. The enhancement of mortgage loans' affordability to people should be achieved through creating conditions for the growth of household incomes, stabilization of housing prices and reduction of interest rates on mortgage loans based on positive macroeconomic development, rather than through an artificial improvement of mortgage loan standards based on expectations of an uninterrupted market growth. Shrinking housing prices as such are a factor of high risk for mortgages. Reduction of housing prices, as a rule, occurs during the overall economic meltdown, and is therefore accompanied by reduction of borrowers' incomes.

Affordability of housing mortgage lending directly depends on the housing market prices. Therefore, it is difficult to achieve higher housing affordability only through expanding opportunities for obtaining mortgage loans. If housing demand is increased through mortgage lending development and enhancement of other various housing finance mechanisms, without changing other conditions in the housing market and housing construction market, it objectively contributes to the growth of housing prices. It is necessary to enhance housing affordability, first of all, through differentiation of the housing market and creation of a new housing segment that will be affordable to middle- or moderate-income households.

Generally speaking, the amount of down payment on mortgages cannot be less than 20–30 percent of the value of the pledged housing, and only in the event of availability of an additional mortgage insurance can it be reduced to 10 percent. Mortgage payments (and other obligatory payments) to income ratio cannot be more than 40–50 percent. Securitization of mortgage assets has considerable limitations and can be carried out only for highly reliable mortgage assets (in the absence of mortgage insurance, LTV ratio should not be higher than 70 percent).

Establishment of a reasonable system of distribution of risks between various participants of the mortgage market (borrowers, creditors, insurance companies, refinancing institutions and secondary market vehicles, investors and the state) should become an important factor for the development of mortgage lending. As regards assisting borrowers with getting a mortgage loan, such assistance should focus on creating proper conditions for borrowers without increasing the risks of other participants of the mortgage market. From this point of view, state assistance in the form of subsidizing down payments under mortgages (used in Russia within the framework of the federal program of assisting young families with housing purchase) is, in our opinion, much more reasonable than subsidizing mortgage loan interest payments, which not only creates long-term budget liabilities, but also increases the risks of creditors and borrowers due to non-implementation of budget liabilities, especially during the crisis (this problem had to be faced by the authorities within the framework of regional programs).

The process of mortgage market development in Russia has been accompanied by an imbalance between certain market segments and objective difficulties, which are worth immediate attention. These difficulties are as follows:

- Critical dependence of the mortgage market on availability of resources in the domestic market at prices that ensure acceptable rates on mortgage loans.
- High dependence of mortgages on the efficiency of the judicial system: an excessively prolonged term of foreclosure and sale of the pledged housing, possibility of eviction of a borrower only subject to a special court ruling after the sale of the pledged housing—all this implies increased losses for creditors and increased debt burden for borrowers after the foreclosure.
- Inefficiency of mass foreclosures and sales of collaterals in the regions that have a high share of mortgaged housing: pressure on the market leads to the growth of creditors' losses.
- Lack of motivation for regional and municipal authorities to increase a maneuverable housing stock for temporary occupancy by insolvent borrowers.
- Absence of a differentiated regional and local approach within the state support of the mortgage market development via reasonable socio-economic typology of municipalities.
- Imbalance between dynamic development of mortgage lending in the secondary housing market, and considerable deceleration of housing construction debt finance, including financing of owner-builder housing construction, repairs, renovations, and rehabilitation of housing buildings and units.
- Discrepancies between the increased affordability of housing to people and higher risks of mortgage lending against the backdrop of reduced housing prices.
- Insufficient development of infrastructure that supports mortgage transactions: low efficiency of operations of state registration of real estate titles and state real estate cadastre; absence of a private mortgage insurance system; poor development of the system of monitoring the housing and mortgage markets.

The housing market, and in particular the mortgage market in Russia, is nascent: We have gained our first experience of development and that of a serious crisis. The planned strategic goals and objectives can be met, in our opinion, only in the event that the lessons of this very first serious crisis in the housing and mortgage markets in Russia are thoroughly investigated, evaluated, and remembered, which is probably the most important.

APPENDIX

Official Exchange Rates of U.S. Dollar and Euro to Ruble, at the Year End

Year	U.S. Dollar, Rubles per One Dollar	Euro, Rubles per One Euro
1998	20.65	24.09*
1999	27.00	27.23
2000	28.16	26.14
2001	30.14	26.49
2002	31.78	33.11
2003	29.45	36.82
2004	27.75	37.81
2005	28.78	34.19
2006	26.33	34.70
2007	24.55	35.93
2008	29.38	41.44
2009	30.24	43.39
1.04.2010	29.50	39.57
1.07.2010	31.26	38.21

*Data as of January 1, 1999.
Source: Data from the Bank of Russia.

NOTES

1. See Struyk (1997).

2. Hereinafter, unless otherwise specified, we use the data of the Federal Service of State Statistics of the Russian Federation (Rosstat)—www.gks.ru. Statistics on housing units are not well enough developed in Russia, and data on the total floor space are the most widely applied. Therefore, whenever possible, we operate with housing units and their total floor space parameters, and if data on housing units are not available, we use only total floor space parameters.

3. Based on the Census of 2002, there were 488,500 communal apartments in the country, and 1.56 percent of Russian citizens resided in them (see Census 2005).

4. "Amenities" are cold and hot water supply, sanitation, heating, bathtub or shower unit, and gas or electric stove.

5. Authors' calculations based on the data of Rosstat. The regions of the Central and North-Western Russia include the constituent entities of the Russian Federation from the Central Federal District and the North-Western Federal District.

6. Calculation of this indicator, detailed statistics and description of research methods can be found at www.doingbusiness.org.

7. See IUE (2004).

8. Ibid.

9. Hereinafter a "primary housing market" means the market of newly built housing units.

10. This indicator is calculated similarly to widely used house price-to-income ratios (for example, UN Habitat Global Urban Indicators Database). However, due to

unavailability of data on median household income and median free-market price of dwelling units in Russia, the house price-to-income ratio is calculated on the basis of the following indicators: average annual per capita monetary income multiplied by three (of a household of three), and social standard of total housing floor space corresponding to that size of a household (54 m^2) multiplied by an average price of one square meter of total housing floor space.

11. It is calculated the same way as the HAI (Housing Affordability Index) applied by the National Association of Realtors of USA (www.realtor.org) with only one adjustment: Average or standard indicators are used instead of median indicators (due to the lack of statistics on the latter).

    The impact on the value of HAR and HAI indicators calculated base on average values and median values could be significant as showed by Struyk (2006).

12. This indicator (designed by IUE) is calculated by determining the minimum aggregate average monthly income of a household of three that is required for purchasing a standard housing unit with family savings and bank loans, and subsequent comparison of the obtained result with the data on households' distribution by the level of average monthly incomes. Currently, this indicator is one of the target indicators applied within the Federal Target Program "Housing."

13. Data from the Bank of Russia on mortgage lending and situation in the financial market of Russia are used in this and the next section, unless otherwise specified (www.cbr.ru).

14. For more detail about mortgage lending development in Russia before 2005, see Kosareva and Struyk (1996), Suchkova and Klepikova (1997), Klepikova and Rogozhina (2006).

15. Information about the AHML is available at www.ahml.ru.

16. In 2004, a package of Federal laws was adopted to enhance housing affordability, including enhancement through mortgage lending development.

17. Foreign currency-denominated loans are loans either made or denominated in foreign currency. Accordingly, the payments to be made under such loans are calculated in the same currency as the currency of the loan. Such loans accounted for 28 percent of the total volume of housing loans made in 2006, for 14 percent made in 2008, and for 7 percent made in 2009. The most popular loans were those denominated in U.S. dollars and Euro.

18. According to the Bank of Russia, as of January 1, 2009, bank deposits of natural persons for a term of three or more years accounted for 5.3 percent of the total volume of natural persons' deposits.

19. In 2003, the law "On Mortgage-Backed Securities" was adopted (#152-FZ, dated November 11, 2003), which established the rules for the issuance of MBS in Russia. It envisages the possibility of issuing three types of MBS:

    1. Collaterized mortgage obligations (CMO), which are issued through SPV and collaterized by mortgages.

    2. Mortgage-backed bonds (MBB), in which banks use mortgages as collateral for a bond issue. The mortgage remains on the balance sheet of the bank as an asset.

    3. Participation Certificates, which are very similar to mortgage pass-through securities. This type of MBS is still a novelty in Russia.

20. Issuance of MBS abroad in accordance with the rules applied in the country of issue.

21. According to the data of Rusipoteka: www.rusipoteka.ru.

22. Until March 2010, Federal law #152-FZ, dated November 11, 2003, "On Mortgage-Backed Securities" prohibited banks from issuing MBS if LTV ratio was more than

70 percent. On March 9, 2010 this law was amended and the maximum level of LTV ratio was increased up to 80 percent. Our evaluation of this decision will be given further on.

23. According to the data of Rusipoteka: www.rusipoteka.ru.

24. See Bank of Russia (2009).

25. Data of Rosstat.

26. As of January 1, 2010, mortgage loans supervised by the AHML accounted for 8.9 percent of the outstanding mortgages in Russia. (Data of the Bank of Russia and the AHML). Hereinafter "mortgage loans portfolio supervised by the AHML" means mortgage loans on the AHML balance sheet and mortgages put by the AHML on SPV for CMO issues.

27. Data of quarterly reports of the issuer of securities are placed on the AHML web site: www.ahml.ru/ru/investors/reporting/Quart reporting/.

28. Federal law "On Mortgage (Pledge of Real Estate)" envisages the necessity of conducting a reappraisal of the value of a collateral at least once a year. Reappraisal was conducted with the help of regional indices of price changes in the housing market published by Rosstat.

29. According to amendments made on December 30, 2008, to Federal law "On Mortgage (Pledge of Real Estate)," foreclosure on pledged residential premises belonging to natural persons is now possible only through court proceedings.

30. For example, the AHML considerably revised its standards in July 2009: it abolished the possibility of confirming a borrower's income with a certificate issued at his place of work (now only Income Tax Returns prepared in accordance with officially approved forms are accepted) and reduced the maximum value of the payment-to-income ratio from 50 percent to 45 percent and the maximum LTV ratio from 90 percent to 70 percent.

31. By the "secondary mortgage market," we tentatively mean both the refinancing and securitization of mortgage loans.

32. In 2009, the AHML primarily refinanced mortgages originated in 2009.

33. According to the data of the AHML and Rosstat.

34. Details about the activity of these institutions are available at the following web sites:

> www.ahml.ru—Agency for Housing Mortgage Lending
> www.fondgkh.ru—Fund for the Promotion of the Housing and Utility Sector Reform
> www.fondrgs.ru—Russian Housing Development Foundation
> www.veb.ru—Vnesheconombank

35. For more detailed information about the program go to www.veb.ru/ru/agent/mrtg/.

36. Information about the program of AHMLR can be found at www.arhml.ru.

37. By "company towns" we tentatively mean towns where the larger part of the local population is in the employ of only one enterprise. During a crisis, borrowers-employees of such an enterprise find it extremely difficult to repay mortgage loans due to job cuts or reduction of wages.

38. Maternal capital—a one-off inflation-indexed sum of 250,000 rubles paid by the state to mothers at the birth of their second or next children that could be put toward healthcare, education, or improvement of housing conditions, but not earlier than three years after the birth of the child.

39. For more details about the activity of OAO (Insurance Company of the Agency for Housing Mortgage Lending), go to www.ahml.ru/ru/participants/IpStrax/.

40. Federal law #161-FZ, dated July 24, 2008, "On Promotion of Housing Construction."

41. See Stiglitz (1990).

42. See Poterba (1984).

43. For example, see, Case, Cotter, and Gabriel (2010).

44. See Egert and Dubravko (2007).

45. See Stepanyan, Poghosyan, and Bibolov (2010).

46. See Toda and Nozdrina (1998), Jaffe and Kaganova (1996), Struyk and Winterbottom (1995), Kosareva et al. (2004), Styrin and Zamulin (2003), Stepanyan, Poghosyan, and Bibolov (2010), Trade Marketing Research (2009).

47. See Trade Marketing Research (2009).

48. See Doing Business (2010), Doing Business (2009).

49. See Styrin and Zamulin (2003).

50. See Stepanyan, Poghosyan, and Bibolov (2010).

51. The draft strategy was drawn up by the Agency for Housing Mortgage Lending with active input by the financial and expert communities. The authors of this article took part in designing the draft strategy.

REFERENCES

Bank of Russia. 2009. "On the Situation in the Housing Mortgage Market in 2009." Report by the Bank of Russia. Available at www.cbr.ru/statistics/ipoteka/am_2009.pdf.

Case, Karl, John Cotter, and Stuart Gabriel. 2010 (February 11). *Housing Risk and Return: Evidence from a Housing Asset-Pricing Model.* Available at www.finance.unimelb.edu.au/Research/seminars/2010/Gabriel_Stuart_2_CCG%2002-13-10.pdf.

Census. 2005. Volume 11. *Russia's Statistics, vol. 11: Housing Conditions. Results of the All-Russia Census Conducted in 2002.* Moscow: Information-Publishing Center .

Doing Business in Russia 2009. Subnational publication. The World Bank and IFC.

Doing Business in Russia 2010: Reforming through Difficult Times. The World Bank, IFC, and Palgrave MacMillan.

Egert, Balazs, and Mihaljek Dubravko. 2007. "Determinants of House Prices in Central and Eastern Europe." BIS Working Papers No. 236, Basel.

Jaffe, D., and O. Kaganova. 1996. "Real Estate Markets in Urban Russia." *Journal of Transforming Economies and Societies* 3:3.

Klepikova, Elena, and Natalia Rogozhina. 2006. "Residential Mortgage Lending, Risk Management, and Affordable Housing Market Development in Russia." In *Housing Finance: New and Old Models in Central Europe, Russia, and Kazakhstan,* eds. Jozsef Hegedus and Raymond J. Struyk. Budapest: Open Society Institute.

Kosareva, N., N. Rogozhina, A. Tumanov, and M. Yakoubov. 2004. *Evaluation of the Scale and Dynamics of Changes in Effective Housing Demand and Housing Construction in Russia.* Moscow: Institute for Urban Economics.

Kosareva, N., and R. Struyk. 1996. "Emerging Long-Term Housing Finance in Russia." *Housing Finance International* 10:3.

Poterba, J. 1984. "Tax Subsidies to Owner-Occupied Housing: An Asset-Market Approach." *The Quarterly Journal of Economics* 99:4, 729–752.

Stepanyan, Vahram, Tigran Poghosyan, and Aidyn Bibolov. 2010. "House Price Determinants in Selected Countries of the Former Soviet Union." IMF Working Paper WP/10/104.

Stiglitz, J. E. 1990 (Spring). "Symposium on Bubbles." *Journal of Economic Perspectives* 4:2, 13–18.

Struyk, Raymond J., ed. 1997. *Restructuring Russia's Housing Sector: 1991–1997.* Washington, DC: The Urban Institute.

Struyk, Raymond J. 2006. "Table 3.1: Home Purchase Affordability and Mortgage Finance." In *Housing Finance. New and Old Models in Central Europe, Russia, and Kazakhstan*, eds. Jozsef Hegedus and Raymond J. Struyk, p. 71. Budapest: Open Society Institute.

———, and C. Winterbottom. 1995. *Housing Demand in a Traditional Market: Moscow*. Prepared for Housing Sector Reform Project, Russian Federation/City of Moscow. Washington, DC: The Urban Institute.

Styrin, K., and O. Zamulin. 2003. "Estimating Price Rigidities in the Russian Real Estate Markets." NES+CEFIR Working Paper.

Suchkov, Andrey, and Elena Klepikova. 1997. "Housing Finance Reform in Russia." In *Restructuring Russia's Housing Sector: 1991–1997*, ed. Raymond J. Struyk. Washington, DC: The Urban Institute.

Toda, Y., and N. Nozdrina. 1998. *The Regional Difference in Housing Price: Russia in 1993–1996*. Department of Economics University of Florida and Institute for Economic Forecasting, Russian Academy of Sciences, Moscow, Russia.

Trade Marketing Research. 2009 (September). "Model of Market Equilibrium in Regional Housing Markets in Russia." Research Paper. Trade Marketing Research. Moscow. Available at www.grouptmr.com/publications/index.html.

ABOUT THE AUTHORS

NADEZHDA KOSAREVA, PhD, Economics, is the President of the Institute for Urban Economics (Moscow, Russia), an independent think tank with a mission to provide analysis and assistance to cities and regions in social and economic development. Kosareva is a professional expert and an author of numerous publications in housing policy, housing finance, real estate development, local governance, and urban socioeconomic development. She actively participates in housing and housing finance policy development in Russia as a member of the Commission under the RF President on Priority National Projects Implementation and Demographic Policy, and is a member of the Collegiate Board and the Public Council under the Ministry for Regional Development of the Russian Federation. She has made a major contribution to drafting a considerable number of legislative documents, including the Housing Code, Town Planning Code, and Land Code of the Russian Federation, as well as the Federal laws "On Mortgage (Pledge of Real Estate)" and "On Mortgage-Backed Securities."

ANDREY TUMANOV, PhD, Economics, is a Project Manager within the Real Estate Reforms Department of the Institute for Urban Economics (Moscow, Russia). He is an expert in housing finance and real estate development, specializing in housing affordability issues, housing supply and demand modeling, and participating in the development of housing finance policy in Russia. As a UN ECE expert, he has contributed to designing the Housing Sector Profile for several CIS countries. Tumanov also has been published internationally in journals focused on housing issues.

CHAPTER 10

The Housing Market and Housing Finance in Russia and Its Regions

A Quantitative Analysis

CARSTEN SPRENGER
ICEF, Higher School of Economics, Moscow, Russia

BRANKO UROŠEVIĆ*
Faculty of Economics, University of Belgrade, Serbia

In the past decade Russia has experienced a period of sustained economic growth. Russia's economy is largely based on natural resources, most notably oil and gas. Exhibit 10.1 shows the change in Russia's GDP since 2000 as well as the strong correlation between oil price levels and Russia's GDP. This does not imply, however, that Russia's GDP is influenced entirely by revenue from oil and gas exports. First of all, other sectors such as transport, financial services, construction, steel, parts of manufacturing, and food, as well as wholesale and retail trade, have also grown strongly. Second, high capital inflows, based on the expectation of further resource-driven growth, have facilitated much-needed investment in the outdated capital stock in Russia. Third, a number of reforms such as a tax reform, setting up a stabilization fund to absorb part of the windfall gains from high oil prices, and prudent monetary and fiscal policies have contributed to trickling down of oil revenues through the economy and a general increase in living standards. These qualifying remarks do not, however, contradict the fact that the Russian economy remains highly susceptible to volatile world market prices for natural resources, in particular oil and gas.

*The authors thank Anna Margolina for providing excellent research assistance, funded under the Program of Fundamental Research of the Higher School of Economics. Carsten Sprenger gratefully acknowledges support from the Scientific Fund of the State University—Higher School of Economics, Grant No 10-01-0158. Branko Uroševiá gratefully acknowledges support by the Serbian Ministry of Science and Technology Grant No OH 179005.

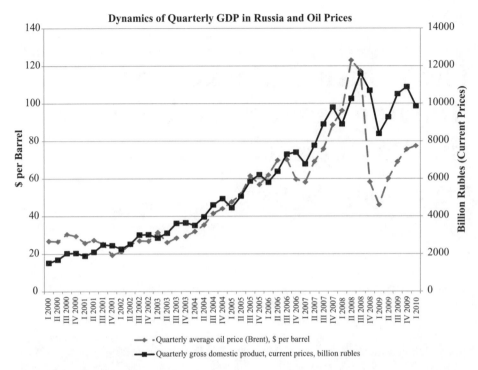

Exhibit 10.1   GDP and Oil Price
Sources: Oil price: Finam; GDP: Federal Statistical Office (Rosstat).

The economic growth since the beginning of the 2000s has been accompanied by an unprecedented increase in house prices. The price-to-income ratio of the Russian housing market is now one of the highest in the world: The ratio of the price of a 100-square-meter apartment to annual GDP per capita is 140 according to the latest data from the Global Property Guide.[1] Comparable numbers are 46 in the United Kingdom, 35 in the United States and in Poland, and 9 in Germany. During the mass privatization of apartments, residents who used to rent their apartments from the state were transferred ownership rights at almost no cost. This has led to a high degree of owner-occupied housing. The rental market is, therefore, less developed, apart from an elite segment.

Since 2005, mortgage lending has shown strong growth, both in volumes and numbers of loans, but the use of mortgage financing is still relatively modest. In Moscow, Russia's most developed housing market, in 2008 less than 30 percent of the transactions in the primary and secondary markets involved mortgage financing.

The main providers of mortgage loans are large Russian banks controlled by the government. In general, the Russian banking system is dominated by banks that are directly or indirectly controlled by the government. Vernikov (2009) estimates that the share of state-controlled banks in total assets is about 56 percent (as of July 1, 2009). The five largest banks, Sberbank, VTB Group, Gazprombank, Rosselkhozbank, and Bank Moskvy—all of them state-owned—account alone for 49 percent of total banking assets in 2009. The market share of these five banks in mortgage lending, in 2008, was 47 percent.

While in the United States the decline in house prices preceded the outbreak of the financial crisis in 2007 and was one of its primary triggers, in Russia the situation was different. Namely, the crisis there was caused primarily by the slowing world economy, the corresponding reduction in oil revenues, and the reversal in capital flows that previously entered emerging markets. In turn, this negatively affected housing and housing finance markets. The crisis reached Russia with some delay: During 2007 it was still seen as a safe haven since Russia's direct exposure to subprime mortgage-backed securities was low.[2]

Many Russian banks had been relying on external borrowing as an important source of funding. This is reflected in the high loan-to-deposit ratio of more than 120 percent in 2008, which is high for emerging market standards. At the beginning of the crisis, more than 40 percent of external borrowing by banks was short-term (World Bank 2008). This entailed a considerable rollover risk, which has led to liquidity problems once international capital started to withdraw from emerging markets. For Russia, the falling oil price accelerated the capital outflow. In the last months of 2008, liquidity problems were growing throughout the domestic banking sector.

Many banks reacted by curtailing their lending programs, in particular mortgage lending. If they did not abandon their mortgage lending programs altogether they increased down-payment and income requirements, increased interest rates and shortened the maturity of mortgage contracts. With decreased demand due to the overall economic uncertainty, prices in the primary housing market stopped increasing in the fourth quarter of 2008 and were falling all throughout 2009. The secondary market moved in the same direction with some delay.

In this chapter, we focus on a quantitative analysis of the housing and housing finance markets in Russia and its regions. We describe the development of housing prices, volumes of construction and mortgage loans, interest rates, and maturity terms in the next section. We focus on the regional dimension since in Russia there are large discrepancies in the development of markets and of house prices across various regions. In the section "An Econometric Model of Regional House Prices," we exploit this regional variation and variation over time to identify the main drivers of housing prices. We use more than seven years of quarterly data on house prices and regional economic indicators for almost 80 Russian regions. The section "Currency Denomination of Mortgage Loans, Ruble Depreciation and Defaults" discusses in detail the default experience on mortgage loans during the crisis and two related issues: the currency denomination of loans and the ruble-dollar exchange rate. It is often thought that the denomination of loans in foreign currency (usually U.S. dollars) reduces the risk of banks that attract funds from international capital markets by eliminating the exchange rate risk. However, as a result of a spillover of the exchange rate risk into credit risk a much higher default rate on loans denominated in foreign currency has been observed since the large ruble depreciation of 2008–2009. The last section summarizes our findings and concludes.

DEVELOPMENT OF THE HOUSING MARKET AND HOUSING FINANCE IN RUSSIA

In this section we present data on the developments on the Russian housing market (prices and square meters of newly constructed residential buildings) as well as

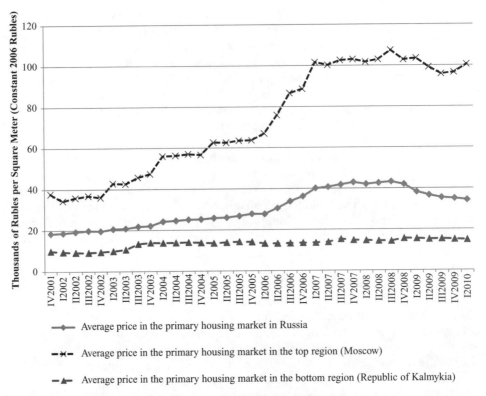

Exhibit 10.2   Real House Prices on the Primary Market
Sources: Federal Statistical Office (Rosstat), authors' calculations.

data on the market for housing finance (amount of new loans, currency denomination, average mortgage contract term, and interest rates).

In the second quarter of 2010, the average price of one square meter of a newly constructed apartment in Moscow was 142,800 rubles (4,720 dollars). The equivalent numbers for the secondary market were 166,930 rubles (5,720 dollars). This is approximately three times more than the national average. These prices are the result of a recovery of housing markets in 2010 after the decline in 2009 due to the financial crisis. To get a correct picture of the price evolution on the housing market in Russia one needs to look at real prices since general inflation has been around 10 percent annually in the past decade. We have computed real house prices using regional consumer price indices as deflators. As the base period, where nominal and real prices coincide, we have chosen the last quarter of 2006.

Exhibits 10.2 and 10.3 show the evolution of average real prices of housing on the primary and secondary markets, respectively. Nominal prices are published by the Russian Federal Statistical Office (Rosstat) on the basis of pricing data reported by real estate agencies on the housing markets of the most important cities in each region. Data is then aggregated across regions using new construction and population as weights for the primary and secondary market, respectively. All data is reported in Russian rubles. After a prolonged period of appreciation of the ruble vis-à-vis the U.S. dollar, by 2007 the ruble had replaced the U.S. dollar as

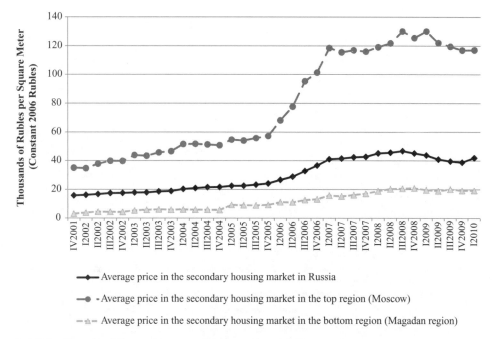

——◆—— Average price in the secondary housing market in Russia

——●—— Average price in the secondary housing market in the top region (Moscow)

——△—— Average price in the secondary housing market in the bottom region (Magadan region)

Exhibit 10.3   Real House Prices on the Secondary Market
Sources: Federal Statistical Office (Rosstat), authors' calculations.

the currency of most transactions in urban residential properties (Institute for the Economy in Transition 2010).

We can observe the strong increase in house prices until 2008. Russia has been and still is a country with a largely unsatisfied housing demand. The housing stock per capita was 22 square meters in 2008, compared to around 70 square meters in the United States. Construction activity, which practically collapsed in the 1990s, has recovered in the first decade of the twenty-first century. But even in the years preceding the recent crisis it has still been below the level of the last years of the Soviet Union.

The decline in prices started at the end of 2008. The slump in house prices in the last quarter of 2008 and the first quarter of 2009 would be even more pronounced if we had expressed prices in U.S. dollars because of the 35 percent depreciation of the ruble during this period. The decline in prices was accompanied by a sharp decline in the volume of transactions on the housing market and by an almost complete freeze in mortgage lending.

We also observe considerable regional variation in the evolution of real prices of housing units. The city of Moscow, the most expensive city in the country, exhibits also a high volatility of real prices of housing units. On the other hand, there are regions with practically flat real house prices.[3] It is instructive to compare the house prices data to rental prices and to compute rent-to-price ratios (cap rates). Unfortunately, data on rents in Russian cities are not readily available. We use data on rents for Moscow and Saint Petersburg from the Economist Intelligence Unit's Worldwide cost-of-living survey. This survey concentrates on living costs for expatriates, and is therefore biased toward the high end of the real estate market.

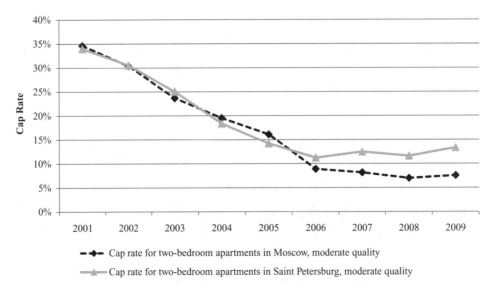

Exhibit 10.4 Cap Rates for Apartments in Moscow and Saint Petersburg
Sources: Economist Intelligence Unit, Federal Statistical Office (Rosstat), authors' calculations.

We therefore compare these data to the high quality categories of our Rosstat house price data. Exhibit 10.4 present the evolution of cap rates from 2001 to 2009.[4]

At the beginning of the last decade cap rates were exceptionally high due to high rents in the expat segment of the market. Nowadays this is not a separated market any more, and cap rates approached normal values around 2006. Since then they have stabilized even though there is a remarkable gap between the two cities of Moscow and Saint Petersburg. The cap rate in Saint Petersburg in 2009 was 13.3 percent, while in Moscow it was 7.5 percent. (For the high (elite) quality standard we have computed 10.9 and 6.8 percent, respectively.) This points to a still excessive price level in the Moscow real estate market.

Next, we turn to the supply side of the market. Exhibit 10.5 shows the dynamics of residential housing construction as well as its regional variation.

There is a strong seasonal component since many objects are commissioned toward the end of each calendar year. Certain stagnation in the commissioning of new houses can be observed already in the first months of 2008 compared to the previous year. Sternik (2009) argues that this is due to the peculiar financing scheme of residential construction that evolved in Russia in the 1990s. In the absence of a functioning banking system, a large part of new houses were financed by direct equity contributions of the future homeowners. Consequently, homeowners had to bear all of the risk. Episodes involving fraudulent construction companies abound. Share equity financing of residential housing was regulated starting only in 2005. Typically, construction companies used bank credit as an additional source of funds, mostly for the acquisition of land. This credit was usually short-term since banks were unable to use land as collateral. This situation has not significantly improved since the adoption of the land code in 2001. Large construction companies also had access to international capital markets. It is the lack of funds along with

→ ‑Total residential housing construction in Russia

‑‑■‑‑ Total residential housing construction in the top region (Moscow region)

—▲—Average total residential housing construction in three bottom regions (Murmansk region, Magadan region, Republic of Ingushetia)

Exhibit 10.5   Residential Housing Construction
Source: Federal Statistical Office (Rosstat).

specific risks (corruption, bureaucratic procedures in establishing legal ownership of land) that constrained greater construction activity in residential housing.

The financial crisis contributed to a further slowdown in construction. Construction companies were unable to refinance short-term loans and went bankrupt in several cases, abandoning many construction projects. Construction activity continued to decrease throughout the crisis.

We now turn to the housing finance market. The Russian market for mortgage lending is rather young. Even though the Federal Agency for Home Mortgage Lending, a government-owned secondary mortgage provider, was established in 1997, mortgage lending took off only around 2005. In 2006, the Central Bank of Russia started to collect data on banks' activities in housing finance. Since then, mortgage lending had been increasing until the onset of the crisis.

The global financial crisis has hit the Russian market of mortgage lending with some delay but very hard. At the end of 2008 and the beginning of 2009, many commercial banks started to reduce or abandon their mortgage lending programs, decreasing the maximum loan to value ratios and increasing interest rates. As a result, in 2009, with respect to 2008, the total number of mortgage loans granted fell by 62 percent, while the total ruble volume of extended loans decreased by 76 percent. Exhibit 10.6 presents the volume of mortgage loans in per capita terms across Russia.

The region with the highest loan amount per capita is the oil-rich Tyumen region, followed by Moscow and Saint Petersburg. On the other extreme, in several republics of the Northern Caucasus banks virtually do not grant *any* mortgage loans.

We now turn to the currency denomination of mortgage loans. The only important foreign currency in this market is the U.S. dollar. For a long time real estate prices were quoted exclusively in dollars. Exhibit 10.7 shows that there is

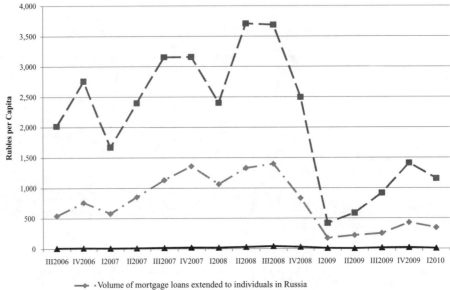

Exhibit 10.6   Volume of New Mortgage Loans per Capita
Sources: Central Bank of Russia, authors' calculations.

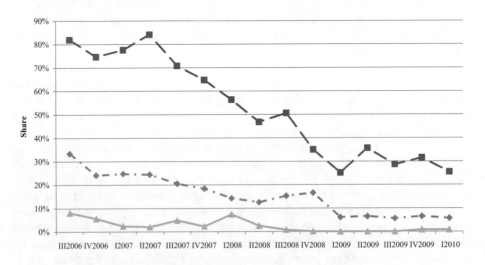

Exhibit 10.7   Currency Composition of Mortgage Loans
Sources: Central Bank of Russia, authors' calculations.

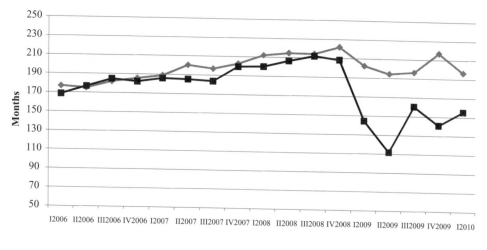

Exhibit 10.8   Weighted Average Maturity of Mortgage Loans
Sources: Central Bank of Russia, authors' calculations.

a relatively stable decreasing trend in the share of loans denominated in foreign currency. In 2009, the share of foreign currency–denominated mortgage loans, in the total volume of mortgage loans, fell to about 6 percent. This decrease was a result of the change of the macroeconomic situation and the depreciation of the ruble at the end of 2008 and in the beginning of 2009. Both banks and borrowers were apparently more aware of the credit risk inherent in foreign currency loans. This had already shown up in the higher incidence of non-payment on foreign currency–denominated loans.

The regional variation in the fraction of foreign-currency denominated loans is remarkable. In Moscow it was more than 70 percent still in 2007 and has come down to around 25 percent according to the latest data. In several regions this fraction has come close to zero in the past two years.[5]

The Central Bank of Russia reports quarterly data on the average maturities and interest rates of mortgage loans since 2006. Weighted average indicators are calculated on the cumulative basis from the beginning of the year. This makes the comparison between quarters problematic. For example, a significant increase of interest rates combined with strongly decreasing volumes of mortgage loans as it occurred in the financial crisis of 2008–2009 would lead to only a small increase in the average cumulated interest rate. A similar effect occurred for strongly decreasing maturities of new mortgage contracts during the crisis.

The numbers on weighted average maturities and interest rates that we report in the following two figures are reduced using an approximate methodology to recover weighted average maturities and interest rates during a quarter.[6,7]

Until the end of the year 2008 weighted average maturities of both ruble denominated and foreign currency-denominated mortgage loans were close and ranged between 170 and 230 months (See Exhibit 10.8). In 2009, weighted average maturities on mortgage loans decreased; the average maturity of foreign

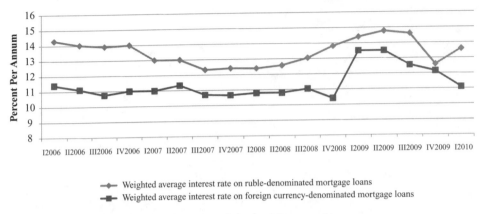

Exhibit 10.9   Weighted Average Interest Rates on Mortgage Loans
Sources: Central Bank of Russia, authors' calculations.

currency-denominated loans decreased more sharply than domestic currency-dominated loans. This was presumably one device applied by banks to control the higher perceived risks in the market for mortgage loans, especially for foreign currency loans after the major ruble devaluation of 2008–2009. Banks did not only grant fewer loans, but also issued loans with shorter maturities.

The growth of weighted average interest rates from 2008Q2 to 2009Q2 can be explained mainly as a consequence of the world financial crisis. Interestingly, interest rates went up already before the virtual breakdown of the mortgage market at the beginning of 2009. Since the Lehman breakdown and the subsequent liquidity crisis in global financial markets, the Central Bank of Russia has supported liquidity in the domestic banking sector by lowering reserve requirements, extending funds, guaranteeing interbank loans and, at some point, even through direct lending without collateral. In 2009Q2 it started to decrease the refinancing rate, which led to a gradual reduction in weighted interest rates on mortgage loans since 2009Q3.

Note that the interest rate spread between foreign-currency and ruble denominated loans has been decreasing during the crisis. While in the past high inflation expectations for the ruble contributed to higher ruble interest rates, now the higher default risk inherent in foreign-currency loans after the considerable ruble devaluation is priced in. We discuss the default experience in Russian mortgage loans after the following section, which presents an econometric analysis of Russian house prices.

AN ECONOMETRIC MODEL OF REGIONAL HOUSE PRICES

In this section, we report econometric evidence on the driving forces behind house price formation in the regions of Russia utilizing a panel data model. Using regional data for estimating determinants of house prices has several advantages over using international data: One does not need to account for differences in regulations, taxation, and financing of construction and purchase of houses (Koetter and Poghosyan 2010).

We use quarterly data of house prices and a wide range of explanatory variables.[8] In order to perform the estimation we use the pooled mean group estimator of Pesaran (1999). Previously, the approach was used to find the determinants of house prices across countries (Kholodilin et al. 2007; Stepanyan et al. 2010) and across German regions (Koetter and Poghosyan 2010). This estimator is appropriate for the nonstationary nature of house prices and some of their determinants, such as income per capita. It integrates the estimation of a long-run (equilibrium) relationship and a short-run adjustment equation. The coefficients in the long-run relationship (except for a constant term) are assumed to be homogeneous across all regions, while the speed of adjustment and the coefficients of all variables in the adjustment equation can vary across regions. The homogeneity restriction seems adequate given that we are using data of one country. Appropriate unit root tests have been applied to the data before running the model.[9]

Our model specification in error-correction form reads:

$$\Delta RHP_{it} = \phi_i \left(RHP_{i,t-1} - \theta_{i0} - \sum_h \theta_h X_{ih,t} \right) + \sum_h \delta_{ih} \Delta Z_{iht} + \varepsilon_{it}$$

where RHP_{it} denotes the real house price in region i and period t, Δ denotes the first difference, θ_{i0} is region-specific constant term in the long-run equation, $X_{ih,t}$ are factors in the long-run equation, and $\theta_1, \theta_2, \ldots$ are the corresponding coefficients, equal for all regions, ΔZ_{iht} are first differences of the factors in the short-term equation and $\delta_{i1}, \delta_{i2}, \ldots$ are their corresponding coefficients. The error correction term (in parentheses) can be interpreted as the deviation of house prices from their fundamental value. The coefficient ϕ_i denotes the adjustment parameter. It can be shown that the half-life of a shock; that is, the time that elapses until a deviation from the long-run equilibrium is halved, equals $\frac{\ln(0.5)}{\ln(1+\phi_i)}$.

We report results for two specifications. In each of them, sets of variables in the long-run equation (X) and the short-run equation (Z) are identical. In the first specification we include the logarithm of the real monthly disposable income per capita and the real interest rate (in percent), which is computed as a national loan rate minus regional inflation. Income per capita is expected to increase house prices while the real interest rate as an opportunity cost of an investment into housing is expected to have a negative effect.

In a second specification we include additional variables, such as population growth, the unemployment rate, and the change in the volume of outstanding consumer loans. For these time series we have more than seven years of quarterly data (2002Q4 to 2010Q1). Instead of consumer loans, we would ideally like to use a series for the volume of newly granted mortgage loans, but this is available only since 2006. We present estimation results for the two specifications in Exhibit 10.10. Since we are mostly interested in the coefficients of the long-run relationship, only these and the adjustment coefficient are reported.

As expected, income per capita has a positive effect on house prices, with elasticity close to unity in specification 1. The real interest rate has a negative, but small effect. When we introduce population growth, unemployment, and the

Exhibit 10.10   Pooled Mean Group (Panel) Estimations for the Logarithm of Average House Prices on the Secondary Market in Russian Regions, 2003Q1–2010Q1

Variable	Specification 1		Specification 2	
Log income per capita	0.958	28.72*	0.512	6.10
Real interest rate	−0.016	−9.69	−0.006	−5.25
Population growth			0.209	2.08
Unemployment rate			−16.946	−12.23
Log change in outstanding consumer loans			0.083	4.96
Adjustment coefficient	−0.130	−11.98	−0.159	−12.28
Log likelihood	3037.3		3180.9	
Number of observations	2251		2173	

*The italic numbers are Z statistics.

change in consumer loans on banks' balance sheets, income per capita, and interest rates continue to be important long-run determinants of house prices. In addition, the volume of loans to consumers has an independent positive effect on house prices. We can therefore conclude that the development of the banking system with a larger market for housing finance contributes to the price dynamics of the housing markets. The unemployment rate is both statistically and economically highly significant in explaining house prices and enters with a negative sign, as expected. Overall population growth is identified as another factor that increases the price level on the housing market.

The adjustment coefficient is –0.13 and –0.16 in the two specifications, respectively. The negative sign implies that after deviation from the long-run equilibrium, there is a tendency that these deviations are reduced in the following quarters. This suggests that there is indeed a cointegration relationship between house prices and the other nonstationary variables of the model. The corresponding half-lives of adjustment after a shock in the two specifications are five and four quarters, respectively.

A preliminary conclusion from this analysis is that house prices in Russia follow an expected pattern as for their dependency on traditional driving factors such as income per capita, interest rates, population growth, and the unemployment rate. The volume of consumer loans as an indicator of the development of the banking system (and which is highly correlated with the volume of mortgage loans) has a positive effect on house prices.

CURRENCY DENOMINATION OF MORTGAGE LOANS, RUBLE DEPRECIATION, AND DEFAULTS

The financial crisis of 2008–2009 has brought about a sharp increase in defaults on bank loans. We focus first on consumer loans since a longer time series is available than for mortgage loans. Exhibit 10.11 presents the fraction of overdue loans in consumer loans—for ruble-denominated loans, foreign currency–denominated loans and their weighted average. In addition, we plot the ruble-dollar exchange rate in the same graph.

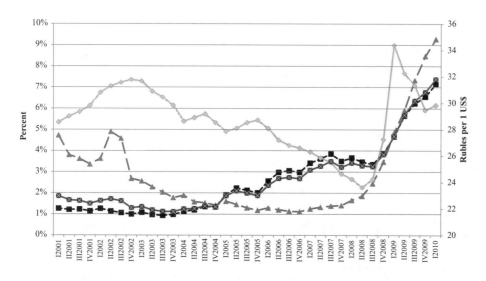

- ━■━ Share of ruble-denominated overdue consumer loans in total volume of ruble-denominated
outstanding consumer loans, %

- ━▲ ·Share of foreign currency–denominated overdue consumer loans in total volume of foreign
currency–denominated outstanding consumer loans, %

- ━⊗━ Share of overdue consumer loans in the total volume of outstanding consumer loans, %

- ━◆━ Quarterly average ruble–dollar exchange rate, ruble per one U.S. dollar

Exhibit 10.11 Fraction of Overdue Loans in Total Outstanding Consumer Loans and the
Ruble–Dollar Exchange Rate
Sources: Central Bank of Russia, authors' calculations.

One observes a sharp increase in defaults since the fourth quarter of 2008. The
default rate among foreign currency–denominated loans has increased the most.
Note that there is a strong correlation between depreciation of ruble with respect
to dollar and an increase in default rates of dollar-denominated loans. As outlined
above, the funding strategy of many Russian banks involved a large portion of
foreign funds. Issuing loans in U.S. dollars has been traditionally perceived by
these banks as a hedge against exchange rate risk. As the crisis experience now
shows this risk has simply been transferred into credit risk.

Spillover of the exchange rate risk into default risk is, of course, not a new
phenomenon, especially in the emerging markets (recall, for example, the Asian
crisis of the late 1990s). Suppose that a loan is issued in a foreign currency (or is
pegged to it). A depreciation of the domestic currency leads to a reduced ability
of a borrower to pay off the loan (in terms of the foreign currency) since her salary
is typically issued in domestic currency and is not pegged to the foreign currency.
This, in turn, leads to a greater probability of borrower's default (see Božović,
Urošević, and Živković, 2009). An increased number of defaults reduces the readi-
ness of banks to lend money or, alternatively, they lend at less favorable terms. As
a result, the economy shrinks. This, in turn, may lead to a further deterioration in
loan quality.[10]

The same argument holds for mortgage loans. Unfortunately, data on overdue
mortgage loans in Russia is available only since the beginning of 2009. Exhibit 10.12

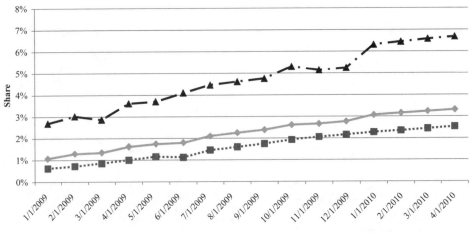

Exhibit 10.12 Fraction of Overdue Loans in Total Outstanding Mortgage Loans: Ruble and Foreign Currency Denominated Loans and Total
Sources: Central Bank of Russia, authors' calculations.

shows the fraction of overdue loans denominated in rubles, foreign currency, and the weighted average of the two. Note that the increasing trend in defaults continues until present even though there are already signs of recovery in the Russian economy in terms of the GDP.

Exhibit 10.13 studies the regional variation in default rates. While there are regions with virtually no defaults (at a small basis of outstanding loans), as of April 1, 2010, default rates have reached 7 percent in the Moscow region (areas neighboring to the city of Moscow). Also, the city of Moscow and the Kaliningrad regions are high up in the ranking with 6.5 and 6 percent default rates, respectively. All these regions have a high fraction of mortgage loans denominated in foreign currency. Default rates on ruble-denominated mortgage loans (not in the graph) are among the highest in Volgograd and Kemerovo regions (above 5 percent), but also Moscow region and Kaliningrad (above 4 percent) and Moscow (above 3 percent) are relatively high.

CONCLUSION

In this chapter we have summarized the developments in the Russian markets for housing and housing finance in the last decade, with a particular focus on the effects of the global financial crisis. While Russia was not immediately affected by falling house prices in the United States and the subprime crisis, the spillover of the crisis into the banking and insurance sector and falling stock markets did affect Russian housing and housing finance markets. The value of the Russian stock market (represented by the RTS composite index) fell by 80 percent between

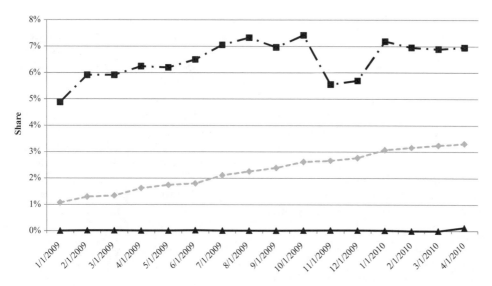

- - ◆ - - Share of overdue mortgage loans in total volume of outstanding mortgage loans extended to individuals in Russia, %

- ■ · Share of overdue mortgage loans in total volume of outstanding mortgage loans extended to individuals in the top region (Moscow region), %

- ▲ - Share of overdue mortgage loans in total volume of outstanding mortgage loans extended to individuals in the bottom region (Kamchatka region), %

Exhibit 10.13   Fraction of Overdue Loans in Total Outstanding Mortgage Loans, Regional Variation

Sources: Central Bank of Russia, authors' calculations.

the peak in May 2008 and the trough in January 2009, compared to a loss of value of 50 percent of the U.S. stocks (S&P 500). The Russian government used its accumulated oil wealth in the stabilization fund to support the economy; the Central Bank injected liquidity into the banking sector and used a sizable fraction of its large currency reserves to prevent a crash of the exchange rate of the ruble with U.S. dollar and euro. Nevertheless, Russia experienced a severe contraction of its economy starting at the end of 2008 and continuing throughout 2009. The two major shocks that the Russian economy faced were the global liquidity crisis with capital flowing out of emerging markets and the sharp decline in the oil price. Russian banks reacted by freezing or reducing their mortgage lending programs in late 2008–early 2009. House prices started to decline significantly in 2009. The housing market was characterized by a much-reduced number of transactions, but is recovering since the beginning of 2010. The number of newly constructed apartments commissioned to homeowners is still decreasing in 2010 since many construction projects were stopped during the crisis.

   We have presented evidence on house prices, residential property construction, the volume of mortgage loans, their currency denomination, average mortgage contract terms, and interest rates, as well as default rates highlighting signifi-cant regional differences. The econometric evidence shows that the variation in Russian house prices can be well explained by traditional driving factors such as income per capita, unemployment rate, interest rates, and population growth. The development of the banking system in a region (which we proxy by the volume of consumer or mortgage loans) is an additional driving force leading to higher house prices.

There are signs of recovery in the Russian economy in 2010, which are already reflected in higher house prices. The main policy challenges are to introduce a functioning regulation of urban land use together with a removal of exceptional bureaucratic barriers to establishing property rights on urban land, as well as improvements in regulations to foster the use of land as collateral in the financing of construction. This could lead to construction activity that would better satisfy large pent-up demand for housing. Moreover, such measures should have a greater effect on affordability of housing than offering more and cheaper mortgage loans. In fact, the expansion in the volume of mortgage lending could lead to a further skyrocketing of price-to-income ratios in Russia.

NOTES

1. See www.globalpropertyguide.com, data retrieved on July 20, 2010. The Global Property Guide uses the prices for upscale apartments, namely the price of 120 square meter apartments in the center of the most important city of the country. If we use instead the average square meter price on the Moscow secondary market and national GDP per capita in 2008, the ratio is still 62.

2. Russia held, however, bonds of the large U.S. mortgage refinancing organizations.

3. The following section investigates in more detail how differences in house prices across regions relate to differences in economic and demographic indicators.

4. Rental data from EUI is given for typical two-, three-, and four-bedroom apartments of either moderate or high quality. We compare this to the "improved" and "elite" categories in the Rosstat house price data for the secondary market. Exhibit 10.4 shows cap rates for two-bedroom apartments assuming an average size of 70 square meters.

5. Note that, in contrast, in most countries in Eastern, Central, and Southeastern Europe mortgage loans are almost entirely pegged to foreign currency, usually the euro. See, for example, the chapter on the Serbian housing market in this volume.

6. In order to be able to recover quarterly maturities and interest rates, at least approximately, we make the simplifying assumption that each bank grants one loan per quarter.

7. This means, however, that the coefficients are not comparable across years.

8. Some of the variables used in the cross-section regressions are, however, not available at quarterly frequency.

9. Following Holly et al. (2010) and Kholodilin (2007), we first test for cross-sectional dependence (using the test of Pesaran, 2004) and find that the residuals of individual augmented Dickey-Fuller regressions for the variables of our model are significantly correlated across regions. We therefore apply the panel unit root test of Pesaran (2007) that allows for cross-sectional dependence. We find that real house prices, real disposable income per capita, change in the volume of outstanding consumer loans and even unemployment rates are I(1) over the sample period; that is, the hypothesis of a unit roots cannot be rejected for levels, but is rejected for first differences. Population growth and real interest rate are found to be stationary.

10. In countries of Emerging Europe the situation is particularly dangerous since there, in contrast to Russia, most loans are pegged to foreign currency (typically the euro).

REFERENCES

Agency for Home Mortgage Lending. 2010. "Rynok zhilya I ipotechnogo kreditovania: Itogi 1 kvartala 2010g." ("The Market for Housing and Mortgage Lending: Results of the First Quarter 2010"). Available at www.ahml.ru, in Russian.

Božović, Miloš, Branko Urošević, and Boško Živković. 2009. "On the Spillover of Exchange-Rate Risk into Default Risk." *Economic Annals* 183, 32–55.

Holly, Sean, M. Hashem Pesaran, and Takashi Yamagata. 2010. "A Spatio-Temporal Model of House Prices in the USA." *Journal of Econometrics* 158:1, 160–173.

Institute for the Economy in Transition. 2010. "The Russian Economy in 2009, Section 5.7.2, the Russian Housing Market in 2009: From the Crisis Downfall to Stagnation," by G, M. Sternik. Available at www.iet.ru.

Kholodilin, Konstantin A., Jan-Oliver Menz, and Boriss Siliverstovs. 2007. "What Drives Housing Prices Down?" Evidence from an International Panel, German Institute of Economic Research, DIW Discussion Paper No. 758.

Koetter, Michael, and Tigran Poghosyan. 2010. "Real Estate Prices and Bank Stability." *Journal of Banking & Finance* 34:6, 1129–1138.

Pesaran, M. Hashem. 2004. "General Diagnostic Tests for Cross Section Dependence in Panels." IZA Discussion Paper No. 1240.

Pesaran, M. Hashem. 2007. "A Simple Panel Unit Root Test in the Presence of Cross-Section Dependence." *Journal of Applied Econometrics* 22, 265–312.

Pesaran, M. Hashem, Yongcheol Shin, and Ron P. Smith. 1999. "Mean Group Estimation of Dynamic Heterogeneous Panels." *Journal of the American Statistical Association* 94:446, 621–634.

Stepanyan, Vahram, Tigran Poghosyan, and Aidyn Bibolov. 2010. "House Price Determinants in Selected Countries of the Former Soviet Union." IMF Working Paper WP/10/104.

Sternik, Gennadi M. 2009. "Spad na rynke stroitel'stva I prodazhi zhilya v Rossii" ("Decline on the Market for Construction and House Sales in Russia"). *Journal of the New Economic Association* 3–4, 185–207, in Russian.

Vernikov, Andrei. 2009. "Russian Banking: The State Makes a Comeback?" Bank of Finland, BOFIT Discussion Paper No. 24/2009.

World Bank. 2007. "Russian Economic Report No. 17." Available at www.worldbank.org.ru.

ABOUT THE AUTHORS

CARSTEN SPRENGER holds a PhD in Economics from Universitat Pompeu Fabra in Barcelona, Spain. He is a Lecturer in Finance at the International College of Economics and Finance of the Higher School of Economics Moscow. He is also Head of the International Laboratory in Financial Economics at this university. His research has been published in the *Journal of Comparative Economics, Journal of the New Economic Association, Journal of the Institute of Public Enterprise, Russian Economic Trends,* and the *European Investment Bank Economic and Financial Reports.* His research interests include corporate finance and governance, real estate, and credit risk management.

BRANKO UROŠEVIĆ holds a PhD in Finance from the University of California–Berkeley, and a PhD in Phyisics from Brown University. He is a Professor of Operations Research and Financial Economics at the Faculty of Economics, University of Belgrade, Serbia. Recently, he has been appointed Special Advisor to the Governor of National Bank of Serbia, in charge of research. He is also Chairman of the Board of Dunav dobrovoljni penzijski fond, the largest private pension fund in Serbia, and a Member of the Board of the Institute for Economic Studies, Belgrade, Serbia. In addition, he is a member of the Visiting Faculty at the Univeritat Pompeu Fabra, where he was an Assistant Professor in Finance from 2002 to 2005. He is the Director of the International Masters in Quantitative Finance (IMQF), the premier finance education program in Southeastern Europe. His research is published in *Journal of Political Economy, Management Science, Economic Theory, Real Estate Economics, Journal of Real Estate Finance and Economics,* and several other journals. In addition, he is the author of four books in finance. He has led and participated in various projects financed by the European Commission, Spain, the United States, and the BBVA Foundation. As a consultant he worked with McKinsey & Company and KPMG, among other firms. His research interests cover a wide range of topics in financial economics and real estate economics, with a focus on risk management, real estate finance, and the connection between corporate finance and asset pricing.

CHAPTER 11

The Housing Market in Serbia in the Past Decade

DEJAN ŠOŠKIĆ
National Bank of Serbia; Faculty of Economics, University of Belgrade

BRANKO UROŠEVIĆ
Faculty of Economics, University of Belgrade; National Bank of Serbia

BOŠKO ŽIVKOVIĆ*
Faculty of Economics, University of Belgrade

MILOŠ BOŽOVIĆ
Center for Investments and Finance; Faculty of Sciences, University of Novi Sad

In this chapter we describe development of the housing market in Serbia in the past 10 years, including the recent period of global financial and housing crisis. Serbia has, in some ways, a unique transition experience. Located in Southeastern Europe, Serbia was the largest republic of the former Yugoslavia. After World War II, Yugoslavia was one of the most advanced and the most open socialist countries with an economic system that incorporated elements of the market economy into a system of socialist self-management. Individuals could own a limited amount of land and housing. While owning an apartment in a city was legal, a vast majority of city dwellers lived in socially owned apartments. As in many other socialist countries, the government considered providing housing units to its citizens as one of its key functions. Consequently, in times of socialist development the country has seen construction of a great number of housing units.

Yugoslavia's tentative transition toward the market economy started in the late 1980s. At that time the first privatization program for government-owned companies was introduced. In addition, a massive drive to privatize the stock of socially owned apartments was undertaken in the early 1990s. Violent disintegration of Yugoslavia in 1991–1992 disrupted the transition process. In Serbia, crippling economic sanctions imposed by the United Nations, world-record hyperinflation in

*The authors gratefully acknowledge support by the Serbian Ministry of Science and Technology Grant No 179005.

1991–1994, and the subsequent war over Kosovo in 1999 against NATO forces led to near-destruction of the country's economy and institutions. At the same time, Serbia became the recipient of the largest number of refugees and internally displaced people in Europe, furthering the strain on meager country resources.

In October 2000, years of violent struggles ended as democratic forces bent on free-market reforms took over the country. In many ways, the year 2000 represents a symbolic new beginning for Serbia, a structural break in the economic and social development of the country. Starting from highly unfavorable initial conditions, Serbia's economy and institutions have been gradually rebuilt. Its institutions and markets, while still relatively underdeveloped, increasingly resemble those of other transition economies. The housing market is no exception. Several years of solid economic growth and the introduction of mortgages and government mortgage insurance schemes that made mortgages more affordable led, in the period prior to the global economic crisis, to a significant increase in housing construction and higher housing prices.

The global crisis severely impacted the construction industry and the demand for housing. As in many other countries, new construction dropped significantly after the onset of the crisis. Several construction companies either filed or are on the brink of declaring bankruptcy. On the other hand, prices have not dropped markedly thus far. Most owners seem to be waiting for the crisis to pass and are not offering significant price reductions. As a result, liquidity of the secondary housing market has practically disappeared. The government is now undertaking measures aimed at propping up the market.

The chapter is organized as follows. We first discuss the evolution of the financial sector, financial markets, and the real economy of Serbia after the year 2000. This information sets the background for understanding the subsequent analysis of the housing market and Serbian real estate. We continue with an overview of the housing market in Serbia. This is followed by a section dedicated to an overview of the institutions and government policies that impact the housing market. Next, we discuss how bank financing affects the demand for housing and the pricing of housing units in Serbia, after which we study the risks facing investors interested in the Serbian housing market. The final section summarizes and offers conclusions on the problems of the housing market.

EVOLUTION OF THE FINANCIAL SECTOR AND REAL ECONOMY IN SERBIA IN THE PAST DECADE

Key Macroeconomic Indicators

Serbia was the largest of the six federal units in the former Yugoslavia, but experienced a rapid economic meltdown at the beginning of the 1990s, during the breakup of the country that led to a civil war and economic sanctions by the United Nations. As a consequence, a high level of non-performing loans and record-high hyperinflation in 1991–1994 produced a widespread insolvency throughout the banking industry. Traditional government financing of real estate development from the pre-1990s socialist era lacked funding, no mortgage lending was available, and the construction industry almost halted. Loss of traditional markets, mismanagement of companies and lack of available financing crippled Serbia's industrial output. Sluggish recovery was yet again hit hard by the Kosovo war and NATO intervention of 1999. Industrial production has not recovered ever since. Despite unfavorable inflation heritage, with 1993 hyperinflation being one of the world's worst in history with an annual inflation rate of 10 to 11 percent (see Hanke and Kwok 2009), political changes at the end of year 2000 brought the country out of isolation and led to a gradual stabilization of inflation.[1] Throughout 2000s, the overall economic situation has been gradually improving. Gross domestic product was increasing at a steady pace. The budget deficit has been relatively modest. Foreign exchange reserves of the central bank, the National Bank of Serbia (NBS), were increasing. Household savings have risen almost 20 times. The exchange rate, until the global economic crisis hit, was relatively stable.

Development of Financial Institutions

At the beginning of the 2000s, the inherited financial system in Serbia was in a state of disarray. The banking sector was undercapitalized and illiquid, with hidden insolvencies (especially among the six largest, state-owned banks), and with low profitability. State (or so-called "social") ownership of the banks was characterized by a low level of investments. Politically influenced decision-making, rather than proper credit analysis, produced a high level of contaminated assets and underestimated loan loss provisions with self-dealing and other fraudulent practices. Household deposits were "frozen," and banks could not service the retail crediting and real-sector financing. Supervision was inadequate and weak.

The banking reform of 2001 started with the screening of the banking sector as a whole. Total net assets of the banking sector were negative in the amount of €4.2 billion, even if one excludes the so-called "frozen old foreign-currency savings" as well as the country's debt to the London and Paris club, World Bank, and IFC (National Bank of Yugoslavia 2001). Most of the liabilities were concentrated in six "too big to fail" banks. But fail they did. In a bold move by the National Bank and the government, the four largest banks were closed in the beginning of 2002 (National Bank of Yugoslavia 2001, 2002, 2003). The reform of the banking sector did not end there. New legislation was put in place, supervision by the National Bank was vastly improved, and much more realistic assessments of asset quality were imposed. A number of banks have been rehabilitated, balance sheets were cleaned up, and debt-to-equity swap was conducted in 16 banks. Liabilities from frozen foreign-currency savings were resolved by issuing euro-denominated medium- and long-term government bonds. A number of European financial institutions entered the market through acquisitions of existing Serbian banks.

Banking reforms were directed to only one round of restructuring with the goal to create sustainable and profitable private banks, and with a strong involvement of foreign financial institutions. The agenda for reform included regaining confidence in the banking sector and starting to provide a full spectrum of financial services to the real sector and households, based on free-market principles.

The level of financial resilience of Serbian banks has increased substantially throughout the past 10 years (Exhibit 11.1), while the banking sector's capital grew significantly above international standards (Exhibit 11.2).

Strong involvement of European financial institutions has been present throughout the past decade in all sectors of the financial system, with the largest

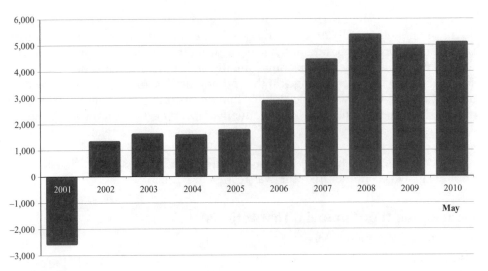

Exhibit 11.1 Capital and Reserves (Millions of EUR)
Note: The last data point refers to May 2010.
Source: National Bank of Serbia.

inflow of investments being made in the banking sector in 2006, 2007, and 2008.
After 2008, foreign direct investments in the Serbian financial industry significantly
dropped. Coincidentally, the drop is largely unrelated to the onset of the world
financial crisis. Namely, by 2008, most of the banks in Serbia had been privatized
and were in the hands of foreign investors. Banks with predominant foreign ownership are dominating the financial institutions arena: While at the year 2000 foreign

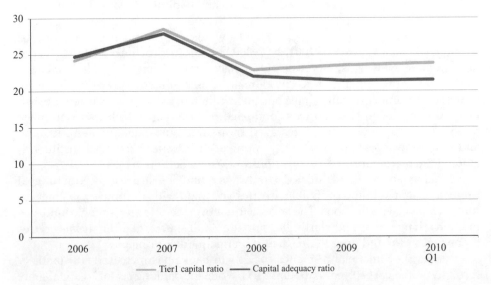

Exhibit 11.2 Capitalization of Serbian Banking Sector (Billions of EUR)
Note: The last data point refers to the first quarter of 2010.
Source: National Bank of Serbia.

banks were not present in the market, currently they own more than 85 percent of Serbian banking assets. On the other hand, development of other financial institutions, such as insurance companies (particularly those specialized in life insurance), mutual funds, and private pension funds is lagging behind the development of the banking sector. One of the main reasons for such a situation is that securities markets are still underdeveloped and characterized by a lack of instruments and liquidity.

Structure of Financial Markets and Trading Volumes

Like in many countries of continental Europe, the financial system in Serbia is strongly bank-centric. This has its positive as well as negative consequences. On one hand, stringent capital requirements imposed by the NBS, absence of secondary mortgage markets and virtual absence of derivatives transactions allowed Serbian banks to avoid, thus far, problems faced by many Western financial institutions. On the other hand, the financial market in Serbia, already quite weak at the time of crisis, was hit hard both in terms of market capitalization and liquidity after foreign portfolio investors virtually withdrew from the market.

The most prominent market in Serbia is the Belgrade Stock Exchange (BSE). The BSE was established in November 1894 and had a relatively thriving history until World War II. In the socialist era, beginning in 1945, it was not allowed to operate. It was reestablished in 1989. In unfavorable circumstances during the 1990s, BSE operated as a primary market for short-term papers issued by corporations and banks. Between 2001 and 2008—when global crisis hit the market—things were gradually improving. First, the government euro-denominated "frozen foreign-currency bonds" were issued at the end of 2001 and have been traded on the stock exchange ever since. In addition, most companies that were undergoing privatization had to be sold through the stock exchange by law. This led to a temporary spike in trading volumes and a small number of stocks began trading in the continuous trading regime. Soon after, stock exchange indexes were formed. A new set of legislation was put in place in 2006. It allowed the establishment of mutual funds and private pension funds. Banks with their trading books, alongside insurance companies, mutual funds, and private pension funds provided a reasonable institutional structure dedicated predominantly to local portfolio investing. A modest number of foreign portfolio investors began testing waters in the market. However, new public issues of securities with subsequent stock exchange listings failed to materialize. After the initial issuance of "frozen foreign-currency bonds" in 2001, the government did not issue any other long-term securities (for more details, see Drenovak and Urošević 2010). Private corporations in search of capital borrowed from banks (including the ones abroad), instead of raising money through the local capital market. Sporadic corporate bond issues have been conducted via private placements, with relatively short maturities, and without centralized secondary trading. The volume of secondary trading of stocks had been increasing initially, but the trading was predominantly governed by corporate takeover transactions. After stabilization of core corporate ownership share, trading has substantially declined, with some healthy companies completely taken off the exchange. Since 2008, prices and trading volumes have additionally been pushed down by the global financial crisis (Exhibit 11.3).

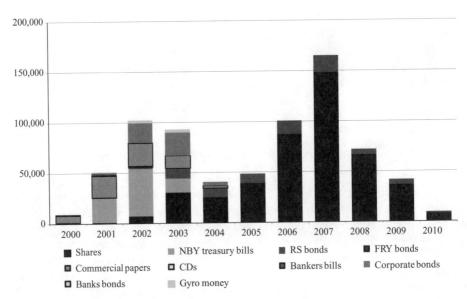

Exhibit 11.3 Trading Volume of Securities (Millions of RSD)
Source: Belgrade Stock Exchange.

Banks had alternatives in short-term transactions with the National Bank of Serbia, first through the Central Bank Bills, and then through repo transactions. Recently, the government started issuing Treasury Bills on a regular basis. The ongoing problem that the investors are facing is the substantial exchange-rate risk between the Euro and the local currency—the Serbian dinar (RSD). In 2009, NBS started entering into currency swaps with commercial banks in order to initialize and promote hedging with currency derivatives. Treasury, on the other hand, is currently trying to increase the marketability of its bonds denominated in RSD, especially the ones with longer maturities.

The securities market in Serbia is still burdened with disclosure issues, the structure of listing on the BSE, and high transaction costs. Lack of long-term debt securities and illiquidity of the BSE are obvious shortcomings. The absence of rating agencies in the market that are available to rate new securities hampers the efforts to increase the assets of insurance, private pension and other portfolio investors.

Growth of Construction Industry

The construction industry in the 2000s fared rather well until the onset of the global financial crisis. It shared the overall gradual recovery; yet it was falling substantially behind the housing production levels at the end of the 1980s (Exhibit 11.4).

Major impetus for construction industry growth was given by widespread introduction of mortgage lending in 2003 and establishment of the National Mortgage Insurance Corporation (NMIC) in October 2004. Both factors have contributed to steady growth in the number of completed housing units, with stagnation and setback initiated by the global crises and recession of 2009.

The same trend is visible with the value of construction work done (Exhibit 11.5, left axis). Overall the construction industry share of GDP in years of growth throughout 2000s has been relatively constant at around 3 percent (Exhibit 11.5, right axis).

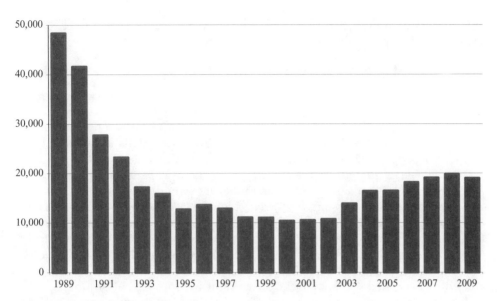

Exhibit 11.4   Number of Completed Housing Units
Source: Statistical Office of the Republic of Serbia.

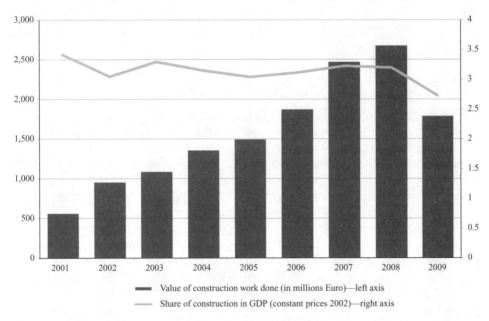

Exhibit 11.5   Value of Construction Work Done (Millions of EUR): Construction Work as a Share of GDP (%)
Source: Statistical Office of the Republic of Serbia.

HOUSING MARKET AND REAL ESTATE SECTOR IN SERBIA IN THE PAST DECADE

Structure of Housing Ownership in Serbia

Housing ownership in Serbia is somewhat specific. Unlike other countries with a similar level of GDP per capita and overall economic activity, Serbia has a relatively high level of home ownership. Out of a total of around 2.7 million housing units, 97.88 percent are in the ownership of private individuals (Statistical Office of the Republic of Serbia 2002). While official information about housing rentals in Serbia is not available (it is largely in the area of gray economy), there is strong anecdotal evidence that a large majority of housing units are owner-occupied.

There are several reasons for such a high level of home ownership. First, throughout the socialist era, private home ownership was never illegal. To a certain extent, even in those times, mortgage lending was conducted and private homeownership was possible and inheritable. However, a vast majority of housing units were given to the employees by their government-owned companies,[2] and with a so-called "tenancy right." This right was permanent and inheritable and was de facto quasi-private ownership. There was no down payment and no monthly mortgage payments. Tenants were obliged to pay only symbolic monthly rents. Second, at the beginning of the 1990s, privatization of apartments by their tenants was conducted, with merely symbolic payments to the state.[3] Hence, most of the real estate built in the socialist era gradually became privately owned by their tenants. Third, a vast majority of the real estate development during the 2000s was conducted with the intention of selling to the homeowners rather than for rental purposes. That additionally increased the number of homeowners.

Real Estate Prices and Mortgage Financing

In the past 10 years the Serbian housing market has developed along lines similar to many other East and Southeast European economies, with some specific features. Since the banking system was in disarray prior to 2001, mortgage lending, as a rule, was limited to "privileged individuals" and was treated more as a favor and a partial gift than as a legitimate and profitable banking business. As the banking reform and macro-economic stabilization started yielding results, mortgage lending started modestly in 2002 and 2003 and then progressively increased in the rest of the years of the past decade. The prices per square meter of housing units in the past 10 years had two periods of a more pronounced increase. The first period (2002–2003) coincided with the introduction of the euro and the beginning of mortgage lending banking activities.[4] The second period (2007–2008) coincided with high capital inflows into the country. An additional factor leading to an increase in housing prices in that period are activities of the National Mortgage Insurance Corporation (NMIC). In Exhibit 11.6 we depict evolution of the average prices of newly constructed housing units in Serbia. The prices are determined based on contractual values gathered in regular six-month surveys conducted by the Statistical Office of the Republic of Serbia.[5]

Yet another factor leading to a pronounced growth in housing prices in 2007–2008 has been nominal and real appreciation of the local currency, RSD,

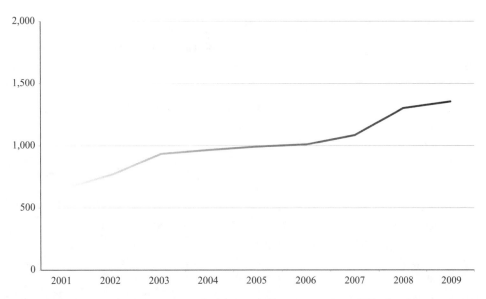

Exhibit 11.6   Average Prices of Newly Constructed Housing Units (EUR per Square Meter)
Source: National Bank of Serbia.

against the EUR. This made mortgages more affordable. Since the hyperinflation period (1991–1993), confidence in the local currency RSD was never fully regained. Long-term mortgages are being issued in RSD indexed to exchange rate of RSD mainly against EUR or Swiss francs (CHF). Since the borrowers rely on income denominated in RSD and have mortgage payments linked to a foreign currency, the exchange rate risk is being taken by the borrowers. This proves to be of systemic importance since more than 99 percent of the mortgage loans have been extended with a foreign currency clause (Exhibit 11.7).

Repossession and Foreclosure Practices

The new Law on Mortgage enacted in 2005 has prescribed a relatively simple and feasible out-of-court procedure for foreclosure by the mortgage lender (Official Gazette of the Republic of Serbia 2005). If the mortgage loan has been issued with a contract containing all the necessary clauses prescribed by the law, in case of default by the mortgage borrower (with his payments past due) an out-of-court procedure can be conducted in the following six steps:

1. The mortgage lender issues a written warning to the borrower and offi-cially initiates the out-of-court foreclosure procedure. This warning, among other things, stipulates the mortgage contract and mortgaged real estate payments are past due, and also stipulates the time frame for fulfillment of obligations of the borrower in order to avoid a real estate sale.
2. If the borrower has not fulfilled his obligation within 30 days after re-ceiving the warning, the mortgage lender issues a written warning of sale to the borrower. This warning of sale, among other things, stipulates the

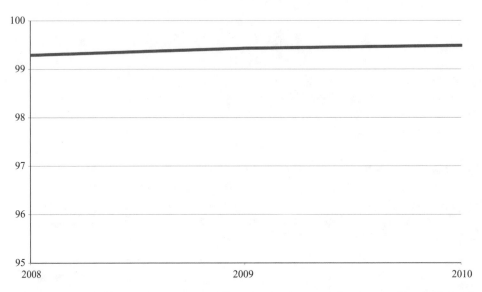

Exhibit 11.7   Foreign Currency–Denominated Mortgage Lending as a Share of Total Lending (%)

Note: The last data point refers to the first half of 2010.

Source: National Bank of Serbia.

         mortgage contract and mortgaged real estate, information that the whole mortgage loan is past due, chosen method of sale, and time frame for fulfillment of obligations of the borrower in order to avoid a real estate sale.

3. Simultaneously, the lender will issue a notice of mortgage sale to the Real Estate Cadastre, where it will be noted with restriction of sale to the owner of the real estate and permission for sale by the lender in 30 days if the borrower cannot prove otherwise.
4. Value of the real estate is then assessed by the court-appointed appraiser as a benchmark for a sale value of real estate.
5. Lender can then proceed with the auction of the real estate or with direct negotiation with potential buyers of the real estate.
6. If the amount received by the sale exceeds the outstanding value of the mortgage loan, the residual must be paid to the borrower. If the value is below the amount owed, the borrower remains liable for the remaining part of the loan. If necessary, the police are obliged to assist the lender in the out-of-court procedure.

Secondary Mortgage Market Prospects

The secondary mortgage market in Serbia has not been established yet. For some time now, the Law on Securitization has been in the pipeline. However, the recent global crisis and the role of securitization in its initiation have raised considerable concerns about the implementation of off-balance-sheet securitization in Serbia. Given the overall underdevelopment of securities markets in the country, the idea of a more conservative step toward securitization, through covered bonds

(*Pfandbriefe*), that is, on-balance-sheet securitization, seems to be more appropriate for Serbia. However, even for covered bonds, related legislation, especially concerning Serbian Bankruptcy Law and the Law on Banks, should be submitted to certain changes in order to fulfill the necessary prerequisites. As for the off-balance-sheet securitization of the mortgage-backed securities type, one has to bear in mind that current legislation in Serbia does not allow the possibility of avoiding double taxation of cash flows through the special purpose vehicles. In addition, the financial system does not fully recognize the function of instruments for credit risk mitigation, such as credit derivatives.

GOVERNMENT INTERVENTION IN THE HOUSING MARKET

Real Estate Registry Reform of 2003

Registration of ownership over real estate in Serbia has been traditionally diverse:

- Land books (Central European *Grundbuch* system), kept and maintained by land registry departments of municipal courts, may be found in major parts of Northern and Central Serbia.
- The Deed System existed in relatively limited areas of the country where land registries have not been introduced, mostly Southern and Western Serbia.
- Land Cadastre records on real estate and the owner/beneficiary, kept by Land Surveyor Authority (LSA).

Traditionally, Serbia had a considerable number of unregistered real estates, and those that were registered were frequently not updated. This resulted in a discrepancy of data between Cadastre and Land Books.

At the beginning of the reform process following the political changes of 2000, Serbian government realized that for mortgage lending development there needed to be a substantial improvement in the area of real estate ownership registration. The registration was not standardized on the whole territory of Serbia, it was incomplete and, to a large extent, not harmonized with the data from the land Cadastre. Where there were Land Books, they were held within the municipal courts and land Cadastre was within the municipal administration, producing additional costs for owners wishing to register their ownership by both means.

Since 2003, the reform process concerning real estate registration is ongoing in Serbia. With the assistance of the World Bank, the idea was to produce a new, unified, and more efficient real estate ownership registration system on the territory of the entire country.[6] All information on real estate registration is kept with the LSA. The major reform impetus was given by the amendments to the Law on State Survey and Cadastre and Registration of Rights over Real Estate from May 2002 (Official Gazette of the Republic of Serbia, 2002). With these amendments, preconditions were made for more efficient development of Real Estate Cadastre (REC) in municipalities without land books, and with a specific time frame for completion (three years). Another important feature of the Law was the possibility for development of licensed private land surveyor companies and for their active and important role in the future registration system. The aim was to improve customer service and to produce digital maps for Cadastre municipalities.

Legal professionals raised their doubts concerning the effectiveness of the new system (Orlić 2000). Namely, they questioned whether there was a step back by moving the land books from courts (as an independent branch of the government) to the LSA. Despite the theoretical disputes, project of implementation of a unified Real Estate Cadastre has been conducted, and by 2008 REC has been operational on more than 84 percent of the total number of Cadastre municipalities in Serbia.

Following the new Law on Mortgage, the Central Mortgage Registry (CMR) database was established in 2006 and kept by the LSA (Official Gazette of the Republic of Serbia 2005). In their mortgage lending procedures, banks in Serbia regularly use the facilities of the CMR and the Credit Bureau.[7]

The main goal of creating the CMR was to create a centralized database of all mortgages in the country. However, mortgages are not registered directly in the CMR by the parties in a mortgage contract. Instead, initial registration of the mortgage is done in the authorized real estate register (land book, real estate cadastre, or deed book). In practice, the CMR gathers data from initial mortgage registration sources in a unified database. The CMR database on real estate and mortgages can be browsed through the Internet.

Data on real estate in the CMR database include:

- Political municipality
- Cadastre municipality
- Number and sub-number of land plots
- Number of building structures within land plots
- Entrance number, floor number
- Number of separate parts within the building structure
- Address (street, house number)
- Purpose of the building structure
- Purpose of the separate parts of the building structure
- Floor space of the part of the building structure

Data on mortgages in the CMR database include:

- Date of the mortgage registration
- Date of the mortgage closure
- Duration of the mortgage
- Comments concerning the duration of the mortgage

National Mortgage Insurance Corporation (NMIC)

National Mortgage Insurance Corporation (NMIC) has been formed according to the Law on National Mortgage Insurance Corporation with a primary purpose of making mortgage loans more affordable to the population of Serbia. Starting its operations in October 2004, NMIC proved to become one of the pillars of the increasing mortgage penetration in Serbia. It is based on the Canadian model and accordingly created with the assistance of Canada Mortgage and Housing Corporation. NMIC provides insurance on mortgage loans approved by banks to citizens for the purpose of construction, purchase, or renovation of housing units. Commercial banks first conclude a mortgage insurance agreement with the NMIC. Following that first step, banks offer eligible individual loans for insurance by the NMIC. If NMIC approves an individual mortgage loan insurance request, it takes on 75 percent of the loss incurred by the bank given default of an insured mortgage loan. Substantially absorbing the default risk, the NMIC significantly reduces the total risk of the bank. This leads to a reduction of interest rates charged by the bank thus making mortgages more affordable. NMIC has a policy of capping the interest rates that could be charged by the bank for specific types of mortgage loans.

NMIC prescribes certain eligibility criteria for a mortgage loan, client, and a real estate. Total amount of NMIC insured mortgage loans on September 2010 was 1971 million euros, of which more than 282 millions were mortgage loans with government subsidy for young couples (couples below the age of 45).

Government Mortgage Loan Subsidies and Bank Reserve Requirements

In recent years, the Serbian government has been actively involved in promoting and subsidizing mortgage lending. All of the subsidy programs have a similar structure. Eligible applicants would finance their real estate purchase 75 percent with a bank loan, 20 percent with a government mortgage loan and 5 percent with a down payment.[8] Mortgage loans would be insured by NMIC. The government-provided loan portion is either interest-free or nearly interest-free. In addition, it has a large grace period. Some of the programs request a life insurance policy to be purchased by the applicant, property insurance policy for the real estate, and interest rate ceilings (expressed in absolute terms or relative to EURIBOR interest rate) for the bank loan. Most recent models provide two-year government coverage of an interest rate portion of the monthly annuity mortgage loan payment.

The following list provides examples of programs sponsored in recent years:

- Government subsidy for young couples' first housing unit purchase (2005–2008).
- Program for long-term mortgage financing in 2008.
- Program for long-term mortgage financing for professionals in health care industry in 2008.
- Program for long-term mortgage financing for military personnel in 2008 and 2010.
- Measures to support construction industry through subsidizing mortgage loan interest rates and long-term mortgage financing in 2009 and 2010.
- Eligibility groups in these programs were determined by age or profession. The loans were limited to 30 years of maturity, and could be granted up to a maximum amount of €100,000.

Apart from subsidies, there has also been a specific NMIC insured mortgage lending promotion measure. Namely, from April 2004, by the decision of the National Bank of Serbia, the amount of extended mortgage loans insured by NMIC is to be subtracted from the amount of deposits, credits and other liabilities of banks

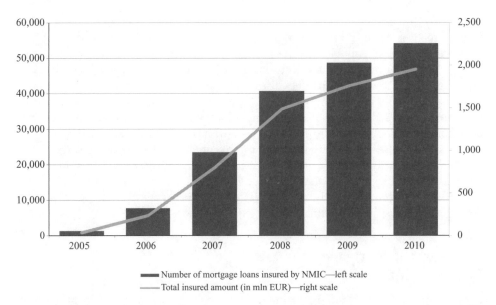

Exhibit 11.8 The Number of Subsidized Mortgage Loans: Total Amount Insured by NMIC (Millions of EUR)
Note: The last data points refer to July 2010.
Source: National Mortgage Insurance Corporation.

for the purpose of calculation of reserve requirements. It is expected that this atypical measure will be abandoned in 2010.

During 2010, government subsidies in mortgage lending are proving to be vital for the severely hampered mortgage lending. Exhibit 11.8 shows the number of mortgage loans insured by NMIC between 2005 and 2010, while Exhibit 11.9 displays the total subsidized amount (with respect to the total amount) of mortgage loans issued in Serbia in the same period. Clearly, there was an increasing pattern in both the number and the amount of loans issued. Moreover, the fraction of subsidized loans was also gradually increasing. However, there is an obvious effect of the crisis past 2008, exhibited in a reduced rate of growth of mortgage loans in general, again both in number and the amount.

IMPACT OF BANK ACTIVITIES ON PRICES OF RESIDENTIAL REAL ESTATE

Égert and Mihaljek (2007) have shown that residential real estate prices in Europe depend strongly on the lending activity of banks. They have found a positive correlation between real estate prices and credit expansion in OECD countries as well as in transition countries of Central and Eastern Europe (CEE). The price elasticity of mortgage credit demand in OECD countries is more than double that in CEE countries, 0.96 versus 0.41, respectively. Also, a well-known stylized fact is that a decrease in interest rates is typically positively related to demand for housing and, thus, to the growth of real prices of housing units. Price sensitivity of real estate prices to interest rate changes is higher in transition countries than in

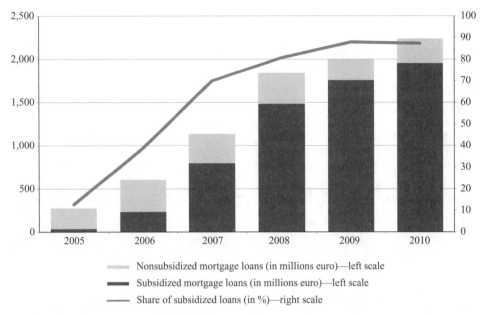

Exhibit 11.9 The Loan Amount of Subsidized and Non-Subsidized Mortgage Loans (Millions of EUR): Share of Subsidized Loans
Note: The last data points refer to July 2010.
Source: National Bank of Serbia and Ministry of Finance of the Republic of Serbia.

OECD countries by a factor of approximately 2.5. It is reasonable to assume that qualitatively similar relationships exist in the case of Serbia, although they are hard to quantify due to a lack of data.

After 2000, the initial level of total loans offered by banks was very low. At the end of 2001 it amounted to only 10.5 percent of GDP. An intense growth in lending activities started in 2003 after the entrance of foreign banks into the market. By the end of 2004, the total amount of extended loans reached 20 percent of GDP (Vuković 2009). A credit boom, primarily in the segment of retail banking activities was registered between 2004 and 2007. In the second half of 2008, as a result of the world financial crisis, the overall credit activity decreased dramatically. At the same time, real estate loans continued to grow both as a fraction of total retail loans and in absolute terms, although at reduced rates.

Continued growth of mortgage loans even through the crisis time is, in part, related to the fact that mortgage loans have received preferential treatment from the National Bank of Serbia. The average annual rate of growth for mortgage loans was 88 percent in the period between 2005 and 2008. During this period, the total amount of mortgage loans has increased by a factor of 6.6, while the total amount of retail loans increased by only around 44 percent.

Importantly, the increase in mortgage loans has been largely concentrated on a relatively small segment of newly constructed real estate. The main reason for this phenomenon is the institutional environment, which made the secondary trade of older housing units difficult. As explained above, all government-owned real estate was privatized during the 1990s according to a massive privatization

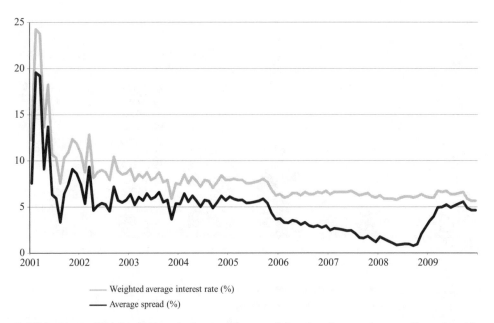

Exhibit 11.10 Weighted Average Interest Rates on Mortgage Loans: Average Spreads with Respect to Six-Month EURIBOR (in Percentage Points)
Source: National Bank of Serbia and EURIBOR-EBF.

scheme and with extremely low prices. The main problem of introducing this segment of real estate demand into the market is related to unclear ownership rights. Consequently, banks have largely been avoiding financing transactions in that segment of the market. Newly constructed housing units, on the other hand, typically do not face such difficultly. Under such circumstances, people who want to finance their real estate purchase prefer to buy new housing units to used ones.

Interest rates on mortgage loans in Serbia have a broadly decreasing trend. Exhibit 11.10 displays the evolution of weighted average interest rates on euro-denominated mortgage loans, between 2001 and 2009. As the graph shows, prior to 2006, most of the variation in the interest rates can be explained by variation in the average spread that the banks charge. Here, the spread was calculated as the difference between the weighted average interest rate and the six-month EURIBOR rate, the latter being the most common reference rate for euro-denominated mortgage loans. The average spread started to decline gradually in 2006, with the first significant takeoff of government subsidies on mortgage loans (cf. Exhibit 11.10). At the same time, banks kept their interest rates at relatively stable levels, accounting for the increase in EURIBOR rates. In 2008, as the global crisis spilled over into the Serbian financial sector, the spreads began to rise sharply, accounting for the greater default risk perceived by the banks. Meanwhile, the EURIBOR rates declined significantly, which absorbed the negative effect of increase in spreads, keeping the overall interest rates steady at their pre-crisis levels.

It is interesting to note that the combined effect of market and regulatory factors also kept the real estate prices in 2009 practically at their pre-crisis levels. In that respect, Serbia is an exception from a common trend of decreasing prices of real estate, especially for residential properties. At the same time, fundamental factors such as GDP growth rate, interest rates on commercial credits, and factors that influence credit and currency risk all moved in unfavorable directions. In fact, Minić (2010) shows that apartments in Belgrade, the capital, and the largest real estate market in Serbia, were on average overpriced by over 23 percent with respect to prices based purely on fundamentals. While there is no hard data on that, anecdotal evidence suggests that prices of housing units in 2009 stayed roughly unchanged in the segment of used housing (secondary trading) as well. It should be noted, however, that the number of transactions in that segment was negligible with respect to pre-crisis levels. It seems, therefore, that Serbian owners of real estate preferred not to complete a transaction rather than to offer a significant price reduction. It is questionable, however, whether this trend can be sustained in the future.

RISKS RELATED TO INVESTMENTS IN HOUSING MARKET IN SERBIA

The key risk related to investments in the Serbian housing market is legal risk (Bardhan et al. 2006). The first type of legal risk is represented by unclear property rights. First of all, there are still a substantial number of housing units in the country that are not properly registered. While a significant progress toward rectifying the problem has been made in the past few years, it is not completely resolved. In addition, the government has not yet addressed the demands for restitution of property rights stemming from the post–World War II nationalization drive. The Law on Restitution is being discussed but it is unclear when the restitution will take place and which forms it will take. This is an issue that can potentially impact the housing market in a serious way. Yet another type of legal risk, especially important when an investor plans to construct a new property, are slow and costly procedures required to secure the appropriate permits and complete the paperwork. Again, anecdotal evidence suggests that this cost is around 10 to 20 percent of the cost of the project. The government is currently working on a legislation that would address this problem and significantly streamline and speed up the procedures.

Liquidity risk is significant in Serbia. The bulk of transactions on the secondary housing market (i.e., trade in the existing properties) cannot be easily financed by a mortgage loan. That means that the buyer either needs to purchase an apartment with cash or in exchange of some other property. Clearly, this makes it difficult to complete a transaction, leading to low trading volumes. The volume of transactions on the secondary market is further eroded by a downward pressure by the macroeconomic fundamentals of the country since the global financial crisis commenced. Namely, while most people, whose principal asset is the housing units they possess, do not want to lower their asking price, they may not be finding any buyers at such prices. Many sellers apparently expect that the crisis will be relatively short-lived and that the demand on the secondary market will recuperate. Thus, they wait. On the other hand, if the crisis is prolonged (which is increasingly likely), they may start running out of cash (and patience). In that case, a fall in prices in that segment of the market would be imminent. On the new housing segment, the impact of the crisis is immediately apparent. New construction is all but halted and most developers are facing a severe liquidity crisis. While no hard data is available, some developers facing a liquidity crunch are starting to lower their asking prices. The government scheme to help boost the demand for new housing, described above, helped sustain price levels throughout 2009 but it is unclear to what extent this will be the case in 2010 and beyond, especially since the government itself is facing severe budget constraints.

Another risk worth addressing is the currency risk. In Serbia, prices of real estate are quoted (and transactions completed) in euros. The same is true with rents. As explained earlier in this chapter, mortgage loans are mostly indexed to euros. On the other hand, people's salaries are typically paid in RSD, the local currency. The salaries are typically not pegged to euros. As a result, while a euro-based investor may have the feeling that she is perfectly hedged from the exchange-rate risk, this risk creeps back as a default risk of a borrower (renter). Namely, in that case of a significant decrease in the value of Serbian currency with respect to the euro, the borrowers' ability to pay would be greatly diminished, leading them to default on their obligations. In a recent article, Božović et al. (2009) present a formal model describing this effect of the spillover of the exchange rate risk into default risk.

For a while, between 2003 and 2008, a strong influx of foreign investments, especially in the financial sector, kept the local currency strong. With the inception of the crisis new investments are harder to come by and banks are much more reluctant to lend. As the Serbian economy has been mostly import-oriented, this led to a 30 percent drop in the value of the currency, making it much more difficult for people to honor their obligations. While the number of borrowers' defaults in the housing market is still quite small (people would often do anything possible to keep the property of their residence as other residences are hard to come by), this effect, if continued, may put a substantial downward pressure on housing prices. The problem is likely to get greater as a result of an (expected) increase in EURIBOR rates.

In order to reduce the problem, the National Bank of Serbia recently initiated a drive to reduce dependence on hard currency–pegged loans. However, with small amounts of long-term RSD-denominated liabilities on banks' balance sheets, and hardly any foreign currency hedging instruments available, this will undoubtedly prove to be a challenge. High-risk premia in RSD-denominated loans make them still very unattractive. Whether any positive movement can be made in this area remains to be seen.

CONCLUSION

In the past decade, Serbia, the largest of the former Yugoslav republics, underwent a profound change. From a war-ravaged country with a world-record hyperinflation facing punishing international economic sanctions, it is increasingly becoming a modern society integrated into the world economy. Its institutions and markets, while still relatively underdeveloped, largely resemble those of other transition economies. The housing market is no exception. On the other hand, there are some interesting peculiarities of the Serbian housing market. In particular, most of the housing stock is privately owned, free and clear of any loans, as a result of a massive privatization drive 20 years ago. While new housing purchases are typically financed via mortgage loans, trade in the older housing units is often conducted via cash-only transactions. In this way, the market is divided into two distinct segments. The global financial crisis impacted the Serbian economy in significantly negative ways. On the other hand, curiously enough, thus far there was no appreciable reduction in housing prices as a result of the crisis. Whether such price stability will continue is uncertain, however, as an increasing number of people face reduced salaries, loss of jobs, and depletion of their cash reserves. The principal risks facing investors in the Serbian housing market are uncertain property rights and complicated and costly bureaucratic procedures, very low liquidity of the secondary market, and the possible spillover of the exchange into default risk due to an increasingly unstable local currency. As a positive consequence of the crisis, the Serbian economy is slowly but inevitably entering into a profound change of focus—from non-tradable to tradable goods. An increasing number of foreign companies are starting to open export-oriented businesses in the country. Employment growth and infusion of hard currency is likely to stabilize currency and have a positive impact on the housing market and financial institutions in the medium run. In addition, the accession process toward EU membership is likely to further improve Serbian institutions and regulatory regime.

NOTES

1. Inflation in this figure is expressed with available data on retail prices. A consumer price index (CPI) constructed in line with EU standards (Harmonized Index of Consumer Prices) is available since 2007.
2. Depending on their family situation, years of employment, level of education, and so forth.
3. Additionally reduced in real terms by the hyperinflation of 1993–1994.
4. Introduction of the euro at the beginning of 2002 had led to a real estate price increase in the Eurozone and other countries with deep penetration of the euro.
5. Note that prices in central districts of Belgrade and other larger cities have been 20 to 50 percent higher than the country average presented here.
6. World Bank Real Estate Cadastre & Registration Project (Serbia), Project ID P078311.
7. Serbia has a centralized database of overall indebtedness of physical and legal entities with financial institutions in Serbia. All commercial banks and leasing companies are members of the centralized Credit Bureau run by the Association of Serbian Banks. The Credit Bureau in Serbia was recently awarded the highest grade by the OECD publication index of investment reforms 2010 (for more information see www.ubs-asb.com).
8. In certain programs a down payment was not needed.

REFERENCES

Bardhan, A., R. Karapandža, and B. Urošević. 2006. "Valuing Mortgage Insurance Contracts in Emerging Market Economics." *Journal of Real Estate Finance and Economics* 32:1, 9–20.
Božović, M., B. Urošević, and B. Živković. 2009. "On the Spillover of Exchange-Rate Risk into Default Risk." *Economic Annals* 183, 32–55.
Drenovak, M., and B. Urošević. 2010. "Modeling the Benchmark Spot Curve for the Serbian Market." *Economic Annals* 184, 29–57.

Égert, B., and D. Mihaljek. 2007. "Determinants of House Prices in Central and Eastern Europe." BIS Working Papers, No. 236.

Hanke, S. H., and A. K. F. Kwok. 2009. "On the Measurement of Zimbabwe's Hyperinflation." *Cato Journal* 29:2.

Minić, B. 2010. "The Analysis of Real Estate Market in Belgrade for 2002–2009." In B. Živković and S. Stamenković, eds., *Economic Policy of Serbia in 2010*, pp. 291–297. Belgrade: Scientific Society of Economists and Faculty of Economics of the University of Belgrade.

National Bank of Yugoslavia. 2001. "Report on the Banking Sector in Federal Republic of Yugoslavia for 2001."

National Bank of Yugoslavia. 2002. "Report on the Banking Sector in Federal Republic of Yugoslavia for 2002."

National Bank of Yugoslavia. 2003. "Report on the Banking Sector in Federal Republic of Yugoslavia for 2003."

Official Gazette of the Republic of Serbia. 2002. No. 25/2002. See also No. 83/92, 53/93, 67/93, 48/94, 12/96, 15/96, and 34/2001.

Official Gazette of the Republic of Serbia. 2005. No. 115/05.

Orlić, M. 2000. "Introduction and Restoration of the Land Books—A Proposal for the Most Suitable Form of Public Real-Estate Registries in Serbia for the 21st Century." *Annals of the Faculty of Law, University of Belgrade* 1–6.

Statistical Office of the Republic of Serbia. 2002. "Population Census of 2002: Apartments. Book 2: Type, Property and Equipment—Data by Municipalities."

Vuković, V. 2009. "Structural Breaks and Performance of Banking in Serbia During 2002–2008." Institute of Economic Sciences, Belgrade.

ABOUT THE AUTHORS

DEJAN ŠOŠKIĆ was born in Belgrade in 1967. He graduated in 1989 from Belgrade University, Faculty of Economics, and obtained his MSc in monetary economics in 1993, and PhD in finance in 1999 from the same university. He is a Fulbright alumnus and member of the Presidency of the Scientific Association of Economists in Serbia. He was an Associate Professor at the Faculty of Economics in Belgrade. In 2002 he lectured at graduate and MBA courses at the University of Nebraska. For years he lectured on regional undergraduate courses organized by Vienna University of Economics and Business, and in Italy on Unicredit graduate courses in Banking. In 2002, he gave a series of guest speaker lectures at the universities of New Haven, Rhode Island, and Berkeley, California. He authored the book *Securities: Portfolio Management and Investment Funds* and co-authored *Financial Markets and Institutions, Economic Statistics*, and *Stock Exchange Glossary*. He has published more than 40 articles and papers in the field of financial markets and institutions and transition in Serbia. He served as a special financial markets advisor in the National Bank of Yugoslavia (2000–2002), economic policy advisor in the EU Policy and Legal Advice Centre (2002–2003), and was a member of the Council of the National Bank of Serbia (2003–2004) and its Chairman (2009–2010). He was appointed Governor of the National Bank of Serbia on 28 July 2010.

BRANKO UROŠEVIĆ holds a PhD in Finance from the University of California–Berkeley, and a PhD in Phyisics from Brown University. He is a Professor of Operations Research and Financial Economics at the Faculty of Economics, University of Belgrade, Serbia. Recently, he has been appointed Special Advisor to the Governor of National Bank of Serbia, in charge of research. He is also Chairman of the Board of Dunav dobrovoljni penzijski fond, the largest private pension fund in Serbia, and a Member of the Board of the Institute for Economic Studies, Belgrade, Serbia. In addition, he is a member of the Visiting Faculty at the Univeritat Pompeu Fabra, where he was an Assistant Professor in Finance from 2002 to 2005. He is the Director of the International Masters in Quantitative Finance (IMQF), the premier finance education program in Southeastern Europe. His research is published in *Journal of Political Economy, Management Science, Economic Theory, Real Estate Economics, Journal of Real Estate Finance and Economics,* and several other journals. In addition, he is the author of four books on finance. He has led and participated in various projects financed by the European Commission, Spain, the United States, and the BBVA Foundation. As a consultant he worked with McKinsey & Company and KPMG, among other firms. His research interests cover a wide range of topics in financial economics and real estate economics, with a focus on risk management, real estate finance, and the connection between corporate finance and asset pricing.

BOŠKO ŽIVKOVIĆ is a Full Professor of Finance at the Faculty of Economics, University of Belgrade. His areas of research and teaching interests are Financial Markets, Investments and Financial Economics. In his academic career he has published several noted papers in Serbian and international journals, as well as several monographies and textbooks. Živković was Chairman of the Security and Exchange Commission of the Federal Republic of Yugoslavia and the Republic of Serbia. He was, also, Deputy Minister of Finance of the Republic of Serbia as well as member of the Council of the National Bank of Serbia and member of the Economic Council to the Prime Minister of Serbia. In July 2010, Serbian national parliament elected him Chairman of the Board of Governors of the National Bank of Serbia.

MILOŠ BOŽOVIĆ holds a PhD in Economics from the University Pompeu Fabra, Barcelona, Spain (2009) and a PhD in Physics from the University of Belgrade, Serbia (2005). He is currently CEO of the Center for Investments and Finance, a Belgrade-based company specializing in risk management research, development, and consulting. Furthermore, he is Professor of Finance at the University of Novi Sad, Serbia, lecturer at the International Masters in Quantitative Finance program at the University of Belgrade, and Visiting Professor at the European Business School (Frankfurt metropolitan area, Germany). As a professional in the financial world, Dr. Božović has worked as a consultant on a number of projects in Europe and the Middle East, including projects for the World Bank, European Commission, Government of Catalunya, Department of Treasury of the Republic of Serbia, and the National Bank of Serbia. He also participated in or led several multiyear research projects in Serbia, Spain, and Greece. His research interests cover a range of topics in financial economics, with a focus on risk management, banking, and financial markets.

PART IV

Asia Housing Bubbles Past, Present, and Future: Contrasts among Asian Economic Giants

CHAPTER 12

Irrational Prosperity, Housing Market, and Financial Crisis

An Empirical Study of Beijing

LU PING
School of Public Administration, Renmin University of China, Beijing

ZHEN HUI
School of Public Administration, Renmin University of China, Beijing

XU YUEHONG
School of Finance, Renmin University of China, Beijing

In 1998, China's housing system entered into a rapid development stage after the country's all-around reform. In 2009, China's real estate investment occupied a proportion of 10.64 percent in GDP and 16.11 percent of the aggregate fixed-asset investment separately, and the real estate industry became one of the pillar industries for the Chinese macro-economy, and obviously made a great contribution to economic growth. As an important part of the real estate industry, with a dual attribute of the consumable and the investment goods, residential real estate is closely linked with the macro-economic situation.

The financial crisis that first burst out in the United States in 2007 and gradually spread to the whole world had a great impact on the Chinese economy and also made the Chinese housing market suffer an unprecedented downturn, which otherwise never occurred during the first decade of the twenty-first century. However, in conformity to the economic goal of "maintaining growth" established by the Chinese government, by virtue of a series of policies initiated to address the financial crisis, the Chinese housing market rebounded quickly in early 2009 and presents a status that is totally different from many other countries and districts at the present time.

This paper, by taking the Beijing housing market as an example, analyzes the different development tendencies of the Beijing housing market before, during, and after the financial crisis from three aspects—housing prices, sale of housing, and housing development and construction. Our study points out the problems and hidden troubles that possibly exist; analyzes and distinguishes the unreasonably high price of the housing market in Beijing at the present time, reveals the irrational factors that cause unreasonably high housing prices from the angle of behavioral economics, and, in the end, makes an evaluation of the targets and effects of the major regulation measures and policies adopted by the government in each market stage.

CHARACTERISTICS OF BEIJING HOUSING MARKET AND PRELIMINARY JUDGMENT

Housing Price Variation—before, during, and after the Global Financial Crisis

Exhibit 12.1 shows the monthly housing price in Beijing between 2005 and 2010. Generally speaking, it presents a fluctuant rise and can be divided into three stages: before, during, and after the global financial crisis. These stages differ largely in the variations in housing prices and the amplitude of variation.

Housing Price Continued to Rise (2005–2007)
The variation of housing price in Beijing was relatively mild in 2005 and 2006. The housing price rose from ¥6,820 per square meter in January 2005 to ¥8,759 per square meter in December 2006, and the rate of growth was 28.43 percent. But in 2007, the housing price presented a fluctuant rise and the amplitude of price fluctuation was large. The housing price was ¥13,746 per square meter at the end of 2007, which doubled the price in early 2005.

Housing Market Was in Downturn Stage and Housing Price Somewhat Declined (2008)
The financial crisis obviously has a great impact on the housing market in Beijing. The housing price has substantially declined for the first time in recent years. In September 2008, the housing price reached the lowest point, which was ¥8,548 per square meter. It has reduced by 37.65 percent from the highest point in September 2007, and it was nearly equivalent to the price at the end of 2006. Although the price slightly rebounded at the end of 2008, it still did not restore the level in 2007.

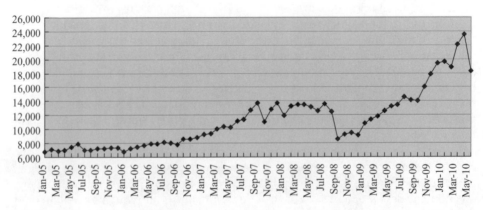

Exhibit 12.1   Housing Price in Beijing between 2005 and 2010 (¥/m²)
Source: Real estate database of SouFun.com.

Housing Price Has Rebounded Swiftly and Dramatically (Since 2009)
There has been a dramatic rebound in the housing market in Beijing ever since 2009, with the rate and amplitude of growth reaching a historical new high. Ever since early 2009, the housing price has surpassed the historical highest level within seven months, rose substantially thereafter, and broke ¥20,000 per square meter on average in early 2010. In the face of the continuously rising house prices, both the Central Government and Beijing Municipal People's Government have issued a series of regulations and control measures to restrain the rapid rise in housing prices. Hence, with the intervention of the regulation policies, housing prices slightly declined in the recent two months, but still maintained a high level of ¥18,000 per square meter.

Sales Volume Declines

The sales unit and sales area of housing in Beijing are basically synchronous; both have gradually reduced in recent years. As shown in Exhibit 12.2, especially in 2008, due to the influence of the global financial crisis, the housing sales unit and the sales area reached a low valley and reduced by 27.63 percent and 39.91 percent, respectively, from 2005 levels. Although there was a drastic rebound in the housing sales in 2009, the sales unit and the sales area were still lower than those in 2005.

At the end of 2009, the resident population of Beijing was 17.55 million, an increase of 10.21 percent from 2005; specifically, the registered population was 12.458 million, an increase of 5.51 percent above 2005. The swift growth of urban resident population and migrant population objectively creates more demand for housing, and, in addition, residents demanded improved housing conditions; this demand does not match with a decline in housing sales volumes. There are mainly two explanations for the situation: (1) the housing price is too high for the majority

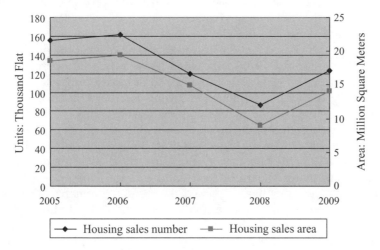

Exhibit 12.2   Units and Area of Housing Sales in Beijing between 2005 and 2009
Source: Real estate database of SouFun.com.

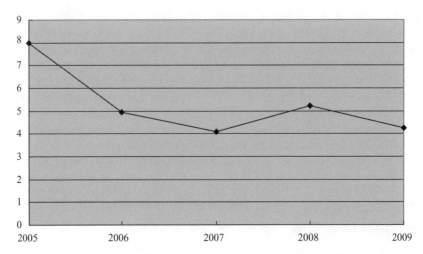

Exhibit 12.3 Housing Vacancies in Beijing between 2005 and 2009 (Million m^2)
Source: Real estate database of SouFun.com.

of potential buyers, and (2) many investors are playing wait-and-see and anticipating market variations.

A Large Quantity of Vacant Dwellings and a High Housing Price Coexist

Exhibit 12.3 shows the housing vacancies in Beijing between 2005 and 2009; we can see in the exhibit that the amount of vacant housing in Beijing has continually decreased since 2005. Although the vacant area increased due to a real estate market downturn under the influence of the financial crisis in 2008, it has somewhat dropped owing to the swift market rebound ever since 2009 and has reached 4.26 million square meters; this means that probably 47,333 flats were vacant (provided that the average flat area was 90 square meters). According to Beijing Statistical Yearbook, the city's registered population was 3.639 million households in 2008. Based on the result of the investigation on 5,000 urban households, the urban residents' self-owned house rate is 80.9 percent. On these grounds, approximately 695,049 households don't have a house with ownership rights. Presently, the vacant dwellings in Beijing can solve the dwelling problem of about 6.8 percent of the households with ownership rights.

Under the background of the quick recovery and warm-up of the Beijing real estate market in 2009, there are three possible explanations for the high rate of vacant housing: (1) as the housing price continually rises, some developers care only for their self-interest, hoard property, and wait for a top price before selling; (2) the high housing price has surpassed the resident's purchasing power, and some residents who really have a residential demand can only bemoan the high price; and (3) the continuous rise in housing price offers speculators a positive expectation: they buy a lot of house property, wait for price hikes, and resell at a profit, and they don't buy houses as primary residence—hence a lot of housing is left vacant.

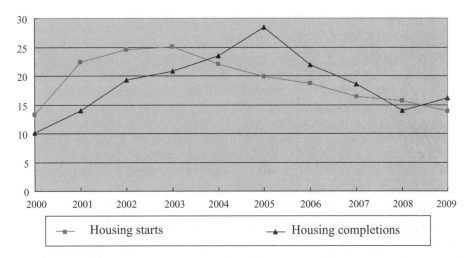

Exhibit 12.4   Housing Starts and Housing Completions in Beijing between 2000 and 2009 (Million Square Meters)
Source: Real estate database of SouFun.com.

Both Housing Starts and Completions Decrease

Exhibit 12.4 presents the housing starts and completions in Beijing ever since 2000. They reached their highest point in 2003 and 2005 separately, and gradually declined thereafter. There are two major reasons for this: land and funds. On February 11, 2004, Beijing Municipal People's Government issued the *Supplementary Provisions on the End of Contracted Transfer of Profit-Oriented State-Owned Land Use Right*, according to which all profit-oriented land transfers should be acquired through bid invitation, public offering, and auction in Beijing after August 31, 2004. Prior to the decline, there was a sharp rise in the volume of land-related business in 2003, along with a rise in land price. Subsequently, land transactions obviously declined, while housing starts reached the historical low point. Providing that construction time for an average dwelling is two years, after the real estate development summit in 2003 housing completions reach their maximum value in 2005, and this can explain why the housing vacant areas are far higher than that of other years (see Exhibit 12.3). In 2008, under the influence of financial crisis, due to the tense capital chain and the slow capital circulation speed of many real estate enterprises, a lot of housing under construction or otherwise being developed was in a shutdown state, and there was a substantial drop in both housing starts and completions.

Causes for Variations in Housing Market

Judging from the variations in housing prices, housing sales, and housing construction, Beijing's housing market is closely related to the country's economic situation and is greatly influenced by the international financial crisis. However, judging from the price level, the negative influence of the financial crisis on Beijing's housing market lasted less than six months. The high recovery speed and the strong rebound strength found in Beijing since 2009 are very rare all over the world. The unique response of the Beijing housing market primarily stems from the following four factors.

The Domestic Real Estate Finance Market Isn't Mature

The Chinese real estate finance market is still in a growth stage. Lenders give priority to a buyer's credit history, and the other modes of financing—such as financing from stock market funds, REITs, bonds financing, fund financing, and so forth—occupy only a small proportion of real estate financing. What's more, either for mortgages extended to home buyers or for loans granted to real estate development enterprises, banks conduct a strict examination prior to granting the loan, and this guarantees financial security to a certain extent.

The Real Economy Is Damaged, and a Lot of Funds Flow into the Real Estate Industry

The international financial crisis has a great influence on the Chinese real economy. In particular, in the southeastern coastal areas, many export-oriented processing industry factories have either closed or been bankrupted due to reduced orders and capital flow, and a great number of workers are unemployed. Under these circumstances, a large quantity of the funds invested in the real economy have flowed into the real economy or real estate industry. As a capital city, Beijing is a preferred area for real estate investors.

International "Hot Money" Flows into China in Large Quantities

In recent years, the swift growth of the Chinese economy has bolstered the prosperity of the securities market and the real estate market, the prices of various assets have continually risen, and all this activity has attracted international "hot money." Besides, given the continuous depreciation of the American dollar and the expectation for a continuous appreciation of RMB (renminbi, or yuan), a large amount of "hot money" represents arbitrage in the domestic market, whereas the hot money mostly flows into the real estate investment field with a rapid increase in value and a high profit margin.

A Lot of "Bailout" Policies Are Issued

As one of the pillar industries for the national economy, the decline of the real estate industry will surely influence the overall economic development level. Moreover, as the finance of local government relies heavily upon income from the land, the depression of the real estate industry will surely have an influence on the local finance. To guarantee continuous economic growth, the Central Government and the local governments have issued a series of credit and taxation policies that can stimulate a resurgence of the real estate industry. Of course, while promoting the rapid recovery of the Beijing housing market and the stabilization of social and economic development, these policies are partly responsible for the swift growth of housing prices and the irrational prosperity of the Beijing housing market since 2009. The section titled "Analysis of Irrational High Housing Price" later in this chapter introduces in detail the main regulation policies that the government has implemented in each stage and the problems that possibly exist.

STUDY OF THE UNREASONABLY HIGH HOUSING PRICE IN BEIJING

A Coordinated Analysis of Housing Price and Economic Fundamentals

The housing price is closely linked with the macroeconomy. In an efficient housing market, the housing price is dependent upon economic fundamentals. There are many economic indexes that influence the housing price but, among them, GDP, per capita disposable income, the resident population, and land price are the most important indexes that influence housing price. The GDP reflects the overall prosperity of the local economy; the residential population reflects the rigid demand for housing; the per capita disposable income reflects the resident's ability to purchase housing; the land price reflects the land supply situation, whereas the land supply will influence the supply of dwellings. These indexes are closely related to the housing price.

The analysis is based on the data between 2001 and 2009. As Exhibit 12.5 shows, in Beijing between 2001 and 2009 the growth rate of GDP basically remained stable

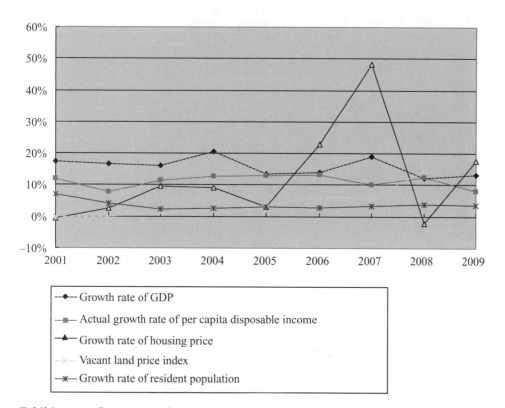

Exhibit 12.5 Comparisons between the Growth of Housing Price and the Growth of Related Economic Indexes in Beijing

Sources: Real estate database of SouFun.com (housing price growth rate, vacant land price index), statistical database of www.cei.gov.cn (growth rate of GDP, actual growth rate of per capita disposable income, growth rate of resident population).

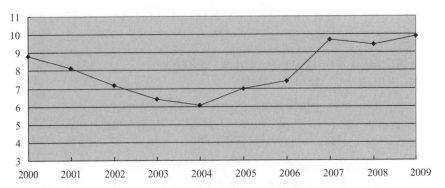

Exhibit 12.6   Price-to-Income Ratio in Beijing's Housing Market between 2000 and 2009
Sources: Real estate database of SouFun.com; statistical database of www.cei.gov.cn.

and was 10 percent to 20 percent; the growth rate of resident population decreased to 3.54 percent in 2009 from 6.93 percent in 2001 because of the family planning policy of China and the restrictions of the household registration system in Beijing. The stable growth of resident population indicated that there was a stable growth in demand for housing. The growth rate of per capita disposable income was also stable. The growth rate of land prices was substantial, and they maintained a steady upward trend.

However, there was a big fluctuation in the growth rate of housing price in Beijing; in particular there was a negative effect in 2008. But the variation of the factors that influence the housing price is very stable, so the fluctuation of housing price can hardly be explained by the economic fundamentals. The different variation tendencies of housing price and economic fundamentals show that the housing price in Beijing is not only under the influence of the economic fundamentals, but also under the interference of other factors.

A Comparison between Housing Price and Resident's Income

Exhibit 12.6 shows the housing price-to-income ratio ever since 2000 with the assumptions that a household consists of three family members, the per capita income is the per capita disposable income of the urban population in Beijing, and a 60-square-meter house is to be purchased.

Compared with the reasonable range of the world housing price-to-income ratio, which is three to six times, the housing price-to-income ratio of Beijing is obviously higher. In particular, it has risen substantially after 2004 and approached 10 in 2009. What's more, in China, the allocation of income is not ideal, the Gini coefficient is high, there is a big gap between the rich and the poor, low-income population is substantial, and the housing price has far surpassed the affordability of the low-income group and the ordinary working-class.

A Comparison between Housing Price and Rental Price

In an efficient housing market, the housing price is the capitalization of future rent. Thus, the housing price and the rent price have a positive correlation and maintain

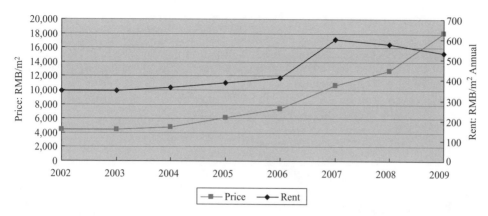

Exhibit 12.7 Comparison of Housing Price and Rental Price in Beijing between 2002 and 2009

Sources: Real estate database of SouFun.com (housing price); statistical database of www.cei.gov.cn (data on renting).

a similar change tendency; otherwise, a discrepancy indicates a deviation either in housing price or rental price.

According to Exhibit 12.7, housing price has continually risen ever since 2002, even during 2008 when the housing market was affected by the global financial crisis. Before the financial crisis, the change tendencies of rental and housing prices were almost consistent with each other, but after that, rent in Beijing experienced an apparent decrease, and this trend didn't change until 2009. Relative to rental price, housing price in Beijing is continuing to increase and is unreasonably high, as it jumped to about ¥18,000 per square meter in 2009.

Study of the "Over-fluctuation" of Housing Price

"Over-fluctuation" means that the actual price fluctuation of assets exceeds the theoretical price fluctuation. This phenomenon was first identified by Shiller (1981) and LeRoy and Porter (1981), almost simultaneously. We merely make a comparative analysis of the theoretical price fluctuation and actual price fluctuation of the Beijing housing market.

Shiller (1987) obtained the "theoretical stock price" method by means of the restoration of the stock dividend while studying the irrational fluctuation of stock price. We can use this method for reference, and utilize the rental price to restore the "theoretical price" of housing. The theoretical price can be understood as the rational market price. As the rental price reflects the real demand for housing, we can obtain the theoretical price of housing by means of the restoration of rent. Moreover, this theoretical price can vividly reflect the housing price that is dependent upon the true housing demand. By comparing the fluctuation parameters of the theoretical price that is calculated on the basis of the rental price with the fluctuation parameters of the actual housing price, we can make a judgment on the rationality of the actual housing price.

The parameters that can measure the fluctuation of asset price include the fluctuation ratio, coefficient of dispersion, and so forth. As all data are in the exponential form, it is best to adopt the coefficient of dispersion for measuring the fluctuation of housing price.

According to the traditional real estate appraisal theory, the housing price is a discount of the future rent income of house property. Provided that P_t^* represents the theoretical price of house at t moment, D_i represents the actual rent from t moment to i year, r represents the ratio of income capitalization, this thinking can be expressed in the following equation:

$$P_t^* = \sum_{i=1}^{\infty} \frac{D_i}{(1+r)^i} \tag{12.1}$$

We herein assume that the house rent array satisfies the independent identical distribution condition, and get the dispersion coefficient of theoretical price $V(P_t^*)$:

$$V(P_t^*) = \frac{\sigma(P_t^*)}{\mu(P_t^*)} = \frac{\sigma(D)}{\mu(D)} \sqrt{\frac{r}{r+2}} \tag{12.2}$$

Among which, $\sigma(P_t^*)$ represents the standard deviation of the housing theoretical price P_t^*, $\mu(P_t^*)$ represents the mean value of the theoretical housing price P^*. $\sigma(D)$ represents the standard deviation of the actual rental price, $\mu(D)$ represents the mean value of the actual rental price.

$\sigma(D)$ and $\mu(D)$ can be directly calculated through the data sample; the main content of the ratio of income capitalization r is the rate of risk return on real estate investment, namely the rate of return on the investment in real estate. The rate of return can be obtained through the real estate market survey. According to the result of investigation on the real estate appraisal enterprises in Beijing, income capitalization ratio of the Beijing real estate industry is about 8 percent between 2005 and 2009.[1]

View the monthly data of the housing price index and rental price index in Beijing between 2005 and 2009 that are quoted from SouFun China real estate index system and used as the sample data. Calculate on the basis of the above formula:

Dispersion coefficient of theoretical housing price fluctuation: $V(P_t^*) = 0.0275$.

If in formula (2), we replace theoretical housing price P_t^* with actual housing price P_t, dispersion coefficient of actual housing price will be calculated: $V(P_t) = 0.1403$.

It shows that, between 2005 and 2009, the dispersion coefficient of the theoretical housing price that is calculated through rent restoration is 0.0275. It is far lower than the dispersion coefficient of the actual housing price, which is 0.1403. Therefore, we can say that there is an over-fluctuation in the actual housing price with respect to the actual housing price, but the variation of the rental price can hardly provide an explanation for the overfluctuation.

The above analysis shows, by utilizing the universally acknowledged measuring indexes, that the housing price in Beijing is not only unreasonably high, but also presents the features of overfluctuation, and that these features cannot be explained by the economic fundamentals; therefore, the causes must be complex and difficult to ascertain.

CAUSES FOR IRRATIONAL HIGH HOUSING PRICE

What are the root causes for unreasonable price hikes? What about the influence of financial crisis on housing price? Exhibit 12.8 gives a possible explanation of irrational effects in the housing market. Three market subjects are included: individual investors, companies, and local governments. It attempts to analyze the root cause for the over-fluctuation of housing price in Beijing from the irrational angle.

Speculators' Irrational Behavior Accelerates the Growth of the Housing Price Bubble

The Effect of "Myth" in the Housing Market

As the housing price in Beijing has presented a double-digit growth in recent years, it has formed a myth that the housing price "merely rises but seldom falls" and even "continually rises and never falls." It is very similar to the myth that has prevailed in society before the burst of the American real estate bubble and was summarized by the American economist Shiller (2009).[4] As a matter of fact, ever since 1998 when the housing market was formed in the real sense, till the subprime crisis, the Chinese housing market has almost never undergone any obvious fall in the housing price. That is to say, the Chinese housing market has not yet undergone a complete cycle of rise and fall, and the same is true for the Beijing housing market. This is a major reason for the number of investors who swarm into the housing market. On the other hand, the housing market attracts a lot of funds, investors, and even common people, and it seems that "everyone who has enough money engages in real estate speculation." Apart from individual investors, a lot of production enterprises, including state-owned enterprises, invest the capital that ought to be used in the production field into the real estate industry.

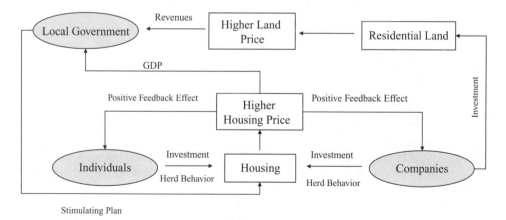

Exhibit 12.8   Irrational Causes of High Housing Price

As some people make a profit by investing in housing, more and more people are attracted to the housing market investment and speculation.

The "Positive Feedback Effect" of Housing Price

When owing to either inadequate or a complete lack of information investors cannot make a rational judgment of the direction of a market, they usually resort to observing the behavior of the people surrounding them. Because many people will be responding to limited information in roughly the same ways or they will tend to mutually reinforce one another's opinions, herding behavior emerges. When people "buy at a price hike and sell at a price fall," the violent ups and downs in the real estate market price will be exacerbated. Given this kind of situation and long-term continuous price hikes, the public cognition that the housing price will continue to rise is strengthened; people will think they are meeting an unprecedented favorable market investment opportunity. This impression is reinforced by the further rise in housing price, which further encouragese herd behavior. The feedback effect of viewpoint and fact will go on and further intensify the faith in the continuous housing price hikes. In the long run, a great number of people swarm into the market and buy real property, and consequently form a great pool of investment demand and speculative demand.

Local Government's Irrational Behavior Makes Housing Bubble Impervious to Financial Crisis

In 2008 and the first half of 2009 when the global financial bubble burst, housing price stopped rising and even dropped somewhat. This was the first time that the housing price in Beijing dropped in the past 10 years.

This was supposed to be the best chance to pierce the housing market bubble and force the housing market to behave in a rational manner. However, the continual rise of housing price had garnered huge political and economic interests, reflected not only in the GDP but also in revenues from land transfers. Therefore, the local government quickly made a bailout plan to stimulate the real estate market. The funding was used to resume production in the housing market; housing price rose quickly after a temporary fall, and the growth rate of housing price even surpassed the rate prior to the financial crisis. The influence of the financial crisis on the Beijing housing market was swiftly erased by the bailout policy issued by the local government, whereas the price risk of that housing market had been further increased.

The accumulation of housing stock was sustained until April 2010, when the price markup surpassed the public's yield limit. In face of the high pressure from public opinion, the government issued restrictive measures on the granting of housing loans and the number of flats purchased, and spread the news that a real estate tax would be imposed on those involved in hoarding and speculation. These measures have caused a change in the people's expectations of housing price. The behavior of a lot of real estate investors and speculators has been effectively restrained and the housing price has stopped rising and begun to slightly decline.

However, the housing price bubble in Beijing has not yet burst, and there isn't a tide of underselling at the present time.

CENTRAL GOVERNMENT'S REGULATION POLICIES AND HOUSING MARKET

Land, credit, and taxation are three major measures for the regulation of the real estate market by the Chinese government. In light of the variations in housing market and the regulation objectives in each stage: Before, during and after the financial crisis, the Central Government and Beijing Municipal Government have issued some policies to restrain the high price markup and guarantee the healthy development of the real estate market. The following summarizes the related policies issued by the Central Government and offers a brief evaluation of the implementation effect together with the problems presented by these policies.

Stabilizing Housing Market by Increasing Land Supply and Regulating Land Supply Structure

The acquisition of land is a key link in the housing construction. For a city like Beijing with a large population, high housing demand, and real estate investment fever, an inch of land is worth an inch of gold and there is a keen competition among real estate developers who strive to win the right to land use. The competition expedites the formation of high-priced land blocks and boosts the pressure on price markup. In order to relieve the pressure, increase the housing supply, and solve the housing shortage, when the housing price rose quickly before the global financial crisis and then rebounded substantially soon afterward, the Central Government issued many effective land supply policies. For example, "In the city where ordinary housing and the affordable housing are in short supply and the housing price rises substantially, appropriately increase the land supply and heighten the proportion of the land used for residential purpose in the land supply, according to relevant provisions".

Exhibit 12.9 shows the variations in the total planned supply of residential land in Beijing between 2005 and 2010. It indicates that the total planned supply of residential land has continually decreased in recent years. However, due to the high markup rate in 2009, the planned supply of residential land increased in 2010, the total supply reached 2,500 hectares, which almost doubled the total supply in 2009.

In order to solve housing difficulties for low and medium income families, the Central Government has consecutively issued a series of land policies to regulate the land supply structure, which includes reducing land supply for high-grade residential buildings and giving priority to the land supply for medium and small-sized flats. According to relevant polices, the government will continue to stop the supply of land for building villas and strictly control the supply of land for high-grade residential buildings. Ever since June 1, 2006, for the construction projects of the newly approved and newly started housing, the proportion of the dwellings with a unit building area that is less than 90 square meters (including affordable housing) must be over 70 percent of the total floor space. A priority shall be given to the land supply for medium and low-priced, medium and small-sized flat-type ordinary housing (including affordable housing) and the low-rent housing. The

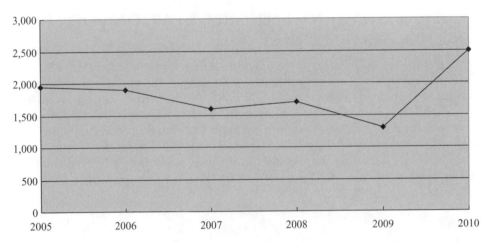

Exhibit 12.9 Planned Supply of Residential Land in Beijing between 2005 and 2010 (Hectare)
Source: Data available at www.bjgtj.gov.cn/publish/portal0/.

annual land supply of these kinds houses shall be no less than 70 percent of the total land supply of residential houses.

Meanwhile, along with the progress of the "Project for People's Well-being," a lot of affordable housing has been completed, and the land supply for this kind of housing has been continually increased. As shown in Exhibit 12.10, the total land supply for affordable housing accounts for 50 percent of the total residential land supply in 2010. As affordable housing is in limited quantity and is available to only a certain urban group, and there is a certain restriction on the transactions, its

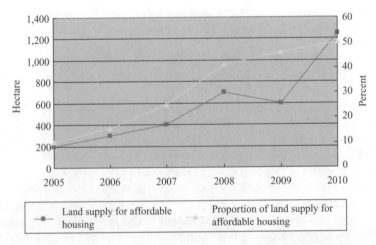

Exhibit 12.10 Planned Supply and Supply Ratio of Land for Affordable Housing in Beijing between 2005 and 2010
Source: Data available at www.bjgtj.gov.cn/publish/portal0/.

Exhibit 12.11   Premium Price Rate of the Transfer of Housing Estates in Beijing

Sample Size & Premium Price Range Year	Total Sample Size	Premium Price Rate 0	0~0.3	0.3~0.5	0.5~1	1~2	>2
2005	29	51.72%	31.03%	3.45%	6.90%	3.45%	3.45%
2006	56	23.21%	46.43%	10.71%	14.29%	5.36%	0.00%
2007	55	10.91%	32.73%	12.73%	14.55%	16.36%	12.73%
2008	49	22.45%	40.82%	6.12%	6.12%	14.29%	10.20%
2009	51	21.57%	23.53%	9.80%	17.65%	23.53%	3.92%
Grand Total	240	23.33%	35.42%	9.17%	12.50%	13.33%	6.25%

Source: Beijing Land Coordination and Reservation Center (www.bjtd.com).

affect on stabilizing housing price is limited. Nonetheless, this plays an important role in solving the housing problems of medium and low-income families.

Control Land Supply Price and Restrain Land Speculation

Exhibit 12.11 shows the land premium price rate of 240 housing estate samples (within eight districts), as published by the Beijing Land Coordination and Reservation Center between 2005 and 2009. It is calculated on the basis of the ratio of the last transaction price and the base transfer price.[2] We see that in the past few years, 76.67 percent of land transactions were concluded at a transfer price that was higher than the base price, and that the premium price rate of nearly 20 percent of the pieces of land was over 100 percent, and was far in excess of the base transfer price. In 2007, 2008, and 2009, land transactions with over 100 percent premium price rate account for 29.09 percent, 24.49 percent, and 27.45 percent of the total transaction volume, respectively. Especially in 2007, the final transaction price of 12.73 percent of the housing estate doubled the base transfer price.

In order to control the high markup rate of land price and prevent land transfers at unreasonably high prices, on the basis of restricting the flat type and controlling the housing price, the Central Government and the local government adopted measures to introduce land price competition and housing price competition. These measures explore new land transfer models, such as "comprehensive bid evaluation,"[3] "one-off quotation,"[4] "two-way quotation,"[5] and so forth; avoid the shortcomings of the traditional land transfer mode, for example, "the one who offers the highest price obtains the land"; and to feasibly restrain the unreasonable markup of the transfer price of housing estate.

To crack down on land speculation, the local government issues the strictest policies. The developers competing for land must provide a performance bond that is not less than 20 percent of the lowest transfer price, sign the land transfer contract within 10 workdays after the transaction is concluded, provide an down payment that accounts for 50 percent of the total transfer price within one month after the signing of contract, pay the remaining sum in a timely manner according to the contract, and ensure that they will pay up no later than within one year.

After the acquisition of land, to prevent developers from hoarding and to avoid having land lie idle, the government applies a system of declaration of the development and utilization of housing estates. Ever since April 1, 2010, developers must send a written application to the land and resources administration department at the commencement and completion date of construction projects, and the land and resources administration department shall carry out effective supervision and control. If the developers are unwilling to execute this declaration system, they must make this fact public and cannot take part in land purchase activities for one year, at the least.

Realize a Rise or Drop in the Temperature of Housing Market by Regulating Down Payment Ratio, Required Reserve Ratio, and Loan Interest Rate

Regulation of the Down Payment Ratio for Housing

Ever since 2005, the proportion of the down payment for housing has been regulated during several time periods. Exhibit 12.12 shows the regulation time of the ratio of down payment for a first house property and a second house property, and indicates a comparison between the down payment and the housing price. In a word, the down payment ratio shall be raised when the housing market is overheated and the price markup rate is too high, and be lowered in a downturn of the housing market during a financial crisis.

In March 2005, the People's Bank of China stipulated that the minimum down payment ratio for housing shall be heightened from 20 percent to 30 percent in the cities or regions with high price markup rates. With the same original intention of cracking down on housing speculation and restraining high markup rate, in September 2007, the ratio of down payment for the second house property was heightened to 40 percent. However, due to the financial crisis, the down payment ratio was lowered to 20 percent again in 2008, so as to guarantee stable economic growth. The down payment ratio for the second flat shall refer to the policy on the

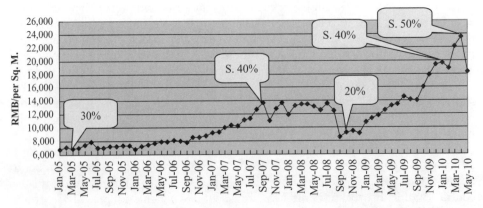

Exhibit 12.12 Policy on the Ratio of Housing Loan and Down Payment and the Housing Price in Beijing
Sources: Real estate database of SouFun.com; The People's Bank of China (www.pbc.gov.cn).

down payment ratio for the first house property, and the second house property loan policy is altered. Presently, in consideration of the quick substantial rise of housing prices since 2009, the Central Government has consecutively heightened the down payment ratio twice this year and stipulated that the down payment ratio for the second house property must not be lower than 50 percent. Based on the policies promulgated by the Central Government, Beijing Municipal People's Government has also issued new provisions on housing loans and stipulated that a family can purchase only one new flat in the city since May 1, 2010.

Judging by the relationship between the regulation of down payment ratio and the variation of housing price, the down payment ratio policy has a certain function on the housing market regulation, but the effect is not ideal. As shown in Exhibit 12.12, after the down payment ratio for the second house property is heightened three times, obviously there is a fall in the housing price, but the effect does not last long; it undergoes a new round of price markup and fluctuation soon afterward. Besides, during the financial crisis in 2008, the loosening of the loan for the second house property is helpful for releasing partial housing demand and makes a lot of speculators swarm into the market for "bottom fishing," but the policy is not tightened in a timely manner after the resurgence of the housing market in 2009, because of the big market rebound in the later stage.

Regulation of Required Reserve Ratio and Loan Interest Rate

Exhibits 12.13 and 12.14 show the relation between the required reserve ratio, the ratio of interest on five-year and above loans, and the variations in the housing market since 2005.

From 2005 to the outbreak of the global financial crisis, China basically implemented a tight monetary policy. Especially in 2007, in light of rapid economic growth, the central bank regulated upward the required a reserve ratio 10 times and heightened the interest rate five times. During the financial crisis, in order to eliminate the negative influence of the international environment on China,

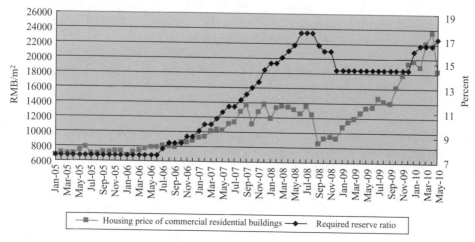

Exhibit 12.13 Required Reserve Ratio and Housing Price in Beijing
Sources: Real estate database of SouFun.com; The People's Bank of China (www.pbc.gov.cn).

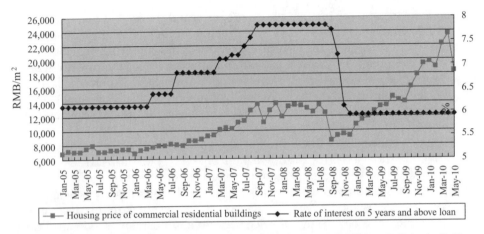

Exhibit 12.14 Rate of Interest on Five-Year and Above Loans and Housing Price in Beijing
Sources: Real estate database of SouFun.com; The People's Bank of China (www.pbc.gov.cn).

stimulate the economic resurgence and guarantee the stable economic growth, the central bank regulated downward the required reserve ratio four times and the interest rate four times and proposed to adopt the "moderately loose monetary policy." In 2010, there was an overheating of real estate investment again, the credit size even reached ¥1.39 trillion[6] in January 2010. In order to maintain the stability of finance and prevent the financial risk, the central bank has regulated upwards the required reserve ratio three times.

The regulation of required service ratios and loan interest rates undoubtedly have a great influence on the housing market. Presently, the real estate development loan and the personal housing loan have accounted for approximately 20 percent of the loans and the balance of loans. Due to the imperfect Chinese financial market and insufficient financial innovative products, either for real estate developers or purchasers, the bank loan is the main source of funding. The upward regulation of the required reserve ratio reduces financial fluidity and heightens the difficulty in the acquisition of capital in the housing market to a certain extent. The regulation of the loan interest rate before a financial crisis heightens the cost of capital and cracks down on the partial investment and speculation in the housing market. But we can also see that the monetary policy has a minor influence on the housing price, the housing price even continually rises along with the upward regulation of required reserve ratio and loan interest rate. A possible reason is that the upward regulation of a required reserve ratio and loan interest rate greatly heightens the cost of real estate development, and the final result of the concrete market feedback is the price markup.

Stabilizing Housing Market by Issuing a Differential Taxation Policy

Exhibit 12.15 shows taxation policy changes from 2005 to 2010. According to the housing market variation, there are mainly four times taxation policy changes. In 2005, the government tightened the regulation and control of the real estate

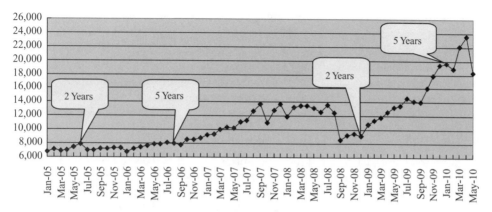

Exhibit 12.15   Policy on Housing Sales Taxes and the Housing Price in Beijing
Sources: Real estate database of SouFun.com; www.law110.com. (Four taxation policies are issued by
State Administration of Taxation, NO.89(2005), NO.108(2006), NO.174(2008), NO.157(2009).)

transaction concerned with speculative and investment house property. If an individual resells a dwelling within two years after purchase, a transaction sales
tax is levied according to the full sum of sales income; if an individual resells an
ordinary house after two years, it is free from sales tax; if an individual resells
an ordinary house within two years, a sales tax is levied on the balance of the
earnings after deducting the purchase cost from the sales income. In 2006, the tax
regulation policy was further strengthened, in that two years was modified to five
years. Meanwhile, ever since August 1, 2006, a tax has been levied countrywide on
personal income from the transfer of second household properties.

During the financial crisis, along with a taxation policy aimed at stimulating
housing consumption, the government began to encourage the consumption of ordinary property, issued the preferential tax policy, released the tentative provisions
on the exemption of the one year's housing transaction sales tax, and changed the
specification of five years back to two years again, in relation to the housing transaction sales tax. (See Exhibit 12.15) Meanwhile, the Central Government adopted
a series of preferential tax policies to stimulate the real estate market in a period
of downturn. The concrete policies include: Ever since November 1, 2008, if a first-
time buyer purchases ordinary house property, the deed tax rate is temporarily
regulated downward to 1 percent; if an individual sells or purchases the house
property, it is free from the stamp duty; if an individual sells the house property,
it is free from the land value-added tax. The local government can establish tax
reduction and exemption policies to encourage housing consumption.

In 2010, in the face of the overheated real estate investment, the specification
of two years was restored to five years again, in relation to the tax on the sales
of ordinary house property by individuals and the tax on the transfer of house
property by individuals.

The taxation policy aims to crack down on investment and speculative behaviors in the housing market, but as it stresses circulation and neglects possession,
the differentiated tax rate policy can hardly play an important role in market regulation and control. Presently, the real estate tax is not levied in China, and the cost
of possessing housing is very low. As long as the purchasers have confidence in the

market and believe that the price will go up in the future; even if the transaction cost is heightened, they cannot control real estate investment and speculation, and the effect of the differentiated tax rate policy can hardly be attained. Thus, we must expedite the levying of the housing possession tax at the present stage, research and establish detailed rules for the implementation of the real estate tax, and truly realize the function of tax policy on the housing market regulation.

Evaluation Housing Market Regulation Policies

Through the summarization of the land, monetary, and taxation policies issued by the Central Government and Beijing Municipal People's Government before, during, and after the financial crisis and the implementation effect of these regulation policies, we can see that the current regulation policies adopted by the Chinese government have some of the following problems.

Economic Growth Goal Guides Policy Making

During the development of China, economic growth is at the core; the government regulation policies are mostly founded on the premise of economic growth. The real estate industry is a pillar industry for the national economy, so the Central Government and the local government rely heavily on the real estate industry while guaranteeing economic growth. The issue of a lot of market bailout policies by the Central Government and the local government is the most obvious manifestation of it. During the financial crisis in 2008, the Central Government put forward the 8 percent protection economic growth goal. To attain this goal, there was a fundamental change in the Central Government's policy orientation for the real estate industry, an important component part of the national economic development.

In the face of the housing market depression, the policy of restraining the price markup, which has been implemented for many years, is changed to stimulate the housing market development. The series of market stimulation policies, such as the loosening of loan restrictions for a second house property, the lowered ratio of initial payment and the preferential tax policies, and so forth, make the oppressed investment and speculation demand release promptly, with the result that the Beijing housing market quickly recovers, and there is a big price rebound in 2009 and 2010.

Policies Cannot Simultaneously Control Housing Price and Enable Citizens to Own Homes

The Chinese people have traditional ideals such as "to live and work in peace and contentment," "to live in our own house," and so forth. For the Chinese people, a house is not only a dwelling place, but also a symbol of stability and wealth. Hence, the housing market management and the solution of the housing problem are not only an economic issue but also social and political issues for the Chinese government. During the course of the price markup, the resident's ability to afford housing has continually been reduced; the notions of the "ant tribe" and of "dwelling narrowness" emerge in big cities like Beijing, at the same time that high housing price becomes the center of attention and the focus of public opinion.

In view of this, the government regulation strategies and policies all aim at forcing the housing price down, solving the housing difficulty for the public, and relieving the pressure of public opinion. However, in Beijing, the total population is 17 million, there are big gaps in residents' incomes, the per capita disposable income of the low-income group that accounts for 20 percent is only ¥11,729 per year, and an average family cannot buy a house at the price of ¥20,000 per square meter—therefore, it is unrealistic to enable all residents to purchase a home. Further, it's not advisable for the government to concentrate on enabling everyone in the big city to have his or her own house according to controlled housing price. Along with price control regulations, the affordable housing policy, together with the housing of the poor (in particular, migrant workers) in cities should be paid more attention.

The Establishment of a Long-Acting Mechanism Is Neglected

It is obvious that the government's housing market regulation has been emphasized frequently when the housing price rises fast. When the housing price continually rises before financial crisis and the market rebounds quickly after financial crisis, both the Central Government and the local government issue a lot of policies regarding land, credit, and taxation in order to slow down the growth rate of housing price and even try to force price down. On the one hand, as the policy changes frequently, it disturbs the expectations for a stable housing market. On the other hand, the fact that the housing price rises continually despite the upward regulation of tax rates enhances purchasers' and investors' confidence in the housing market. Whenever there is market turbulence and a slight decline in the housing price, more and more purchasers will swarm into the market for bottom fishing, hence there is a new round of the price markup.

Judging from the credit and taxation policy, the government's housing market regulation policies are very sensitive to the abnormal variation of market data, as well as changing frequently in different stages. Meanwhile, as regulation policies are a remedy only for existing market problems, and pursue excessively the short-term market effect, they neglect the establishment of a long-acting market operation mechanism, and can hardly realize the anticipated effect at the same time. Therefore, it is necessary for the future housing market regulation policies to lay a special stress on the establishment of long-acting market mechanisms, so as to promote the long-term healthy and sustainable development of the Chinese housing market.

CONCLUSION

The Chinese housing market is in a stage of rapid development and has not yet undergone a complete cycle, which is the biggest difference from the experiences of other countries following the global financial crisis. Housing price continues to rise quickly in the continually rising market environment, especially in Beijing. Even if the financial crisis had a great impact on the whole world in 2008, housing price markup has only slowed down. After the financial crisis, Beijing almost immediately entered into a new round of swift price markups.

If we use the prevailing measures used in Western countries, it is obvious that the housing market price in Beijing is unreasonably high. As GDP and the finances of local governments in China mainly rely on the real estate market and land transfers, local governments' short-term, profit-driven behaviors accompanied by speculators' irrational behavior are the root causes of such high housing price. These factors, which are common in the market, usually make real estate prices materially deviate from the real value of property. This is a major reason for the violent price fluctuation of the real estate market, just as for other investment goods.

In any case, we can draw a lesson from Japan, which suffers from a long-term economic depression due to the bursting of a real estate bubble, and from America, which suffers from the subprime mortgage crisis. The Chinese government must be careful while facing the fluctuations of the housing market. In the past year, the implementation of restrictive housing credit and taxation policies had a great impact on the real estate market speculation behavior. From April 2010 to July 2010, the volume of housing market transactions in big cities like Beijing shrank quickly, and the transaction value also slightly declined. This further proves our conclusion, drawn on the basis of the above analysis, which is that real estate market speculation behavior is the main reason for the unreasonably high housing price in China and the frequent price fluctuation. The land, credit, and taxation policies crack down on the investment and speculation behavior in the housing market to a certain extent, and play a positive role in preventing the risk factors of the housing market and finance that arise temporarily from the irrational factors.

With regard to the future housing market and housing prices, the government at all levels should judge dynamically the present situation and the future tendencies of the national and regional housing supply and demand, so as to formulate both short-term and long-term development programs for the housing industry. The regulatory program will include putting forward the planning and program of residential land and affordable housing supply, based on the full-scale correct evaluation of the land and housing market, and releasing the market information and the policy signals in order to avoid large rises and falls of housing prices arising from irrational factors.

Besides, it is important to change from the present policy regime of "frequent regulation" to "long-term supervision" policy, by establishing and perfecting land, finance, and taxation policies, including strict control and crack down on speculative behavior in the housing market and guaranteeing healthy development of the housing market and of other closely related fields, such as housing finance. At the same time, it needs to dispose correctly of the responsibility of government between market and non-market interests. It should emphasize the responsibility of the government to ensure social security and to pay more attention to the housing supply of low-income groups, in order to form a housing supply gradient that covers the whole region, and feasibly solves the housing problem, which is the key issue regarding the national economy and the livelihood of China's citizens.

NOTES

1. It's the average value of profitability of real estate companies in Beijing from 2005 to 2009.
2. Base transfer price is the lowest land transfer price evaluated by the government before a land transaction.
3. In the old land transfer mode, the company that could offer the highest price would get the land. But in the new land transfer mode, land price is not the only matter, other factors such as housing planning, housing price, etc. will be considered.

4. A company only can bid once in the land-bidding competition process.

5. Not only the land price but also the housing price will be considered by the government. The lower housing price is, the bigger the chance for companies to get the land.

6. Quoted from http://news.sohu.com/20100303/n270535138.shtml. For the original text, see the *First Financial Daily*, dated March 3, 2010.

7. Quoted from http://money.163.com/10/0113/10/5STDGQ9E0025431 7.html.

REFERENCES

Akerlof, George A., and Robert J. Shiller. 2009. *Animal Spirits: How Human Psychology Drives the Economy, and Why It Matters for Global Capitalism*. CITIC Press: Beijing.

Beijing Municipal Construction Committee. 2009. *Beijing Real Estate Year Book*. China Metrology Publishing House.

Cheung, Steven N. S. 2009. *The Economic System of China*. CITIC Press: Beijing.

DiPasquale, Denise, and William C. Wheaton. 1996. *Urban Economics and Real Estate Markets*. Saddle River, NJ: Prentice-Hall.

Green, Richard K., and Stephen Malpezzi. 2003. *A Primer on U.S. Housing Markets and Housing Policy*. The Urban Institute Press: Washington, D.C..

LeRoy, Stephen F., and Richard D. Porter. 1981. "The Present Value Relation: Tests Based on Implied Variance Bounds." *Econometrica* 49, 555–574.

Lin, Yifu. 2008. *Special Topic about Economy of China*. Beijing: Peking University Press.

Shiller, Robert J. 1981. "Do Stock Prices Move Too Much To Be Justified by Subsequent Changes in Dividends?" *American Economic Review* 71: 421–436.

Shiller, Robert J. 1987 (January 2). "The Volatility of Stock Market Prices." *Science*, 235: 4784, 33–37.

Yukio, Noguchi. 2005. *Bubble Economy*. Sdxjoint Publishing Company: Shanghai.

ABOUT THE AUTHORS

PING LU is Professor in the School of Public Administration at Renmin University of China. Her research interests include real estate economics, real estate price and market, and real estate policy analyses. She received her PhD in Economics from Renmin University of China, and MSc in Management from the same university. In 2000 she spent one year on post doctoral research at Tel Aviv University, Israel. During 1994–1995, she studied at Greenwich University in the United Kingdom, with support from the Sino-British Land Pricing project. Dr. Lu is the director of the Asian Real Estate Society (AsRES), the director of the China Land Society (CLS), a qualified member of the China Land Valuation Association (CLVA), and the commissioner of Housing Policy Committee of Ministry of Housing & Urban-Rural Development. She has taken charge of many research projects financed by the National Natural Sciences Research Foundation, National Social Science Fund, Beijing Philosophy-Social Science Planning Project, Ministry of Land & Resource, Ministry of Education, and the UNDP, which related to land and housing markets. Dr. Lu has published books including *Real Estate Economics*, *Real Estate Development and Management*, and *Land Administration*. Her research is published in *China Soft Science*, *China Land Science*, *Urban Studies*, *Urban Problems*, *China Rural Survey*, and *Urban Policy and Research*.

ZHEN HUI is studying for a PhD degree in the Department of Land and Real Estate Management, School of Public Administration, Renmin University of China. She holds a Masters in management from Renmin University of China and a Bachelor's degree in engineering from Wuhan University. Her research interests cover real estate economics, affordable housing, and asset pricing.

XU YUEHONG is studying for a doctoral degree in Finance Engineering in the Finance School of Renmin University of China. He holds a Masters of Real Estate economics, from the Public Administration School of Renmin University of China, and a Bachelor's degree in Business and Administration, from the Economics School of Central China Normal University. During August–October 2010, he studied at the Finance School of the Univeristy of Colorado–Boulder as a visiting scholar. His research interests cover real estate finance, economics, and pricing.

CHAPTER 13

Home Mortgage and Real Estate Market in Shanghai

JIE CHEN
Associate Professor, School of Management, Duty Director of Center for Housing
Policy Studies

Since the end of the welfare-oriented urban home distribution system in the late
1990s, China's home mortgage business has witnessed a tremendous growth and
currently it is the primary funding resource for urban residents' home purchases.
But how the development of home mortgage business is related to the boom of the
real estate market in China has not received much empirical examinations. This
chapter utilizes the most recent data in Shanghai to examine this relationship. The
impact of mortgage loans on the evolution of the real estate markets are studied
through both documental review and statistical analysis. A particular focus is the
association of mortgage terms and home market performance during 2008–2009,
the time period of global financial crisis. It finds that the availability of mortgage
credit plays a significant role in driving the quick recovery of the Shanghai real
estate market in 2009.

INTRODUCTION

Since the outburst of the subprime mortgage crisis, the topic of the relationship
between mortgage credit and real estate price dynamics once again attracts extensive attention (Coleman et al. 2008; Duca et al. 2009). But it is still unclear what
emerging economies can learn from lessons of mortgage development in developed countries. Sustained growth in China's house prices has coincided with a
surge in mortgage lending. As a result, the possibility of a reinforcing relationship
between mortgage lending and house prices has received increased attention.

Notably, for past few years there have been persistent vehement controversies
in China regarding whether a rapidly growing speculative bubble is emerging
in the real estate market.[1] The residential sector constitutes the biggest chunk in
China's real estate industry. Given China's growing role in the global economy,
such a topic has been lifted to a worldwide concern.[2]

Amid fears of a devastating real estate crash, in early January 2010 the State
Council (China's cabinet) attempted to cool down the real estate market by instruct-
ing banks that the down-payment ratio of a second home mortgage should be in
no case less than 40 percent (General Office of the State Council [GOSC] 2010a).[3]

Nonetheless, this policy had little impact on the market, and property prices continued to race upward at a furious pace. Under great pressures from both the populace and the need for economic stability, in early April 2010 the State Council issued a new series of radical policy measures to curb speculation in the scorching property market. A central element of this policy package was to raise the down payment ratio for people buying their second homes from a minimum of 40 percent to at least 50 percent (GOSC 2010b). Moreover, in areas with soaring property prices, the central government instructed banks to reject mortgage loan applications for people buying their third house and also demanded banks halt issuing mortgages to those who could not prove they had lived and paid taxes for at least one year in the city. Judging by these observations, it looks as though easy money from mortgage finance sources is blamed for the surge of property prices in the average policymaker's view. However, little is known about the effect of the availability of mortgage credit on the pace of appreciation of home prices in China.

Using data on the real estate market and home finance market in Shanghai, the biggest city and leading industrial hub of China, this paper analyzes how the development of the real estate market and home financing are correlated to each other during the past decade, with a focus on their association during the global financial turmoil period. The long-run trend and policy suggestions thereof are also discussed. The rest of the paper is organized as follows. The next section reviews the existing literature. The third section introduces the background of the Shanghai real estate market and home finance business. The following section discusses the correlation of the two sectors during the global financial crisis period, and the last section concludes this chapter.

LITERATURE REVIEW

Theoretical and empirical studies of house price dynamics typically emphasize the importance of income and interest rates; however, there is little evidence that house prices can be explained by fluctuations in these two variables alone. For example, Muellbauer and Murphy (1997) stress that credit constraints should enter the home price function with similar importance as income, housing stock, and the real user cost of housing. Further, using the home price-to-rent approach to model home prices, Kim (2007) shows theoretically that down-payment constraints can significantly affect home prices.

Empirically, the coincidence of cycles in bank credit and property prices has been widely documented in policy-oriented literature (IMF 2000; BIS 2001). Thus, the inclusion of a measure of mortgage credit as a fundamental determinant of fluctuations in house prices has become a common approach in international studies.

For example, Egert and Mihaljek (2007) include credit growth as a potential determinant of house prices alongside the typical fundamentals to explain the differences of housing price dynamics patterns between central and eastern European countries with OECD countries. Tsatsaronis and Zhu (2004) examine the importance of mortgage credit for house price fluctuations in 17 countries and find that fundamentals relating to mortgage finance, including bank credit and the real interest rate, could explain approximately one-third of the long-run variation in house prices. Gerlach and Peng (2005) suggest that there exists a long-run relationship between house prices, bank credit, and GDP in Hong Kong. In the short run, they believe that the relationship is a one-way street; a change in house price causes changes in bank credit. Collyns and Senhadji (2002) find that credit growth has a significant contemporaneous effect on residential property prices in a number of Asian economies. Using the U.S. national data, McGibany and Nourzad (2004) find that mortgage credit affects the demand for houses through the transmission mechanism of interest rates. However, Berlinghieri (2008) used inflation-adjusted U.S. national data and found that house price growth responds immediately to a change in mortgage credit and mortgage credit responds contemporaneously to the change in house prices, suggesting the relationship is bidirectional. In addition, there is evidence that the relationship reinforces itself in the short run. The discovery of a two-way relationship between mortgage credit and house prices in the United States parallels what Fitzpatrick and McQuinn (2007) suggested for Ireland.

In summary, the existing literature indicates that housing prices and mortgage credit are linked in the long run. In addition, there is also some evidence of a short-run relationship between housing price changes and credit growth, although the direction of the relationship is not completely clear.

BACKGROUND

The Real Estate Market in Shanghai

Shanghai is probably the most famous city in mainland China and its name will become even more well-known to the world because of the recent Expo 2010. For more than 150 years, Shanghai has been the most prosperous city in mainland China. High mean incomes with right-skewed income distributions, high housing prices that reduce home ownership chances for low-income households, high and escalating price-to-income ratio and price-to-rent ratios are characteristics defined by Gyourko et al. (2006) for "superstar cities" and are clearly visible in Shanghai.

Nonetheless, housing was freely supplied in Shanghai 30 years ago. However, as the state budgetary funding was the only funding sources for this housing system, the supply of housing could not be sustained on economic terms (Zhang, 2000). In Shanghai, as in all other major cities in China, investment of residential dwellings were scarce (see Exhibit 13.1).[4] To demonstrate the inadequacy of

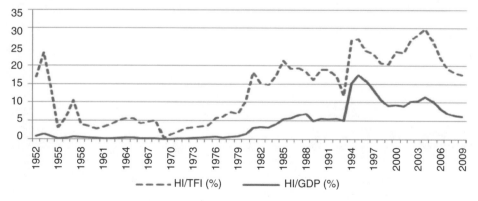

Exhibit 13.1   Housing Investment in Shanghai, 1952–2009
Note: HI: housing investment; TFI: total fixed investment; GDP: gross domestic product.
Sources: Shanghai Statistics Yearbook 2000–2010; "Shanghai Statistics Bulletin 2010."

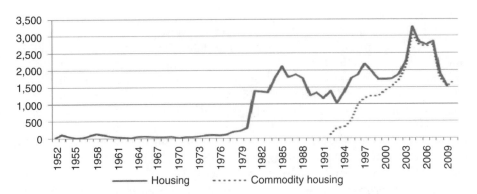

Exhibit 13.2 The Supply of Newly Completed Housing in Shanghai, 1952–2010 (10,000/m²)

Sources: Shanghai Statistics Yearbook 2000–2010; "Shanghai Statistics Bulletin 2010."

housing investment, the annual average of newly completed residential construction space in Shanghai was as low as 0.61 million square meters, or 0.06 square meter per inhabitant for this period (see Exhibit 13.2). Consequently, the acute crowding conditions of urban residents in Shanghai were not addressed during this period (see Exhibit 13.3).

Under grave pressures of both housing shortage and budgetary burden, China initiated market-oriented housing reform in 1978. Commodity housing that was built for sale appeared in Shanghai in the late 1980s but most buildings were sold to either overseas Chinese or domestic firms and institutions. Anyhow, the ratio of commodity housing in total newly constructed housing rose steadily from 8.1 percent in 1992 to 54 percent in 1997 (see Exhibit 13.2).[5]

Nonetheless, until 1998 the traditional welfare housing regime continued to prevail in the Chinese urban housing sector and most employees in state-owned enterprises (SOEs) and government agencies still got free housing from their employers (Zhao and Bourassa 2003). Therefore, real estate developers had limited incentives to build residential housing, as the market was small and the return was

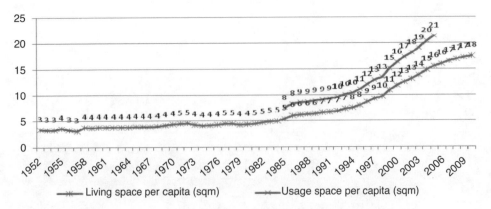

Exhibit 13.3 The Living Conditions of Shanghai Residents, 1952–2010

Sources: Shanghai Statistics Yearbook 2000–2010; "Shanghai Statistics Bulletin 2010."

low (see Exhibit 13.1 and 13.2). Thus, the shortage of residential dwelling remained an acute issue in Shanghai and the improvement of urban residents' living conditions lagged substantially behind achievements in economic and income growth (see Exhibit 13.3).[6]

But in summer 1998, as a key measure to counter the negative shocks of the 1997 Asian financial crisis on Chinese economic growth, the welfare housing regime was formally terminated (GOSC 1998). By a series of policy reform, the residential real estate industry was completely liberalized within a few years of 1998 and quickly became one of most profitable business in China. By 2003, the majority of residential dwelling were supplied through the market and the segment of welfare housing constituted only a small margin in Shanghai: less than 7 percent of new construction space (see Exhibit 13.2). The construction speed of new housing in Shanghai increased considerably (see Exhibit 13.2), and living space per capita doubled within 12 years and rose to 17.2 square meters by the end of 2009 (see Exhibit 13.3).

Between summer 2002 and spring 2005, the Shanghai real estate market encountered its first boom. The trading value of firsthand residential property experienced a steep increase of 50 percent in 2003 and continued to soar to 86 percent in 2004 (see Exhibit 13.4). Nonetheless, the selling space did not grow much for the same period (see Exhibit 13.5). Based on official data, the mean price of first-home residential property grew 19 percent in 2003 and another 28 percent in 2004, much larger than income growth for the same period (see Exhibit 13.6).

To cool down the apparently over-heated real estate market, the State Council (China's cabinet) issued a series of regulation policies. On March 26, 2005, the General Office of the State Council (GOSC) circulated a notification to all government agencies and expressed their concern about property speculation. For the first time, the State Council placed a priority on the stability of real estate prices above of the development of the real estate industry (GOSC 2005a). This document was usually referred to as the "*lao guo ba tiao*" (the former State Council's "eight points"). On April 27, 2005, the Standing Committee of the State Council (SCSC)

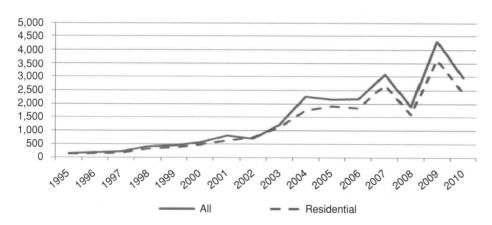

Exhibit 13.4 The Selling Value of Firsthand Real Estate in Shanghai, 1995–2010 (RMB 0.1 Billion)

Sources: Shanghai Statistics Yearbook 2000–2010; "Shanghai Statistics Bulletin 2010."

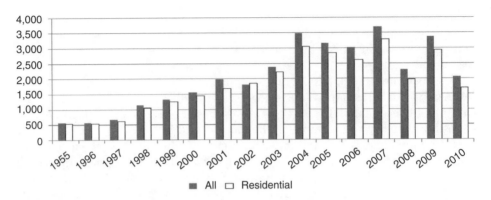

Exhibit 13.5 The Selling Space of Firsthand Real Estate in Shanghai, 1995–2010 (10,000/m^2)

Sources: Shanghai Statistics Yearbook 2000–2010; "Shanghai Statistics Bulletin 2010."

announced the "*xin guo ba tiao*" (the new "eight points") to reinforce the government's bid to crack down on property speculation (*Xinhua News* 2005). On May 9, 2005, by approving and circulating the real estate market regulation policies suggested by seven ministries, including the Ministry of Construction (MoC) and People's Bank of China (PBC), GOSC stressed again the importance of curbing raging housing prices (GOSC 2005b). During this process, the PBC had increased the interest rate twice and tightened the rules regarding down payments and mortgage terms.[7] Further, since June 1, 2005, a transaction tax was imposed at the effective rate of 5.5 percent of gross resale price for sellers who have owned their properties for fewer than two years.

After this series of regulatory blows, the Shanghai real estate market was brought to a sudden cool-down and the escalating price growth encountered a sharp halt in spring 2005. Between May 2005 and July 2007, the mean residential property prices slumped consecutively for eight months with an accumulated fall of 13 percent and took 17 months to return to the original levels (see Exhibit 13.7).

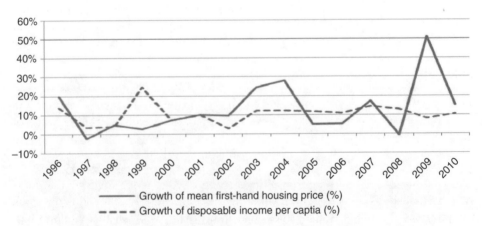

Exhibit 13.6 The Annual Growth of First-hand Residential Property Prices and Comparison with Income in Shanghai, 1995–2010 (%)

Sources: Shanghai Statistics Yearbook 2000–2010; "Shanghai Statistics Bulletin 2010."

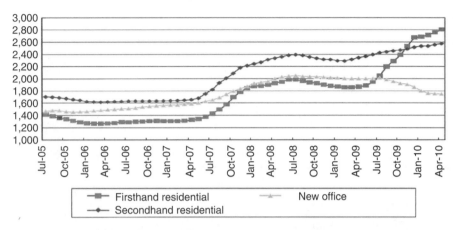

Exhibit 13.7   The ZF Monthly Real Estate Price Index for Shanghai, March 1999–April 2010
Note: The ZF (ZhongFang) real estate price index is compiled by CREI (China Real Estate Institute) and has been computed for Shanghai's property market since February 1995. It is currently well-recognized as a leading indicator of China's real-estate market, although it is not quality-adjusted.

Despite the government's various attempts to stabilize the market, an unprecedented real-estate boom unexpectedly hit Shanghai and most other major cities in the second half of 2007. According to official data, the mean price grew by 17 percent in this year (see Exhibit 13.6). However, the CREI data suggested that, at the end of 2007, the mean residential property price in the downtown area of Shanghai was 40 percent higher than one year earlier (see Exhibit 13.7).[8]

The State Council did not intervene directly this time but People's Bank of China acted as the fire marshal again. Spiraling prices finally spurred new rigid rules on lending. On September 27, 2007, PBC tightened the mortgage terms for applicants who already held loans, requiring a minimum down-payment ratio of 40 percent and setting the mortgage interest rate to 1.1 times that of benchmark loan rates (PBC 2007a).[9] As it was the first time that the phrase "the number of loans by borrowers" was added to loan regulations, commercial banks were confused about whether the "number" was based on a household level or an individual level.[10] On December 5, 2007, PBC issued a supplementary directive clarifying that the number of loans to a borrower shall be determined on the basis of loans to the borrower's family (including the borrower, his/her spouse, and his/her underage children) (PBC 2007b).[11]

The property market in Shanghai and other major cities rapidly lost vigor in early 2008, and the Shanghai property market encountered a severe crash in the latter half of 2008 and early 2009. The trading space as well as trading value of firsthand property in the whole year of 2008 plummeted 40 percent compared to 2007, but the fall of mean price was negligible, less than 1 percent (see Exhibits 13.1–13.7).

Anyhow, Shanghai's experience in housing development suggests that market mechanism is effective in promoting housing supply: the housing stock in 2009 was 2.5 times that of 2000 and more than 10 times that of 1978 (see Exhibit 13.8). The current situation in Shanghai is one whereby overall affordability appears to have been maintained whilst the shift toward market provision has been achieved. Among permanent residents, 79 percent owned their homes in

Exhibit 13.8 The Construction Space of Housing Stock in Shanghai (10,000 m²)

Year	All Housing	Residential Housing	Residential Share (%)
1978	8,653	4,117	47.58%
1990	17,256	8,901	51.58%
1995	22,094	11,906	53.89%
2000	34,206	20,865	61.00%
2005	64,198	37,997	59.19%
2008	81,121	47,195	58.18%
2009	87,327	50,211	57.50%

Source: Shanghai Statistics Yearbook 2000–2010.

2009 (see Exhibit 13.9). However, we can expect that there are serious affordability pressures of market prices on new market entrants, who are forming a growing proportion of the permanent resident population (Chen et al. 2010).

The Home Mortgage Business in Shanghai

The first home mortgage in China was issued in 1986 (Chen, 2009), but until 1997 this business was heavily constrained and grew very slowly (PBC 1995; 1997).[12] It is only since the 1998 housing reform that the mortgage market has grown significantly. To provide necessary financial preparation for the State Council's planned abolishment of the urban welfare housing system in the summer of 1998, the People's Bank of China liberated the home-mortgage business in April 1998 (PBC 1998).

The development performance of the Chinese mortgage business since 1997 is truly spectacular. According to the People's Bank of China, the outstanding balance of home mortgages has increased more than 250 times between 1997 and 2009, soaring from RMB 19 billion to RMB 4,760 billion. At the end of March 2010, the home mortgage loan consisted of 12.52 percent of all banking loan balances

Exhibit 13.9 Housing Tenure in Shanghai (Permanent Residents), 2004–2009 (%)

Tenure Type	2004	2005	2006	2007	2008	2009
Rental	26.6	26.6	25.1	22.0	21.6	20.0
—Public rental	25.9	25.5	23.8	20.4	17.4	16.3
—Private rental	0.7	1.1	1.3	1.6	4.2	3.7
Home Ownership	72.9	73.3	74.1	77.6	77.6	79.2
—Owned: inherited from pre-reform era	2.2	2.4	1.3	0.9	0.7	0.7
—Owned: from public housing privatization	42.9	40.4	40.4	37.3	37.8	37.2
—Owned: purchased from market	27.8	30.5	32.4	39.4	39.1	41.3
Other	0.5	0.1	0.8	0.4	0.8	0.8
Total	100	100	100	100	100	100

Source: Shanghai Statistics Yearbook 2008–2010. In summary, the real estate market in Shanghai had experienced large swings before 2008, with at least two episodes of booms and two episodes of sharp slumps. Besides movements in fundamentals, changes in the availability of mortgage credit have been identified as a key driver of property cycles.

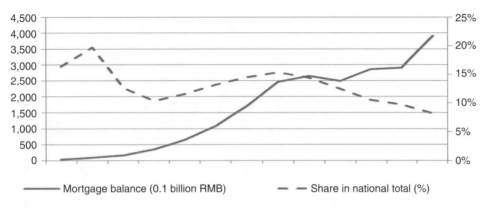

Exhibit 13.10 Home Mortgage in Shanghai and Its National Share, 1997–2009
Sources: Shanghai Statistics Yearbook 2000–2009; "Shanghai Statistics Bulletin 2010."

and its share in long-term banking loans was 21 percent. In the early 2000s, the non-performing rate of home mortgages was around 0.15 percent, substantially lower than the non-performing rate of other loan services (PBC 2005).

The home-mortgage market in Shanghai developed much earlier than that of any other city in China (Chen 2009). For this reason, the scale of its expansion since 1997 is relatively smaller than that of the national level, although its outstanding value also achieved a 125-fold growth between 1997 and 2009 and comprises a significant share in the national total (see Exhibit 13.10). At the end of 2009, the outstanding balance of home mortgages in Shanghai was RMB 391 billion, consisting of 13 percent of all banking loans issued in RMB and 28 percent of all long-term banking loans (see Exhibit 13.11).

In the literature, the mortgage depth, or the ratio of mortgage balance as a percentage of GDP, is often employed to assess the risk status of the home mortgage business. At the end of 2009, the mortgage depth in Shanghai was 26 percent, which was in sharp contrast to only 0.91 percent in 1997 (see Exhibit 13.11). However, compared to advanced economies with average mortgage ratios of 50 percent (see

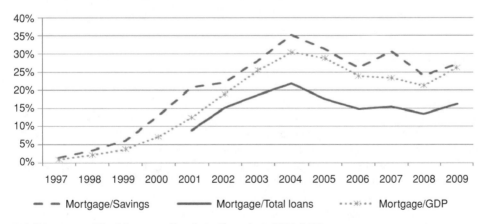

Exhibit 13.11 The Mortgage Depth in Shanghai, 1997–2009
Sources: Shanghai Statistics Yearbook 2000–2009; "Shanghai Statistics Bulletin 2010."

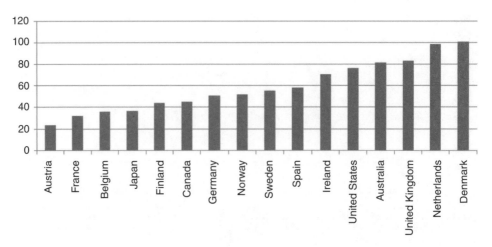

Exhibit 13.12 The Mortgage Depth of Selected OECD Countries in 2006
Source: World Economic Outlook: Housing and Business Cycle, IMF 2008, Chart 3.1.

Exhibit 13.12), the mortgage market in Shanghai still has room to grow. In addition, taking into account the low ratio of mortgage to household savings, the mortgage business in Shanghai is fairly safe (see Exhibit 13.11).

The terms of mortgage loans are currently regulated as follows: The maximum loan-to-value ratio is 80 percent (of the lower of the appraisal value or purchase price), and the maximum mortgage term is 30 years. Mortgage interest rates are controlled and set to track central bank rates. While new products are emerging, the self-amortizing mortgage remains the most common.

Since the opening of the mortgage business, with funding coming mainly through retail deposits, commercial banks dominate the primary home mortgage market in China and the four major state-owned banks—"the Big Four"[13]—are the market leaders. However, the mortgage market in Shanghai is much more competitive. The Big Four altogether takes only slightly more than 60 percent of the market share, and they are facing fierce competition from other national banks as well as local banks (see Exhibit 13.13).

Housing Provident Fund in Shanghai

In addition to the Western-type commercial home mortgage business, China's home finance system is complemented with the Housing Finance Provident (HPF) scheme, which was first introduced in Shanghai in 1991 and spread across the nation in a few years. Since 1994 the implementation of HPF to all urban employees has been adopted as a national policy (Yeung et al. 2006).

The HPF scheme is based on the Singapore Central Provident Fund and operates in a very similar manner (Duda et al. 2005). Basically, it is a compulsory saving plan with social security purposes, requiring both employees and employers to provide equal contributions of a certain percentage of an employee's salary on a monthly basis. In Shanghai, the compulsory contribution rate was initially 5 percent and has been fixed at 7 percent since 1999, but employees and employers

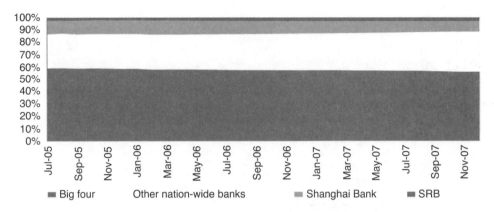

Exhibit 13.13 The Market Structure of Home Mortgages in Shanghai, 2005–2007
Note: SRB: Shanghai Rural Cooperative Bank.
Sources: The People's Bank of China; Shanghai Head Office.

are encouraged to contribute additional savings: complementary HPF with rates ranging from 1 to 8 percent.[14] The HPF savings are deposited in the participating employee's personal accounts and all the funds, including interest, belong to the employee. However, if used before the employee retires or dies, the fund is strictly restricted to housing-related needs, for example, purchases, self-construction, major housing repairs, renovation, and paying rent (under certain conditions).

With the HPF plan, participants have the right to obtain home loans with preferential interest rates. Actually, until 1998, the HPF home loan was the dominant or maybe the only virtual funding source for personal home purchase in urban China and its development proceeded much earlier than the commercial home mortgage. In some sense, the advance of the HPF home loan in the 1990s paved the way and encouraged the later development of commercial home mortgages. The business of HPF home loans was developed much earlier in Shanghai than in any other city in China. Until early in the first decade of the twenty-first century, the HPF loans in Shanghai still comprised one-third of the nation's total loans.[15] In recent years the ratio has dropped to around 10 percent. Currently the outstanding balance of HPF loans in Shanghai is only one-fifth of that of commercial mortgages (see Exhibit 13.14).

Given soaring home prices, the credit from HPF loans is often insufficient for the entire financial needs of purchasing a home (see Exhibit 13.15). Therefore, most households apply for HPF loans and commercial mortgages simultaneously. In addition, since 1998, the interest rate of an HPF home loan does not have too much advantage compared to a commercial mortgage (see Exhibit 13.16).

HOME MORTGAGE AND REAL ESTATE IN SHANGHAI DURING THE FINANCIAL CRISIS

Which Came First? A Chicken-or-the-Egg Puzzle

It is widely admitted that there exists a positive statistical relationship between house price and mortgage credit. Same as in other countries, mortgage lending

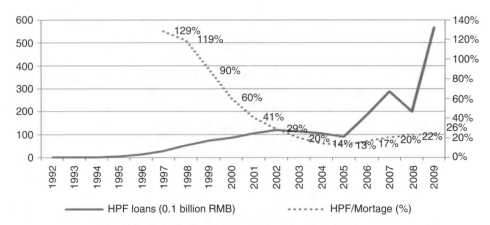

Exhibit 13.14   The Size of HPF Home Loans in Shanghai, 1992–2009

Note: "HPF/Mortgage" refers to the ratio of the outstanding balance of HPF home loans in relation to commercial mortgages. Before November 2007, nearly all borrowers could get mortgages at preferential interest rates, as long as their credit risks were assessed low by issuing banks. After November 2007, banks could issue mortgages at preferential rates only if the borrowers are buying their first-home (PBC 2007).

Source: The Shanghai Housing Provident Fund Management Center.

in China is assessed on market-based collateral values. Therefore, the amount of mortgage credit available to borrowers is likely to increase in response to escalating house prices. But lenders' willingness to provide mortgage credit is dependent on their liquidity, the gap of mortgage interest rates in relation to other loan services, and their own assessment of the financial risks of the home market. Rising prices, by sending positive signals of asset value, likely promote the supply of mortgage credit. Therefore, an increase in the amount of credit available, either exogenous or endogenous, has the potential to spur the demand for home buying, causing house prices to further increase. Therefore, the causal relationship between home mortgage credit and house price is something like a "chicken or the egg" puzzle, in which it is very difficult to determine which comes first (Gerlach and Peng 2005).

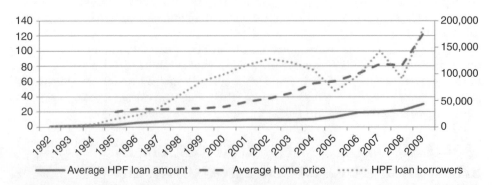

Exhibit 13.15   The Average Amount and Number of Borrowers of HPF Home Loans in Shanghai, 1992–2009

Note: Both average HPF loan amount and average home prices are measured in RMB 10,000 (left *y*-axis). The number of borrowers is measured in terms of household (right *y*-axis).

Source: The Shanghai Housing Provident Fund Management Center.

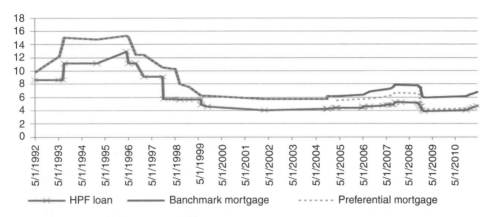

Exhibit 13.16 The Comparison of the Interest Rate of HPF Home Loans and Commercial Mortgages, 1998–2011 (percent points)
Source: People's Bank of China.

However, during the global financial crisis the Chinese government introduced a series of emergency attempts to bolster housing demand through the relaxing of mortgage regulations. The result can be regarded as a social experiment and thus provide us a good opportunity to identify the causal relationship between mortgage and housing prices in the short run. Thus, this paper utilizes monthly data of mortgage loans and property sales in Shanghai during 2008–2009 to explore how property market is affected by mortgage supply.

The Impacts of the Global Downturn on the Real Estate Market in Shanghai

In the year 2009, with FDI as low as 22.3 percent and exports stumbling by –17.4 percent, Shanghai's GDP grew at a speed of only 8.2 percent. Although such growth performance may be regarded as outstanding in any other country at any time, for Shanghai it was a 20-year record low and it was lower than the national average level for the first time since 1991, the year the development of Pudong New Area was initiated.[16] As officially admitted by the Shanghai municipal government in the gazette of 2009 (a social-economic statistical report), "2009 was the hardest year since 1991."

As shown in Exhibit 13.17, it is clear that the industrial outputs of both China and Shanghai were performing very well in 2007 but suddenly experienced severe difficulties in the second half of 2008 and the first half of 2009. They both experienced gradual recoveries in the second half of 2009. Their trends coincide with the evolution of the global financial turmoil.

In accordance with the aggregate economic trend, after the zeal in the second half of 2007, the real estate market in Shanghai was plunged into a deep recession in 2008 (see Exhibits 13.18 and 13.19). The latter half of 2008 saw a deep dampening in the sales of property as well as housing investments across all major cities in China. In Shanghai, the trading value of firsthand residential property in the third quarter of 2008 slumped to only one-third of that one year earlier, a record low since 2005 (see Exhibit 13.18).[17] A highly influential household questionnaire survey that was regularly conducted by the People's Bank of China hinted that housing

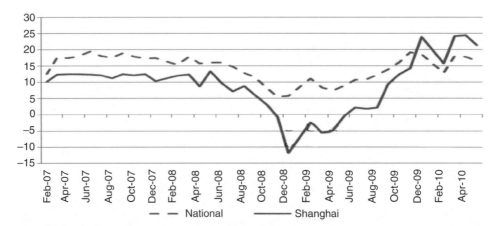

Exhibit 13.17 The Growth Rate of Industrial Output in China and Shanghai, January 2007–May 2010 (% Change Year-on-Year)
Source: Online Database of National Bureau of Statistics of China.

demand was bleak and the real estate market would continue to be sluggish for a particularly long period. This survey suggested that only 13.3 percent of the polled intended to purchase houses in the last quarter of 2008, a record low since 1999. Further, several experts insisted that, in this round of macro-control measures, the government should still stick to its previous policy of containing the rocketing housing prices until they returned to reasonable levels.[18] Until early October 2008, the market outlook was still very gloomy (see Exhibit 13.18 and 13.19).

Chinese Government's Policy to Boost Housing Demand

Under the immense pressures of massive job losses, the Chinese central government chose to accept that the revival of real estate sales and quick recovery of housing investment were central to shoring up the national economy amidst the global and domestic economic slowdowns.[19] To combat the economic crisis and to

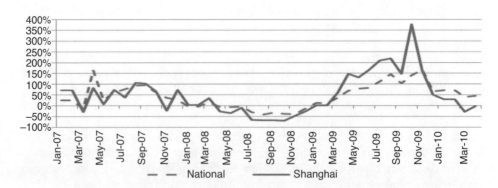

Exhibit 13.18 The Growth Rate of Trading Value of Firsthand Housing in China and Shanghai, February 2007—April 2010 (% Change Year-on-Year)
Source: Online Database of National Bureau of Statistics of China.

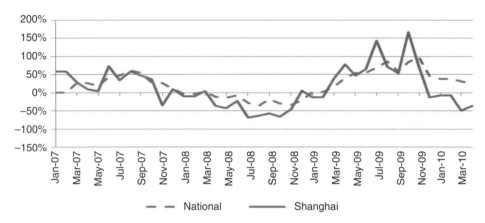

Exhibit 13.19 The Growth Rate of Trading Space of Firsthand Housing in China and Shanghai, February 2007—April 2010 (% Change Year-on-Year)
Source: Online Database of National Bureau of Statistics of China.

stoke domestic demand, the central government reversed the housing policies it implemented in late 2007.

In October 2008, the State Council stepped in to bolster the sagging real estate market by lowering transaction taxes, reducing requirements for down payments, and lowering mortgage rates (GOSC 2008).

First, beginning November 1, 2008, property purchase tax was lowered to 1 percent for people buying their first home if the housing was smaller than 90 square meters. The previous rate was 3 percent, with those buying houses smaller than 140 square meters paid 1.5 percent.

Second, for people buying their first home, the down payment ratio would be lowered to 20 percent, and banks would be allowed to charge as low as 70 percent of benchmark lending rates for such mortgages.

The Shanghai municipal government promptly enforced this series of policies (SMGO 2008). In addition, the HPF center in Shanghai increased the cap of HPF home loans from RMB 400,000 to RMB 600,000. Following the government's instructions, Chinese banks loosened their purse strings for mortgage financing and prepared to create ample liquidity. The growth of real estate sales measured over four quarters turned positive in January 2009, for the first time since January 2008 (see Exhibit 13.18 and 13.19). But with the looming uncertainty regarding further economic downturns, the property market in Shanghai was still sluggish in the spring of 2009 (see Exhibit 13.18 and 13.19).

Since April 2009, housing prices in Shanghai started to climb unabated and the real estate sector began attracting buyers at a frenetic pace (see Exhibit 13.7 and 13.18). The second quarter of 2009 observed a moderate increase of 5 percent in the housing prices but the third quarter witnessed a unprecedented surge of 18 percent in three months, followed with another spectacular soar of 17 percent in the fourth quarter (see Exhibit 13.7).

Meanwhile, the rapid rush of property prices spurred the demand amidst fears of further increases. It also clearly incurred renewed speculation: According to the PBC's Shanghai headquarters, in the latter half of 2009, about 35 percent of

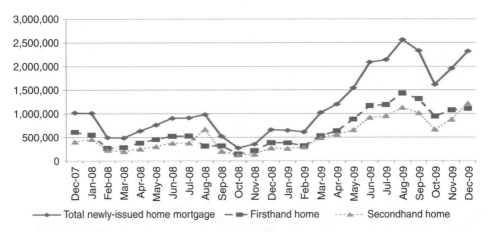

Exhibit 13.20   The Newly Issued Mortgage in Shanghai, December 2007—December 2009
Source: The People's Bank of China, Shanghai Head Office.

new mortgages in Shanghai were issued to non-local home buyers and another 10 percent was used to foreign buyers. Thus, the trading volume of housing soared in line with the surge of prices; the selling value and transaction space of new housing in the latter half of 2009 were RMB 240 billion and 18.03 million square meters, respectively. These figures were about 2.69 times and 1.65 times those of one year earlier, respectively (see Exhibit 13.18 and 13.19).[20] The fever spread to the secondhand housing market, too. There are no data on the transaction values of secondhand housing in Shanghai available yet. But according to the mortgage data, for the whole year of 2009, new mortgages used to finance the purchase of secondhand housing increased at the same speed as mortgages for firsthand housing (see Exhibit 13.20). Within a few months, the downturn trend of the real estate sector was completely reversed.

The quick recovery and new boom of the real estate market in Shanghai and other major cities in mainland China surprised all observers.[21] How much of the unexpected resurgence of the real estate market in 2009 could be attributed to the government rescue in late 2008, particularly, the changes in regulations of mortgage supply? This is the key issue to be investigated in this chapter.

Gauging the Importance of Mortgage Credit to the Real Estate Revival

Given the short span of the intervention event and the limited available data, it is not yet possible to perform rigorous econometric regressions on the impacts of mortgage credit on real estate prices in Shanghai. Instead, we attempt to explore the statistical association between the two series.

Exhibit 13.21 suggests that households in Shanghai are conservative with borrowing and rely moderately on mortgages when buying homes. For firsthand housing, the leverage ratio (defined by the share of new mortgages in relative to home purchases) was on average 29 percent during 2008–2009. Interestingly, the exhibit also shows the leverage ratio for firsthand housing was considerably higher in 2009 than 2008: 30 percent versus 27 percent. Particularly, the average leverage

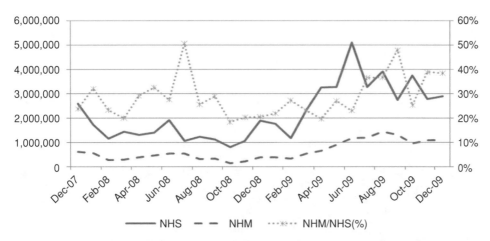

Exhibit 13.21 The New Mortgage and Housing Sales in Shanghai, December 2007—December 2009

Note: NHS: Selling value of firsthand housing; NHM: Newly-issued mortgage for firsthand home. Due to the lack of monthly-level data, the newly issued HPF home loan is not included in this measure of mortgages. But considering that HPF home loans constitute only 20 percent of total home credit in Shanghai, this omission should not be significant. Both NHS and NHM are measured in RMB 10,000 (left *y*-axis).

Source: The People's Bank of China, Shanghai Head Office.

ratio in the latter half of 2009 reached as high as 37 percent, compared to 27 percent one year earlier.[22]

For the whole year of 2009, the total of new mortgages issued for all types of home buyers in Shanghai amounted to RMB 200 billion, which was 2.5 times that of the amount in 2008 (see Exhibit 13.20). If comparing the numbers in only the second halves of the years, the expansion of home credit is more remarkable: New mortgages issued in the latter half of 2009 were 3.4 times greater than one year earlier (see Exhibit 13.20). Further, the mortgages issued in the latter half of 2009 comprised 64 percent of the total for that year (see Exhibit 13.20). Evidently, the evolution patterns of new mortgage credit perfectly mirrored the trading trends of residential housing between 2008 and 2009 (see Exhibit 13.18 and 13.20).

As an attempt to investigate the causality between newly issued mortgages and property prices, the time-series movements of the two series (for firsthand residential housing) between 2008 and 2009 are plotted in Exhibit 13.22.[23] It can be seen that the two series are tied to each other very closely and both turned from negative to positive sharply in March 2009; thus, it appears that the two series are moving simultaneously even in the short run.

Interestingly, the data also suggest that an increase of 1 percentage in housing prices over a previous month is, on average, associated with a 2 percent rise in new mortgages over the earlier month (see Exhibit 13.22); this appears to imply that the elasticity of mortgages with respect to housing prices is around 2 percent in Shanghai. However, as our data is drawn from a short and very special period, this observation that strong market recovery is associated with ample liquidity is, of course, only for inspiration. Also note that the mortgage rate was reduced heavily and the minimum down-payment requirement was cut from 30 percent to 20 percent in late 2008 (see the third section in this chapter and Exhibit 13.16).

Exhibit 13.22 The Month-to-Month Growth Rates of Mortgage and Housing Prices in Shanghai, December 2008—December 2009
Note: In order to avoid the seasonal bias, the monthly mortgage data was converted to its 12-month moving average before obtaining the month-on-month growth rate. Both series refer to only firsthand residential housing. To control for the measurement error, the monthly price series is using the CREI Shanghai Housing Price Index rather than the average sale price computed from dividing the selling value by selling space.
Sources: The People's Bank of China, Shanghai Head Office; CREI.

They may contribute to the outburst of mortgage credit too. But how much the proportion of mortgage growth is attributed to the price growth and how much is due to relaxing mortgage terms is not easy to assess. A robust estimate of the elasticity of new mortgages with respect to home price growth in China requires sufficiently long intervals of data and is left for further research.

Discussions and Policy Implications

From a theoretical point of view, a finding of simultaneous short-run movement between new mortgages and home prices makes sense. Increases in home prices positively affect mortgage borrowing via various wealth effects (Hofmann 2004; Gerlach and Peng 2005). First, due to asymmetric information in credit markets, both the borrowing capacity and credit demand of households are positively affected by changes in home prices. Second, upward-trending home prices may induce households to change their perceptions of their lifetime wealth and expand their borrowing with the aim of evening out their consumption patterns over the life cycle. Third, rising home prices will cause more optimistic expectations about future economic prospects and then induce a higher level of borrowing.

On the other hand, rising prices positively affect banks' capital positions, risk-taking capacity, and credit availability, and induce them to be more willing to lend. Therefore, additional mortgages from banks will be used to buy more homes, pushing home prices even further, which then creates more demand for mortgages among households and at the same time more supply of credit from banks. Thus, the mutually reinforcing cycles in banking loans and the home market may evolve in the long run due to the two-way causality between mortgage credit and home prices.

The connection between mortgage credit and housing price that we observed in Shanghai during 2008–2009 seems to provide a new piece of empirical support to the theoretical discussion earlier. The short-run causality between mortgage credit and home prices appears at best to be a two-way street. There is no clear evidence that the unexpected property recovery in 2009 is due primarily to the government's fine-tuning of mortgage policy.

However, until now a key question in this chapter remains unanswered: If mortgage policy has a limited role in explaining the recovery of the property market in Shanghai since early 2009 or in other places in China, what else can explain the performance of the real estate market?

From our perspective, the Chinese government's overall massive economic stimulus package, by bringing up the economic outlook and upholding household confidence, appears to be a significant factor for the property boom. One may note that both home prices and mortgages in Shanghai were continuing to decline several months after the government's announcement of a new mortgage policy in October 2008 (see Exhibit 13.22). Month-on-month changes of home prices turned positive in April 2009 and this happened one month after Shanghai's industrial output reversed its downtrend to an uptrend for the first time since July 2008 (see Exhibit 13.17 and 13.22). Further, the surge of money supply in China during the global financial crisis period, by triggering households' widespread worry of high inflation, has been pointed to as the main driving force of the property price surge. Data suggests that M2, the widely used indicator of money supply, soared 28 percent in China during 2009. Although the Chinese government's officially published CPI data was still negative in 2009 (–0.6 percent), it is evident that many Chinese households hold different views.

The experiences from other countries during the global financial crisis may provide support for our analysis. China is not the only country to lower interest rates and relax mortgage terms during this period. The United States passed several bills to stimulate homebuyers' confidence and most were enacted through changes in mortgage policies, but the effect was at best marginal. The same experiences were observed in most EU countries and other nations. The property market generally did not show signs of recovery when mortgages became more available. It usually turned positive only after the aggregate economy sent out clear signals of climbing out of the recession.

Therefore, there are reasons to believe that the recovery or the boom of the property market is often a by-product of a government's economic stimulus policies, where lower interest rates and a looser money supply are usually the central elements of such a stimulus package. Nonetheless, it is tempting to recall U.S. history between that nation's 2001 recession and 2006 subprime crisis. Alan Greenspan has now publicly regretted relying on the self-interest of investors; nevertheless, while a loose monetary policy can solve some urgent problems in the short run, it is destined to nurture a long-building asset bubble. Once an asset bubble is formed, ultimately it will force the whole economy to pay a huge cost to resolve it. China is on such a path now. Many prominent Chinese economists have called for immediate correction of the previous loose monetary policy, but it is difficult to judge whether it is too late to rectify the economic situation.

CONCLUSION

The development of China's real-estate industry has its roots in the process of economic growth as well as fast-paced urbanization, which was set in motion in 1978. During the past three decades, the real estate market in Shanghai has experienced several large swings. The newest round of rising property prices in this city and other major cities, since late 2009, prompted the central government to issue new regulation policies in April 2010 to rein in escalating prices and guard against a devastating housing collapse. Again, tighter control of mortgage credit was the key tool.

While there are numerous studies of house price dynamics in China, few of them have considered the direct role of mortgage lending. This analysis first introduces the historical development of the real estate sector and mortgage business in Shanghai, and then uses monthly data of mortgage and housing sales during 2008–2009 to examine how mortgage credit affects the real estate market in this city. It has found that the availability of mortgage credit plays a significant role in explaining fluctuations of housing prices in Shanghai. The mortgage credit should be considered as a critical factor for understanding housing prices in China. Further, there is clear evidence that, in the short run, the causality between mortgage credit and home prices runs in both directions.

This finding has important policy implications. Loosening the terms of mortgage credit will bolster housing demand only when the market trend turns from downward to upward. On the other hand, without major changes in the market fundamentals, one should not expect that tightening the mortgage supply could effectively curtail the pace of home prices. Government's fine-tuning of mortgage policy in general has only limited effect in either boosting or dampening the housing market.

We also briefly discussed other potential driving forces behind the surge of property prices in China since 2009 and concluded that the economic stimulus policy, with a loose monetary policy at its core, is the main reason for surging property prices. Warning of a possible long-building bubble under loose monetary policy is given. Of course, further analysis is needed to shed more light on the relationship between monetary policy, mortgage credit, and home prices in China.

NOTES

1. "China Real Estate Time Bomb Ticking," *China Daily*, April 19, 2010.

2. "Skyrocketing Prices May Point to a Real Estate Bubble in China," March 4, 2010; "Is China Another Real Estate Bubble?" CNNMoney.com, March 15, 2010; "China: Red-Hot Real Estate," *Economist*, April 26, 2010.

3. This order in effect rescinded the policy announced in late 2008 that second-home mortgage applicants could get preferential terms and rates as first-home buyers as long as they could prove their home purchase was to upgrade their living conditions (GOSC 2008). Interestingly, the policy enacted in 2008 was delivered with a clear purpose to spur depressive housing demand under the background of global financial turmoil.

4. For the similar period, the world average of housing investment as percentage of total fixed investment and GDP is 20 percent and 6 percent, respectively (World Bank 1993).

5. Until 2000, the commodity housing market in Shanghai was operated in a two-track system: One was high-standard dwelling targeting overseas Chinese and another was ordinary dwellings reserved for only domestic buyers. Among the latter group, prior to the 1998 reform the majority of buyers were institutions and firms and individual buyers comprised a small part; nevertheless it grew from 5.6 percent in 1988 to 46.3 percent in 1996 (Chen 2010). The two tracks of the commodity housing market were merged in 2001.

6. Between 1979 and 1997, the average annual salary of a worker in Shanghai achieved a three-fold growth (after taking inflation into account) (¥784 in 1979 vs. ¥11,425 in 1997).

7. On March 17, 2005, PBC lifted the preferential treatment of mortgage interest rates for the first time since 1999 and unified it with the benchmark long-term loan interest rate: for mortgages longer than five years, the rate was increased from 5.31 percent to 6.12 percent. But at the same time PBC allowed commercial banks to give borrowers a maximum discounted rate of 10 percent of the benchmark rate. The minimum ratio of down payment was also increased from 20 percent to 30 percent in the cities with a rapid growth of property prices.

8. "Shanghai Property Market Keeps Pace," *China Daily*, August 20, 2007.

9. First-home buyers can get a preferential treatment of a 20 percent down payment only if they buy homes smaller than 90 square meters; otherwise they need to pay at least a 30 percent down payment.

10. "Spiraling Prices Spurred New Rules on Lending," *People's Daily Online*, September 29, 2007.

11. "China to Curb Property Loans," *China Daily*, December 14, 2007.

12. For example, by 1995 the maximum length of a mortgage was only 10 years, and the regulations asked borrowers to supply a double guarantee when applying for a home mortgage and to deposit no less than 30 percent of the amount they were planning to borrow (PBC 1995). The 1997 regulations lifted the two requirements but a home mortgage was still restricted to only the purchase of housing financed by a government subsidy (PBC 1997).

13. The Big Four includes: IBBC (Industrial and Commercial Bank of China), AB China (Agriculture Bank of China), BOC (Bank of China) and CCB (China Construction Bank).

14. As the HPF savings are tax-exempted, both employees and employers have incentives to deposit complementary HPF savings.

15. "The HPF Loan in Shanghai Exceeded 10 Billion RMB," Xinhau News January 10, 2002. Available at http://news.xinhuanet.com/fortune/2002-01/10/content_233195.htm.

16. Pudong New Area is a district in eastern Shanghai along the HuangPu River; its development since 1991 signals the revival of Shanghai's role as the economic center in China.

17. "China Cuts Taxes, Rates to Boost Housing Market," *China Daily*, October 23, 2008.

18. "Govt Should Not Rush in to Aid Housing Market," *China Daily*, October 20, 2008.

19. "China Cuts Taxes, Rates to Boost Housing Market, *China Daily*, October 23, 2008.

20. For the whole year of 2009, the selling value and transaction space of new housing were 360.2 billion RMB and 29.28 million square meters, respectively. These figures were about 2.22 times and 1.46 times those in 2008, respectively.

21. "Property Market Recovery Strong," *China Daily*, September 14, 2009.

22. It will be ideal to compare whether this figure is significantly larger than historical average levels. But the problem is that we did not have mortgage data that distinguished

between firsthand and secondhand housing before 2008. There is also no data on the selling value of secondhand housing in Shanghai for any year.

23. As potential home buyers usually compare the current home price with the latest one, it is reasonable to depict the price movement by using month-on-month changes. But for new mortgages, which are governed by home purchases with strong seasonal patterns, we need to convert the original level to a 12-month moving average before obtaining its month-on-month growth rate.

ACKNOWLEDGMENTS

The author thanks Peking University–Lincoln Institute of Land Policy and the Fudan University 211 Project (211XK06) for financial support of the research for this paper.

REFERENCES

Ahearne, Alan G., John Ammer, Brian M. Doyle, Linda S. Kole, and Robert F. Martin. 2005. *House Prices and Monetary Policy: A Cross-Country Study.* Board of Governors of the Federal Reserve System, International Finance Discussion Papers, Number 841.

Allen, Jason, Robert Amano, David P. Byrne, and Allan W. Gregory. 2006. "Canadian City Housing Prices and Urban Market Segmentation." Bank of Canada, Working Paper 2006.

BIS. 2001. The 71st Annual Report. Bank for International Settlements.

Berlinghieri, Laura. 2008. "House Prices and Mortgage Credit Availability: Is the Relationship Reinforcing?" Job Market Paper, Department of Economics, Washington University.

Chen, J. 2009. "The Sixty Years of China's Housing Sector" (in Chinese). Working Paper No.0902, Center of Housing Policy Studies (CHPS), Fudan University.

Chen, J., Q. J. Hao, and M. Stephens. 2010. "Assessing Housing Affordability in Post-Reform China: A Case Study of Shanghai." *Housing Studies* 25:6, 877–901.

Coleman, Major D., Michael LaCour-Little, and Kerry D. Vandell. 2008. "Subprime Lending and the Housing Bubble: Tail Wags Dog?" *Journal of Housing Economics* 17:4, 272–290.

Collyns, C., and A. Senhadji. 2002. "Lending Booms, Real Estate Bubbles, and the Asian Crisis." IMF Working Paper No. 02/20. Washington DC: International Monetary Fund.

Duca, John V., John Muellbauer, and Anthony Murphy. 2008. "House Prices and Credit Constraints: Making Sense of the U.S. Experience." Federal Reserve Bank of Dallas.

Duda, Mark, Xiulan Zhang, and Mingzhu Dong. 2005. "China's Homeownership-Oriented Housing Policy: An Examination of Two Programs Using Survey Data from Beijing." Harvard Joint Center for Housing Studies Working Paper Series: W05-7.

Edward, H., K. Ng, and Rosaline Chow. 2004. "Availability of Bank Credit and the Residential Property Price Level: Evidence from Singapore." *Asian Real Estate Society Annual Conference.*

Eddie, Hui C. M., and Y. Shen. 2006. "Housing Price Bubbles in Hong Kong, Beijing, and Shanghai: A Comparative Study." *Journal of Real Estate Finance and Economics* 33, 299–327.

Egert, B., and D. Mihaljek. 2007 (September). "Determinants of House Price Dynamics in Central and Eastern Europe." *Comparative Economic Studies* 49:3.

Fitzpatrick, T., and K. McQuinn. 2007. "House Prices and Mortgage Credit: Empirical Evidence from Ireland." *The Manchester School* 75:1, 82–103.

General Office of the State Council. 1998 (July 3). Notice on Further Deepening of the Urban Housing Reform and Fastening the Housing Construction (No. 23 [1998] of the General Office of the State Council).

General Office of the State Council. 2005a (March 26). Circulation on Effectively Stabilizing Housing Price (No. 8 [2005] of the General Office of the State Council).

General Office of the State Council. 2005b (May 9). Notice of the General Office of the State Council on Forwarding the Opinions of the Ministry of Construction and Other Departments on Efforts to Stabilize Housing Prices (No. 26 [2005] of the General Office of the State Council).

General Office of the State Council. 2006 (May 24). Notice of the General Office of the State Council on Forwarding the Opinions of the Ministry of Construction and Other Departments on Adjusting the Housing Supply Structure and Stabilizing the Housing Prices (No. 37 [2006] of the General Office of the State Council).

General Office of the State Council. 2007 (August 7). Opinions of the State Council on Solving the Housing Difficulties of Urban Low-Income Families (No. 24 [2007] of the General Office of the State Council).

General Office of the State Council. 2008 (December 20). Several Opinions of the General Office of the State Council on Promoting the Healthy Development of the Real Estate Market (No.131 [2008] of the General Office of the State Council).

General Office of the State Council. 2010a (January 7). The Notice on Promoting the Stable and Sound Development of the Real Estate Market (No. 4 [2010] of the General Office of the State Council).

General Office of the State Council. 2010b (April 17). The Notice on Resolutely Curbing the Soaring of Housing Prices in Some Cities (No. 10 [2010] of the General Office of the State Council).

Gerlach, S., and W. Peng. 2005. "Bank Lending and Property Prices in Hong Kong." *Journal of Banking and Finance* 29:2, 461–481.

Gyourko, Joseph E., C. J. Mayer, and T. M. Sinai. 2006. Superstar Cities. NBER Working Paper, No. W12355.

Hofman, Boris. 2004. "Bank Lending and Property Prices: Some International Experience." University of Bonn, Working Paper.

IMF. 2000. World Economic Outlook. May 2009.

Kim, Yong. 2007. "Rent-Price Ratios and the Earnings Yield on Housing." University of Southern California, unpublished manuscript.

Krainer, John. 2009. "House Prices and Bank Loan Performance." FRBSF Economic Letter, Number 2009.

Li, Si-Ming, and Zheng Yi, 2007. "Financing Home Purchase in China, with Special Reference to Guangzhou." *Housing Studies* 22:3, 409–425.

Mayer, Christopher, and R. Glenn Hubbard. 2007. "House Prices, Interest Rates, and the Mortgage Market Meltdown." Columbia Business School, Working Paper.

McGibany, J., and F. Nourzad. 2004. "Do Lower Mortgage Rates Mean Higher Housing Prices?" *Applied Economics* 36:4.

Muellbauer, John, and Anthony Murphy. 1997. "Booms and Busts in the U.K. Housing Market." *The Economic Journal* 107:6, 1701–27.

People's Bank of China. 1995 (July 31). Provisional Regulations of Commercial Bank's Self-Operating Home Loan Business (No. 220 [1995] of the People's Bank of China). People's Bank of China. 1997 (April 28). Notice on Issuing the Provisional Regulations of Personal Home Guarantee Loan (No. 171 [1997] of the People's Bank of China). People's Bank of China. 1998 (April 7). Notice on Increasing Home Credit to Support Housing Construction and Consumption (No. 169 [1998] of the People's Bank of China).

People's Bank of China. 2005. China Real Estate Finance Report 2004. Beijing: China Financial Press.

People's Bank of China. 2007a (September 27). Notice of the People's Bank of China and China Banking Regulatory Commission on Strengthening the Administration of Commercial Real Estate Credit Loans (No. 359 [2007] of the People's Bank of China).

People's Bank of China. 2007b (December 5). Supplementary Notice of the People's Bank of China and China Banking Regulatory Commission on Strengthening the Administration of Commercial Real Estate Loans (No. 452 [2007] of the People's Bank of China).

SMPG. 2008 (December 27). Notice of the General Office of Shanghai Municipal People's Government on Transmitting the "Implementation Suggestions on Promoting the Healthy Development of the Real Estate Market of This Municipality by Carrying Out the Spirit of the Document of the General Office of the State Council" Made by Five Departments Including the Municipal Housing Administration (No. 55[2008] of the General Office of Shanghai Municipal People's Government).

Tsatsaronis, K., and H. Zhu. 2004 (March). "What Drives Housing Price Dynamics: Cross-Country Evidence." *BIS Quarterly Review* 1: 65–78.

Warnock, Veronica Cacdac, and Francis E. Warnock. 2008. "Markets and Housing Finance." *Journal of Housing Economics* 17:3, 239–251.

World Bank. 1993. *Housing: Enabling the Markets to Work.* Washington, DC: World Bank. Xinhua News. 2005 (April 27). China's Cabinet's Notice on Housing Market. http://news.xinhuanet.com/house/2005-05/19/content_2974234.htm.

Yeung, Stanley Chi-Wai, and Rodney Howes. 2006. "The Role of the Housing Provident Fund in Financing Affordable Housing Development in China." *Habitat International* 30:2, 343–356.

Zhang, X. Q. 2000. "The Restructuring of the Housing Finance System in Urban China." *Cities* 17:5, 339–348.

Zhang X. Q. 2006. "Institutional Transformation and Mercerization: The Changing Patterns of Housing Investment in Urban China." *Habitat International* 30:2, 327–341.

Zhao, Y., and S. Bourassa. 2003. "China's Urban Housing Reform: Recent Achievements and New Inequities." *Housing Studies* 18:5, 721–744.

ABOUT THE AUTHOR

JIE CHEN is Associate Professor of the Department of Industrial Economics, School of Management, Fudan University, China, and Duty Director for the Center for Housing Policy Studies, Fudan University, China. His research covers various fields in regional, urban, and housing-related economic issues. In 2005 he received a PhD in Economics from Uppsala University, Sweden. He also holds a master's degree in Development and Environmental Economics from Oslo University, Norway, and a bachelor's degree in Economics from Fudan University, China. His publications have appeared in the *Journal of Housing Economics, Urban Studies, Housing Studies, International Real Estate Review,* and other international peer-reviewed journals. Professor Chen has received several national-level research grants and has published voluminous articles on influential Chinese media. He is active in Chinese housing policy debate and has also worked as policy advisor for World Bank as well as several government agencies including the Chinese Ministry of Housing and Rural-Urban Construction. He also provides consulting services for leading firms such as Goldman Sachs, Morgan Stanley, Credit Sussie, Fidelity, and other businesses.

CHAPTER 14

Evolution of the Indian Housing Finance System and Housing Market

R. V. VERMA
Chairman and Managing Director, National Housing Bank, India

This chapter traces the evolution of the housing finance system/market in India, its various constituents, and their inter-connections. It also analyzes the weaknesses and the vulnerabilities of the housing finance market, and what the economic and the financial sector reforms have meant for the housing sector, in the context of the global meltdown triggered by the subprime mortgage crisis in the United States. The chapter describes the role of different players in this market space and attempts to present a holistic overview of the mortgage market, as it has developed in India.

EVOLUTION OF THE HOUSING FINANCE SYSTEM IN INDIA

The 1990s were very eventful for the country as a whole, and most particularly for the financial sector, which saw groundbreaking changes involving institutions, policies, systems, and practices. The government's "hands off" approach provided greater freedom to the market and private enterprises in almost all sectors. The developmental objectives of the government, however, always occupied an important place, even in the midst of market imperatives. "Housing" has been long identified as a social priority, but there has been a chronic deficiency of funds (particularly long-term funding) for meeting the housing needs of the people. The government's policies in the past were largely based on grants and subsidies for special housing schemes for the lower-income segments of the population (now known as the "subprime" market). Important lessons have since been learned in the process of the economic reforms. The subsidies approach is not a long-term solution and is often inspired by short-term objectives. Subsidies carry hidden costs (in terms of fiscal impacts), targeting the subsidies is always a challenge, subsidies are vulnerable to distortions, and the housing sector is particularly susceptible to them. There is a limit to policy interventions, which often counter or mitigate the efficiencies of the underlying market forces. At one extreme end of the spectrum, the market inadequacies, particularly in the emerging economies, may encourage a generous dose of policy interventions, which can at times be more counter-productive than the market inadequacies themselves. At the other end, absence of timely policy interventions, including regulatory measures, may trigger potential market failures that could otherwise be prevented. In certain measure, these factors also did contribute to the subprime crisis in the United States, which eventually led to the global crisis. In hindsight, we see that the crisis partly emerges from a very disproportionate mix of the market and the policies regarding it, or lack thereof, in a close-to-nonexistent regulatory environment. The housing sector in India historically had significant gaps in terms of credit flow and market infrastructure. The market reforms and liberalization throughout the 1990s contributed substantially to the productivity and efficiency of this sector in terms of credit flow and its absorption in the market. The supply responses, however, have not been as smooth, and are marked by rigidities. While some sectors responded quickly to the reform measures, others have experienced prolonged adjustments. The housing sector has built-in rigidities in terms of inflexible supply responses in the "real" sector domain. As a result, the smooth integration of the financial market with the real housing sector was a challenge when the reforms began. Though the banking sector is now contributing significantly to the growth of housing in the country, disconnects with the real sector continue to limit the impact of financial sector reforms on housing. However, the lack of complete integration helps in decoupling or circuit breaking, in the event of volatilities experienced in one segment of the market (not transmitted to other segments in the absence of full integration).

The housing finance sector has seen very high growth rates over the past five years. The main factors driving this growth are:

- Fiscal concessions provided by the government in successive budgets.
- Regulations of the Reserve Bank of India (RBI) and National Housing Bank (NHB) encouraging banks and housing finance companies (HFCs) to extend credit in this sector.
- Decline in interest rates on housing loans during the years 2003 to 2008–2009.
- Higher competition and increase in product offerings.
- Rapid construction, increasing supply, and stable/declining property prices for most years.
- Steady increase in urbanization levels.
- Increase in disposable income for large sections of the population.
- Change in attitude toward debt for purchase of a house (one of the largest individual investments).
- Confidence-building measures and positive sentiments have also played an important role.

India's experience, over the past decade or so, has been very encouraging and the investments in housing have registered a compounded annual growth rate (CAGR) of nearly 28–30 percent, despite recession in different segments of the economy from time to time. The commercial banks that are the major players in the financial market have stepped up their housing loan advances significantly over the years, achieving an annual growth of nearly 25–30 percent. The growth in their housing loan portfolios is largely demand-driven. Similarly, a separate set of funding institutions, the specialized Housing Finance Companies (HFCs), are the other significant players in this market. They have also experienced similar expansion in their housing loan business. A supportive tax regime by way of fiscal incentives and an enabling regulatory (financial sector) framework until about 2006–2007 has led to a sustained increase in demand for housing loans. The borrowers of housing loans have definite preferences for tax savings through housing loan repayments (principal and interest), which are provided for under the existing taxation laws.

For the lending agencies, the banks and the housing finance companies, tax shelters continue to act as added incentives for their lending. The regulatory risk weights on individual housing loans backed by the mortgage of property was brought down from 100 percent to 50 percent in the year 2002. This reflected a lower risk outlook on the housing loans, as the lenders will be required to provide less capital (an effect of lower risk weight on the capital-to-risk weighted-assets ratio [CRAR], a regulatory requirement) against their housing loan portfolio. As a result of these regulatory relaxations and incentives, the banks and the HFCs scaled up their housing loans to the individuals. The banks' lending for individual housing up to Rs.2 million per borrower is part of the priority lending, required under the directions of the central bank. The credit policy regime has gradually shifted from a "directed" regime to an "incentive-based" approach. Also, the switch-over from the administered interest rate regime to a more liberalized lending regime has brought about the benefits of competition and efficiency in the housing finance market, which have been visibly witnessed in recent years. In short, there has been a paradigm shift in favor of a liberalized market combined with prudent regulations based on global best practices.

Homebuyers in India were traditionally debt-averse and opted for external funding only as a last resort. Consequently, formal external funding of home purchase has accounted for a relatively small proportion of housing finance in the three decades since this business activity formally began in India in the 1970s. The remaining amount has usually been met from sources such as personal savings, sales of assets, and borrowing from informal sources. However, a steady change in India's housing finance sector is currently underway, with mortgage financing being available more easily and debt being increasingly seen as an acceptable means of financing home purchase. This trend is expected to gather further momentum in the next three to five years.

Economic development in India has brought increased urbanization in its wake. In 1961, only 18 percent of the country's households were in urban areas. Four decades later, the figure had risen to 28 percent (according to the census that year). Urban population is expected to increase further with a rise in the urbanization levels and in population. This implies that demand for housing would increase at a faster pace in urban India in the short to medium term as the cultural barrier to debt is further breached.

Over the past six to seven years, property prices have fluctuated while income levels, particularly among the middle class, have more than proportionately increased. The cost of a house has dropped from 20 times the annual gross income of a typical borrower to around just 5.5 to 6 times over this period, making housing more affordable.

Although the housing finance industry in India has been growing at an impressive rate for the past few years, financing through the organized sector continues to account for only 25 percent of the total housing investment in India. The amount of a loan is dependent on the debt-repayment capacity of the borrower, which, in the case of many self-employed individuals, is under-assessed, as a measure of caution. The general loan-to-value (LTV) ratio practiced in the industry is about 70 percent. In the absence of mortgage guaranty and insurance, the high LTV loans are not prevalent. Also, high LTV loans carry higher regulatory risk weights, thus acting as a disincentive for the lenders. Measures such as the rationalization of stamp duty (statutory charges and levies payable to the state government as a percentage of the value of the property being transacted) and the launch of innovative housing finance products would help the industry tap the segments currently catered to by the unorganized sector. Although the self-employed individual segment offers good growth potential for mortgage players, success in the segment would hinge on the use of risk-based pricing methods and the credit appraisal skills of lenders.

With the rising demand for housing loans, the banking sector started expanding their housing finance operations, and with the help of its vast reach and cheaper financial base, the banking sector has now taken a lead role in the Indian housing finance market. The transition started in 2002–2003 and, as a result of this, the share of HFCs has declined to approximately one-third of the housing finance market.

Presently, the Indian housing finance market is oligopolistic in nature and the major players are banks, HFCs, and the cooperative sector institutions. These three kinds of financial institutions account for over 95 percent of the Indian housing finance market. However, their geographical coverage has not reached the interiors of the urban and rural areas that accommodate a large section of the poor and vulnerable masses. As a result, a large number of other small-scale institutions such as micro-finance institutions (MFIs), community-based organizations (CBOs), self-help groups (SHGs), and so forth have emerged to cater to the housing and housing finance needs of these segments of the population. Although the costs of housing finance from these small sources are high compared to those of the banks, HFCs, and co-operative sector institutions, the easy, quick, and timely availability of finance are supporting the growth and development of these small-scale institutions. Today, the banking sector in India is experimenting a new kind of approach to strengthen their presence and base among the poor masses through both formal and informal linkages. The bank–SHG linkage is an example of this and has been quite successful in fulfilling the housing finance needs of the informal sector of low-income borrowers.

Exhibit 14.1 presents the institutional profile of the housing finance market and their interlinkages through the financial and the "real" sector agencies.

The Indian housing finance market involves a wide range of institutions operating at different levels of the economy. The housing finance market, in this regard, can be said to be of a diverse nature as it has stakeholders operating at its top level as part of a formal system and at the grassroots level as part of an informal system. These stakeholders are, however, governed at a different level by a different set of guidelines and regulations. A brief snapshot of the stakeholders as well as governing bodies is placed in Exhibit 14.2.

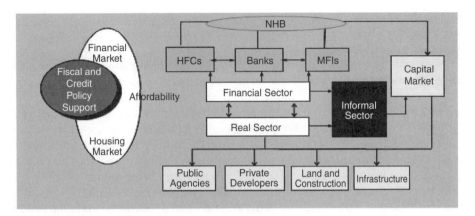

Exhibit 14.1   Housing Finance Market

Exhibit 14.2   Housing Finance Institutions, Regulators, and Target Groups

Institutions	Regulated by	Target Groups
1 All India level financial institutions such as NHB, NABARD	Reserve Bank of India	Refinancing institutions catering to all segments of the society; however, focus is on EWS/LIG and rural
2 Banks including regional rural banks and state co-operative banks as well as foreign banks	Reserve Bank of India NABARD	A cross-section of society in both urban and rural areas, but concentrating on large size loans above Rs.500,000 in recent years. Have taken major steps toward linking the informal sector with the formal sector.
3 Housing finance companies (54 in number, as of November 26, 2010)	National Housing Bank	Dedicated institutions lending for housing. Catering largely to the middle- and higher-income groups, particularly in the urban and semi-urban areas. Limited presence and reach in rural areas.
4 Cooperative sector institutions	State Cooperative Acts	A sector that has deep roots in the country; however, on account of poor financials, it has had limited success in lending for housing in the recent years.
5 Microfinance institutions/ NGOs/SHGs	Unregulated (An act will be introduced for regulating these)	Recent foray into housing, particularly in home improvement finance, catering to the poor and lower-income segments.

THE ROLE OF THE NATIONAL HOUSING BANK (NHB)

The National Housing Bank (NHB) was established by the National Housing Bank Act, 1987, as an apex housing finance institution in India to develop a sound, healthy, and sustainable housing finance system in a holistic manner. It has been mandated to promote housing finance institutions both at local and regional levels and to provide financial and other kinds of support to such institutions. NHB has three broad functions—promotion and development, financing (refinance, direct finance, and equity), and regulation and supervision.

The regulatory framework established by the National Housing Bank coupled with its financing and promotional support has led to widening and deepening of the housing finance system along sound and sustainable lines. NHB exercises regulatory and supervisory authority over the HFCs in the matter of acceptance of deposits by them, pursuant to the powers vested in it under the act. Amendments in effect from June 12, 2000, vest NHB with the power to grant Certificates of Registration to companies to carry on the business of a housing finance institution. Besides, NHB regulates the deposit acceptance activities in the matter of a ceiling on borrowings (including public deposits, rate of interest, period, liquid assets, etc.). NHB has also issued directives on prudential norms in regard to capital adequacy, asset classification, concentration of credit, income recognition, provisioning for bad and doubtful debts, and so forth.

The regulations for the HFCs have helped them in mobilizing funds from the public as depositors, corporations as investors in their bonds, and banks lending funds to the HFCs. Even though in recent years the banks have increasingly and aggressively resorted to direct financing for housing, their indirect lendings through HFCs have also steadily expanded. The commercial banks have a wide presence across the country and are well located in the system to deliver housing credit. There has been a significant shift in the approach of the lending institutions as well as of the policy makers, who now recognize "housing" not purely as a social need, but as a viable and good business proposition and engine of economic growth.

Moreover, as the regulations relate to nearly all aspects of HFCs functioning, the potential promoters also feel comfortable and protected in taking higher equities in these institutions. Regulations have also controlled the proportion of nonperforming assets (NPA) in the industry, which has remained at 1.5 percent and below (currently 0.83 percent), the expansion in housing credit notwithstanding. With enhanced confidence in the HFCs, the banks' lending to the housing finance companies have gone up quite significantly, growing 25 to 30 percent between 2003–2004 and 2009–2010. This has further added to the depth and reach of the housing finance system. With greater funding by the banks for the HFCs, there is greater integration of the housing finance system with the broader financial market.

The housing finance sector in India continues to be driven by the larger national policy and the market. While sizeable segments of the market are still untapped, the lending agencies are looking to these segments for potential business to increase their market share. The lending institutions, at the same time, recognize the risk in lending to such segments such as non-salaried, non-conventional borrowers, and so forth; they tend to price these risks accordingly to maintain their profitability levels. As this market segment is quite huge and is rapidly growing, it offers an enormous untapped potential for the lending institutions. There is also a huge segment of borrowers on the margin who can be reached profitably by the credit institutions, provided their level of confidence and comfort is enhanced through an appropriate institutional mechanism. The Government of India had announced measures for introducing a mechanism for a mortgage guarantee to support and expand lending to these segments of the population. NHB is exploring the introduction of a mortgage guarantee product in collaboration with some international partners, including the IFC and the ADB. This venture will seek to improve accessibility and affordability of housing finance for the newer segments of the population. This venture will also promote the market for MBS in the country and bring about efficiencies in practices and operations.

THE EXPANSION OF PRIVATE FINANCING INSTITUTIONS

The entry of commercial banks in housing finance business is relatively recent. Historically, the housing finance companies have played an important role in funding the housing sector. The Housing Development Finance Corporation (HDFC) and Housing and Urban Development Corporation Ltd. (HUDCO) were the first few leading players in the housing sector, with the former in the private sector and the latter in the public sector. While HDFC's leading profile has been largely for individuals (although it includes corporations and public agencies), HUDCO's lending was mainly to the public agencies at the state level. The setting up of the National Housing Bank at the apex level as a multi-tasked development financing institution in 1988 was an important landmark in the growth of this sector. The objective was to expand and deepen the institutional mechanism for channeling funds into the housing sector. The regulatory framework for the HFCs has resulted in enhanced confidence, evident in the entry of new housing finance companies and growth and expansion among the existing ones. A number of banks and corporations have ventured to set up specialized housing finance outfits. A total of 55 housing finance companies are currently registered with the National Housing Bank.

Recent trends in disbursement of housing finance by the institutions indicate that housing is becoming an "engine of growth" in India, too, as in most of the developed nations of the world. The Government of India and the Reserve Bank of India have attached priority to the housing finance sector and continue their support to the sector through fiscal and regulatory measures for home purchases. The burgeoning middle class, their increasing purchasing power, the changing demographics, and the increasing number of nuclear families, stable real-estate prices, and softer interest rates, coupled with a low delinquency rate resulting in a low number of non-performing assets as compared with other sectors, also enabled the sector to grow at a phenomenal rate and attracted many institutional players.

Housing finance in India is growing rapidly. With the intervention of the banking sector and the emergence of more specialized financial institutions, the sector is attracting a wide range of customers ranging from individuals to corporations to groups. A snapshot of the trend in housing finance disbursements during the past few years by various stakeholders in the housing finance market is displayed in Exhibit 14.3.

With the entry of banks in a large measure since 2002–2003, the scenario has changed dramatically. The growing competition has aggravated the turf war in this segment, with banks accounting for more than 60 percent of the total market of about Rs.503 billion in the year 2003–2004. In a growing, deregulated environment, the competition has resulted in innovations in resource mobilization and lending.

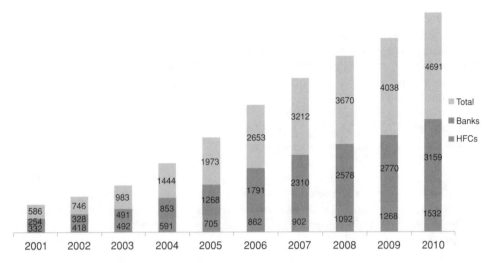

Exhibit 14.3   Housing Loans Outstanding (Rs./Billion)

Lending rates dropped from 15–16 percent per annum until about 2002–2003, to 7–8 percent per annum in the years up to 2008–2009. Competition also led to greater awareness among the borrowers about the opportunities and different ranges of market products. With the expectation that the decline in the interest rates would continue, nearly 80 percent of the loans in the recent past have been contracted at floating rates of interest. Interest rates fluctuate in the housing finance segment, because of increased competition and the undercutting of rates, and at times this has led to under-pricing of risk. Recent years have also witnessed, for the first time, a large take-over of loans (refinancing) among the lending institutions, which has a significant effect on the balance sheet if the numbers are too large. In order to attract customers, the loan size as well as loan-to-value (LTV) ratios have also increased from earlier levels, easing the conditions for borrowers. The aggressive market conditions have imposed a greater need for closer monitoring of the balance sheet and more diligent management of liabilities and assets.

AVAILABILITY AND AFFORDABILITY OF HOUSING CREDIT

The emerging atmosphere of economic development has highlighted significant affordability-related issues. Government-owned public agencies that have been the major providers of subsidized housing were stretched beyond their means, which was a drag on government fiscal health. They have had to gradually withdraw from their traditional construction activities and make room for the more efficient market players in the private sector. For the sake of affordability for low- and moderate-income households, however, the public and private sector agencies are seeking to work in partnership and supplement each others' efforts, deploying their resources to their areas of comparative strengths. The process of reforms has witnessed unification of the various market segments in the formal sector. The linkages between the formal and the informal sectors have also been strengthened, facilitating a free and unobstructed flow of capital. More recently, though, the informal sector agencies, for example, the micro-finance institutions (MFIs) are in the midst of a raging controversy, and the sector is likely to see new legislations and regulatory frameworks. In the emerging scenario, there does appear to be a necessary expanded role of the non-governmental organizations (NGOs), to act as the critical link between the formal and informal sectors in the new institutional format.

The phenomenal growth in mortgage disbursements in recent years has been supported by the availability of alternative distribution channels. Over the last few years, not only has there been a significant increase in the number of banks' own distribution points, but also a proliferation of direct sales agents (DSAs), which have contributed greatly to the expansion of their reach.

Increased competition has led to the introduction of new mortgage products in the market. These products include variable interest rate loans and customized products with features like ballooning equated monthly installments (EMI) or reducing EMIs, depending on the need and eligibility of the borrower. In addition, some banks and HFCs are offering home equity loans (loans against the mortgage of existing property), which may be used for non-housing purposes.

Positive developments notwithstanding, there are still wide gaps in the existing housing finance system as the resources required to meet the country's housing needs are colossal. In a demand-driven sector like today's, the needs of the lower-income populace often do not convert into effective demand. These segments of the population are outside the income-tax brackets and the tax benefits are not availed of by them. On the other hand, they are perceived as higher risk by lending agencies, which often charge higher interest rates and demand higher equity (borrower's contribution in the project) for the loan. The challenges are of two sorts: (1) the housing needs of these segments are "least revealed" to the market, both on the demand (credit) and the supply side; and (2) even if identification of demand were possible, affordability is a key challenge.

In order to meet the housing needs of this segment of the population, the governments, at the union and the state levels, have implemented special schemes from time to time through their own budgetary support and subsidies. Though these schemes reflect the political and social commitment to affordable housing on the part of the government, the ability to fund such programs remains limited and, therefore, proves to be clearly unsustainable, with the government's growing commitment to economic reforms. While specific steps were taken in the past to direct credit through subsidized packages to the people in the low-income category, both transparency and the targeting of subsidies were always a challenge.

In the current scenario, both the government's policy interventions as well as the market as an allocator of funds determine the flow of funds compared to the demand. Government continues to play an important role in ensuring that the affordability component merges well with the overall sectoral strategy. At the macro level, this involves an interactive and a progressive integration between the financial market and the housing market at the policy level, institutional level, and product level. These integrations, though in a limited way, are starting to show up at the union, state, and local levels.

Two factors that have clearly emerged as key drivers in the Indian housing market are (1) a wider group of stakeholders and a multiplicity of institutions, and (2) enhanced confidence in the housing finance industry. It has been recognized that the housing sector is a critical economic sector and can potentially leverage large-scale economic development at the local and the national level.

For the government, which is a major stakeholder, housing is recognized as a powerful contributor to the economy, as it can stimulate industrial activity through its strong links with a number of industries. The contribution of Indian housing and the housing finance sector to GDP of India is expected to rise as the Indian housing and housing finance sector are in the growth stage and are rapidly moving toward the maturity state.

The government also recognizes the revenue-generating potential (through taxation) of increased investments in housing and expansion in housing construction. The employment potential of housing construction activities is also recognized by the policy makers. The government of India, Reserve Bank of India, and the National Housing Bank as policy makers, as well as industry representatives, recognize the multiplier effect of housing production on the economy. Changes in the effective demand for housing have been brought about through innovative loan products offered by various lending agencies in a competitive environment. This has been possible because of a conducive and largely supportive taxation and regulatory system. Besides the housing finance segment, there is also an equally strong imperative for an enabling and supportive framework for the real sector—that is, land and infrastructure and construction activities.

A plethora of laws governing the transactions in the land and housing market have led to complexities and inefficiencies in the functioning of the housing market. These, in turn, increase the transaction costs and adversely affect the confidence of various stakeholders, including the financiers. These obstacles have been long recognized, and include the system for maintenance of land records, rationalization of high and widely different stamp duties levied across the states, registration laws, approval procedures, and so forth. Regulation of the housing market brings attendant costs on the system not only in terms of higher transaction costs but also because of an inadequate flow of institutional funds into the sector on the supply side, for example, through the construction and production of housing.

With the growth of specialized housing finance institutions—currently 55 are registered with the National Housing Bank—and the banking sector's growing interest in housing finance, the market is witnessing new financial depths. The composition of funds for the housing sector—a mix of short- and medium-term funds—are somewhat a concern, while institutions are giving out long-term loans. Measures are being considered for channeling long-term pension and provident funds as well as external funds into the housing sector. A securitization market has also begun to operate, as a measure for better matching of assets and liabilities.

The housing finance sector has enormous developmental impact in terms of social stability and economic empowerment at the individual level and larger economic development at the sector level. The extent of integration of the housing finance system with the broader financial market, however, is a determinant of the leveraging effect and implications. However, as evidenced in different economies, the higher level of integration of the housing market with the rest of the economy can also result in greater pro-cyclicality, which can lead to an immensely magnified effect of any disturbance or stress in any part of the circuit.

Many of the emerging economies, including India's, still don't have fully integrated and unified sectors. In a well-functioning housing finance market in a developed economy, there are significant linkages of the housing finance sector with the financial and the capital market and, in large measure, the growth of securitization and secondary mortgage market have been responsible for this integration. Significantly, in all such markets, supportive regulatory and fiscal regimes have catalyzed these developments. The Indian housing finance market is characterized by a deep and vibrant primary mortgage market. However, the secondary market has not fully developed as the regulations are considered to be rather conservative, not providing adequate incentives for the securitization and development of the secondary mortgage market. This disconnect, which is also a feature of several emerging economies, may also have limited the impact of the financial sector crisis, domestic and global, on the mortgage market.

The incidence of substandard assets against individual housing loans is significantly low and continues to remain so, ensuring sustained and continued flow of funds into the sector. The primary mortgage market has the required infrastructure and depth for continued supply of appropriate, demand-led housing supply in the country.

Taxes and subsidies, like anywhere else, have played an important role in stimulating the demand for housing and the growth of the housing sector in India. In the environment of directed credit and an administered interest rate regime, the banks' lendings were mostly (loan) slab-based. More expensive loans were provided at a higher rate of interest and lower loan amounts at lower rates. The slab structure had a built-in mechanism for internal cross-subsidization. The lower end of the slab could be even lower than the cost of funds for the bank or provide minimum spread to the bank. This could limit the funding by the bank for the lower loan segments and was therefore not in sync with the market reforms and the financial sector developments witnessed since 1991. The administered interest rate structure was eventually dismantled and gave place to independent policies by different banks. This resulted in greater freedom to the banks in their lending operations and offered opportunities for diverse structures and innovative products, both market-friendly and customized. The market has witnessed big-ticket housing loans, going up to Rs.10 million and more. Further, the tax structure also encourages people to place their houses in the market for rent and increase the rental housing stock in the country. The tax provision for borrowings seeks to promote rental housing, recognizing the demand for such housing in the country and the lack of ability amongst those with economic limitations to own a house of their own. While this can result in greater housing production and capital formation in the economy, it also requires rationalization of rent-control provisions, which tends to discourage rental housing. The Rent Control Act imposes rental ceilings, which is a disincentive for rental housing. Rentals should be allowed to work themselves out depending upon the market for allocating funds toward rental and ownership housing and depending upon the relative costs, returns, and fiscal benefits or the lack of it.

While tax incentives are targeted at taxpayers (which implies subsidies), various direct subsidy schemes have been implemented for those who belong to the non-tax-paying category in the lower-income segment of the population. The subsidies implemented in the past have included direct and indirect subsidies, 100 percent subsidies, loan-cum-subsidies schemes, and so forth. Thus, the scope of the housing and the housing finance market in the country is quite extensive, covering various segments of the population through a blend of market-oriented and government-supported programs and initiatives. This has also added to the depth and stability of the housing market, both the "real" and the "financial" subsystems.

OTHER ASPECTS OF HOUSING AFFORDABILITY

"Affordable Housing for All" has been a stated national policy of the government of India. The efforts of the Central Government are being supplemented by housing schemes of several state governments Although many of the programs of the government are designed to provide affordable housing to lower-income households through the subsidy-cum-loan schemes, the NHB, working with support from World Bank, explored the scope of a market-based solution for lower-income households. The study, conducted by the Monitor Group for NHB, found that it is commercially viable to build houses for low-income groups. These results led to a number of projects currently in the pipeline of builders and housing finance companies.

In this format, the subsidies schemes of the government for the lower-income populace have varied from a 100 percent subsidy (the cost of the entire housing units including building materials, construction costs, and basic infrastructure, etc.) to partially subsidized programs with some equity contributed by the borrowers themselves. These schemes have been more in the nature of public housing programs carrying direct subsidies out of the government budget. In some cases, this is done on a sharing basis between the central and the state government, and in some cases is shared with the financial intermediaries. There is growing acceptance among policy makers that the stakeholding of the individual in his housing project is important and the government can play a facilitating role in providing title/tenure to the property in favor of the individual. The right to the property sustains the interest of the lending institutions, thereby leveraging institutional financing for individual housing. A fully or largely subsidized housing unit without the matching economic capabilities of the beneficiary is always exposed to the risk of transfer by way of sale to others for ready cash. Under the social housing program, reasonable subsidy is an integral component that should typically not be loaded to the financial system but should be exclusively held outside the financial system and targeted with transparency and clarity. Notably, in India the Urban Land Ceiling Act, which began in 1976, was aimed at making housing affordable for the lower segment of the population, as excess land above the ceiling would be acquired by the state for undertaking such programs. However, the result has been quite to the contrary, since the act, as it turned out, was premised on assumptions that didn't prove to be correct, and the entire process had built-in snags and inefficiencies. The Urban Land Ceiling Act essentially restricted landholdings and their transfers and thus obstructed the free supply of land and efficient functioning of the market. Out of 220,674 hectares of land declared surplus under the act, only 19,020 hectares could be taken for construction of dwelling units. The remaining area was locked up in litigation leading to scarcity of land and an increase in land prices. In order to release the remaining land and make it available for housing purposes, the Union Government enacted the Urban Land (Ceiling and Regulation) Repeal Act, 1999. The repeal of the act seeks to free up the supply of usable urban land for housing construction, which can also lead to moderation in prices and greater availability of land in the market for large-scale public housing programs.

LAND AVAILABILITY AND LAND MARKETS

Land markets in India are highly affected by regulations, controls, and limitations. The land markets have seen limited reforms. Consequently, there has been a general lack of flexibility in the supply of land, which results in price distortions. Moreover, there has been general lack of land development initiatives, resulting from poor administration and an inappropriate legal structure. The poor quality of land has resulted from a lack of urban infrastructure, poor city planning, poor land records, and cumbersome procedures for buying and selling land. These, in turn, have led to speculation in real estate, the uneven spread of cities, bad environmental outcomes, and high costs of providing municipal services.

Urban land is mostly reclaimed from erstwhile agricultural land situated on the fringes of a growing city. This often means that much of the land around cities is likely to be fragmented, increasing the costs of large-scale housing construction as well as those of developing complementary infrastructure.

The current system is one where the government or its agency takes over the land and compensates the original owners. It then develops the land and sells it. The key problem with this model is that original owners gain little, and frequently such takeovers become embroiled in legal controversies. Most important, the necessary infrastructure investments are constrained by the (local) governments' inability to allocate requisite amounts of funds.

The obvious alternative is to allow private initiative, with some government support or action to facilitate rezoning of agricultural land. These include the planning and zoning regulations, the municipal and building by-laws and codes, planning laws for infrastructure and municipal services, the establishment of a simplified and easily verifiable system of land title (clear and unencumbered), and stamp and registration acts (features of a well-functioning housing and property market). Here, the private developer identifies the area that he or she feels has good market potential. The government helps in transferring the property to the private entity, which in turn compensates the owners. The private entity can then develop the consolidated land.

There have been some instances of public-private partnerships in urban land development, such as the Public Private Partnership for financing water supply or municipal bodies raising funds through their own bonds from the primary market to fund infrastructure projects, on a build-own-operate (BOO) model or build-operate-transfer (BOT) model.

In short, the government can best ensure progress in the housing sector by creating conditions where private entities take on the investment, construction, and service provision roles. Bringing in the private sector in a major way would be eased if a thorough Land Assessment Survey precedes every project. Land assessment surveys identify what part of the urban landscape should be used for which purpose—this depends on surrounding land usage, geological character-istics, infrastructure availability and the cost of creating new infrastructure, and so forth.

Urbanization and rural development policy also must be considered in pro-moting a more competitive land market. According to the Census of India, urban lands (i.e., lands under municipal jurisdictions) constitute about 2.7 percent of the country's land area. There is no doubt that more land will need to be brought into the fold of urban use unless we are able to reverse the impact of economic growth and prevent migration of people to the urban centers or are able to de-centralize and disperse the economic activity to the rural centers. In such a scenario more land will need to be brought under economic, residential, and infrastructure uses in urban, semi-urban, and rural centers.

Initiatives such as land pooling, land banks, and town planning schemes need to be scaled up, to integrate and create synergies among the different pieces of policy interventions. To make these interventions more effective and efficient, there is a need to assess them in a broader perspective in the context of a medium-to long-term plan for town and regional growth. The exercise must involve an assessment of the quantum of developed land as part of the town planning process and identify channels for mobilizing such land for timely delivery in the market. Proactive measures may be taken to ensure that there is no psychology of shortage of developed land. The policy should enable public agencies together with their private sector counterparts to maintain an active supply chain of developed land.

Some of the state governments have sought to address this issue through either direct acquisition of agricultural and rural land in adjoining villages and providing infrastructure *or* allowing the private developers and builders to acquire such land with the government providing the approvals for land use conversion and construction of houses. This could be done more efficiently if the government and planning authorities draw up a regional plan for the development of housing that includes such areas (presently agricultural and rural land) as part of the regional plan.

In order to provide adequately for the economically weaker section (EWS) and lower-income group (LIG) housing, the public agencies should make it mandatory for a certain percentage of housing to be constructed for EWS/LIG at a prefixed price determined by the government for projects where the land is acquired by the public agency and given to the private sector for construction.

The present initiatives should be particularly targeted at the EWS/LIG, for industrial workers, and also slum redevelopment programs. Since market-based solutions are best suited for the middle-income group (MIG) and higher-income group (HIG) categories, the government or its outfit should focus on ensuring adequate housing supply for the lower-income households. The public agencies may gainfully use their land bank as a good resource for the EWS/LIG housing. The capital value of the land may be converted into subsidized housing for these segments by way of predetermined lower-than-market price for the segments and also as a resource for incentivizing the private sector to capture the embedded value in the land and generate their own profit against the subsidized pricing of the lower-income housing.

It is widely believed that the problems of the housing sector, and in particular housing for the urban poor are due to the various acts and legislations enacted by the government. Whether it be the Urban Land (Ceiling and Regulation) Act of 1976, the rent-control laws, the Land Acquisition Act of 1894, stamp laws, property titling laws, or the acts under which various agencies (Development Authorities, Housing Boards, Slum Clearance and Improvement Boards, Planning Acts, etc.) function, none of them have led to an increase in the supply of land and/or housing.

Land has competing uses from different sectors. The financing policies through the banking sector, the financial institutions, the non-banking financial institution, and the capital market are determined by the union policies at the center. On the other hand the land-related policies and also the housing and construction sector are governed by the state and local authorities and the policies are determined at the state level. Often the direction and trends in the housing market (which comprises the land market and construction market, etc.) are not in sync with the financial market. The reasons are that the two markets are driven by different sets of objectives. There is a need to reconcile or integrate the two markets through suitable legislations and amendments.

The legislation or a policy to reduce the stamp duty, substantially, to the level of 4–5 percent across the country will bring in greater efficiency in the housing market. There is a strong case for it at this time: The government's expenditures are expected to come down significantly as part of the financial and fiscal reforms. A large part of the government's responsibilities and investments in different sectors are gradually being taken over by the private sector. As a result the government's expenditures are likely to come down. Even social sectors such as health and education and power are witnessing larger private sector participation. The higher level of prudence and fiscal discipline on the part of the state governments provides a good environment for reduction in the stamp duty (even if it is presumed that lower stamp duty will result in lower revenue, which may not be true). It is reasonable to assume that a reduction in stamp duty can result in higher disclosures and greater transparency in market-oriented valuation and all these can result in higher revenue.

The market forces alone, devoid of a suitable policy environment and public objective and programs, will not serve the housing needs of the urban poor. Such interventions will not come directly or independently from the market unless this business segment has high profit potential. Given the constraints on the land supply, distortion in valuation, lack of and vagaries of income among the urban poor, low comfort among the lending agencies, and above all the social issues involved, the objective of any such program will need the collective efforts of the public and private sectors, the local government, the state government, and the central government. The private sector, comprising the market forces, will be largely driven by profit-motive and business prospects (safety, marketability, and return on funds). It is unlikely that the private sector, through the market forces, will be encouraged to take up such projects through the use of venture funding. The public agencies, with their mandate to pursue social objectives, will do well to unlock the value of the land in the interest of the project and will make the project viable and internally cross-subsidized.

OTHER CHALLENGES OF THE REAL ESTATE SECTOR

The development of a suitable environment in the form of favorable demographics, increasing purchasing power, existence of customer-friendly banks and housing finance companies, professionalism in real estate, and legal reforms are aiding in the growth of the real estate sector as a whole. However, it does face some challenges.

> **High-Density Area Pressures:** Due to the short supply of developed land, housing is in greater demand and has had exorbitant price increases, making housing costs too expensive for the poor. The existing Floor Area Ratio (FAR) and Floor Space Index (FSI) policies across many cities are considered to be obsolete given the scarcity of land and the ever-increasing competing demand for the same. This will place more pressure on high-density areas. It is considered that a portion of the housing needs in the affordable housing category can be met by upward revision in the FAR and FSI.

> **Restricted Market on Affordable Housing:** "Affordable Housing for All" is an important policy agenda of the Government of India. The government has sought to create an enabling and supportive environment for expanding credit flow to the housing sector and increasing home ownership in the country, since the market-based credit system provides credit mainly to the top of the pyramid. Recently, the Ministry of Housing and Urban Poverty Alleviation (MH&UPA) has launched an Interest Subsidy Scheme as an additional instrument for addressing the housing needs of the EWS and LIG segments in urban areas, with the NHB as Nodal Agency.

> **Absence of Real Estate Regulator:** There is no regulator for the land and housing market in India. The MH&UPA is planning to establish a Regulatory Authority and an Appellate Tribunal to regulate, control, and promote planned and healthy development, construction, sale, transfer, and management of residential areas and pockets of residential buildings, apartments, and other similar properties. In addition, the MH&UPA is planning to host and maintain a web site containing all project details, with a view to protecting, on one hand, the public interest in relation to the conduct and integrity of promoters and other persons engaged in the development of such colonies and to facilitate, on the other hand, the smooth and speedy construction and maintenance of such colonies, residential buildings, apartments, and properties and for matters connected therewith or incidental thereto. This will pave the way for consumer protection and fair pricing for housing in India.

> **Nonexistence of Rental Housing Market:** Prime reasons for land market distortions include inflexible zoning and rent and tenancy laws. Zoning laws, rent controls, and protected tenancies restrict the availability of land in cities that would otherwise be made available for new housing and retail construction. The different states and union territories have enacted their own rent control legislation to regulate the chargeable rents, recovery and possession of property, and tenancy rights. These laws have acted as a

disincentive toward investments in housing for rental purposes. Public agencies must provide for rental housing for the EWS, LIG, and migrant industrial workers. The public agencies may engage the private sector to construct such housing on identified and earmarked public land through a Special Purpose Vehicle (SPV) mechanism, and the rental may be managed by the SPV while the maintenance and services are provided by private-sector-estate and property-management agencies. A second approach is that the public agencies can undertake the program in partnership with the private sector. The state government, in exchange for land for commercial, MIG and HIG housing, can make it mandatory for the private builders to construct rental housing stock. Tax incentives would be a third approach to encouraging investment.

Registration Fees and Stamp Duties: Most states in India charge very high registration fees and stamp duties on property transactions. The rate of stamp duty varies from 5 percent in Andhra Pradesh to 14.7 percent in Orissa. High stamp duty and registration costs lead to under-reporting of the agreed-upon value of properties. As a result, a large portion of the real estate market does not remain in the purview of the formal housing finance sector (banks, HFCs, and institutions). The reduction in stamp duty rates applicable for securitized mortgage instruments, to 0.1 percent, by five states has resulted in providing an impetus to the mortgage-backed securities (MBS) market in India.

To facilitate investments in housing, a number of measures have been undertaken recently, from the investors', savers' and lender's points of view. The recently enacted Securitisation and Reconstruction of Financial Assets and Enforcement of Security Interests (SARFAESI) Act will help the lending agencies to foreclose on properties and recover non-performing loans.

With housing finance now contributing to the development of financial depth in the market and in the post-reform scenario, there has been a significant change in approach on the part of the government. The new National Housing and Habitat Policy of the Government of India clearly identified the role of the Government as a facilitator rather than as a builder or a financier. This is likely to have an impact on the partially public housing program undertaken by the public agencies in different states where a certain portion of housing projects was intended to be earmarked for the EWS populace. In recent years, public agencies have had to depend largely on the market for meeting their funding needs rather than resort to the government's budget. Commercial banks and housing finance institutions are playing an important role in funding these agencies for their projects. This has, in large measure, resulted in better interfacing and integration of the housing sector with the financial system.

Exhibit 14.4 represents different institutions operating in the housing sector and their roles and inter-linkages.

SUBPRIME MORTGAGE CRISIS AND INDIA

Although the subprime mortgage crisis turned into a global financial crisis and had its greatest impact on developed economies such as the United States, United

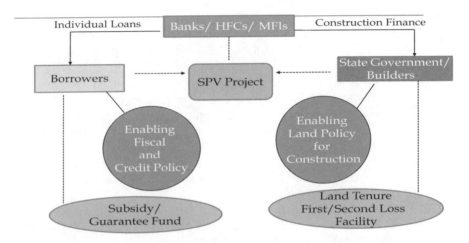

Exhibit 14.4   Institutional Stakeholders

Kingdom, European Union nations, and so forth, its effect on developing countries cannot be ignored. However, this impact was softened by the limited exposure and connection of developing countries with those of the developed world. India, for instance, felt the shockwave of the financial earthquake, but was less affected compared to nations at the epicenter. The primary reason behind the limited impact was the different structure of the housing and housing finance markets in India.

The Indian mortgage market was relatively safer than the U.S. mortgage market. In general, the loan-to-value ratio is modest, the Indian housing lender is by and large cautious, financial regulations are proactive, and many risky products, such as interest-only, teaser, and negative amortization loans are not offered. Furthermore, complex innovative financial instruments have not yet penetrated the Indian mortgage market.

Financial contagion occurred through global economic links. Being the largest economy of South Asia, India is the second-fastest growing economy in the world after China. The economic reforms of India in the 1990s opened the door for globalized standards for the Indian economy. With rising foreign direct investment (FDI) and increasing share in global trade, India has established its place in the global financial system. The link between the Indian economy and the global system is based on a full float in current accounts (trade and services) and partial float in capital accounts (debt and equity).

The impact of the subprime mortgage on India occurred because of two links between the Indian financial system with that of the U.S. economy; specifically, through trade in goods and the flow of capital. The immediate impact of the crisis was plummeting stock prices, net outflow of foreign institutional investors and investments (FII), reduced foreign reserves and tightening of the domestic liquidity situation. As a result, short-term interest rates started to strengthen and a fluctuation in the exchange rate was noticed. Further, the domestic demand in organized sectors such as construction, housing, information technology, and so forth also experienced a decline due to a liquidity crunch in the system. Exports were also affected, but the combined effect of imports and exports was nearly zero. Overall, the subprime mortgage crisis had a limited impact on the Indian economy.

IMPACT AND POLICY MEASURES

The policy response in India to the crisis was quick and steady, in order to tackle the situation and stabilize the overall financial market. Central banks across the globe started to infuse liquidity support in their respective economies as a short-term measure to soften and mitigate the impact of the crisis. The long-term as well as short-term policy responses of the central banks and their respective governments were also customized to their specific national contexts, and to that extent varied in nature based on their prudential norms and characteristics, the functioning and structure of their economy, the extent of their integration with the global economy, and their dependence on the external sector. However, recognizing the global nature of the crisis, the individual policy responses of the central banks soon coalesced in coordinated and collective measures for tackling the crisis at the global level. The Indian banking system was not so much affected by the incidence of the crisis; and the policy response of the Reserve Bank of India (RBI), in this regard, was quite different from that of other central banks. The focus of RBI, while conducting its monetary response, was on preserving financial stability, maintaining price stability, and sustaining the momentum of economic growth through a number of measures. Besides, the effort also took into consideration the augmentation of domestic and foreign exchange liquidity and enabling banks to continue lending quality credit for productive purposes. A synopsis of the measures taken by the RBI to heal the operations of the financial institutions plagued by the crisis and to stabilize the overall economy is shown in Exhibit 14.5.

IMPACT OF THE RECENT ECONOMIC CRISIS ON THE INDIAN ECONOMY AND HOUSING SECTOR

The outlook for India, going forward, is mixed. There is evidence of economic activity slowing down. The Indian banking system was not directly exposed to the subprime mortgage assets. It has very limited indirect exposure to the U.S. mortgage market, or to the failed institutions, or stressed assets. Indian banks, in both the public and private sectors, are financially sound, well-capitalized, and well-regulated. Even so, India is experiencing the knock-on effects of the global crisis, through the monetary, financial, and real channels.

The real estate market in India has been affected due to the global economic slowdown. A slowdown has been observed on both the supply and demand side. Sales have dropped significantly due to the high interest rates. The demand for property has slackened and direct housing loans have also decelerated. In response to emerging global developments, the government of India and the Reserve Bank of India have taken a number of measures since mid-September 2008. Besides the financial sector measures, the "real" sector issues also need to be addressed. In all such crises, the lower segments of the population are affected the most. The governments at the union and the state levels together with the central bank are playing an important role in mitigating the effect of the crisis on the existing system and the people.

In the aftermath of the global economic downturn, various institutional and policy responses have helped the revival of the sector. These have included stimulus packages, liquidity infusion and growth impulses. The combined impact of the

1. Advance allocation of amounts from SCBs to NHB and SIDBI for housing and micro and small enterprises, refinance facility to NHB, SIDBI and EXIM Bank
2. Counter-cyclical prudential measure—provisioning requirement—reduction of all standard assets provisioning to 0.4 percent
3. Reduction of risk weights—all unrated claims on corporations by 100 bps
4. Loans granted by banks to HFCs for on-lending for housing up to Rs. 20 lakh per dwelling unit clasified as priority sector
5. SPV for addressing temporary liquidity constraints of NBFC-ND-SIs.

Rupee Liquidity

1. Gradual reduction in CRR by 400 bps
2. Reduction in SLR by 100 bps
3. Gradual reduction in REO under LAF by 350 bps
4. Gradual reduction in Reverse Repo under LAF by 200 bps
5. Term repo facility of RS. 60,000 crore for NBFCs and MFs under LAF
6. Agricultural debt waiver of Rs. 25,000 crore
7. Special refinance facility up to 90 days with a limit for SCBs up to 1.5 percent of NDTL.
8. Buyback of MSS
9. Prescribed interest rate as applicable to post-shipment rupee export credit (not exceeding BPLR (-) 2.5 percentage point) extended to overdue bills up to 180 days

Subprime Crisis

Foreign Exchange Liquidity

1. Sale of US dollars
2. Special Market Operations to meet public sector oil companies' requirements against oil bonds
3. Enhancing interest rate ceiling on FCNR (B) and NR(E)RA deposit accounts
4. Enhancement of ECBs—quantum USD 500 million per borrower per year—cost ceiling enhanced 200/300/500 bps over LIBOR
5. NBFCs-ND-SI and NHB—permitted to raise short-term foreign currency borrowings
6. Buyback/pre-payment of FCCBs
7. Extension of period of entitlement of first slab of pre-shipment rupee export credit up to 270 days
8. Eligible ECR limit tp 50 percent of outstanding export credit
9. Raise in ceiling rate on export credit in foreign currency to LIBOR+350 bps subject to condition that banks will not levy any other charges (decided by RBI in consultation with GoI) correspondingly, the ceiling interest rate on the lines of credit with overseas banks has also been increased from six months LIBOR/EURO LIBOR/EURIBOR + 75 bps to six months LIBOR/EURO LIBOR/EURIBOR + 150 bps from February 5, 2009.

Exhibit 14.5   Prudential Measures
Source: Reserve Bank of India.

various measures are summarized here, in the particular context of the housing and the housing finance industry:

1. There are definite signs of the market picking up with buyers now coming into the market. The past couple of months have seen good growth in the demand for housing loans. What has caused this more than anything else is the shift in focus of the construction industry from the high-end segment to the middle and the lower segments of the market. This visible shift has the potential to improve the supply of housing as well as cause a reduction in price. The current pick-up in demand shows that the market is

more sensitive to the price of a unit in contrast to interest rates on housing loans. We expect that there is enough latent demand in the system for housing units as well as for housing loans. However, the trigger has to come from the price of the unit. The announcement of projects at lower cost by builder communities across the country, together with lower interest rates on housing loans, have generated positive sentiments in the market. However, the pick-up in the demand should not suggest that the market is ready for a hike in property prices yet. The construction industry must sustain the supply of housing at a lower cost and should operate on a larger scale. This will generate confidence among the various stakeholders, including the lenders, and will induce greater stability in the market, and at the same time sustain the profit-driven (based on volume rather than value) housing and real estate industries.

2. The revival package included liquidity infusion and regulatory forebearance on the restructuring of debts for the cash-strapped real estate sector, an outcome of the global crisis and the economy-wide liquidity crunch. There was seemingly a crisis of confidence and apprehensions about the economy in recession. The increasing incidents of job losses in various segments of the economy affected the credit sentiments, bordering on risk averseness on the part of the lenders. The lenders perceived higher risk in lending for projects (deteriorating the financial positions of over-stretched construction corporations) as well as for individuals (feared impact of recession and job losses). However, with timely and proactive policy interventions, both liquidity and confidence have been somewhat restored. The rapid reduction in the policy rates, involving the cash reserve ratio, repo, and the reverse repo rates, during the period between September and December of 2008 (announced by the Reserve Bank of India) has seen improved liquidity in the system, while signaling an environment of lower interest rates. It is important that the market should respond adequately to the policy inputs, through the actions of the suppliers of credit as well as the suppliers of housing units. A lot depends on how the market players respond to the external stimulus provided by the government and the central bank.

3. Aggregate outstanding housing loans account for only about 7 percent of the country's GDP. This is woefully inadequate and highly inconsistent with the scale of the housing shortage in the country at 24.7 million in the urban areas and nearly 45 million units in the rural areas as estimated for the eleventh five-year plan. If anything, the housing sector needs a big-bang approach. For this to happen, there is a need for a coordinated approach among all the stakeholders—the central government, state government, the private sector construction agencies, and the financing institutions—including banks and housing finance institutions. Fiscal incentives are an important adjunct of the market and are known to stimulate the market more than any other intervention, because investments in housing construction stimulate economic activities that generate income and revenue in their turn. Thus fiscal incentives for promoting investments in housing are widely known to be revenue-neutral to the fiscal authorities. Considering the leveraging effect of fiscal incentives on the demand for housing, any policy measure in this field will be extremely timely and potent, given the current state of the market.

Rather than marginal tweaking, a quantum jump in the fiscal concessions for home-loan borrowers will indeed move the market visibly, in my view. The demand for credit, supported by fiscal benefit, will determine and drive lending in the market. The time for such interventions is very critical, since the market is just about beginning to look up, with the builder community coming to terms with the middle segment of the market, which is a large consumer market (not an investing market) and a safer segment to serve. Creating enough space for fiscal concessions on repayment of principal and interest on their housing loans is likely to make a difference in the size of the housing market and its contribution to the country's GDP.

4. While speaking of the big bang approach, there is clearly a need for stimulating housing demand as well as the supply of housing and housing investments. The housing finance market is fairly well regulated. The fiscal policies on housing should relate to both the demand and supply sides of the sector. Providing incentives to the lending institutions for extending loans to the buyers as well as builders of the properties (within certain limits) consistent with the government's broader policy paradigm, could better serve the social mandate as a market stimulant, and in any case leading to higher levels of home ownership in the country.

The lending institutions must also be incentivized through appropriate risk mitigating instruments to lend for lower-income housing. This is necessary for ensuring adequate credit flow to the segment, which is largely underserved by the market. An explicit or implicit support of the government will improve the risk perception of lenders and encourage them to reach out to the lower segments of the market. While supporting the market through such measures, this will also be consistent with the public policy of the government.

THE ROLE OF THE NHB AND SECURITIZATION IN THE NEAR FUTURE

The National Housing Bank has been playing a lead role in starting up mortgage-backed securitization and development of a secondary mortgage market in India. NHB launched the pilot issues of mortgage-backed securities (MBS) in August 2000 in the Indian financial market, followed by other MBS issues aggregating to Rs.8,622 million. Securitization can be a very powerful instrument for augmenting funds for the housing sector. With the broadening and deepening of the capital market, and given the expansion in the primary housing finance market, there is an opportunity for promoting the secondary mortgage market. The home loan portfolios are good quality assets, and these securitized portfolios will have high acceptability among the investor community. The benefits of securitization are well recognized: liquidity, capital relief, leveraging, and better ALM opportunities. While the NHB is looking at opportunities to kick-start the RMBS market in coordination with the industry participants, the capital market regulator, SEBI, is working on guidelines for listing and trading of the RMBS papers (following the amendment to the Securities and Contract Regulations Act, which now includes the securitized papers as eligible securities). Pension and Provident Funds are natural investors in the RMBS papers, which will help in channeling long-term funds for housing. NHB has offered 14 issues of RMBS in the past and the bank will be expanding its role. It must be emphasized that there are no short-cuts to securitization and the process must go through the rigors that are required to ensure a robust and sustainable RMBS market. After the subprime episode, there is a need to revive the confidence and interest of the various stakeholders in the securitization market, including the regulators. We envisage NHB's role to be very central to this whole process. Ownership of the RMBS transactions and partnership among the various stake holders has been the cornerstone of NHB's securitization issues in the past and will continue to be so. Out of the 14 issues that were offered by NHB, six have successfully closed without any default in payment to the investors.

In the emerging scenario, the growth of the MBS market and securitization of the assets have offered new opportunities to HFCs to improve their liquidity and at the same time better manage their risks through this mechanism. NHB is playing a key role in promoting the MBS market in the country under the provisions of the NHB Act. To facilitate the growth of the MBS market in India, the Reserve Bank of India has issued guidelines for investment by banks in the MBS. The capital market regulator, SEBI, has also permitted mutual funds to invest in the MBS. Efforts are underway to tap the Provident Fund for investments in the MBS. As a significant measure, a number of state governments (six at the time of this writing) have reduced their stamp duty on the securitized instruments, backed by housing loans as low as 0.1 percent *ad valorem*, together with the registration fee for such instruments. Other state governments are also being encouraged to take similar measures, which will expand the market for MBS, facilitating the transfer and liquidity of such instruments and creating a foundation for efficient pricing.

CONCLUSION

The market mechanism to ensure the supply of affordable housing and housing finance as compared to demand is still far from fully developed. The rising population and rapid urbanization are further putting an immense pressure on the housing stock of India. Presently, about 30 percent (328 million) of the population are living in urban centers, and this estimate is expected to further rise to about 40 percent by 2025. Nothing short of concerted and proactive efforts on the part of all stakeholders is going to work.

Further, the fear of a housing bubble growing in the market has often placed all the stakeholders, including regulators, on the defensive with a preference for more conservative and counter-cyclical regulatory prescriptions. With regard to the government's role toward provision of affordable housing, a coordinated approach between the government, regulators, and lending institutions, together with the real sector participants including the construction agencies in the private and public sectors, is now being explored. A collaborative and partnership approach is considered as a more robust and sustainable model, in contrast to a pure lending phenomenon, à la subprime lending. Fresh new thinking has emerged on formulating and designing bankable schemes for the lower-income market. The lenders and the regulators alike are adopting a cautious approach in lending to lower-income households, particularly those in the informal sector. A parallel intervention from the government side is also forthcoming as a response to the financial sector interventions and regulatory prescriptions. The underlined objective is to serve the low-income market efficiently and sustainably, through interventions and support from the financial system as well as the real sector (land and infrastructure, tax, stamp duty, subsidies, etc.). As this segment continues to grow, they need to be served through measures of financial inclusion and inclusionary housing. However, they will need to be protected/hedged against the inbuilt uncertainties and volatilities in the financial and housing sectors. The regulators of the financial market and the housing finance entities—the Reserve Bank of India and the National Housing Bank—are very alive to the potential for bubbles in the market and the need for proactive measures of regulations and signaling.

Lastly, in order to expand the market to the lower-income segment of the populace, the availability of mortgage guarantee products is ensured by the launching of mortgage guarantee companies, for which the Reserve Bank of India has already issued the necessary guidelines. The NHB is working on the project in partnership with some international entities.

ABOUT THE AUTHOR

R.V. VERMA is the Chairman and Managing Director of India's National Housing Bank. The NHB regulates, supervises, and supports the development of a sound and sustainable housing finance system in India. At the National Housing Bank, Mr. Verma is extensively engaged in designing and guiding developments in the country's mortgage market and works in close association with policy making bodies. He is a leading participant at the national and international level on dialogues relating to regulatory issues of housing finance. Mr. Verma was instrumental in NHB's initiative on securitization and development of the secondary mortgage market in India, and has headed the Committee on the "Development of Mortgage Guaranty" in India set up by the Reserve Bank of India. Prior to joining NHB, until 1988, Mr. Verma worked with the Reserve Bank of India in various capacities. He has a Master's in Economics from Delhi School of Economics, a Master's in Business Administration (Finance) and is a Certified Associate of the Indian Institute of Bankers.

CHAPTER 15

The Housing Market and Housing Finance under Liberalization in India

C. P. CHANDRASEKHAR
Professor, Centre for Economic Studies and Planning, Jawaharlal Nehru University

Since the launch of the program of economic liberalization in India in the early 1990s, there has been a huge expansion of the market for housing in the country. However, while India has experienced a housing boom, it was not affected by a crisis similar to the one that was seen in the housing finance and residential property market in the United States and Europe during 2007–2008. In fact, after a brief lull during the worst phase of the global financial crisis, housing prices seem to be once again on the rise. This warrants an examination of the kind of trajectory the housing market in the country has taken.

Five factors are seen as underlying the housing boom in India. The first is the shift since 1980, and especially in the current decade, to a trajectory of growth marked by rates of expansion of GDP well above those recorded during the first three decades after Independence. Consistent and moderately high GDP growth rates during most years of the 1980s and 1990s had encouraged optimistic projections about the housing sector's future growth potential. These projections have been seen as being conservative because of the close to 9 percent growth rate recorded during much of the current decade. The second factor is the evidence that much of this growth in income is accruing to urban residents, with the urban share of national income having risen from 46 percent in 1990 to close to 60 percent currently. Associated with this has been a process of urbanization, with the share of urban population (based on the census definition of urban areas) having risen from 26 percent in 1991 to 28 percent in 2001 and an estimated 30 percent currently.

Third, the effects of high growth are expected to be amplified because of a potential source of new dynamism. This is the *demographic* advantage that India currently has relative to the developed countries and also countries like China (Chandrasekhar et al. 2010). India is and will remain one of the youngest countries in the world. A third of India's population was below 15 years of age in 2000 and close to 20 percent were young people in the 15–24-year-old age group. The population in the 15–24 age group grew from around 175 million in 1995 to 190 million in 2000 and 210 million in 2005, increasing by an average of 3.1 million

Exhibit 15.1   Housing Shortage in India

		1961	1971	1981	1991	2001
Population (in crore*)	Urban	7.89	10.91	15.95	21.76	28.61
	Rural	36.03	43.91	52.38	62.87	74.25
	Total	43.92	54.82	68.33	84.63	102.86
Housing shortage in crore	Urban	0.36	0.3	0.7	0.82	1.06
(10 million)	Rural	1.16	1.16	1.63	1.47	1.41
	Total	1.52	1.46	2.33	2.29	2.47
Shortage as a percentage	Urban	20.4	12.29	19.62	16.84	16.56
of total H/H (in % age)	Rural	16.58	13.61	16.03	12.04	9.78
	Total	17.35	13.31	16.96	13.41	11.86

Note: Shortage includes houseless households as well as dilapidated houses.
*One lakh is equal to one hundred thousand and one crore is equal to 100 lakhs.
Source: Census of India and National Buildings Organisation figures quoted in Roy et al. (2008).

a year between 1995 and 2000 and 5 million between 2000 and 2005. In 2020, the average Indian will be only 29 years old, compared with an average age of 37 in China and the United States, 45 in Western Europe, and 48 in Japan. This demographic process implies that those who are entering, are scheduled to enter, or are currently in the workforce constitute an overwhelming majority. This feature and the associated low dependency ratio provides the potential for a sharp rise in housing investment financed with credit, since faith in their ability to service that debt can be high for a substantial section of the population. Bandyopadhyay et al. (2008) estimate that due to the demographic effect, around 68 million Indians will require independent housing by 2015 (assuming an average household size of three).

Fourth, there is evidence of a significant increase in the size of the middle class, a group that is earning incomes, relative to house prices, that are adequate to sustain purchases financed with housing credit. And, finally, the government has facilitated the housing expansion by bringing down interest rates and offering significant tax deductions against housing investments.

The census for 2001 had identified close to 250 million houses in the country. This must have increased substantially over the past decade because of the factors noted above. So must have the housing shortage, which has been estimated at 24.7 million units in 2001 (Exhibit 15.1). Not surprisingly, the Planning Commission estimated the investment requirements for housing during the 11th Plan (2007–2012) at $108 billion. The demand for housing has, therefore, been increasing and will continue to increase.

This increase in demand for housing is accompanied by an increase in the share of the population that can afford modern housing. An examination of trends in housing conditions using data from the periodic surveys of the National Sample Survey Organization (NSSO) points in two directions. First, the share of the population residing in *pucca* buildings[1] has been rising over time (Exhibit 15.2). The percentage of households living in what is termed a *pucca* structure increased from 32 percent in 1993 to nearly 48 percent in 2002, and further to nearly

Exhibit 15.2   Distribution (per 1,000) of Households by Type of Structure

		All-India		
		Type of Structure		
Sector	Pucca	Semi-Pucca	Katcha	All
		49th round (January–December 1993)		
Rural	323	360	317	1,000
Urban	738	179	83	1,000
Rural & urban	432	313	256	1,000
		58th round (July–December 2002)		
Rural	484	303	213	1,000
Urban	877	90	32	1,000
Rural & urban	596	242	162	1,000
		65th round (July 2008–June 2009)		
Rural	554	276	170	1,000
Urban	917	62	21	1,000
Rural & urban	661	213	126	1,000

Source: Housing Finance and Housing Demand.

55 percent in 2008–2009 in rural areas. The proportion of urban households living in pucca structures increased from 74 percent in 1993 to nearly 88 percent in 2002 and 92 percent in 2008–2009. Second, the proportion of individuals living in rented accommodation in urban areas has remained more or less constant with rapid urbanization, suggesting that the demand for owned accommodation in urban areas must be rising.

The expansion in the volume and improvement in the quality of housing has been facilitated by the expansion of the housing finance industry. Globally, a significant component of the process of financial expansion and an important site for financial innovation has been the housing finance or mortgage market. The reasons for this are obvious. In most contexts, individuals or families would like to own a house if it can be afforded. Given the relative costs of housing within the desired asset basket of a household, it constitutes one among the larger investments or the single largest investment that many households ever make. Given the lifespan or durability of that investment and its liquidity characteristics, this is an asset that is most eligible for debt financing, since foreclosures due to default can in most circumstances be followed by easy liquidation to compensate the lender.

This makes housing finance one of the largest feasible mass markets for debt. That market can be made even larger if explicit or implicit government guarantees of housing loans are provided, as happened for example with the creation of Fannie Mae in 1938 and Freddie Mac in 1970 in the United States.

These characteristics notwithstanding, housing finance demand depends on the market for housing, or the number of individuals or families with not only the desire but also the characteristics that make them eligible for such credit. This number depends also on the ability of individuals and households to use potential future income as the basis for acquiring a housing asset, since saving to

accumulate the lump sum required for the purpose would postpone the acquisition substantially. Changes in finance are also therefore an important influence
on housing demand at any given point in time. As in other emerging markets,
in India too, these factors have combined to deliver a housing boom, especially
in urban areas. Moreover, despite the almost synchronized collapse of the boom
in many economies across the world in the wake of the U.S. subprime mortgage
crisis, this has not yet happened in India. The issue in India, therefore, is not the
nature of the crisis affecting the housing market but whether risks of the kind that
precipitated the housing collapse in the United States and elsewhere are being
accumulated in India as well, even though as of now the market shows signs of
robust growth.

Growth of the Housing Finance Industry

In India, official efforts to direct credit to meet the housing finance needs of private
investors gathered momentum with the establishment of the National Housing
Bank (NHB) in 1988. The NHB was set up as a wholly owned subsidiary of the
Reserve Bank of India that was to both serve as a regulator for the dedicated housing
finance companies (HFCs) as well as an institution providing refinance facilities
to the HFCs. At that time nearly 80 percent of the housing stock in the country
was reportedly financed by informal sources. There were even then, however,
a number of housing finance companies (HFCs) that were non-bank financial
companies (NBFCs), but were regulated by the Reserve Bank of India (RBI). They
included small companies with localized operations and companies engaged in
construction and/or development, which also offered housing credit. Several of
the companies relied on public deposits for their resources. A notable exception
was the Housing Development Finance Corporation (HDFC).

The creation of the National Housing Bank was an attempt to make housing
finance companies significant financial intermediaries. Its mandate included helping create new housing finance companies and regulating and supervising them
as per the provisions of the NHB Act of 1987 and the Housing Finance Companies
(NHB) Directions of 2001. While soon thereafter many new HFCs were set up,
including several sponsored by banks and financial institutions and some with
equity support from the National Housing Bank, the independent housing finance
industry was even recently by no means the dominant player. In fact, according to
the Committee on Financial Sector Assessment (CFSA) set up by the government
and the RBI that submitted its report in 20009, the number of HFCs had by 2008
fallen to around 43, and of these, 12 accounted for 90 percent of the business of
these firms as a group.

However, HFCs are among the more fragile of financial firms. Having to mobi-
lize a large proportion of their resources in the form of short-term deposits, while
being engaged in an activity involving long-term lending, these firms are prone
to liquidity problems arising from maturity mismatches. This makes asset liability
management (ALM) crucial to these firms, wherein they are at a disadvantage vis-
à-vis the commercial banks, which have been allowed over time to expand their
presence in the housing finance market.

Given their sheer scale it is to be expected that commercial banks, which are
the principal depository institutions in a system dominated by banking, are in a

better position to deal with the problem of maturity mismatches. Hence, if these banks were encouraged to diversify into the housing finance sector, they would be in a position to dominate the market. Driven by the objective of encouraging private investment in housing and of reforming finance to create universal banks that were not constrained within narrow functional spaces, the government did allow them to enter the housing finance industry.

Subsequently, the emphasis shifted to incentivizing the provision of housing finance by the banks. The Reserve Bank of India's *Statement on Monetary and Credit Policy for the Year 2002–2003* noted that The Basel Capital Accord of 1988 and the New Capital Adequacy Framework, which was at the consultative stage, envisaged a risk weight of 50 percent and 100 percent for claims secured by residential property and commercial real estate. Taking a cue from there the *Statement* declared that: "With a view to improve flow of credit to the housing sector, it has been decided to liberalize the prudential requirement on risk weight for housing finance by banks and encourage investments by banks in MBS (mortgage-backed securities) of HFCs, which are recognized and supervised by NHB." In May 2002, the RBI issued a notification allowing banks extending housing loans to individuals against mortgage of residential housing properties to assign a risk weight of 50 percent instead of the then-existing 100 percent. As a result, scheduled commercial banks remained the dominant players in the housing loan market. According to estimates from the Investment and Credit Rating Agency (ICRA), the total mortgage debt outstanding in India as on December 31, 2009, was over Rs.4,137 billion, with 71 percent in the books of the scheduled commercial banks and the balance in that of the HFCs (Exhibit 15.3).

This dominance of banks was not without adverse implications. The first was the concentration of housing market exposures in a few banks. According to ICRA (2010): "HDFC (along with HDFC Bank), State Bank of India (SBI), ICICI Bank (along with ICICI Home Finance), and LIC Housing Finance (LIC HFL) clearly

Exhibit 15.3 Break-Up of Home Loan Portfolio among HFCs and Banks

	March 2004	March 2005	March 2006	March 2007	March 2008	March 2009	December 2009
HFCs	354	468	598	734	912	1,082	1,219
SCBs	894	1,347	1,852	2,310	2,557	2,724	2,918
Total	1,248	1,815	2,450	3,044	3,469	3,806	4,137
Credit growth: HFCs	27%	32%	28%	23%	24%	19%	17%
Credit growth: Banks	158%	51%	38%	25%	11%	7%	11%
Credit growth: Total	100%	45%	35%	24%	14%	10%	12%
HFC share in total housing credit	28%	26%	24%	24%	26%	28%	29%
Bank share in total housing credit	72%	74%	76%	76%	74%	72%	71%

SCBs: Scheduled Commercial Banks
Note: Amounts in Rs. billion; growth rates for December 2009 are on an annualized basis over March 2009 levels.
Source: RBI, Annual Reports of Mortgage Lenders and ICRA estimates quoted in ICRA (2010), *Housing Finance Companies and the Indian Mortgage Finance Market*, New Delhi.

dominate the domestic mortgage market, together accounting for 53 percent of the total housing credit in India (as of December 31, 2009). Apart from these big market participants, there are some HFCs with relatively smaller credit portfolios operating in their respective geographies or serving niche customers."

But liquidity problems similar to those faced by the HFCs plague banks, as well. According to the CFSA, there has been an increase in recent times of banks' dependence on bulk deposits to fund credit growth. On the other hand, there has also been an increase in the volume of housing loans provided by banks as a share of their advances, and an increase in their exposure to the real estate and infrastructure sectors, which has resulted in an elongation of the maturity profile of bank assets.

Banks were also indirectly exposed to the mortgage market. The increased importance of banks in the housing finance market was also because of developments akin to those in the developed countries. There, financial innovation that had permitted the transfer and spread of risk had also helped expand the mortgage business. Securitization by transferring risk, while allowing investors in securities to choose the bundle of risks considered appropriate, facilitated the expansion of the housing finance market. It encouraged the relaxation of lending norms, so that the threshold ratio of house prices to annual incomes at which a household becomes eligible for credit is lowered. In India too, the government permitted securitization.

The first mortgage-backed securitization in India was for Rs.507 million in 2000, as part of a pilot project undertaken by the National Housing Bank, in which the originators of the mortgages were the HDFC and LIC Housing Finance. Furthermore, in the 2002 notification referred to earlier, investments by banks in mortgage-backed securities (MBS) of residential assets of housing finance companies were also declared eligible for risk weight of 50 percent for the purpose of capital adequacy. The intention was clearly to encourage such investments and facilitate the parallel growth of the housing finance industry. By 2006 the issue of MBS had risen to $50.1 billion. It must be noted, however, that for a variety of reasons the growth has been volatile. During financial year 2007 the Indian securitization market stood at Rs.370 billion. Of this, residential mortgage-backed securities amounted to Rs.16 billion, or less than 5 percent of the total issuances.

Banks were important investors in mortgage-backed securities generated by HFCs. This also meant a different kind of concentration of their exposure. As of March 2009, about 69 percent of the total portfolio of ICRA-rated HFCs was concentrated in the top two states of operation. As ICRA (2010) notes: "Such geographical concentration makes these HFCs sensitive to adverse movements in property prices in specific regions (following oversupply, demand slowdown, or other events), and can cause asset quality concerns in the future." If HFCs are prone to financial difficulties because of such concentrated exposure, so would be the banks and other institutions that buy into the securities generated on the basis of the credit assets they originate.

To partly reduce the risk carried by the banking system, the regulatory system required the transfer of the right to generate and sell MBSs to a Special Purpose Vehicle (SPV)/Trust (Kothari 2007). Towards that end, the law requires the irrevocable transfer of the right, title, and interest of an HFC in securitized housing loans and receivables underlying them to the SPV, which must hold the securities exclusively on behalf of and for the benefit of the investors by the SPV/Trust. The SPV then is entitled to the receivables under the securitized loans with an arrangement for the distribution of this to the investors as per the terms of the MBS. The loans to be securitized should be loans advanced to individuals for acquiring or constructing residential houses, which should have been mortgaged to the HFC by way of exclusive first charge. They must also have been accorded an investment grade credit rating by any of the recognized credit-rating agencies.

Using mechanisms such as these, the regulatory framework sought to underplay the risks associated with rising bank exposure to the housing finance market. This helped expand the universe of borrowers to cover some borrowers who were earlier considered not so creditworthy. Given the consequent increase in the number of less-affluent borrowers in the housing finance market, the demand for housing credit tends to be sensitive to the interest rate. Hence an easy credit regime with low interest rates or a policy of quantitative easing that expands credit, triggers a sharp increase in the demand for housing and the volume of debt. The consequent increase in housing investment and the derived demands it generates contributes in turn to overall growth. When the central bank pumps liquidity into the system, credit financed housing investment increases and serves as the transmission mechanism to effect growth. When liquidity is squeezed, on the other hand, housing credit, demand, and growth can be affected adversely. In other words, the effectiveness of monetary policy as an instrument to drive demand and growth increases when financial innovation helps expand the share of credit diverted to the housing market. This encourages government to find ways of expanding the market for housing as part of a strategy of promoting growth.

Implications for Prices

There is, however, one difficulty. Since housing requires land, a scarce resource, as an input, and housing demand tends to be unevenly distributed geographically, with a concentration in urban areas as urbanization proceeds, increases in demand often result in sharp increases in prices. This, on one hand, increases the ratio of house prices to annual incomes and dampens housing demand. Bandyopadhyay et al. (2008) found that: "An increase in house prices by 10 percent, *ceteris paribus*, results in a 4.6 percent decrease in housing demand as affordability comes down." On the other hand, housing price inflation encourages speculative investments in housing, especially since the pre-existing stock of housing, the value of which is rising, can to differing degrees be used as collateral. Most often the speculative impact dominates, resulting in spiraling prices, till a debt overhang, government action, or a change in investor sentiment halts or reverses the rise.

One fall-out of these features of the housing market is that financial liberalization that permits securitization and the creation of complex instruments that help transfer and distribute risk, and thereby expand the universe of borrowers with access to the housing finance market, could trigger a housing boom and a speculative spiral. If such liberalization is accompanied by a loosening of monetary policy and an engineered reduction in interest rates, this tendency is only strengthened. Often, therefore, these elements combine to transform the boom into a bubble that must finally burst, as happened in the run up to the subprime mortgage crisis in the United States. When that happens the value of the housing stock that constitutes the collateral for much of this lending collapses, with extremely adverse consequences for the financial system and the real economy.

Financial liberalization, however, is not restricted to the developed countries. Over the past two to three decades most developing countries have liberalized their financial policies and transformed their financial structures in ways that make those structures approximate the Anglo-Saxon model created through liberalization in the United States and United Kingdom since the 1980s. The reasons for this are well known. Starting from the mid-1970s, a combination of surpluses generated by the oil shocks, savings accumulated by the baby-boomer generation in pension funds, and liquidity generated by the excess global spending of the United States (which had the benefit of the dollar being the world's reserve currency), encouraged financial firms to find new targets for lending and investment in the emerging markets. This gave developing countries an opportunity in the form of increased access to international liquidity. When these countries chose to exploit this opportunity by attracting foreign capital inflows, they had to invite the foreign financial firms that were the carriers of such capital as well. They therefore reformed their financial regulations, to provide these firms the space to undertake their activities as well as function according to the norms that they were used to in their own home countries. As a result the nature of markets, institutions, and instruments in the financial sectors of developing countries and the regulatory framework governing them were transformed and reshaped in the image of financial structures in the Anglo-Saxon world. As a result of this structural contagion, many of the financial practices characterizing the developed nations have also come to characterize the developing countries. Thus, just as much as the mortgage market and its derivatives have come to play a role in the metropolitan countries, so have they in the developing countries. This has been true in India as well since the early 1990s.

This has led to an acceleration of the transformation of banking in India, with growing exposure of commercial banks to the retail credit market with no or poor collateral and a growing tendency to securitize personal loans. The growth in retail credit occurs when credit provision is expanding and at the margin much of the new credit is diverted to the retail sector. Total bank credit grew at a scorching pace from 2004–2005 till 2007–2008, at more than double the rate of increase of nominal GDP. As a result, the ratio of outstanding bank credit to GDP (which had declined in the initial post-liberalization years from 30.2 percent at the end of March 1991 to 27.3 percent at the end of March 1997) doubled over the next decade to reach about 60 percent by the end of March 2008. Thus, one consequence of financial liberalization was an increase in credit dependence in the Indian economy, a characteristic imported from developed countries such as the United States. The growth in credit out-performed the growth in deposits, resulting in an increase in the overall credit-deposit ratio from 55.9 percent at the end of March 2004 to 72.5 percent at the end of March 2008. This increase was accompanied by a corresponding drop in the investment-deposit ratio, from 51.7 percent to 36.2 percent, which indicates that banks were shifting away from their earlier conservative preference to invest in safe government securities in excess of what was required under the statutory liquidity ratio (SLR) norm. (Data in this and the subsequent paragraphs are from CFSA 2009.)

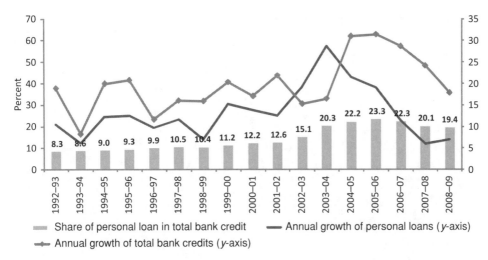

Exhibit 15.4   Trends in Personal Loans

Not surprisingly, these changes were not primarily driven by an increase in the commercial banking sector's lending to the productive sectors of the economy. Instead, retail loans became the prime drivers of credit growth. The result was a sharp increase in the retail exposure of the banking system, with personal loans increasing from slightly more than 8 percent of total bank credit in 1992–1993 to more than 23 percent by 2005–2006 (Exhibit 15.4). Though there has been a decline in that ratio subsequently, it still stood at 19.4 percent at the end of 2008–2009. The decline appears to be the result of an overall correction in bank lending growth, which also declined in this period, with the adjustment being much sharper in the case of personal loans when the transition occurred in 2004–2005.

Of the components of retail credit, the growth in housing loans was the highest in most years. As Exhibit 15.5 indicates, the rate of growth of housing loans gathered momentum at the end of the 1990s and remained at extremely high levels right up to 2006–2007. As a result the share of housing finance in total credit rose from 5 percent in 2001–2002 to 12 percent in 2006–2007 and was still at 10 percent in 2009–2010. The increase is often attributed to the low level of penetration of the mortgage market in India, standing at 7 percent in 2006, as compared to 12 percent in China, 17 percent in Thailand, 26 percent in Korea, 29 percent in Malaysia and a huge 80 and 86 percent respectively in the United States and United Kingdom. But these differential penetration rates have to be seen in the light of differentials in per capita income and the degree of income inequality, both of which do not favor a significantly large mortgage market in India.

By all accounts, the credit-financed boom in the housing market has triggered a spiral in housing prices, which then feeds the boom even more. Unfortunately, till recently India had no reliable index of housing prices, with available figures being from stray private sector real estate consulting firms. But the Residex, now being collated by the National Housing Bank with 2007 as base (=100), shows that even during the period when the boom was tapering off, prices in most metropolitan centers (Delhi, Mumbai, Kolkata, and, more recently, Chennai) were

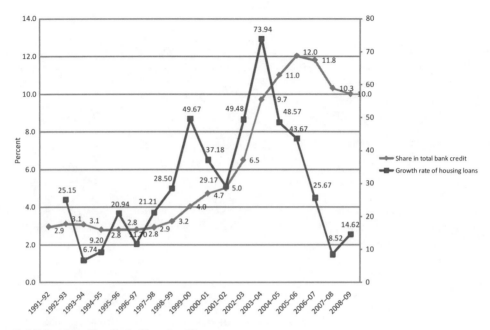

Exhibit 15.5   Trends in Housing Finance

rising quite significantly. Thus, the conclusion derived from experiences elsewhere in the world that easy credit accompanied by low interest rates leads to a sharp increase in housing finance and increases in house prices fed by speculation seems to be true of India as well, in its new liberalized financial environment.

One study (Lall 2006) relating to the city of Delhi tracks the movement in housing prices since 1997, when prices had peaked, driven by an acute shortage of land and speculative investments. According to the study: "The burst of the bubble in 1998 was an outcome of over valuation of property prices and liquidation of speculative holdings. Prices fell by 40–80 percent, virtually wiping out the entire capital of speculative investors. First signs of recovery were evident in 2003 and prices spiraled thereafter due to easier access to housing finance, and general improvement in economic conditions."

The increase in prices was estimated at 19 percent during 2001–2002, 32 percent in 2003, 58 percent in 2004, and 105 percent in 2005. Lall argues that during the period up to 2003, which set the foundations for the subsequent spiral, price increases were based on genuine and not speculative demand. Subsequently, however, housing price increases were driven by speculation. The increase in demand was across all price segments. High incomes, affordable home loan rates, and a stable economy are seen as having contributed to increasing affordability and rising effective demand for housing units. Thus this evidence seems to suggest that boom-bust cycles in the housing market seem to have been true of much of the period of liberalization.

As a former Deputy Governor of the RBI has noted (Mohan 2007): "Demand for housing finance has emerged as a key driver of bank credit in the past few years. As incomes grow further and the pace of urbanization picks up, and, in view of the substantial backlog, demand for housing and housing finance can be expected to record continuous high growth over the next few years. In view of the expected high demand, pressure on real estate prices may continue. Moreover, real estate markets are characterized by opacity and other imperfections in developing countries, and certainly in India. Such developments can easily generate bubbles in the real estate market, because of problems in the elasticity of supply, and information asymmetries. Strong demand for housing and buoyancy in real estate prices in an environment of non-transparency, thus, could potentially pose risks to the banking system. In conjunction with interest rate cycles, the banking system as well as the regulator would need to be vigilant to future NPAs and the U.S.-like subprime woes."

This is a recognition of the possibility that the rapid increase in credit and retail exposure would have brought more tenuous borrowers into the bank credit universe in India, as well. A significant (but as yet unknown) proportion of this could be subprime lending. To attract such borrowers, banks had offered attractive interest rates below the benchmark prime lending rate (BPLR). More recently banks, including public sector banks, have been opting for the scheme of initial teaser rates on housing loans, which tends to attract borrowers of doubtful repayment capacity into the housing market. The share of BPLR loans in the total rose from 27.7 percent in March 2002 to 76.0 percent at the end of March 2008. This increase was especially marked for consumer credit and reflected a mispricing of risk that could affect banks adversely in the event of an economic downturn.

Further, rapid credit growth meant that banks were relying on short term funds to lend long. From 2001 there was a steady rise in the proportion of short-term deposits with the banks, with the ratio of short-term deposits (maturing up to one year) increasing from 33.2 percent in March 2001 to 43.6 percent in

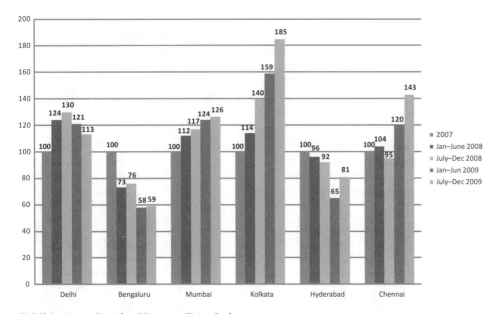

Exhibit 15.6   Residex Housing Price Index

March 2008. On the other hand, the proportion of term loans maturing after five years increased from 9.3 percent to 16.5 percent. While this delivered increased profits, the rising asset-liability mismatch increased the liquidity risk faced by banks.

Faced with these risks the central bank has been periodically warning banks against excessive increases in exposure to the housing finance market. In its Annual Policy Statement for 2006–2007 the Reserve Bank of India increased the general provisioning requirement for residential housing loans exceeding Rs.20 lakh from 0.40 percent to 1.0 percent. Subsequently, the RBI warned banks against resorting to teaser interest rates, given the experience with the consequences of such rates in the United States and other contexts. However, the risk weight on bank exposure to housing loans continued to be kept low and a substantial segment of home loans falling below Rs.20 lakhs were kept within the ambit of the priority sector, which consists of a combination of sectors like agriculture and small-scale industries to which a specified minimum percentage of total lending is required to be directed by the banks (40 percent for the scheduled commercial banks). This treatment of housing as a priority sector is partly because the government has not been able to provide adequate volumes of affordable housing, especially in urban areas where the demand from a burgeoning middle class is substantial. But it is also substantially because credit-financed housing demand is seen as an important driver of growth in the new context, creating a lobby in its favor within the government. However, in the process India may be encouraging a trend that increases the fragility of the housing market and therefore of the financial and the real economy.

That such a trend is underway emerges from the Reserve Bank of India's monetary policy review for the second quarter of 2010–2011 (Reserve Bank of India 2010), in which it sent out a strong signal that it wants the commercial banking system to rein in the boom in housing finance. The RBI's concern stems from the evidence of a spike in lending for housing. Over the period of April 1 to September 25, 2010, housing credit increased by Rs.16,195 crore[2] as compared to Rs.7,891 crore over the corresponding period of the previous financial year. What is more, during the five-month April to August period, net credit provided by the housing finance companies also rose by Rs.7,519 crore, as compared with Rs.3,581 crore during six months stretching from April to September 2009. Banks have adopted a number of techniques to expand this market. This included the practice of offering these loans at lower teaser interest rates during the first few years, with the rates being subsequently reset to much higher levels.

Realizing that such practices tend to attract subprime borrowers who do not have the ability to meet their future commitments, the RBI has chosen to rein in the housing finance lending spree. It has done this with four sets of measures. First, it has put a ceiling of 80 percent on the loan-to-value (LTV) ratio, which reduces leverage by requiring borrowers to commit their own equity to the extent of at least 20 percent of the value of the asset at the very beginning. This reduces the risk burden on the lender. Second, in a reversal of policies adopted earlier it has decided to raise the average risk weight associated with larger housing loans. A higher risk weight requires banks to set aside a larger volume of regulatory capital for a given loan size. When the risk weight on a particular credit type is 100 percent and the capital adequacy requirement is 12 percent, capital equivalent to 12 percent of the loan has to be invested in specified regulatory assets. Since regulatory capital is supposed to be in forms that are safe and relatively liquid, the return on such assets is lower and reduces average bank revenues. So increasing risk weights on any kind of lending is expected to discourage that kind of lending.

Till the recent policy review, the risk weights on residential housing loans with LTV ratios of up to 75 percent was 50 percent for loans up to Rs.3 million and 75 percent for loans in excess of that amount. For loans with LTV ratios greater than 75 percent, the risk weight was 100 percent irrespective of the size of the loan. In addition to capping the LTV ratio at 80 percent, the RBI has now decided to increase the risk weight for residential housing loans of Rs.7.5 million and above to 125 percent, irrespective of the loan-to-value ratio associated with any particular loan of that size.

Third, the RBI has sent out a strong cautionary signal with regard to the practice of offering teaser rates. In its view, "This practice raises concern as some borrowers may find it difficult to service the loans once the normal interest rate, which is higher than the rate applicable in the initial years, becomes effective. It has been observed that many banks at the time of initial loan appraisal do not take into account the repaying capacity of the borrower at normal lending rates." Finally, having recognized that loans offered with teaser interest rates have higher risk associated with them, the RBI has decided to increase the provisioning required for these assets categorized as standard assets from 0.40 percent to 2 percent, so as to take care of that subset of loans that turns non-performing.

Put together these measures constitute a significant effort at prudential regulation of a banking sector that is increasingly diversifying into retail lending involving personal loans of various kinds. The message from the central bank is clear. India may have avoided a crisis of the subprime mortgage type, but it remains prone to such crises. Regulation and control are, therefore, a must.

NOTES

1. A *pucca* construction is one that includes varying combinations of the following materials: cement; concrete; oven-burnt bricks and/or hollow cement/ash bricks; stone and/or stone blocks; jack boards (cement plastered reeds); iron, zinc, or other metal sheets; timber; tiles; slate; corrugated iron; asbestos cement sheet; veneer; plywood; artificial wood of synthetic material; and polyvinyl chloride (PVC) material.

2. One lakh is equal to one hundred thousand and one crore is equal to 100 lakhs.

REFERENCES

Bandyopadhyay, Arindam, S. V. Kuvalekar, Sanjay Basu, Shilpa Baid, and Asish Saha. 2008. *Study of Residential Housing Demand in India*. Pune: National Institute of Bank Management.

Chandrasekhar, C. P., Jayati Ghosh, and Anamitra Roychowdhury. 2010. "Reaping the Demographic Dividend." In A. K. Shiva Kumar, Pradeep Panda, and R. Rajani Ved, *Handbook of Population and Development in India*. 22–31 New Delhi: Oxford University Press.

Committee on Financial Sector Assessment (CFSA). 2009 (March). *India's Financial Sector Assessment: Overview Report*. Mumbai: Government of India and Reserve Bank of India.

ICRA. 2010. *Housing Finance Companies and the Indian Mortgage Finance Market*. New Delhi: ICRA.

Joshi, Himanshu. 2006. "Identifying Asset Price Bubbles in the Housing Market in India—Preliminary Evidence." *Reserve Bank of India Occasional Papers* 27: 1–2.

Kothari, Vinod. 2007. *India Securitisation: Regulatory and Market Scenario* (mimeo). Kolkata: Vinod Kothari Consultants Private Limited.

Lall, Vinay D. 2006. *Development of House Prices in India: Experiences with a Weak Database*. Paper 9, OECD-IMF Workshop on Real Estate Price Indices, 6-7 November, Paris: OECD.

Mohan, Rakesh. 2007 (December). "India's Financial Sector Reforms: Fostering Growth While Containing Risk." *Reserve Bank of India Bulletin*.

Reserve Bank of India. 2002 (May). *Statement on Monetary and Credit Policy for the Year 2002–2003*, Reserve Bank of India, Mumbai.

Reserve Bank of India. 2010 (November). *Second Quarter Review of Monetary Policy 2010–2011*, Reserve Bank of India, Mumbai.

Roy, Uttam K., Madhumita Roy, and Subir Saha. 2008. "Mass-Industrialized Housing to Combat Consistent Housing Shortage in Developing Countries: Towards an Appropriate System for India." Paper presented at World Congress on Housing, November 3–7, Kolkata, India.

ABOUT THE AUTHOR

C. P. CHANDRASEKHAR is currently Professor at the Centre for Economic Studies and Planning, Jawaharlal Nehru University, New Delhi. His areas of interest include the role of finance and industry in development, and the experience with fiscal, financial, and industrial policy reform in developing countries. He is the co-author of *Crisis as Conquest: Learning from East Asia* (Orient Longman), *The Market That Failed: Neo-Liberal Economic Reforms in India* (Leftword Books) and *Promoting ICT for Human Development: India* (Elsevier). He is a founding Executive Committee Member of International Development Economics Associates, and a regular columnist for *Frontline* (titled *Economic Perspectives*) and *Business Line* (titled *Macroscan*).

CHAPTER 16

The Recent Financial Crisis and the Housing Market in Japan

MIKI SEKO
Keio University, Faculty of Economics

KAZUTO SUMITA
Kanazawa Seiryo University, Department of Economics

MICHIO NAOI
Tokyo University of Marine Science and Technology, Faculty of Marine Technology

This chapter offers an overview of the housing and housing finance markets in Japan, discusses the causes and consequences of the international propagation of the 2008 U.S. financial crisis to the Japanese market, and suggests directions for future policy reforms. We compare the differences between the consequences of the 2008 U.S. subprime loan problem and the bursting of Japan's asset bubble in the early 1990s for the overall economy with a focus on the housing and housing finance markets in Japan. The Japanese housing bubble in the early 1990s and the current financial crisis have had similar macroeconomic consequences, involving a sharp decline in housing prices and housing starts, increased housing foreclosures, and rising unemployment. Even as Japan reels from the current economic crisis, the potential benefits of market-oriented reforms for real estate securitization, housing finance system, private and public rental housing, and the second hand housing market in Japan are evident.

INTRODUCTION

The housing and housing finance markets in Japan and the consequences for these markets of the 2008 financial crisis are examined in this chapter. We examine the institutional structure of the housing market and housing finance system in the United States and Japan and then discuss the impact of the current financial crisis on the Japanese housing market and some policy implications. The second section, presents an overview of the Japanese economy and its housing and housing finance markets. In the third section, we discuss the causes and consequences of the current financial crisis, and also suggest possible reforms, while our conclusions are featured in the last section.

OVERVIEW OF THE JAPANESE ECONOMY, HOUSING MARKETS, AND HOUSING FINANCE

This section overviews the Japanese economy in the post–World War II period focusing on the role of the housing market and the housing finance system. Our particular interest is in the magnitude of the impact of the recent global recession on the Japanese economy. In this regard, we examine market consequences of the current financial crisis resulting from the U.S. subprime loan problem, and compare them with those resulting from the bursting of Japan's asset bubble in the early 1990s.

The Japanese Economy

Japan achieved sustained economic growth in the post–World War II era, but is now entering the third decade of the Lost Decade of economic stagnation. Since the end of 2008, it has been battered by the global recession resulting from the U.S. subprime crisis. Exhibit 16.1 shows the trends in real GDP and per capita real GDP in Japan between 1980 and 2009. Until the late 1980s, the Japanese economy enjoyed steady growth, both in terms of total GDP and its per capita value, registering annual growth of 4.5 percent in GDP between 1981 and 1991.

The Japanese economy moved from a land and stock-price bubble in the late 1980s to an implosion of asset prices in the early 1990s (see the section titled "Housing Prices, Housing Equity and Possible Reforms" for details). There is no denying that the collapse of the economic bubble and subsequent government

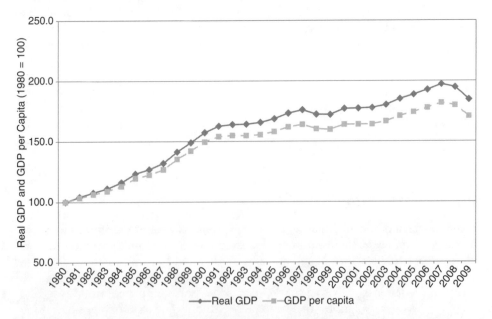

Exhibit 16.1 Trends in Real GDP and GDP per Capita in Japan, 1980–2009
Note: Real GDP is calculated based on 93SNA (2000 price).
Source: "System of National Accounts," Cabinet Office.

policy errors exacerbated and prolonged Japan's economic malaise in the 1990s and into the twenty-first century. Since the early 1990s, Japan's economy stagnated, registering an annual growth rate of only 0.7 percent between 1992 and 2009.

The financial sector has gone through a series of painful adjustments since the mid-1990s, driven by bad loans. This bad loan problem reflects poor risk management by Japanese banks and the absence of due diligence. In Japan, loans were approved using land as collateral. The inflated land prices during the bubble era facilitated higher levels of lending, a house of cards that came crashing down when land values plummeted in response to a series of interest rate hikes initiated by the Bank of Japan in 1989. As a result, Japan's financial system was placed on life support requiring inter alia, government bailouts and bank mergers.

Exposure of the subprime loan crisis in 2007 and the collapse of Lehman Brothers investment bank in September 2008 hammered global markets and caused a sharp downturn in the Japanese economy. As a result, the global recession caused Japanese GDP to decline in real terms by 1.2 percent in 2008 and 5.2 percent in 2009, a far sharper contraction than in the post-bubble 1990s. The global recession also hit the Japanese labor market as unemployment rose from 3.9 percent in 2007 to 5.1 percent in 2009, a relatively high figure in Japan, where the historical high of 5.4 percent was registered in 2002. As discussed below, the post-crisis impact on the housing market has also been substantial, involving sharp declines in housing prices and housing starts and increased housing foreclosures.

Obviously, there are various channels through which the U.S. subprime crisis can be transmitted internationally. Among these potential transmission channels, previous studies suggest that the cross-market linkages through trade and finance can be particularly important. In fact, the recent global recession caused a sharp and sudden drop in Japanese exports. Exhibit 16.2a clearly shows that negative GDP growth in 2009 stemmed mainly from the decline in exports (and also private investment), which is indicative of the importance of trade links as a transmission channel. The Lost Decade of the 1990s, by contrast, was driven by domestic factors such as the decline in private investment and consumption.

Exhibit 16.2b shows the shares of housing and non-housing investment in real GDP over the period 1980–2008. As can be seen from the figure, the share of housing investment was relatively large in the late 1980s (i.e., bubble period), and then fell throughout 1990s and 2000s.

Cross-national financial linkages also play an important role as a transmission mechanism. For example, cross-national investment of subprime-related securities and bonds has a significant contagion effect. Banks outside the United States that had a significant exposure to subprime-related securities booked large losses. As a result, financial markets in many European countries deteriorated, while Japan had relatively limited exposure and therefore suffered only a minor impact (Kurahashi and Kobayashi, 2008).

Land and Housing Markets

Real estate is a crucial component of the Japanese economy and therefore it is important to understand a number of distinctive aspects of this market.

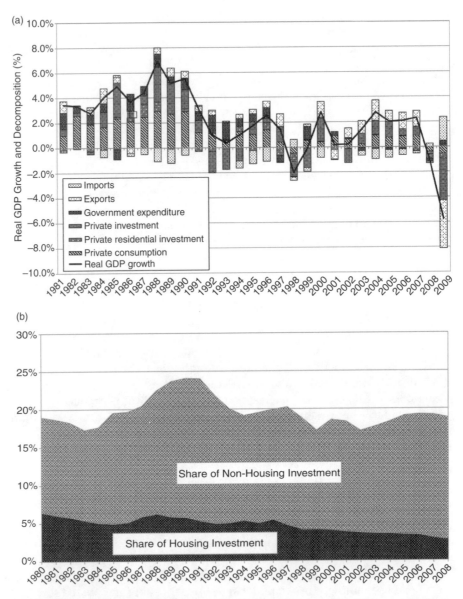

Exhibit 16.2 (a) Factor Decomposition of Real GDP Growth, 1981–2009, and (b) Share of Housing and Non-Housing Investment in Real GDP
Note: Real GDP is calculated based on 93SNA (2000 price).
Source: "System of National Accounts," Cabinet Office.

Over the past two decades, Japan has seen a rise and fall in land value that rivals that of any period in modern history. Exhibit 16.3a shows the trends in land prices together with the stock price index between 1970 and 2009. Stock prices began increasing in 1983, and it was around 1986 when the rise began accelerating rapidly. The rise in land prices followed that in stock prices, spreading from Tokyo to major cities such as Osaka and Nagoya, and then to other cities.

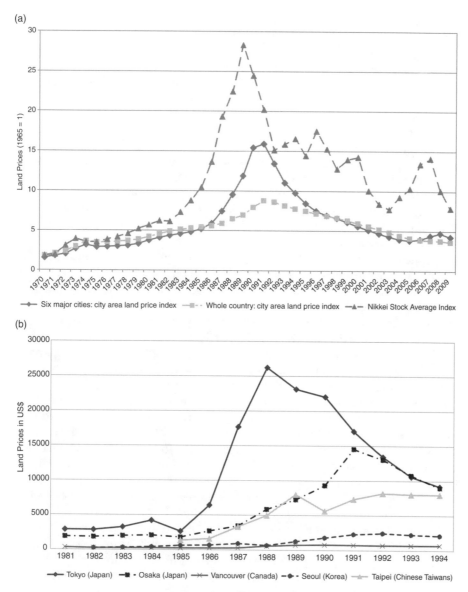

Exhibit 16.3 (a) Trends in Land and Stock Prices in Japan, 1970–2009, and (b) Trend in Residential Land Prices for Selected Countries, 1981–1994

Note: Real GDP is calculated based on 93SNA (2000 price).

Sources: (a) "Real Estate Related Statistics," Mitsui Fudosan Co, Ltd. and (b) "Comparative Economic and Financial Statistics: Japan and Other Major Countries," Bank of Japan, 1996.

The rise in land prices in the late 1980s was significant as compared with other countries. Exhibit 16.3b shows the trend in land prices for selected countries.

Exhibit 16.3a shows that land prices in Japan have continuously declined since 1991 until now. While the price index in six major cities recorded slight increases between 2005 and 2008, after the global financial crisis land prices declined by about 10 percent in 2009 alone.

The real estate sector plays an important role in stimulating economic growth. As has been observed in Japan since 1991, a reduction in land prices led to an overall lower level of economic activity. This continuous decline in land prices during the 1990s and until now has depressed consumer demand and suddenly highlighted to consumers the risks associated with purchasing housing in a country where the land myth—prices always rise—enjoyed considerable sway.

Exhibit 16.4a shows the actual housing price and the price of a 75-square-meter dwelling in the Tokyo metropolitan area between 1975 and 2009. Average prices rose sharply until 1990 and then fell throughout the 1990s. In the first decade of the twenty-first century, housing prices rose moderately, and this uptrend reflects an adjustment to the proper market value rather than a housing boom. In fact, the appreciation of housing prices during this decade was about 20 percent, which is much smaller than in the United States and other countries, where housing prices nearly doubled in the same period.[1] Exhibit 16.4b shows the quality adjusted condominium price index of the Tokyo Metropolitan area between 2005 and 2010.

Despite the recent decline in housing prices, owner-occupied housing in Japan is still not affordable for average households. Exhibit 16.5 shows the price/income ratio for the typical condominium units and built-for-sale houses in the Tokyo metropolitan area between 1985 and 2010. The exhibit shows that purchase of owner-occupied housing had been particularly difficult for Japanese households during the bubble era (i.e., late 1980s). Especially during this period, housing prices were much higher than in most other industrialized nations, due in large part to the much higher price of land compared to almost all other countries. There is an absolute shortage of suitable land because some 85 percent of the terrain is very mountainous while economic activity is concentrated mostly in large conurbations extending from Tokyo to Osaka, putting a premium on land in this region. Although housing prices continuously declined throughout the 1990s, the price/income ratio still remains at relatively high levels, at least for built-for-sale detached houses. This is due to the sustained price level of detached housing and the fall in the average income level over the past two decades. As a result, the purchase price of built-for-sale housing is approximately 7.2 times the average worker's pre-tax annual income (2010) compared to the United States, where this ratio is 4.0 as of 2007.

The proportion of owner-occupied housing in Japan is 61.2 percent,while private rental tenure accounts for 29.9 percent of the housing market as of 2008.[2] About 5.9 percent of Japanese households live in public housing that is provided at greatly subsidized rates to low- and middle-income households, while 2.8 percent of households live in employer-provided housing that is provided free or at subsidized rents to employees, irrespective of their incomes.[3] Although the home ownership rate in Japan remains relatively stable at roughly 60 percent, the proportion of households living in public rental housing is decreasing. The average floor spaces of typical housing units are: 50.48 square meters for public rental housing, 44.65 square meters for private rental housing, 53.17 square meters for employer-provided housing, and 122.38 square meters for owned housing. The contrast in living space is remarkable and corroborates the generally poor image of affordable rental housing in Japan where most units tend to be old, shabby, and poorly maintained. Given declining household income and the high price of purchasing housing, there is a dire need to improve the overall quality and space of public and private rental housing. As we discuss below, incentives have been skewed towards owned-housing.

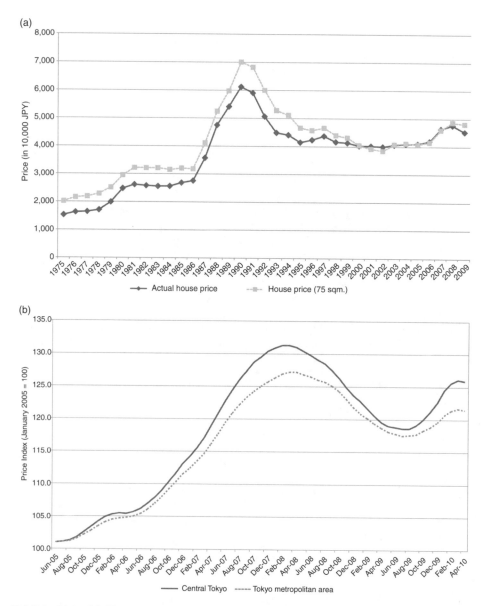

Exhibit 16.4 (a) House Prices in Tokyo Metropolitan Area, 1975–2009, and (b) Condominium Price Index in Tokyo Metropolitan Area, 2005–2010
Source: (a) "Housing Economy Databook," Housing Industry Newspaper Company. And (b) Recruit Co., Ltd

Japan has maintained a very high-level of housing construction after World War II, reflecting and feeding economic growth. Trends in housing starts in Japan between 1985 and 2009 are shown in Exhibit 16.6. Housing starts dropped sharply in 2009 (particularly for condominium units), by an even greater magnitude than in the early 1990s when the Japanese housing bubble popped.

The impact of the Lehman Shock is especially evident in the foreclosure market. Foreclosures dramatically increased in September 2008, just after the Lehman

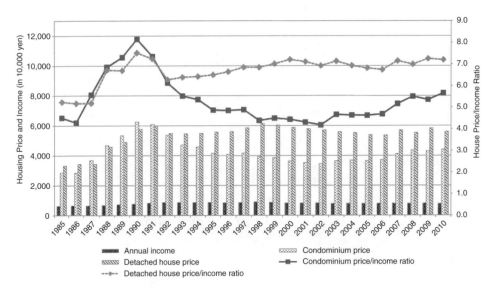

Exhibit 16.5 Price/Income Ratio for Condominium and Built-for-Sale Houses in Tokyo Metropolitan Area, 1985–2010

Note: Date for 2010 is based on the half-year figures. Both of the housing prices are calculated based on their average floor spaces from 1975 to 2010: 67 square meters for condominiums and 171 square meters for detached houses.

Sources: "Trends in Condomium Market," "Trends in Built-for-Sale Housing Market," Real Estate Economic Institute Co., Ltd., "Survey of Household Economy," Statistic Bureau of Japan.

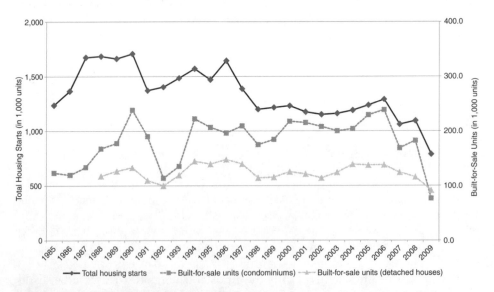

Exhibit 16.6 Housing Starts in Japan, 1985–2009

Note: Housing starts for built-for-sale detached houses are not reported before 1987.

Source: "Building Construction Survey," Ministry of Land, Infrastructure, Transport and Tourism.

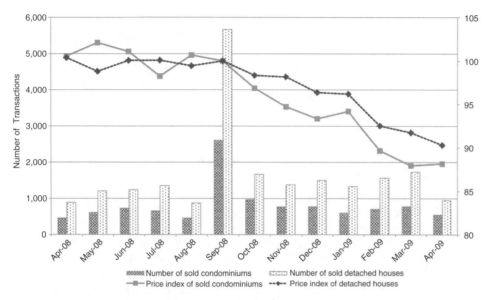

Exhibit 16.7   Foreclosure Transactions and Prices of Condominiums and Detached Houses
Source: Sumita et al. (2010), *Econometric Study of Sold Prices in the Real Estate Foreclosure Market.* Tokyo: Zenkoku Keibai-Hyoka Network.

Brothers collapse. Exhibit 16.7 shows the number of sold condominiums and detached houses and their price indices transacted in the foreclosure market all over Japan from April 2008 to April 2009. In September 2008, the number of condominiums and detached houses sold in the foreclosure market dramatically increased and rather more than usual sold during the following months. On the other hand, the price indices for foreclosed condominiums and detached houses decreased from September 2008, reflecting an increased supply and stagnant demand in the housing foreclosure market.[4]

The Housing Finance Market in Japan

Until recently, the Japanese housing finance systems involved an unusual combination of private and public lending. Government subsidized lending has played an important role in the Japanese housing finance system. The Government Housing Loan Corporation (hereafter GHLC) is the largest single mortgage lender in Japan and accounts for some 25–35 percent of housing loans in Japan in 2003.[5] The GHLC was established in 1950 as a special public corporation that provided long-term capital at a low rate of interest for the construction and purchase of housing. The GHLC obtained funds from the Fiscal Loan and Investment Program, which mainly obtained funds from postal savings deposits. Unlike other advanced industrialized nations, Japan has no major private-sector institutions that specialize in housing finance, like the savings and loan associations in the United States and building societies in the United Kingdom. In Japan, there were bank-affiliated housing-loan companies called jusen. These were first established in 1971 under the guidance of the Ministry of Finance. The jusen served to channel funds from financial institutions to individuals and firms, but were displaced by banks from the home mortgage market in the 1980s. Essentially, the jusen were in-house bank operations specializing in real estate lending and became involved in speculative investments. The jusen ended up with many non-performing loans and in 1996 seven out of eight jusen went bankrupt as part of a taxpayer-funded liquidation administered by the Housing Loan Administration Corporation at an initial cost of $6.8 billion, with secondary losses estimated at $12 billion (Felson, 1997; Kanaya and Woo, 2000) Moreover, until recently there has been no active secondary mortgage market.

In financing housing purchases, Japanese consumers typically self-finance about 35.6 percent of the purchase price, two-thirds of which comes from personal savings.[6] To cover the remaining housing cost, almost two-thirds of households take out loans.[7]

We examine the reasons for restructuring the Public Housing Loan Corporation and sketch some of the possible consequences thereof. Although households benefited from access to GHLC lending at low, long-term interest rates, the provision of subsidized lending ran counter to government efforts during the Koizumi era (2001–2006) to promote privatization, deregulation, and market-oriented reforms. In addition, the GHLC was becoming a financial burden.

As a result of the low interest rate policy in the 1990s, with private housing loan rates available at extremely low interest rates, borrowers were refinancing their GHLC loans, which were contracted at higher interest rates. As a result of these increases in advanced redemption of higher cost GHLC loans and the low prevailing private sector rates of interest on housing loans, GHLC's financial situation deteriorated gradually during the 1990s. Aggressive lending policies for housing by private financial institutions also affected the position of GHLC. Previously a significant proportion of bank's profits depended on lending to companies for their capital investment programs, but since the late 1980s firms increasingly resorted to direct financing by issuing stocks and bonds. This trend toward direct financing is especially true with the least risky, most creditworthy large firms. Due to these conditions, private financial institutions have focused on tapping the retail housing loan sector, where there is relatively small risk and stable returns. As a result, the operating conditions for the GHLC grew increasingly difficult, leading to its demise.

As of April 2007, the successor organization of the GHLC, the Japan Housing Finance Agency (JHF) was established. The already issued loans by GHLC are managed by JHF. Basically, commercial banks became the primary lender of mortgage loans after the abolition of GHLC. In 1990, the share of GHLC in outstanding mortgages was 31.5 percent, while private banks accounted for 35.0 percent. In 2009, GHLC's (and JHF's) share fell to 16.6 percent, while private bank's share rose to 58.2 percent. It is desirable to craft a new housing finance system based on market principles in the future.

THE FINANCIAL CRISIS, THE JAPANESE HOUSING MARKET, AND SOME POLICY REFORMS

As discussed in the previous section, the 2008 financial crisis emanating from the United States has had a substantial impact on the Japanese housing market and its overall economy. In some respects the impact was similar to the situation in the early 1990s when Japan's asset bubble burst. In this section, we examine the institutional structure of the housing market and housing finance system in the United States and Japan. We then discuss the impact of the current financial crisis on the Japanese housing market and some policy implications.

Comparison of Japanese and U.S. Housing Finance

The Japanese housing bubble in the early 1990s and the current financial crisis carried similar macroeconomic consequences. As discussed in the second section, the crisis in both cases either directly or indirectly resulted in sharp declines in housing prices and housing starts, increased housing foreclosures, and rising unemployment. It is also important to note that the collapse in real estate prices in the early 1990s was driven by domestic factors while the post-Lehman Shock crisis resulted from international financial and trade linkages. In addition, there is a key difference between the mortgage financing systems in the United States and in Japan. Compared with the United States and other European markets, mortgage financing in 1980s' Japan was generally based on traditional residential mortgages, where mortgage securitization was virtually non-existent, at least until the beginning of the twenty-first century (see the previous section for detail). On the other hand, the subprime mortgage crisis in the United States occurred under a hierarchical arm's-length (market-based) indirect financing system. This hybrid system involves both market and financial institutions as mediators between sources of capital and borrowers. It is a new system for channeling money from the providers of capital to the users of capital. In this system, the providers of capital, in many cases households, enter the capital market via financial products and financial service companies that transfer their capital to securitization vehicles and companies in need of capital, promising relatively high rates of return.[8] Since these securitized mortgage products are spread across global markets, these cross-national investments result in wider repercussions, as is evident in the aftermath of the subprime loan debacle in the United States.[9] In the following sections, we discuss the impact of the recent financial crisis on the Japanese housing market.

Housing Prices, Housing Equity, and Possible Reforms

As shown in Exhibits 16.3a and 16.4a, there was a sharp decline in land and housing prices in the Japanese housing market after the recent financial crisis. During the 2005–2007 periods, land prices in six major cities experienced a slight recovery from the continuous downturn after the bubble burst in the early 1990s. In 2009, however, the price dropped by about 10 percent, and several other housing indicators showed a similar tendency. For example, the condominium housing price index in Exhibit 16.4b shows that the condominium price reached its peak in April 2008, and then fell throughout the year, resulting in a 7.6 percent decline in July 2009. Given the importance of housing in the average household asset portfolio, plummeting housing prices undermined household wealth and consumption.[10]

Regarding the potential consequences of housing price fluctuations, recent studies focus on the relationship between housing equity and the residential mobility of homeowners. The sharp decline in housing prices caused low or negative housing equity for many homeowners, which constrained residential mobility.

This has important policy implications because residential mobility is an equili-brating factor in the housing market, and any institutional constraints that impede residential mobility disrupt the allocating role of housing markets.

For example, Seko, Sumita, and Naoi (2011) investigated the effect of housing equity constraints on own-to-own residential moves in Japan.[11] We found that housing equity constraints deterred residential mobility, especially for positive equity households.

In Japan, the negative effects of the housing equity constraint on residential mobility are certainly amplified by the mortgage loan system. Housing loans for residential houses in Japan are based on a recourse loan contract system. Under this system, when the value of the mortgage (housing loans) exceeds the value of the housing, and the borrower is unable to service the loan, borrowers have to surrender any unencumbered assets to cover the loan outstanding. On the other hand, under a non-recourse loan system, even if the value of the mortgage exceeds the value of the housing, and the borrower is unable to service the loan, they do not need to surrender unencumbered assets. Therefore, under a non-recourse loan system, borrowers may default and retain their other assets. As a result, the negative effects of housing equity constraints on residential mobility should be much more severe under a recourse loan system than under a non-recourse system. Hence, in terms of public policy implications it is important to lessen regulatory barriers to residential mobility such as the severe equity constraint of negative net equity in housing. A non-recourse loan system would facilitate greater mobility by lessening equity constraints and thus would help limit housing price volatility in Japan by encouraging adjustments in the price and supply of housing. Introducing non-recourse loans is a sensible policy response, but this depends on curtailing strategic defaults by devising some regulations to prohibit or penalize such defaults.

In addition to introducing a non-recourse loan system, it is also important to establish a well-functioning rented housing market in Japan. The focus of hous-ing policy in Japan should switch from promoting the homeownership rate to encouraging rental housing. One of the lessons of the U.S. subprime loan crisis is that too much emphasis on promoting home ownership is highly risky given the volatility, complexity, and lack of transparency in derivative markets. The problem in Japan is that rental housing is undesirable, especially for family use, because it is cramped, low quality, and poorly maintained. As a result, renters are eager to purchase their own housing, and are ready to assume very high debts in order to do so. Highly leveraged households, however, are very vulnerable to economic fluctuations and volatility in housing prices, with significant negative implications. Thus, there are good reasons to promote an increase in the supply of good quality, larger-size public, as well as private, rental housing to make this a more attractive option. In order to do so, it is crucial to ease strong legal protections for renters in terms of renewal rights and rent increases, as landlords prefer to rent smaller-sized housing to singles or tenants with smaller families because there is a relatively high turnover rate among such tenants.[12]

In addition, Japanese housing policy should create incentives to nurture a more vibrant secondhand housing market. For a variety of reasons, the market for used houses is small in Japan. For example, the share of secondhand housing transactions is only 13.1 percent of all housing transactions in 2003 and 12.7 percent in 2008. Again this means reducing legal protections for renters, a reform that would shift incentives for landlords and boost the supply of secondhand housing for sale. A well-developed secondhand housing market combined with a non-recourse loan system would help negative equity households sell their old houses, repay their mortgages, and begin a new chapter in their life.

Another reform involves foreclosure properties sold at Japanese judicial auctions. Under present circumstances, rental properties are often delivered to buyers with an unclear title as existing renters retain their rights. Amendment of protection laws for both short-term and long-term leaseholds is desirable to address this problem and increase the overall efficiency of the real-estate market where landlords' rights are strictly constrained.

Real Estate Securitization in Japan and Possible Reforms

Securitization in Japan includes investment vehicles such as J-REITs for individual investors. The J-REIT market drastically declined in 2008 because of worldwide financial anxieties and the global business recession stemming from the subprime loan problem in the United States. As of FY 2007, the Ministry of Land, Infrastructure, Transport and Tourism estimated the "value of real estate, subject to securitization" to be about ¥8.4 trillion, equivalent to about 2.6 percent of the aggregate market value of the Tokyo Stock Exchange, and J-REITs account for 19.9 percent of this total.[13] At the end of FY 2007, of this securitized real estate the ratio for office use was 35.8 percent, residential use 19.5 percent, commercial use 14.2 percent, industrial use 3.8 percent, hotel use 5.3 percent, and other uses 21.5 percent.[14] Exhibit 16.8 shows these ratios between 1997 and 2007.

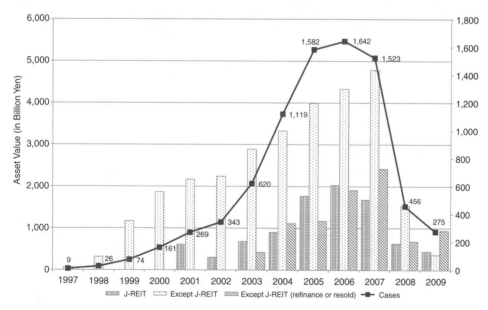

Exhibit 16.8   Real Estate Securitization in Japan, 1997–2009
Source: "Fact-Finding Study of Real Estate Securitization," Ministry of Land, Infrastructure, Transport and Tourism.

The public sector is also developing securitized investment products in order to supply long-run fixed-rate housing loans. GHLC's mortgage housing loans (debt-purchase type) were introduced October 1, 2003.[15] In this case, the GHLC repackages mortgages held by private financial institutions and issues residential mortgage-backed securities (RMBS) based on them. Through the repackaging and sale of mortgage-backed securities, the GHLC is enhancing the flow of funds from capital markets to the housing market. The GHLC purchases housing loans provided by private sector financial institutions and other organizations. These are used as collateral for issues of RMBS that are sold to investors to raise funds. In 2004, RMBS of approximately ¥2.45 trillion were issued, reaching a peak in 2006 of approximately ¥5.12 trillion.[16] The RMBS market in Japan, however, has been drastically reduced with the recent global recession. The total amount of RMBS issued in 2009 was less than ¥2 trillion, well below the 2004 level.

The subprime loan problem in the United States has taught us several lessons. Securitization is located midway between the traditional indirect financing system and the direct financing system. The advantage of securitization is to facilitate individual investment in new assets like real estate. However, five disadvantages of securitization highlighted by the subprime loan problem are: (1) traders advanced funds although they knew repayment was unlikely from the outset, (2) grading of loan quality reflected inadequate monitoring, (3) corner-cutting was done in the pooling of housing loans, (4) sometimes risk was not explained properly to investors at the time of sale and, (5) incentives for loan officers were skewed by linking loan volume to bonuses without due diligence regarding the quality of the loans.[17]

It is important to rectify these problems of securitization, especially from the viewpoint of investors. In order to regain trust in real estate securitization products among investors, it is crucial to enhance transparency about what is being sold and accountability on the part of those packaging and selling these products. There is also a need to monitor practices and ensure the ethical conduct of securitization specialists by establishing benchmarks for best practices and penalties for noncompliance.

The post–Lehman Shock and Japan's two-decade-long period of stagnation have highlighted the need for basic transformation in Japan's economic structure. In recent years, there has been a growing consensus in business and government circles that Japan should revive its economy by implementing market-oriented structural reforms driven by the principle of competition. Securitization of real estate is a good example of this type of reform. In recent years, J-REITs (Japan-style real estate investment trusts) have grown in number and the securitization of housing loans has steadily grown. The recent economic malaise has raised questions about the advisability of deregulation and about some of these financial innovations, but even if reform initiatives have lost some of their shine, there is also recognition that they are essential because the usual ways and means of Japan, involving collusive relations between government and business, managing competition and policies aimed at minimizing and mitigating risk, are unsustainable. Policy makers are examining ways to address the evident problems, most notably by focusing on improved monitoring and transparency in markets and a shift from the rule by law involving extensive discretionary powers of the bureaucracy (gyosei shido), to the rule of law nurturing a level playing field where rules are uniformly enforced (Kingston 2004; 2010).

CONCLUSION

The recent financial crisis emanating from the United States has had a substantial impact on the Japanese housing market and its overall economy. Compared with other Asian and European countries where significant housing booms and busts took place during the 2000s, the Japanese housing market was relatively stagnant. The Lehman Shock, however, led to a global economic meltdown, and the repercussions remain powerful in Japan and much of the rest of the world. Our analysis suggests that the recent downturn in the Japanese housing market has been driven primarily by the consequences of the U.S. subprime crisis.

Comparison of the Japanese and U.S. bubbles shows that the consequences of the U.S. subprime crisis have been fairly large. Japanese GDP declined in real terms by 1.2 percent in 2008 and 5.2 percent in 2009, respectively, exceeding the declines registered in the post-Bubble 1990s. The impact on the housing market has also been substantial: Land prices in metropolitan areas dropped by about 10 percent in 2009, condominium prices fell about 7.6 percent between the recent peak on April 2008 and the recent bottom on July 2009, and housing starts dropped about 30 percent in 2009.

Until the 1990s, real estate was a relatively risk-free investment in Japan, but after the asset bubble burst in the early 1990s, Japanese households, and those who lend to them, have learned the costs of risk. The fairly large impact of the current financial crisis highlights the potential importance and benefits of market-oriented reforms for real-estate securitization, the housing finance system, private and public rental housing, and the secondhand housing market in Japan. In order to help manage and mitigate this risk, we propose various reforms.

For example, the sharp decline in housing prices undermined homeowners' portfolios, resulting in constrained residential mobility due to low or negative housing equity. Introducing non-recourse loans is a sensible policy response because it would facilitate greater mobility by lessening equity constraints and thus would help limit housing price volatility. It would also enable households to hit the reset button on their finances, and counter deflationary trends. We also believe that there are good reasons to revise tenant rights in order to promote the development of good-quality rental housing and stimulate a secondhand housing market because owned-housing is currently out of reach of many households.

The Japanese housing finance system remains immature, as evident in the absence of both an active mortgage market for used houses and private-sector institutions specializing in housing finance. While deregulation remains crucial, the subprime loan problem emanating from the United States highlights the need for caution in terms of securitization of mortgages. We recommend stricter reporting and monitoring requirements, greater market transparency, and a recalibration of incentives to focus on the quality rather than the quantity of loans.

Even as Japan reels from the current economic crisis, it is important to recognize the potential benefits of market-oriented reforms, and the need to proceed cautiously with deregulation while sustaining momentum in the process of financial deepening as a way of hedging risk.

NOTES

1. For example, the Halifax housing price index shows that UK housing prices rose 90 percent between 2000 and 2009, the RPX/IEIF housing price index shows housing prices in Paris rising more than 140 percent, and the median house price in Sydney rose about 63 percent between 2002 and 2009 (Australian Bureau of Statistics).

2. See Housing and Land Survey of Japan (Statistics Bureau, Ministry of Internal Affairs and Communications, 2008). The home-ownership rate in Japan is almost equal to that of the United States and higher than in some European countries.

3. See Seko and Sumita (forthcoming) for further details about the Japanese housing and land market.

4. These price indices are quality-adjusted by the hedonic methods by using the real estate assessor's opinion of value, as in Clapp and Giaccotto (1992).

5. See Quick Look at Housing in Japan (2003), Building Center of Japan, Tokyo.

6. See Seko (1994) for details about the Japanese Housing Finance System.

7. See "Report on the Survey of Housing Market Trends, 2007" (Ministry of Land, Infrastructure, Transport, and Tourism 2007; hereafter cited as MLIT 2007).

8. There are many reasons why the subprime loan problem occurred in the United States, but certainly one of the most important ones involves the problem of adverse selection. Since mortgages of varying quality were bundled together, it was difficult to properly assess risk associated with each securitized mortgage product. The spread of defaults among less credit-worthy borrowers had a domino effect that brought the house of cards crashing down (Yoshino and Yano 2009). Miyao (2010) compared the U.S. subprime crisis and the Japanese bubble in the late 1980s and early 1990s.

9. The impact of the subprime loan problem in the financial industry spread to the overall U.S. economy, sparking a sharp contraction that adversely affected trading partners and undermined business sentiments.

10. See, for example, Leung (2004) for the macroeconomic consequences of the fluctuations in housing price.

11. For empirical evidence outside Japan, see Ferreira et al. (2010) for the United States and Henley (1998) for the United Kingdom.

12. Renters are protected by the Japanese Tenant Protection Law. Iwata (2002) argues that the small size of Japanese rental housing is caused by the implicit rent control system that resulted from the law. In March 2000, this law was revised and rental housing with a fixed rental term was introduced in order to increase the supply of good quality rental housing. Seko and Sumita (2007) analyzed the Japanese housing tenure choice and welfare implications after the revision of the law. Seshimo (2009) also discusses the problems of strict tenant rights under the Japanese Tenant Protection Law.

13. These figures are cited from the Fact-Finding Study of Real Estate Securitization (Ministry of Land, Infrastructure, Transport and Tourism, 2008).

14. Ibid.

15. The mortgage housing loan (guarantee type) was introduced in October, 2004.

16. Japanese Bankers Association, Trends in Securitization Markets. Although the share of securitized mortgages rose significantly in the early 2000s, securitization is still limited in Japan compared with the United States and other markets. In 2006, the share of securitized mortgages was only 4 percent on total mortgage lending.

17. See Ohta (2009).

REFERENCES

The Association for Real Estate Securitization. 2008. *Real-Estate Securitization Handbook 2008–2009.* Tokyo: TP Publishing.

Clapp, J. M., and C. Giaccotto. 1992. "Estimating Price Trends for Residential Properties: A Comparison of Repeat Sales and Assessed Value Methods." *Journal of the American Statistical Association* 87:417, 300–306.

Felson, Howard M. 1997 (December). "Closing the Book on Jusen: An Account of the Bad Loan Crisis and a New Chapter for Securitization in Japan." *Duke Law Journal* 47, 567–611.

Ferreira, F., J. Gyourko, and J. Tracy. 2010. "Housing Busts and Household Mobility." *Journal of Urban Economics* 68:1, 34–45.

Henley, A. 1998. "Residential Mobility, Housing Equity and the Labour Market." *Economic Journal* 108, 414–427.

Housing Policy Division, Housing Bureau, Ministry of Land, Infrastructure, Transport and Tourism, ed. 2008. *A Quick Look at Housing in Japan*, 6th ed. Tokyo: Building Center of Japan.

Housing Industry Newspaper Company (2008). *Housing Economy Data Book* (in Japanese). Tokyo: Housing Industry Newspaper Company.

Iwata, S. 2002. "The Japanese Tenant Protection Law and Asymmetric Information on Tenure Length." *Journal of Housing Economics* 11: 2, 125–151.

Kanaya, A., and D. Woo. 2000. "The Japanese Banking Crisis of the 1990s." Washington, D.C.: IMF Working Paper, 2000.

Kingston, J. 2004. *Japan's Quiet Transformation: Social Change and Civil Society in the 21st Century.* London: Routledge.

Kingston, J. 2010. *Contemporary Japan: History, Politics and Social Change Since the 1980s.* London: John Wiley & Sons.

Kurahashi, T., and M. Kobayashi. 2008. *Understanding the Subprime Loan Problem.* Tokyo: Iwanami (in Japanese).

Ministry of Land, Infrastructure, Transport and Tourism. 2004. Report of the Committee about Future Housing Finance System Based on Actively Adopting Market Mechanisms (in Japanese). Available at www.mlit.go.jp/jutakukentiku/house/juukinkon.htm, accessed March 6, 2009.

Ministry of Land, Infrastructure, Transport and Tourism. 2007. "Report of the Committee about Adjustment of the Housing Finance Market" (in Japanese). Available at www.mlit.go.jp/jutakukentiku/house/torikumi/jyutakukinyu/dai3kai/dai3.html, accessed March 6, 2009.

Ministry of Land, Infrastructure, Transport and Tourism. 2008. "Fact-Finding Study of Real Estate Securitization, 2007" (in Japanese). Available at www.mlit.go.jp/common/000016935.pdf, accessed March 6, 2009.

Ohta, Y. 2009. *Land Price Dissolution* (in Japanese). Tokyo: Nikkei.

Leung, C.K.Y. 2004. "Macroeconomics and Housing: A Review of the Literature." *Journal of Housing Economics* 13, 249–267.

Miyao, T. 2010 (Spring). "Learn from the Subprime-Financial Crisis" (in Japanese). *The Quarterly Journal of Housing and Land Economics* 76, 2–9.

Seko, M. 1994. "Housing Finance in Japan." In Y. Noguchi and J. Poterba, eds., *Housing Markets in the United States and Japan*, pp. 49–64. Chicago: NBER and the University of Chicago Press.

Seko, M., and K. Sumita. 2007. "Japanese Housing Tenure Choice and Welfare Implications after the Revision of the Tenant Protection Law." *Journal of Real Estate Finance and Economics* 35, 357–383.

Seko, M., K. Sumita, and M. Naoi. 2011 "Residential Mobility Decisions in Japan: Effects of Housing Equity Constraints and Income Shocks under the Recourse Loan System." *Journal of Real Estate Finance and Economics*. Doi: 10.1007/s11146-011-9322-3.

Seko, M., and K. Sumita. Forthcoming. "Trends and Prospects in Japan's Mortgage Market." In *International Encyclopedia of Housing and Home*. Elsevier.

Seshimo, H. 2009. "U.S. Housing Finance and Suggestions for Japan from the Viewpoint of the Subprime Loan Problem" (in Japanese). *Urban Housing Sciences* 65, 4–10.

Sumita, K., T. Kuroda, M. Seko, T. Kuroda, and M. Naoi. 2010. *Econometric Study of the Sold Prices in the Real Estate Foreclosure Market* (in Japanese). Tokyo: Zenkoku Keibai-Hyouka Network.

Statistics Bureau. Ministry of Internal Affairs and Communications. 2008. *2008 Housing and Land Survey of Japan* (in Japanese). Tokyo: Japan Statistical Association.

Yoshino, N. M. Yano, and Y. Higuchi. eds. 2009. *Subprime Loan Problems and an Increase in Financial Market Quality* (in Japanese). Tokyo: Keio University Press.

ABOUT THE AUTHORS

MIKI SEKO is Professor of Economics at Keio University, Japan. Her research on topics relating to housing has appeared in the *Regional Science and Urban Economics*, the *Journal of Housing Economics*, the *Journal of Real Estate Finance and Economics*, and the *Journal of Property Research*, amongst others. Her research interests are in housing demand, housing price dynamics, and policy. Currently, she serves on the Editorial Boards of five real estate and urban economics journals. She was president of the Asian Real Estate Society and co-authored *A Companion to Urban Economics* (Blackwell Publishing, 2006).

KAZUTO SUMITA is Associate Professor at Kanazawa Seiryo University, Japan. He received his PhD from Keio University. His research interests include house price dynamics and applied econometrics. Recent publications have appeared in *Journal of Real Estate Finance and Economics* and *Journal of Housing Economics*, among others.

MICHIO NAOI is Assistant Professor at the Tokyo University of Marine Science and Technology. His research interests include tenure choice and housing demand, house price dynamics, and housing market regulation and institutions. Recent publications have appeared in *Regional Science and Urban Economics*, *Journal of Real Estate Finance and Economics*, and *Journal of Property Research*, among others.

PART V

Managing Housing Bubbles and Housing Markets in Diverse Asian Economies

CHAPTER 17

Comparing Two Financial Crises

The Case of Hong Kong Real Estate Markets

CHARLES KA YUI LEUNG
City University of Hong Kong

EDWARD CHI HO TANG
City University of Hong Kong

Hong Kong is no stranger to bubbles or crisis. During the Asian financial crisis (AFC), the Hong Kong housing price index dropped more than 50 percent in less than a year. The same market then experienced the Internet bubble, the SARS attack, and recently the global financial crisis (GFC). This chapter provides some "stylized facts," follows the event-study methodology to examine whether the markets behaved differently in the AFC and GFC, and discusses the possible linkage to the change in government policies ("learning effect") and the flow of Chinese consumers and investors to Hong Kong ("China factor").

INTRODUCTION

Real estate, once a necessary good, has become an investment vehicle and, if not properly managed, the consequences can be serious. For instance, real-estate-related financial products, such as mortgage-backed securities (MBS) and collateralized debt obligations (CDO), are associated with the recent global financial crisis (GFC) of 2008. Even without these products, the housing market deserves policy attention. A typical example is provided by the Hong Kong experience during the Asian financial crisis (AFC) in 1997. Speculators aimed at huge profits by participating in both Hong Kong's foreign exchange market and financial market. The Hong Kong Monetary Authority (HKMA) defended the fixed exchange rate by increasing the interest rate, which triggered a large reaction in the asset markets. A decline in real estate value hindered the renewal of small business loans and, as a result, a contraction of the aggregate economy and an increase in the unemployment rate were observed, and, in some extreme cases, suicide followed bankruptcy.[1]

With such important consequence in mind, it is natural to ask a series of questions. Why did HKMA need to defend the exchange rate? Why defend it by increasing the interest rate? Why would the real estate price drop so dramatically? Was it too high before the crisis? How could it become too high in the first place? Did the Hong Kong market as well as the government make changes so that the economy would become less vulnerable to financial crisis?

A small but emerging literature attempts to address these questions. On the empirical front, Ho and Wang (2006, 2008, 2009), Ho, Ma and Haurin (2008), and Wong (2010), among others, attribute the recession after the AFC to the change of the public housing policy. They provide evidence that there is a housing ladder in Hong Kong: When people living in public rental housing, which is not means-tested, accumulate enough savings, they will move to subsidized ownership schemes provided by the Hong Kong government. People who earn more will then move to the private market for even higher quality housing units. When the Hong Kong government allowed residents in the public rental housing to purchase their own houses (privatization of public housing), the demand for subsidized ownership quickly and significantly shrank. The price of those units fell, and subsequently the price of private sector units fell as well. Aggregate consumption and investment contracted, leading to a recession. Their empirical works verify the collateral-based housing ladder theory proposed by Ortalo-Magne and Rady (2006).

While the above series of papers is very insightful, it seems to be more specific to the Hong Kong experience. Yet many Asian economies experienced adverse effects of the AFC. Therefore, there are several attempts to deepen the understanding of the relationship between a financial crisis and the real estate market on the theoretical front. For instance, Tse and Leung (2002) observed that during the AFC period, closed and small economies such as Taiwan experienced a much smaller impact than open and small economies such as Hong Kong and Singapore. They therefore propose a simple theory in which the collateral constraint will have a much larger impact on aggregate output when capital flows are free. Their theory also predicts that as small economies grow, they will allow for more capital flows and hence experience higher economic growth (and more volatility). Chen and Leung (2008) and Jin, Leung, and Zeng (2010) emphasize the spillover effect between commercial real estate and residential real estate. When real estate prices drop, bank credit directed to the producers contracts, especially for small and medium-size businesses. That leads to further reduction of real estate demand and hence leads to a further drop in real estate prices. Evidence based on aggregate data (e.g., Chen and Leung 2008; Jin, Leung, and Zeng 2010) and micro data (e.g., Leung, Lau, and Leong 2002; Leung and Feng 2005), among others, find that this positive feedback mechanism seems to be able to account for the experiences of Hong Kong, Japan, and even the recent history of the United States.

On the other hand, Chen, Chen, and Chou (2010) emphasize the consumption channel of the collateral effect. In their model, consumers would like to smooth out consumption over time. However, when the collateral value of their houses drop, the consumer credit they can receive decreases. The aggregate consumption drop will then be more significant than when consumers can freely borrow without any borrowing constraint. The researchers find support from the Taiwan data.

In the media, AFC is often described as a bubble period and the following recession is interpreted as a correction. The theoretical analysis of Leung and Chen (2006, 2010) suggests another possibility. They construct an overlapping-generations model in which the land price and stock price can fluctuate over time even with invariant economic fundamentals. In other words, it may not be easy to dictate what the fundamental-determined asset price is and hence the term bubble could be confused with normal fluctuations of asset prices.

In sum, it seems that the relationship between the aggregate economy and real estate markets can be quite complicated and it takes more than a single theory to provide the full picture. In light of the development of the literature, this chapter attempts to provide a more updated review on the Hong Kong experience during the financial crises and hopefully it can shed light on the future development of the related theoretical literature and enable us to deepen our understanding. It is organized as follows: It first reviews the historical background of the Hong Kong economy, and then recalls the incident of currency attack in 1998. To enrich the understanding of the housing market, discussions on land sale procedures and mortgage market follow. Next, it compares the performance of the housing market during the AFC and the GFC, using event study techniques. Conclusions are made at the end of this chapter.

BACKGROUND

Hong Kong's development history can be traced since the nineteenth century, when it was a fishing village. The wide and deep Victoria Harbor was probably the only natural resource of the region. In 1842, the Qing Dynasty was defeated in the First Opium War, and Hong Kong Island was ceded to Britain under the Treaty of Peking. In 1860, the Qing Dynasty was again defeated in the Second Opium War, and the Kowloon Peninsula and Stonecutters Island were ceded to the British under the Convention of Peking. Finally in 1898, the British obtained a 99-year lease of the New Territories under the terms of the Convention for the Extension of Hong Kong Territory.

The British government turned Hong Kong into an entry port in the early twentieth century. Trade between South China and foreign countries had to pass via Hong Kong. Many refugees and corporations came to Hong Kong in 1949, after the People's Republic of China was established. The sudden increase in labor created favorable conditions for Hong Kong to develop its textile and manufacturing industries. With the open policy of mainland China in 1979, and the increasing labor cost in Hong Kong, manufacturing companies moved their operations to China in waves. Hong Kong's role in the manufacturing industry eventually declined, and it had to reposition itself as a service center. The service industry increased from 68 percent of GDP in 1980 to 86.5 percent in 2000. With its free-market policies, low corruption rate, highly educated and productive labor force, and strong financial infrastructure, Hong Kong developed into an international financial center and achieved significant economic growth. Starting from HK$26,094 of per capita GDP in 1961 (expressed in constant dollars, 2008 level), it increased 9.2 times to HK$240,096 in 2008. Population also exhibited continuous growth, from 3,168,000 in mid-1961 to 6,988,900 in the year-end of 2008. The continuing growth in population and the per capita income naturally lead to an increasing demand for housing. The real housing price index in Hong Kong increased from 100 in 1979 to 162.5 in 2008, despite some downturns in between (see Exhibit 17.1). Hong Kong's scarce land resources led to expectations of a general increase in the real housing prices. Yet the housing price drop after the AFC was so great that even when the GFC

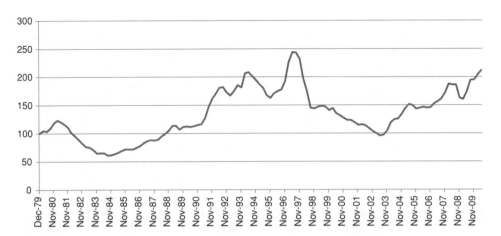

Exhibit 17.1   Time Plot of Real Housing Price Index (Base Year: December 1979)
Source: Rating and Valuation Department.

happened in 2008, the (average) level of housing price in Hong Kong had not re-covered to the level it had attained before AFC (more systematic comparison will be provided in a later section).

CURRENCY ATTACK (1998) IN HONG KONG

Expecting more capital coming from China, Hong Kong experienced a sharp in-crease in real estate prices during the first half of 1997, just before the handover.[2] In hindsight, an asset bubble was created at that time. From January 1990 to March 1997, the real wage index increased by only 3.8 percent, but the inflation rate was 80.0 percent. Also, the real aggregate GDP, real Hang Seng Index, and real housing price increased by 32.6 percent, 153.1 percent, and 101.4 percent respectively. These figures revealed a few facts. First, income distribution became more unequal (the aggregate GDP increase was much higher than that of the real wage). Clearly, those who could take advantage of the economic growth of China (such as lawyers, ac-countants, and entrepreneurs) would have income growing much faster than those who provided routine labor in Hong Kong. Second, asset prices (stock and hous-ing) became more expensive. In fact, the ratio of the housing price index relative to wage index doubled from 100 in 1982 to 200 at the housing price peak in 1997 (Exhibit 17.2). If those who earned higher incomes also saved more, which seems to be true in many countries, then wealth inequality between the high-income group and the low-income group would also increase.[3]

Real prices of both office and retail property also increased significantly before the AFC, from 100 in 1986 to more than 350 before the AFC.[4] This led to an increase in business operating costs within that period, and translated into higher selling prices of the finished products (see Exhibit 17.3). The competitive power was then weakened. To regain its competitive power, obviously Hong Kong had to reduce production costs by either devaluing the currency or, perhaps painfully, devaluing real estate prices.

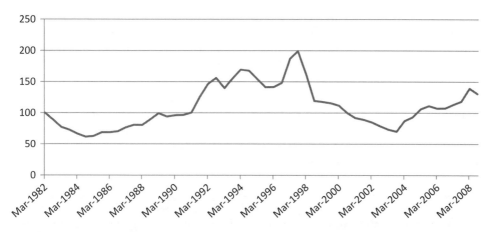

Exhibit 17.2 Time Plot of Housing Price Index Relative to Wage Index (Recalculated as 100 at March 1982)

Source: Rating and Valuation Department (for housing price series) and Census and Statistics Department (for wage index series).

The importance of the manufacturing industry diminished in Hong Kong since 1980, and the real price of factories therefore dropped from around 250 in 1993 to around 70 in 2003.[5] Recently, the high price of office and retail properties has motivated more redevelopment. As a result, the real price of factories climbed back to around 200 before the GFC.

Speculators understood the conditions of Hong Kong, and were trying to make money by taking double market play[6]: They simultaneously sold short Hong Kong dollars, both spot and forward, on the foreign exchange market and shorted

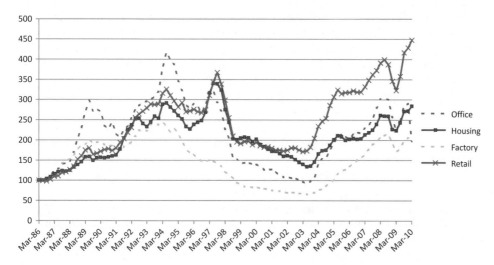

Exhibit 17.3 Time Plot of the Quarterly Real Estate Price Index, Recalculated at March 1986, in Real Terms

Source: Rating and Valuation Department.

Hong Kong stocks on both the spot and futures markets. If the Hong Kong dollar peg was given up, speculators would make substantial amounts of money from the foreign exchange market; if the interest rate rose, they could also make profits from the securities market. It seemed that with this strategy, the speculators would make a huge profit at the expense of the Hong Kong residents.

The government's official defense from such systematic speculation was first to protect the currency from devaluation, fearing that abandoning the 15-year-old linked exchange rate system would be a shock to the economy and could lead to loss of confidence about the domestic currency. With free capital control in Hong Kong and unstable Asian financial markets, further speculation on the currency was very likely, risking currency over-devaluation. Second, they had to prevent the financial market from collapse. The financial industry is one of the most important economic pillars in Hong Kong. A sudden fall in asset value would cause the problem of negative equity. It would then affect the banks, as the loans can never be repaid. The local economy would be severely affected.

On August 14, 1998, the Hong Kong Monetary Authority (HKMA) unexpectedly used the official reserves to purchase stocks, aiming to prevent speculators from profiting from market manipulation. The intervention process stopped on August 28, 1998. After that, the increased stability in the financial market attracted the inflow of funds and the Hang Seng Index caught up to above 10,000 points in October 1998. Moreover, in order to dispose the shares with minimal disruption to the market, the Tracker Fund of Hong Kong was launched in November 1999. It replicates the performance of the Hang Seng Index, so investors can gain immediate diversification and exposure to the largest stocks in the Hong Kong market.

Definitely, the intervention taken in August 1998 did not reflect the "positive non-intervention" policy adopted since 1971. Donald Tsang, the Financial Secretary of Hong Kong, explained that if the government did not intervene, the stock market would fall between 2,000 and 3,000 points and the interest rate would rise by 50 percent. Asset value would fall below the fundamental value, and the market crash would trigger serious actions by other investors. The local economy would then be sent into recession quickly.[7] Therefore, the government had to intervene in the market directly in order to restore the confidence of the public.

Together with the intervention of the financial market, HKMA took seven measures on September 5, 1998 to strengthen the currency board arrangements in Hong Kong[8]:

1. To demonstrate the government's commitment to the linked exchange rate system, HKMA provided a clear undertaking to all licensed banks in Hong Kong to convert Hong Kong dollars in their clearing accounts into U.S. dollars at the fixed exchange rate of HK$7.75 to US$1.
2. As the improved efficiency of the interbank payment system facilitated liquidity management of licensed banks, the bid rate of the Liquidity Adjustment Facility was removed.
3. Replacing the Liquidity Adjustment Facility by a Discount Window with a base rate. (The base rate would be responsive to capital flows and is determined by HKMA from time to time to dampen excessive and destabilizing interest rate volatility.)

4. By removing the restriction on repeated borrowing with respect to the provision of overnight Hong Kong dollar liquidity through repo transactions using Exchange Fund Bill and Notes, it can make the monetary system less susceptible to manipulation and dampen excessive interest rate volatility.
5. To ensure that all new Exchange Fund papers are backed by foreign currency reserves, it will be issued only when there is an inflow of funds.
6. Introducing a schedule of discount rates applicable for different percentage thresholds of holdings of Exchange Fund paper by licensed banks for the purpose of assessing the Discount Window.
7. Retaining the restriction on repeated borrowing in respect to repo transactions involving debt securities other than Exchange Fund paper.

On October 14, 1998, Joseph Yam, Chief Executive of HKMA, announced in a speech[9] that after the government intervened in the market, speculators suffered considerable losses in the short position in the currency and stock market futures, and there had been no indication of further market manipulation since August 1998. HKMA was successful in defeating speculators from attacking Hong Kong monetary and financial systems. Nevertheless, the defense of the peg exchange rate comes with a price, which includes a significant drop in real estate value.

As a comparison, during the GFC in 2008, the source of the shock was the United States, followed by Europe. There is no significant speculation against Hong Kong dollars. On the contrary, there is an inflow of capital. Thus, the Hong Kong Monetary Authority did not need to raise the interest rate, and the Hong Kong government did not use the fiscal reserve to intervene in the stock market. Market forces mainly drove the asset market during the GFC.[10]

LAND SIZE AND SALE PROCEDURES

It is not an overstatement that the rise and fall of the real estate value in Hong Kong is tied to a sequence of historical events. When Hong Kong was a British colony in 1898, the boundary of Hong Kong was already fixed with a size of 1104 square kilometers. With scarce land resources and a growing population, the need for accommodations were by and large satisfied. As shown in Exhibit 17.4, there is, on average, a housing unit for each household. More attention has been paid to the high land price policy maintained by the government. Since the government owned all of the land and sold it to property developers at a high price, the government was able to maintain a low income tax rate and fiscal balance over the years. On the other hand, profit-maximizing property developers sold their properties at an even higher price to the buyers.

Before April 1999, a regular sale of land was adopted, which provided the government with a stable source of income. The government then used the funds to provide free education, maintain a high standard of medical services, and create jobs. In the fiscal year 1996/97, land sale revenue accounted for 8.63 percent of the total government revenue. In April 1999, Chief Executive Tung Chee-Hwa introduced the application list system. Under this system, the government published a list of land available for sale upon application. Property developers who are interested in sites need to state the minimum amount they are willing to pay in

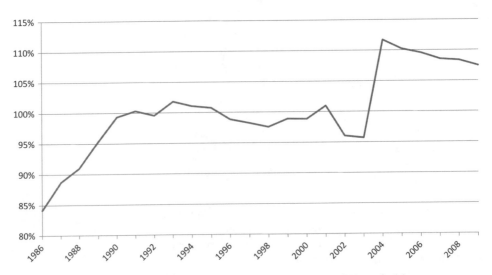

Exhibit 17.4   Time Plot of Total Housing Units Relative to Total Households
Sources: CEIC (for total housing units' series); Census and Statistics Department (for total households' series).

the application. If the government approves it, the land will be offered for sale at a public auction. In January 2004, the regular sale of land system was completely replaced by the application list system.[11] However, because recently there have been fewer pieces of land sold through the application list system, the government can no longer rely on this source of income.

Citizens criticized the high land price policy. Since private housing is unafford-able to most of the people, the government is under pressure to build more public housing to satisfy their living needs. For those who buy a house, mortgages take a large portion of the total income. Hence, investment in real estate may become a burden under unfavorable economic conditions. A typical example is the Asian Financial Crisis. During this period assets declined in value and people lost their jobs, yet they still had to repay their mortgages.

In addition, government and property developers might have incentives to jointly push up house prices. The government can control the land supply by fixing the amount of land released for application. Since the Hong Kong housing market is dominated by a small number of developers, they could simultaneously decrease the total new supply and push up the unit price.[12] Therefore, it seems that the land policies work unfavorably for the citizens, and hence there are more voices calling for policy replacements.

MORTGAGE MARKET

Given the high price of housing, it is unlikely that a typical household would purchase a home with cash. A mortgage loan is the most likely alternative. In Hong Kong, mortgage lending has been regarded as a low-risk business, because of the upward trend in real estate prices and low default rate. As financial institutions became willing to offer mortgages with lower interest rates to customers, there

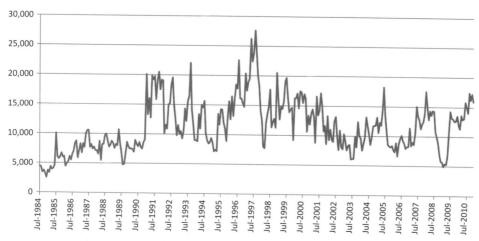

Exhibit 17.5 Time Plot of Monthly Issued Mortgages
Source: CEIC.

was a large increase in mortgage lending. For example, between July 1984 and September 1993, the monthly mortgage deeds received by the Land Registry of the Hong Kong government, which includes both mortgage re-finance cases and the newly issued mortgage cases, rose sharply from 4,525 cases to 22,055 cases (see Exhibit 17.5). However, a heavy reliance on the mortgage business brings underlying problems. The first is a typical maturity mismatch problem of financial intermediations. Assets of the financial institutions are usually long-term, while the liabilities are short-term. Financial institutions depend on foreign capital to fund all the loans. When the foreign short-term capital (or so-called hot money) withdraws from the Hong Kong market, there is a danger that the Hong Kong banking system is unable to provide enough funding for the credit. Since the mortgage loans are long term (10 to 20 years) and in a sense precommitted, the banking system will be forced to reduce other loans that are relatively short term, including loans to small and medium business, which can result in a credit crunch. The economy becomes vulnerable to the external funding shocks. Exhibit 17.6 is consistent with this hypothesis. The total loan amount actually drops from more than HK$4 trillion (1997) to about HK$2 trillion (2002). At the same time, the ratio of residential loans to total loans increases from slightly above 6 percent to more than 30 percent. The banking sector as a whole may have become over-exposed to housing loans.

Clearly, similar problems have been experienced by advanced economies such as the United States. With the examples of Fannie Mae and Freddie Mac in the mind of some regulators, the Hong Kong Mortgage Corporation Limited (HKMC) was established in March 1997. This corporation is wholly owned by the government through the Exchange Fund. Its Guaranteed Mortgage-Backed Pass-Through Programme aims to provide an efficient and cost-effective way for the banks to convert their illiquid residential mortgage loans into liquid mortgage-backed securities (MBS). In principle, the program can improve the stability of the banking and monetary system. In practice, however, none of the major banks joined this program as they expected that house values would continue to follow an upward trend and that there would be a continuing inflow of capital from China and other

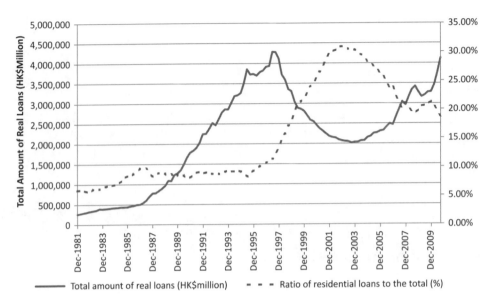

Exhibit 17.6 Ratio of Residential Loans to the Total Loans in all Financial Institutions
Source: CEIC.

countries. This leaves the Hong Kong banking system vulnerable to potential exchange rate and interest rate shocks.[13] In that sense, the Hong Kong economy as a whole has not learned as much as they could from the AFC. If the Hong Kong economy fares better than the GFC, it seems that the direction of capital flows plays a more important role than institutional changes.

HOUSING MARKET PERFORMANCE IN THE ASIAN FINANCIAL CRISIS (AFC)

As mentioned previously, Hong Kong has been developing its service industry since 1980. Between 1981 and 1992, its real GDP (in chained [2008] dollars) nearly doubled from HK$121,915 million to HK$238,107 million, while the unemployment rate dropped from 3.1 percent to 2.0 percent. Wealth started to accumulate among households, and that led to an increase in housing prices. The increase in house price relaxed the collateral constraints of those who owned small houses. As in the model of Ortalo-Magne and Rady (2006), those households now could trade-up (i.e., sell the small units and buy bigger ones), and we would expect an increase in the number of mortgage loans and an even higher house price in the economy.

In the first half of 1997, the asset bubble was inflated to the extreme. The real Hang Seng Index reached a peak of 14,677 points in July 1997 (Exhibit 17.7). The housing price index stayed at the peak in the second quarter of 1997 (Exhibit 17.3). The increasing trend of the asset markets attracted more investment.[14] In August 1997, the turnover value (in real terms) and volume in stock market reached historic highs: HK$569,774 million and 312,900 million shares, respectively (see Exhibit 17.7). In the housing market, 27,611 registered mortgage cases were recorded (see Exhibit 17.5).

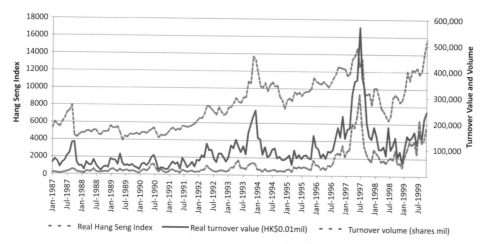

Exhibit 17.7   Time Plot of Real Hang Seng Index (Base Year: July 1964) and Its Turnover
Source: Hong Kong Exchanges and Clearing Limited.

Good market sentiment was maintained until Hong Kong experienced the financial crisis in late 1997. The interest rate was raised by the HKMA to defend the peg exchange rate. After that, Hong Kong experienced a recession: Within a year, the real stock market index dropped by more than 50 percent, housing prices declined by 40 percent, the unemployment rate rose by 3 percent, and the real GDP declined by 9 percent. As a consequence, the wealth of existing homeowners was dramatically reduced. They had to face the problem of negative equity, where the amount of outstanding mortgage loan was greater than the value of asset. Some homeowners continued repayment of the mortgage loan, and hoped that the housing price would rebound in the future. Others deferred mortgage payment, sold the home at a discount, or declared bankruptcy. As shown in Exhibit 17.8, both

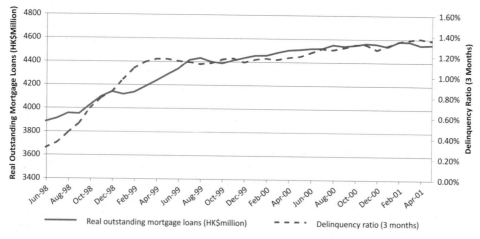

Exhibit 17.8   Time Plot of Real Outstanding Mortgage Loans and Delinquency Ratio
Source: CEIC.

the real amount of outstanding loans and the delinquency ratio increased during the period of 1998 to 2001.

EVENT STUDY

The Asian Financial Crisis (AFC) was a very painful experience for Hong Kong. Before the AFC, the positive expectation in Hong Kong was so extreme that some people quit jobs to work as full-time speculators. When the AFC hit Hong Kong, many people, even government officials, were caught by surprise. In the Hong Kong Year Book 1998, Donald Tsang, the Financial Secretary at that time, wrote: "Now that we can look back on it, 1998 was surely a year to remember. Many of the lessons were far from pleasant but, so long as we learn from them, we can only grow and improve." [15] In fact, the government imposed many policy measures to guard against another financial crisis. Equally important, investors in Hong Kong changed their expectations. In December 2009, the same Donald Tsang, now the Chief Executive, comments that the "Financial Tsunami is different from the Asian Financial Crisis, where it starts from the United States of America and affects globally. To defend us from the attack of the crisis, one basic strategy is to have a certain level of foreign reserves. Countries or nations cannot solely depend on financial industry, but have to develop other industries."[16] On top of the institutional changes that the Hong Kong government has implemented after the AFC learning effect is the emergence of China and its close relationship with Hong Kong and the possibility the relationship would reduce the impact of the GFC to Hong Kong.

To assess whether Hong Kong does behave differently, this section employs event-study graphs for illustration. The choice of the frequency of data matters. Most economic variables do not have high frequency data. On the other hand, if an annual frequency is chosen, some of the impact of the crisis will be hidden as the impact period is averaged out by the subsequent period.[17] As a compromise, we use quarterly data, and monthly when it is available. We can get most of the macroeconomic time series from the Hong Kong government web site, with a few exceptions, such as the wage index. We use the IMF data for the wage index, in quarterly frequency. To facilitate the comparison, all variables are recalculated as 100 at the time of the AFC (December or fourth quarter of 1997) and GFC (September or third quarter of 2008). Pre- and post-crisis performances can then be easily observed.

Beginning with asset markets, as shown in Exhibit 17.9a, real housing prices dropped by 40 percent after 10 months of the AFC, and still had not recovered after 24 months. Compared to the case of the Financial Tsunami, housing prices took a shorter period (11 months) to return to pre-crisis level. The situation for real office price is similar (Exhibit 17.9b). It took a much shorter time to recover during the GFC than during the AFC. The real retail property price dropped significantly during the AFC (Exhibit 17.9c). During the GFC, however, it dropped shortly but then actually surpassed the level before the GFC! It is quite possible that the continuing economic growth in China brings many tourist-shoppers to Hong Kong. Their spending capacity is strong enough that the retail property price does not suffer any loss after adjusting for inflation. Similarly, in the stock market, the Hang Seng Index dropped dramatically at the beginning of the crisis. The effect of the AFC is more long-lasting, in which the Hang Seng Index took about 15 months to reach the pre-crisis level (Exhibit 17.9d). The data seems to be consistent with the notion that Hong Kong investors were better prepared this time (for instance, with better risk management through different financial instruments), and hence the asset markets took a shorter period to recover.

Economic activity as a whole dampened with each financial crisis. As shown in Exhibit 17.9e, real GDP declined more than 10 percent after the two financial crises. However, real GDP did not recover after seven quarters of the AFC, while it took five quarters to recover after the GFC. The employment market seemed to be badly affected by the AFC. The unemployment rate was 2.5 times more than the pre-crisis level and there was no tendency for it to fall after eight quarters. In contrast, the Hong Kong labor market seems to be much less affected during the recent GFC (Exhibit 17.9f). The continuing economic downturn and inappropriate housing policies during the AFC were two of the main reasons for Tung Chee-Hwa to step down on March 10, 2005.

Because of a fall in income during poor economic conditions, the housing market was seriously affected. People were cautious about purchasing houses and the real value of housing transactions in the secondary market did not improve after the crisis. On the contrary, secondary market transactions in Hong Kong actually increased since the outbreak of the global financial crisis. Part of the reason may be due to the continuous economic growth of China and the willingness of Chinese investors to diversify their portfolios in the Hong Kong housing market (Exhibit 17.9g).[18] Outstanding mortgage loans rose by 15 percent after 20 months of the AFC. At that time, real estate developers provided some secondary mortgages to buyers in order to liquidate their inventory (i.e., the housing units ready for sale). Also, the government launched many policies to encourage people to participate in different subsidized ownership schemes as a way to stabilize the housing market. As a result, the total amount of mortgages can actually increase when the total value of secondary market trading decreases. However, these policies were no longer in place. The outstanding mortgage loans remain more or less the same after the recent financial tsunami (Exhibit 17.9h). In addition, the ratio of residential loans relative to the total rose by 60 percent after two years of the AFC, while its ratio stabilized after the financial tsunami, which suggests that financial institutions are more prudent in making loans (Exhibit 17.9i).

In summary, the lessons that the AFC brought to us are memorable. Through a series of rectifications and improvements, the housing market became better behaved. Banks are better at managing their loan portfolio, as the proportion of residential loans is kept stable after the GFC. In addition, relative to GDP, the transactions in the secondary housing market were very active after two quarters of the GFC (Exhibit 17.9j), while the outstanding mortgage loans were much smaller than those in the AFC (Exhibit 17.9k). All these factors suggest that the economy as a whole may be less vulnerable to another financial crisis.

CONCLUSION

If home ownership is a dream for the working class, then the continuous economic growth in Hong Kong between the 1960s and 1990s made this dream apparently tangible. Hard work and rising wages made this possible. Although the house prices rose even faster than wages, this confirmed the conventional wisdom that

(a) Real Housing Price

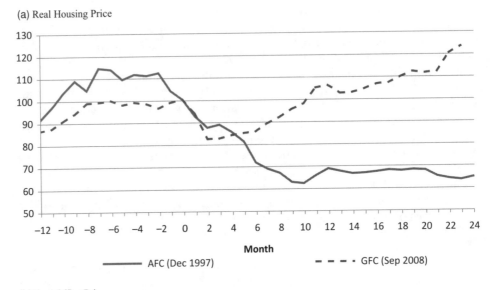

(b) Real Office Price

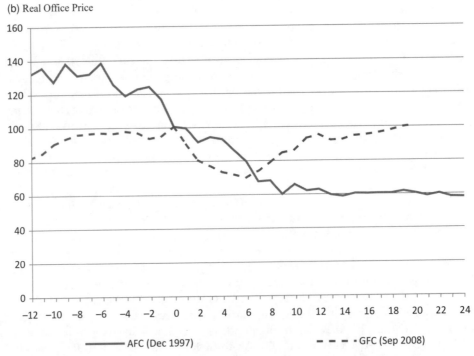

Exhibit 17.9 (a–k) Event Studies Comparing Hong Kong Economic Indicators with the AFC and the GFC

Sources: Valuation Department, Hong Kong Government (a–d); Hong Kong Exchanges and Clearing Limited (e); Census and Statistics Department (f–g); CEIC (h–k).

(c) Real Retail Property Price

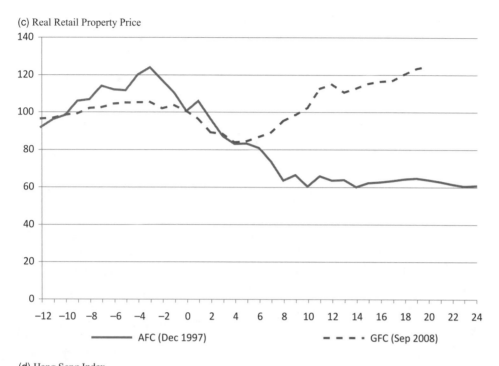

AFC (Dec 1997)   GFC (Sep 2008)

(d) Hang Seng Index

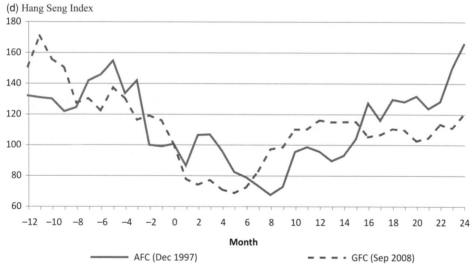

Month

AFC (Dec 1997)   GFC (Sep 2008)

Exhibit 17.9 (*Continued*)

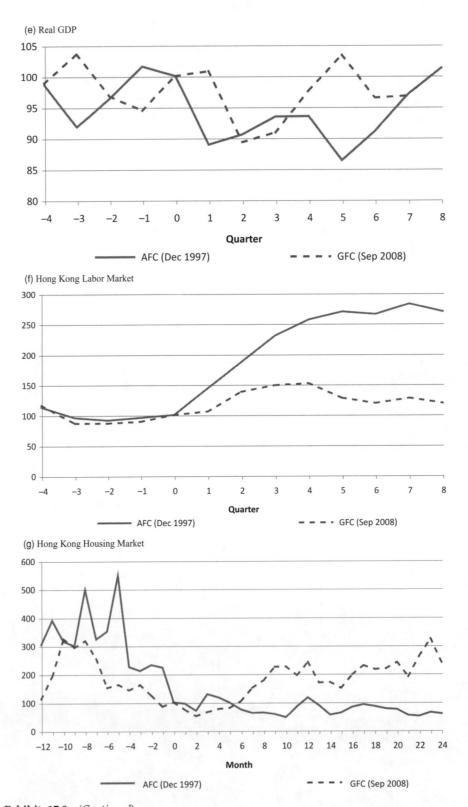

(e) Real GDP

(f) Hong Kong Labor Market

(g) Hong Kong Housing Market

Exhibit 17.9 (*Continued*)

(h) Real Outstanding Mortgage Loans

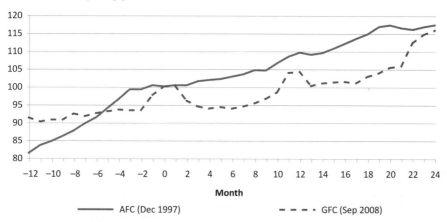

(i) Ratio of Residential Loans to the Total Loans in All Financial Institutions

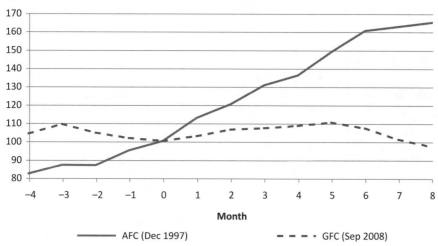

(j) Ratio of the Value of Trading in Secondary Housing Markets Relative to the GDP

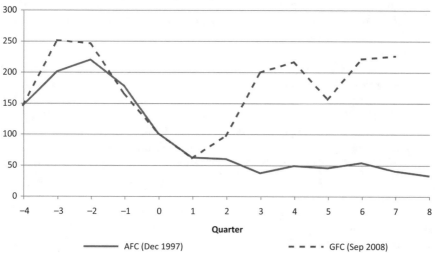

Exhibit 17.9 (*Continued*)

(k) Ratio of the Value of Outstanding Mortgage Loans Relative to the GDP

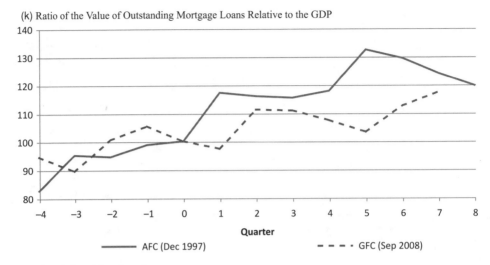

Exhibit 17.9 (*Continued*)

house prices would only increase. This gave people even more incentives for home ownership, and perhaps more than one home for each household. The AFC changed these perceptions and behaviors. Households experienced negative equity and since mortgage loans in Hong Kong are recourse by nature, people were trapped in their underwater houses. At the same time, the banking sector faced the external shock of the AFC and found itself being over-exposed to risk in the residential loan sector. The government also experienced a fiscal deficit, which has rarely happened since the 1970s. Hong Kong was in great distress.

Lessons were painfully learned and policy measures were implemented. For instance, to improve market efficiency, the Hong Kong Mortgage Corporation was established in 1997. This gives an additional option to an individual bank. In addition, some government interventions and strengthening measures were undertaken during the AFC, including using the fiscal reserve to purchase stock in the financial market, and imposing more stringent rules on short-term capital flow (hot money). All these seem to contribute to the stabilization of the market.

Our event study seems to suggest that the Hong Kong economy did behave differently during the AFC and the recent GFC. In particular, it seems that the adverse effect of external shocks on different aggregate economic variables are much smaller, and take a much shorter time to have their effects die out. It could be due to government policy (the learning effect). It may also be due to the China factor. Of course, it can be argued that the learning effect is so significant that Chinese investors have perceived that the Hong Kong market has become safer than before and hence are more willing to invest in Hong Kong. It will take another careful empirical study to investigate the relationship between the learning effect and the China factor. An alternative explanation is related to a possible change in the perception of the investors. The AFC experience clearly illustrates that the housing price can decrease, and decrease dramatically. This may lead to a revision of the investment strategy for local investors. Econometrically, it would mean a structural change in the system. Recent research such as Leung, Wong, and

Cheung (2007) and Leung, Cheung, and Tang (2009), among others, has taken some preliminary steps in this direction. Clearly, more research efforts are needed to gain a better understanding of how the real estate market, financial crisis, and general economic structure of an economy interact with one another.

ACKNOWLEDGMENTS

The authors are grateful to (in alphabetical order) Ashok Bardhan, Nan-Kuang Chen, Bob Edelstein, Cynthia Kroll, and Francois Ortalo-Magne, among many other seminar participants for many inspiring discussions over the years. The financial support from the City University of Hong Kong is gratefully acknowledged. The usual disclaimer applies.

NOTES

1. Among others, see Chan et al. (2005) and Chang et al. (2009).
2. Among others, see Chow et al. (2002) on this point.
3. Unfortunately, the government does not provide data on wealth inequality in Hong Kong.
4. Interestingly, before the GFC in 2008 occurred, the office price in real terms was restored to the level of 1997, before the AFC. For the case of real retail property, it even surpassed its 1997 value before the GFC.
5. See Leung, Wei, and Wong (2006) for more details.
6. See Goodhart and Dai (2003) for more details.
7. For more details, see Goodhart and Dai (2003), Leung, Wong, and Cheung (2007), Leung, Cheung, and Tang (2009), among others.
8. Hong Kong Monetary Authority, 5 September 1998. Strengthening of Currency Board Arrangements in Hong Kong, press release. Details are available at www.info.gov.hk/hkma/eng/public/qb9811/pdf/qbfa02.pdf.
9. Yam, J., October 14, 1998. "Defending Hong Kong's Monetary Stability." Speech at TDC Networking Luncheon, Singapore. Details are available at http://www.info.gov.hk/hkma/eng/speeches/speechs/joseph/speech_141098b.htm.
10. See Yiu et al. (2010) for more details.
11. Even though the government took an active role in selling the land located at Ho Man Tin in June 8, 2010, there is no further evidence that the current land sale arrangement will be replaced shortly.
12. For more discussion on the oligopolistic structure of the Hong Kong housing market, see Renaud, Pretorius, and Pasadilla (1997), among others.
13. The failure to securitize the mortgage debts as well as to "dollarize" foreign debt seemed to be common across Asian countries during the AFC, and may contributed a significant part in the large impact of the AFC. Among others, see Choi and Cook (2004) and Chue and Cook (2008) for more details.
14. There are many justifications for "trend-chasing." Among others, see Orosel (1998) for a rational foundation for trend-chasing behavior in the financial market.
15. Hong Kong Yearbook 1998. Details are available at www.yearbook.gov.hk/1998
16. Commercial Radio, December 29, 2009. Details are available at: http://881903.com

17. The time aggregation bias has been studied by Christiano and Eichenbaum (1987) and Christiano, Eichenbaum, and Marshall (1991).
18. See Leung and Tang (2010) for further discussion.

REFERENCES

Case, K. E., J. M. Quigley, and R. J. Shiller. 2005. "Comparing Wealth Effects: The Stock Market versus the Housing Market." *Advances in Macroeconomics* 5:1, 1–32.

Census and Statistics Department. Available at http://censtatd.gov.hk.

Chan, K., P. Yip, J. Au, and D. Lee. 2005. "Charcoal-Burning Suicide in Post-Transition Hong Kong." *British Journal of Psychiatry* 186, 67–73.

Chang, S. S., D. Gunnell, J. Sterne, T. H. Lu, and A. T.A. Cheng. 2009. "Was the Economic Crisis 1997–1998 Responsible for Rising Suicide Rates in East/Southeast Asia? A Time–Trend Analysis for Japan, Hong Kong, South Korea, Taiwan, Singapore, and Thailand." *Social Science and Medicine* 68:7, 1322–1331.

Chen, N. K., S. S. Chen and Y. H. Chou. 2010. "House Prices, Collateral Constraint, and the Asymmetric Effect on Consumption." *Journal of Housing Economics* 19, 26–37.

Chen, N. K., and C. K. Y. Leung. 2008. "Asset Price Spillover, Collateral, and Crises: With an Application to Property Market Policy." *Journal of Real Estate Finance and Economics* 37, 351–385.

Choi, W. G., and D. Cook. 2004. "Liability Dollarization and the Bank Balance Sheet Channel." *Journal of International Economics* 64:2, 247–275.

Chow, Y. F., C. K. Y. Leung, N. Wong, E. H. F. Cheng, and W. H. Yan. 2002. *Hong Kong Real Estate Market: Facts and Policies*. Hong Kong: Ming Pao Publisher (in Chinese).

Christiano, L., and M. Eichenbaum. 1987. "Temporal Aggregation and Structural Inference in Macroeconomics." Carnegie-Rochester Conference Series on Public Policy 26, 63–130.

Christiano, L., M. Eichenbaum, and D. Marshall. 1991. "The Permanent Income Hypothesis Revisited." *Econometrica* 59, 397–424.

Chue, T. K., and D. Cook. 2008. "Sudden Stops and Liability Dollarization: Evidence from Asia's Financial Intermediaries." *Pacific-Basin Finance Journal* 16:4, 436–52.

Commercial Radio. Available at http://881903.com.

Fu, Y., 2000. "Hong Kong: Overcoming Financial Risks of Growing Real Estate Credit, in Asia's Financial Crisis and the Role of Real Estate." In Koichi Mera and Bertrand Renaud, eds., *Asia's Financial Crisis and the Role of Real Estate*, 139–158. New York: M. E. Sharpe.

Goodhart, C. and L. Dai. 2003. *Intervention to Save Hong Kong*. Oxford: Oxford University Press.

Gyourko, J., and D. Keim. 1992. What Does the Stock Market Tell Us about Real Estate Returns? *Journal of the American Real Estate and Urban Economics Association* 20, 457–485.

Haldane, A. G., Executive Director, Financial Stability, Bank of England. 2009 (May 8). "Small Lessons from a Big Crisis." Available at www.bankofengland.co.uk/publications/speeches/speaker.htm#haldane.

Haldane, A. G., Executive Director, Financial Stability, Bank of England. 2010 (January 27). "The Debt Hangover." Available at www.bankofengland.co.uk/publications/speeches/speaker.htm#haldane.

Ho, L. S., and G. Wong. 2006. "Privatization of Public Housing: Did It Cause the 1998 Recession in Hong Kong?" *Contemporary Economic Policy* 24:2, 262–273.

Ho, L. S., and G. Wong. 2008. "Nexus between Housing and the Macro Economy: The Hong Kong Case." *Pacific Economic Review* 13:2, 223–239.

Ho, L. S., and G. Wong. 2009. "The First Step on the Housing Ladder: A Natural Experiment in Hong Kong." *Journal of Housing Economics* 18, 59–67.

Ho, L. S., Y. Ma, and D. Haurin. 2008. "Domino Effects within a Housing Market: The Transmission of House Price Changes across Quality Tiers." *Journal of Real Estate Finance and Economics* 37:4, 299–316.

Hong Kong Monetary Authority. 1998 (September 5). "Strengthening of Currency Board Arrangements in Hong Kong."

Hong Kong Mortgage Corporation. 1997. "Guaranteed Mortgage-Backed Pass-Through Programme." Available at www.hkmc.com.hk.

Hong Kong Yearbook 1998. Available at www.yearbook.gov.hk/1998.

Housing Department. Available at www.housingauthoriy.gov.hk.

Jin, Y., C. K. Y. Leung, and Z. Zeng. Forthcoming. "Real Estate, the External Finance Premium, and Business Investment: A Quantitative Dynamic General Equilibrium Analysis." *Real Estate Economics*.

Kothari, S. P., and J. B. Warner. 2007. "Econometrics of Event Studies." In *Handbook of Corporate Finance, Vol. 1*. Elsevier.

Lands Department. Available at www.landsd.gov.hk.

Leung, C. K. Y., and N. K. Chen. 2006. "Intrinsic Cycles of Land Price: A Simple Model." *Journal of Real Estate Research* 28:3, 293–320.

Leung, C. K. Y., and N. K. Chen. 2010. "Stock Price Volatility, Negative Auto-correlation and Consumption-Wealth Ratio: The Case of Constant Fundamentals. *Pacific Economic Review* 15:2, 224–245.

Leung, C. K. Y., P. W. Y. Cheung, and E. C. H. Tang. 2009. "Financial Crisis and the Co-Movements of Housing Sub-Markets: Do Relationships Change after a Crisis?" Working Paper.

Leung, C. K. Y., and D. Feng. 2005. "What Drives the Property Price-Trading Volume Correlation: Evidence from a Commercial Real Estate Market." *Journal of Real Estate Finance and Economics* 31:2, 241–255.

Leung, C. K. Y., G. C. Lau, and Y. C. F. Leong. 2002. "Testing Alternative Theories of the Property Price-Trading Volume Correlation." *Journal of Real Estate Research* 23:3, 253–263.

Leung, C. K. Y., and E. C. H. Tang. 2010. "Speculating on China's Economic Growth through Hong Kong? Evidence from the Stock Market IPO and Real Estate Markets." City University of Hong Kong, mimeo.

Leung, C. K. Y., P. Wei, and S. K. Wong. 2006. "Are the Markets for Factories and Offices Integrated? Evidence from Hong Kong." *International Real Estate Review* 9, 62–94.

Leung, C. K. Y., S. K. Wong, and P. W. Y. Cheung. 2007. "On the Stability of the Implicit Prices of Housing Attributes: A Dynamic Theory and Some Evidence." *International Real Estate Review* 10:2, 65–91.

Ming Pao. Available at www.mingpao.com.

Orosel, G. O. 1998. "Participation Costs, Trend Chasing, and Volatility of Stock Prices." *Review of Financial Studies* 11, 521–557.

Ortalo-Magne, F., and S. Rady. 2006. "Housing Market Dynamics: On the Contribution of Income Shocks and Credit Constraints." *Review of Economic Studies* 73, 459–485.

Rating and Valuation Department. Available at www.rvd.gov.hk.

Renaud, B., F. Pretorius, and B. Pasadilla. 1997. *Markets at Work: Dynamics of the Residential Real Estate Market in Hong Kong*. Hong Kong: Hong Kong University Press.

Tsang, J. 2010. "Budget Speech 2010–11." Available at www.budget.gov.hk/2010.

Tse, C. Y., and C. K. Y. Leung. 2002. "Increasing Wealth and Increasing Instability: The Role of Collateral." *Review of International Economics* 10:1, 45–52.

Wessel, D. 2010 (April 8). "Did 'Great Recession' Live Up to the Name?" *Wall Street Journal*.

Wong, G. 2010. *Three Essays on Housing Market in Hong Kong: Implications for Public Policy and Macro Economy*. Hong Kong: Lingnan University.

Yam, J., Chairman of Hong Kong Monetary Authority. 1998 (October 14). "Defending Hong Kong's Monetary Stability." Available at www.info.gov.hk/hkma.

Yiu, M., A. Ho, Y. Ma, and S. K. Tsang. 2010. "Hong Kong Linked Exchange Rate System and Hong Kong Dollar Exchange Rate Dynamics under Strong Capital Inflows." Hong Kong Monetary Authority, mimeo.

ABOUT THE AUTHORS

CHARLES KA YUI LEUNG received his PhD at the University of Rochester. He is currently an associate professor of the Department of Economics and Finance at the City University of Hong Kong. He received the Fulbright Scholarship (Research) in 2004–2005 and has been a visiting scholar at both the Fisher Center for Real Estate and Urban Economics at Haas School of Business, University of California, Berkeley; and Hoover Institution, Stanford University. He has served as a guest editor of *Journal of Housing Economics* and an editorial board member of the *International Real Estate Review*. He also serves as a member of the Board of Directors of the Asian Real Estate Society (beginning in 2007). He was selected as one of the Weimer School of Advanced Studies in Real Estate and Land Economics Post Doctoral Honorees (2008) and received the Red Pen Award from the American Real Estate Society (2010).

EDWARD CHI HO TANG received his BBA (Finance) at the City University of Hong Kong in 2006 and Mphil in 2008. He is currently a PhD candidate of the Department of Economics and Finance at the City University of Hong Kong. He has presented at Asian Real Estate Society (AsRES), Global Chinese Real Estate Congress (GCREC), Asia-Pacific Real Estate Research Symposium, and Brown Bag Seminar. In 2009, his joint paper with Dr. Charles Leung won the Third Best Paper Award at GCREC.

CHAPTER 18

The Global Financial Crisis and the Korean Housing Sector

How Is This Time Different from the 1997 Asian Financial Crisis?

KYUNG-HWAN KIM
Professor of Economics, Sogang University

Following a brief introduction, this chapter presents an overview of housing market trends and government policies in Korea since the mid-1990s. It then describes the key elements and characteristics of the housing sector, such as the changing consumer sentiments, the behavior of developers, the responsiveness of new supply, and mortgage market innovations. The chapter also provides a comparison between the global financial crisis (GFC) and the Asian financial crisis (AFC) in terms of the economic and housing market environment, the behavior of housing price and quantity variables, and government intervention. The key findings include: that the housing sector was the victim of the economic crisis rather than a major cause of the crisis in each case, that the impact of the GFC on the housing sector was moderate compared with that of the AFC, and that the GFC failed to serve as important a platform for policy reform as the AFC did. Some explanations for these findings are offered. The chapter concludes with a discussion of policy issues going forward.

INTRODUCTION

Housing is a major sector of the Korean economy. Housing comprises 72 percent of the nations' total wealth and 83 percent of household assets as of 2007, and housing investment has accounted for over 5 percent of the gross domestic product (GDP) since 1970 (Cho and Kim 2010). Extensive government intervention has been a key feature of the Korean housing sector. Government has micromanaged the various aspects of the supply of developable land and housing over the years (Kim and Kim 2000). Mitigating the fluctuations of housing price has been an overarching objective of housing policy in Korea. Specific policy packages were introduced for that purpose at different phases of the market cycle, which resulted in an alternation of suppression and boost measures in a counter-cyclical manner.

Over the past two decades or so, the Korean economy has been hit by two major crises, the Asian financial crisis that broke out in November 1997 and the global financial crisis that started in September 2008. The economic environment surrounding the housing market preceding the first crisis was significantly different from the environment of the second one. A major difference is that the 1997 crisis broke out after a period of declining house price, whereas the global financial crisis followed the house price boom in some submarkets in Seoul and the existence of a sizeable stock of unsold houses in some other cities. Another difference was that the mortgage-lending sector became much larger and the terms of mortgage finance more diverse during the intervening years. In both crises, however, the housing sector was a victim of the economic crisis, not a major contributor to it. This distinguishes the case of Korea from that of Thailand for the Asian financial crisis (Kim 2000) and from that of the United States for the ongoing global financial crisis.

The Korean government responded to both crises with comprehensive stimulus packages in an attempt to prevent the collapse of the price of housing and the residential construction activity. Each crisis also served as a catalyst for policy reform in the housing sector, although to different degrees. The mortgage market was liberalized, a secondary mortgage market facility was established, and many regulations were removed or improved upon in the wake of the Asian financial crisis. Some deregulation measures were reversed and new regulations were introduced during the intervening period between the two crises. Such moves were made to respond to the actual or anticipated house price increases. Efforts were made to fix the legacies of past regulations in recent years in the wake of the global financial crisis, but the outcome was not as impressive as it was in the case of the Asian financial crisis.

This chapter is organized into four sections following the introduction. The next section presents an overview of housing market trends since the mid-1990s and government response to the Global Financial Crisis. The second section describes important aspects of the housing markets such as the role of consumer sentiments, the behavior of developers, the supply elasticity, and mortgage market innovations. The third section draws a comparison between the global financial crisis and the Asian crisis in terms of the economic and housing market environment, and the behavior of price and quantity variables. Several conjectures are offered to explain the differences. The last section offers suggestions concerning policy issues going forward into the future.

AN OVERVIEW OF HOUSING MARKET TRENDS AND HOUSING POLICY

The Price of Housing

Korea has experienced several housing cycles since the late 1980s. There was a massive run-up in house price between 1988 and 1990. It was caused by accumulated shortages of housing combined with the surge in demand following a period of rapid income growth during 1986–1988. The housing price peaked in April 1991 and started declining thereafter. The turnaround of housing price increase was mainly attributable to the government drive to build two million new houses between 1988 and 1992. The plan represented a landmark in government housing policy in that the whole government was mobilized to increase housing supply on an unprecedented scale.[1] The annual target of 400,000 units was almost double the level prior to 1988 but the actual supply figures (on a permit base) far exceeded the target. The momentum of supply increases carried on until the outbreak of the Asian economic crisis in November 1997.

It is well documented that the bust of a real-estate price bubble was responsible for damaging the financial sector and hence became a cause of the economic crisis in some Southeast Asian countries, such as Thailand. However, the real-estate sector was not a cause but a victim of the 1997 Asian crisis in the case of Korea. In fact, housing price had been falling steadily since May 1991 in both nominal and real terms, until it took a nosedive in 1998. A large number of housing construction companies went bankrupt, and residential construction activities shrunk dramatically in the wake of economic crisis.[2] Government responded to the totally unanticipated economic disaster with various measures to stimulate the real estate sector, hoping that it would spearhead the overall economic recovery. Thanks to those measures and the quick recovery of the macroeconomy, housing price started bouncing back in 1999. Exhibit 18.1 illustrates the close linkages among the changes in nominal GDP, nominal housing price index, and land price index around the Asian financial crisis.

Housing price started rising at a more rapid pace from late 2001, and developed into a major run-up by 2002. The record-low interest rate, rapid expansion of mortgage lending, and the lagged impact of the reduction of new supply in the wake of the Asian financial crisis were its drivers. A major feature of the 2002–2003

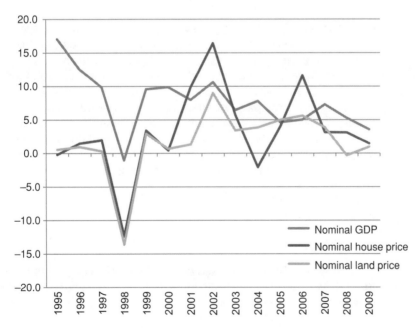

Exhibit 18.1   The Growth of Nominal GDP and the Prices of Land and Housing
Source: Bank of Korea, KB.

Exhibit 18.2   Real House Price Trends Since 1995
Source: KB.

house price run-up was that its magnitude varied across cities and their submarkets, housing types and size categories. The Seoul metropolitan area experienced a much higher rate of appreciation than elsewhere, and the medium and large condominiums located in the three districts of Seoul enjoyed the largest price gain.[3] This can be seen from Exhibit 18.2, which traces the trends of the real house price index with 1995 as 100, and confirms parts of such a pattern. The administration that took office in February 2003 made various attempts to contain the price hike. Despite the extensive policy intervention covering taxation, regulation, and finance, however, housing price rose sporadically until 2007.[4] It was not until September 2008 when housing price took a downturn as the global financial crisis set in. But the spell of falling housing price was brief and housing price stabilized, thanks to the government stimulus package.

The Quantity of Housing

Housing supply statistics in Korea are based on approval of development projects. Exhibit 18.3 illustrates the trend of new housing supply since 1995 for Korea, Seoul, and the Capital Region consisting of Seoul and the province surrounding it. Several points can be made using the chart. First, new housing supply averaged around 500,000 per year. Second, there was a substantial reduction in supply during the three years 1998–2000 following the Asian financial crisis and a similar decline in

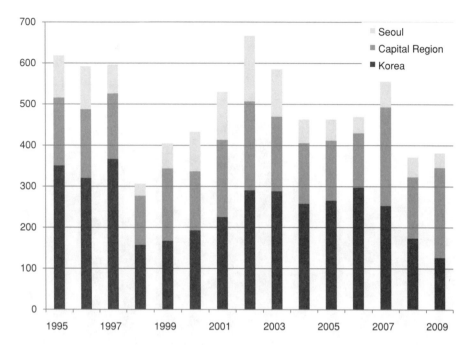

Exhibit 18.3   Housing Permits by Region
Source: MLTM.

the wake of the global financial crisis of 2008–2009. Third, the amount of new supply in Seoul was very small during the period 1998–2000 and since 2004. One more important point that cannot be seen from the chart is a sharp withdrawal of the private sector from housing supply in recent years. This is a result of the sluggish demand and the expansion of the government program for direct provision of housing since 2008.

Data on trading volume are available only from 1998. Exhibit 18.4 presents the trend of the number of transactions in housing between 1998 and 2009. The trading volume started low in 1998 right after the Asian crisis, started rising in 1999, and then peaked in 2002–2003 and again in 2005–2006. These were the years of rapid appreciation of housing prices. A weak but positive correlation between the rate of increase in housing price and that of trading volume can be seen from Exhibit 18.5.

The inventory of unsold condominiums (called apartments in Korea) is another key indicator of the Korean housing market. Condominiums are the dominant housing type and most condominiums are presold. The data graphed in Exhibit 18.6 include unsold units at the time of initial presale up to the completed ones that remain unsold. The inventory of unsold condominiums fell steadily from 1995 till 2002 and increased again, but not rapidly, until 2006. The inventory increased sharply in 2008 and peaked at the end of 2008 at 164,000, before it fell to 123,000 by December 2009 and further to 100,000 units, which is about the 15-year average level, by September 2010. An important fact to note is that the completed and unsold units were as much as 50 percent of the inventory at that time.

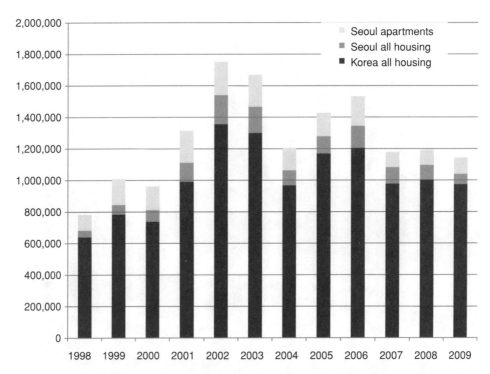

Exhibit 18.4   Trading Volume of Housing
Source: MLTM.

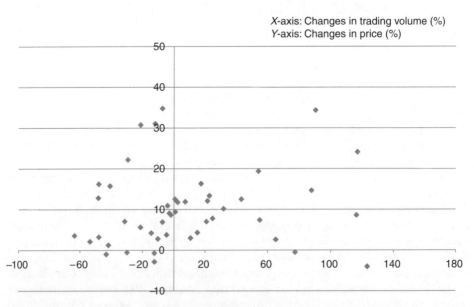

Exhibit 18.5   Changes in Housing Price and Trading Volume
Source: MLTM, KB.

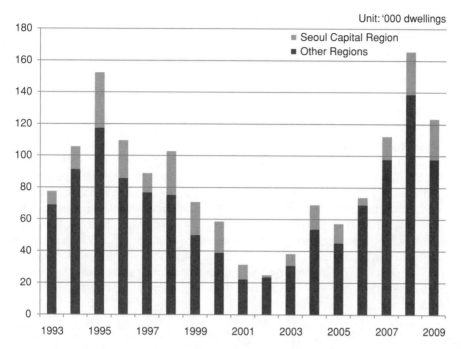

Exhibit 18.6 Inventory of Unsold Apartments by Region
Source: MLTM.

Government Response to the Global Financial Crisis

The current Lee Myung-bak government took office in February 2008, when the housing market was already sluggish and the stock of unsold apartments was rising fast. The government tried to boost the housing market by cutting the rate of the acquisition tax and the registration tax by 50 percent. The time span for a household to own two or more houses without being subject to the higher rate of the capital gains tax was extended from one year to two years. The government also announced a new program of supplying 1.5 million small apartments for owner occupation and rental for middle- and lower-income households by 2018 with government initiative. In addition, some regulations on redevelopment of condominiums in Seoul were relaxed. As the shockwave of the global financial crisis impacted the Korean economy, the government introduced a comprehensive fiscal stimulus package of KRW 14 trillion in November 2008.[5] In addition, the government introduced measures to preempt the fallout of the real-estate market and the consequent detrimental impact on the financial system. They included lifting the designation of speculation-watch areas in which mortgage lending was regulated. Early in 2009, the government announced a five-year exemption of capital gains tax for those who purchased new houses within one year, as well as lowering the penalizing high rate of capital gains tax on those who owned two or more houses. As the housing price recovered and started rising again later in 2009, the government tightened the reins on mortgage lending by lowering the maximum loan-to-value (LTV) ratio from 60 percent to 50 percent, as well as introducing a ceiling on the debt-service-to-income (DTI) ratio in Seoul and the Capital Region.

A few points are worth noting about the government responses to the global financial crisis. First, the top priority of the government intervention, immediately following the outbreak of the crisis, was to mitigate a sharp decline in housing price. Consequently, the government changed the course of policy as housing price started rising after falling for six months. Second, the government employed regulations on mortgage lending to contain a possible housing price run-up. Thirdly, the government made efforts to normalize the taxation of real estate by lowering the burden of the capital gains transactions taxes and the property-holding taxes, while offering temporary tax breaks to boost the housing market. The previous government of Roh Moo-hyun that was in office from 2003 to 2007 had raised the overall burden of local property tax and introduced a new national tax called Comprehensive Real Estate Tax on the owners of expensive houses. It had also strengthened the capital gains tax on the owners of two or more houses, raising the tax rate to 50 percent (55 percent including a surtax) on the former and to 60 percent (66 percent including a surtax) on the latter. The current government attempted to reverse the tax policy changes of the previous government, but it only partially succeeded.

KEY ELEMENTS AND STRUCTURAL CHARACTERISTICS OF THE HOUSING MARKET

Consumer Sentiments and Over-valuation in the Hottest Markets

Consumer expectation is a key factor in shaping the housing price path during a boom and a downturn (Case and Shiller 2010). Chung's analysis of Korean data (2010) suggests that housing price is affected by consumer confidence in addition to market fundamentals such as income and interest rate. He estimated an error correction model and found that consumer sentiment affects both the long-run equilibrium price and the short-run price adjustments.

The possibility that excessive optimism might have exacerbated the house price hike of 2002–2003 and 2005–2006 led to a debate over whether there was a housing bubble in Korean cities. Contrary to the widespread belief that there was a bubble, empirical research suggests that housing price hike was concentrated in selected submarkets of Seoul and that housing price was not far off from its long-run path. Kim and Cho (2010) estimated a long-run equilibrium housing price equation and computed the deviation of the actual house price from the level forecast by the model. They found a moderate overvaluation of around 10–20 percent in Seoul but no sign of overvaluation in four other provincial cities as of 2007.

Once house price started rising in the spring of 2009, after a six-month decline, and the price increase continued into the summer, government tightened mortgage supply in September to contain a possible run-up in house price in some submarkets. This policy move froze the market and the trading volume fell sharply. By that time, pessimism about the long-term housing market had taken over.[6] The prediction of a long-term decline in housing prices suddenly emerged as a dominant view of the market. The story of decelerating population growth, the retirement of the baby boomers, and so forth had been known to market participants for some time, but the argument for a further decline in house price gained momentum. The pessimistic view of the market induced would-be home buyers to postpone home purchases until housing prices fell further. The slowdown of the housing market activities made the government introduce a partial relaxation of the LTV-DTI regulation in August 2010. Housing price remains stable as of December 2010, with a sign of turning around.

Behavior of Developers and Overbuilding

Home builders are known to behave with myopic and overly optimistic expectations about market demand and the future course of the price, and that such behavior can lead to overbuilding (Wang and Zhou 2000). This tendency is observed in Korea where overbuilding has been a cyclical issue since the 1990s. The developers ended up supplying quantities of new housing in the provincial cities where the growth of population and employment was very sluggish. There is a failure of coordination amongst developers, each of whom believes that he will do just fine. This can be aggravated by changes in government policy in some cases. For example, the announcement made in January 2007 of the government plan to expand the coverage of the price control on new apartments (effective in September 2007) forced the home builders to rush and pre-sell their projects to avoid the regulation. Three years later, this led to a large increase in the completed new units in 2010, and, combined with weak demand, exercised a downward pressure on housing price.

Supply Elasticity and Volatility of Housing Price and Quantity

The elasticity of supply of new housing is known to be determined by the elasticity of the supply of developable land, the share of the land cost in total cost of housing production, and the elasticity of substitution between land and non-land inputs in housing production (Kim et al. 2010). In Korea the share of land cost is substantial, as great as 45–61 percent of the cost of new apartments built in recent years, and the quantity and the terms of supply of developable land are tightly controlled by the government. It has been argued that Korea has an inelastic housing supply system and that the government has responded to housing price hikes caused by increasing demand by shifting the inelastic housing supply curve to right over the years (Green et al. 1994). Malpezzi and Mayo (1997) and Mayo and Sheppard (1996) confirmed that the supply elasticity of housing in Korea is close to zero for the period up to the 1980s. Estimation using the same model suggests that the price elasticity of housing supply has been consistently small in more recent years.

One implication of inelastic supply is high volatility of housing price in response to a shift in demand. In empirical terms, housing price in Korea exhibits larger volatility compared with other developed economies, while Korean housing price increases have been moderate. In fact, Korea was an under-performer in terms of the average rate of increase in real house price next only to Japan, Germany, and Switzerland (Kim and Renaud 2009). On the other hand, Korea tops the list of OECD countries in terms of the volatility of real housing price changes over the period 1991–2007 measured in the coefficient of variation (Kim and Cho 2010).[7]

Mortgage Market Innovation, Risk Management and Macro-Prudence Regulation

The real estate finance system was a major beneficiary of government policy in the aftermath of the Asian financial crisis. In February 1998, the Bank of Korea lifted the regulation that prohibited financial institutions from lending to finance land purchases, and the purchases and construction of houses larger than 100 square meters of floor space. The removal of the regulation and the interest rate liberalization opened the door for commercial banks and non-bank deposit-taking financial institutions to enter the mortgage business. The liberalization of the interest rate also enabled the establishment of a secondary mortgage market facility and hence allowed for the capital market funding of mortgage lending. As a result, the size of the mortgage market has expanded enormously since 2000. The landscape of mortgage market also changed from one dominated by the Korea Housing Bank (a state bank) and the National Housing Fund (a government fund), two special-circuit public sector housing finance institutions, to one dominated by commercial banks with national branch networks.

A typical loan product in the Korean mortgage market is a short-term adjustable rate with balloon payment. Exhibit 18.7 summarizes the key characteristics of mortgage products. The table shows a recent trend toward lengthening of maturity and principal amortization. The share of loans with a term of 10 years or longer jumped from 20.7 percent to 59.6 percent while the share of loans with principal amortization rose from 23.2 percent to 60.9 percent between 2004 and 2008. On the other hand, the adjustable rate mortgages (ARMs) currently account for more than 90 percent of loans. To the extent countries with larger shares of ARMs are associated with greater volatility of house price,[8] the current composition of mortgage products could impair housing market stability. Moreover, a typical ARM contract in Korea has a prepayment penalty but provides no cap on periodic or lifetime rate reset, which places a disproportionate burden of risk on borrowers[9] (Cho and Kim 2010). However, the rate of delinquency on household loans in general and that on housing loans in particular shows no sign of significant deterioration since 2008 as can be seen from Exhibit 18.8. This might be attributable to the fact that the average loan-to-value ratio on existing loans is just under 50 percent and that increases in mortgage lending were concentrated among high-income and high-wealth households.

Exhibit 18.7   Rate of Delinquency on Consumer Credit (%)

	Dec-04	Dec-05	Dec-06	Dec-07	Dec-08	Jun-09	Dec-09	Jun-10
Consumer credit	1.8	1.2	0.7	0.55	0.6	0.6	0.48	0.57
Housing loans	1.9	1.2	0.6	0.43	0.47	0.4	0.33	0.44

Source: Financial Supervisory Service.

COMPARISON BETWEEN THE GLOBAL FINANCIAL CRISIS AND THE ASIAN FINANCIAL CRISIS

Macroeconomic Environment and Housing Sector Performance

Unlike the Asian financial crisis (AFC hereafter), the global financial crisis (GFC hereafter) originated from the West and Asia suffered from its ramifications. Macroeconomic conditions and the housing market environment at the outbreak of the 2008 global financial crisis were substantially different from that of the 1997 Asian financial crisis. Exhibit 18.8 provides the GDP growth rates for two years around each crisis. The rate of change figures over the previous quarter and that over the same period of the previous year are reported. It is clear that the aggregate output shock was milder during the GFC compared with the AFC on both measures.

Exhibit 18.9 summarizes the key statistics of the housing sector as of one year prior to each crisis. First, Korea had a housing shortage in 1996 but there was a nationwide surplus of housing by 2007. The housing supply ratio, defined as the ratio between the number of housing units and the number of households (excepting the one-person households), was 92 percent in 1996 but it surpassed 100 percent in 2002 and rose further to 108 percent in 2007. This dramatic improvement was possible because housing stock increased 30 percent against a 5 percent increase in population and a 10 percent increase in the number of households between 1996 and 2007. Second, there was a much larger inventory of unsold condominiums in 2007 than in 1996. Moreover, most of the unsold inventory in 2008 comprised large units exceeding 85 square meters of net floor space and supplied by the private sector, while the vast majority of unsold inventory in 1997 consisted of smaller units supplied by the public sector. Therefore, the unsold inventory was expected to last longer this time around. Third, housing prices had fallen 22 percent in real terms during the five years prior to the AFC, whereas housing price had risen 12 percent during the five year period preceding the GFC. As a result, the house-price-to-income ratio (PIR) was substantially higher in 2007 than it was in

Exhibit 18.8   GDP Growth Rates around AFC and GFC

Year/Qtr	QOQ	YOY	Year/Qtr	QOQ	YOY
1997/1	0.7	5.5	2008 1	1.2	5.5
1997/2	2.9	7.1	2008 2	0.3	4.4
1997/3	1.0	6.6	2008 3	−0.1	3.3
1997/4	−0.4	4.0	2008 4	−4.5	−3.3
1998/1	−7.0	−3.5	2009 1	0.2	−4.3
1998/2	−1.0	−7.3	2009 2	2.4	−2.2
1998/3	1.3	−7.1	2009 3	3.2	1.0
1998/4	2.5	−4.7	2009 4	0.2	6.0
1999/1	3.0	6.4	2010 1	2.1	8.1
1999/2	4.1	11.2	2010 2	1.4	7.2
1999/3	2.3	11.9	2010 3	0.7	4.4

Source: Bank of Korea.

Exhibit 18.9 Housing Market Conditions One Year Prior to the AFC and GFC

	December 1996	December 2007
Population ('000)	45,954	48,297
Population Growth Rate	0.94%	0.33%
Share of Age 65 and Older	6.40%	9.90%
Per Capita GNI ($)	11,205	21,695
Number of Households ('000)	11,542	12,760
Housing Supply Ratio	92.0%	108.1%
Housing Stock ('000)	10,627	13,793
Unsold Units	88,867	112,254
PIR	4.6	6.6
Five-year house price change	21.8%	11.6%
Five-year CPI change	21.8%	11.6%
Five-year real house price change	−21.8%	11.9%
MDO/GDP	10.0%	33.0%
Household Loan Lending Rate	12.30%	6348%
LTV on KB Mortgages	22.7%	35.3%

Source: MLTM, BOK, KB.

1996. Finally, the mortgage market had expanded during the intervening period between the two crises. The ratio between mortgage debt outstanding (MDO) and nominal GDP was around 10 percent in 1996 but it jumped to 33 percent by 2007. Mortgage terms were more favorable in 2007 than in 1996. The average lending rate was 6.5 percent in 2007, much lower than 12.3 percent that prevailed in 1997. The loan-to-value (LTV) ratio on new loans made by KB, the largest commercial bank, was much larger in 2007.

The home builders were in better financial shape at the time of the GFC. Thanks to the restructuring of the construction industry in the aftermath of the AFC, the surviving construction companies had a much lower debt ratio than before. As a result, the number of housing construction companies that went bankrupt in the wake of the GFC was much smaller than that at the time of the AFC. Exhibit 18.10 shows that the rate of bankruptcy, or the number of companies that went bankrupt as a share of all housing contractors, was 1.17 percent in 2008, much lower than 13.02 percent in 1998.

On the other hand, the major home builders were exposed to a new type of potential risk in the aftermath of the GFC. Prior to 2000, most home builders were both developers and contractors, but the two functions were separated since 2000. This shift was made because the large construction companies found it difficult to purchase land from private land-owners at reasonable prices since the latter tended to charge higher prices once they learned that major contractors were trying to purchase land. The new division of labor required new financing schemes for small developers. The lenders required a guarantee by the contractors to provide the bridge loans to the developers. This financing scheme is known as project finance but it is not a pure project finance scheme since the lenders' origination decisions are dependent on the third-party guarantee and not solely on the financial feasibility

Exhibit 18.10 Bankruptcy among Housing Construction Companies

Year	Total	Bankrupt	Bankruptcy Rate
1995	4,144	168	4.05
1996	3,900	179	4.59
1997	3,626	221	6.09
1998	3,195	416	13.02
1999	3,555	91	2.56
2000	3,835	141	3.68
2001	3,929	79	2.01
2002	4,848	46	0.95
2003	5,967	78	1.31
2004	6,336	109	1.72
2005	6,794	98	1.44
2006	7,118	66	0.93
2007	6,980	64	0.92
2008	6,171	72	1.17
2009	5,360	56	1.04

Source: MLTM.

of the development project. The third-party guarantor is a major contractor that will take over the development project once the site is secured and the approval procedure is completed. This scheme encouraged the mutual savings banks to take excessive exposure to real estate development finance. Exhibit 18.11 shows that the outstanding balance on project finance loans shrank after the outbreak of the GFC and that the rate of delinquency has been rising. The government had to move in to arrange for the KAMCO (Korea Asset Management Corporation) to purchase KRW 3.5 trillion of non-performing loans in 2009, but the problem lingered on as the housing market remained sluggish. Government suspended the operation of some savings banks with negative net worth in January/February 2011.

Exhibit 18.11 Outstanding Balance and Delinquency Rate of Project Finance (Billion KRW, %)

Lender	Category	Jun-08	Dec-08	Jun-09	Dec-09	Jun-10
Commercial	Balance	47,912	52,512	54,135	50,959	44,900
banks	delinquency	0.68	1.07	2.62	1.67	2.94
Savings	Balance	12,210	11,523	11,049	11,808	11,900
banks	delinquency	14.28	13.03	9.56	10.6	12.0
Insurance	Balance	5,324	5,519	5,474	5,736	5,395
companies	delinquency	2.37	2.41	4.06	4.55	7.9
Securities	Balance	2,960	2,858	2,829	2,747	2,457
companies	delinquency	6.57	13.92	24.52	30.28	25.17

Source: Financial Supervisory Service.

Exhibit 18.12   Comparison of the Behavior of Two Indexes of Housing Price

	KB House Price Index				MLTM Price Index	
	Korea, All	Seoul, All	Korea, Apt.	Seoul, Apt.	Korea, Apt.	Seoul, Apt.
Oct-97	67.6	52.4	55	40.9		
Nov-98	58.7	44.5	46.7	33.5		
% change	−13.2	−15.1	−15.1	−18.1		
Aug-08	101.2	101.5	101.9	102.8	129.3	142.6
Mar-09	99	98.8	99	98.7	118.4	116.9
% change	−2.2	−2.7	−2.8	−4.0	−8.4	−18.0
Aug-10	102.3	101.7	102.5	100.8	130.9	132.7

Source: MLTM, KB.

The Behavior of Housing Price and Quantity

The magnitude of the housing price decline in the wake of the global financial crisis was much smaller than during the Asian financial crisis. There are several data sources for housing price in Korea. The most widely used index is the KB housing price index compiled by the KB, which became the largest commercial bank since it merged the former state-owned Korea Housing Bank. The KB index is based mostly on real estate agents' estimates of the current market price and is known to have a smoothing problem. The MLTM (Ministry of Land Transport and Maritime Affairs) repeat-sales index is constructed using the data on transactions of apartments only. The index is available monthly from 2006, and it has a built-in time lag of two months since buyers are given 60 days to report their transactions to the relevant local government office. The MLTM index exhibits much greater volatility than the KB index of apartments, as can be seen from Exhibit 18.12 In addition, there are several private providers of property price data including the average price per square meter of apartment space.

Exhibit 18.12 summarizes the behavior of the asset price of housing around the two crises. The index in the month preceding each crisis, and that for the month just prior to the reversal of the fall in price, are presented for the AFC and the GFC. The figures for the KB index are provided for both crises, while the MLTM index is available only for the GFC. The data in the table clearly show that the magnitude of the fall in housing price was much larger during the AFC than during the GFC. The national index fell 13.2 percent during the 11 months from the outbreak of the AFC, while the comparable figure for the GFC was only 2.2 percent. A similar pattern is found for apartment prices and for Seoul. Exhibit 18.13 exhibits this pattern. The level of the index in August 2010 is about the same as its pre-GFC level.

The MLTM index peaked in August 2008 and started falling in September 2008 for the whole nation, while the price in Seoul started to decline one month earlier. But the price decline lasted for only six months, and stabilized thereafter. The cumulated price decline from the peak was 8.6 percent for Korea and 18.9 percent for Seoul. The housing price index bounced back to its peak by September 2009, which invited government intervention to cool off the market. As the government tightened its grip on mortgage lending, housing price fell again, but only slightly

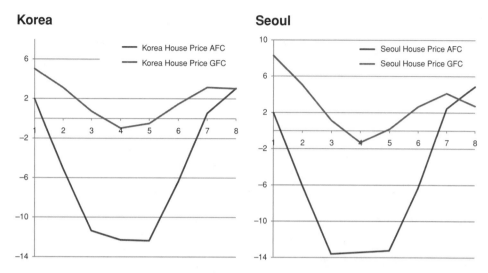

Exhibit 18.13 The Magnitude of House Price Fall: AFC versus GFC
Source: KB.

this time. The August 2010 level is just about the 2008 peak for the whole country and 8 percent lower for Seoul.

As for the rental sector, the dominant form of rental contract in Korea is *chonsei*. Under a chonsei contract, the tenant leaves a lump sum deposit at the start of the lease and pays no monthly rents during the lease period.[10] The deposit is fully refundable at the conclusion of the lease. The ratio between the chonsei deposit and the asset price of a house reflects the market expectation about house price appreciation.[11] With no expected capital gain, the ratio will be one, and it will fall as the expected capital gain increases. Exhibit 18.8 presents the data on chonsei deposit index in the same format as that of the asset price of housing reported in Exhibit 18.14. Again, the magnitude of the price decline was much smaller during the GFC than during the AFC. Exhibit 18.15 illustrates the pattern.

Several conjectures can be offered as to why housing price decline was relatively moderate in the wake of the global financial crisis.[12] First, the amount of

Exhibit 18.14 The Trend of Chonsei Price Index

	KB Chonsei Price Index			
	Korea, All	**Seoul, All**	**Korea, Apt.**	**Seoul, Apt.**
Oct-97	69.7	69.1	59.2	59.8
Nov-98	55.9	51.6	45.8	43.5
% change	−19.8	−25.3	−22.6	−27.3
Aug-08	101.5	102.9	101.8	104.6
Mar-09	98.8	99.1	98.5	98.5
% change	−2.7	−3.7	−3.2	−5.8
Aug-10	107.2	109.3	109.3	111.9

Source: KB.

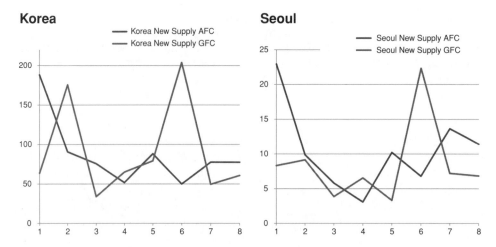

Exhibit 18.15 The Trends of Residential Building Permits: AFC versus GFC
Source: KB.

house price appreciation in Korea during the global housing boom was much smaller than in most developed economies (Kim and Renaud 2009). Second, there was no subprime mortgage problem in Korea and the loan-to-value (LTV) ratio was kept below 50 percent in most cases. Consequently, there was no surge in delinquency on mortgage loan repayment as documented above. Third, the government intervened promptly with a comprehensive stimulus package to avoid a collapse of the housing market. Fourth, consumers might have learned a lesson from the Asian financial crisis and believe that housing price will bounce back once the economy recovers from the crisis.

Finally, Exhibits 18.15 and 18.16 compare the fluctuations in the supply of new housing and the volume of housing transactions around the two crises. Housing

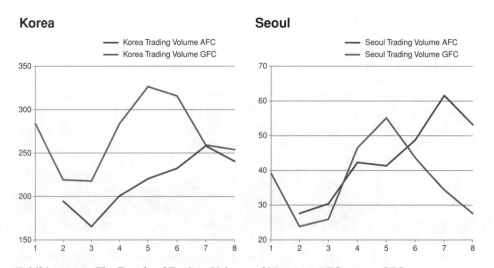

Exhibit 18.16 The Trends of Trading Volume of Housing: AFC versus GFC

supply decreased much more sharply during the Asian financial crisis compared with the global financial crisis. Trading volume for the whole country exhibits a similar pattern in both cases. On the other hand, the data for Seoul suggests that trading volume recovered sooner during the GFC but dropped below the level during the AFC.

CONCLUSION

Just as was the case in 1998 in the wake of the Asian financial crisis, the Korean housing sector suffered from the abrupt economic downturn in 2008 caused by the global financial crisis. But there are some important differences between the two cases. One key difference is that the malfunctioning corporate and financial sectors were responsible for the 1997 crisis whereas these sectors were functioning better at the time of the GFC. In neither instance was the housing sector a cause of the crisis. Although the GFC was expected to inflict more serious damage on the economy at the time of its outbreak, the Korean economy came out strong, surpassing expectation. Housing price declined for only six months and bounced back to such an extent that another price run-up was feared by September 2009. Government responded with bold measures to boost the property market and the home building activity as an integral part of the comprehensive economic stimulus package in the early phase of the GFC and then reversed its course of action to cool off the market in July and September 2009. The market turned around again in March 2010, and housing price softened. Trading volume dropped sharply and the housing market froze. The government came up with a stimulus package again, though a less drastic one. This sequence of government responses confirms that housing price stability is the overarching goal of housing policy in Korea.

Another difference is that the GFC failed to serve as a platform for housing policy reform as much as the AFC did. It is true that many key financial reforms had been implemented prior to the 2008 crisis. However, reform was not so impressive on the real side of the housing market, and some reform such as the lifting of the price control on new apartments, implemented in the wake of AFC, was reversed in 2003 (Cho and Kim 2010). The system of real estate taxation was further distorted during the Roh Moo-hyun government. The current Lee Myung-bak government had planned to rationalize the price control and the real estate taxes but it failed on the former, and succeeded only partially on the latter. These cases suggest that policy makers continue to follow a risk-averse, lukewarm, and piece-meal approach and the political environment affecting the policy-decision process remains unfavorable to a more market-driven approach (Kim and Kim 2000).

The proposed tax reform involved normalizing the real estate tax system featuring the "comprehensive real estate tax," a net wealth tax levied on expensive housing, and a punitive burden of capital gains tax on households owning more than one house, both introduced by the previous government. The initial proposal was to integrate the comprehensive real estate tax, a national tax, into the local property tax, as well as reducing the burden on capital gains tax on the owners of two or more houses. The plan was thwarted by political arguments that such reform might end up benefiting the wealthy households and inviting speculation. The reform of the comprehensive real estate tax proved to be even more difficult because the revenue of the tax had been distributed to local governments with weak fiscal bases and the removal of the tax would take away such windfall revenue to the local governments benefiting from the transfer. Consequently, the initial plan for a fundamental reform of the property holding tax was dropped and the capital gains tax reform was framed in a finite time line to be reviewed in two years time.

On the other hand, the regulation on mortgage lending in the form of a ceiling on the loan-to-value ratio (LTV) and debt-service-to-income ratio (DTI) emerged as a new policy instrument at the time of the GFC. As Cho and Kim (2009) document, however, the regulation is unique in several key aspects. First, the regulation is applicable only to specific areas and specific size categories of houses. Second, a uniform ceiling applies regardless of the creditworthiness of the potential borrowers. Third, it was adjusted back and forth within a short period of time. These features suggest that the regulation is more about promoting housing price stability than improving risk management in mortgage lending or guarding against systemic risks that can be caused by housing market disruptions. Such frequent changes in the mortgage lending parameters are counter-productive as they create uncertainties in the property market and make monetary policy more difficult to conduct when a property cycle does not coincide with an overall business cycle.

There is debate as to whether the current softening of housing price is of a cyclical nature or the beginning of a long-term trend of steady decline. The argument in favor of the latter is based on the assumption that housing demand will decrease due to demographic shifts such as the falling population growth rate, increasing share of one- and two-person households, and rapid aging of the population. Mankiw and Weil (1989) predicted that the exit of the baby boom generation from the U.S. housing market would lead to a sharp decline in housing demand, which would cause the housing price to fall 47 percent in real terms or 3 percent per annum between 1987 and 2007. The paper spawned a series of papers criticizing the methodology of the paper as well as case studies of other countries such as Canada, Japan, and the United Kingdom using a similar model.[13] The Mankiw-Weil prediction went off the mark and U.S. housing price actually rose at 3 percent per annum during the same period. Similar studies carried out by Korean researchers provide somewhat different findings for Korea. First, income growth appears to matter more than the demographic changes. Second, housing consumption in Korea rises up to 70 years of age as opposed to the mid-50s in the United States. Third, the increase in one- and two-person households may not necessarily result in a proportionate decrease in housing demand, since some basic spaces, such as kitchen and dining area, are required. Under a reasonable set of assumptions about income growth and user cost, housing demand is predicted to increase until 2020 for the whole country, and up to 2030 in the Seoul Capital Region. Whether or not this prediction proves to be accurate, it is important to secure a supply system that is responsive to the changing demand, which is uncertain. This raises the question of whether the current regulatory structure governing the supply of developable land established to address the problem of housing shortages and speculation remains valid in the changing environment.

The global financial crisis demonstrated the importance of close monitoring of the mortgage market and the housing market as well as the need for quality data on key variables of the housing sector. The availability and the quality of data on housing has improved over time in Korea, but substantial gaps still exist. The time series data on the construction of new housing is based on the approval of development projects, rather than on housing starts or completions. The data on trading volume are available since 1998 but are sensitive to the large-scale redevelopment projects. The data on mortgage lending also needs improvement. First of all, the data on housing-related loans does not distinguish between mortgage loans and home equity. Secondly, there are no data on mortgage origination except on fixed rate loans underwritten by the Korea Housing Finance Corporation. The existing data are based on the loans outstanding, which make it impossible to trace the performance of mortgage loans of different vintages with different loan terms. Even the time series data on mortgage loans outstanding fails to cover all the originating institutions. As a result, it is difficult to establish the relationships between housing-related lending and housing price,[14] and this poses a problem since regulation on mortgage lending is based on the presumption that expansion of mortgage lending leads to housing price increases. Such data gaps need to be filled to allow better market analysis and more informed housing policy.

NOTES

1. See Cho and Kim (2010) for a more detailed description.
2. See Kim (2000) for details.
3. Another important aspect of housing price increase is the role of condominiums up for redevelopment. Low-density condominiums built in the 1970s and early 1980s were eligible for high-density redevelopment after 20 years from the time of construction. This involves large capital gains on existing units, and is capitalized in their market prices (Lee et al. 2005). The rate of appreciation was much smaller once the condominiums near redevelopment were excluded.
4. See Kim and Cho (2010) for details.
5. The total fiscal stimulus amounted to KRW 23.3 trillion (US$23.3 billion), or 3.6 percent of GDP in 2009 (Kim 2010). Additional measures were taken, such as establishing a US$20 billion bank recapitalization fund.
6. It is known to be very difficult to predict when and how market sentiment will turn around (Shiller 2008).
7. The volatility of housing price changes, measured by the coefficient of variation of monthly rate of change, does not exhibit a clear pattern of increase over time.
8. See IMF (2004).
9. Mortgage loans in Korea are full-recourse loans.
10. See Chung and Lee (2010) for a detailed analysis of the chonsei market.
11. In short, chonsei is an asset-based rental scheme and as such it imposes a serious burden upon those with inadequate income and wealth.
12. Housing markets in Asian countries, especially China, Singapore, and Hong Kong, did quite well in the current global financial crisis.
13. See Makiw and Weil (1992) for references.
14. Kim and Kim (2010) find that the direction of causality between housing loans and housing price varies across cities.

ACKNOWLEDGMENTS

The author acknowledges research assistance by Sera Kye, the support of a research grant from Sogang University, and the helpful comments of Bertrand Renaud.

REFERENCES

Case, Karl E., and Robert J. Shiller. 2010 (May). "What Were They Thinking? Home Buyer Behavior in Hot and Cold Markets." Mimeo. Wellesley College.

Cho, Man, and Kyung-Hwan Kim. 2009 (December). "Three Pillars of Mortgage Credit Risk Management: A Conceptual Framework and the Case of Korea." *Housing Finance International* XXIV, 17–23.

Cho, Man and Kyung-Hwan Kim. 2010. "Housing Sector Reform: Contrasting Real Sector vs. Financial Sector." In Youngjae Lim, ed., *Making Reform Happen: Lessons from Korea since the 1987 Democratization*, pp. 131–160. Seoul: Korea Development Institute.

Chung, Eui-Chul. 2010. "Consumer Sentiment and Housing Market Activities: Impact on Sales Price of Housing." *Journal of the Real Estate Analysts Association* 16:3, 5–20 (in Korean).

Chung, Eui-Chul, and Chang-Moo Lee. Forthcoming, 2010. "Monthly Rent with Variable Deposit: A New Form of Rental Contract in Korea." *Journal of Housing Economics*.

Green, Richard, Stephen Malpezzi, and Kerry Vandell. 1994. "Urban Regulations and the Price of Land and Housing in Korea." *Journal of Housing Economics* 3:4, 330–56.

International Monetary Fund (IMF). 2004 (September). *World Economic Outlook*.

Kim, Chung-Ho, and Kyung-Hwan Kim. 2000. "Political Economy of Government Policies on Real Estate in Korea." *Urban Studies* 37:7, 1157–1169.

Kim, Joo Hyun. 2010 (July 7–8). "The Global Financial Crisis and Lessons Learned: Korea's Key Success Factors." *Presentation at the Global Recovery: Asia and the New Financial Landscape*, Federal Reserve Bank of San Francisco,.

Kim, Jun-Hyung, and Kyung-Hwan Kim. 2010 (July). "Relationships between Housing and Household Loans in Korea: Do They Vary across Cities?" Paper presented at the AsRES Annual Conference, Caoshiung.

Kim, Kyung-Hwan. 2000. "Could a Price Bubble Have Caused the Korean Economic Crisis?" In Koichi Mera and Bertrand Renaud, eds., *Asia's Financial Crisis and the Role of Real Estate*, pp. 99–114. New York: Sharpe.

Kim, Kyung-Hwan. 2004. "Housing and the Korean Economy." *Journal of Housing Economics* 13, 321–341.

Kim, Kyung-Hwan, and Man Cho. 2010 (November). "Structural Changes, Housing Price Dynamics, and Housing Affordability in Korea." *Housing Studies* 25:5, 835–852.

Kim, Kyung-Hwan, and Bertrand Renaud. 2009 (January). "The Global Housing Price Boom and Its Unwinding: An Analysis and a Commentary." *Housing Studies* 24:1, 724.

Kim, Kyung-Hwan, Sock Yong Phang, and Susan M. Wachter. Forthcoming, 2010. "Supply Elasticity of Housing." *International Encyclopedia for Housing and Home*. Elsevier.

Lee, Bun Song, Eui-Chul Chung, and Yong Hyun Kim. 2005. "Dwelling Age, Redevelopment, and Housing Prices: The Case of Apartment Complexes in Seoul." *Journal of Real Estate Finance and Economics* 30:1, 55–80.

Mankiw, Gregory N., and David N. Weil. 1989. "The Baby Boom, Baby Bust, and the Housing Market." *Regional Science and Urban Economics* 19:2, 235–258.

Mankiw, Gregory N., and David N. Weil. 1992. "The Baby Boom, Baby Bust and the Housing Market: A Reply to Our Critics." *Regional Science and Urban Economics* 21:4, 573–579.

Malpezzi, Stephen, and Stephen K. Mayo. 1997. "Getting Housing Incentives Right: A Case Study of the Effects of Regulation, Taxes, and Subsidies on Housing Supply in Malaysia." *Land Economics* 73, 372–391.

Malpezzi, Stephen, and Susan M. Wachter. 2005. "The Role of Speculation in Real Estate Cycles." *Journal of Real Estate Literature* 13, 143–165.

Mayo, Stephen K., and Stephen Sheppard. 1996. "Housing Supply under Rapid Economic Growth and Varying Regulatory Stringency: An International Comparison." *Journal of Housing Economics* 5, 274–289.

Quigley, John M. 2001. "Real Estate and the Asian Crisis." *Journal of Housing Economics* 10, 129–161.

Shiller, Robert J. 2008. "Historic Turning Points in Real Estate," *Eastern Economic Journal* 34:1, 1–13.

Wang, Ko, and Youqing Zhou. 2000. "Overbuilding: A Game-Theoretic Approach." *Real Estate Economics* 28:3, 493–522.

ABOUT THE AUTHOR

KYUNG-HWAN KIM is a professor of economics at Sogang University, Seoul, Korea. He is a fellow at the Weimer Graduate School of Advanced Studies in Real Estate and Urban Land Economics, and a research affiliate at the Centre for Asset Securitisation and Management in Asia of the Sim Kee Boon Institute for Financial Economics at Singapore Management University, and a scholar at the Institute for Urban Research of the University of Pennsylvania. He has taught at Syracuse University and worked at the UN Habitat. Dr. Kim is a past president of the Asian Real Estate Society, a member of the editorial board of the *Journal of Housing Economics*, and a member of the management board of the *Housing Studies*. He holds a PhD in economics from Princeton University.

CHAPTER 19

Government Policy, Housing Finance, and Housing Production in Singapore

LUM SAU KIM

This paper explains how policy developments that affected both the public and private segments of the Singapore housing sector have led to their dramatic price trajectory over the past five years. Before the Asian financial crisis, strong economic expansion and the liberalization of the public housing market created excess demand for housing. With demand destruction, the state curtailed public housing production and the supply of state-owned land for private housing. Concurrently, Singapore pursued policies to develop its financial sector and enhance its status as a global city. As fundamentals improved amid ample liquidity and as pro-immigration policies gained traction in the mid-2000s, consumption and asset demand for housing grew rapidly. Without a commensurate supply-side response, house price appreciation in Singapore was among the highest worldwide, both before and after the global financial crisis. Since September 2009, the state has instituted several rounds of market cooling measures and boosted the supply of land and public housing. It is unclear if these policy interventions are sufficient to ensure a more sustainable housing sector.

INTRODUCTION

Singapore is a prosperous city-state with a gross domestic product of S$265 billion or US$182 billion in 2009.[1] It is densely populated: 5.1 million people comprising 3.7 million residents (citizens and permanent residents) and 1.3 million foreigners live on a land mass of only 710 square kilometers. With a high owner-occupation rate that has exceeded 80 percent since the mid-1980s, housing has traditionally been one of the most important assets for households in Singapore. Through deliberate and pervasive state intervention in the housing sector as well as monopolistic control of both housing and land supply, a vertically segmented housing market has developed. It is characterized by the coexistence of a dominant public housing sector where dwellings are developed by public agencies and a small, growing private segment with relatively higher quality housing built by private firms. Except for a minor social housing component, 95 percent of public housing in Singapore has been privatized through home ownership. These units are initially

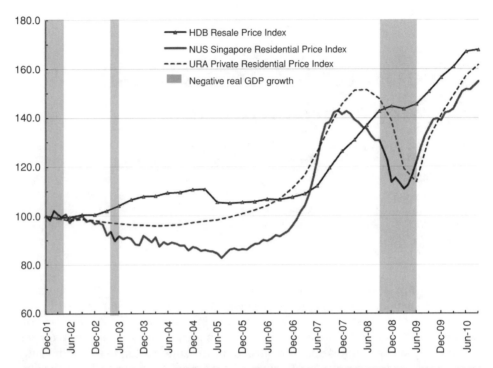

Exhibit 19.1   The HDB Resale Price Index (Q4:2001 = 100), the NUS SRPI (Dec 2001 = 100), and the URA Private Residential Price Index (Q4:2001 = 100)

sold at a discount by the state but can be traded at open market prices subject to rules that circumscribe ownership rights and that prevent excess profiteering.

To create a home-owning democracy in Singapore, the government has supported housing asset inflation and has leveraged on the formation of both gross and net housing wealth, particularly in the public housing sector, to achieve various socio-economic and political goals. At the same time, economic expansion, the availability of onshore financing and large capital inflows have made residential property an attractive investment proposition. In fact, the Singapore private residential market has been identified as one of the "frothiest" in the world both before and after the global financial crisis (GFC).[2] Exhibit 19.1 shows that from July 2005 to November 2007, nominal house prices appreciated 73 percent (26.5 percent CAGR) as measured by the NUS Singapore Residential Price Index (SRPI).[3] The private housing market subsequently declined 22 percent (−17.3 percent CAGR) and hit a post-GFC low in March 2009 before rebounding about 40 percent (25.9 percent CAGR) by September 2010. These movements are also broadly reflected by the URA Private Residential Price Index.[4] In the secondary public housing market, capital appreciation as measured by the HDB Resale Price Index[5] was equally impressive: Prices grew 50 percent between mid-2007 and mid-2010 with only a 1 percent fall in the first quarter of 2009.

As with many other countries, investment and speculation in residential property have been implicated in the economic vicissitudes of Singapore during the recent GFC. The purpose of this chapter is to provide a perspective on developments in both the public and private segments of the Singapore housing sector that have led to their dramatic price trajectory over the past five years. The next section introduces the salient features of the Singapore housing system. As there are many parallels between the housing boom-bust experience during the Asian financial crisis (AFC) and the recent GFC, the third section reviews key events associated with the earlier crisis and the subsequent interventions undertaken to stabilize the residential market. Various policies implemented post-AFC provide the institutional context for understanding the run-up in the Singapore housing sector prior to the GFC and the subsequent fallout of the private, but not the public, housing market as the crisis took hold. This is presented in the fourth section. Since early 2009, there has been a remarkable upturn in the Singapore private residential market. The fifth section examines the causes of the sharp recovery and the ongoing efforts by the government to moderate house price inflation. While it is still premature to assess how well the latest market cooling measures would work, the chapter concludes with some thoughts on the policy levers available to the state and potential issues for the Singapore housing sector.

THE SINGAPORE HOUSING STORY

Since attaining self-governance in 1959, housing for the masses has been an important engine of social development and economic growth for the city-state. Faced with a chronic shortage of decent and affordable housing then, the ruling government established the Housing and Development Board (HDB) in 1960 as the national public housing authority to plan, develop, allocate and manage public housing units called HDB flats. While its initial mandate was to provide basic rental accommodation for the poor, the HDB introduced a Home Ownership Scheme (HOS) in 1964 through which eligible households could purchase a 99-year leasehold interest in their flat, but not in the land or common areas, at a subsidized price.

Although unpopular at first, the HOS received a boost in 1968 when the government allowed citizens to withdraw the savings in their Central Provident Fund (CPF) accounts to pay the down payment, stamp duties, and debt service of the flats bought from the HDB instead of relying solely on their take-home pay. The CPF is essentially a national state-managed social security savings scheme set up in 1955 to ensure the financial security of all workers. It requires mandatory contributions from both the employer and employee, of a defined percentage of the employee's monthly contractual salary,[6] and is placed into his or her personal account within the fund. As the economy prospered and wages rose, these forced tax-exempt savings accumulated rapidly but could not be withdrawn until retirement. Between 1968 and 1981, public housing was the only avenue by which a substantial portion of CPF savings could be used and this steadily increased the home ownership rate of HDB units from 14 percent in 1964 to 95 percent at present.

In tandem with state policies that strongly promoted owner-occupation, the HDB began to focus on the large-scale production of affordable, standardized high-rise housing for the lower-income groups. During its first decade of operation, the HDB built only one- to four-room flats. Over time, the role of the HDB evolved to cater to middle-income and upper-middle-income households as well.

Five-room flats were introduced in the 1970s and executive apartments[7] in the 1980s in response to the demand for larger units. Periodic improvements were also made to each flat type in terms of size and design. For example, private firms were invited to design and build HDB flats to inject greater variety and choice in public housing, and studio apartments designed to meet the needs of Singapore's ageing population were unveiled in 1997. Not only was there greater emphasis on providing a higher quality and wider selection of flats, but beyond the flat itself, the HDB paid increasing attention to enhance the overall quality of the housing estate in terms of the amenities provided, aesthetic appeal, and visual identity.

The prices of new flats are fixed by the government, having regard to the general state of the economy and affordability levels for the different flat types. Initially, these selling prices were set without reference to either secondary market transactions in the resale market for HDB flats or land costs incurred by the HDB. Hence, there was no price differentiation between similar-sized flats based on location and a public housing subsidy was given for the difference between the selling price and construction cost of a unit. This changed in 1987: A market-based approach was introduced to price new HDB flats that factored in all land costs, location premiums and amenities. Indeed, the government benchmarked new flat prices to comparable resale flat prices in the vicinity and priced new HDB units below the resale prices so that buyers would enjoy a housing subsidy.[8] As the subsidy decreased in flat size, the one- and two-room flats were mainly rented on short leases to the lowest income groups while the larger flats were designated for outright sale.

From the time CPF funds were liberalized for the purchase of public housing till the onset of the Asian financial crisis, there had been excess demand for new HDB flats. To regulate demand, the HDB used various eligibility rules such as citizenship status, non-ownership of private properties, a minimum household size of two persons, and amount of household income; while flats were allocated through waiting lists, balloting, and queues. In line with economic growth and the HDB's projected ambition in 1985 of housing 90 percent of the total population, the government kept raising the income ceiling such that no fewer than eight out of every ten Singaporeans would qualify for a subsidized flat.[9] This resulted in long waiting lists of applicants for new flats. Especially in the mid-1990s, queuing periods for a subsidized unit could stretch beyond five years. Those who could not wait for a flat directly from the HDB and households that either had exceeded the income limit or were otherwise excluded from subsidized public housing had two options: They could buy a resale HDB flat in the secondary market or a dwelling in the private residential sector.

There has been a resale market for HDB flats since 1971 in which owners who have fulfilled a stipulated minimum occupation period (MOP) could sell the residual leases in their units at market-determined prices to anyone eligible for public housing. Initially, the regulations governing the secondary market were onerous to prevent profiteering from the capitalization of state subsidies at a time when the housing stock was low: Owners who wished to sell their flats must have resided in them for at least three years but were barred from applying for another new flat for a year. As the HDB stock increased and the housing market became more mature, the resale regulations were relaxed to enable upgrading to newer flats. The debarment period was abolished in 1979 but sellers had to pay a 5 percent levy on the transacted price of the flat. Subsequently, the levy was tweaked into a more progressive system of claw-backs to ensure that the subsidy enjoyed by a household buying a second new flat would be less than that for its first unit.[10]

In 1989, the HDB began easing its ownership eligibility criteria for *resale* flats to facilitate residential mobility: The income ceiling was lifted and Singapore permanent residents as well as private housing owners could buy resale HDB flats for owner-occupancy. The eligibility rules for buying *new* flats remained unchanged but HDB-flat-owners were allowed to invest in private dwellings as long as they resided in their flats. Also, in a bid to shorten the queues for new units and improve affordability, the state began offering various CPF housing grants to qualifying households for the purchase of resale units in 1994. However, it was the revision of the HDB mortgage financing policy for resale flats in March 1993 that had the greatest impact on demand and resale prices: A buyer could borrow 80 percent of the market valuation of the resale flat or its declared resale price, whichever was lower, instead of the 1984 posted price of the new flat. Given that new flat prices had risen some 58 percent between 1984 and 1992,[11] marking-to-market the loan quantum for resale flats provided a huge credit boost to the secondary market.

With more than 82 percent of the resident population being housed in HDB flats currently, private housing developers play a limited role of supplying expensive dwellings to the higher income groups as well as expatriates and foreign investors. In the past, private housing was built on land of predominantly freehold or long-leasehold (999-year) tenure. From the mid-1960s to the early 1980s, the state embarked on a massive exercise of land reclamation and compulsory acquisition for public housing, urban renewal, and other national development projects that raised its ownership of the total landmass in Singapore from around 40 percent in 1960 to about 76 percent by the mid-1980s. As the limited amount of privately held land was insufficient to accommodate the demand for private housing from an increasingly affluent population, the state began to auction state-owned land on shorter leaseholds of 99 years via its Government Land Sales (GLS) program for these developments. The GLS program has become an important revenue generator for the state as well as the key source of private land supply. Unlike public housing leases however, buyers of private units built on these state-owned land parcels own an undivided share of the rights in the land as well.

Exhibit 19.2 shows the structure of the Singapore housing sector as a multi-tiered hierarchy. The bottom layer represents the social housing component comprising the smallest HDB flats that are rented to disadvantaged households. Above that in ascending order are the smaller owner-occupied flats, the larger and newer public housing units, entry-level private housing, medium-level private housing, and finally luxury properties. Private residential properties can be divided into two categories: non-landed properties consist of apartments and condominiums while landed properties can be terraced (or linked) housing, semi-detached houses, or bungalows. (Studio Apartments do not fall neatly into the hierarchy but have been included for completeness. The Executive Condominium, a hybrid form of housing, is discussed in the third section.) Over time, the proportion of the total stock in private housing has been edging up and the planning intent is to have it rise to 25 percent in the long term.

Exhibit 19.2　The Stock of Residential Units

	Number of Units as of End of Year			
	1997	2004	2009	Percentage of Total Stock*
Public Sector Housing				
1-room	25,182	20,142	20,041	1.7%
2-room	34,610	29,351	29,680	2.6%
3-room	239,562	227,125	220,696	19.2%
4-room	267,517	325,794	339,782	29.6%
5-room	134,051	206,614	209,764	18.3%
Executive	50,320	65,158	65,076	5.7%
Studio Apartments	—	936	1,239	0.1%
HUDC Apartments	4,071	1,865	1,865	0.2%
Total	755,313	876,985	888,143	77.4%
Executive Condominiums	—	8,856	10,430	0.9%
Private Residential Properties				
Apartments	49,678	59,349	64,513	5.6%
Condominiums	48,364	94,916	115,478	10.1%
Terraced houses	33,496	37,031	38,101	3.3%
Semi-detached houses	19,597	20,702	21,128	1.8%
Detached houses	10,138	9,905	10,269	0.9%
Total	161,273	221,903	249,489	21.7%
Total Stock	916,586	1,107,744	1,148,062	100.0%

Notes: The public sector stock refers to units under HDB management, including apartments built by the Housing and Urban Development Company (HUDC) that were transferred to the HDB for management in 1982.
*The percentages are computed for 2009 only.
Sources: Department of Statistics, Singapore, *Singapore in Figures, 2010*; and Urban Redevelopment Authority, REALIS.

HOUSING FINANCE

Public policy in Singapore is clearly biased toward financing the housing sector. The nation's high savings rate and much of the funding for public housing resulted in large measure from compulsory contributions to the CPF as well as voluntary deposits in the Post Office Savings Bank (POSB).[12] When the Home Ownership Scheme (HOS) began, private sector financial institutions were unwilling to offer mortgages for low-income housing given the economic uncertainties and regulated interest-rate environment of the time. Without credit, private developers had no incentive to provide low-cost housing. Allowing the use of forced savings in the CPF for financing HDB flats in 1968 created a closed financial loop (Chua 2000). CPF monies were used to buy government debt, part of which was used as annual grants for the HDB's operations, housing development loans for financing public housing construction programs, and mortgage financing loans that funded the mortgage loans granted to end-purchasers of HDB flats. The flats were sold to households who obtained mortgages from the HDB, which, in turn, deducted the debt service from the households' CPF accounts. To ensure the stability of this loop, the HDB pegged the interest rate of its concessionary mortgage at 10 basis points above the prevailing CPF savings rate,[13] which was also the rate at which the HDB could borrow from the government.

At the outset of the HOS, the HDB provided concessionary loans for 80 percent of the purchase price of a new flat. Over time, these loans were made available for resale flats as well. CPF savings could be used to pay up to 100 percent of the valuation or purchase price of the flat, whichever was lower, or to fund the down payment and transaction costs with the balance of the purchase price financed by a HDB loan. Depending on prevailing economic conditions, the loan-to-value (LTV) ratio could reach 90 percent while the maximum loan repayment period was 32 years or when the borrower reached 65 years of age, whichever was earlier. To facilitate social mobility, flat owners could obtain more than one concessionary loan and were not subjected to any credit assessment. For the most part, HDB concessionary loans were subsidized in that the mortgage contract rate, which was tied to the CPF savings rate, was below the commercial housing loan rate. Households that were ineligible for HDB concessionary loans could obtain market rate loans from the HDB for buying public housing[14] or from private players.

While the HDB-CPF scheme successfully addressed the market failures associated with financing both the provision and purchase of public housing, it also promoted home-ownership in the public housing sector at the expense of the private housing market. To mitigate this and to stimulate the property market after the oil crisis, the state-owned POSB established a subsidiary, Credit POSB, in 1974 to extend housing loans at rates that were lower than the prevailing market rates.[15] The main private sector lenders then were local commercial banks and finance companies that offered fixed rate loans for tenors of up to 20 years. Over time, adjustable-rate mortgages with upfront teaser rates and longer repayment periods (of up to 35 years) have become prevalent. In 1981, the liberalization of CPF savings for financing private residential properties drove up private housing prices and amplified the boom-bust property cycle during the mid-1980s. Its longer-term impact was the growth of housing loan originations to finance private housing consumption and investment in tandem with house price appreciation. Exhibit 19.3 shows the flow amounts contributed to and withdrawn from the CPF including the monies withdrawn under the public housing and private housing schemes.

CPF monies withdrawn for housing purchases must be restituted with accrued interest when a property is sold to ensure adequate savings for retirement. Since 1984, the government has incrementally allowed the withdrawal of CPF savings for other approved investments and merit goods. While this has gradually reduced the CPF's sectoral bias toward the housing sector, Exhibit 19.3 shows that housing remains the single largest use of CPF funds. With the CPF as an instrument of housing finance, Singapore has become not only a nation of homeowners but often, excessive consumers of housing as well (Lim et al. 1986).

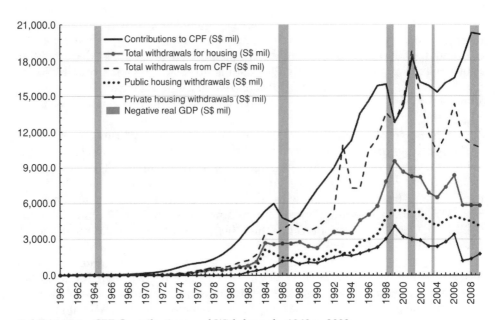

Exhibit 19.3   CPF Contributions and Withdrawals, 1960 to 2009

Note: Large withdrawals in 1993 and 1996 were for the investment share scheme and the purchase of Singapore Telecom shares.

THE 1995–1996 HOUSING BOOM AND THE ASIAN FINANCIAL CRISIS

In the decade prior to the AFC, robust economic growth, rapid household formation, and a favorable housing finance environment underpinned strong demand for both public and private housing. Sentiment was further heightened by a spectacular bull run in the Singapore stock market during the early 1990s and ample liquidity from hot money flowing into the region. Over the same period, the government raised the income ceiling for new HDB flats four times and the withdrawal limit for CPF funds to buy private housing twice.[16] It also implemented a series of policy measures to privatize public housing that included:

- From 1988, market-based pricing of new HDB flats. The prices of new four-room flats rose by an average of 12 percent per annum between 1988 and 1992 compared to only 2.5 percent per year between 1981 and 1988.
- From 1989, allowing HDB owners who had stayed in their units for at least five years to invest their excess CPF savings in private residential properties.
- In 1989 and 1991, the relaxation of home ownership restrictions in the public resale market.
- From 1993, extending larger loans for resale flat buyers that were pegged to market values rather than historical prices. From the end of March (when the measure was introduced) to the end of December 1993, the HDB resale price index rose 62 percent.

This confluence of fundamental and policy-related demand drivers supported strong resale price inflation. Since new HDB flats were subsidized but could be re-sold at higher prices in the open market, ownership of public housing became a source of tax-free "fortuitous" wealth (Lum 1996). A seller could keep all the un-taxed capital appreciation, and realize substantial financial gains by downgrading (since each eligible household is entitled to buy subsidized flats directly from the HDB twice) or exiting the public housing market. Alternatively, the seller could upgrade to another new larger HDB flat using a second HDB concessionary loan or buy a private dwelling with the net sales proceeds. Through the resale mechanism, public housing served as a launching pad for upward social mobility and became an investment good for the masses in Singapore to build up equity.

Exhibit 19.4 shows the HDB Resale Price Index in relation to an index of season-ally adjusted real GDP, the demand for new HOS flats, and HDB flat completions. Until 2001, new flats were allocated using a registration system where demand was measured by the number of applications in the new flat queue. By the end of 1993, long queues had developed. However, many lower-income households could not afford buying a four-room flat, the smallest flat type being built by the HDB then, due to the HDB's market-based pricing of new units. This prompted a three-pronged response in 1994. First, the HDB attempted to pare down excess

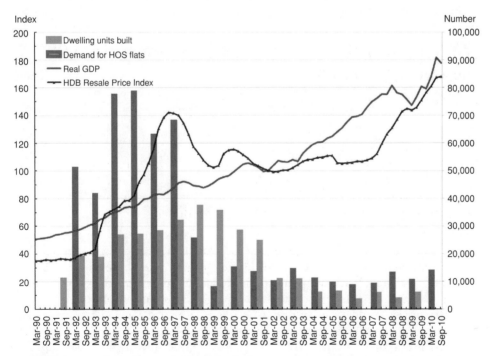

Exhibit 19.4   The Demand for and Completions of HDB Flats (March 1991 to March 2010) and the HDB Resale Price Index (Q4:2001 = 100) and real GDP (Q4:2001 = 100)

Note: Demand for HOS flats refer to new demand in a fiscal year while flat completions are for a calendar year. 1990 data were omitted as they were computed on a different basis.

demand by requiring applicants for a second new flat to satisfy a longer minimum occupation period in their first flat and to pay a higher resale levy. Second, the government transferred some of the demand for new HDB flats to the secondary market by offering eligible homebuyers demand-side subsidies in the form of CPF housing grants[17] to partially defray the cost of buying HDB resale flats.[18] Third, the HDB began to repurchase three-room flats from the open market for allocation to households earning below S$3,000 per month.

Both the housing grants and the buy-back operations exacerbated the demand for resale flats with prices far outpacing fundamental economic growth. The measures directed at moderating new flat demand also failed as the waiting list for new flats continued to grow. In particular, the queue for executive flats (the largest flat sold by the HDB) had grown eight-fold between 1992 and 1995. To tackle this, an intermediate class of housing called the Executive Condominium (EC) was introduced in 1995.[19] It also sought to fulfill the housing aspirations of "sandwich" households whose incomes exceeded the HDB income ceiling but were insufficient for private housing. To be built and sold by private developers, ECs would bridge the gap between HDB flats and private condominiums by offering living standards comparable to those of the latter but at lower prices due to a land cost subsidy. Ownership was restricted; households must meet eligibility criteria similar to those for new HDB flats but could have a higher monthly income ceiling of S$10,000. ECs must be financed by commercial loans and although they would eventually be privatized, resale would be subject to a minimum occupation period requirement.

Given the hierarchical structure of the Singapore housing market, excess demand for public housing spilled over into the lower-end private residential segment. However, land for private housing development was in short supply as the state had suspended its GLS program since 1982 and private land banks were increasingly becoming depleted. Concerned with the steep run-up in house prices, the government resumed selling state-owned sites in 1991. Despite annual increments in the land supplied, the GLS program failed to cool down the overheated housing market. Instead, benchmark prices for state land continued to be set at each successive sale, due to intense market competition, and the government came under criticism for exacerbating the real estate price cycle.

Despite the imposition in 1994 of a 5 percent booking fee for the option-to-purchase, that was raised to 10 percent of the property price a year later, demand grew unabated as capital gains were untaxed and mortgage financing was readily available: Some loans were geared at an LTV ratio of 103 percent to cover not just the purchase price of the property but the stamp duty as well. Between 1986 and 1996, the private residential market experienced a nominal price growth of 540 percent that far outpaced rental increases (Exhibit 19.5) and the conventional wisdom was that prices could only continue to appreciate in a land-scarce, booming city-state.

To dampen speculation in private housing, the government announced a package of measures in May 1996. For every sale of residential property within three years of purchase, the capital gains would be taxed as income[20] and stamp duty would be levied on the vendor (in addition to the buyer).[21] Financing was limited to 80 percent of the purchase price or valuation, whichever was lower, and the 20 percent down payment must be cash-funded. Non-residents and non-Singapore

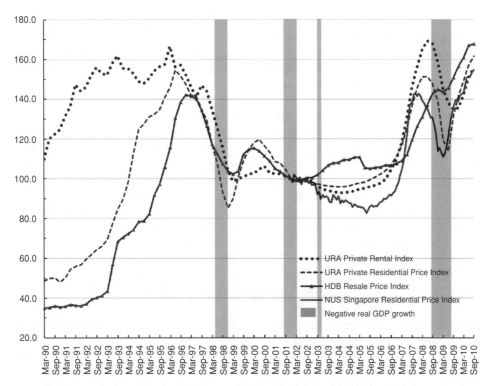

Exhibit 19.5 The HDB Resale Price Index (Q4:2001 = 100), the NUS SRPI (Dec 2001 = 100), and the URA Private Residential Price and Rental Indexes (Q4:2001 = 100)

companies were prohibited from Singapore-dollar housing loans while a permanent resident was limited to one such loan to purchase a property for owner-occupancy. The anti-speculation measures decreased both the transaction volume and prices in the private residential market while the prudential limits on housing loans moderated credit growth from 20 percent per annum before the curbs to 14 percent in 1997.

Investor confidence was further eroded with the onset of the AFC and funds flowed out from the region. As an oversupply situation began to build up in the private housing segment, the government undertook measures to resuscitate the market. It reduced the supply of state land for 1997, allowed developers who had bought state-owned sites to defer housing completion[22] and exempted sellers of private dwellings from payment of stamp duty. Under a Deferred Payment Scheme (DPS) introduced in October 1997, developers were also allowed to offer purchasers of uncompleted properties the option to defer progress payments till completion.[23] In practice, buyers need not prove that they had sufficient funds or were able to secure adequate loans from banks before they bought a property. As this presented adverse selection problems, default risk would be more concentrated in developers and, in turn, their lenders, if prices were to collapse.

As part of the cooling measures in 1996, the government also reduced the flexibility of public housing owners to upgrade. The time-bar to reapply for another new flat was doubled[24] and access to HDB concessionary loans was tightened to prevent abuse: A borrower was limited to two subsidized loans and was subject to credit assessment for the first time.[25] Unlike in the private housing market however, these measures had no appreciable impact on demand or resale prices in the short term. Since the queue for new HDB flats had still not materially shortened in 1997, the quantum of land for ECs was doubled.

As the AFC propagated through the region, Singapore faced the full brunt of its spillover effects in 1998. To avert a precipitous drop in real estate values from negative GDP growth and rising unemployment, the government instituted various off-budget measures and reversed many of its earlier policies including deferring stamp-duty payments and suspending the GLS program. As conditions in crisis-hit countries began to normalize, the Singapore economy staged a V-shaped recovery from 1999 through 2000. Exhibit 19.5 shows that private house prices began to recover in early 1999 after falling 45 percent from the first quarter of 1997 to the end of 1998. Resale prices also turned up in the second quarter of 1999 after a 28 percent decline from their peak.

THE 2006–2007 HOUSING BOOM AND THE GFC

The period post-AFC leading up to the GFC can be characterized as one of financial liberalization amidst wider economic restructuring efforts to diversify and grow Singapore's economic base. At the same time, the openness of its trade-oriented economy and capital markets meant that Singapore was particularly exposed to the vagaries of a very fluid global economy. In particular, loose American monetary policy was transmitted to Singapore through financial market linkages and an exchange rate that is managed in part against the U.S. dollar. As a result, the housing sector became increasingly volatile and saw frequent policy interventions that are described further on.

With improved sentiments and lowered real financing costs after the AFC, buyers were drawn to the HDB resale and private property market where prices had declined substantially during the crisis compared to only marginal corrections in new flat prices. From the end of 1998 to mid-2000, private housing prices rebounded by 40 percent, an increase that was sufficient for the state to resume its GLS program and to require HDB owners to seek its approval before buying private housing.[26] Over the same period, the resale flat market also recovered but to a lesser extent due to reductions in the quantum of CPF housing grants and a ruling in October 1999 that restricted the second HDB concessionary loan to only borrowers who upgraded to larger flats. However, the primary HDB market suffered the greatest impact from the AFC: Demand fell sharply in 1998 as applicants dropped out of the new flat queue or opted to buy resale flats instead of waiting. Exhibit 19.4 shows that while the demand for new flats did increase in late 1999, it was substantially lower than pre-crisis demand levels and could not absorb the completions from a pipeline that had been ramped up by the HDB in the mid-1990s. By the end of 1999, there was an overhang of about 31,000 unsold flats that not only curtailed new construction but would take another seven years to whittle down.

In 2001, a global electronics slump and a sharp slowdown in the U.S. economy following the dot-com bust precipitated a synchronized downturn across most countries. The Singapore housing sector was hit by one of the worst recessions on record. This triggered a revamp of the GLS program in June: In addition to a confirmed list of sites that have been earmarked for periodic sale based on medium term projections, stand-by parcels would be placed on a reserve list to cater to demand shocks. A reserve site would only be triggered for sale if the state received a bid that exceeded its (undisclosed) reserve price.[27] With a reserve supply, the quantum of land released under the confirmed list was reduced. The HDB also changed the way new flats were sold from a first-come, first-served queue system to a build-to-order (BTO) system under which building would commence only if most of the flats to be built on proposed sites had been booked.[28] The BTO system allowed supply to be better calibrated to demand and has been the main mode of sale for new flats since its introduction. Following September 11, the government attempted to boost demand by lifting the capital gains tax on private housing and allowing foreigners access to Singapore dollar loans for buying private residential properties. In addition, the sale of sites under the confirmed list was suspended in October.

The Singapore economy rebounded in the first half of 2002 but external conditions quickly deteriorated again from increased geopolitical uncertainties, financial market volatility and weak economic activity. Still, the amount of mortgage loans grew due to keen competition among established lenders and new bank entrants that drove down home loan rates. Housing demand was also supported by new CPF rulings that allowed CPF monies to be used for paying half of the down payment instead of an all-cash payment.[29] In addition, the priority of claims over mortgaged properties was changed so that banks held the first charge for a property ahead of the CPF.[30] However, concerns about the excessive use of CPF savings for housing consumption led to a reduction of the total amount of CPF savings that could be withdrawn for servicing new or refinanced loans secured by private housing.[31]

Between 2003 and mid-2005, the Singapore housing sector remained moribund as the economy vacillated between growth and weakness following a series of demand shocks. Throughout this period, the sale of confirmed land sites remained suspended and stamp duty rates were reduced by 30 percent. The HDB further relaxed its restrictions on both the subletting and resale of flats[32] with the most notable being the reduction of the minimum occupation period for buyers who had not received any form of subsidy: They could resell their units after a year rather than 2.5 years. This would have important consequences later since shortening the holding period reinforced the attractiveness of public housing as a low-risk investment and even speculative vehicle, particularly for those without credit constraints. Due to weak labor market conditions then, much of the housing demand was for small units and consequently, the prices for three-room flats rose. As these flats were only available in the resale market, the HDB resumed building them in 2004 (and two-room flats in 2006) to improve affordability.

In 2005, a resilient United States lifted the world economy and Asian bourses were boosted by foreign capital flows into emerging markets in search of higher yields. This and an announcement in April that two mega integrated resorts would be built in Singapore renewed investor interest in properties. However, private housing prices were still declining, albeit slowly, and the downtrend was arrested only when a package of measures to inflate the market was announced in July that included:

- Raising the maximum LTV ratio of housing loans from 80 percent to 90 percent and reducing the cash down payment from 10 percent to 5 percent.
- Lowering the minimum lease period of properties that could be purchased with CPF savings from 60 to 30 years.[33]
- Allowing non-related CPF members to use their CPF savings to jointly purchase private housing units.
- Relaxing restrictions on foreign ownership of units in low-rise apartments.[34]
- Reinstating private residential properties as allowable investments under the state's Global Investor Program for a foreigner seeking to qualify for permanent residence.

Based on the SRPI, private house prices bottomed in July and appreciated 4 percent by year-end. Although resale HDB prices remained weak, the demand for bigger flats had also increased reflecting an improving job market.

With strong growth of the global economy in 2006, Singapore experienced record job creation, robust economic expansion, and the highest rate of private house price appreciation of 11 percent in Asia. In late 2006, the government withdrew an earlier concession to defer payment of stamp duty and announced the resumption of confirmed land sales for 2007, six years after it had been suspended. As demand in the public housing segment remained muted, the HDB made additional CPF housing grants available to improve affordability. It fixed the amount of resale levies payable instead of pegging them to resale values, re-introduced two-room flats for sale and allowed elderly flat owners to reverse mortgage their flats with financial institutions on commercial terms. Reverse mortgages first appeared in 1994 for private property owners but have been unpopular due to their high cost. Indeed, the take-up rate amongst public housing owners was far lower and would necessitate other measures to monetize housing equity.

By early 2007, Asian economies with strong fiscal positions were seeing large speculative capital inflows. This stemmed from three factors: bullish sentiment on the back of sustained growth and low inflation expectations, abundant liquidity in the global financial system, and increasing concerns about the sustainability of U.S. economic growth given its cooling housing market. The capital inflows kept domestic interest rates and risk premia low and encouraged more risk-taking in property markets. Another two key demand drivers for housing were record job creation and the rapid influx of foreigners as a direct consequence of Singapore's liberalized immigration policies to attract a highly skilled workforce. Particularly after 2006, the pace of immigration picked up as the government made it easier for foreign workers to gain PR status and for permanent residents to become citizens. Exhibit 19.6 shows the substantial growth in the non-resident population from 2006 to 2008. Non-citizens accounted for 25 percent of the total residential sales in 2007, the highest level in 13 years. Finally, urban development policies and the sale of state land for iconic projects aimed at branding Singapore as a culturally vibrant global city have also boosted the housing market.

In the 12 months to end November 2007, private house prices increased a massive 53 percent according to the SRPI. Exhibit 19.6 shows that the price inflation was generally in line with rental growth, unlike the earlier pre-AFC boom. Buying

Exhibit 19.6 Singapore Population Size and Growth by Residential Status

| Year | Number ('000) | | | | | | Average Annual Growth (%) | | | | |
| | | Singapore Residents | | | Non-Residents | | Total | Singapore Residents | | | Non-Residents |
	Total	Total	Citizens	PRs		Total		Total	Citizens	PRs	
1990	3,047.1	2,735.9	2,623.7	112.1	311.3	2.3	1.7	1.7	1.7	2.3	9.0
2000	4,027.9	3,273.4	2,985.9	287.5	754.5	2.8	1.8	1.3	9.9	9.3	
2005	4,265.8	3,467.8	3,081.0	386.8	797.9	2.4	1.6	0.8	8.6	5.9	
2006	4,401.4	3,525.9	3,107.9	418.0	875.5	3.2	1.7	0.9	8.1	9.7	
2007	4,588.6	3,583.1	3,133.8	449.2	1,005.5	4.3	1.6	0.8	7.5	14.9	
2008	4,839.4	3,642.7	3,164.4	478.2	1,196.7	5.5	1.7	1.0	6.5	19.0	
2009	4,987.6	3,733.9	3,200.7	533.2	1,253.7	3.1	2.5	1.1	11.5	4.8	
2010	5,076.7	3,771.7	3,230.7	541.0	1,305.0	1.8	1.0	0.9	1.5	4.1	

Notes: For 1990 and 2000, growth rate refers to the annualized change over the past 10 years.

"Total" refers to the total population, comprising Singapore residents and non-residents. Resident population comprises Singapore citizens and permanent residents. Non-resident population comprises foreigners who were working, studying, or living in Singapore but not granted permanent residence, excluding tourists and short-term visitors.

Source: Singapore Department of Statistics, *Population Trends 2010.*

activity was also less frenzied than before the AFC, probably because a larger proportion of the buyers in 2006–2007 were high-net-worth individuals and foreign
institutional investors. Still, resale activity had picked up and banks had become
more cautious in lending. Hence, it was somewhat surprising that only two measures were implemented to keep private house prices in check and that these came
in October when there were already signs of an incipient economic slowdown. The
first was the withdrawal of the deferred payment scheme, which immediately depressed builder stocks but boosted bank equities. The second was the enactment of
more stringent rules governing collective or *en bloc* sales of housing developments
owned by multiple parties.[35] Escalating house prices, particularly of high-end
properties, had created strong demand for prime land. This triggered a wave of
collective sales in the first half of 2007 of older, centrally located residential projects
for redevelopment. *En bloc* sales not only set increasingly higher benchmark prices
for land but, by removing existing stock from the market amidst a fast-growing
immigrant demographic, created excess demand for accommodation. As a result,
rents increased by 41 percent in 2007 and led many to buy rather than lease. However, the new rules to moderate *en bloc* sales activity had limited efficacy as they had
been generally anticipated and an unexpected increase in betterment tax earlier in
July had already reduced expected profits.

The short-supply situation was exacerbated by the suspension of sales of confirmed state-owned land since 2001. When the program was resumed in 2007, the
key sites released were intended to advance the prevailing planning intent of developing new non-CBD commercial regions. Unlike the prime land sold through
collective sales, most of the state-owned residential sites offered for sale were not
centrally located and were placed on the reserve list. Triggering a reserve site for
auction was onerous as a developer needed to submit a minimum bid above the
state's reservation price and, if accepted, place a deposit of 5 percent of the bid
amount. This focused attention and intense competition on a few select plots that
set record prices for suburban land, which in turn fueled expectations of higher
future selling prices. Although the amount of residential land was increased in
October, the reception was dampened by the removal of the DPS and increased
uncertainty about profit margins given escalating building costs amidst a global
commodity boom.[36] Further, there were resource constraints due to the synchronized construction of various landmark projects that had been deferred to the
mid-2000s when economic recovery was expected to be on a firmer footing.

The public resale market had been languishing for several years but began to
pick up in the second quarter of 2007. Indeed, a key impetus for the capital appreciation came from the HDB itself, when it substantially relaxed its flat subletting
policy in March. By reducing the minimum occupation period before a flat could
be rented out to five years (three years) for subsidized (non-subsidized) units and
by delinking the eligibility to rent from the loan status,[37] the HDB directly fueled
investment demand for its flats. The excess demand from expatriates and middle-
income families who had been priced out of the private market filtered down to the
HDB sector in the second half of 2007. Given the tight housing market conditions
then, HDB flat rentals rose (by as much as 21.2 percent for five-room flats in the
third quarter), but their lower prices meant higher rental yields compared to those
for private housing, making HDB flats an attractive play. In August, the government gave a further boost to the public housing sector with more generous housing
grants for HDB flat buyers. As a result of the high resale prices and a public housing

supply program that had been substantially scaled down, the HDB cleared much of its remaining unsold stock in 2007. By year-end, resale prices had risen 17 percent while applications for new flats had increased about 50 percent. Increasing concerns about housing affordability led the government to announce that more new HDB flats with a larger proportion of smaller units would be released for sale over the next six months.

Just as the government stepped up its GLS and HDB building program for 2008, the U.S. subprime mortgage crisis precipitated a credit squeeze that marked the onset of the GFC. Strong inflationary pressures in the first half of 2008 further depressed growth. Amidst widespread financial turmoil following the collapse of Lehman Brothers, the global economy plunged into its worst recession in the post-war period in late 2008 into early 2009. Due to the synchronized nature of the downturn and as the contagion from an impaired global financial system spilled over to the real economy worldwide, global demand slumped and trade collapsed. Given its strong external orientation, the impact on Singapore was severe and its economy contracted 10.1 percent during the year to the first quarter of 2009. Over the same period, no state-land sales were concluded and the private housing market fell 20 percent to hit a post-GFC low in March 2009. As mitigation, the state suspended the confirmed list for its 2009 GLS program and allowed various concessions for residential developers to phase the construction and sale of their private sector projects[38].

In contrast, the public housing sector remained firm throughout the GFC with demand for new-build units overwhelming the limited supply. According to brokerage reports, market rents of HDB flats continued to rise while the official HDB Resale Price Index gained 10 percent in the year to the end of March 2009, buoyed by relatively stronger demand for larger units. The main concern among policy makers then was on providing assistance to targeted groups affected by the recession. The measures included implementing a lease buyback scheme for low-income elderly lessees that would pay them an annuity stream, providing rental rebates and enhancing grants that now reached the middle income group and that boosted demand for the smaller flats.

Although the GFC led to the default or early redemption of several structured products in Singapore, the exposures of domestic financial institutions to the U.S. housing market, toxic instruments, and failed or distressed institutions elsewhere were not significant relative to their assets and did not pose any systemic risk. The incidence of credit defaults did not increase drastically because the balance sheets of the end-customers, especially those of the households, remained robust. In particular, the resilience of the banking sector was underpinned by the strong capital and liquidity position of banks, which helped to absorb any increases in non-performing loans and pressures on profits. This allowed the Singapore financial system to generally function in an orderly manner in the midst of increased volatility and wealth destruction in other economies.

THE POST-GFC HOUSING BOOM AND ITS SUSTAINABILITY

Since mid-2008, global inflation had decelerated significantly in tandem with falling commodity prices due to weak demand. Following concerted fiscal, monetary and other stimulus measures by governments across the world, second-order effects began to ease in early 2009. Given the sound macroeconomic and financial fundamentals of Asian economies, the region was expected to outperform the global economy and attracted capital flight to quality. Singapore was a beneficiary of these developments, having built up its wealth management capabilities in line with its ambition to be a financial hub. This, coupled with an earlier move by the MAS (Monetary Authority of Singapore), the *de facto* central bank, that raised the pace of Singapore dollar appreciation to counter imported inflation, helped attract foreign funds to flow back into the local market and kept interest rates and borrowing costs low. Indeed, the excess liquidity helped to fuel an even stronger bull run in the Singapore property market post-GFC that would make it one of the frothiest in the world.

Rebounds of the Singapore private housing sector had always lagged wider economic recovery in the past. However, the prospect of a V-shaped economic upturn combined with ample liquidity and expectations of continued low interest rates set off a sharp increase in private house prices in April 2009 ahead of positive GDP growth. By then, escalating resale flat prices had narrowed the price gap between the largest HDB units and entry-level private housing. This, coupled with developer discounts, boosted transaction volumes of private units that were perceived to be reasonably priced.[39] The sector also benefited from credit-tightening measures in China and Hong Kong that diverted some buying attention to Singapore. Unlike the pre-GFC boom when luxury units dominated transactions, the majority of the new private sector units sold comprised either small- or mid-market homes for middle-income buyers, many of whom capitalized on high resale flat prices to upgrade. Such entry-level private housing is often built on state land parcels in suburban areas, but the state elected to suspend the confirmed list of the GLS program for the rest of the year as there were ample reserve sites. However, only two reserve sites had been triggered for sale in mid-2009 and this indicated that either the reserve list system was not well primed to respond to demand shocks or that reservation prices may have been too high relative to bids.

Only after private house prices had surged 19 percent from March to August 2009 did the government intervene to cool the housing market in mid-September. It announced that the confirmed list would be reinstated for the 2010 GLS program, a move that did not immediately change the status quo in terms of land supply. Further, the MAS banned financial institutions from offering interest-absorption and interest-only housing loans, both variants of the former DPS, to buyers of uncompleted private housing units:

- In interest absorption schemes offered by a developer and his partner bank(s), purchasers would make the upfront down payment and commit to a loan with the developer's partner bank but could defer further installments payments until their units were completed. Prior to completion, the bank required only interest payments to be made, which were borne by the developer.
- In an interest-only housing loan, a borrower made only interest payments for a period of time. Compared to payments under a standard payment scheme, installments in the interest-only period were lower but subsequent payments would be higher when amortization of the loan principal resumed.

As the loans either entirely eliminated or substantially lowered regular installment payments for private housing buyers in the first few years before the properties were completed, they could encourage speculation. Their removal was intended to encourage prospective buyers to consider carefully their long-term affordability.

Despite these measures, the speculative momentum in the property market continued to escalate and necessitated a new round of measures in February 2010. First, sellers of residential properties or land bought on or after February 20 and sold within one year from the date of purchase were required to pay stamp duty. Second, the MAS lowered the LTV limit for housing loans from 90 percent to 80 percent, but HDB concessionary loans were exempted to promote home ownership amongst first-time flat buyers and upgraders. Third, a record quantum of state land was made available for sale in the GLS program for the first half of 2010 although the bulk was in the reserve list. To facilitate triggering reserve sites for sale, in March the government reduced the deposit payable by a successful applicant. It would also auction a site if it attracted sufficient market interest, which meant that at least two bids had to be received that were within the ballpark of the state's reservation price. By the end of May, only four of 34 reserve sites had been sold and this prompted the government to increase the supply of land for the rest of the year and to raise the proportion of land offered under its confirmed list.

In March, the HDB also announced new measures to curb speculation in the HDB resale market. Most notable was the reversal of its long-standing policy of granting a second HDB concessionary loan to those who bought a larger unit only: Due to concerns that this had encouraged leveraged overconsumption of housing, a second subsidized loan would be extended to all eligible buyers regardless of flat size but a requirement to use the sale proceeds from the first flat translated into lower loan quantums. To reduce the incidence of flipping resale flats, buyers must now occupy their flats for at least three years rather than a year (for unsubsidized units) or two and one-half years (for unsubsidized units bought with a concessionary loan). Although market evidence did not support the perception that demand from non-citizens had caused the inflation of resale flat prices, the rapid influx of immigrants had generated tension. In a bid to appease the electorate, the HDB imposed a quota cap on the number of flats that could be bought by permanent residents (PRs) and reduced the housing grant for couples that consist of a citizen and a PR.

An interesting development that accompanied high resale flat prices and which also underscored how far the marketization of public housing had come was the increasing use of HDB flats as security for cash loans from licensed moneylenders. Under the prevailing legislation, a HDB flat could not be pledged as collateral for any debt, obligation, or claim except for financing its purchase. Flat owners circumvented this by entering into agreements to assign the sales proceeds from their HDB flats as repayment of monies owed. To claim an interest in the sales proceeds, the moneylenders would lodge caveats against the borrower's flat. This allowed them to demand repayment before they agreed to withdraw the caveat for the sale transaction to go through. In July, the legislation was revised to disallow the practice and to introduce a new rule that voids any contract or agreement to use HDB flats, including the sales proceeds, as security or collateral. In addition, caveats against HDB flats for the payment of debt could no longer be lodged. These amendments were not only intended to deter the premature sale of HDB flats to raise cash but would help keep Singaporeans rooted to the state through holding HDB flats as long-term assets.

While Singapore had enjoyed strong economic growth in the first half of 2010, growth was expected to moderate in the second half of the year. However, property price inflation continued and it became clear that the market cooling measures in February and March had failed again: Private house prices rose 6 percent while HDB resale flat prices grew 4 percent—its eighth straight quarter of growth—to achieve record levels in the second quarter of 2010. To quell increasing disquiet about housing affordability, a slew of new policies were announced a day after the Prime Minister assured Singaporeans in a National Day Rally speech that the government would prevent housing prices from rising beyond their reach. The latest measures introduced on August 30, 2010 include:

- Extending the holding period for the imposition of stamp duty on sellers of residential land and houses from a year to three years.[40]
- Raising the minimum cash payment from 5 percent to 10 percent of the lower of property value or property price and lowering the LTV cap for housing loans from 80 percent to 70 percent for buyers with at least one outstanding housing loan at the time of the new housing purchase.
- Barring HDB flat owners from owning both private property and an HDB flat at the same time during the minimum occupation period (MOP).
- Increasing the MOP for non-subsidized flats from three to five years.

The immediate impact of the policies was uncertainty about the ambit of the measures pertaining to ownership of public and private housing. It appears that private residential property owners who buy resale HDB flats must now dispose of their house(s), in or outside Singapore, within six months of the purchase of the HDB flat—a rule that had not existed before but that would apply for locals and foreigners alike. This effectively bans private property owners from buying HDB resale flats for investment purposes. Those who had bought a non-subsidized HDB flat were required to sell off their private property, wherever it was located, within six months from August 30, 2010. Similarly, buyers of non-subsidized HDB flats would not be allowed to invest in any private property before the MOP is up, although they were previously allowed to do so. The new rules were meant to "ensure equitable treatment" of all flat owners during the stipulated occupancy period, although the rationale for prohibiting ownership of overseas properties to moderate house price inflation in Singapore, even when the houses were bequests, was inscrutable to many.

Besides dampening speculative and investment demand for housing, the government has promised more help for first-time home buyers and significantly raised the supply of new HDB flats and state land for premium public housing units and ECs. Indeed, record private housing and resale flat prices have obliged the state to continue affordable housing provision and even expand housing concessions in the interest of securing continued political support. However, there is a practical limit to how much the government can afford to give to producer and demand subsidies, particularly when the capital subsidies that were originally intended to benefit select groups have been transferred (eventually) to private housing and other assets. In order to comply with various affordability benchmarks[41] and yet keep subsidy levels manageable, the HDB may build marginally smaller units in the future. This would mirror the recent trend in the private housing market where developers have been selling shoebox dwellings of less than 600 square feet to ensure that the absolute price remains affordable to buyers.

CONCLUSION

The government's objective is to ensure a stable and sustainable property market where prices move in line with economic fundamentals. How well it can achieve this would depend on its ability to conduct timely surveillance and the effectiveness of its policy levers. Curtailing demand has proven to be difficult given the openness of the Singapore economy and property market to foreign capital inflows. Further quantitative easing by the Fed could potentially be transmitted to Singapore directly through funds that acquire assets and via a cheaper real cost of finance that also would stimulate more property buying. In this regard, policy makers have expressed confidence that the Singapore financial system is capable of handling the capital flows. What the government has done recently, in part to address discontent among citizens about the large influx of immigrants and housing affordability, is to perceptibly tighten its immigration policies while ramping up flat production. While total population growth has slowed this year, residential rents have not materially softened due to delays in new home launches and construction bottlenecks over the past two years as a result of projects to pump-prime the economy. The future rent trajectory would depend on the rate of housing completions in the short term but an aggressive HDB building program and competition between private sector and public infrastructure projects for capacity this year may result in a lower quantity of ready-built private housing units than earlier projected.

Besides flat production, the state has another policy lever in its land sale program. Its track record in managing residential land supply to accommodate demand shocks and moderate house price volatility has been criticized by private developers. Although the GLS is a market-driven instrument for housing market stabilization, policymakers enjoy unfettered latitude in determining the quantum and location of land to be sold and the timing of the sale. Each year, the land sales program is planned carefully based on national development imperatives and an assessment of the mid- to long-term demand for the various types of properties. This being the case, the assumptions about market conditions that prevailed when the plan was initially conceived and which justified its provision may have materially changed by the time the land was actually released. The synchronization of land supply with housing demand will become more difficult given the growing interconnections among financial markets across different economies and the swiftness with which changes in financial market conditions are transmitted to the housing sector.

The state also decides on the selling price of each parcel but, without a transparent land sales rule, discretionary land supply may be problematic in a manner raised by Kydland and Prescott (1977). Ostensibly, the state favors gradual house price appreciation and will combat any surprise inflation by releasing more land for housing. However, land sales provide a substantial source of revenue and in

the absence of a rule, there may be a temptation to generate a little more price inflation to boost public coffers. In setting bid prices for land, developers may build
in inflationary expectations, as would other market participants, in their decisions.
In the past, the timing of public land sales often coincided with boom episodes in
the property market, when record prices for residential land have been set by keen
market contests for state land releases. As private land banks in Singapore become
more depleted and housing supply becomes more dependent on state-owned land,
policy makers must guard against supply-side rationing in the land market that
could increase price pressures on the housing sector.

Housing has appreciated faster than GDP expansion since the GFC with house
price levels at the end of October 2010 exceeding their historical maxima in the
second quarter of 1996 as well as their pre-GFC peaks. Such rapid price growth has
significantly eroded affordability levels and is probably unsustainable. Despite
three sets of cooling measures, the Singapore housing market remains buoyant,
supported in part by record-low housing finance costs. In a country where the
homeownership rate of resident households is close to 89 percent and in which
housing purchases are often leveraged, many households are potentially vulnerable to house price corrections and/or increases in the cost of debt. While such
shocks are not expected to severely threaten the financial system in Singapore
given its prudent lending standards and the good asset quality of housing loans,
they could potentially exert adverse wealth and income effects. Negotiating these
risks would require continued vigilance from as well as more effective policy coordination among state agencies.

NOTES

1. Ministry of Trade and Industry (MTI), *Singapore in Figures 2010*. The annual GDP figure
   is in current nominal dollars with an exchange rate in December 2009 of approximately
   S$1.45 to US$1.

2. See *The Economist*, July 5, 2007, May 22, 2008, and April 15, 2010.

3. The Singapore Residential Price Index is a quality-controlled transaction price index
   produced by the National University of Singapore (NUS) that tracks price movements
   in the Singapore private residential market on a monthly basis using a basket-based
   approach. For details, see www.ires.nus.edu.sg/srpi.aspx.

4. The URA Private Residential Price Index is a median transactions price index that tracks
   the overall price movement of the private residential market using the fourth quarter of
   1998 as the base period.

5. The HDB Resale Price Index is a median transactions price index that tracks the overall
   price movement of the secondary or resale HDB market from the first quarter of 1990
   with the fourth quarter of 1998 as the base period.

6. Contribution rates for the employer and the employee can differ and vary with economic
   and labor market conditions. For details, see www.cpf.gov.sg.

7. A flat is named according to the number of rooms it has. The sitting-dining room and
   bedrooms are counted but not the kitchen and washrooms. The executive apartment
   has five rooms but is larger than the five-room flat.

8. This generated controversy, particularly when new flat prices rose in sync with escalating resale prices. As HDB units were built on state-owned land, much of which had been

compulsorily acquired at below market prices from private owners, buyers questioned if the HDB had been making profits rather than providing subsidies.

9. As a matter of government policy, three-room flats are priced such that at least 90 percent of new Singaporean households would be able to pay their HDB mortgage repayments using only their CPF contributions without having to use cash. Four-room flats would be similarly priced to be affordable to 70 percent of Singaporean households. When the income ceiling was last revised in late 1994, 94 percent of all Singaporean households became eligible for new flats.

10. With effect from September 1982, sellers could pay either a graded resale levy on the sale price of their first unit based on the flat type or a standard 10 percent premium on their second flat purchased from the HDB. In July 1985, the resale levy was waived for the first flat if the seller did not repurchase another subsidized unit.

11. Ministry of Trade and Industry, *Report of the Cost Review Committee, 1993.*

12. POSB began as a postal savings scheme in 1877 and evolved into a major state-owned savings bank offering low-cost banking services.

13. Savings in the CPF Ordinary Account earn a market-related interest rate based on the 12-month fixed deposit and month-end savings rates of the major local banks, subject to a minimum of 2.5 percent per annum.

14. The HDB ceased granting market rate loans with effect from January 1, 2003.

15. This came to an end in 1998 when POSB was acquired by a state-controlled commercial bank DBS.

16. In 1988, CPF members could withdraw up to 100 percent of the lower of the purchase price or valuation of the dwelling instead of 80 percent previously. The withdrawal amount was raised to cover mortgage interest payments in 1993.

17. An eligible household would receive a S$30,000 grant in its CPF account when it applied to buy a resale flat within two kilometers of the buyers' parents'/married children's homes. In August 1995, this was raised to S$50,000, while all first-time buyers who purchased a resale flat were eligible for a S$40,000 grant.

18. In February 1995, resale procedures were revised to ease the payment of cash upfront by moving flat valuations closer to transacted prices and reducing the down payment from 20 percent to 10 percent of the selling price.

19. 80 percent of the ECs would be allocated to existing executive flat applicants in the HDB queue and eligible households would get a S$40,000 grant. With the introduction of the EC, the HDB phased out the executive flat (Lum 1997).

20. 100 percent, 66 percent and 33 percent of the capital gains were taxable if a property was sold within one, two, and three years of its purchase respectively.

21. This was payable on signing the Sales & Purchase Agreement instead of at completion.

22. In November 1997, the stipulated completion time for projects where units had not been launched for sale was extended to eight years (up from 30 months imposed in May 1996), subject to a premium of 5 percent of the land price payable per year of extension.

23. Under a normal progress payment scheme, buyers normally secure a housing loan early, as they are billed by the developer in stages, according to the progress of the project's construction. With the DPS, buyers paid only 10 percent, or more typically 20 percent, of the house price with the next payment due on completion, a few years down the road.

24. The time bar was increased from 5 to 10 years to shorten the HDB queue. The resale levy was simplified to only the graded resale levy scheme, with buyers of new flats and ECs having to pay higher levies.

25. The credit assessment imposed a 40 percent ceiling on the debt service to income ratio. In September 1997, HDB owners could book a private unit only after a five-year occupation period in their flats.

26. In June 2000, land was released for 6,000 units of private housing and 3,000 units of ECs. HDB owners required approval for buying private housing even if they met the five-year MOP.

27. Under the Reserve List system, the government would only release a site for sale if an interested party submits an application to release the site with an offer of a minimum purchase price that is acceptable to the state. The successful applicant must undertake to subsequently bid for the land in the tender at or above the minimum price offered in the application.

28. Under this system, buyers ballot for the chance to select a flat and pay a down payment to secure a booking. The HDB proceeds to build when the majority of flats are booked.

29. The cash down payment for private residential properties and ECs was cut to 10 percent of the purchase price, down from the 20 percent imposed in May 1996, and the balance could be paid by CPF funds.

30. Before September 1, 2002, a lender taking a mortgage over the property ranked second behind the borrower's own CPF claims.

31. As interest payments were an expense item and did not increase the value of property, lowering the amount of CPF funds for interest by 6 percent a year from 150 percent to 120 percent in 2008 would reduce housing over-consumption.

32. Since October 2003, flat owners could sublet their whole flat after a 15-year MOP or after 10 years if they had paid off their home loan. In March 2005, these time bars were reduced to 10 years and 5 years respectively. The MOP before buying another subsidized flat was decreased from 10 to 5 years.

33. CPF withdrawal limits will be pegged to the age of the purchaser and the remaining lease of the property.

34. Foreigners could buy any non-landed property but all other properties such as vacant residential land, landed homes, and whole buildings or condominiums were restricted and required state approval.

35. In an *en bloc* sale, owners of fragmented interests in land would amalgamate their combined interests in either strata-titled units or adjoining single-family units for sale and eventual redevelopment (Lum et al. 2000).

36. Construction costs increased by 20 to 30 percent in fourth quarter of 2007 (year-on-year) and by early 2008, had overtaken the land cost for some 99-year leasehold sites. To ease inflationary pressure on the construction sector, the government shelved S$4.7 billion of public sector projects until 2010 and beyond.

37. This was a major change from the HDB's prevailing policy (see note 32) and was intended to help home owners monetize their homes as well as to enlarge the rental market.

38. The measures in the 2009 budget included: allowing developers who bought GLS sites and foreign developers who owned private residential land a one-year extension to commence development, allowing developers to resell the land or dispose of their interest in it before January 21, 2010, and giving foreign developers two more years to dispose of the units or up to four years to rent out unsold apartments. (In the past, they were required to sell all the units in their project within two years of completion and were not allowed to rent out unsold units.)

39. From 953 housing units in fourth quarter of 2008, sales soared to 10,120 units in second quarter of 2009 and 11,518 units in third quarter of 2009.

40. This applies to any transfer or disposal of interest (including sale and gifts) on or after August 30, 2010 within three years of purchase. Specifically, the full stamp duty rate (1 percent for the first $180,000 of the consideration, 2 percent for the next $180,000, and 3 percent for the balance) will be levied if the properties are sold within the first year of purchase. This goes down to two thirds (one third) of the full rate for a sale within the second (third) year of purchase.

41. The HDB sets new flat price at between five to six times household income. The proportion of income and the CPF savings utilized to pay for both the down payment and mortgage installments should be around 25 percent to 30 percent of household income. A third indicator of affordability is the application pattern.

REFERENCES

Central Provident Fund, Singapore. *Annual Report*, various years.

Chua, B. H. 1997. *Political Legitimacy and Housing: Stakeholding in Singapore*. London: Routledge.

Chua, B. H. 2000. "Public Housing Residents as Clients of the State." *Housing Studies* 15:1, 45–60.

Department of Statistics, Singapore. *Yearbook of Statistics*, various years.

Housing and Development Board, Singapore. *Annual Report*, various years.

Housing and Development Board, Singapore. www.hdb.gov.sg.

Kydland, F. E., and E. C. Prescott. 1977. "Rules Rather Than Discretion: The Inconsistency of Optimal Plans." *Journal of Political Economy* 85:3, 473–491.

Lim, C. Y., et al. 1986. "Report of the Central Provident Fund Group." *The Singapore Economic Review* 31, 1–103.

Lum, S. K. 1996. "The Singapore Private Property Market: Price Trend and Affordability." Conference on The Singapore Dream: Private Property, Social Expectations & Public Policy, September 6, 1997, National University of Singapore.

Lum S. K. 1997. "Executive Condominiums in Singapore: Housing Gap Solution or Stop-Gap Measure." Working Paper, Department of Real Estate, National University of Singapore.

Lum, S. K. 2002. "Market Fundamentals, Public Policy, and Private Gain: Housing Price Dynamics in Singapore." *Journal of Property Research* 19:2, 1–23.

Lum, S. K., L. L. Sim, and L. C. Lee. 2004. "Market-Led Policy Measures for Urban Redevelopment in Singapore." *Land Use Policy* 21:1, 1–19.

Monetary Authority of Singapore, Singapore. *Annual Report*, various years.

Ministry for National Development, Singapore. Available at www.mnd.gov.sg.

Phang, S. Y. 2001. "Housing Policy, Wealth Formation and the Singapore Economy." *Housing Studies* 16:4, 443–459.

Phang, S. Y. 2005. "The Creation and Economic Regulation of Housing Markets: Singapore's Experience and Implications for Korea." Korea Development Institute Conference on Residential Welfare and Housing Policies, Seoul, Korea, June 2–3, 2005.

ABOUT THE AUTHOR

LUM SAU KIM is program director of the MBA (Real Estate) that is offered jointly by the Department of Real Estate and the NUS Business School. She obtained her PhD in Business Administration, co-majoring in Finance and Real Estate, from the Haas Business School at University of California–Berkeley. A former Asean and British Commonwealth scholar, she is a recipient of the Homer Hoyt post-doctoral award and NUS Teaching Excellence awards. She has consulted for various public sector agencies and private corporations. Her research interests are in the areas of urban and housing economics, land policy, and index construction. As a joint appointment holder of the Institute of Real Estate Studies at NUS, she recently led a project that created price indices for the Singapore private housing market.

CHAPTER 20

Taiwan: Housing Bubbles and Affordability

CHIN-OH CHANG
Distinguished Professor, Department of Land Economics, National Chengchi University, Taiwan

MING-CHI CHEN
Professor, Department of Finance, National Sun Yat-Sen University, Taiwan

This chapter begins with a general description of Taiwan's housing development and finance systems that influence the evolution of the housing market. Four periods of housing price jumps occurred in the past 40 years. We describe how these jumps occurred and how the government responded. We also show the sizes of housing bubbles in relation to housing prices, indicating a serious housing affordability problem in Taiwan. We present the current status of the housing market and discuss the major concerns for the current housing policy. We also present two important progresses in the Taiwan housing market: real estate securitization and reverse mortgage.

INTRODUCTION

Taiwan, officially named the "Republic of China," is an island located in the western Pacific Ocean, off the southeastern coast of mainland China. The area of Taiwan is only 36,000 square kilometers, but it has a population of approximately 23 million people (2010 figures). On average, there are 639 people per square kilometer and 3.3 people per household. Approximately two-thirds of the total area is unfavorable to land development due to site gradients. The island is roughly divided by the Central Mountain Range from north to south, with most settlements developed in the western Taiwanese plain. There are four major cities: Taipei, Taichung, Tainan, and Kaohsiung. Taipei is the capital and the largest city, with a population of 2.6 million. The second largest city is Kaohsiung, which has a population of 1.5 million. However, the population distribution is unbalanced in Taiwan. The Taipei metropolitan area (Taipei city and county) has a population of 6.5 million, accounting for almost one-third of the Taiwanese population.

During the past 40 years, the average annual population growth rate in Taiwan reached a peak of over 3 percent, but then declined to less than 1 percent after 1990.

447

Taiwan now has a 0.83 percent birth rate (2010), which is among the lowest rates in the world. On the other hand, life expectancy (for male) at birth in Taiwan increased from 62 in 1970 to 76 in 2009. The population aged over 65 made up 10.5 percent of the total population in 2009. Taiwan has begun to face severe population aging, as in other developed countries.

Taiwan's economy underwent a rapid transition and industrialization led by export growth during the post-war period. Economic growth recorded an impressive rate of increase, with an average of 9 percent per annum during the 1960s and 1970s. Although two oil crises and recessions occurred in the 1980s, Taiwan recovered faster than most other countries, with a peak economic growth rate of 12 percent in 1987. However, Taiwan's economy began to show signs of maturity, and economic growth began to slow down after the 1990s. Because of a conservative financial system, Taiwan suffered little compared with many of its neighbors in the 1997 Asian financial crisis. After 1997, economic growth rates fell below 6 percent. The global economic downturn, political turmoil, and an increasing amount of bad debt in the banking system pushed Taiwan into recession in 2001, the first full year of negative growth since 1947. Currently the electronics industry is the most important industry in helping to maintain Taiwan's economic growth. Exports, led by electronics and machinery, generate 70 percent of Taiwan's GDP growth and have provided the primary impetus for industrialization. This heavy dependence on exports made the economy vulnerable to the downturns in world demand resulting from the U.S. subprime crisis in 2007. However, Taiwan has shown signs of recovery, with an economic growth rate of 13.27 percent in the first quarter of 2010. Taiwan currently still runs a large trade surplus, and its foreign reserves are the world's fourth largest, behind China, Japan, and Russia. Recently, opened cross-strait travel, transportation, and tourism links are likely to increase Taiwan and China's economic interdependence.

HOUSING DEVELOPMENT, FINANCE, AND MORTGAGE

We briefly describe the development of the housing, finance system, housing finance system, and mortgage market as the background for understanding why housing price cycles have occurred for the past 40 years.

Housing Development

Investment in housing as a percentage of the gross domestic product has not been very stable, varying from 1.15 to 4.21 percent over the past 40 years. There is evidence of a significant decrease from the past decade, dropping below 2 percent since 1997. The housing stock closely matches the household number. The ratio of housing stock to household number is generally slightly higher than one, indicating no sign of a housing shortage. During the early years, new housing completions were occurring at around one hundred thousand units per year, whereas the ratio of completions to housing stock in Taiwan was approximately 2 to 3 percent. However, this ratio has dropped below 2 percent over the past 10 years, as in other developed countries where the population growth rates are decreasing.

In terms of housing space, the living standards have improved gradually over the past few years. The average floor area of a household increased from 106 square meters in 1987 to 142 square meters in 2008. According to the "2005 Report of Housing Status Survey," 32.10 percent of households were accommodated in apartments, 24.58 percent in town houses, 5.91 percent in duplexes, 18.86 percent in single-family houses, and 8.55 percent in farmhouses. This report also indicated that 31.44 percent of houses were built before 1980, 31.72 percent were built between 1970 and 1980, 29.42 percent were built between 1980 and 1990, and 7 percent were built after 1990.

The proportion of owner-occupied dwellings in Taiwan increased significantly from 66.3 percent in 1970 to 87.4 percent in 2008, corresponding with a decline in the number of privately rented properties. One important characteristic of Taiwan's housing market is its comparatively large number of owner-occupied dwellings and a relatively small rental sector. Exhibit 20.1 shows the Taiwan housing market development in recent years.

Financial System Development

Taiwan's financial institutions can be classified into two groups. One group is established under laws, whereas the other is not based on laws and involves underground financial institutions. Legal financial institutions include commercial banks, specialist banks, savings banks, and so forth. One commercial bank, Taiwan Land Bank, specializes in real estate and handles real estate loans pursuant to government policies to enhance national economic development. However, Taiwan Land Bank is still a full-scale financial institution, and all other financial institutions can provide loans for real estate. The principle government agency responsible for the supervision of financial institutions is the Central Bank, which is responsible for implementing monetary policies and handling a considerable amount of financial supervision.

The financial system in Taiwan transformed slowly, from a backward and controlled system to a modernized and liberalized system. Before 1975, the interest rate was wholly determined by the Central Banks. All of the banks were either entirely or partly owned by the government and had to accept the designated interest rate. In 1980, the "Essentials of Interest Rate Adjustment" was promulgated and implemented with the purpose of allowing banks more flexibility in determining interest rates during times of change in the money-market situation. A loan rate liberalization policy was further implemented in 1985, in which 10 leading banks were required to set their own prime rate according to their own position and the market position. This so-called "basic lending-rate system" was followed by other banks in September 1987.

Some other important financial changes also occurred in the late 1980s. Before 1987, Taiwan adopted a fixed exchange-rate regime. Because of its huge export surplus from the early 1980s, market forces exerted a strong upward pressure on the exchange rate. After the Central Bank adopted a managed floating exchange rate regime in 1987, the exchange rate began to rise rapidly, from NT\$36 = US\$1 to NT\$25 = US\$1 from 1987 to 1989. Furthermore, foreign exchange control was abolished in 1987. The restrictions on capital flows were lifted, enabling capital to move freely in the foreign exchange market, which resulted in higher speculative

Exhibit 20.1 The Taiwan Housing Market and Development

	2004	2005	2006	2007	2008
Housing Demand and Supply					
Households	7,179,943	7,292,879	7,394,758	7,512,449	7,655,772
Housing stock (dwelling-unit)	7,297,358	7,409,953	7,531,797	7,659,643	7,767,945
Housing supply ratio (%)	101.64	101.61	101.85	101.96	101.47
Housing surplus (dwelling-unit)	117,415	117,074	137,039	147,194	112,173
Number of units by building permit	110,981	121,622	116,165	106,197	70,318
Number of units by occupancy permit	96,614	114,904	123,853	130,515	111,057
Housing Market					
Transaction registered buildings	418,187	434,888	450,167	414,641	379,326
Auction registered buildings	54,717	33,295	25,467	25,596	24,954
Price-income ratio (house-owners)	6	6.9	6.6	7	7.1
Mortgage payment-to-income ratio (%)	27.1	28.4	30.9	30.8	29.6
Outstanding construction loan (million NTD)				694,838	708,350
Outstanding house loan (million NTD)				4,069,802	4,677,643
Loans (including NPL) (million NTD)				4,542,354	4,737,824
The amount of NPL (million NTD)				67,621	68,435
NPL ratio (%)				1.49	1.45
Housing tenure					
Ownership (%)	86.8	87.33	87.83	88.14	87.36
Dwelling level (m^2)					
Average living space per household	140	139	131	143	143
Average person per household	3.5	3.42	3.41	3.38	3.35
Average living space per person	40.0	40.7	41.4	42.3	42.5

Source: Housing Statistics Annual Report (2007), Construction and Planning Agency, Ministry of the Interior.

movements during this period. All of these financial changes caused an imbalance in the macroeconomy in the late 1980s, which can be gauged from the increase in the money supply, which was as great as 50 percent per annum during the late 1980s. It seems that financial liberalization and loose monetary policy unleashed investment activity in both the stock and real-estate market, causing dramatic booms.

After 1990, Taiwan's bubble economy began to collapse. Economic growth tended to decline, and the trade surplus began to decease. The new Taiwanese dollar also began to depreciate against the U.S. dollar. Missile tests and other military activities conducted by mainland China in 1997 and the Asian financial crisis in 1997 further caused capital outflow and NT dollar depreciation. The Central

Bank had to release U.S. dollars into the foreign exchange market to stabilize the fluctuations. On the other hand, as a step toward financial liberalization, the government lifted its ban on new establishments of commercial banks in 1991, creating a competitive situation in the banking sector.

Housing Finance Development

Whereas private housing accounts for most of the housing stock in Taiwan, Taiwan did not have mature housing finance until 1990. The financial system in Taiwan before the 1990s was criticized as being underdeveloped and inefficient. Due to the underdeveloped finance system of the early years, private developers usually obtained loans for land acquisitions with land as collateral because they had difficulty obtaining loans during the construction stage. Private developers had to devise various strategies, such as cooperative construction and pre-sales systems, to solve the problem of funding. These strategies were proven to be successful in the development of the Taiwanese housing system.

The pre-sales system, which was developed in the 1960s and is still very popular in the Taipei area, can be thought of as a kind of self-financing system for house-buyers and developers. Once a building permit is obtained, the developer can pre-sell the property before construction to real estate buyers who will then pay based on an agreed schedule according to the construction progress. From the speculative buyer's viewpoint, because only 5 percent of the housing price or even less is required in cash, the leverage is very high. There is also no transaction tax before the property is completed because the property has no record on the official property registrar. Pre-sale contracts have therefore served as popular investment vehicles.

Mortgage Market

Financial institutions are the main sources of construction and housing loans. Because of their conservative economics, Taiwan's financial institutions tend not to engage in risky construction and housing loans. The government is another source of housing loans, but only for public housing, which accounts for less than 5 percent of the total housing stock. In recent years, the government has tended to subsidize mortgage rates instead of providing housing loans.

Exhibit 20.2 illustrates the house-purchasing and construction loan trends for the past 20 years. Both loans show rapidly increasing trends. Construction loans show strong cyclical behaviors because of the boom-and-burst cycle in the housing markets. Following the authorization of 16 new banks in 1991, stiff competition has caused the banking industries in Taiwan to loosen their lending requirements. The growth of mortgage loans is largely driven by private banks. However, after the 1997 Asian financial crisis, the macroeconomy declined and the real estate market became sluggish, leading to increases in the non-performing loans ratio in Taiwan's banking industries. Housing, renovation, and construction loans were equal to about half of Taiwan's gross domestic product. Household mortgage loans accounted for 38.4 percent of the GDP, whereas the proportion of household total debt to the GDP was 54 percent, the highest in the Asian region.

Exhibit 20.2 House-Purchasing and Construction Loans (million NTD)
Sources: Financial Statistics Monthly 2010; the Central Bank of China.

The debt burden of households is heavy in Taiwan, especially for the Taipei area. Mortgage payments for Taipei households may be up to 40 percent, whereas households in other cities have relatively lower percentages, around 30 percent. Owner-occupied residential loans usually have a term of 20 years, but favorable bank customers may obtain a loan of maturity for 30 years. The term of maturity is influenced by the borrowers' credit record or investment relationship with the bank and appears to be a measure of distinguished borrower segments rather than borrowers' self-selection behaviors, as in the U.S. market.

Mortgage contracts in Taiwan were mostly nominated adjustable rates, which are adjusted according to the basic rate of mortgage determined by the Central Bank. However, this basic rate is sticky so Taiwan mortgage contracts were fixed rates in nature before 2000. During the late 1990s, the market interest rates spiraled down, but the overall banking industries in Taiwan tended not to mark down mortgage rates to earn extra spread to cover their substantial mortgage losses. Therefore, the Central Bank improved the basic point mortgage and asked banks to make the mortgage rate more flexible in 2001. There have been many banks offering adjustable-rate mortgages since then. In term of the loan-to-value ratio (LTV), 70 percent is the average figure, whereas the max LTV was 80–90 percent. The LTV varied according to the market situation.

Government Housing Policy Using Mortgage

Starting in 1999, Taiwan's government introduced a series of policies to encourage households and housing developers to enter the housing market. The most important policy for promoting housing market growth is the mortgage-interest-rate subsidy to first-time home buyers. In 1999, the government provided a budget of 150 billion NTD (about 4.5 billion USD) to subsidize first-time home buyers with a lower mortgage interest rate. All qualified first-time home buyers were allowed a mortgage of 2 to 2.5 million NTD with a subsidized interest rate about 0.25 percentage points lower than the market rate. These subsidies remained in place until 2008. The goal of the Taiwanese government's housing policies was to make owner-occupied housing more affordable by subsidizing the mortgage interest rate, increasing the maximum amount of mortgage loans eligible for subsidy, and relaxing the requirement that only lower-income households would be eligible for subsidies. These subsidies enhanced and strengthened the linkage between housing and credit markets.

The housing subsidy policy in Taiwan has for a long time overwhelmingly concentrated on promoting home ownership, but has done very little to subsidize renters, whose income is usually lower and who also need more subsidies than home-buyers. As a result, many studies have indicated the inequality of housing subsidies, which is a critical issue in Taiwan.

Housing Cycles and Policy against Bubbles

Taiwan has experienced high growth rates in housing prices over the past 40 years. Exhibit 20.3 shows Taipei's household disposal income and pre-sale housing prices in real term from 1973 to 2010. During this 38-year period, the nominal average annual price increase was 9.96 percent, but the real price increase was 5.53 percent. The standard deviation of average nominal housing prices was almost 25.34 percent over the sample period, indicating that housing prices were highly volatile and that there were periods of remarkable fluctuations in their rate of growth.

There were four cycle periods: 1972–1974, 1978–1980, 1987–1989, and 2004–2010. Nominal housing prices doubled during the first and second cycle,

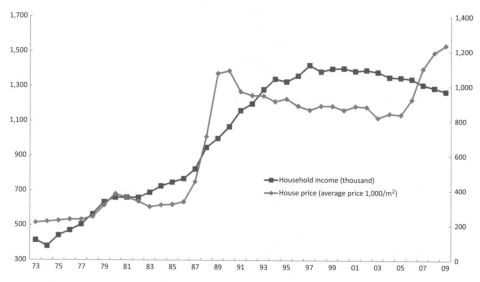

Exhibit 20.3 Taipei Household Incomes and Housing Prices from 1973 to 2010 (in Real Terms)

Sources: Household Income: Taipei City Statistical Abstract and Taipei Country Statistics; Housing Prices: Taiwan Real Estate Research Centre, National Chengchi University.

tripled in the third, and have almost doubled so far in the present cycle. The last year of the first cycle period was 1974, which was followed by three years of recession. During the second cycle, the real price increases were 27.5 percent and 20.3 percent in 1979 and 1980, respectively. Prices then declined by an average of 3.6 percent per annum over the next six years. In 1987, 1988, and 1989, real prices increased by 33.3 percent, 69.5 percent, and 43.2 percent, respectively. During the third cycle the rate of real price increase peaked in the third quarter of 1989 and then declined by 14.1 percent in 1991. The housing market went into a very long recession of about 13 years after the third boom and then began to rise again after 2004. Thus far (up to 2010), housing prices have increased by almost 70 percent in the city of Taipei.

In terms of periods of expansion and contraction, we can see that the first and second cycles had an approximately two-year expansion period and a seven-year contraction period. The third cycle had a three-year expansion period and a 13-year contraction period, and the recent cycle so far has had a five-year expansion period. One phenomenon found in the Taiwan housing market is that expansion periods are short, whereas contraction periods are long. This appears to be different from the housing markets in other developed countries, such as the United States, where there are long expansion and short contraction periods. If this phenomenon continues to persist, one might expect the Taiwanese housing market to go into a long recession period after this boom. Furthermore, when periods of expansion and contraction increase, it means that the degree of volatility is decreasing. This appears to suggest that the Taiwan housing market is becoming more stable, which has been observed in other developed countries.

The First Cycle (1972–1974)

The rise in housing prices in the early 1970s was commonly understood as caused by the oil embargo. Being a small open economy, Taiwan is rapidly affected by external shocks caused by changes in international prices and currencies. The effects of the oil embargo were worldwide and were especially severe in oil-importing countries. Because 75 percent of energy and all oil is imported, the housing market as well as the whole economy was seriously affected by this crisis. The sudden increase in oil prices led directly to high inflation in most commodities. The oil embargo caused inflation rates to jump around 80 percent from 1973 to 1974. It also led to a sharp rise in the cost of construction and the cost of capital on the supply side, and triggered the expectation of housing price increases.

Money supply is believed to be an important factor behind the housing price rise. Money supply increased rapidly in the early 1970s. Before the oil embargo, Taiwan had a few years of high economic growth, which maintained a high rate of around 12 to 13 percent from 1971 to 1973. The trade surplus caused foreign money expansion and also led to increases in the domestic money supply. In this period, lower interest rates further caused an expansion of domestic money supply of more than 30 percent and stimulated investment in the housing market.

Controlling inflation has always been a primary objective of Taiwan's macroeconomic policy. In order to stabilize the inflation caused by the oil embargo, the government proposed some programs. In 1973 and 1974, the government announced the "Economic Stabilization Program" in order to control the negative effect of inflation on economic growth. Programs relating to the housing market included credit restrictions and termination of permits on vacant development land. Because some developers hold vacant land and delay the timing for development, this program forced them to release vacant land in the market in order to increase housing supply. Mortgage interest rates also rose from 11.3 percent in 1973 to 16.5 percent in 1974. These policies successfully stabilized the economy as well as housing prices.

The Second Cycle (1978–1980)

After four to five years of recession in the housing market, housing prices began to rise again in 1978. The factors that stimulated the increase in housing prices were similar to those that caused the first boom. Inflation caused by oil price increases again resulted in higher costs on the supply side and expectations of price increases on the demand side. Money supply was also considered as a secondary factor. The causes behind the money supply expansion were the low interest rates, high economic growth, and the trade surplus. These are also the same causes as the causes of the first boom.

Again to dampen the real estate boom, the government proposed programs similar to those in the first boom period, such as termination of construction permits, an increase in land value for tax base, and so forth. In addition, zoning was approved in the councils of the cities of Taipei and Kaohsiung, which caused developers to build more houses ahead of these changes. These measures again successfully brought the boom to a halt. Unfortunately, worldwide economic recession began after this boom and affected the Taiwanese economy. This economic slump affected the investment demand and also severely damaged the construction industry. About 13 percent of property developers declared bankruptcy by 1981.

The Third Cycle (1987–1989)

The main cause of housing price increases during this boom was the rapid expansion of the money supply. The inflation rate on the general price level was relatively stable and did not play a significant role in this boom compared with the previous booms. The primary reason behind the increase of the money supply was the consistently high economic growth rate of around 12 to 13 percent. First, credit restrictions were relaxed in 1987, causing the expansion of lending volume to the housing sector by banks. Second, a change in the foreign exchange rate regime and the liberalization of foreign exchange control (removal of foreign exchange limitations) induced speculative activity in the foreign exchange market, causing foreign money to flow into and out of domestic financial markets. Taiwan's currency finally appreciated by almost 40 percent, and this raised the level of domestic money supply. Foreign exchange reserves increased rapidly during 1985–1987 and clearly displayed a jump just before the third housing price boom. The increase in foreign exchange reserves reflects the rapid economic growth in Taiwan and appears to show a higher correlation with housing prices than the GNP. Third, expropriation for reserved land for public facilities caused large amounts of compulsory purchase cash to go into the investment market. The government reserved large amounts of land for public facilities, which were supposed to be mandatorily purchased within 15 years of 1973. However, because of budget shortages, the government had difficulty in purchasing during these years. The government finally prepared a budget in 1989 and gave a large amount of cash to the owners of reserved land. The owners of reserved land invested this cash in the asset markets. In addition, due to the fewer investment assets in Taiwan, the expansion of money supply flowed into the stock market and the property market as a store of wealth and created this amazing boom in both markets. Real housing prices increased threefold and the stock price index dramatically rose from 2,000 to 12,000 points during this period.

The government again proposed programs such as raising interest rates and loan controls to reduce the money supply in 1989. The Central Bank adopted selected credit control measures, including stopping uncollateralized loans for land and restricting the amount of construction loans and LTV below 50 percent. This helped to push the economy into recession and weakened the housing market considerably. Despite success in smoothing out the housing price increases, housing prices increased three-fold, reaching a peak in 1989 and then settling down into a long quiet period until 2004.

The Fourth Cycle (2004–2010)

After 13 years of recession from 1990 to 2003 in the Taiwan housing market, housing prices began to rise again in 2004. However, the difference of this cycle from the previous cycles is that it occurred in the major metropolitan areas but was not widely spread out in Taiwan. The Taipei metropolitan area had a much higher housing price growth rate than the other cities. This phenomenon is fundamentally related to unbalanced resource distribution in Taiwanese regional development because Taipei is the political and economic center and has more job opportunities than other cities. Another difference is that this cycle has lasted much longer in terms of expansion and contraction as compared with the previous cycles. This cycle is basically fueled by low interest rates, which give business conglomerates and speculators leverage to play the market. This record-low interest-rate environment may prolong the bubble-to-burst cycle.

Other factors attributed to Taipei's rising housing prices may include the surging stock market, reduced estate and gift taxes, an easing of cross-Taiwan Strait regulations and a lack of confidence in derivatives or other sophisticated financial instruments. This long-lasting cycle may be partly driven by expectations of Chinese investments. In 2010, Memorandums of Understanding (MOUs) on financial supervisory cooperation signed by Taiwan and China and the Economic Cooperation Framework Agreement (ECFA) between the two countries widened market openings for Taiwan and China. These closer trade ties with China have increased investors' expectations.

In June 2010, the Central Bank raised the re-discount rate and secured the financing interest rate and short-term interest rate by 0.125 percent respectively. The Central Bank also adopted targeted credit tightening measures in specific areas (including the city of Taipei and 10 cities in Taipei County). Under these measures, if those who are already homeowners want to apply for mortgages for newly acquired residential properties in those specific areas, the mortgages are subject to the following three stipulations: (1) approved loans must not exceed 70 percent of the value of the collateral, (2) no grace periods can be allotted, and (3) no additional loans such as home renovation loans against the same collateral can be taken. Other anti-bubble measures taken by the government included increasing the supply of low-cost housing and discontinuing the sale of government-owned lands. The

Ministry of Finance is also contemplating the implementation of a progressive real-estate tax system.

Because of such measures, there were signs that housing prices would decline as transaction volume began to contract. However, none of these steps were found to be very effective in taming Taipei real-estate prices, and housing prices remained resilient. This is also probably due to historically low interest rates. In addition, at the same time, the government carried out a series of stimulus measures, such as extending the expiration of construction license permits and offering additional preferential mortgage loans for home buyers as well as opening local real estate to investors from China. Housing prices are still increasing.

An Estimation of Housing Bubbles

Chang, Chen, Teng, and Yang (2009) and Chang, Chen, and Yang (2010) quantitatively analyzed bubbles for the Taipei housing market. These two studies derived the market fundamental housing price as the sum of the expected present values of rent or permanent housing income. Then they used a state space model to estimate the exact bubble values. The underlying hypotheses are that deviations from the fundamental outcome are bubbles. The rent model assumes that the present value of rent is the fundamental value of housing. The income model assumes that the affordable values are the fundamental values of housing.

By using the housing prices in Taipei from the first quarter of 1973 to the first quarter of 2010, it can be seen that bubbles are statistically significant in Taipei for 1988 to 1990 and 2004 to 2010 for their models. Exhibit 20.4 shows the estimation of the housing bubbles. The bubble accounts for 57 percent of the housing price from the housing rent and income models. The bubble prices estimated by the two models for the present are close to 43 percent of the housing price.

A Survey of the 2010 Housing Market

Based on a 2010 housing demand survey conducted in five major urban areas by the Construction and Planning Agency, the Ministry of the Interior stated that new homeowners and first-time self-use buyers composed the largest portion

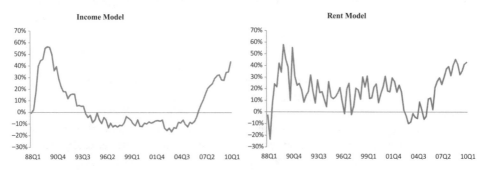

Exhibit 20.4 Percentage of Housing Bubble to Housing Price
Source: Chin-Oh Chang, Ming-Chi Chen, Chih-Yuan Yang (2010), "Re-examination of Taipei Housing Bubbles," Taiwan Real Estate Center, National Chengchi University.

(58 percent), and owners for investment purposes accounted for 17 percent. The Taipei County area has the largest portion of first-time self-use buyers, whereas Taipei City has a higher percentage of buyers for investment purposes; Kaohsiung has a higher percentage of buyers for replacement purposes. Among all purchases, secondhand houses/apartments accounted for the largest portion (62 percent), followed by newly built (31 percent), pre-sale (6 percent), and foreclosure properties (1 percent). Taichung has the highest pre-sale percentage as compared with the others, whereas Kaohsiung has the highest foreclosure percentage. The price is negotiable for up to 11 percent on average below listing price and Taipei has the largest price negotiation range (13 percent). The average searching period was six and one-half months, and the average number of houses viewed by the purchaser was 13. In these five major urban areas, the average housing price-to-income ratio (PIR) was 7.7 for homebuyers, and the monthly mortgage payment over income ratio was 31.6 percent. Taipei City has a higher PIR (10.9) and mortgage-payment-over-income ratio (43.0 percent), whereas Kaohsiung has a lower PIR (6.4) and mortgage-payment-over-income ratio (25.1 percent).

HOUSING AFFORDABILITY AND POLICY

Housing affordability problem is always a major concern for housing policy in Taiwan. Rapid economic growth in Taiwan has resulted in both income growth and monetary growth. The growth in income has increased residential demand for houses, and monetary growth has caused further investment demand for houses. These strong demands for houses have caused housing prices to rise quickly and have produced heavy housing cost burdens for households. This burden is especially heavy in the Taipei area, where strong investment demand for housing persists.

Housing Affordability

There are several possible underlying causes of Taiwan's affordability problem. First, its high population density is the fundamental cause, as is the case in other Asian cities. Second, the Chinese traditional preference to own property could be another reason. One characteristic of Taiwan's housing market is its comparatively large number of owner-occupied dwellings and a relatively small rental sector. Third, housing policy has been considered as a low priority in Taiwan's development agenda, with public housing comprising less than 5 percent of the total housing in the market. Fourth, financial liberalization and loose monetary policy might have caused the PIR to shift even higher. Domestic monetary growth has been considered as an important factor in explaining housing price fluctuations in Taiwan. In a rapidly growing economy, economic growth will certainly cause income and housing prices to rise. However, it is questionable that housing price will climb faster than income in the long run because houses will eventually become unaffordable.

    Chen, Tsai, and Chang (2007) examined the relationship between housing prices and income in Taiwan over the past few decades. They found that the

PIR has varied from 5 to 13 because income shows a steady growth, but housing prices shoot up every other time. Their empirical analysis provides evidence of a long-term equilibrium between housing prices and income, although short-run deviations exist, explaining why the PIR ratio sometimes climbs up to 13. This study suggests that housing and income may not always correspond to each other but will return to an equilibrium level in the long run. This study also suggests that, due to inefficiency in the Taiwan housing market, the market may take quite a long time to recover. If the housing affordability problem becomes very serious, the government should act more quickly to intervene with policies to help the ratio recover sooner. In recent years, the housing bubble has widened the gap between the real estate haves and have-nots. Wealthy people with substantial capital can buy luxury condominium units, whereas workers with average salaries cannot buy even a regular apartment unit. However, Taiwan's government is still hesitating to dampen the real estate boom because of its low economic growth since the U.S. financial crisis.

Housing Policy

As a result of the increases in housing prices over the past five years, there have been considerable differences in housing prices in Taiwan's main metropolitan regions. Prices have risen most sharply in Taipei due to strong demand. The sharp increases in housing prices in the Taipei metropolitan area have created a heavy burden for low- and middle-income earners and salaried employees. This phenomenon is closely related to factors such as limited land supply, regional development, and the spatial distribution of industries. Because the real-estate sector is an important part of the overall economy, the Council for Economic Planning and Development (CEPD, Cabinet) has drawn up a proposal for a Plan to Enhance the Soundness of the Housing Market, with the aim of promoting socioeconomic stability and meeting the basic housing needs of low- and middle-income earners and the salaried class. This plan is based on the six core principles of (1) tailoring measures to the needs of localities and populations, (2) acting moderately but effectively, (3) stressing soundness and stability, (4) pursuing social equity, (5) maintaining information transparency, and (6) taking relevant complementary measures. It contains 21 working principles and 44 specific measures to address the six tasks of achieving a balance of housing supply and demand in the Taipei metropolitan region, helping low- and middle-income earners and salaried employees increase their ability to purchase or rent a home, improving housing information, enhancing risk management for real estate loans, enhancing social fairness, and taking relevant complementary measures.

In February 2011, the Finance Ministry proposed a luxury tax, which targets real-estate speculation and expensive goods and services. The plan calls for a luxury tax of 15 percent on properties sold within a year of purchase. Although this luxury tax will be not launched until mid-2011, it has already exerted a strong influence and is now cooling down the housing market. On the other hand, Central Bank is also trying to strengthen the central bank's audits to block speculative funds from flowing into the housing market.

FUTURE MARKET REVOLUTION IN TAIWAN

Two important policies came into effect recently for the long-term development of the housing market. The first concerns real-estate securitization, which helps to liquidate mortgages for financial institution and to provide an effective channel for real-estate developers. Real-estate securitization also helps to direct investment demand for real estate from the real-asset market to the financial-asset market. The policy of real-estate securitization aims to regulate the fluctuating real-estate market. Reverse mortgage is another important housing policy. The population in Taiwan is aging rapidly and reverse mortgage can solve the problems of senior citizens for both residential and living expense.

Real-Estate Securitization

Taiwanese real-estate finance has made substantial progress since 2000, when the secondary-mortgage market and real-estate securitization policies began to take effect. The Financial Asset Securitization Act was promulgated in 2002, and Taiwan's Real Estate Securitization Act was enacted in 2003. The Financial Asset Securitization Act allows Taiwan's financial institutions to create mortgage-backed securities (MBS). On the equity side, the Real Estate Securitization Act allows two types of real estate securitization structures to be created: Real Estate Investment Trusts (REITs) and Real Estate Asset Trusts (REATs).

The creation of mortgage-side securitization of real estate was intended to help Taiwanese financial institutions transform their mortgages into liquid and tradable capital market instruments to replenish their funds. Cash flows from mortgages should become the focus of the banking and securities industries for mortgage pricing in the secondary mortgage markets. However, the liquidity of mortgages is not a major concern for current Taiwanese financial institutions because credit has over-expanded. Thus far, there have been very few MBSs created in Taiwan.

Taiwan's REITs are basically similar to those of other countries but with some major differences. For example, Taiwanese REITs only allow the operation type of investment trust, not the corporation type. In addition, Taiwanese REITs do not allow investing in real-estate development activities. The first REIT, FuBon REIT number one, was listed on the exchange in 2005; thereafter, seven other REITs were listed consecutively, which increased market capitalization to US$1,588 million by the first quarter of 2009. This activity is nonetheless small compared with other Asian countries. On the other hand, the REATs were established to first hold defined real estate for specific periods of time, and then to raise funds in exchange for the properties. Rental and other incomes generated from the properties are also distributed to investors during the holding periods.

Although real-estate securitization opens up new sources of capital through public market listing (providing a good channel for developers or real-estate owners to raise funds), the impact of securitization in the real-estate capital markets is not strong. This is because Taiwan only allows REITs/REATs to invest in the properties that have produced income, but not in real-estate developing projects. In addition, because the low property rental rates have caused very low yields of Taiwanese REITs/REATs compared with other countries, current Taiwanese REITs/REATs are not attractive investments.

Reverse Mortgages

The Taiwanese government plans to design a feasibility and implementation plan for a reverse mortgage program for senior citizens. The CEPD plans to introduce this program in 2011, with "house-rich, cash-poor" senior citizens being the main targets. Chang (2009) proposed three reverse mortgage models. The first reverse mortgage design allows a homeowner to defer his obligation to repay the loan until he dies or leaves or the home is sold. The second one is sale-and-leaseback, which requires that a homeowner sell his or her property. However, the original homeowner can pay a small rent to remain in the house. The third mode is a social-care scheme, in which a homeowner donates his property to social welfare organizations, or the home-owner's property is held in trust and a social-welfare organization is the beneficiary. The organizations must then take care of the home-owner until he or she dies.

Reverse mortgages, sale/leasebacks or social-care schemes are very useful for helping senior citizens who have low incomes but a house of their own to boost their disposable income. Reverse mortgages are simply loans made to a homeowner against the property's equity. The money can be released in one lump sum or in multiple payments and is repaid when the property is sold or refinanced by the borrower's heirs after he or she dies. The mortgage allows seniors, when needed, to use their own properties as guarantees to obtain funds for post-retirement expenses including medical care fees. The sale/leasebacks option would allow the elderly to sell their homes to insurance firms, which in turn offer the seniors annuities based on the value of their property, while still allowing them to reside in their own homes as tenants. The social-care scheme, which was developed by Chang (2009), combines social care and donations or a trust system. Social-welfare organizations will take care of the elderly and keep their property in either a donation or trust system.

Taiwan has a rapidly aging population. At the end of 2009, the number of people who were 65 years and older reached 10.5 percent of the overall population, and this figure may rise to 14.7 percent in the next 10 years, according to estimations by the CEPD. Mortgages allow homeowners, usually retirees, to borrow money in the form of annual payments that are charged against the equity of their property. By offering a reverse-mortgage system, the Taiwanese government provides an opportunity to help property owners aged 65 and above in difficult financial situations to enjoy a higher standard of living.

However, reverse mortgages may cause the next subprime crisis. Some of the same U.S. lenders that helped drive the real estate boom with loans to home buyers who could not afford the payments are now targeting seniors. Taiwan should treat schemes that help the elderly live off the equity built up in their homes as commercial products rather than social-welfare benefits to ensure that the system can be sustained. The policy could be cost-free for the government except that it would be obliged to take over a property when most of its value has been converted into payments to the borrower, who will continue to receive subsidies from the government for as long as the borrower lives.

This extra cost, however, should not be seen as a burden since it has long been one of the government's responsibilities to look after the nation's financially marginalized groups, especially elderly citizens who may be homeless and penniless. It is never too early for the government to begin with the creation of a social welfare safety net for Taiwan's growing population of seniors. Another question that needs to be addressed is whether the government should invite the private insurance or banking sectors to participate in the system. The answer in the foreseeable future may not be possible since private companies generally seek a profitable business model when deciding whether to enter a potential market.

The great incentive behind the growing popularity of reverse mortgages, at least in the United States, is that if a borrower outlives the loan's term, he or she can continue to stay in the property while being entitled to government subsidies. However, when a borrower sells his or her home, he or she can use part of the proceeds to repay the lender's loan plus interest and other fees, whereas the remaining equity in the property still belongs to the borrower or his or her estate. This is a losing deal for private companies.

Additionally, the U.S. experience shows that more than 90 percent of reverse mortgage borrowers prefer a safe plan, such as that provided by the federal-government-insured U.S. Home Equity Conversion Mortgage program. Therefore, it is generally agreed upon that full government support will be key to the success of this initiative in Taiwan.

CONCLUSION

The Taiwan housing market has been quite volatile with four booms having occurred over the past 40 years. Measures by the government have successfully dampened price increases during the first three booms. However, housing prices have continued to rise during the current boom since 2004. The U.S. financial crisis occurred in 2007 and hit Taiwan's economy resulting in low and negative economic growth in 2008 and 2009. However, the Taiwan housing market appears to be intact and housing prices continue to climb. The government, so far, has not used strong policy measures to dampen housing price increases. Economic growth slowdowns over the past 20 years and the U.S. financial crisis have caused the government to hesitate using strong measures during the current housing market boom. Historically low interest rates might have sustained housing prices, preventing them from bursting. As the price-to-income ratio increased to a new high in the Taipei area, the government needed to take effective action to reduce the housing burden. For a long time, the Taiwan housing market has come under pressure from demographic influence, scarcity of land, and fast economic growth. However, a low birth rate and the slow economic growth over recent years should lead the housing market toward different developments. For the future housing market, the government should establish housing policy from a new line of thinking.

REFERENCES

Central Bank of China. 2010. "Financial Statistics Monthly" (in Chinese).

Chang, Chin-Oh. 2009. "The Three Designed Models of Reverse Mortgage for Taiwan" (in Chinese). Paper presented at Reverse Mortgage Conference, Taipei.

Chang, Chin-Oh. 2009. "Housing Demand Survey Second Half Year of 2009" (in Chinese). Construction and Planning Agency, Ministry of the Interior.

Chang, Chin-Oh, Ming-Chi Chen, and Chih-Yuan Yang. 2010. "Re-examination of Taipei Housing Bubbles" (in Chinese). Taiwan Real Estate Center, National Chengchi University.

Chang, Chin-Oh, Ming-Chi Chen, Hsiao-Jung Teng, and Chih-Yuan Yang. 2009. "Is There a Housing Bubble in Taipei? Housing Price vs. Rent and Housing Price vs. Income." *Journal of Housing Study* 18:2, 1–22 (in Chinese).

Chen, Ming-Chi, I-Chun Tsai, and Chin-Oh Chang. 2007. "House Prices and Household Income: Do They Move Apart? Evidence from Taiwan." *Habitat International* 31, 243–256.

Construction and Planning Agency, Ministry of the Interior. 2005. "2005 Report on the Housing Status Survey" (in Chinese).

Construction and Planning Agency, Ministry of the Interior. 2007. "Housing Statistics Annual Report" (in Chinese).

ABOUT THE AUTHORS

DR. CHIN-OH CHANG is Distinguished Professor in the Department of Land Economics and the Director of Taiwan Real Estate Research Center, National Chengchi University, Taipei, Taiwan. He received his Architecture Master's degree at MIT (Massachusetts Institute of Technology) in 1980, and a City and Regional Planning PhD degree at the University of Pennsylvania in 1986. He was President of the Asian Real Estate Society (AsRES) in 1997–1998, and the President of Global Chinese Real Estate Congress (GCREC) in 2009–2010. His research is published in *Urban Studies, Housing Studies, Journal of Property Research, Habitat International, International Real Estate Review,* and several other journals. He has concentrated his research in areas related to housing and land policy, real-estate investment, and financial analysis.

DR. MING-CHI CHEN is a Professor of Finance at National Sun Yat-sen University in Taiwan. He received his MS degree in Business Administration from Pennsylvania State University in 1993 and his PhD degree in Land Economy from the University of Cambridge in 1999. His primary research interest is in real-estate finance, economics, and investment; applied econometrics; and project financing. He has published in many international journals such as the *Journal of Risk and Insurance, Journal of Real Estate Finance an Economics, Journal of Housing Economics, Journal of Real Estate Portfolio Management, Journal of Property Investment and Finance,* and so forth. He currently serves as an editor of *Journal of Housing Study* (Taiwan).

PART VI

Avoiding Contagion in Other Markets

CHAPTER 21

Australia's Economic Response to the Global Financial Crisis and Its Housing Markets

DOGAN TIRTIROGLU
Professor and Chair of Banking, The University of Adelaide Business School

This chapter first provides a summary of the Australian banking and real-estate markets and then discusses policy developments to fight off the adverse observed and expected consequences of the global financial crisis (GFC), and concludes with a review of the current state of both markets.

Australia's geography has direct and indirect influences on its financial and, especially, housing markets. Australia sits mainly on an unusual island continent, which is wide, large, far away from the other landmasses of the Earth, and is fundamentally structured as a desert with limited water but rich mineral and mining resources. With a population of about 22 million, a great majority of its people are immigrants. Immigration is still and will continue to be an important source of new blood and richness in culture and wealth for Australia. While the earlier immigrant generations were of European descent (due to the state's immigration policy and preferences), immigration from several Asian countries has been the dominant trend within the past 20 years. The number of Australian residents with an Asian background is expected to overtake that with a European background within a few decades.

A vast territory of Australia is comprised of a wild, arid, harsh, and even deadly desert, raising major obstacles for human settlement and also restricting the supply of usable/feasible land for real-estate development, among other consequences. Therefore, Australia's population has been thickly settled around cities, established nearby the oceans that surround the continent. These cities enjoy relatively easy access to the much-needed water resources. The main five historically visible cities, in the order of highest to lowest current populations, are Sydney, Melbourne, Brisbane, Perth, and Adelaide. About 13 million people, out of approximately 22 million, live in these cities. The first three are located on the eastern seaboard by the Pacific Ocean; Perth is on the western seaboard with access to the Indian and Southern Oceans, and Adelaide is on the southern seaboard facing the Southern Ocean. The Timor and Arafura seas also envelope Australia from above in the north, with the cities of Darwin and Cairns situated in the middle-north and northeastern parts of the continent, respectively. Canberra is the capital and maintains a small population.

From a political viewpoint, Australia has expressed clearly its choice of being a member of the Asia-Pacific community of nations for some time now. This explicitly stated choice has substantial and immense implications for Australia's current and future economic performance/development and its political reach in the world. Given that consensus is growing for the view that Asia will be the center and leading force of economic growth and development in the world in this century, Australia's choice to be a key member of this region has to be kept in mind for analyzing its economic and political performance. Commentators point out that reliance on China's and, to a lesser extent, India's economic performance, as both countries keep demanding more of Australia's resources every day, has been an important protective shield for Australia so far during the GFC. However, this direct reliance also poses future risks and requires not only strategies to hedge against value fluctuations in the mineral markets but also spillovers that can arise from economic bust cycles in these and other surrounding countries in this region.

Australia's experience with the GFC has so far been recognized as one of the few stories of success. The response of the Labor Party government, headed by then-Prime Minister Kevin Rudd, by engaging in fiscal stimulus is today being credited for the country's almost full employment, still increasing property values, and its vibrant economy.

Lending Sector in Australia: Before the GFC

The Australian banking sector is highly concentrated and observes a universal banking system. Its main residents, in the order of highest to lowest total assets as of June 2009, are Commonwealth Bank of Australia (CBA), National Australia Bank (NAB), Westpac Banking Corporation (Westpac), and Australia New Zealand Bank (ANZ) (see Seeking Alpha 2009).

As of September 2008, the Australian banking system did not have an explicit deposit insurance system. Instead credit rating agencies, such as Standard and Poor's or Moody's, provided, on a regular basis, default ratings for the Australian banks. Thus, the market discipline, not the regulatory supervision, appeared to be a key ingredient of the architecture of the banking system in Australia. Of course, a curse or blessing of the GFC—depending on one's views—has been the introduction of 100 percent deposit insurance and the reincarnation of the "too big to fail hypothesis" (TBTF) for the banks and other large financial institutions in Australia.[1]

The variable rate mortgages (VRMs) are by far the most dominant mortgage contracts in Australia. While the monthly mortgage payments on VRM contracts are amortized over a relatively long period, such as 20 years, the coupon interest rate of a VRM contract varies over time. It responds immediately to the regularly scheduled monthly announcements, by the Reserve Bank of Australia (RBA), of changes in the term structure of the Treasury securities. The changes in the coupon interest rate trigger re-amortization of the outstanding mortgage balance over the remaining time period. Therefore, a VRM mortgage holder faces the risk of increases or decreases—sometimes substantial and sudden—in his or her cash outlays for monthly mortgage payments. The VRMs are recourse (i.e., without limited liability) contracts and do not offer a put option to the borrowers (see the following section). This aspect of VRMs resembles that of Canadian mortgage contracts.[2]

Australia's legal system is based on English common law. The legal system does not allow for the tax deductibility of interest payments on residential property, but allows for that on investment properties.

THE LOAN-TO-VALUE RATIO: INTERSECTION OF HOUSING AND LENDING MARKETS

The loan-to-value (LTV) ratio is where the banking (or lending) market meets the housing market and allows one to examine the interdependence or co-existence between both markets in response to a policy development or a shock in one or both of the markets. Our analysis begins with the fixed-rate mortgage (FRM) loan contracts, which are very common in the United States,[3] to establish a benchmark for the movements of the LTV ratio.

The market value of any FRM loan moves inversely in response to a change in the term structure of interest rates. The time-path of the market value of a FRM loan is dynamic and volatile over the life of the loan. Holding all else constant, the time path of the *book value* of a FRM loan is, however, pre-determined, smoothly declining, and not a market-driven variable. Of course, any sufficiently large difference between the market and book values of loans is a source of risk and requires careful risk management techniques and means.

The U.S. legal system endows mortgage loan borrowers with a set of embedded options.[4] These options affect both borrowers' and lenders' behavior. Refinancing and default are the most obvious and recognized options. When the term structure of interest rates shifts sufficiently down, the borrowers can exercise their refinancing (i.e., call) option to be able to obtain a new mortgage loan at the new and reduced coupon rate. Down movements in the term structure of the interest rates correspond *usually* to excess liquidity in financial markets and an economic boom cycle. The default option arises from the *non-recourse* (i.e., limited liability) characteristic of mortgage loans in the United States. This option enables a borrower to walk away (i.e., put) from the outstanding balance of a mortgage loan and the pertinent collateral property without lender recourse on the borrower's other assets. The exercise of the default option occurs mainly during sufficiently deep bust cycles.[5]

Both embedded options have the power to alter or terminate abruptly, albeit for different reasons and under different economic conditions, the pre-determined and smoothly declining time path of the outstanding book value balance of an FRM loan. Lenders need to be alert about these options and the risks that they may induce on lenders and also need to price their products in view of these potential risks.

In the meantime, the denominator of the LTV ratio refers to the *market value* of a property. It should be large enough, as the collateral, to secure the outstanding book value of any kind of mortgage loan. Value is entirely sensitive to any market factor. Its fluctuations are unpredictable, even sudden, sometimes wild, and are rooted in the underlying demand and supply factors with an effect on the housing markets at any time.[6]

From a risk-management perspective, left not hedged, the combination of the smooth and pre-determined time path of the book value of a FRM loan and the dynamic, volatile, and unpredictable time path of the value of a property *can* pose substantial and potentially deadly risks. The richly informative history of repeated bank failures and their consequences in the United States and elsewhere is a reminder of these risks.

The VRM Loans and the Inter-temporal Behavior of the LTV Ratio

As indicated above, a great majority of the Australian mortgage contracts is of the VRM type.[7] Further, VRMs also constitute a large proportion of Australian lenders' loan portfolios. These contracts are not endowed with either the refinancing or the default options. The coupon interest rates adjust fast to both up or down changes in the term structure of Treasury securities. Such fast coupon rate adjustments preempt naturally any need for refinancing. Thus, the Australian lenders do not assume the risks from the loan refinancing activity and also do not have to worry about finding risk management solutions for keeping the market and book values of loans within a reasonable distance to each other.[8] Further, the recourse characteristic of the VRMs removes, to a very large extent, the default option from these mortgage contracts. Thus, the architecture of the Australian credit market has traditionally offered the Australian lenders a considerably more stable lending environment than their counterparts in the United States and, to a lesser extent, Canada. But one must be aware of the risk-shifting role of the VRMs. These contracts generate dynamic time paths as a function of the shifts in the term structure of interest rates. Coupon adjustments, while maintaining the market value of the loan at or close to its par value, periodically induce changes in the outstanding book value of mortgage loans. Hence, these contracts help ultimately to pass the burden of the interest-rate risk from the lenders' shoulders to the borrowers' shoulders, rendering the need for risk management at the homeowner level. This is currently missing in Australia as it is missing almost everywhere else in the world (see Shiller 1993). This inadequacy and shortcomings in addressing the risk management of the interest-rate risk for the borrowers may expose any similarly structured financial system to systemic risks, especially under severe duress conditions.

The VRMs substantially help lenders with their asset-liability management issues (i.e., immunization) in their balance sheets. Thus, the inter-temporal behavior of the *numerator* of the LTV ratios in Australia is highly likely to be free from potentially abrupt distortions and risks that stem from refinancing and/or default activities. This observation also underlies the obvious conclusion that the Australian policymakers' efforts to ward off against the adverse consequences of the GFC must have *mainly* targeted the inter-temporal behavior of the *denominator* of the LTV ratio. That, I believe, has indeed been the case in Australia and is explored further next.

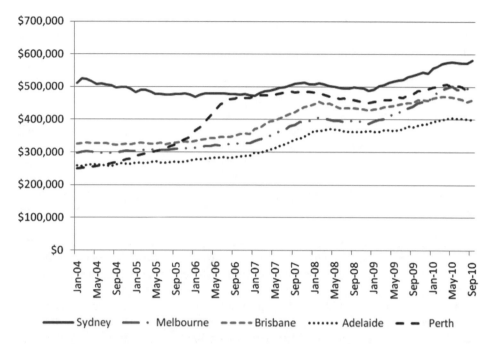

Exhibit 21.1 RP Data-Rismark Home Value Index, Recalculated at September 2010 Median Price in Australia's Five Major Cities
Source: RP Data—Rismark Home Value Indices.

AUSTRALIAN HOUSE-PRICE DYNAMICS

Australia's rental yields are consistent with those of developed economies; yet, Australia has the least affordable housing market among the six surveyed (developed) countries (Fifth Annual Demographia International Housing Affordability Survey 2009). Whether the house price patterns in Australia are consistent with a bubble phenomenon is without any rigorous empirical evidence so far.

Exhibit 21.1 provides a graphic view of the recent dynamics of the housing prices in five Australian cities. The time paths of the house prices in Melbourne, Brisbane, and Adelaide resemble, to some extent, one another while those for Sydney and Perth exhibit considerable differences from each other and from others'. The volatility appears to be the lowest for Sydney and the highest for Perth during this period. In all five cities, house prices appear to have declined between the third quarter of 2007 and first quarter of 2009. Starting around late 2008 and early 2009, house prices in Sydney and Melbourne exhibit sharp recovery, followed by declines in late 2009; house prices in Brisbane exhibit first a recovery and then a decline in late 2009 and 2010. House prices in Adelaide continue to decline and remain flat well into 2010.

House prices in Sydney and Perth exhibit visibly different characteristics over time. House prices in Sydney are never below those in other cities and were almost twice as high as others' in early 2004. Perth prices make a steep jump between early 2004 and third quarter of 2006. The difference in the house prices for

Sydney and Perth was less than AU$7,000 in October 2006 and increased in favor of Sydney beyond that. Price patterns in Perth between mid-2004 and mid-2006 were breathtaking. Perth has experienced an unprecedented boom in its mining and minerals sector. Harvesting natural resources and exporting them, especially copper, to China and other resource hungry economies in the region was the root cause of this boom. The substantial jump pattern in Perth prices is consistent with the growth option arguments (Myers 1977). I explore this matter further later.

Exhibit 21.2 provides further and recent movements of house and unit prices.[9] While the 12-month property value changes from March 2009 to March 2010 show a strong performance, the same changes from September 2009 to September 2010 provide evidence of cooling in house prices. This downward movement is not surprising and reflects both policymakers' concerns and the risks that might have been growing within the Australian economy. One must acknowledge the sharp (considerable) turnaround in Perth (Brisbane) prices, respectively, and the strong performance, in spite of the cooling process, for properties in Melbourne and Sydney from September 2009 to September 2010. The sharp decline in the recent Perth prices is consistent, once again, with the growth option (out-of-the-money) arguments (Myers 1977).

Further, publicly available information (not reported in this paper) from the Australian Bureau of Statistics (ABS) demonstrates overall, strong, and continued recent growth in house prices, outperforming other asset classes, and growth rates in both CPI and GDP. One may take this growth pattern as a formation of a bubble in house prices, especially at a time when risk aversion all over the world has remained very high.[10] In fact, the RBA has been signaling cautiously its concern for the bubble phenomenon by repeatedly raising interest rates since late 2009.

THE GFC AND POLICY DEVELOPMENTS IN AUSTRALIA

Between July 2008 and September 2008 (right before the collapse of the Lehman Brothers), some key members of the Labor government—including then–Prime Minister Kevin Rudd—repeatedly made the point that high inflation, which they claimed was inherited from the previous Howard government of Conservatives (known as Liberals), had been the main economic concern confronting the Australian economy. During this period and perhaps even earlier, the Rudd government also repeated that Australia had a budget surplus and that interest rates were likely to go up. These comments came at a time when the rest of the world was grappling with the increasingly devastating adverse effects of the GFC, and it sounded as though Australian politicians were above, far away, and far removed from the GFC. Of course, the spectacular collapse of Lehman Brothers delivered to Australian politicians the reality of the reach, depth, and breadth of the GFC and forced them to change immediately their economic course.[11] Gone overnight was the talk about high inflation and budget surplus. The government took immediate steps and formulated policies to stimulate fiscally the economy to either avoid or minimize the observed (elsewhere) devastating consequences of the GFC. The spending programs of the government have quickly swallowed the budget surplus, pushed it into a large deficit over a short period of time, and resulted in full

Exhibit 21.2 Largest Australian Capital Cities, Median Dwelling Prices and Change in Values, March and September 2010

City	Median House Price	Median Unit Price	12-Month Change in House Values September 2010	12-Month Change in Unit Values September 2010	12-Month Change in House Values March 2010	12-Month Change in Unit Values March 2010
Sydney, NSW	$585,000	$426,000	8.90%	10.37%	+12.8%	+10.6%
Melbourne, Vic	$482,000	$410,000	13.16%	11.09%	+19.0%	+17.7%
Brisbane, Qld	$463,000	$375,000	1.93%	3.12%	+6.2%	+9.1%
Adelaide, SA	$405,000	$325,000	6.10%	5.69%	+9.1%	+7.5%
Perth, WA	$495,000	$412,500	0.36%	-3.25%	+7.9%	+7.9%

Note: "Units" in Australia are usually apartments.
Source: RP Data—Rismark Home Value Indices.

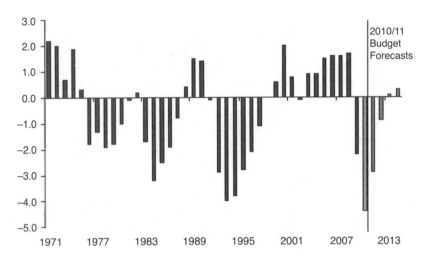

Exhibit 21.3   Australian Budget Deficit Patterns as a Percent of GDP
Source: Commonwealth Treasury.

employment. Exhibit 21.3 provides an inter-temporal perspective of Australia's budget deficit.

Currently, Australia has a relatively large budget deficit and is facing the economic and political aftermath of deficit spending.[12] Of course, the possibility of a delayed but effective hit of the GFC is not an unlikely outcome.

So, what fiscal stimulus policies had the Australian government implemented to avoid a collapse in the value of properties in the face of the GFC?

There have been mainly three policy measures (or modifications of existing policies) with a relatively direct impact on the Australian housing markets: (1) modifying an existing government program of financial incentives for first-time home-buyers, (2) substantially moving down the term structure of the interest rates on Treasury securities, and (3) introduction of 100 percent deposit insurance. All of these policy implementations aim at keeping stable the inter-temporal behavior of LTV. In particular, boosting or supporting property values—the denominator of the LTV ratio—has been a key policy objective and also success, at least so far, in Australia.

Boosting Financial Incentives for First-Time Homebuyers[13]

The first initiative expanded the scope of financial incentives (i.e., grants) of an existing housing program, known as First Home Owner Grant (FHOG) and first introduced on July 1, 2000, to first-time homebuyers. Under the original program, first-time homebuyers could receive a AU$7,000 once-off payment; this was to offset the cost of goods and services tax (i.e., GST). This incentive program was offered nationwide, but was funded by the states and territories.

In October 2008, the federal government boosted the incentives to stimulate the housing industry and to increase home affordability. The modified program offered an extra AU$14,000, available to first-home owners buying or building a

Exhibit 21.4   Australia's First-Home-Owner Grant Scheme Since Its Inception

Type	Scheme	Eligible Dates	Benefit
Established homes	First-home-owner Grant	July 1, 2000–present	$7,000
New homes/construction	First-home-owner Grant	July 1, 2000–present	$7,000
Established homes	First-home-owner boost	October 13, 2008– September 30, 2009	$7,000
New homes/construction	First-home-owner boost	October 13, 2008– September 30, 2009	$14,000
Established homes	First-home-owner Boost	October 1, 2009– December 31, 2009	$3,500
New homes/construction	First-home-owner boost	October 2009– December 31, 2009	$7,000

Source: Office of State Revenue (www.osr.nsw.gov.au/benefits/first_home/).

new home, as well as an extra AU$7,000 made available for established homes. The modified program was effective between October 14, 2008, and September 30, 2009. An extension to this program made it effective between October 1, 2009, and December 31, 2009. According to this extension, home-owners who were buying new homes or building a new home would be paid an extra AU$7,000 on top of the regular AU$7,000 once-off payment. Further, home-owners who were buying established homes were given AU$3,500 during this period. On January 1, 2010, the scheme returned to its default state of giving AU$7,000 to all first-time home-owners. Exhibit 21.4 summarizes this incentive program's evolution.

   All first-time home buyers are eligible irrespective of their income levels. Further, they do not pay any tax on this grant. There is, however, a cap on the maximum property price a first-time home buyer can pay and still be eligible for the grant. The cap is mostly around AU$750,000 across Australian states (with Australian Capital Territory and South Australia being the main exceptions with no limits).

Pushing Down the Term Structure of Interest Rates on Treasury Securities

The RBA compiles a lot of historical statistical data and makes it publicly available on its web site www.rba.gov.au/statistics/. I borrowed from the RBA's web site some exhibits and data to discuss the changes in the term structure and their effects on VRM rates. The RBA's cash rate (i.e., the overnight money-market interest rate used to express Australian monetary policy decisions) moved from 7.25 percent in August 2008 (first almost reached in March 2008) to 3.00 percent in May 2009 and remained there until September 2009. Exhibit 21.5 provides a comparative view of the relation of the rate on VRMs and the RBA's cash rate since 1994.

   It is clear from this exhibit and the RBA data (available at its web site) that the spread between the rate on banks' standard VRM contracts and the cash rate were stable and about 180 basis points between January 2002 and December 2007. It jumped to 195 basis points in January 2008 and exhibited a volatile and steeply

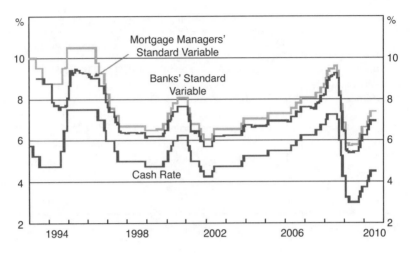

Exhibit 21.5   Australian Housing Interest Rates
Source: The Reserve Bank of Australia.

increasing time path, reaching 290 basis points in December 2009 and stabilizing around that point since then.

Exhibit 21.5 and the RBA data offer four additional pieces of anectodal and deductive evidence. First, the financial markets were far ahead—by at least nine months—of the Australian government in detecting and reacting to the GFC. Second, which follows from the first, banks had not passed one-for-one the RBA's cash rate reductions to their clients. This point is in spite of a huge effort by politicians and taxpayers to secure stability for banks.[14] Third, the increasing trend of the cash rate from 2002 until around 2008 suggests the persistent presence of inflationary pressures in Australia during this period. Fourth, Australia's experience with the GFC has not been as severe as the experience of the United States. The lowest for the RBA's cash rate was 3 percent in May 2009 (also the lowest since 1986). This rate has been on a steady rise since October 2009, reaching its current level of 4.75 percent in November 2010.

Introduction of 100 Percent Explicit Deposit Insurance

As indicated above, Australia was one of the few exceptions, among the world's wealthy nations with well-developed capital markets and financial intermediation, without an explicit deposit insurance scheme. Especially the Australian Prudential Regulation Authority (APRA) and also the Australian Securities and Investments Commissions (ASIC) have mandates to monitor deposit-taking authorities. This mandate is to be able to minimize the risks against the safety of depositors' funds (see www.apra.gov.au/).

The global credit crunch and several spectacular failures of financial institutions all over the world, including Australia, have been some of the key outcomes of the GFC. Thus, governments have been implementing policies that either attract capital from other markets to the domestic markets and/or avoid capital flight from the domestic markets to other markets. The deposit insurance scheme and direct capital infusion to those financial institutions under financial duress offer such policy measures.

On October 12, 2008, then–Prime Minister Kevin Rudd announced that, as part of the Australian government's response package to the GFC, 100 percent of all deposits and wholesale funding to Australian banks would be protected over the subsequent three-year period (*Australian Financial Review* 2008). Mr. Rudd pointed out that Australian banks were well capitalized and well regulated and that the measures were needed to help Australian banks compete with others in the international market.[15] While the reductions in the cash rate have supplied a cheaper price for capital in Australia, the introduction of a 100 percent explicit deposit insurance scheme has offered much-needed security and guaranty for this cheaper capital.[16] Both policy measures have had the effect of keeping the market and book value of mortgage loans, in the numerator of the LTV ratio, close to each other.

A Synthesis

Next, I focus my attention on whether and how policy implementations and some other fundamentals might have affected house prices in Australia.

Affordability
Unlike house prices in several developed countries with substantial declines during the GFC, house prices in Australia have shown some volatility but been remarkably high across main Australian cities. Meanwhile, housing in Australia remains much less affordable than that of other developed countries. For example, an international survey finds that "Of the 27 Australian markets included in the survey, 24 markets were rated as 'severely unaffordable' (with Median Multiple of 5.1 and above), while three markets were regarded as 'seriously unaffordable' (Median Multiple between 4.1 and 5.0)."[17]

The median house (unit) values move from less than AU$350,000 (about AU$300,000) in June 2004 to about AU$500,000 (slightly more than AU$400,000) in June 2010, respectively. Meanwhile, the median income figures (available publicly) are robustly moving at a level close to the AU$40,000–AU$50,000 range during this period. Substantial rises in property prices in Australia appear to press the median income earners gradually, but surely, out of this market and provide further concerns for the future stability of Australia's financial markets.

Financing Patterns
Exhibit 21.6 shows that mortgage lending has dominated others in Australia since early 2000s.

Meanwhile, the RBA data (not reported in this chapter) for the annual percentage change in credit lines for housing, personal, and business loans, between 1995 and 2010, show a steep and rapid deterioration of the personal and especially business loans since the GFC has hit the world markets. The start of housing loans' deterioration dates back to 2004/2005. But its deterioration is not that steep and is smaller than those for the other two credit sectors. In 2007, the percentage change for housing sector's credit fell below the 10 percent level for the first time since 1998. The recourse nature of mortgage contracts, the government's financial

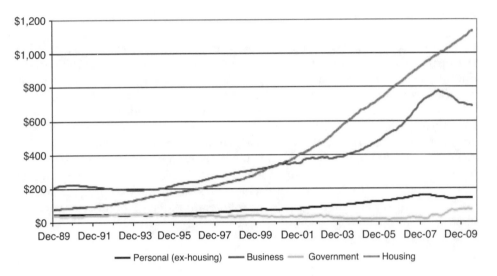

Exhibit 21.6   Australian Finance and Lending (AU$Billion S.A.)
Source: Data Diary (www.datadiary.com.au/2010/09/01/australian-july-credit-growth-last-of-the-true-believers-buys-another-house/australian-finance-lending/).

incentives for first-time home-buyers, and the collateral nature of the property are likely reasons for the better performance of the housing credit sector.

Exhibit 21.7 shows the inter-temporal patterns for household leverage. The debt amount, for both leverage related ratios in this exhibit, includes outstanding mortgage loans. Given the patterns for personal loans in Exhibit 21.6, the inference that the mortgage loans are the fundamental ingredient of household leverage

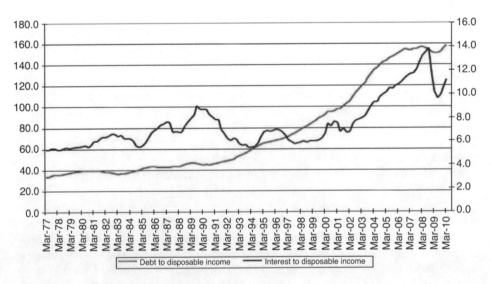

Exhibit 21.7   Household Leverage
Source: Data Diary (www.datadiary.com.au/2010/06/18/australian-household-finances-disposable-income-just-cant-keep-up/household-finances-mar10/).

appears to be reliable. The debt-to-disposable income (left axis of the exhibit) ratio has been increasing steeply since the mid-1990s. This steeply increasing intertemporal behavior hints that the Australian economy may be nurturing a leverage crisis for the near future. The interest-to-disposable income ratio (right axis of the exhibit) diverges from a range of 6 to 7.5 and assumes an increasing trend between early 2001 and late 2008. This indicates increased borrowing at increasing rates of interest under inflationary conditions. The effects of the GFC-related policy interventions, which, as shown in earlier exhibits, push the term structure of interest rates down, sharply pull this ratio down from around 14 to less than 10 between late 2008 and late 2009. There have been more than eight increases in the RBA's cash rate since late 2009. Consistent with this increasing trend of the term structure of interest rates, this ratio picks up another momentum of increase since late 2009. Once again, there is a warning sign for a leverage crisis in these patterns. As indicated earlier, these upward interest rate movements have been a source of increasingly painstaking financial burden on all existing VRM borrowers. Borrowers have been facing hardening difficulties in meeting their monthly mortgage payments. Some borrowers even claim that they have been reducing their food and other necessity consumption to be able to meet the higher monthly mortgage payments.[18]

Exhibits 21.6 and 21.7 also suggest that the Australian lending institutions lack sufficient diversification in their loan portfolios. This is, in my opinion, a weakness for this sector, especially in the long run, and may affect adversely their competitiveness in an increasingly globalizing world economy. Of course, the collateral nature of property with recourse loans and the fact that a great majority of mortgage contracts are VRMs in Australia currently help these institutions in an easy way with their asset-liability management problems. But, any sufficiently large downturn in house prices may lead to bitter economic consequences for the banks and the economy.

Results in Exhibit 21.8 offer an opportunity for a back-of-the-envelope inference on the dollar magnitude of such risks. An eyeballing examination reveals a homeowner percentage of approximately 75 percent (25 percent) with (without) a mortgage, respectively, between 1995 and 2006. Of this distribution, approximately 59 percent (35 percent) of mortgage borrowers are between 15 to 44 years old (15 and 34 years old), respectively. Let's assume the same patterns remain intact today. Given that 98 percent of the contracts are of the VRM type in Australia (see endnote 7), about 58 percent of the outstanding mortgage contracts are likely to feel the pinch, in increased mortgage payments, of the interest-rate increases every time they occur. The left tail of the distribution covers young and younger borrowers with potentially limited income and other financial wealth, and commands a weight of 35 percent. This suggests that default risk, which may stem from interest-rate increases, on about 34 percent of the outstanding mortgage contracts is considerably high. Global Property Guide (2009) reported that the Australian mortgage market grew from around 15 percent of GDP in the 1970s to 84 percent of GDP in 2008, and that in 2008, total mortgage debt was around AU$995 billion (US$912.4 billion), about 83 percent (i.e., about AU$825 billion) of which was housing loans. The dollar amount at risk, corresponding to the left tail of the distribution above, is about AU$280 billion. This is not small at all for any economy.[19]

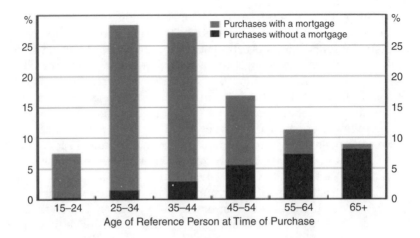

Exhibit 21.8 Dwelling Purchases by Age (Owner-Occupiers, Share of Total)
Note: Sample includes purchases between 1995 and 2006.
Source: Data Diary (www.datadiary.com.au/2010/06/10/housing-turnover-and-first-home-buyers/dwelling-purhcases-by-age/).

First-Time Home Owners

Exhibit 21.9 exhibits the first-time home-owner transactions as a percent of the total number of transactions since December 1990. The steepest climb-up, ending with the peak in this exhibit, occurs during the GFC. The graph clearly exhibits the immediate positive effect of the financial boosts in the grants for first-time homeowners, introduced as part of policy measures against the GFC in October 2008. Starting in late 2009, a sudden and steep plummet occurs. This behavior is

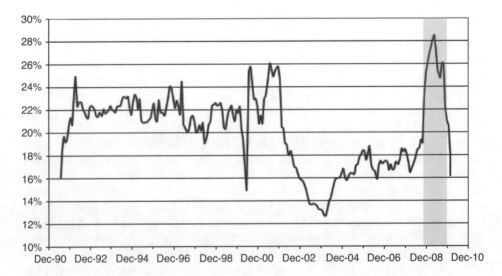

Exhibit 21.9 First-Home Buyers as Percent of Total
Source: Data Diary (www.datadiary.com.au/2010/05/14/australian-housing-finance-mar10/).

consistent with the pull-back of some of the financial incentives in the scheme and also with repeated increases in the cash rate since late 2009.

While this scheme has been claimed to help keep property prices high during the GFC,[20] one must consider its potential side effects, which are likely to cause headaches. There is anecdotal evidence that the positive effect was only for the low end of the housing market and that the scheme did not help the high-end properties. In fact, the high-end was affected adversely by the GFC.[21]

The timing of the cooling in house prices, observed in Exhibit 21.2, appears to follow from the timings of both the sharp decline in the number of first-time home-owners and the upward movements in the term structure of interest rates.

Supply Patterns and Demographic Changes

Supply constraints of land for development, net immigration gains, and changes in lifestyle are frequently expressed factors for the hot property market in Australia and persistently high prices. Exhibit 21.10 provides information that appears consistent with the potential for excess demand effects of supply constraints[22] and lifestyle changes.

The data for the change in building approvals run a stable course between 30,000 and 50,000 units between 1986 and 2010. Meanwhile, the change in population is almost always above the change in building approvals and exhibits a persistent trend of increase since 2003. Australia has been going through a process of net additions to its population.

Whether changes in population due to newly arriving family members or newly arriving immigrants should trigger further demand for housing is an

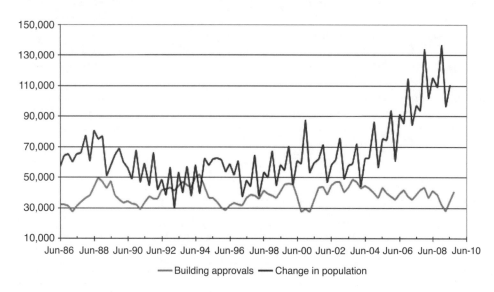

Exhibit 21.10 Change in Population and Residential Building Approvals
Source: Data Diary (www.datadiary.com.au/2010/04/27/how-much-above-trend-are-australian-house-prices/).

open-ended question.[23] The upward change in housing density since 2004 is consistent with a process in which more babies are arriving in Australian households and a density of less than 2.75 in 2009/2010 is far less than that of about 3.07 in 1986 (see www.datadiary.com.au/2010/04/27/how-much-above-trend-are-australian-house-prices/). It is not unlikely that home-owners have sufficient room to accommodate their new family members without demanding further housing. Similarly, whether immigrants would have the financial means upon arrival to demand relatively expensive housing is also an open-ended question. An Australian Government Department of Education, Employment, and Work Relations report (2010) shows that the arrival of skilled workers to Australia has been in a declining trend since mid-2002. Thus, it is not clear whether changes in the population dynamics may be the root cause of house price dynamics in Exhibits 21.1 and 21.2.

Growth in the Resource Sector and Home Prices

The soaring prices of resources (in particular, precious goods and minerals) have provided a substantial amount of wealth for Australia and Australian regions, especially Western Australia, for some time by now. Home prices in Perth, in particular, have also soared during the same period. Whether the price patterns of commodities and resources are related to those of homes in Australia and Perth arises as a relevant question (Myers, 1977).

The Bank of Canada provides on its web site the most comprehensive monthly commodity price index that I could locate on the Internet (see www .bankofcanada.ca/en/rates/bcpi_month.html).[24] Exhibit 21.11 shows the correlation coefficients between the commodity price indexes—one based on the U.S. dollar and one based on the Australian dollar after applying the average monthly AUD$/US$ parities—and the home price indexes for Australia and Perth (see Exhibit 21.1 for home prices and www.oanda.com/currency/average for foreign-exchange rates). House prices in Perth are very highly correlated with the commodity price movements irrespective of the currency effects. House prices across Australia, on the other hand, show much less correlation with the commodity indexes and instead exhibit sensitivity to currency movements. These correlations, in my view, provide some preliminary evidence for the effect of soaring commodity prices on Perth's soaring home prices.

Exhibit 21.11 Correlation Coefficients between Commodity Prices and Home Prices: January 2004–September 2010

	Perth	Australia
Comm Ind US$	0.876	0.676
Comm Ind AU$	0.873	0.530

Source: Author's own calculations.

CONCLUSION

There is a general consensus that Australia's response to the GFC has been a success story so far. As for housing, the policymakers have implemented policies as part of a massive fiscal response package to the GFC, which has aimed to sustain high property values in Australia. In my view, Australian housing markets are more locally driven than those in other developed countries. High population density, which arises from the business establishment, in Sydney and, to an increasing extent, in Melbourne, has helped house prices to maintain an upward mobility. Perth, on the other hand, has benefited from the growth option in the resources/mining sector. China remains a healthy and hungry interested party in Western Australia's mines and minerals, providing unprecedented wealth and population movements to that region. Adelaide, meanwhile, enjoys its own—yet dormant so far—growth options, which arise from the large uranium and gold deposits in South Australia. Of course, relatively low mortgage rates on VRM contracts, as a function of low interest rates on Treasury securities since the mid-1990s, have allowed all potential home-owners, irrespective of their localities, to maintain a healthy appetite for purchasing houses.

Given the unaffordability patterns, remaining concerned about future aftershocks—especially in the background of substantial inflation pressures and the ensuing upward interest rate adjustments in Australia—has to be in the minds of policymakers and citizens alike. The current risky decomposition of Australian banks' loan portfolios with a need for further diversification and the substantial outstanding household debt, especially mortgage debt by those with relatively low income (such as the majority of first-time home-owners), also add to these concerns.

Australian banks have been sourcing their financing needs mainly from the international markets for some time now. Inflationary pressures are a likely outcome of the massive budget deficits around the world, once the world economies pull themselves out of the GFC. Further, the Australian economy has its own homemade concerns for inflation. Thus, increasing borrowing costs, both domestically and internationally, for Australian banks and, consequently, for all Australian mortgage borrowers with a VRM contract, are not unlikely in the near future. As inferred above, the amount of highly risky mortgage debt in Australia is in the neighborhood of AU$280 billion. A future realized 10 percent default rate will translate into a foreclosure process with a minimum total cost of AU$20 to AU$30 billion. So, given the current large budget deficit, assumed in response to the GFC, any derailment in the Australian economy may cause severe and potentially lengthy financial trouble ahead.

Of course, the presence of rich mining and mineral deposits appear to provide a cover for such risks. But, one must remember the very interesting recent political duel, played out very much in and for the public, between the Rudd government and the mining industry in response to the government's proposed tax policy on these companies. Several daily TV and other media commercials, with an accusation targeting the other side, and several dramatic press conferences by government ministers—including the Prime Minister—or by mining industry spokespeople, took place in early to mid-2010, ending with the political coup-d'état that ousted then–Prime Minister Kevin Rudd after only two years in office and after winning a landslide election (see endnote 12). The bargaining between the newly formed Labor government, with Julia Gillard as the new Prime Minister, and the mining industry took place mostly behind closed doors and has ensured an end to this political duel and installed a lasting peace (at least so far). One may interpret this episode as evidence for the mining industry's deep reservations and hesitation to be a source of current and future funding for the budget deficit.[25] That is, whether the presence of rich mining and mineral deposits will provide a cover for the budget deficit and any future financial burdens remains an open-ended question in the author's view. It may be that the Australian taxpayers, just like the American taxpayers, will have to shoulder the substantial and potential bail-out costs.

Finally, given this background, watching for China and/or India's economic performance and moves should be a key priority for Australia and for all countries in the region.

NOTES

1. Right after migrating to Australia in July 2008, I discovered with fascination that the Australian banking system did not have an explicit deposit insurance system. While opening my first-ever Australian bank account, I inquired about the parameters of the deposit insurance in a branch of one of these four banks. Much to my surprise, I learned that even the bank manager of this particular branch had no idea about the meaning of deposit insurance.

2. The coupon rate adjustments of this mortgage structure contrast with those of the adjustable rate mortgages (ARM), commonly observed in USA, and of the typical Canadian mortgage contracts. The changes in the coupon rate of an ARM occur at regular intervals, such as every six months. The revision period for updating an ARM's coupon rate, the interest-rate updating process (i.e., the relevant interest rate index for measuring the interest rate changes), and the upper and lower limits of the amount of change (i.e., interest rate floors or caps) are all specified in each ARM contract. The typical Canadian mortgage contract, on the other hand, has a contractually specified coupon adjustment period of usually either three or five years (or even seven years) and relies for the coupon adjustments on the term structure of the Treasury securities that prevails at the expiry of an adjustment period (see Courchane and Giles, 2002).

3. For a review of the evolution of mortgage contracts with response to their inherent risks, with an emphasis on the U.S. market, see Geltner et al. (2006, ch. 16).

4. See Ambrose and Buttimer (2000) for a detailed analysis of options in mortgages.

5. Meanwhile, it appears that borrowers are not fully aware that the IRS is also a partner in such put options. It taxes borrowers for the gain on exercising the put option and, hence, effectively increases the exercise price of the default option (see Opdyke, J., *WSJ*, May 8, 2010). I thank Bob Edelstein for bringing this point to my attention for the first time over an informal conversation in 2009.

6. The inter-temporal behavior of the LTV ratio (for a FRM) may be characterized by one of three possibilities. In the (hypothetical) case of a straight-line time path for the property value over the life of the mortgage contract, the time path of the LTV ratio will be smoothly declining and dictated by the pre-determined time path of the outstanding book value of the mortgage loan. Such a declining, preferably smooth, time-path pattern in the LTV ratio is within a lenders' risk appetite and poses negligible and manageable

default risks for the lending industry. In a boom cycle and holding all else constant, the property value path usually exhibits an increasing trend, leading to persistent reductions in the inter-temporal behavior of the LTV ratio and benefiting the home owners without harming the lenders. On the other hand, in a bust cycle and holding all else constant, the property-value path exhibits a declining trend, leading to persistent increases in the inter-temporal behavior of the LTV ratio, gradually pushing home-owners toward the dreaded default (i.e., foreclosure) decisions/actions, raising downside risks and potentially severely harming the lenders.

7. Hemingway (2010) reports that 98 percent of all Australian mortgages are VRMs.

8. These adjustments follow the RBA's cash-rate announcements and are evident in Exhibit 21.5.

9. I thank Tim Lawless of the RP Data for his personal correspondences to explain that "the RP Data–Rismark Home Value Index uses median prices as the index base to show the relativity of pricing in the market, and that the index does not track median prices over time (median prices can be very much compositionally biased). The index tracks value movements in the market. I have used the median price as a base (rather than an arbitrary index number such as 100) to provide some level of relativity of pricing." The details of the index methodology can be seen at www.rpdata.com/property_indices/property_indices.html.

10. Global Property Guide (2009) reported: "In September 2009, all eight Australian capital cities recorded strong annual house price increases. Darwin recorded the highest house price increase of about 12.3 percent from a year earlier. Melbourne and Canberra followed, with price rises of 8.4 and 7.8 percent over the same period. Sydney registered a house price increase of 5.9 percent in September 2009 from a year earlier. House prices have also risen in Brisbane (5.6 percent), Hobart (5.4 percent), Perth (4.4 percent), and Adelaide (3.7 percent)." Similarly, the ABS reported on its web site (www.abs.gov.au/) that, in the third quarter of 2009, the average established home price index for eight capital cities rose nominally by 4.2 percent, or 3.2 percent when adjusted for inflation, following a 4.1 percent rise in the second quarter of 2009 and a 0.7 percent decline in the first quarter of 2009.

11. There was a direct and early hit, warning of the exploding GFC, on Australia. Basis Capital Fund Management failed in July 2007 (see http://money.cnn.com/magazines/fortune/storysupplement/subprime_global).

12. GlobalPropertyGuide.com (November 22, 2009) noted: "In response to the crisis, the government introduced a huge stimulus package, worth AU$10.4 billion (US$7.24 billion), around 1 percent of GDP, in October 14, 2008." Also, Forbes.com (May 13, 2009) stated: "Whatever the final form of Australia's proposed budget, one thing is clear: in an effort to spend its way out of recession, Australia will wind up with a record budget deficit . . . . [The] government on Tuesday night unveiled a budget with the largest Post-War budget deficit Australia's ever had." The Labor government ousted Kevin Rudd, who was both its leader and Prime Minister of Australia, on June 24, 2010. Ms. Julia Gillard, the new Labor Prime Minister, pointed out that the Rudd government had lost its way. She called an early election, and the election results led to the first hung parliament in Australia. The political uncertainties and weaknesses of this newly elected parliament have been of interest to all observers of Australia.

13. There are also additional grants that some state governments are providing to first-time buyers. Coverage under this scheme and its details are available at *fhogonline* (www.firsthome.gov.au/).

14. This has been a good example of Kane's (1977) regulatory dialect framework.

15. Several governments have subscribed to both measures. For example, the United States increased temporarily its deposit insurance limit from $100,000 per account to $250,000 per account. Similarly, the United Kingdom, United States, and French governments, among others, transferred giant amounts of taxpayers' funds to financial institutions under duress in an effort to stabilize not only them but also the financial systems.

    Mr. Rudd reportedly stated that "I don't want a first-class Australian bank discriminated against because some other foreign bank, which has a bad balance sheet, is being propped up by a guarantee by a foreign government." (*Sydney Morning Herald* 2008). The move to guarantee deposits followed a week of investor panic. The Australian dollar went from a stable range, fluctuating around 95 U.S. cents right before September 2008 to a level of 65 U.S. cents with a lot of volatility in Oct 2008. It has climbed to a stable range around US$1 for about more than a year by now. APRA considered the introduction of explicit deposit insurance on savings up to AU$20,000 since the failure of a major financial institution in early 2000s. Further, the Australian government also announced that it would double the funds available for mortgage-backed securities to AU$8 billion to help maintain liquidity for non-bank lenders. The Opposition also welcomed this measure (see *The Sydney Morning Herald*, 2008).

16. One should be mindful of the *forbearance hypothesis*. Kryzanowski and Roberts (1993) document, for example, that it was the political interventions with back-door capital infusions (i.e., forbearance) but not the economic efficiency that kept several insolvent (in market-value terms) Canadian banks and insurance companies alive during the Great Depression. Taxpayers, whose consent is not sought after and received for such interventions, end up with the entire and highly costly financial burdens for such capital infusions from governments to private establishments. The GFC provides fertile grounds to examine empirically and internationally this hypothesis.

17. The norm value for the Median Multiple, computed by dividing the median house price by the median household income, is three times the annual household income or less; the Median Multiple in Australia is 6 (see Fifth Annual Demographia International Housing Affordability Survey, 2009).

18. Aussie Home Loans chief John Symond reportedly stated in a news item (see Andersen 2010): "That's the unfortunate downside in borrowing money, particularly at a cycle where we were having interest rates at historic lows and now very rapidly interest rates have been increased by the Reserve Bank. Six increases in the past seven meetings is very rapid and it's probably faster than the RBA or banks expected interest rates to rise and it certainly caught a lot of borrowers unawares. There's a lot of pain out there at the moment and the conception of the consumers is that these rates—if they go up further and they probably will—we could end up in trouble." I note that recent RBA meetings in October/November 2010 witnessed further rate increases. In view of these difficulties, the Commonwealth Bank introduced a program, as early as March 2009, by which its unemployed customers were given the opportunity to defer repayments on their mortgages. This bank has offered a six-month break from repayments and up to 12 months in cases of extreme hardship (ABC News 2009).

19. Global Property Guide (2009) stated further: "Total housing loans have increased by 13.7 percent annually from 2004 to 2008. . . . Around 70 percent of the total outstanding housing loans to households were for owner-occupied homes while the remaining 30 percent were for investment homes, according to ABS. The Australian mortgage market is highly concentrated. Australia's "big four" banks. . . . had an almost 100 percent share of the country's new mortgage market in July 2009, according to the Australian Prudential Regulation Authority (APRA). Larger banks benefited as smaller lenders exited the market due to financial difficulties caused by the global credit crunch."

20. Global Property Guide (2009) indicated: "By the end of August 2009, the FHOB had helped more than 153,000 Australians buy their first home. By July 2009, first home buyers had risen 73 percent from the same period last year. New home sales rose 11.4 percent in August 2009 (or by 25 percent up on last year), from anemic monthly increases of 0.1 percent in July and 0.5 percent in June 2009, according to the Housing Industry Association (HIA). Detached home sales rose 11.8 percent, while apartment sales rose 7.5 percent in August 2009 from the previous month. Victoria registered the highest increase in detached home sales of about 21.8 percent, followed by Queensland (20.9 percent) and Western Australia (15.1 percent). On the other hand, sales fell by 11.3 percent in New South Wales and 2.5 percent in South Australia. 'A late surge in sales to first home buyers ahead of the step-down in the new home boost, propelled new home sales. . . . [making] August the best monthly result for over three and a half years,' said HIA chief economist Harley Dale."

21. See Zappone (2009). Further, the question of who might have benefited the most from this scheme is important and has not even entered the economic and political discussions so far. Economic theory and empirical evidence for similar schemes tell us that capitalization of the tax benefits—due to the increased demand—into the property prices should follow under this scheme. In such a case, the developers, but not the first-time homeowners, are likely to be the main beneficiaries. Of course, especially late-moving first-time homeowners end up with a higher valued property and higher amount of mortgage debt.

22. However, an analyst expresses reservation about supply constraints: "This is fluff. The major home builders manage the supply of new houses coming out of their landholdings to optimize demand and price—none of them (to my knowledge) is short of supply." (See www.datadiary.com.au/2010/04/27/how-much-above-trend-are-australian-house-prices/.)

23. An ABS report, entitled "Births as a component of population growth," states "Since 1976 Australian fertility has been below replacement level of 2.1 babies per woman; that is, below the number of births required to replace a woman and her partner . . . . Despite this, natural increase is still positive because of the relatively young age structure of Australia's population . . . . there are relatively few people at older ages, resulting in a relatively low number of deaths per year.

24. The Bank reports that this is a chain Fisher price index of the spot or transaction U.S. dollar prices of 24 commodities produced in Canada and sold in world markets, with weights updated on an annual basis.

25. These events also constitute interesting evidence for Kane's (1977) political dialect framework.

ACKNOWLEDGMENTS

I would like to thank and express my gratitude to Bob Edelstein for inviting me to write this manuscript and Ashok Bardhan and Cynthia Kroll for their patience and guidance in the preparation of this manuscript. All errors in the paper are mine. I thank the members of the Institute of Applied Mathematics at the Middle East Technical University, Ankara, Turkey, for their kind hospitality during the preparation of this manuscript. I also thank very much both Rohan Clarke of *DataDiary* and Tim Lawless and the Research Department of *RPData* for granting their permissions to use their data and graphs as well as for their constructive comments with my inquiries. Burak Ata provided excellent research assistance. Upon request, I will be happy to provide further data and information not reported to save space in this chapter.

REFERENCES

ABC News. 2009 (March 17). "CBA Announces Mortgage Deferments for Unemployed." Available at www.abc.net.au/news/stories/2009/03/17/2518687.htm.

Ambrose, B. W., and R. J. Buttimer. 2000. "Embedded Options in the Mortgage Contract." *Journal of Real Estate Finance and Economics* 21:2, 95–111, DOI: 10.1023/A:007819408669.

Andersen, B. 2010 (May 5). "Mortgage Stress Rising along with Rates." Available at www.abc.net.au/news/stories/2010/05/05/2891259.htm.

Australian Prudential Regulation Authority. Available at www.apra.gov.au/.

Australian Bureau of Statistics. Available at www.abs.gov.au/AUSSTATS/.

Australian Bureau of Statistics. "Births as a Component of Population Growth." Available at www.abs.gov.au/ausstats/abs@.nsf/Products/B5586A7AAE821089CA25766A001211 AE?opendocument.

The Australian Financial Reviews. 2008 (Oct. 13). "Rudd Guarantees Bank Deposits." Available at www.afr.com.au/p/national/item_UrJ1ZHMiOnK6QXSr2wnBZN?hl.

Australian Government Department of Education, Employment and Work Relations. 2010. Available at: Skilled Worker Index, www.deewr.gov.au/, accessed on September 13, 2010.

CNNMoney.com. Available at http://money.cnn.com/magazines/fortune/storysupplement/subprime_global, accessed September 2010.

Commonwealth Treasury. Available at www.cfsgam.com.au/uploadedFiles/CFSGAM/PdfResearch/100512%20Budget2010.pdf, accessed September 5, 2010.

Courchane, M. J., and J. A. Giles. 2002. "A Comparison of U.S. and Canadian Residential Mortgage Markets." *Property Management* 20:5, 326–368.

Bank of Canada, Monthly Price Indexes. Available at www.bankofcanada.ca/en/rates/bcpi_month.html, accessed January 2011.

Fifth Annual Demographia International Housing Affordability Survey. 2009. Available at www.demographia.com/dhi2009.pdf, accessed July 11, 2011.

First Home Owner Grant General Information. Available at www.firsthome.gov.au/, accessed January 2011.

Forbes.com. 2009 (May 13). "Deficit for Australia with New Budget." Available at www.forbes.com/2009/05/13/australia-record-deficit-markets-economy-tax.html.

Geltner, D. M., N. G. Miller, J. Clayton, and P. Eichholtz. 2006. *Commercial Real Estate Analysis and Investments,* Upper Saddle River, NJ: SouthWestern.

GlobalPropertyGuide.com. 2009 (November 22). "Australian House Prices Surge!" www.globalpropertyguide.com/Pacific/Australia/Price-History.

Hemingway, T. 2010 (June 21). Available at www.ozcarguide.com/business-money/real-estate-investment/810-mortgages-fixed-variable-rate.

Data Diary. Various figures and data. Available at www.datadiary.com.au/, accessed September 2010.

Kane, E. J. 1977. "Good Intentions and Unintended Evil: The Case against Selective Credit Allocation." *Journal of Money, Credit, and Banking* 9:1, 55–69.

Kryzanoswki, L., and G. Roberts. 1993. "Canadian Banking Solvency, 1922–1940." *Journal of Money, Banking, and Credit* 25:3, 361–376.

Myers, S. 1977. "Determinants of Corporate Borrowing." *Journal of Financial Economics*, 5:2, 147–175.

OANDA. Average Monthly Currency Rates. Available at www.oanda.com/currency/average, accessed January 2011.

Opdyke, J. 2010 (May 8). Available at WSJ, http://online.wsj.com/article/SB10001424
052748703686304 575228783947789118.html?mod=WSJ_article_related.

Office of State Revenue. "First Home Buyer Grant Scheme." Available at
www.osr.nsw.gov.au/benefits/first_home, accessed January 2011.

Seeking Alpha. 2009 (August 25). Available at http://seekingalpha.com/article/
158189-top-10-banks-of-australia-by-assets-and-deposits.

Shiller, R. J. 1993. *Macro Markets: Creating Institutions for Managing Society's largest Economic
Risks.* Clarendon Lectures in Economics. New York: Oxford University Press. RP Data.
RP Data—Rismark Home Value Indices. Personal Communication. November 23, 2011.

RP Data. *RP Data—Rismark Home Value Indices - Methodology*, http://www.rpdata.com/
property_indices/property_indices.html. Personal Communication, accessed November
23, 2010.

The Reserve Bank of Australia. Various graphs and data. Available at www.rba.gov.au/
statistics/, accessed September 2010.

The Sydney Morning Herald. 2008 (October 12). "Bank Deposits Guaranteed for 3 Years."
www.smh.com.au/business/bank-deposits-guaranteed-for-3-years-20081012-4z07.html.

Zappone, C. 2009 (May 15). "Crisis Hits Millionaires' Row." Available at
www.theage.com.au/business/crisis-hits-millionaires-row-20090515-b56i.html.

ABOUT THE AUTHOR

DOGAN TIRTIROGLU is currently a Professor of Finance and the Chair of Banking at the Business School, the University of Adelaide, Australia. He has a PhD in Finance from the University of Connecticut and has held academic posts in the United States, Canada, the United Kingdom, and Turkey. He is a fellow of the Homer Hoyt Advanced Studies Institute (United States) and an affiliated researcher of the Financial Mathematics group of the Institute of Applied Mathematics at the Middle East Technical University (Turkey). His research has been published in the *Journal of Banking and Finance;* the *Journal of Money, Credit, and Banking; Financial Management;* the *Journal of Economic Behavior and Organization; Advances in Financial Economics; Real Estate Economics; Journal of Financial Services Research; Journal of Regional Science; Journal of Housing Economics; Journal of Real Estate Literature; Quarterly Journal of Business and Economics; Journal of Economics and Finance; Applied Economics; Journal of Property Finance; Appraisal Journal; Canadian Journal of Administrative Sciences;* and *Studies in Economics and Finance.* He has been a long-standing member of AREUEA, FMA, and AFA, and co-organized the 2011 Asia-Pacific Real Estate Research Symposium.

CHAPTER 22

The Financial Crisis and Brazil's Expanding Housing Market

EMILIO HADDAD AND JOÃO MEYER
University of São Paulo, Brazil

The purpose of this chapter is to provide a picture of and briefly discuss the impact of the 2008 international financial crisis upon housing markets in Brazil. With the purpose of providing a more complete context, the chapter initially provides some background information on Brazil, and the evolution of its housing policies and financing. After a discussion at the national level, the study focuses on the case of the São Paulo, the largest city and housing market in Brazil. Because more detailed real-estate information is available for this city, it is possible to better detail and analyze recent market behavior. Finally, some conclusions and perspectives for housing in Brazil are presented.

BACKGROUND ON BRAZIL

With 8,500,000 square kilometers, Brazil is the fifth largest country in the world, and the largest nation in Latin American. According to the 2010 Census, Brazilian population in 2010 was estimated as 190.700 million inhabitants, constituting 67.550 million households,[1] with 84 percent living in urban areas.

With a GDP of over US$2 trillion, Brazil is the world's eighth biggest economy. Per capita income is US$11,000; however, this average might be misleading as Brazil has been well known for the unevenness of its income distribution. According to the U.S. Central Intelligence Agency's *World Factbook* (CIA), amongst 134 countries Brazil ranks the tenth in the Gini index of family income distribution, meaning that only nine among all countries have more skewed distribution. Yet, in 2007, the highest 10 percent of Brazilian households received 43 percent of the national income, while the lowest 10 percent received only 1.1 percent. Only 1.7 percent of the families had a monthly income that was equal to more than 10 minimum wages in 2007 (US$1,974 in 2007).

The quality of the housing stock is probably the most conspicuous evidence of the distribution of income in any society. Yet, family income distribution is at the core of Brazilian housing conditions, with an historic accumulated deficit, estimated in 7.9 million dwellings in 2005, mostly for families with monthly incomes below US$200, the condition of 78.5 percent of Brazilian families.

Families that live in inadequate dwellings (slums, tenements, improvised dwellings, excess density dwelling, lack of infrastructure, inadequate titling, lack of exclusive bathrooms, or high-depreciate building) represent 45 percent of this deficit. The other 55 percent is composed of families sharing the same dwelling with one or more other families, a housing arrangement that is characteristic of countries in development.

It must be mentioned that those numbers refer only to inadequacy of buildings: Brazilian cities do present serious problems in urban infrastructure provision. For example, it is estimated that 56 percent of all houses do not have access to sewer treatment.

From the demographics point of view, there has been strong pressure over housing demand. The country doesn't have a younger profile population anymore; now, it has a predominance of adults. The estimated population aged between 25 and 64 years, where the housing demand is concentrated, is expected to grow from 43.4 million (36.6 percent) in 1980 to 112.6 million (54 percent) in 2020. This means that, if in the 1980s, 920 thousand households were formed each year, it is expected that more than 1.2 million new households per year will be formed in the decade of 2010.

Thus, present Brazilian demand for mortgages and formal housing production is concentrated in 5 to 10 minimum wages monthly family income bracket, which means 8.4 percent of the total families. This demand is well known and led to the creation of the government program Minha Casa, Minha Vida (My House, My Life) launched in 2009 to deliver partial subsidies to housing purchasers to enable them to afford mortgage payments, as will be discussed later in this chapter.

HOUSING FINANCE IN BRAZIL

In the case of Brazil, a better understanding of more recent behavior of the housing market requires some knowledge of the recent history of housing finance in the country.

Before 1964, home loans and public initiatives in housing provision were few and far between: Only 143,000 units of social housing were provided between 1937 and 1964, with more than 85 percent being produced by investments through the pension funds of major unions (Bonduki 1998), which was hardly adequate given the country's need. For one thing, inflation discouraged the formation of saving funds because there was no mechanism to adjust debt to inflation.

Created in 1964, the Brazilian Housing Finance System (SFH) introduced a monetary correction for inflation in contracted loans, allowing the formation of saving funds to long-term finance.

SFH consisted of two sources of funds:

1. A compulsory one, the Employees Guarantee Fund (Fundo de Garantia por Tempo de Serviço [FGTS]), to be managed by a government finance institution, the Banco Nacional da Habitação (BNH, or National Housing Bank)
2. A voluntary one, the Brazilian Savings and Loan System (SBPE), operated by private banks and other lending institutions under strict governmental regulations.

SFH has soon become the most important component of the Brazilian financial system, and a centralized and hegemonic source of housing finance in Brazil.

Fundo de Garantia por Tempo de Serviço (FGTS)

FGTS collects 8 percent tax on all private sector wages, accumulating funds to provide unemployment insurance. The fund was initially coordinated and managed by the National Housing Bank until 1986, when the Caixa Econômica Federal (CEF) assumed part of operations control. CEF is a government financial institution that provides housing loans, beyond other commercial bank operations.

FGTS priority is financing low-income housing. Basically, FGTS was designated to finance homes up to R$80,000 (about US$36,000),[2] and in cities where land prices were higher, R$130,000 (about US$58,000). The highest monthly income to qualify for this credit is R$3,900 (about US$1,700), around nine minimum wages. In those places where the house value is higher, the limit increases to R$4,900 (about US$2,200), around 11 minimum wages.

As well as subsidizing housing mortgages, FGTS has been used to finance sanitation projects, urban infrastructure, and urban transport, but at least 60 percent of resources have been earmarked for housing.

Sistema Brasileiro de Poupança e Empréstimo (SBPE)

The SBPE, geared toward middle-income families, provides funds based on savings deposits in commercial banks and the CEF. The saving deposits receive a fixed 6 percent annual interest rate plus TR (a reference interest rate that is a floating and partial inflationary correction adopted by the SFH), income-tax free. It can finance homes up to R$350,000 (about US$156,000). The maximum amount of funding is R$245,000 and the maximum interest rate is 12 percent by year. After 2004, bank competition for mortgage supply improved the credit conditions, mainly by decreasing interest rates and increasing loan maturity. Depending on the value of the property and form of payment, the CEF interest rates varied from 8.4 to 11.5 percent in April 2009.

In Brazil, the interest rate of housing loans is fixed during the contract. The FGTS accounts balance can be used for payment of SBPE mortgage. An SBPE mortgage covers the construction or the acquisition of both new and used homes. The law requires setting aside at least 65 percent of the saving deposits for housing loans, of which 80 percent is for the SFH rules and 20 percent for housing mortgages in the free market. The saving deposits balances have quickly increased, from R$51 billion in 1995 to R$215 billion in 2008 (US$96 billion), a 13.5 percent per year geometric growth rate. Investment in housing has grown at an accelerated pace from R$3 billion to almost R$29 billion (about US$13 billion) between 2004 and 2008 (see Exhibit 22.1).

SFH PERFORMANCE

From its beginning in 1964 until 2008, SFH has financed almost 9.84 million housing units, 63.3 percent of them by the FGTS. But these mortgages were distributed very unevenly over the period.

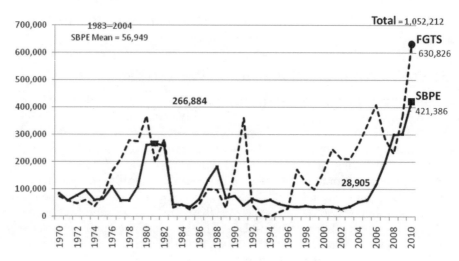

Exhibit 22.1   Housing Mortgage Evolution: Units (Brazil 1970–2010)
Sources: ABECIP; Central Bank; CEF.

The evolution of the system went through three phases: (1) consolidation and growth, (2) crisis and destructuring, and (3) restructuring and recovery, as described next.

Consolidation and Growth (1964–1982)

The period from 1964–1982 corresponds to a larger growth of the economy, known as the Brazilian Miracle. The average GDP growth rate was 8.7 percent between 1971 and 1980. The legal and institutional apparatus was organized in this period. The BNH has become the central body, controlling the system. At the beginning, in 1971, it acted only for resource allocation, forming an agents' network of financial intermediation in fundraising and funds application. The mortgages grew quickly until reaching the historic record of 627,000 units in 1980. Around 4.1 million units were financed until 1982. The system had an important role in the housing market, in the structuring of cities and in the economy.

Crisis and Dismantling of the Housing Finance System

The housing finance system began to collapse in 1982, with the coming of the Brazilian external debt crisis: First because of an increase in withdrawals from the FGTS and savings accounts due the fast unemployment growth, and then because of an explosion in insolvencies resulting from the rising inflation and wage crunch. The number of new loans fell sharply. The solution found was financially unsustainable: Mortgage payments were indexed to borrowers' wages, lower than the mortgage index. In 1985, while the mortgage indexation was 246 percent, the installment one was 112 percent and the insolvency reached 25 percent.

A Wage Variation Compensation Fund (FCVS) was created in 1967 to guarantee the discharge of the balances due at the end of contracts from mortgage borrowers in the SFH system. Due to that index mismatch, the FCVS liabilities quickly grew to gigantic proportions. The system could not cope, leading to the demise of the National Housing Bank in 1986. The operations of the FGTS were taken over by CEF. The other functions were redistributed: the housing policy to the Environment and Urban Ministry, the regulation of the SFH to the National Monetary Council, and the SBPE supervision and rules to the Brazilian Central Bank.

To smooth the losses incurred by the banks, the government has made an exception to allow them to count the FCVS funds as mortgage loans, to comply with the reserve requirement rule, where 65 percent of saving deposits had to be directed to mortgages. Since then, the banks started to avoid providing mortgage loans. This explains why for more than two decades the provision of loans for the formal production of housing was minimal, contributing to the degradation of housing conditions. The SBPE remained practically paralyzed, restricted to CEF loans. Between 1983 and 2005 the SBPE financed an average of only 56,949 units a year in the entire country, 5 percent of the annual new households formed in the 1990s. New loans during this period came mainly from the resources of the FGTS, which responded for twice as many loans as the SBPE.

Restructuring and Recovery (Since 2001)

The conditions for the recovery of SFH had been built gradually over many years; initially by the economic stabilization and, years after, by the restructuring of the new regulatory framework, the wage recovery, ending the use of FCVS funds to comply with the reserve requirement rule in SBPE, the decreased interest rate in Brazil, and the easing of financing conditions.

An obstacle to the lowering of interest rates had been a long period of very high inflation. Annual inflation rates that were around 40 percent in the 1960s and 1970s, went up to 330 percent in the decade of 1980, and reached 764 percent in the period between 1990 and 1994. Between 1986 and 1991, the government implemented five drastic economic plans to combat hyperinflation, with ephemeral results due to inflation inertia. Only in 1994, with the Plano Real (Real Plan), named after the new currency, the taming of hyperinflation was successful.

Exhibit 22.2 displays falling interest rates, using as reference the rate paid by the Brazilian Central Bank to finance public debt. Lower interest rates brought reduction of mortgage payments, and therefore enlarged affordability which, in its turn, has created new housing demand.

Besides price stabilization, other important structural changes in the Brazilian economy have worked together for the expansion of the housing activity in Brazil, namely the increase and redistribution of income, the decreasing of household size, and creation of the Real Estate Financial System (SFI), introducing changes in the Housing Financial System (SFH). Each one of these factors is discussed next.

Income Increase and Redistribution

Concerning income redistribution, a most important move was the establishment, in 2004, of Bolsa Familia (Family Allowance), part of the Brazilian governmental

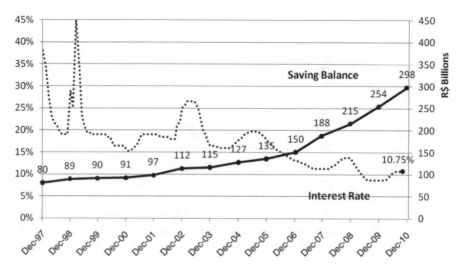

Exhibit 22.2 Saving Deposits Balance Evolution and Central Bank Public Debt Interest Rate (Brazil 1997–2010)
Sources: Brazil Central Bank, available at www.bcb.gov.br; and CBIC, available at www.cbicdados.com.br.

welfare program Fome Zero (Zero Hunger). Bolsa Familia is a program with conditional transfer of direct income, which benefits families in poverty and extreme poverty. The Bolsa Familia serves more than 12 million households nationwide. Depending on family income per person (limited to R$140) and the number and age of children, the benefit amount received by the family can vary between US$22 and US$200.

Several studies point to the contribution of the program toward reducing social inequalities and poverty. The National Monitoring Report of the Millennium Development Goals indicates a fall in extreme poverty from 12 percent in 2003 to 4.8 percent in 2008.

In 2006, Bolsa Familia was estimated to cost about 0.5 percent of Brazilian GDP and about 2.5 percent of total government expenditure. The management of a family allowance is decentralized and shared among federal agencies, state agencies, the Federal District, and municipalities. The list of beneficiaries is public and can be accessed by any citizen.

After 2004, the process of wage improvement progressed. Between 2001 and 2007, the family average monthly income increased by 8.2 percent, adjusted by inflation (National Consumer Price Index [IPCA]). All these factors paved the way to the recovery of mortgage offerings. However, constraints remain on the ability of affordable housing to meet the potential demand: The main housing finance agency, Caixa Econômica Federal, is especially rigorous in its credit analysis. Many families lack the savings for a down payment. And many workers, employed in informal jobs, lack the stable income or the proof of income required to qualify for a loan.

Decreasing of Household Size

The decrease in household size has been a consequence of socio-economic changes in the Brazilian society, following a pattern seen in more developed nations. It has come about because of urbanization, single people being able to afford to move out of their parents' homes, the increasing participation of women in the labor market, and the increase in the rate of divorces. Another cause of decreasing household size is the wish of separate families that share a house to move out and live by themselves.

Average household size in Brazil was 4.8 residents in 1970, 3.68 residents by 2000, and 3.31 according to the 2010 Census. Decreased family size means the formation of new households and new units needed to accommodate them.

REAL ESTATE FINANCIAL SYSTEM

To raise new and more stable funds, outside the FGTS and saving accounts, the Real Estate Financial System (SFI) was created in 1997 through the creation of mortgage receivables (CRI) and the assistance of secondary mortgage market institutions. For this purpose, the new system introduced the deed of trust clause, by which the borrower has the right to the house only after the full payment of the debt, instead of while paying the mortgage. It was an important step to overcome the problem of time spent on foreclosure procedures.[3]

The new system has been denominated by the Real Estate Financial System in lieu of the Housing Financial System, because it was geared to finance any income-generating property, residential as well as non-residential. Yet the aim of SFI was to open the possibility of using market instruments to approximate the SFH of the capital market, displacing the system of state regulation. The SFI does not regulate limits for mortgage value, nor for interest rates or the values of the property.

Due to the SFH's failure to finance the housing activity for decades, developers had limited working capital to finance buyers and thus limited production capacity. The secondary mortgage market, made possible by SFI, was established to help financially relieve the developers allowing them to focus on their core business. However, the interest rates charged by market investors were too high to compete with the financing terms offered by the SFH.

SFI has been a modest tool for fund raising. The peak of registered CRI primary issues achieved almost R$5 billion in 2008 (US$2.2 billion). The accumulated total financial funds in CRI achieved R$7.2 billion in 2008. The financial resources generated have been geared mostly toward investment in commercial real estate. Traditionally there is virtually no investment in rental housing in Brazil, where residential rent control policies have limited the return on investment.

On the other hand, banks have been engaged since 2004 in achieving the goal of expanding the real-estate credit, imposed by the gradual resumption of the reserve requirement rule. Thus, there wasn't an effort to generate mortgage for secondary markets beyond the requirement of 65 percent, because the earnings of banks with this additional resources were much larger if directed to other loans, whose rates were free, or to simple applications in Treasury debt securities, due to the high basic interest rate in force. The SFI may prosper only if the interest rates continue to drop.

RESTRUCTURING OF THE REAL ESTATE INDUSTRY

Another very important element of housing in Brazil was restructuring of the real-estate industry. Seeking a better alignment with new requirements of scale and professionalism, between the second half of 2005 and the end of 2007 many real estate companies went public. By December 2007, 29 were listed on the stock exchange. Initial public offerings of real estate development companies injected more than 12 billion reais (R$) into the sector.

There has been a process of continuing oligopolization of the sector through mergers and acquisition, and these companies are diversifying their activities, moving into new regions and new markets and moving down the income ladder to reach new families.

The Expansion of Housing Activity

Earlier we discussed the conjunction of elements—lowering of interest rates, increase and redistribution of income, new household creation from socio-economic changes—that altogether resulted in an expansion of housing activity, which started around 2006.

Others actions taken continuously improved the new legal landmark, mainly in 2004 by increasing security for creditors and borrowers, tax exemption for developers, and reducing costs and increasing tools for credit securitizations. New regulations resulted in improvement of mortgage conditions, increasing the loan maturity and decreasing the interest rate. Thus family income, necessary to finance the same house, decreased to 50 or 60 percent lower than before, between 2006 and 2007.

Housing financing from the SBPE grew rapidly, increasing from 28,900 units in 2002 to almost 300,000 in 2008, surpassing the historical peak attained in 1981, the year before the crisis began, when 267,000 units were financed. However, as the number of households more than doubled between 1980 and 2008, from 25.2 to 57.2 million, the total units financed by the SFH achieved 540,000 in 2008, 14 percent less than the historical peak of 627,000 units in 1980.

Total mortgages in Brazil were only 4.4 percent of the GDP in 2006. Another indicator of growth is per capita housing investment. In 2005, housing investment in Brazil was US$241.67, adjusted for purchasing power parity, less than half of that in Mexico. By comparison, in the same year South Korea invested US$1,320.24 and Australia invested US$2,246.51. Annual investment in housing is expected to exceed US$100 billion in coming years and US$200 billion in the decade of 2020.

Similarly to what has happened in non-housing sectors, a large foreign investment is steadily growing, attracted by the favorable factors of the Brazilian housing market that we describe earlier: economic, institutional, and legal stability; level and growth of income; the prospect of economic growth; trends in population growth; the wide-horizon of demand; existence of a matured financing system with stronger legal guarantees; and the absence of risk factors that triggered the real estate crisis in developed countries, as conditions for granting credits are much more restrictive in Brazil.

This was the picture at the time of the outbreak of the global financial crisis, the effects of which are the subject of the next section.

THE IMPACT OF THE 2008 GLOBAL FINANCIAL CRISIS

As a result of the 2008 global financial crisis, Brazil experienced two quarters of recession, to the extent that global demand for Brazil's commodity-based exports dwindled and external credit dried up. However, Brazilian finances were virtually not contaminated by investments originating from U.S. securities based on sub-prime mortgages, and ended up being one of the first emerging markets to begin a recovery.

Brazilian housing markets have been in a somehow peculiar situation with respect to the impact of the global financial crisis. Brazil was facing a process of economic growth that flourished in 2006, after years of economic restructuring and stabilization. This process had an important redistributive element.

The expansion of lending capacity reached the limits of available funds in the SFH: FGTS and savings. A quick increase in mortgages due to the SFH recovery spurred the availability of 540,000 units in 2008. Nonetheless, this has not been enough to meet the demand for the annual creation of 1.2 million new household dwellings, on top of the accumulated housing deficit of 7.9 million units. The system expansion to meet the affordable demand depends on a fall of interest rates to encourage the secondary mortgage market.

Growth of the adult population is faster than that of the total population, associated with income increase of the poorest extracts resulted in incorporating into the market a large mass of consumers. As a sign, even after the global financial crisis, the volume of housing loans has continued to grow.[4] (See Exhibit 22.6.)

Impact of the 2008 downturn was felt in Brazilian real estate. The BOVESPA Real Estate index, which started with a nominal value of 1,000 in December 2007, registered 307 in December 2008 and 938 in December 2009, reaching 1,000 in September 2010. Caution should be made concerning using this data for furthering the analysis, given the speculative character of the stock market, in the short run.

In this context, a further restructuring of the real estate industry took place, with more oligopolization, with the merging of companies that were not able to stand in the new economic environment.

Minha Casa, Minha Vida (My House, My Life) Housing Program

In Brazil, there has always been a nationwide discussion of improvements of the housing system, particularly coming from developers' associations. This discussion intensified in late 2008, given the need to take actions to combat the impacts of the global financial crisis.

Most of these proposals were covered, in March 2009, by a comprehensive federal government housing plan, named Minha Casa, Minha Vida (My House, My Life): reducing the tax burden for building materials and housing entrepreneurs, modernizing official property records expansion of land regularization instruments of informal settlements, expansion of subsidies that have been linked to funding for families with lower-class and lower-middle-class incomes, and creating mechanisms of loan guarantees for the lower-income families.

Minha Casa, Minha Vida has been launched as an ambitious program, with around US$30 billion (of up to US$1.4 billion) in subsidies, which, according to the government, expected to produce a million new units[5] (Cardoso and Leal 2010).

The program has focused on the rising demand from families in the five- to 10-minimum-wages income bracket, which means 8.4 percent of the total families. The program also provides for the 11.4 percent of families in the three- to five-minimum-wages bracket. For those with a monthly income of three minimum wages (US$592) or less—78.5 percent of families—the program makes provisions of up to R$2.5 billion (around US$1.4 billion) in kind and in mortgage subsidies.

The Brazilian financial system was at that time relatively sound, and public resources were available partly because they did not need to be allocated to help financial institutions, as happened in the United States and other economies.

Minha Casa, Minha Vida came out as a Keynesian-type response to the impact of the global financial crisis, in a remarkable move in a country that has traditionally approached economic policy using monetary mechanisms. However, because of the hurry to achieve results in combating the financial crisis, this plan was not linked to the actions of urban policy and the National Housing Plan, developed over five years and approved a little earlier.

THE CASE OF THE CITY OF SÃO PAULO

The case of São Paulo, the largest city and housing market in Brazil, is illustrative. A reason for the choice of São Paulo is the availability of more adequate real-estate information,[6] making it possible to better detail and analyze recent market behaviors, including the impact of the 2008 global financial crisis.

In a previous work, Haddad and Meyer (2009) made a descriptive analysis of the São Paulo housing market, using information from a database on housing starts in São Paulo along with data from official sources. With a major focus on the relationship of housing conditions and income distribution in São Paulo, the study analyzed the evolution of housing prices and production by different housing sizes, and explored the behavior of the private sector as one of the major actors in housing development, based on how the formal housing market serves only middle- and high-income families. It also has shown some characteristics of the housing industry, pointing the way to further empirical and comparative studies.

As the study covered a period that ended a year before 2008, it does not show the effects of the 2008 global financial crisis. It nevertheless provided a broad picture of the housing situation in São Paulo that seems to be central to situating the impact of the arrival of the global financial crisis. For this purpose, a few findings of that study are selected to be briefly reviewed in this section of the chapter, after presenting some background on the city.

Background on São Paulo

According to the official census, the city of São Paulo, the core of the Greater São Paulo Metropolitan Region, had a population of 9,527,426 in 1991 and 10,434,252 in 2000. This population comprised 2,539,953 households in 1991 and 2,985,977 in 2000. During 1977–2007 formal housing production in the city of São Paulo averaged 22,257 units a year.

Data on housing conditions detail the inadequacy of housing in São Paulo. In 2000 an estimated 551,815 households (18.5 percent of all households) with income below five minimum wages were living in slums, irregular subdivisions, government-produced housing needing improvements, or tenements—or were homeless. Yet many households with an income of more than five minimum wages, which are expected to be served by the formal market, were also living in slums and/or irregular subdivisions—an estimated 221,348 of them (7.4 percent of the total) in 2000.

The main explanation for this apparent contradiction lies in income distribution: a small number of families buy very large units, while the majority live in inadequate housing. But another factor that must be considered is the lack of mortgages designed for the middle-income group, as will be seen in the next section.

Because of the inadequate supply of affordable housing, lower-middle-income families have had to improvise housing solutions. They are competing for places with low-income households on the extreme periphery, where the fragile environment is being damaged. These families are occupying settlements without infrastructure and located far from employment, causing a saturation of the road system.

Brazil has been known as a most unequal society. São Paulo, a small sample of the country, shows a similar pattern. In São Paulo, after a long decline, average family income has recently shown a recovery. Between 2004 and 2006 it rose by 24.6 percent, as compared with an inflation rate of 10.8 percent (based on the Brazilian Statistics and Geography government agency IBGE's IPCA). While average family income in the Greater São Paulo Metropolitan Region increased by almost 58 percent between 2000 and 2007, the minimum wage value increased by 151.7 percent. Caution must therefore be taken when using the minimum wage as a basis for comparison between years, because families have been reclassified to lower brackets over time.

Davis (2006) documents similar developments in different countries around the world, all of them countries that are being affected by globalization. Davis also describes the consequences for housing, which he portrays as generating "a planet of slums."

Housing Starts in São Paulo

Exhibit 22.3 displays the number of residential starts for both the City of São Paulo and the São Paulo Metropolitan Region, in the period between 1985 and 2010. The

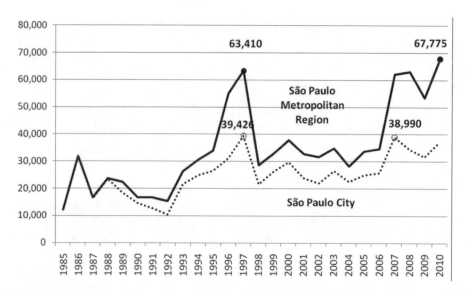

Exhibit 22.3   Residential Unit Starts: São Paulo City and São Paulo Metropolitan Region
Source: EMBRAESP.

cyclical nature of housing starts is recognizable, which can be explained by macro-economic trends and changes in the supply of credit. Indeed, changes in housing starts have been used as a first indicator of whether an economy is heading toward a period of recession or expansion.

Several trends and events can be associated with the behavior of housing starts. For example, the surge in production in 1986 came as a result of the successful implementation of the stabilization policy Plano Cruzado, which had positive effects on income distribution. The more stable rhythm of housing starts since 2000 largely reflects the overall economic stability during the period. And the boom in new starts in 2007 can be accounted for by the capitalization of the biggest developers through initial public offerings, the restructuring of the housing finance system, the decline in interest rates and the lengthening of loan maturities, and the recovery of the economy and the buying power of salaries.

The data illustrates how the uneven income distribution affects housing market production. In the 2001–2005 period, the total residential area offered by the formal market in the city of São Paulo increased by more than 20 million square meters, an average of 66 square meters for each of the new inhabitants, more than enough to shelter them. Yet official statistics reveal a worsening of housing conditions between 2000 and 2005. In that period, the number of people living in favelas (occupied land) increased by 300,000, from 9.4 percent of the population to 11 percent (São Paulo Municipal Government 2003). The population living in irregular subdivisions in 2000 was estimated at 1.46 million, or 14.1 percent.

Issues of Affordability

Studies of housing affordability are usually made on the basis of the relationship between price and income or, whenever there is long-term financing, the relationship between monthly disposable income and the monthly installment payment. The availability of information on income, the main component of demand, has permitted us to build an interesting, and to the best of our knowledge, innovative comparison of the supply of affordable housing and its demand by income bracket. For this purpose two sets of calculations were made:

1. First, we estimated the supply of affordable housing by income bracket, calculating the number of housing starts by income bracket from the price of units and loan conditions from Caixa Econômica Federal.[7]
2. Second, we calculated the distribution of demand by income bracket. Annual demand was calculated from household formation, a vacancy rate (5 percent), obsolescence, and use conversion. This annual demand was then distributed across the income brackets from the sample microdata tabulation, using IBGE's 2000 census.

Using the results of these calculations, an affordability graph was built for 2006 and 2007. Exhibit 22.4 displays the comparison between housing demand and what the formal market has supplied in São Paulo.

The Exhibit includes supply data for 2007 as well as 2006, capturing the shift in the housing supply curve from one year to the next. There was a strong increase in supply, with 25,689 new units in 2006 and 38,990 in 2007—a 52 percent increase. Only families with the income required for the highest ceiling loan value established for the Housing Finance System, R$350,000, were considered. By 2006 the family income required for this highest value was almost 40 minimum wages. In

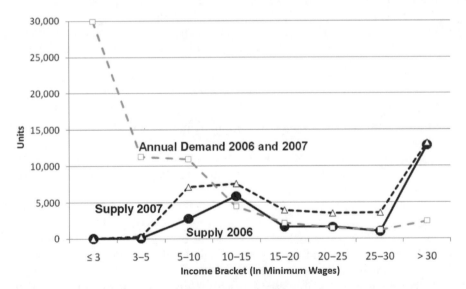

Exhibit 22.4 Housing Production (Units) and Affordability by Income Brackets (São Paulo City, 2006–2007)

Source: Elaborated by the authors with data from EMBRAESP, Caixa Economica Federal, 2000 Census sample micro data from IBGE, PNADs 2001 to 2006 (IBGE household sample annual research), BACEN (Central Bank—IPCA inflation), SEADE 2004 (population and household forecasts), TPCL/PMSP (municipal authority land and building cadastre).

2007 this income requirement dropped to 30 minimum wages, mostly due to the Federal policy of adjusting the value of the minimum wage above the inflation rate.

Exhibit 22.4 clearly shows how great a mismatch there was between supply and demand: While most families are in the lower income brackets, formal market production is geared toward the middle and upper classes. Indeed, the formal market produces almost nothing for families with incomes below five minimum wages—only 0.2 percent of housing starts in 2006 and 0.7 percent in 2007—even though they constitute almost 65 percent of the demand. At the other extreme, 50 percent of housing starts in 2006 and 34 percent in 2007 were produced for families with monthly incomes exceeding 30 minimum wages, which account for only 3.8 percent of the demand.

If the families with incomes above five minimum wages can be used as a proxy for the formal market, it can be said that the formal market is 35 percent of the total market. Half of this formal market is made up of families in the income bracket of 5 to 10 minimum wages. Yet for these families only 10.7 percent of the formal housing supply was affordable in 2006, and 18.2 percent in 2007. The findings also show an unmet demand in the lower-middle class, neglected by formal production as well as by public housing programs.

In 2006 the supply curve had closely adjusted to the demand in the income brackets corresponding to 15 to 30 minimum wages. In 2007 the supply in these brackets was two to three times as large. At brackets above 30 minimum wages the market remained oversupplied. Below this level the supply was sold, reflecting the changes in financial terms that captured part of the latent market. This latent demand can be understood from the inadequacy of housing conditions, accumulated over more than 20 years as a result of the lack of mortgages.

New financial conditions in 2007—and thereafter—opened the way to housing projects affordable to families with incomes below five minimum wages.

Developers' Perspective

In São Paulo, housing development traditionally has not been a concentrated market compared with those in other cities, particularly in the developed world. In 2005, for example, the EMBRAESP database reported that 335 companies had housing starts in the Greater São Paulo Metropolitan Region; the 10 largest of these accounted for 22.64 percent of the market.

Still, a shift toward greater concentration can be observed: In 2000 there had been 360 companies and the 10 largest had a market share of 20.55 percent. The concentration increased since 2007 after a series of mergers and acquisitions following the capitalization of Brazilian real-estate development companies through initial public offerings.

The comparison of quantity and price for housing starts over time in the Greater São Paulo Metropolitan Region gives a picture of developers' behavior. It is remarkable how consistently these indicators move in opposite directions. Exhibit 22.5 shows that the high-income segment operates as a shelter for investment whenever there is a drop in demand, with middle-income housing perceived as a riskier investment.

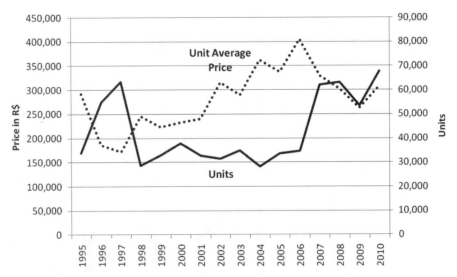

Exhibit 22.5   Residential Unit Starts and Average Total Price (R$): São Paulo Metropolitan Region
Source: EMBRAESP.

The private sector has consistently produced a small number of very large residential units, averaging more than 800 square meters, and virtually no units affordable to those in the lowest income brackets, who have had to find shelter in substandard housing and in informal settlements. This outcome appears to be consistent with the profit-maximizing logic of housing producers.[8]

Impact of the 2008 Global Financial Crisis in São Paulo

In correspondence with what happened at the national level, the impact of the international financial crisis in 2008 was felt in São Paulo: Economic uncertainty led to the halt of housing in October 2008. As expected, this was particularly experienced by housing planning activity; new projects were halted or postponed. However, concession of new financing contracts continued at a steady pace.

In February 2009, a first "after the crisis" residential project was launched in São Paulo, attracting the curiosity of all housing market agents about the outcome. Sales went very well, above expected, which encouraged the launching of old retained projects and new ones as well.

On the other hand, the Minha Casa, Minha Vida program launched in 2009 has boosted the construction of more popular housing, to fill the newly created demand. Indeed, it has been as expected.

In Exhibit 22.5, the presence of the 2008 global financial crisis in São Paulo is displayed with some very interesting insight about its nature. It shows the evolution of past annual residential starts in the period between 2006 and 2010. It clearly indicates an inflection in August 2008, when the financial crisis arrived and a deep fall until July 2009, when the housing activity started increasing again.

Exhibit 22.5 also displays the number of mortgages that has been contracted under the savings and loans (SBPE) system, at the national level. It shows that

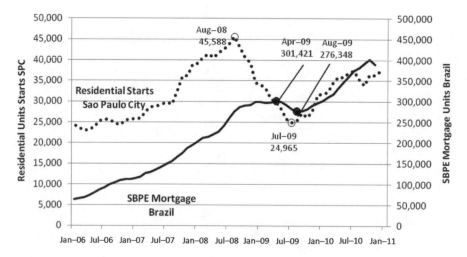

Exhibit 22.6 Impact of the 2008 Global Financial Crisis: SBPE Mortgage: Brazil (Units);
Residential Starts: São Paulo City (Units)
Source: Embraesp, ABECIP, and Central Bank.

the 2008 international financial crisis provoked very little impact over the rhythm
of mortgages, distinctively from what was happened with housing starts. The
comparison leads to an important finding: The fall in the number of housing starts
should be mostly attributed to the conservative attitude of housing developers
whom, facing the new financial outlook, made the decision to stop new projects
and wait. New mortgages in this period were geared to finance used homes.

Another noticeable change has been the move of the housing market toward
lower-income families, as indicated in Exhibit 22.7.

If we take the two-bedroom unit as a proxy, the number of new housing starts
in 2006 were 10,941, and grew to 21,610 (2007), 22,387 (2008), 27,426 (2009), and

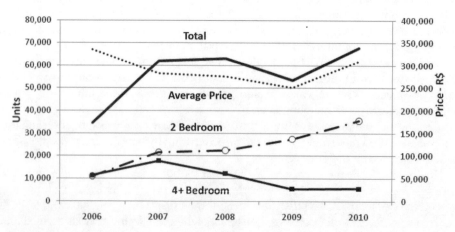

Exhibit 22.7 Average Price of Residential Starts: Two and Four Bedrooms (São Paulo
Metropolitan Region)
Source: EMBRAESP.

29,963 (2010, up until November). On the other extreme, starts for four-or-more-bedroom units went down from 17,770, in 2007, to 12,173 (2008), 5,466 (2009), and 4,634 (2010, up until November).

This realignment of the housing market to attend families in the lower income brackets has been an expected effect of the Minha Casa, Minha Vida program. This shift is also shown by the decrease of the mean value of all new residential starts, which went down from R$334,939 in 2006 to R$250,860 in 2009. Increase in average value in 2010 can be partially explained by the hike in land prices, mostly due to demand pressures for new construction, but also due to restrictions from a new City Zoning regulation.

CONCLUSION

The 2008 global financial crisis has produced impacts that were differentiated among countries, which can be understood only by considering the dynamics of their own socioeconomic conditions and housing situations. Any housing analysis and forecast in developing countries, like Brazil, with a sizeable housing deficit must consider changes in the pattern of income distribution, which dams up an enormously latent housing demand. This partially explains why in Brazil, the impact was limited: It reached the country while the housing sector was booming, as an outcome of a series of structural changes that were taking place in the economy, mostly resulting in an increase of average family incomes, and more availability of mortgage credit.

New economic and financial housing policies and programs have succeeded in moving many families out of housing deficit, to now be part of the solvable demand. This essay is written in 2010, picturing a nationwide flourishing housing activity that has been projected to keep up in the short run, along with the expected permanence of the economic situation. By now, the (improperly named) "housing crisis" seems to have faded away in the memory of the Brazilian housing agents.

New steps have been identified and discussed as necessary to improve the delivery of new housing in Brazil: creation of the register of good borrowers to further ease credit; enlargement of the secondary mortgage market in addition to continuing the reduction of interest rates—which will make saving earnings competitive again, compared to funds that invest in debt securities of government; the standardization of mortgages contracts; costs reduction; simplification of bureaucratic procedures; and the elimination of retention of credit for originators.

A final comment: Housing delivery for most Brazilian people, the poor in particular, will still require a large amount of subsidy. Urban policy and housing policy should have a decisive role, with the lending system, to meet the housing needs of the Brazilian population.

ACKNOWLEDGMENTS

The authors would like to thank Luis Paulo Pompeia, executive director of Empresa Brasileira de Estudos do Patrimonio (EMBRAESP), for his comments and for permission to use information from EMBRAESP database.

NOTES

1. A comment should be made about the term *household* as used in this chapter. Many readers—especially those from developed nations—might equal one household to one family, which is not necessarily the case in Brazil and in other developing nations. Macedo et al. (2007) discusses definitional nuances whenever applying U.S.-based housing analysis models to the Brazilian case: "The definition of certain terms became very important to ensure equivalency and precision of the adapted model, particularly terms not commonly used in American context such as informality, shared households, and late-stayers."

2. The translation of R$ to US$ uses the exchange rate of April 1, 2009: US$1 = R$2.25.

3. Foreclosure in Brazil, is too complex to be properly quantified. In a period of high inflation, payment adjustments—made annually—are very sharp and the risk of delinquency becomes a much politicized issue. With debt renegotiation schemes, the condition of foreclosure becomes fuzzy. On the other hand, new conditions of SFI contracts have been effective in reducing foreclosure, which has been difficult to determine from the available aggregate data.

4. There is a time lag between the signing of a loan contract and the beginning of construction.

5. Almost comparable to Bolsa Familia, Minha Casa, Minha Vida was taken as one of the pillars of President Luis Ignacio Lula da Silva's political strategy. At the end of his mandate, in December of 2010, it was announced that the targeted one million houses was already contracted, although only 247,000 were delivered to that date.

6. A major source of information is one database on new housing in the city of São Paulo, Brazil. With data collected and organized by Empresa Brasileira de Estudos do Patrimônio (EMBRAESP), a local private real-estate consultancy, this database has documented housing starts in São Paulo for almost 30 years.

7. A large number of data were used and for that purpose hypotheses need to be made relating to the index for adjusting prices for inflation and the correction of census microdata to account for income from family members.

8. This part of the chapter is heavily based on Haddad and Meyer's (2009) evidence, which furthers the São Paulo housing market analysis, including the implications of the new Zoning regulation, evolution of prices, and giving details that go beyond the purposes of the present chapter.

REFERENCES

Akiyama, Y. 2002. "The World Land Survey: An Introduction of a Methodology for Comparing Real Estate Values." Available at www.lares.org.br/SL2_akiyama.pdf, accessed April 7, 2007.

Banco Pactual SA. 2006 (January 23). "Mortgage Boom in Brasil: The FCVS effect." Pactual, in *Brazil Equity Update*.

Barbon, A. L. 2003. *Mobilidade residencial intra-urbana em grande centros: Região Metropolitana de São Paulo*. Master's thesis, Pontifícia Universidade Católica de Campinas, State of São Paulo.

Brazil Central Bank. Available at www.bcb.gov.br.

Brasil. 2009. "Medida provisória n. 459 de 25 de Março de 2009—Dispõe sobre o Programa Minha Casa, Minha Vida—PMCMV, a regularização fundiária de assentamentos localizados em áreas urbanas." Presidência da República do Brasil, Brasília.

Brazil, Ministry of Cities, National Secretariat of Housing; Centro de Estudos da Metrópole; CEBRAP (Centro Brasileiro de Análise e Planejamento). (n.d.). "Estudo revela mais 6 milhões de brasileiros vivendo em áreas precárias." Available at www.cidades.gov.br/media/DomiciliosemAssentamentosPrecariosporMunicipio.pdf, accessed January 12, 2008.

Brazilian Statistics and Geography Governmental Agency (IBGE). Available at www.sidra.ibge.gov.br.

Bonduki, N. 1998. *Origens da habitação social no Brasil*. São Paulo: Estação Liberdade.

Cardoso, Adauto Lucio, and José Agostinho Leal. 2010. "Housing Markets in Brazil: Recent Trends and Governmental Responses to the 2008 Crisis." *International Journal of Housing Policy* 10: 2, 191–208.

CIA (Central Intelligence Agency). "Brazil." In *The World Factbook*. Available at https://www.cia.gov/library/publications/the-world-factbook/geos/br.html.

Construction Industry Brazilian Chamber (CBIC). Available at www.cbicdados.com.br.

Davis, M. 2006. *Planet of Slums*. London: Verso.

Duhau, E., and G. Uribe. 2007 (October). "Los nuevos productores del espacio habitable: Breve historia de una mercancía possible." Paper presented at the 30th meeting of Red Nacional de Investigación Urbana, Toluca, Mexico.

Ernest and Young and FGV. 2008. "Brasil sustentável potencialidades do mercado habitacional." Available at www.ey.com.br.

FGV. 2007. "O crédito imobiliário no Brasil: caracterização e desafios." Fundação Getúlio Vargas (FGV) projetos, São Paulo. Available at www.abecip.org.br/sitenovo/arquivos/Trabalho_FGV.pdf.

Haddad, E. 2005 (September). "O Mercado imobiliário antecipa as alterações da estrutura dos bairros? Evidências no caso de São Paulo." Paper presented at the fifth annual meeting of the Latin American Real Estate Society, São Paulo. Available at http://www.lares.org.br/haddad.pdf, accessed May 4, 2007.

Haddad, Emilio, and João Fernando Meyer. 2009. "Housing Conditions and Income Distribution: Evidence from São Paulo." In S. V. Lall et al., eds., *Urban Land Markets: Improving Land Management for Successful Urbanization*. The World Bank. Springer.

IPEA. 2007. "Habitação. IPEA. Políticas sociais—acompanhamento e análise no 14. 2007. Boletins—IPEA. Available at www.ipea.gov.br.

João Pinheiro Foundation and Brazil, Ministry of Cities. 2005. "Déficit habitacional do Brasil". Available in CDSoftware, issue 1.5.

Macedo, Carlos G. 2007 (January 19). "'Your Time Is Gonna Come': Por que o crédito imobiliário não será relevante para os bancos por algum tempo." *Unibanco, relatório*.

Macedo, J., D. Nguyen, W. J. O'Dell, M. T. Smith, M. V. Serra, G. A. Guia, et al. 2007. Affordable Housing Needs Assessment Methodology: The Adaptation of the Florida Model to Brazil. In M. Freire, R. Lima, D. Cira, B. Ferguson, C. Kessides, and J. A. Motta, eds., *Land and Urban Policies for Poverty Reduction: Proceedings of the Third International Urban Research Symposium*, vol. 2, pp. 239–268. Washington, DC; Brasilia, D.F.; World Bank: IPEA.

Meyer, J. F. P. 2008. *Demanda residencial: Adequação da análise de mercado imobiliário—o caso de São Paulo*. PhD dissertation, University of São Paulo, School of Architecture and Urbanism.

Miles, M., G. Behrens, and M. Weiss. 2000. *Real Estate Development: Principles and Process*, 3rd ed. Washington, DC: Urban Land Institute.

Real Estate Saving and Loans Entities Association (ABECIP). Available at www.abecip.org.br.

São Paulo Municipal Government. 2003. *Plano Municipal de Habitação. Versão para debate*. São Paulo: Author.

São Paulo Municipal Planning Department. 2002. "População, renda e categorias selecionadas de uso do solo em São Paulo: 1991–2000." Available at http:// sempla.prefeitura.sp.gov.br/, accessed August 31, 2006.

SEADE (São Paulo State Statistical Office) and SABESP (São Paulo State Water Resources Management Agency). 2004. *Projeções para o Estado de São Paulo: População e domicílios até 2025* (CD-ROM). São Paulo: Author.

SECOVI (São Paulo State Housing Union). *SECOVI.* Available at www.secovi.com.br

Souza, Aline Amaral. 2006. O papel do crédito imobiliário na dinâmica do mercado habitacional brasileiro. I prêmio Abecip de monografia em crédito imobiliário e poupança, Rio de Janeiro.

World Bank. 1993. "Housing: Enabling Markets to Work." World Bank Policy Paper. Washington, DC.

ABOUT THE AUTHORS

EMILIO HADDAD is a Civil Engineer, with a degree from the University of São Paulo–USP (1970), a Master's of Science in Civil Engineering from Stanford University (1973), a Master's of City Planning from University of California–Berkeley (1975), and a PhD from the University of São Paulo (1987). He served as Principal Researcher of the São Paulo Technological Research Institute (IPT) from 1969 to 1997 and as Planning Director for the Greater São Paulo Housing Authority (COHAB) from 1983–1986. Presently Haddad is associated professor of the School of Architecture and Planning of the University of São Paulo and Coordinator of MBA in Real Estate Development, of FUPAM Foundation. He is a past president of the Latin American Real Estate Society, and his fields of interest include Urban Planning, Real Estate Markets, and property and environmental valuation.

JOÃO FERNANDO PIRES MEYER is an architect, with a PhD from University of São Paulo. He is a professor and researcher in the School of Architecture and Planning at University of São Paulo. He is also professor of real estate marketing analysis at the Foundation for Environmental Research (FUPAM). He is a past president of the Latin American Real Estate Society (LARES). His research interests are housing, urban planning, real estate market, and real estate projects.

CHAPTER 23

The Canadian Housing Market

No Bubble? No Meltdown?

TOM CARTER
Professor of Geography, The University of Winnipeg

INTRODUCTION

The impact of housing is far-reaching. It plays a dynamic and crucial role in people's lives and in the economy of countries. The purchase of a home is generally the largest investment people make, usually the largest debt they have to repay, and often the equity in their homes is a tremendous source of wealth. Housing equity accounts for over 40 percent of the assets of households (CMHC 2010a). Affordable quality housing with security of tenure also contributes to positive educational and health outcomes. Housing construction can be the basis for skills development, employment generation, and community development. From an economic perspective housing-related economic activity accounted for $307 billion in 2009 in Canada—over one-fifth of Canada's gross domestic product (Statistics Canada 2010a). Housing generates employment across a wide range of sectors. In 2009 approximately 71,000 residential construction firms and 158,000 specialty trade contractors worked in residential construction (CMHC 2010a).

Given the importance of housing, when there are significant price swings or other shifts in the housing market, the ripple effects filter through the economy and beyond to affect the lives and livelihood of many people. Such has been the case with the housing bubble, and subsequent market meltdown in many countries in the 2007 to 2009 period. The bubble and the bursting of the bubble combined with the subprime mortgage problems in countries like the United States helped trigger a global economic downturn from which most of the world has yet to recover.

The broad objective of this chapter is to address the basic question: Was there a housing bubble and market meltdown in Canada? The discussion begins with an examination of trends in basic elements of housing demand. This is followed by an examination of market trends in recent years to capture changes in housing prices and other key indicators before, during, and since the recent market difficulties. Both national and city specific trends will be highlighted because markets in some Canadian cities deviate substantially from national averages. This section is followed by a discussion of the housing finance sector in Canada, the regulatory framework the government has established, and the role lending regulations and criteria played in preventing a housing meltdown. Within this discussion the role of institutions such as Canada Mortgage and Housing Corporation (CMHC) and their activity in mortgage insurance and provision of mortgage-backed securities and the effect they may have had on market stabilization will be highlighted.

The basic argument throughout the chapter is that, although there was price escalation nationally and particularly regionally (in specific cities) there was no fatal "bubble." Price escalation was significant in some markets, however the collapse (price decline) either did not happen, has yet to happen, or was modest compared to the situation in some other countries. Consumers, lenders, and others in the housing market felt some pain but it was short-lived and not fatal. The discussion examines the evidence that supports this basic argument.

WHAT IS A HOUSING BUBBLE?

Before moving into an analysis of market trends a discussion of the characteristics of a housing bubble is useful. According to MacDonald (2010), a "housing bubble emerges when housing prices increase more rapidly than inflation, household incomes, and economic growth. Several factors tend to contribute to the growth of a housing bubble: low mortgage rates, access to easy credit, net immigration, and the supply of available housing. Bubbles are often accompanied by wild card factors such as subprime mortgage schemes in loosely regulated financial markets."

According to MacDonald there have been geographically isolated bubbles in Canada in the past: two in Vancouver and one in Toronto. The first bubble burst in Vancouver in 1981, the second in 1994. Toronto had one bubble that burst in 1989. However, MacDonald also points out that although there were price corrections associated with all three of these bubbles, the decline stretched over a three- to four-year period—the air escaped gradually from the bubble. Price corrections were gradual and generally less than 20 percent depending on unit type and location in the respective cities. Calgary and Edmonton, in the oil-rich province of Alberta, experienced similar market price declines in the early 1980s, but the trend was very short-lived and prices soon began climbing again. During these bubbles a few people lost homes but the most significant effect was a short-term decline in equity (MacDonald 2010).

Although there have been no bubbles since then, some economists have warned that Canada's housing market is overvalued (Wong 2010). The Canadian Imperial bank of Commerce warns that a housing correction is in the cards (Laduarantaye 2010) and the Canadian Association of Accredited Mortgage Professionals estimates that there are close to 400,000 mortgage holders in Canada who are already challenged by their current payments and may not be able to handle higher interest rates (Grant 2010). The following discussion further develops the evidence around the bubble meltdown scenario.

DEMAND INFLUENCES

Examination of some of the basic factors that influence the demand for housing indicates that there are few trends nationally that would prompt rapid price escalations in housing. These include underlying demand factors such as population and household growth, and interprovincial and international migration. These are factors that affect the number of houses needed to accommodate the population.

Effective demand factors that actually permit households to exercise their housing choices such as income growth are also examined. Some of the trends discussed actually helped protect home owners from exposure to higher prices and mortgage defaults.

Population and Household Growth

Population growth rates in Canada have slowed in recent years. The five-year growth rate in the period 1971–1976 was 9.2 percent; during 2001–2006 it was 3.8 percent. During the 2006–2009 period estimated annual population increase has been 1.1 percent, or roughly 385,000 people annually (Statistics Canada 2010b). The population is aging and fertility rates have continued to decline and are currently below replacement rates. Population growth is driven by a relatively high level of immigration and higher fertility and growth rates amongst some sectors of the population, such as Aboriginals.

Growth rates, however, have varied depending on the region of the country and have been substantially above the national average in some provinces. Over the decade 1999–2009, Alberta has led all provinces in growth and the population has increased 25 percent (Exhibit 23.1). In Ontario and British Columbia growth rates have also exceeded the national average over this timeframe. Some provinces actually experienced population decline during this period and several others grew more slowly than the country as a whole. The West (Manitoba, Saskatchewan, Alberta, and British Columbia) grew more rapidly than the rest of Canada, although much of this growth was concentrated in Alberta and British Columbia. Certain metropolitan centers also grew more rapidly than others. The two major metropolitan centers in Alberta—Calgary and Edmonton—led the way with growth rates of 46 percent and 30 percent respectively over the 1996–2009 period, followed by Toronto at 28 percent, then Vancouver at 22 percent (Exhibit 23.2). Again metropolitan centers in the west grew more rapidly than those in the rest of Canada.

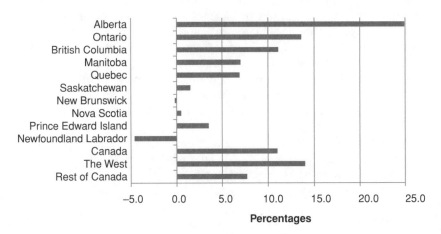

Exhibit 23.1 Population Growth Rates by Province, 1999–2009
Source: Statistics Canada 2010, Cansim Table 51-0046.

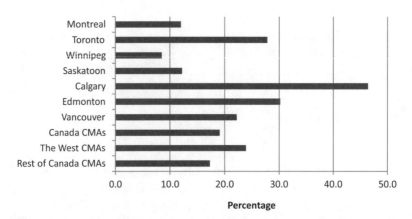

Exhibit 23.2 Population Growth in Selected Metropolitan Centers, 1996–2009
Source: Statistics Canada 2010, Cansim Table 51-0046.

Nationally household growth rates, the basic element of housing demand, have also been declining since 1971. During the period 1971–1976, the five-year increase in households was 18.7 percent (Statistics Canada 2007) but fell to 7.6 percent during the period 2001–2006. Immigration and falling household size (from 3.5 in 1971 to 2.5 in 2006), and growth in smaller household types such as single seniors, childless couples, and single individuals, has continued to generate demand for housing, albeit at lower levels than in the past. In absolute terms the annual growth in households nationally is currently approximately 175,000 (Statistics Canada 2007).

Again, there are region- and center-specific differences in the basic element of housing demand. Drawing on statistics from the period 1996–2006 household growth ranged from 4 percent in the Province of Saskatchewan to 28 percent in Alberta and 68 percent in British Columbia (Exhibit 23.3). Ninety-two percent of total household growth in Canada during the 1996–2006 period occurred in the four provinces of Quebec, Ontario, Alberta, and British Columbia (Statistics Canada 2007). With respect to metropolitan areas, high rates of household growth occurred in Toronto (21 percent), Calgary (36 percent), and Edmonton (27 percent)—all well above the national average of 15 percent. Vancouver and Montreal grew at approximately the national average. When absolute numbers are considered, Montreal was experiencing growth of approximately 18,000 households annually, Toronto 31,000, Calgary 11,000, Vancouver 12,000, and Edmonton 8,500. Fifty percent of annual household growth in the nation occurred in these five centers (Statistics Canada 2007).

From a population and household growth perspective, housing demand was very region- and center-specific and, as a later discussion illustrates, this has the expected effects on other market indicators.

Interprovincial and International Migration

Population shifts within regions of Canada and the arrival of international immigrants have a significant effect on housing markets. Canada has been accepting

Exhibit 23.3 Household Growth: Canada, Provinces, and Selected
Metropolitan Centers, 1996–2006

	Avg. Annual Growth	% Change
Canada	161,742	14.9
Newfoundland and Labrador	1,169	6.3
Prince Edward Island	518	10.8
Nova Scotia	3,425	10.0
New Brunswick	2,481	9.1
Quebec	3,673	13.0
Ontario	63,052	16.1
Manitoba	2,940	7.0
Saskatchewan	1,433	3.8
Alberta	27,703	28.3
British Columbia	66,398	67.8
Montreal	18,435	13.7
Toronto	31,270	21.0
Winnipeg	1,983	7.8
Saskatoon	1,072	12.7
Calgary	11,029	36.1
Edmonton	8,525	26.7
Vancouver	12,407	18.0

Source: CMHC 2010, adapted from Statistics Canada (Census of Canada) Catalogue
#96F0030XIE2001003.

approximately 250,000 international immigrants annually since the late 1990s.
Over the past decade 75 percent of these immigrants chose Toronto, Montreal,
and Vancouver as their destination. Secondary destination points of importance
include Calgary and Edmonton (Citizenship and Immigration Canada 2010). Over
the period 1997 to 2007, provinces that were destinations for interprovincial moves
were Ontario, Alberta, and British Columbia. Alberta, for example, gained on average 27,500 people annually over this period as people moved from other provinces
(Statistics Canada 2008a).

As Exhibit 23.4 illustrates, international immigration is the most significant
driver of population growth in metropolitan areas, contributing 10.65 persons
per thousand to growth in 2008/2009, while interprovincial migration resulted in
a loss of -0.08 persons per thousand. Intraprovincial migration contributed 0.19
and natural increase 4.78 persons per thousand to metropolitan growth. Vancouver led all major metropolitan cities with 19.44 international immigrant arrivals
per thousand, followed by Saskatoon, Calgary, Toronto, Montreal, Winnipeg, and
Edmonton. Most cities, including Vancouver, actually lost people through interprovincial migration but Saskatoon, Calgary, and Edmonton experienced net gains
through interprovincial migration. International immigration has had a significant
influence on housing demand and housing markets in specific regions and centers, and in some centers in the west demand has been further strengthened by
interprovincial moves.

The characteristics of immigrants and their housing choices and opportunities also have an influence on housing markets. Approximately one-half of

Exhibit 23.4 Demographic Growth Factors by Selected Metropolitan Areas, 2008/2009 (Rates per Thousand)

	Natural Increase	International Migration	Interprovincial Migration	Intraprovincial Migration	Total Migration	Total Growth
All CMAs	4.78	10.65	−0.08	0.19	10.76	15.54
Toronto	6.18	15.02	−1.42	−3.13	10.47	16.65
Montreal	5.16	12.17	−2.54	−1.70	7.93	13.09
Winnipeg	3.19	12.05	−2.48	0.84	11.42	14.60
Saskatoon	5.45	16.09	3.66	3.28	23.04	28.49
Calgary	9.02	15.07	7.20	0.42	22.69	31.71
Edmonton	7.23	10.89	4.80	1.68	17.37	24.60
Vancouver	4.32	19.44	−0.17	−2.44	16.84	21.60
Canada	4.02	8.28	0.00	0.00	8.28	12.30

Source: Statistics Canada 2010, Catalogue #91-214-X.

international immigrants over the past decade have been economic immigrants selected for their high level of skills and their ability to fit into skilled positions needed in the labor force. Five percent of the economic immigrants are investor immigrants who come to establish or invest in existing businesses. They come with significant assets. When all immigrants are considered the majority (two-thirds) are married, with 50 percent in the prime workforce age group of 25–44. Approximately 45 percent have university degrees (16 percent a Masters or PhD) and another 20 percent have certificates in the trades (Citizenship and Immigration Canada 2010). Although labor force integration is difficult for some because of credential recognition problems and difficulties getting their foreign work experience recognized, because of their higher levels of education and skills, their earning potential is significant, particularly for the economic immigrants.

With a strong preference for homeownership and the characteristics noted above, immigrants can have significant effect on the demand in the homeownership market soon after they arrive. Carter (2009) found that 39 percent of economic immigrant arrivals to Manitoba under the Manitoba Provincial Nominee Program had bought homes within two years of arrival. At the end of five years 76 percent were homeowners, higher than the average (68 percent) for the total provincial population. Hiebert and Mendez (2008) found that Canada-wide home-ownership rates amongst all recently arrived immigrants increased from about 20 percent six months after arrival to just more than 50 percent four years after arrival. Although still below the national average of 68 percent, this represents a significant demand for homes, particularly in certain major metropolitan centers, where a very large percentage of immigrants settle. Ley (2001) has noted the high correlation between the arrival of international immigrants and increases in house prices in Toronto (0.81) and Vancouver (0.96).

Interprovincial migrants have different population and locational characteristics. They are more likely to move to take jobs in industries located in resource communities than they are to relocate to larger cities. The vast majority are young adults, although there are also older families leaving the more economically depressed regions of the country (Roach 2010). Interprovincial migrants also include seniors seeking retirement locations, particularly in warmer locations in British Columbia. Overall, interprovincial migrants have less effect on housing demand in the major metropolitan centers and are more likely to be renters than owners. This does not mean that their arrival does not drive up housing prices and rents. In resource communities like Fort McMurray in Alberta housing prices and rents have escalated significantly and vacancy rates in the rental market are near zero (CMHC 2010b).

Changes in the Proportion of Homeowners

Another factor important to housing market circumstances in the Canadian context is the level of home ownership. The percentage of households that own in Canada has been climbing steadily since 1971, from 60 to 68 percent in 2006. Rates vary by metropolitan center. It is higher in western cities such as Calgary (74 percent) and Edmonton (69 percent). Vancouver (65 percent) and Toronto (68 percent) are near the national average (Exhibit 23.5). Overall, the level of ownership has increased about 10 percent nationally over the period 1971–2006 but in some metropolitan centers the increase during that time frame has been 10 to 15 percent. In Montreal, normally characterized as a "city of renters," the proportion of owners has jumped almost 20 percent since 1971. As the figures illustrate, a lot of the increase is recent and occurred in the decade 1996–2006.

The significant rise in condominium development has also helped to increase the level of ownership. In centers of 10,000 plus, condominiums constituted 22 percent of all starts in 2000. By 2008 this proportion had risen to 39 percent before falling back to 26 percent in 2009 (Exhibit 23.6). When condominiums and single detached starts (both intended for the ownership market) are combined, approximately 90 percent of all starts in centers of 10,000 people or more were intended for the ownership market over the 2000–2009 period. A minor qualification is required to clarify this discussion. Some of these condominiums are what are known as "investor condominiums." They are purchased by people who then rent them out. However, many of these investors plan to occupy these units themselves at a future date—when they retire for example. They become owner-occupiers. Despite this qualification, from 1981 to 2006 the number of owner-occupied

Exhibit 23.5 Home Ownership Rates, Canada and Selected Centers, 1971–2006

	1971	1976	1981	1986	1991	1996	2001	2006
Canada	60.3	61.8	62.1	62.1	62.6	63.6	65.8	68.4
Montreal	35.5	38.4	41.9	44.7	46.7	48.5	50.2	53.4
Toronto	55.4	56.7	57.3	58.3	57.9	58.4	63.2	67.6
Winnipeg	59.6	59.2	59.1	60.8	62.0	63.9	65.5	67.2
Saskatoon	61.3	65.7	61.8	59.9	61.0	61.4	65.0	66.8
Calgary	56.5	59.2	58.4	57.9	60.6	65.5	70.6	74.1
Edmonton	57.1	58.1	57.9	57.1	59.2	64.4	66.3	69.2
Vancouver	59.8	59.4	58.5	56.3	57.5	59.4	61.0	65.1

Source: CMHC 2010a, adapted from Statistics Canada (Census of Canada).

Exhibit 23.6 Housing Market Indicators Canada, 2000–2009

	2000	2001	2002	2003	2004	2005	2006	2007	2008	2009
Housing Starts	151,165	162,733	205,034	218,426	233,431	225,481	227,395	228,343	211,056	149,081
Single detached starts (%)	61	59	61	56	55	53	53	52	44	51
Intended Market										
Freehold (%)	70	67	69	64	61	59	58	58	51	60
Condominium (%)	22	22	21	26	29	31	32	32	39	26
MLS sales ($)	334,375	381,484	418,948	434,310	459,762	483,663	483,129	521,051	431,823	465,251
MLS average price ($)	163,992	171,743	188,871	207,321	226,561	249,187	277,207	307,094	304,971	320,333
MLS price change ($)	—	4.7	10.0	9.8	9.3	10.0	11.2	10.8	-0.7	5.0
New house price index (% change)	2.2	2.7	4.1	4.8	5.5	5.0	9.7	7.7	3.4	-2.3
Consumer price index	2.7	2.5	2.3	2.8	1.9	2.2	2.0	2.1	2.4	0.3
Unemployment rate	6.8	7.2	7.7	7.6	7.2	6.8	6.3	6.0	6.1	8.3
1-year mortgage rate	7.85	6.14	5.17	4.84	4.59	5.06	6.28	6.90	6.70	4.02
5-year mortgage rate	8.35	7.40	7.02	6.39	6.23	5.99	6.66	7.07	7.06	5.63
Real median household income ($)	46,100	47,600	47,700	47,500	47,900	48,900	49,800	51,200	52,000	N/A
Real median household income (% change)	—	3.3	0.2	-0.4	0.8	2.1	1.8	2.8	1.6	—
Real median income after tax owner households ($)	55,600	58,000	58,100	58,100	58,500	59,600	60,300	62,000	63,800	—
Real median income after tax owner households (% change)	—	4.3	0.2	—	0.7	1.9	1.2	2.8	2.9	—
Real disposable income (% change)	5.0	2.8	1.7	2.2	3.9	2.7	5.9	4.0	3.7	1.2

Source: CMHC 2010a Canadian Housing Observer.

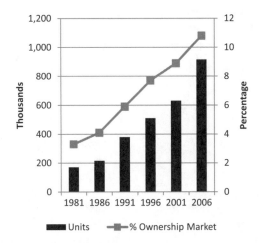

Exhibit 23.7 Condominiums and the Ownership Market, 1981–2006
Source: CMHC 2010a, adapted from Statistics Canada (Census of Canada).

condominiums in Canada increased five-fold from 171,000 to 916,000 and the market share of condominiums rose from 3 to 11 percent (Exhibit 23.7).

These figures suggest a rising number of households with exposure to changes to prices in the ownership housing market. However, many condominiums are purchased by middle-aged and older generations. The home ownership rate for households with maintainers aged 50 or older has risen sharply because of rising condominium ownership rates. In 2006, 57 percent of condominium owners in Canada were aged 50 or older while 16 percent were 75 or older (CMHC 2010a). In the past many of these elderly people would have moved into the rental market and their increased ownership of condominiums has helped raise the overall level of home ownership. Many of the older (50-plus) households purchase condominiums with equity from previous units they have owned—often mortgage-free. When they purchase a condominium they have either a low-value mortgage or no mortgage at all. Their risk exposure to market fluctuations is minimal, except for the effect that price changes may have on equity.

Furthermore, 46 percent of all households in the nation who own a home are mortgage-free and the vast majority are over the age of 50 (CMHC 2010a). The average Canadian homeowner's equity position in 2009 was about 74 percent of home value compared to 43 percent in the United States (Davies and Daniel 2009). Among the subset of mortgage holders in Canada, about 80 percent have at least 20 percent equity in their homes—9 percent have less than 10 percent equity. In the Canadian context, equity increases with age (Exhibit 23.8), rising from a 40 percent equity share for households with maintainers aged 20–29 to over 90 percent for household maintainers aged 60 years and over (Brown and Lafrance 2010).

This trend is affected by the fact that older households are less likely to have a mortgage, as more than three-quarters of household maintainers over 60 years of age are mortgage-free. Rising prices since purchase also affect the equity ratio and older households have the advantage of price appreciation over a longer period of time. The equity position of households has changed only marginally over the past three decades. Generally, the equity position of households with maintainers

Exhibit 23.8 Housing Tenure Owners with and without Mortgages and Equity Share by Age Group

	Tenure		Owner-Occupied Dwellings		
	Rent %	Own	With Mortgage	Without Mortgage	Equity Share
20 to 29	70	30	87	13	40
30 to 39	39	61	88	12	45
40 to 49	30	70	70	30	66
50 to 59	22	78	47	53	79
60 to 69	25	75	26	74	90
70-plus	32	68	11	89	97

Source: Statistics Canada 2010, Survey of Household Spending (2006) and Survey of Financial Security (2005).

under the age of 40 has declined because in recent years the down payment required has been lowered as a proportion of the sales price and prices have been rising. The declines in equity share are on the order of 20 percent (Brown, Hou, and Lafrance 2010). For household maintainers over 40 there has been virtually no change in their equity share (Exhibit 23.9). However, the dollar value of equity has risen considerably in recent years. For example, the value of the equity for all households with a mortgage rose from $93,000 in 1999 to $120,000 in 2005 (in 2005 dollars). Owners without a mortgage have seen the value of their equity rise from $173,000 to $228,000 and for all owners the figures are $125,000 to $169,000 (CMHC 2010a). The Canadian Association of Accredited Mortgage Professionals estimates that in 2010 owners who have a mortgage had equity of $146,000 (2010 dollars) and for owners without a mortgage their equity had risen to $335,000 (Dunning 2010). In 1999 the equity in the home represented about 30 percent of owners' net worth and this had risen to 40 percent by 2005 (CMHC 2010a). No similar figures are available for 2010.

It appears that Canadian home owners may be in a better equity position than their American counterparts. With just one-in-ten owing more than 90 percent of the value of their home, Canadian home owners are in a good position to weather economic turmoil (Davies and Daniel 2009). Younger homeowners, however, have more limited equity and therefore are more exposed to risks associated with price declines than older households, particularly as close to 90 percent of owners under 40 still have a mortgage. Older households are less exposed to risks associated with fluctuations in market price. They have sufficient equity in their home to cover mortgage costs (if they have a mortgage) if they had to sell. However, moving forward, if house prices decline then people's equity will also decline, leaving them more exposed to risks in general and reducing their net worth overall.

Income Growth

Income is another key underlying factor that affects housing demand, people's ability to absorb price increases, and weather market fluctuations. Income growth has been very modest in Canada. Real median household income after tax increased approximately 1.7 percent per annum over the period 2000 to 2008. In some years

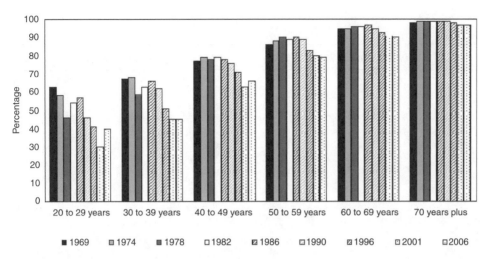

Exhibit 23.9 Equity Shares across Age Groups, 1969–2006
Source: Statistics Canada 2010, Publication 11F0027M, no. 66.

it actually declined, for example in 2003 (Exhibit 23.6). For families, the growth was 1.8 percent per annum and 1.4 percent for individuals. These modest growth rates lag increases in general cost of living (CPI) and increases in house prices (Exhibit 23.6). Increases in the real median income (after tax) of homeowners have also been modest—in some years there has been no increase. Real disposable income increases, however, have exceeded increases in the CPI but have lagged increases in house prices (Exhibit 23.6). Improvements in disposable income have been affected in a positive fashion by changes in the tax system: the reduction of the Goods and Services Tax (GST) by the federal government from 7 to 5 percent, and changes to income tax rates, particularly for moderate and higher income people, that left more money in their pockets (Yalnizyan 2010).

Income, like other indicators, does vary regionally. Ontario, with an annual average real median household income of $56,800 exceeds the national average of $52,000 by almost $5,000. British Columbia has an average real median household income of $53,900, approximately $2,000 above the national average. Alberta at $67,400 exceeds the national average by approximately $14,000. Specific centers exceeding the national average by amounts ranging from $5,000 to $10,000 include Ottawa and Toronto, and a number of smaller metropolitan centers in the Toronto region. Average household incomes in Edmonton and Calgary exceed the national average by more than $15,000 (Statistics Canada 2008b). The more robust income growth in some areas suggests higher purchasing power or at least the ability to afford higher prices.

Unemployment

Unemployment, also a key factor in people's ability to purchase and/or maintain their homes, did increase during the recent recession, although in many centers the increase was modest. Nationally, the unemployment rate increased from 6 percent in 2007 to 6.1 in 2008, and then jumped to 8.3 percent in 2009. Over the period 2007–2009 the rate in Toronto jumped from 6.8 to 9.4 percent, in Calgary from 3.5 to

Exhibit 23.10 Unemployment Rates: Canada and Selected Metropolitan Centers, 1999–2009

	1999	2000	2001	2002	2003	2004	2005	2006	2007	2008	2009
Canada	7.6	6.8	7.2	7.7	7.6	7.2	6.8	6.3	6.0	6.1	8.3
Montreal	9.6	8.1	7.9	7.9	7.5	6.9	7.3	7.9	6.4	6.2	6.9
Toronto	6.1	5.5	6.3	7.4	7.7	7.5	7.0	6.6	6.8	6.9	9.4
Winnipeg	5.8	5.3	5.2	5.3	5.2	5.5	4.8	4.6	4.7	4.3	5.4
Saskatoon	6.7	5.6	6.3	6.1	6.0	6.2	5.0	4.4	4.0	4.0	4.7
Calgary	5.5	4.5	4.5	5.7	5.4	5.0	3.9	3.2	3.2	3.5	6.6
Edmonton	5.9	5.6	5.0	5.2	5.0	4.8	4.5	3.9	3.8	3.7	6.7
Vancouver	7.7	5.8	6.6	7.7	7.3	6.7	5.7	4.4	4.0	4.3	7.0

Source: Statistics Canada 2010 *Labour Force Survey* Cansim Table 71-001-X.

6.6, Edmonton 3.7 to 6.7, and Vancouver 4.3 to 7.0 percent (Exhibit 23.10). These are significant increases but rates in 2010 are again starting to decline, although very modestly. Looking forward, however, if employment rates should increase, or remain high in the higher-priced centers like Vancouver, Calgary, and Toronto and interest rates rise, then more households will have difficulty maintaining their mortgage payments. The risk of defaults may rise and prices may decline.

Summary

In summary, basic elements of housing demand suggest that:

- Population growth rates have been modest in recent years and have been falling continuously since 1971. Fertility rates have fallen below replacement levels and growth is driven largely by international immigration, which is region- and center-specific because of the preferred destination of migrants.
- Household growth rates have also been declining since 1971 but declining household size and growth in smaller household types have kept housing demand relatively robust. One hundred persons today live in 40 homes. In 1971 these same 100 people would have lived in 29 homes. Household growth, like population is also region- and center-specific.
- The proportion of households that are home owners has increased appreciably, but this has not necessarily increased owners' exposure to market bubbles and bursts because a large percentage of households are mortgage free and even most households with mortgages have substantial equity in their homes.
- Increases in incomes have been modest and have lagged increases in the general cost of living and housing price increases, although real disposable incomes have fared better.
- Unemployment rates, although they have increased significantly in some centers over the period 2007–2009, are beginning to moderate again in 2010 and many centers never experienced any significant increases.
- Regional variations in all these basic elements of housing demand are significant in Canada with population growth, household growth, and growth in

incomes being much more robust in the provinces of Ontario, Alberta, and British Columbia, and major metropolitan centers in these provinces, such as Toronto, Edmonton, Calgary, and Vancouver.

On a national basis the key factors underlying housing demand do not illustrate the sort of trends that would support significant and inflationary increases in housing prices. On a regional basis, however, population, household and income growth has been much more significant because of interprovincial and particularly international movements of people. Housing demand, particularly for ownership units, has been significant in selected metropolitan centers and provides the basics for more inflationary increases in prices.

MARKET TRENDS AND SUPPLY SIDE INFLUENCES

How did the Canadian market perform before, during, and since this crisis? Was there evidence of price escalation, steep price declines, and consumer stress? Has the residential mortgage market experienced rising arrears and defaults? The discussion here addresses these questions.

Housing Starts

Housing starts in Canada over the past decade have increased from approximately 150,000 a year at the turn of the millennium, to 210,000 to 233,000 over the period 2002 to 2008, before dropping significantly to 149,000 in 2009, the lowest level since 1999 (Exhibit 23.6). The level of starts over the past decade has been well below the record level of approximately 275,000 set back in 1976 and 1977 (CMHC 2010). Single detached homes destined for the ownership market generally account for more than 50 percent of these starts. Condominiums have accounted for approximately another one-third of the starts, indicating that over 80 percent of the housing starts in major urban centers have been destined for home ownership in recent years.

As one would expect, increases in the supply of housing have been very region- and center-specific, following the pattern of population and household increase. Over the past decade 85 to 90 percent of housing starts have occurred in the four provinces of Quebec, Ontario, Alberta, and British Columbia (CMHC 2010a). Approximately 50 percent of all housing starts over the past decade have occurred in five metropolitan centers: Montreal, Toronto, Edmonton, Calgary, and Vancouver.

Price Increases in New Housing

Increases in the new house price index (NHPI) were lower than increases in the consumer price index (CPI) from 1990 through to the year 2001 (Exhibit 23.6). There were several years during that period when prices actually declined. The NHPI then started to increase faster than the CPI with an annual increase in 2006 of 9.7 percent compared to a CPI increase of 2 percent. The NHPI increase fell to 7.7 percent in 2007, then to 3.4 in 2008, and −2.3 percent in 2009. Canada-wide, prices escalated appreciably between 2002 and 2007 but not in bubble magnitudes. Price increases moderated in 2007 and 2008, and declined in 2009, but not in meltdown proportions. Based on the NHPI, nationally there was no bubble, no meltdown!

National figures, however, hide significant regional variation. Saskatoon, a city of approximately 200,000 people, after experiencing very modest NHPIs over the 2000–2005 period, saw prices jump by 9.1 percent in 2006, 38.8 percent in 2007, 20.6 percent in 2008, and −7.6 percent in 2009. Vancouver, generally considered a hot market, experienced much more modest NHPI increases of 6.9 percent in 2006, 7.1 and 2.3 in 2007 and 2008, and a decline of −6.3 percent in 2009. Calgary, also considered a hot market, experienced an increase of 43.6 percent in 2006, another 16.2 percent in 2007, but only 0.6 percent in 2008, followed by a −6.7 decrease in 2009. New house prices in Toronto increased by 3.8, 2.7, and 3.5 percent in 2006, 2007, and 2008 respectively and declined 0.1 percent in 2009 (Statistics Canada 2010c). Inflationary markets were not widespread—restricted instead to selected markets. Even where prices experienced significant inflation there has, as yet, been no major price declines following the increases.

Price Increases in Existing Housing

Nationally the sale of existing units climbed steadily from 2000 to 2007 increasing from 334,375 units to 523,835 units. Sales dropped off considerably in 2008 to 431,823 units, but increased 7.7 percent to 465,251 units in 2009 (Exhibit 23.6). Historically low mortgage interest rates improved affordability and increased demand, but in 2009 pent-up demand from the downturn in 2008 also played a role. Average sales prices followed a similar trend nationally, rising from approximately $164,000 in 2000 to $306,000 in 2007, then dropping modestly to $303,600 in 2008, but rising again in 2009 by 5 percent to $320,333. Price increases since 2001 have been greater for existing, rather than new units, but also well above the consumer price index, increasing between 9 and 11 percent annually from 2002 to 2007, then recording a decline of −0.7 percent in 2008 before rallying again to post a 5 percent gain in 2009.

As with new house prices, the national figures hide significant regional variations. Toronto's market reflected the national situation with increases of 4.8 and 7 percent in 2006 and 2007, followed by a 0.7 percent increase in 2008 and a rebound to 4.3 percent in 2009. Saskatoon and Calgary were much more inflationary, with increases of 11, 45, and 24 percent in 2006, 2007, and 2008 in Saskatoon followed by a −3.1 percent decline in 2009; Calgary was similar with increases of 38 and 19 percent in 2006 and 2007, followed by decreases of −2.1 and −4.8 percent in 2008 and 2009. Vancouver prices jumped 20 percent in 2006, another 12 percent in 2007, 4 percent in 2008, and declined −0.2 percent 2009 (CREA 2010). Certainly inflationary increases occurred in some centers, however, as yet, no significant meltdown has followed these increases.

Over the longer term there have been significant price increases for existing units in some centers. Exhibit 23.11 illustrates that over the period 2002–2009 the price of existing units in Canada increased 70 percent. Winnipeg, Saskatoon, and Edmonton experienced increases of over 100 percent. Increases in Vancouver and Calgary were just under 100 percent. Exhibit 23.11 also illustrates the significant variation in price levels across the country. The average sales price in Vancouver exceeds the national average by $272,000 or 85 percent. The Vancouver price is $385,000 higher than the Winnipeg price, a difference of 186 percent. Price

Exhibit 23.11 Price Increases for Sales of Existing Units: Canada and Selected Centers, 2002 and 2009

	2002 ($)	2009 ($)	% Change
Canada	188,871	320,333	69.6
Montreal	153,298	274,842	79.3
Toronto	275,887	396,154	43.6
Winnipeg	98,055	207,341	111.5
Saskatoon	118,999	278,895	134.4
Calgary	198,350	385,882	94.5
Edmonton	150,165	320,378	113.4
Vancouver	301,475	592,441	96.5

Source: CMHC 2010a.

increases and price levels vary significantly by center—much more significantly than incomes.

Housing Affordability

Housing affordability is a good test of a crisis situation in the housing market. Eroding affordability is a red flag that something is wrong in the market place. Despite the modest increases in income noted in this paper, the Royal Bank of Canada (RBC) 2010 believes housing affordability is still in the safe range in *most* markets in Canada.

Housing affordability in Canada is measured in a number of ways. In this paper two approaches are highlighted. In the first, used by CMHC, the monthly mortgage payment is calculated using the Multiple Listing Service (MLS) average price for existing units and the five-year fixed posted mortgage rate assuming a 25 percent down payment and a 25-year amortization period. The income used is personal disposable income (after tax) per worker. Using this measure, housing affordability improved in 2008 after a significant deterioration in 2007. At the end of 2008 the ratio of the mortgage payment to disposable income was 33 percent, compared to 39 percent in 2007 (CMHC 2010a). It fell below 30 percent in early 2009, but had risen to 31 percent by the end of 2009. Moderating housing price increases (declines in some centers) and historically low interest rates account for the improvement.

The RBC uses a slightly different measure. It is based on the proportion of median pre-tax household income required to service the cost on an existing housing unit at a going market price, including principal and interest (based on a 25 percent down payment and a 25-year mortgage loan at the five-year fixed interest rate), property taxes, and utilities. The RBC approach includes costs over and above a mortgage where they are available, so the proportion of income required is higher. This affordability indicator follows the same pattern as the CMHC approach, but in 2008 the cost of an average bungalow required more than 45 percent of income—an average condominium about 30 percent. The ratios trended downward in early 2009 but then up again although they have not reached the 2008 levels.

Again there is considerable regional variation. Affordability ratios based on the RBC approach reached 40 percent in Saskatoon in 2008, 40 to 50 percent in

Calgary, and approximately 70 percent in Vancouver for a three-bedroom single detached bungalow. Toronto stood at just over 40 percent in 2008. All centers had much lower affordability ratios for condominiums. In nearly all other Canadian metropolitan centers affordability ratios are much more modest (RBC 2010). All centers followed the national trend with improving affordability ratios in early 2009 followed by modest deterioration since then.

All aspects considered, the affordability situation remains within a safe range in Canada. There are local markets where the share of household income taken by ownership costs is worrisome (RBC 2010), but there have been no meltdowns. Vancouver is a case in point. There have been price increases in Vancouver as noted, but it is the current underlying value of residential properties that generate the high affordability index, not the recent increases in prices. Prices have been rising for years and the city has the highest home values and home ownership costs in the country. The Vancouver market is clearly vulnerable to a price correction but according to leading housing economists a collapse is not imminent (RBC 2010). However, as previously pointed out, unemployment rates have increased since 2007 and should interest rates rise many home owners may well face increased housing stress and the risk of defaults may rise.

Mortgage Arrears and Defaults

Data on Canadian residential mortgages in arrears strengthen the conclusion that there has been no collapse nor is one currently imminent on a national basis. As of December 31, 2009, 0.45 percent (18,059) of Canadian residential mortgages were three months or more in arrears, compared to 0.33 percent (12,914) 12 months earlier (Canadian Bankers Association (CBA) 2010). The annual average rate of mortgage arrears in 2009 was 0.41 compared to 0.28 percent in 2008. Average annual arrears were as high as 0.60 percent in 1996 and as low as 0.25 percent in 2006. Current rates are still below the historical average.

Further strengthening the conclusion there has been no meltdown is the default rate on prime residential mortgages. At the end of the second quarter in 2010 the default rate was 0.42 percent—the same level as a decade ago (CBA 2010). By comparison, United States prime mortgage default rates were slightly below 7 percent. Default rates in Canada on subprime mortgages stood at 4.6 percent compared to 28 percent in the United States (CBA 2010).

These positive figures, however, do not rule out the possibility of center specific housing stress, particularly in such expensive markets as Vancouver and Calgary. As MacDonald (2010) points out there have been bubbles in Canadian centers in the past, followed by major price corrections. This may yet occur, particularly if interest rates rise.

Summary

This review of market trends suggests that:

- Housing construction activity over the last decade in Canada has been characterized by a relatively consistent level of housing starts. The emphasis has been on single detached homes and a rising proportion of condominiums— both destined for the ownership market.

- The price of new homes rose much more rapidly than the CPI from 2006 to 2008, but percentage increases were not in the double digits nationally, although inflationary increases were evident in a few metropolitan markets. Price declines in 2009 were modest.
- Similar trends were evident in the existing resale market.
- Housing affordability indices (the proportion of income people pay for housing) rose significantly in 2007, dropped in early 2009 and since then have trended upward but have not reached 2007 levels. The indices have been higher in the past. In some markets, Vancouver for example, households spend a very significant proportion of their income to purchase a home but affordability is in a safe range in most markets.
- There has been no significant increase in mortgage arrears or defaults over the past three to four years.

Based on this evidence there has been no collapse nor does it appear a collapse is imminent. However, a significant increase in the interest rate or an increase in unemployment could change the circumstances substantially, particularly in high-priced markets such as Vancouver and Calgary where affordability ratios are near stress levels.

FINANCE AND LENDING REGULATIONS: CANADIAN FINANCIAL INSTITUTIONS WEATHER THE STORM

The housing price bubble associated with several foreign housing markets, most notably that of the United States, began to deflate in 2007 and burst in 2008. The fallout reverberated through world financial markets leading to a credit crisis and a global economic downturn. International financial institutions collapsed or had to be bailed out. Some banks were nationalized. A range of financial interventions by governments occurred as countries struggled to get their credit markets functioning again. Large economic stimulus plans were implemented as adverse credit market conditions began impacting nations' economies.

The downstream impacts of the contraction in the global economy trickled through the Canadian economy but Canada's financial institutions weathered the global financial turmoil well. Canada's lending institutions had limited exposure to United States' subprime markets and Canadian banks reported only $12 billion in write-downs by the third quarter of 2008 compared to the $476 billion estimated by the Institute of International Finance for the United States. The write-downs Canadian banks made were not attributable to domestic residential mortgages (Bank of Canada 2008).

This does not mean that Canada's financial system did not face challenges. The Bank of Canada had to make extensive use of its liquidity facilities to support Canadian banks, and banks did not have access to the full range of capital markets normally available to them to support funding/lending purposes. Despite these problems Canadian lending institutions exhibited stability and resiliency throughout the period.

Canada's economy did undergo a short, but marked, recession. The gross domestic product contracted 2.5 percent in 2009, 400,000 Canadians lost their jobs and unemployment jumped 3 percent to 8.3 percent for the year (CMHC 2010a). Despite these weaknesses the housing finance system continued to function and lending to households to finance housing purchases, renovations, and improvements was sustained.

The Canadian Mortgage System

Before discussing finance and lending regulations a brief overview of the housing mortgage system in Canada will provide the reader with some basic information that will facilitate a better understanding of the discussion that follows. In Canada the purchase of a home typically means getting a mortgage. Mortgage lenders include banks, credit unions, and specialized financial institutions such as trust and life insurance companies. About 60 percent of funding for mortgages comes from these institutions' depositors that purchase Guaranteed Investment Certificates (GICs), lenders also get about 30 percent of mortgage funds from mortgage-backed securities and smaller amounts from covered bonds, both of which rely on the capital markets. Almost all mortgages are full recourse loans where the borrower remains responsible for the mortgage even in the case of default and foreclosure.

Mortgages are typically amortized over 25 years, although up to 35 or 40 years has been permitted in the recent past. The most common mortgage is the fixed-rate mortgage where the interest rate is set for a five-year term. About two-thirds of mortgages fall into this category (Dunning 2010). After the five-year term, the borrower typically negotiates another term and interest rate. Three, two, and occasionally 10-year terms are available. In recent years the use of the variable rate mortgage has become more common. Instead of a fixed interest rate for a specific term, the interest rate varies with market rates whenever lenders adjust their rates. Slightly less than 30 percent of current mortgages are variable rate. Prepayment of mortgages is typically allowed but there are often prepayment penalties.

Mortgage loan insurance is provided by CMHC and private insurers. Mortgages with loan-to-value ratios greater than 80 percent require mortgage insurance. Mortgage loan insurance protects mortgage lenders against potential defaults on the part of mortgage borrowers. Mortgage interest is not tax deductible in Canada.

In Canada, mortgage lenders fall into three major categories: chartered banks, credit unions, and specialized financial institutions (trust, mortgage loan, life insurance companies, etc.). In 2009 the six main chartered banks provided about 48 percent of mortgage credit. Another 30 percent was provided through the mortgage-backed securities (MBS) under the National Housing Act (NHA). NHA MBS are distributed mainly through the chartered banks and credit unions (CMHC 2010a). As the figures suggest, approximately 90 percent of residential mortgage funds in any one year come from large national institutions with branches across the country—not a collection of small local banks. This lends considerable strength, and greater capacity, to the mortgage-lending industry in Canada. Because of this the lending industry is better positioned to weather shocks in the housing market. As the subsequent discussion will illustrate, there is also considerable regulation of the mortgage lending system. The strength of the financial industry (based on size), government involvement, and regulatory oversight explain the resiliency of Canada's housing finance system during the recent housing crisis.

Protecting the Vulnerability of the Canadian Housing Finance System

Banking problems in Canada were due more to global liquidity constraints than to domestic market weakness. Nevertheless, the Canadian government acted to strengthen Canada's financial system by introducing a number of new policies and programs. The vulnerability of Canadian banks was protected by a number of factors.

Their High Capitalization

Canada's minimum capital requirements are tougher than those called for by Basel II and all other G7 bank regulators (CBA 2009). The higher levels of capitalization reduce their exposure to risk of write-downs.

Their Improved Liquidity

The Government of Canada also took steps to improve bank liquidity. The government, through CMHC, expanded its Mortgage-Backed Securities (MBS) Program. The Program was initially introduced in 1987 under the NHA in order to increase the availability and reduce the cost of mortgages. NHA MBSs are pools of amortizing residential mortgages insured by CMHC or private mortgage insurers. Investors in NHA MBS purchase interests in pools of mortgages and receive monthly installments of principal and interest as passed through from the cash flow of the underlying mortgages. For mortgage lenders, the proceeds provide a source of funding for their mortgage operations, reducing or eliminating the dependence on retail deposits from consumer savings in Guaranteed Investment Certificates or term deposits. In October 2008, during the height of the financial crisis, CMHC purchased an additional $25 billion in insured mortgage pools to maintain the availability of longer-term credit for consumers, homebuyers, and businesses in Canada. The commitment was subsequently increased to $75 billion in November 2008 and by a further $50 billion in January 2009, for a total of $150 billion (CMHC 2010a).

In July 2008 the Government of Canada also announced an expansion of the Canada Mortgage Bond (CMB) Program. The CMB was introduced in 2001 and has provided a continuing opportunity for investors and a cost-effective source of funding for mortgage lenders. The bonds are issued by the Canadian Housing Trust and are fully guaranteed. The proceeds from investment in the bonds are used to purchase NHA MBS and lenders use the funds for lending to mortgage borrowers. This improves the liquidity and competitiveness of the Canadian mortgage market and the affordability of mortgage financing for home buyers. Because the bonds are fully guaranteed for timely payment of principal and interest, and payments are semi-annual coupon payments and final principal payments, they are appealing to a broad range of investors; hence, funding by CMBs can be achieved at relatively lower rates. The expansion in July 2008 included a 10-year maturity program that built on the previously available five-year maturity option. As well as being attractive to investors, the 10-year maturity date facilitates cost effective funding for mortgage lending institutions and mortgage consumers over a longer term (CMHC 2010a).

Growth in Canadian mortgage credit outstanding slowed in 2008, but still increased by 10.3 percent to a total of $903 billion at December 31, 2008. A year earlier, however, it had increased by 12.3 percent. Residential mortgage credit out-standing reached $965 billion by December 31, 2009, increasing another 7 percent. Fewer home sales and declining house prices brought about the slower growth (CMHC 2010a).

Increased Mortgage Securitization

Mortgage securitization increased substantially, largely because of the expanded NHA MBS mortgage funding available. In 2008 NHA MBS issuances rose to $61.1 billion from $23.3 billion in 2007, and CMB issuances rose to $43.5 billion from $35.7 billion the previous year. NHA MBS issued another $55.1 million in 2009 and CMB added another $3.4 billion. There was a total of $298.3 billion of NHA MBS and $175.6 billion CMB outstanding by year-end in 2009. Increasing securitization in the market further strengthened lenders (CMHC 2010a).

Repeated Reductions in Interest Rates

In addition to improving liquidity for banks during the financial crisis, the Bank of Canada repeatedly reduced its overnight rate, prompting lower mortgage rates. The initial drop in December 2007 was followed by eight other reductions through to January 2009. The cumulative decline was 350 basis points, bringing the rate down to 1 percent. One hundred basis points equals 1 percent. The rate reductions, accompanied by the liquidity injections already mentioned, increased the chartered banks' liquidity, expanded the money supply, and put downward pressure on interest rates and increased consumer confidence in borrowing.

While the overnight rate declined significantly, the decline in mortgage inter-est rates was more modest, because there were increases in some funding costs for lenders. Five-year fixed mortgage rates dropped only 33 basis points. The spread between fixed mortgage rates and variable mortgage rates, however, widened. In 2008 the five-year fixed rate averaged 7.06 percent while the variable rate averaged 4.87 percent. In January 2009, however, the five-year fixed rate fell to 5.79 percent. Mortgage discounting (borrowers negotiating rates lower than those posted) was significant in 2008 with the Canadian Association of Accredited Mortgage Profes-sionals (2009), indicating that five-year fixed-rate mortgages were 159 basis point below the posted rates. By January 2009, however, rate discounting had almost disappeared.

Mortgage lending continued at a healthy pace, facilitated by CMHC's secu-ritization programs and contributions to lenders' liquidity and low interest rates. Lenders were able to weather the financial turmoil and keep housing markets relatively strong.

Tightening Mortgage Lending Criteria

In addition to improving bank liquidity and increasing mortgage securitization the government also took steps to tighten mortgage lending criteria and mort-gage underwriting practices to ensure mortgage borrowers were not placed in positions of very high risk should there be growing market instability and price fluctuations.

More prudent underwriting standards introduced to protect and strengthen the housing market and protect borrowers and lenders alike included:

- Regulations prohibited mortgage loans with no amortization in the initial years. Such mortgages had crept into the system with lower interest rates and relaxed lending standards prior to the recession.
- Maximum loan-to-value ratios are not allowed to exceed 95 percent, and more recently were reduced to 90 percent. Prior to the potential financial crisis no-money-down loans had crept into the mortgage lending field.
- The maximum amortization period is not allowed to exceed 35 years. This will be reduced to 30 years by March 18, 2011. Some amortization periods had crept up to 40 years to help reduce monthly payments and allow lower-income households to qualify for higher mortgage amounts as house prices increased.
- The maximum total debt service ratio of 45 percent was rigidly enforced. The total debt service ratio is the proportion of gross household income that is spent on debt service on housing-related debt and other forms of debt (car payments, for example).
- Minimum loan documentation standards were enforced to ensure evidence of borrower income, job stability, and property value.
- All borrowers had to meet the standards for a five-year fixed rate mortgage even if they choose a mortgage with a lower interest rate and shorter term. Prior to the financial crisis, qualification for a mortgage was based on the rate and term negotiated. Those choosing variable rate mortgages often were qualified on rates that were 2 to 3 percent lower than the five-year rate. This allowed them to take on greater mortgage debt but also put them at greater risk when rates rose.
- A minimum down payment of 20 percent is required in order to obtain government-backed mortgage insurance on non-owner occupied properties purchased for speculation. This helps reduce speculative purchases and reduces purchaser's risk should prices fall. Mortgages on a principal residence with a loan-to-value ratio in excess of 80 percent have always required mortgage insurance. This has always helped stabilize and strengthen mortgage lending and protects lenders against default. Lenders pay an insurance premium that they pass on to the home's purchaser.
- The maximum amount that Canadians can withdraw in refinancing their mortgages was lowered from 95 to 90 percent of the value of their homes. This will be reduced to 85 percent on March 18, 2011. With such low interest rates Canadian homeowners have been using equity in their home as collateral for other borrowing. If interest rates rise and prices fall, this home-equity financing could put many home owners in a tight spot.

In addition to the above prudent lending practices another factor in reducing risk of defaults is the fact that the subprime sector in Canada has always been very small, estimated at less than 5 percent of the Canadian residential mortgage market, compared to 14 percent in the United States. There is no universally accepted definition of subprime mortgages, but in general, a subprime mortgage is one where the borrower has a weak or flawed credit history. The Bank of Canada also pointed out that the subprime sector in Canada is not only smaller, but also characterized by more stringent underwriting standards than those employed in the United States (CMHC 2010a).

Summary

Canada housing financial institutions generally performed better than their international peers through the housing crisis and economic downturn (CMHC 2010a). The banks remained profitable and cumulative write-downs were less than those suffered by major United States and European banks (Bank of Canada 2009). The Federal Reserve Bank of Cleveland investigated why the United States did, while Canada did not, experience the housing bust in the period after 2008. It concluded that relaxed lending standards led to a dramatic rise in subprime lending in the United States and a growing component of this subprime lending had no mortgage loan insurance (MacGee 2009). Canadian banks, however, were operating under much stricter lending guidelines, there were very few subprime mortgages, securitization was much higher, a much larger component of mortgages had mortgage loan insurance and mortgages were provided under much more prudent lending criteria. This had a stabilizing effect on mortgage markets during the economic downturn.

CONCLUSION

No bubble! No meltdown! The evidence in the Canadian situation supports this assertion. As this discussion has highlighted, nationally the underlying factors of demand such as population and household growth and increases in income did not illustrate the types of trends that would generate significant and inflationary price increases. The level of homeownership increased significantly but the good equity position of most owners meant they were less exposed to risks during market fluctuations. Certain regions and centers, however, were characterized by much stronger demand factors.

The evidence based on market trends such as housing starts, price increases, and housing affordability was similar. Nationally, and in most centers, price increases and declines were not significant but inflationary increases in prices did occur in certain centers and housing affordability indices rose to red flag levels, particularly in centers such as Calgary and Vancouver. Nevertheless there have been no significant increases in mortgage arrears or defaults. There has been no collapse, even in those centers with inflationary prices, and a collapse does not appear imminent.

Canada's housing financial system also weathered the housing crisis well. The chapter highlights the fact that there are features of mortgage lending in Canada that helped the nation avoid the type of housing problems that did serious damage to the United States' financial system and housing market (Elliott 2009). Financial institution lending is more conservatively managed and regulated so it operates with less systemic risk than the American system (Booth 2009). Therefore, even in a situation where there was considerable price escalation, a meltdown has been avoided because of prudent lending and mortgage qualification criteria. More stringent mortgage lending practices made a difference. The subprime mortgage market was small and much more regulated than in some countries. Support for the lending institutions in the form of government-backed securitized funding where mortgage insurance is mandatory improved bank liquidity. It ensured a stable supply of low-cost funding for mortgage lenders without any significant risk. Canada's broader, more regulated, and more government-backed financial system helped the financial institutions and the housing market, enabling housing consumers to weather the crisis relatively well.

Canada and Canadian housing consumers were spared the pain that characterized the United States during the housing and global financial crisis. However, Canadians may not be out of the woods yet. Levels of debt are high. The Bank of Canada (2010) points out that Canadians now have the highest domestic debt level burdens in Canada's history. The ratio of household debt to disposable income has reached 148.1 percent or $1.48 for every dollar of disposable income, which excludes what is spent on taxes and other government levies. Canadian homeowners have also been taking on increasing debt through home-equity loans. Still housing prices continue to rise and sales continue to be brisk.

Bankruptcies are also up. Bankruptcies filed in the 12 months ending October 2010 are 22.5 percent higher than the pre-recession levels recorded in 2007–2008 (Bank of Canada 2010). Although few of these bankruptcies are related to mortgage default, should interest rates rise, which is probably just a matter of time; house prices fall; the economic recovery stagger; and unemployment rates increase, many homeowners may face considerable stress and be at much greater risk of mortgage default. There may be tough times ahead, particularly for recent purchasers who have little equity to fall back on if prices fall and interest rates rise. Perhaps it is too early for Canadians to pat themselves on the back and say that we have weathered the storm.

REFERENCES

Bank of Canada. 2010. *Financial Systems Review*. Ottawa: Bank of Canada.

Bank of Canada. 2009. *Financial Systems Review*. Ottawa: Bank of Canada.

Bank of Canada. 2008. *Financial Systems Review*. Ottawa: Bank of Canada.

Booth, L. 2009 (July–August). "The Secret of Canadian Banking: Common Sense." *World Economics* 10:3, 1–17.

Brown, M., and A. Lafrance. 2010. *Incomes from Owner-Occupied Housing for Working-Age and Retirement-Age Canadians, 1969–2006*. Ottawa: Statistics Canada.

Brown, M., F. Hou, and A. Lafrance. 2010. *Incomes of Retirement-Age and Working-Age Canadians: Accounting for Homeownership*. Ottawa: Statistics Canada.

Canada Mortgage and Housing Corporation (CMHC). 2010a. *Canadian Housing Observer*. Ottawa: CMHC.

Canada Mortgage and Housing Corporation (CMHC). 2010b. *Housing Market Report: Province of Alberta*. Ottawa: CMHC.

Canadian Association of Accredited Mortgage Professionals (CAAMP). 2009. "The Elephant in the Room." In Will Dunning, ed., *Mortgage Journal*, June 2009:44–45.

Canadian Bankers Association (CBA). 2010. *Comments on Canadian Residential Mortgage Default Rates*. Toronto: Canadian Bankers Association.

Canadian Bankers Association (CBA). 2009. *Canadian Bank Regulatory Capital Requirements*. Toronto: Canadian Bankers Association.

Canadian Real Estate Association (CREA). 2010. *Residential Prices for the Sale of Existing Units*. Toronto: Canadian Real Estate Association.

Carter, T. 2009. *An Evaluation of the Manitoba Provincial Nominee Program*. Winnipeg: Manitoba Department of Labour and Immigration.

Citizenship and Immigration Canada (CIC). 2010. *Facts and Figures 2009: Immigration Overview*. Ottawa: Citizenship and Immigration Canada.

Davies, K., and R. Daniel. 2009. *Fall 2009 Mortgage Industry Snapshot*. Toronto: Canadian Association of Accredited Mortgage Professionals.

Dunning, W. 2010. *Annual State of the Residential Mortgage Market in Canada*. Ottawa: Canadian Association of Accredited Mortgage Professionals.

Elliott, R. 2009 (October). "Lessons in Mortgage Lending, Canadian Style." *Financial Executive* 25:8, 50–51.

Grant, T. 2010. "Rising Mortgage Rates: Rising Trouble" in *Globe and Mail*. Toronto. Available at www.theglobeandmail.com/report-on-business/rising-mortgage-rates-rising-trouble/article1563265/#comments.

Hiebert, D., and P. Mendez. 2008. *Settling In: Newcomers in the Canadian Housing Market, 2001–2005*. Ottawa: Canada Mortgage and Housing Corporation.

Laduarantaye, S. 2010. "Overvalued Homes, Higher Mortgage Rates Drop Hot Resale Market." *Globe and Mail*. Toronto. Available at www.theglobeandmail.com/report-on-business/economy/nearly-20-of-homes-overvalued-report/articles1580185/#article.

Ley, D., and J. Tutchener. 2001. "Immigration, Globalization, and House Price Movements in Canada's Gateway Cities." *Housing Studies*, 16:2, 199–223.

MacDonald, D. 2010. *Canada's Housing Bubble: An Accident Waiting to Happen*. Ottawa: Canadian Center for Policy Alternatives.

MacGee, J. 2009. "Why Didn't Canada's Housing Market Go Bust?" *Economic Commentary*. Cleveland, OH: Federal Reserve Bank of Cleveland.

Roach, R. 2010. *State of the West 2010: Western Canadian Demographic and Economic Trends*. Calgary: Canada West Foundation.

Royal Bank of Canada (RBC). 2010. *Housing Trends and Affordability*. Toronto: Royal Bank of Canada.

Statistics Canada. 2010a. *CANSIM: GDP Spending on Housing*. Ottawa: Statistics Canada.

Statistics Canada. 2010b. *Population by Year by Province and Territory. CANSIM Table 051-0001*. Ottawa: Statistics Canada.

Statistics Canada. 2010c. *New House Price Index. Catalogue No. 62-007-X*. Ottawa: Statistics Canada.

Statistics Canada. 2008a. *Report on the Demographic Situation in Canada 2005-2007. Catalogue No. 91-209-X*. Ottawa: Statistics Canada.

Statistics Canada. 2008b. *Survey of Labor and Income Dynamics*. Ottawa: Statistics Canada.

Statistics Canada. 2007. *Household Growth Summary: Canada, Provinces, Territories and Metropolitan Areas*. Ottawa: Statistics Canada.

Wong, T. 2010. "Canadian Housing Market Correction in the Cards." *Your Home*. Toronto. Available at www.yourhome.ca/homes/realestate/article/799961.

Yalnizyan, A. 2010. *The Rise of Canada's Richest 1%*. Ottawa: Canadian Centre for Policy Alternatives.

ABOUT THE AUTHOR

TOM CARTER is Professor of Geography and Canada Research Chair in Urban Change and Adaptation at the University of Winnipeg. Tom has served several terms as Director of Urban and Regional Research at the University's Institute of Urban Studies. Prior to joining the University in 1985, Tom was Executive Director of the Research and Policy Development Division with the Saskatchewan Housing Corporation. Tom's research experience covers a wide range of housing, neighborhood revitalization, urban development, and social policy issues. Tom has also been an active researcher and program evaluator on poverty alleviation and other social programs.

CHAPTER 24

Partly Cloudy to Clear

The Israeli Economy and the Local Housing Market under the Storm of the World Financial Crisis

DANNY BEN-SHAHAR
Faculty of Architecture and Town Planning at the Technion–Israel Institute of Technology

JACOB WARSZAWSKI
Faculty of Architecture and Town Planning at the Technion–Israel Institute of Technology

The global financial crisis that started in mid-2007 has caught Israel's economy in a relatively positive condition, with a surplus in the balance of payments and current accounts, relatively low unemployment rate, stable growth in the economic activity, and a continuous decline in the public-debt-to-gross-domestic-product (GDP) ratio (see Bank of Israel 2008). Moreover, not only did housing market prices not show any indication of bubble behavior prior to the crisis (as seemingly experienced by some Western economies),[1] but also, as part of the cyclical nature of the local real estate market, prices generally maintained a stable level over the period 2000–2007—the period that preceded the onset of the world financial crisis.

While the global financial crisis did leave tracks on the financial sector in Israel (and thereby on other related sectors of the local economy as we discuss below), its overall effect was limited in scope and considerably less significant compared to, for example, the U.S. experience. Furthermore, according to the Central Bureau of Statistics (2009), unlike many other housing markets around the world, the local housing market has, interestingly, demonstrated a dramatic average price increase over the period 2008–2009.

Why did the storm of the world financial and housing crisis leave what may presently be judged as only a minor and short-term effect on the Israeli economy and its local housing market? In the first part of this chapter, we examine this question by descriptively focusing on the behavior of major relevant economic variables during the years that preceded the crisis as well as the policy adopted by the decision-makers in response to the crisis. Apparently, the solid economic condition in which Israel has met the world financial crisis, combined with the economic measures carried out in a timely response to the outbreak of the crisis, acted as what currently seem to be effective ingredients to cope with the urgent, intensive, and challenging economic situation that emerged.

As we further discuss in later sections, among the major factors that contributed to the strength of the Israeli economy and the local housing market when meeting the storming world developments were a declining trend of public-debt-to-GDP ratio; relatively low unemployment rate; balanced government budget; per capita GDP in levels comparable to Western economies; increasing ratio of the number of households to the number of dwelling units in the market; relatively strict financial regulations vis-à-vis a strong banking system (entering the crisis, for example, with 11.2 percent of capital adequacy, the highest level since 1992; see Bank of Israel, 2008);[2] absence of a formal institutionalized secondary mortgage market; relatively narrow subprime mortgage market; and, finally, financial institutions (such as pension funds and trust funds) whose assets (per fund) are not only limited in scope, but also mostly invested in local financial assets and government bonds (see also Bank of Israel 2008).

In the second part of the chapter, we concentrate on the local housing market and, in particular, study the pattern of local housing prices and affordability. Using a structural model of supply and demand in the housing market, we derive a reduced form equation of housing affordability, where the affordability variable is measured by the number of average monthly wages per employee job that is required for purchasing an average dwelling unit (referred to as the housing price-to-wage ratio; see, for example, Gan and Hill, 2009). We empirically estimate the model in order to examine the factors that correlate with housing affordability in Israel for the years 1989–2009. Moreover, we compare the actual time series of housing affordability to the fitted values of affordability that arise from the model, thereby studying housing price (and affordability) dynamics prior to and following the world financial crisis.

We find that the housing price-to-wage ratio negatively correlates with the mortgage interest rate and the unemployment rate (with a three-quarter lag). Also, the price-to-wage ratio positively correlates with a six-quarter lag in the number of housing starts, the current change rate in GDP, the current change rate in the price index of inputs in residential construction, and the current exchange rate between the New Israeli shekel (NIS) and the U.S. dollar (USD).

Focusing on the actual housing affordability time-series for the years 1989–2009, we find that two years following the onset of the world financial crisis, the price-to-wage ratio in the Israeli housing market reached its highest level ever. Moreover, comparing the differences between actual housing price-to-wage ratio figures to their fitted values that arise from the model (obtained from the empirical estimation of the affordability equation), we find that, in the last quarter of 2009, the actual price-to-wage ratio deviates from its in-sample fitted value by 2.78 standard deviations. Re-estimating the model for the 1989–2007 period, the deviation of the actual price-to-wage ratio from its out-of-sample fitted value for the last quarter of 2009 rises to 3.42 standard deviations. This implies that the local housing market has not only avoided a slump during the world financial crisis but, as some may argue, might even be showing disturbing preliminary signs of a price bubble phenomenon previously observed elsewhere around the world shortly before the crisis.

THE ISRAELI ECONOMY AND THE LOCAL HOUSING MARKET PRIOR TO AND FOLLOWING THE ONSET OF THE WORLD FINANCIAL CRISIS

With GDP equal to 204 billion U.S. dollars in 2008 (in Purchasing Power Parity—PPP figures) and an international-trade-to-GDP ratio of over 40 percent, Israel's economy is relatively small by Western standards and, accordingly, highly dependent upon foreign trade (see, for example, OECD, 2010). Yet, as we discuss below, the effects of the world financial crisis on the local economy and the local housing market were minor compared to most Western economies. To understand the reasons, we focus in this section on Israel's economy in the period that preceded the crisis and on the measures undertaken by the decision-makers in response to the economic developments. We begin with a brief background of the Israeli economy and the local housing market.

Brief Background of the Israeli Economy and the Local Housing Market[3]

Since the 1985 stabilization program initiated by the Israeli Government (following the hyper-inflation era of the first half of the 1980s), the Israeli economy has experienced an extensive liberalization process that largely opened its financial and real estate sectors to interactions with the global economy. From an economy primarily based on labor-intensive production and agriculture, Israel has developed into a knowledge-based economy, with internationally competitive high-technology industries and per capita GDP comparable with levels prevailing in Western economies (in early 2010, Israel joined the Organization for Economic Cooperation and Development [OECD]).[4]

Exhibit 24.1 depicts Israel's per capita GDP (in PPP figures) from the first quarter of 1996 to the last quarter of 2009. Note from the graph that Israel's per capita GDP numbers have not only reached levels comparable with those of Western economies but also, in general, experienced a continuous positive trend over the period 1996–2009.[5]

The institutional structure of the housing market and housing finance in Israel is rather distinctive by Western standards. The Israel Land Authority (ILA), a governmental agency, owns approximately 93 percent of Israel's entire stock of land.[6] In most cases, it leases land to the private sector for a 49-year period. To engage in new construction, developers thus must acquire land from either the ILA or the relatively small share of private owners. This situation potentially allows the ILA to intervene in the determination of land prices and, thereby, affect housing prices.

Other institutional features of the Israeli housing market worth noting include limited tax incentives for homeownership—once every four years homeowners can sell their dwelling unit exempted from capital gains tax. Nevertheless, there is no deductibility of mortgage interest payments (yet, according to the Central Bureau of Statistics, 2009, even under these circumstances, approximately 70 percent of the housing stock is owner-occupied). Additionally, there is a relatively limited share of public housing in the market (no such construction in recent years)

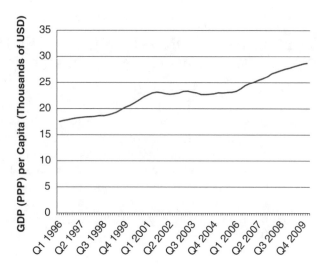

Exhibit 24.1   Per Capita GDP (in PPP) by Quarters, 1996–2009
Source: Bank of Israel, www.bankisrael.gov.il/publheb/dataheb.htm.

and an insignificant share of rent control arrangements—and the latter is slowly disappearing from the market as terminating controlled contracts have not been renewed in recent decades.

The Israeli Economy and the Local Housing Market Prior to the World Financial Crisis

To better understand the solid economic conditions with which the Israeli economy has met the world financial crisis, one must first consider the local economic developments in the years that preceded the crisis. In describing the economic situation that persisted in Israel in 2002, the Bank of Israel (2002) reported that Israel was experiencing the longest recession period since its establishment in 1948. Per capita GDP in 2002 continued its 2001 decline, dropping by an additional 3 percent (see once again Exhibit 24.1), the unemployment rate climbed to 10.3 percent, and the consumer price index reached a 6.5 percent inflation (far above the target then set by the Central Bank).

The roots of this slowdown in the local economic activity (that, in retrospect, commenced in the last quarter of 2000) were planted in a combination of direct-local and indirect-worldwide shocks. On one hand, the local fragile security situation that resulted in from the Second Palestinian Intifada (uprising) that started in September 2000; and, on the other hand, decelerated worldwide economic activity that accompanied, among others, the burst of the high-tech bubble and the sharp price drop in stock markets around the world—both produced uncertain atmosphere and instability in the local markets.[7]

With a concrete threat upon its financial and economic firmness, Israel embarked an economic recovery plan in the second quarter of 2003 that, essentially, dramatically cut the fiscal deficit and further reduced Government expenditures planned for future years (thereby restoring confidence in Government's economic

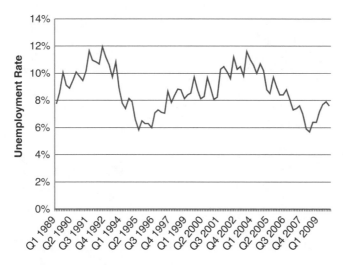

Exhibit 24.2 Unemployment Rate by Quarters, 1989–2009
Source: Central Bureau of Statistics.

policy). In addition, the ticking bomb of pension arrangements was at last restructured along with reforms in National Insurance benefits and revisions in retirement age (see Bank of Israel 2003).

In the years that followed, Israel continued to adhere to strict economic measures leading it to a solid economic environment in 2008. According to the Ministry of Finance (2009) and Bank of Israel (2009), GDP has increased from $22,800 USD in the second quarter of 2002 to almost $28,000 USD (in PPP figures) by the end of the third quarter 2008; public-debt-to-GDP ratio dropped from close to 100 percent in 2003 to about 78 percent in 2008; Government budget deficit decreased from 5.3 percent of GDP in 2003 to a balanced budget in 2007; and external-debt-to-GDP declined from about 62 percent in the third quarter of 2002 to just below 43 percent in the third quarter of 2008. Furthermore, as one can see from Exhibit 24.2, in spite of experiencing fluctuations over the period, unemployment rate altogether dropped from 10.9 percent in the last quarter of 2003 to 5.9 percent in the second quarter of 2008.

Exhibit 24.3 shows the net addition to the number of households versus the number of housing unit completions for the period 1989–2008. As one can see, since 2000, the growth in the number of households was consistently greater than the number of construction completions.[8] Exhibit 24.4 further presents the resulting total number of housing units and the number of housing units occupied for the years 1995–2008. It follows that the inventory of vacant units in the market slowly diminished over the years, reaching historically low vacancy rates in 2008.[9] Accordingly, Exhibit 24.5 depicts the housing price index for the years 1994–2009. Arguably, occupancy acted as a vital factor in the housing price behavior. While housing prices generally maintained a stable level in the years 2000–2007 (a total of almost 5 percent drop over this entire period), since the first quarter of 2008 the demand for housing units exceeded supply and housing prices steadily and sharply increased (see Exhibit 24.5).

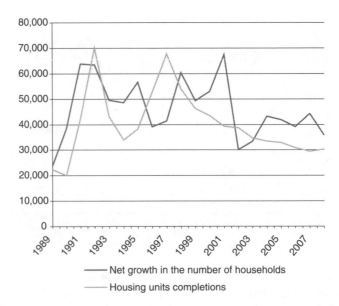

Exhibit 24.3 Net Growth in the Number of Households and Total Housing Units Completions by Years, 1989–2008
Source: Central Bureau of Statistics.

The World Financial Crisis: Israel's Economy, the Local Housing Market, and the Reaction of Policy Makers

The world economic and financial crisis that began in 2007 has had a rolling effect on Israel's foreign trade and foreign direct investments (exports dropped by 30 percent from the third quarter of 2008 to the first quarter of 2009 and imports plummeted by 40 percent over the same period). Exhibit 24.6 depicts the exchange rate of the local currency, New Israeli shekel (NIS) versus USD and EUR. One

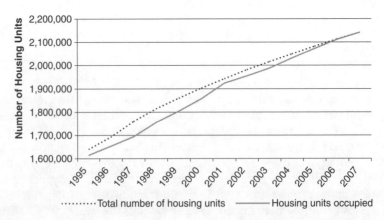

Exhibit 24.4 Total Number of Housing Units and Housing Units Occupied by Years, 1995–2008
Source: Central Bureau of Statistics.

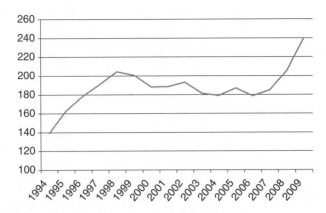

Exhibit 24.5 Housing Price Index by Months, 1994–2009
Source: Central Bureau of Statistics.

can see that in the second half of 2007 and the first half of 2008, the USD and the EUR depreciated by 27 and 12 percent, respectively, compared to the shekel (they were further accompanied by increasing volatility). While the crisis had a gradual negative effect on the local stock market (Exhibit 24.7 shows the behavior of the Tel Aviv 100 Stock Index over the period January 2000 to December 2009), the dramatic price drop was essentially short-term and in 2009 prices effectively climbed back to their pre-crisis regime. At the same time, the financial system and, specifically, the financial institutions remained generally stable; and the profitability of the banking system did, in fact, improved during the year 2009 (see Bank of Israel 2009).

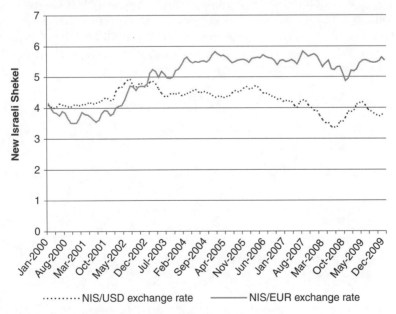

Exhibit 24.6 NIS/USD and NIS/EUR Exchange Rates by Months, 2000–2009
Source: Bank of Israel.

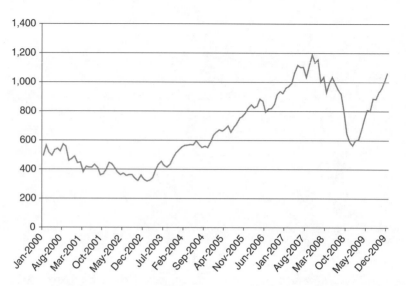

Exhibit 24.7   Closing Prices of the Tel Aviv 100 Stock Index by Months, 2000–2009
Source: Tel-Aviv Stock Exchange.

Policy makers, and, particularly, the Central Bank (Bank of Israel) reacted quickly to the world economic developments by launching anti-cyclical policies. Most importantly, the Bank of Israel decreased the short-term interest rate from 4.25 percent in September 2008 to its all-time lowest level of 0.5 percent in April 2009 (see Exhibit 24.8). Moreover, facing strong criticism, the Central Bank continually intervened in the foreign currency market to prevent the collapse of the U.S. dollar versus the New Israeli Shekel. According to Bank of Israel (2009), this intervention was accompanied by a sharp increase in total foreign currency reserves held by the Central Bank (measured in USD)—from 28 billion in March 2008 to over 61 billion at

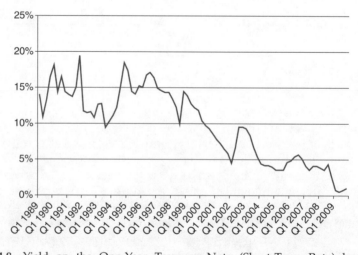

Exhibit 24.8   Yield on the One-Year Treasury Note (Short-Term Rate) by Quarters, 1989–2009
Source: Bank of Israel.

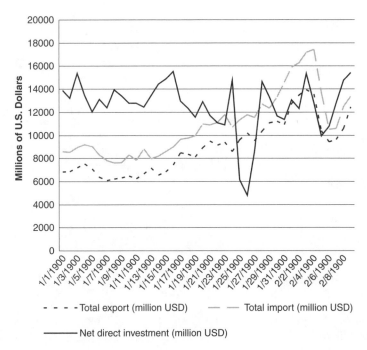

- - - - Total export (million USD)   — — Total import (million USD)

———— Net direct investment (million USD)

Exhibit 24.9 Total Import, Total Export, and Net Direct Investments by Quarters, 2000–2009

Source: Central Bureau of Statistics.

the end of 2009. The latter further produced a secondary effect on the inflation rate as imports maintained a significant share of private consumption—the inflation rate exceeded the target set by the Central Bank reaching 3.8 and 3.9 percent in 2008 and 2009, respectively. (According to Elkayam, 2003, Barnea and Djivre, 2004, and Eckstein and Soffer, 2008, the NIS/USD exchange rate maintained a transmission process of approximately 30 percent to changes in the consumer price index.) Local commercial banks were, at the same time, pressured to raise their capital adequacy, which ultimately reached an average of 13.5 percent by the third quarter of 2009.

Focusing on major macroeconomic variables presented by the Bank of Israel (2009), one can argue that, by the end of 2009, the aforementioned effects of the crisis had largely evaporated. Exhibit 24.9 shows the foreign trade (export and import) and net direct investments from the first quarter of 2000 to the last quarter of 2009. One can see not only that both import and export experienced a sharp increase in 2009, but also that net direct investments returned to their highest pre-crisis levels during the equivalent period. In addition, GDP rose by 0.7 percent in 2009, resulting from a 3.3 percent growth in the second half of the year and a 1.5 percent decline in the first half. The unemployment rate dropped from 7.9 percent in mid-2009 to 7.3 percent by the end of the year, and private consumption recovered rapidly and, in fact, surpassed its pre-crisis level by the end of 2009.

In the housing market, the historically low short-term interest rates, coupled with a low unemployment rate and increasing net direct investments, fueled the demand side of the market. The latter brought a sharp rise in the housing price index from the first quarter of 2008 to the end of 2009 (see again Exhibit 24.5).

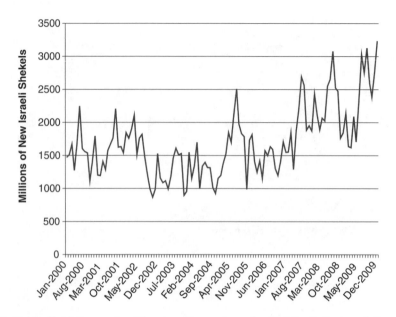

Exhibit 24.10 Total Loans for Housing Granted to the Public (Inflation Adjusted) by Months, 2000–2009
Source: Bank of Israel.

Particularly, average house prices surged by more than 21 percent in 2009. Correspondingly, in contrast to the extreme credit crunch experienced during the crisis by other Western housing markets and, particularly, that in the U.S., changes in the volume of mortgage loans for housing in the local housing market were much slighter (see Exhibit 24.10). Specifically, following a decrease in the volume of loans that were granted for housing from mid-2008 to mid-2009, the second half of 2009 experienced a drastic increase in the volume of loans, which, in effect, reached all-time highest levels by the end of the year.

Finally, the rise in the volume of mortgage loans during the second half of 2009 was further accompanied by significant changes in mortgage interest rates (average interest rate on price-level-adjusted long-term mortgages). Following a slight rise in mortgage interest rate in 2008 (attributed to the uncertainty in world markets associated with the crisis), average market mortgage rates dropped in 2009, reaching historically lowest levels by the end of the year (see Exhibit 24.11).

EMPIRICAL ESTIMATION OF HOUSING AFFORDABILITY IN ISRAEL

An important indication of the behavior of housing prices over time is the pattern of housing affordability. As claimed by Robinson et al. (2006), "affordability refers to the relationship between housing costs and some ability to pay criterion."[10] Gan and Hill (2009) draw a distinction among the concepts of purchase affordability, repayment affordability, and income affordability. While purchase affordability indicates the household's ability to borrow sufficient funds to purchase a dwelling

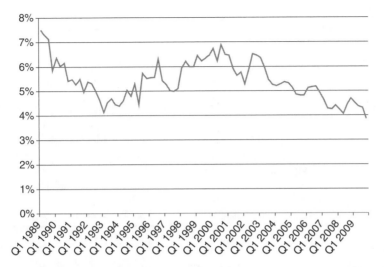

Exhibit 24.11 Fixed-Rate Price-Level-Adjusted Mortgage Interest Rate (20-Year Maturity) by Quarters, 1989–2009
Source: Bank of Israel.

unit, repayment affordability measures the burden imposed by mortgage repayment. Correspondingly, by computing the ratio between the cost of homeownership and income, income affordability measures the household long-run ability to achieve ownership.

In the model below, we adopt the definition of income affordability, namely, measuring affordability by the ratio of housing prices to income (see also Malpezzi 1999, who empirically focuses on the same affordability measure). Based on a structural model of demand and supply in the housing market, we derive and estimate an affordability equation by which we study the factors that correlate with housing affordability in Israel in the years 1989–2009. Moreover, concentrating on the fitted values of affordability that arise from the estimation and comparing them to actual affordability figures, we explore housing price and affordability dynamics in Israel prior to and following the 2007 world financial crisis.

The Empirical Model

Consider the following structural model of demand and supply.

$$Q_t^d = \alpha_0 + \alpha_1 \times \frac{P_t}{W_t} + \alpha_2 \times HH_t + \alpha_3 \times MR_t + \alpha_4 \times GDP_t + \alpha_5 \times UR_{t-j} + \alpha_6$$
$$\times USDEX_t + u_{1t} \tag{24.1}$$

and

$$Q_t^s = \beta_0 + \beta_1 \times \frac{P_t}{W_t} + \beta_2 \times CI_t + \beta_3 \times HS_{t-n} + \beta_4 \times BR_t + u_{2t'} \tag{24.2}$$

Exhibit 24.12 Description of Variables

Variables	Description
P	Average dwelling unit price
W	Average monthly wage per employee job (including workforce only)
P/W	Price-to-wage ratio
BR	Yield on the one-year treasury note issued by the Bank of Israel
CI	Rate of change in price index of inputs in residential construction
GDP	Annualized rate of change in the gross domestic product
HH	Change rate in the number of households in the economy
HS	Number of housing starts
MR	Interest rate on 20-year fixed rate (price-level-adjusted) mortgage
UR	Unemployment rate
$USDEX$	Exchange rate between the New Israeli shekel and one USD.

where the subscript t denotes the time period (in quarters), Q_t^d and Q_t^s respectively denote the demanded and supplied number of dwelling units in quarter t, P is the average price per unit, and W is the average monthly wage per employee job. By focusing on the ratio of P over W (the affordability ratio), we effectively concentrate on the housing cost in terms of average monthly wage units, that is, the average number of employment months required for purchasing an average dwelling unit (see earlier discussion on affordability). Also, HH denotes the change rate in the number of households in the economy, MR is the price-level-adjusted long-term fixed mortgage interest rate, GDP is the change rate in the gross domestic product, UR is the unemployment rate, and $USDEX$ is the exchange rate between the New Israeli shekel (NIS) and one U.S. dollar.[11] Finally, CI denotes the change rate in the price index of inputs in residential construction, HS is the number of housing starts, and BR is the yield on the one-year treasury note issued by the Bank of Israel (representing the short-term interest rate). The subscripts j and n represent the number of lagged quarters, u_1 and u_2 are the random disturbance terms, and α_0–α_6 and β_0–β_4 are estimated parameters. Exhibit 24.12 concludes the description of all variables.[12]

As the price and quantity of dwelling units in equations (24.1) and (24.2) are simultaneously endogenously determined, we further develop these equations (see appendix) to generate the following reduced form equation:

$$\frac{P_t}{W_t} = \lambda_0 + \lambda_1 \times HH_t + \lambda_2 \times MR_t + \lambda_3 \times GDP_t + \lambda_4 \times UR_{t-j} + \lambda_5 \times USDEX_t$$

$$-\lambda_6 \times CI_t - \lambda_7 \times HS_{t-n} - \lambda_8 \times BR + u_{3t'} \tag{24.3}$$

where the price-to-wage ratio (the affordability measure) on the left-hand side of (24.3) is presented as a function of a series of exogenous variables, u_3 is a standard disturbance term, and λ_0–λ_8 are estimated parameters—all of which are functions of α_0–α_6, β_0–β_4, and u_1 and u_2 (see appendix).

Finally, due to multicolinearity in equation (24.3) caused by the significant correlation between the yield on the one-year treasury note (BR) and several other independent variables and, similarly, due to the significant correlation between the

Exhibit 24.13 Correlation Matrix

	MR	HS (−6)	UR (−3)	GDP	USDEX	CI	BR	HH	P/W	P/W (−1)
MR	1.00	0.04	−0.06	−0.06	0.28	−0.11	0.19	−0.07	0.00	0.11
HS (−6)	0.04	1.00	−0.07	−0.08	−0.23	−0.01	0.31	−0.38	0.06	0.00
UR (−3)	−0.06	−0.07	1.00	0.02	0.04	0.17	−0.17	−0.11	−0.43	−0.43
GDP	−0.06	−0.08	0.02	1.00	−0.10	0.23	0.15	−0.10	0.13	0.00
USDEX	0.28	−0.23	0.04	−0.10	1.00	−0.35	−0.76	0.85	0.56	0.56
CI	−0.11	−0.01	0.17	0.23	−0.35	1.00	0.36	−0.35	−0.15	−0.27
BR	0.19	0.31	−0.17	0.15	−0.76	0.36	1.00	−0.90	−0.30	−0.30
HH	−0.07	−0.38	−0.11	−0.10	0.85	−0.35	−0.90	1.00	0.54	0.56
P/W	0.00	0.06	−0.43	0.13	0.56	−0.15	−0.30	0.54	1.00	0.87
P/W(−1)	0.11	0.00	−0.43	0.00	0.56	−0.27	−0.30	0.56	0.87	1.00

change rate in the number of households (HH) and other independent variables (correlation matrix of all variables is presented in Exhibit 24.13),[13] we omit the variables BR and HH from equation (24.3). We therefore maintain the following estimated reduced form equation:

$$\frac{P_t}{W_t} = \lambda_0 + \lambda_2 \times MR_t + \lambda_3 \times GDP_t + \lambda_4 \times UR_{t-j} + \lambda_5 \times USDEX_t - \lambda_6 \times CI_t - \lambda_7$$

$$\times HS_{t-n} + u_{3t}. \tag{24.4}$$

Data and Summary Statistics

We observe quarterly data published by the Israel Central Bureau of Statistics and the Bank of Israel from the first quarter of 1989 to the last quarter of 2009. Exhibit 24.14 shows summary statistics for all variables in the estimated equation (24.4). Notably, the price-to-wage ratio (P/W) has a mean of 92.4 (that is, 92.4 months of average wage per employee job are required for covering the average cost of a dwelling unit) with a minimum of 61.0 and maximum of 116.1. Over the period, the unemployment rate ranges from 5.7 to 12.0 percent with a mean of 8.8 percent. Quarterly growth in GDP reaches a maximum of 7.5 percent and a minimum of −3.8 percent. Mean quarterly GDP growth is 1.1 percent. Also, housing starts range from a minimum of 4,250 and peak at a maximum of 23,487 with a mean of 10,316. The 20-year fixed (price-level-adjusted) mortgage interest rate for the period ranges between 3.9 and 7.5 percent with a mean of 5.4 percent, and the quarterly change rate in the price index of inputs in residential construction ranges between −2.35 and 8.05 percent with a mean of 1.71 percent. Finally, the NIS/USD exchange rate ranges between 1.8 and 4.9 with a mean of 3.6.

Estimation Outcomes

The outcomes from the estimation of equation (24.4) are reported in Exhibit 24.15. We find that the price-to-wage ratio negatively correlates with the interest rate

Exhibit 24.14 Variables and Summary Statistics

Variables	Mean	Standard Deviation	Min	Max
P	542,798	215,506	117,158	937,600
W	5715.7	1994.8	1855.9	8168.7
P/W	92.4	10.2	61.0	116.1
CI	1.71	2.23	−2.35	8.05
GDP	1.1	2.3	−3.8	7.5
HS	10316.6	4009.1	4250.0	23487.0
MR	5.4	0.8	3.9	7.5
UR	8.8	1.6	5.7	12.0
USDEX	3.6	0.9	1.8	4.9

Exhibit 24.15 Factors Correlating with the Price-to-Wage Ratio

$$\frac{P_t}{W_t} = \lambda_0 + \lambda_2 \times MR_t + \lambda_3 \times GDP_t + \lambda_4 \times UR_{t-j} + \lambda_5 \times USDEX_t - \lambda_6 \times CI_t - \lambda_7 \times HS_{t-n} + u_{3t}.$$

Dependent Variable	P/W
Constant	35.03∗∗∗
	(4.47)
MR	−2.11∗∗∗
	(−3.93)
HS(-6)	0.000196∗∗
	(2.05)
UR(-3)	−0.95∗∗∗
	(−3.24)
GDP	0.38∗∗
	(2.28)
USDEX	2.93∗∗∗
	(4.08)
CI	42.6∗∗
	(1.99)
P/W(–1)	0.69∗∗∗
	(9.71)
N	78
R^2	0.85
F-statistic	56.59

Notes: Exhibit 24.15 reports regression results using OLS and correcting for first-order serial correlation. *t*-values are in parentheses below the coefficients. Significant values at 10 percent, 5 percent, and 1 percent significance levels are marked with one, two, and three asterisks, respectively. The number of lags appear in parentheses in the dependent variable column. See Exhibit 24.12 for variable definitions.

on the fixed rate price-level-adjusted mortgage (significant at a 1 percent level). This result is consistent with, for example, Malpezzi (1999) and Schnure (2005). Specifically, this evidence shows that, *ceteris paribus*, for every 1 percent absolute rise in the mortgage rate, the average number of monthly wage per employee job that is required to cover the cost of an average dwelling unit drops by 2.11.

Theoretically, the unemployment rate may, of course, correlate the price-to-wage ratio both directly via the wage and indirectly via housing prices (see, for example, Ortalo-Magné and Rady, 2006). We find that, overall, the price-to-wage ratio negatively correlates with a three-quarter lag of the unemployment rate (significant at a 1 percent level). This is consistent with, for example, Jacobson and Naug (2005), Schnure (2005), and Abelson et al. (2005). In other words, unemployment is, arguably, more substantially associated with lower housing prices than lower wages (as the latter is possibly more sticky than the former—see, for example, Case and Quigley, 2008).

We also find evidence of a positive correlation between the price-to-wage ratio and both the change rate in GDP (significant at a 5 percent level)—consistent, for example, with Sutton (2002)—and the change rate in the price index of inputs in residential construction (significant at a 5 percent level)—consistent, for example, with Poterba (1984). Furthermore, we find that depreciation of the local currency by one NIS in exchange to one USD, *ceteris paribus*, is associated with a 2.93 rise in the price-to-wage ratio (significant at a 1 percent level)—consistent with, among others, Soffer (2006).[14]

Furthermore, we find a significantly positive correlation between the price-to-wage ratio and a six-quarter lag in the number of housing starts (significant at a 5 percent level). It follows that, *ceteris paribus*, every additional 1,000 units of housing construction starts associate with an increase in the price-to-wage ratio by 0.196 some six quarters later. This result might seem somewhat counter-intuitive as one may argue that an increase in housing starts should decrease prices due to the increase in housing supply. Yet, the result is consistent with expectation theories according to which developers and investors in the real estate market act upon their anticipation for future demand and prices (see, among others, Case and Shiller, 1989, Mei and Saunders, 1997, Ling, 2005, Arbel et al., 2009, and Lambertini et al. 2010). Finally, we find evidence of a one-quarter positive serial correlation in the price-to-wage ratio variable, namely, that the current change in the ratio tends to attain the same sign as the previous quarter change (see also, for example, Capozza et al. 2002, Case and Shiller 2003, Terrones and Otrok 2004, Jacobson and Naug 2005, and Lamont and Stein 1999).

Implications for Housing Affordability

In Exhibit 24.12 we compare actual and fitted values of the price-to-wage ratio from the first quarter of 1989 to the last quarter of 2009. Particularly, we focus on the comparison in the difference between actual and fitted values for the post-financial crisis period, 2008(Q1)–2009(Q4). We produce both in-sample fitted values based on the entire sample and out-of-sample fitted values based on the 1989–2007 data for the 2008(Q1)–2009(Q4) period.

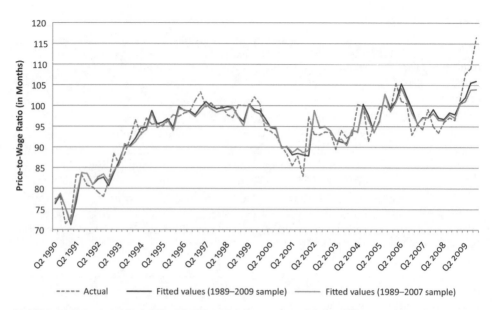

Exhibit 24.16   Actual and Fitted Values of the Price-to-Wage Ratio, 1989–2009 (Based on 1989–2007 and 1989–2009 Samples)

One can see from Exhibit 24.16 that in the last quarter of 2009 the series of actual price-to-wage ratio has crossed the 116 months mark (i.e., 116 months of average wage per employee job are required to cover the cost of an average dwelling unit), reaching an all-time high. Moreover, when comparing the actual levels of the price-to-wage ratio to their in-sample fitted values, we find that, given the economic variables that are included in the empirical model, the actual level of the price-to-wage ratio at the end of 2009 is 8.0 percent higher than its fitted value. This difference is equivalent to 2.78 standard deviations. Comparing the actual values to the out-of-sample fitted values (based on the 1989–2007 data), it turns out that the actual level of the price-to-wage ratio at the end of 2009 climbed up to 10.3 percent higher than its fitted value, which is equivalent to 3.42 standard deviations.[15] Observing Exhibit 24.16, one can see that the price-to-wage ratio originally entered its new highest-ever levels in the third quarter of 2008.

Apparently, the expansionary measures implemented by the Central Bank of Israel—including the record low interest rates, the purchase of government bonds, and the intervention in foreign currency trade (by particularly purchasing USD)—while maintaining the local economy in safe waters during the world financial storm, may have accelerated the demand for housing and, in turn, contributed to the dramatic rise in housing prices.

Our analysis thus leads to the inevitable conclusion that the price-to-wage ratio in the Israeli housing market some two years after the onset of the world financial crisis has not only reached all-time highest levels but also disturbingly deviates from its long-term trend—hence showing signs of overly heated housing prices that may be reminiscent of the phenomena observed in other housing markets on the eve of the world financial crisis.

CONCLUSION

With GDP equal to 204 billion USD in 2008 (in PPP figures), Israel's economy is relatively small by Western standards and highly dependent on foreign trade. Yet, some two years after the onset of the world financial crisis, the effect of the world economic developments on the Israeli economy and the local housing market are relatively minor compared with most Western markets.

In this chapter we described and explained the major factors that evidently prevented the storming world financial crisis from fatally damaging the shores of the Israeli economy and its local housing market. Particularly, two aspects underlie the strength of the local economy: (1) the solid economic variables with which Israel has met the crisis—among others, a declining trend of public-debt-to-GDP ratio; relatively low unemployment rate; balanced government budget; relatively strict financial regulations; absence of a formal secondary mortgage market; and relatively narrow subprime mortgage market; and (2) the measures effectively adopted by the Bank of Israel following the onset of the crisis—among others, dramatically decreasing short-term interest rates; and intensively intervening in the foreign currency market, thus preventing a collapse in the exchange rate of the U.S. dollar to the New Israeli shekel.

We further explored the dynamics in local housing prices and affordability before and after the onset of the world financial crisis. Specifically, we empirically examined the economic variables that correlate with the housing price-to-wage ratio in the years 1989–2009 (these variables include the change rate in GDP, unemployment rate, NIS/USD exchange rate, housing starts, mortgage interest rate, and change rate in the price index of inputs in residential construction). Based on the estimation of a structural demand and supply model, we interestingly found that, by the last quarter of 2009, the actual price-to-wage ratio not only reached an all-time highest level, but, moreover, deviated from its in-sample (out-of-sample) fitted value by 2.78 (3.42) standard deviations. This arguably bubble-like behavior trend, whose preliminary signs could have already been observed in mid-2008, should cautiously be considered by both market participants and policy makers so that the disturbing phenomena observed in some housing markets around the world on the eve of the financial crisis do not re-occur in the framework of the local Israeli economy.

APPENDIX: GENERATING THE ESTIMATED EQUATION (24.4)

Isolating P/W in equation (24.1) produces

$$\frac{P}{W} = \frac{\alpha_0 + a_2 \times HH_t + \alpha_3 \times MR_t + \alpha_4 \times GDP_t + \alpha_5 \times UR_{t-j} + \alpha_6 \times USDEX_t + u_{1t}}{\alpha_1}$$

(A24.1)

Substituting the right-hand side of (A24.1) into equation (24.2) produces:

$$Q_t^s = \beta_0 + \beta_1 \times \frac{[Q_t^d - (\alpha_0 + \alpha_2 \times HH_t + \alpha_3 \times MR_t + \alpha_4 \times GDP_t + \alpha_5 \times UR_{t-j} + \alpha_6 \times USDEX_t + u_{1t})]}{\alpha_1 + \beta_2 \times CI_t + \beta_3 \times HS_{t-n} + \beta_4 \times BR_t + u_{2t}}. \quad \text{(A24.2)}$$

In equilibrium, however, we have

$$Q_t^s = Q_t^d = Q. \quad \text{(A24.3)}$$

We can therefore re-write (A24.2) such that

$$Q = B + \beta_1 \times (Q - A)/\alpha_1, \quad \text{(A24.4)}$$

where

$$A = \alpha_0 + \alpha_2 \times HH_t + \alpha_3 \times MR_t + \alpha_4 \times GDP_t + \alpha_5 \times UR_{t-j} + \alpha_6 \times USDEX_t + U_{1t} \quad \text{(A24.5)}$$

and

$$B = \beta_0 + \beta_2 \times CI_t + \beta_2 \times HS_{t-n} + \beta_4 \times BR_t + u_{2t}, \quad \text{(A24.6)}$$

Isolating Q in (A24.4) generates

$$Q = \frac{\alpha_1 \times B - \beta_1 \times A}{\alpha_1 - \beta_1} \quad \text{(A24.7)}$$

and under the assumption that $(\alpha_1 - \beta_1) \neq 0$ and following (A24.3), we can substitute the right-hand side of (A24.7) with Q_t^d in (A24.1) to obtain

$$\frac{P}{W} = \frac{\left[\frac{\alpha_1 \times B - \beta_1 \times A}{\alpha_1 - \beta_1} - A \right]}{\alpha_1}. \quad \text{(A24.8)}$$

which, in turn, could be simplified into

$$\frac{P}{W} = \frac{B - A}{\alpha_1 - \beta_1}. \quad \text{(A24.9)}$$

Finally, substituting the expressions for A and B from in (A24.5) and (A24.6), respectively, into (A24.9) we get after reduction that

$$\frac{P_t}{W_t} = \lambda_0 + \lambda_1 \times HH_t + \lambda_2 \times MR_t + \lambda_3 \times GDP_t + \lambda_4 \times UR_{t-j} + \lambda_5 \times USDEX_t$$

$$- \lambda_6 \times CI_t - \lambda_7 \times HS_{t-n} - \lambda_8 \times BR + u_{3t}. \quad \text{(A24.10)}$$

where

$$\lambda_1 = \frac{\alpha_0 - \beta_0}{\alpha_1 - \beta_1}, \quad \lambda_2 = \frac{\alpha_2}{\alpha_1 - \beta_1}, \quad \lambda_2 = \frac{\alpha_3}{\alpha_1 - \beta_1}, \quad \lambda_4 = \frac{\alpha_4}{\alpha_1 - \beta_1}, \quad \lambda_5 = \frac{\alpha_5}{\alpha_1 - \beta_1},$$
$$\lambda_6 = \frac{\alpha_6}{\alpha_1 - \beta_1}, \quad \lambda_7 = \frac{\alpha_7}{\alpha_1 - \beta_1}, \quad \alpha_8 = \frac{\alpha_8}{\alpha_1 - \beta_1}, \quad \lambda_9 = \frac{\beta_3}{\alpha_1 - \beta_1}, \quad \text{and} \quad \eta = \frac{u_1 - u_2}{\alpha_1 - \beta_1}.$$

NOTES

1. For more on price bubbles in housing prices, particularly in the United States, see, for example, Wheaton and Nechayev (2008) and Zhou and Sornette (2006).

2. The capital adequacy in Israel is measured according to the Basel II regulations.

3. For further background of Israel's local housing and mortgage markets see Ben-Shahar et al. (2008).

4. Strawczynski and Zeira (1999) analyze the significant decline in the relative size of the Israeli public sector after 1985. They show evidence that fiscal discipline significantly increased after 1985 and that the reduction in public expenditure could be attributed to three main factors: decline in military expenditures, reduction in subsidies to the business sector, and a reduction in interest payments due to declining debt. Also see OECD (2009) for the first OECD review of Israel's economy.

5. According to OECD (2010), per capita GDP for OECD in 2008 was $33,732 USD while the equivalent figure for the European Union at the time was $30,651 USD. Also, it should be noted that during the 1990s, Israel absorbed a large-scale immigration wave, the size of which was almost 20 percent of the population of Israel at the time. These immigrants, coming predominantly from countries of the former USSR, have exhibited higher than average education levels. The new skilled workforce together with the added demand accelerated the economy and reinforced its foundations.

6. See the Israel Land Administration web site: www.mmi.gov.il/envelope/indexeng .asp?page=/static/eng/f_general.html, accessed July 5, 2010.

7. These factors were further accompanied by the government's considerable budget deficit in the years 2001 and 2002, culminating at almost 10 percent of GDP in the last quarter of 2001, while in the last quarter of 2002, the yield on short-term Government bonds reached a rate of about 12 percent (see more in Bank of Israel, 2002). Also, for more on the effect of the Second Palestinian Intifada on the Israeli economy, see Eckstein and Tsiddon (2004) and on the local housing market see Arbel, Ben-Shahar, Gabriel, and Tobol (forthcoming).

8. It may further be seen from Exhibit 24.3 that total housing completions peaked in 1997 as a result of the large-scale immigration wave from the former USSR (more than doubled from its 1994 level). Also, net growth in the number of households has fluctuated between 40,000 and almost 70,000 per year from 1991 to 2001, much above its steadier level ranging within the 30,000–45,000 boundaries since 2002.

9. According to the Ministry of Finance (2010), foreign citizens have purchased only 2.8 percent of the total number of housing units sold in 2009 (in comparison with a peak level of 5 percent attained in the years 2005–2007), one quarter of which has been newly constructed. A drop of 33 percent in the number of housing units purchased by foreign citizens was experienced in 2008 followed by an additional drop of 13 percent in 2009. The ratio between housing units purchased and sold by foreign citizens was down to 1.2 in 2009 from a peak level of 2.9 in the years 2005–2007.

10. In the sociology literature, affordability generally measures the public ability to purchase housing services. Accordingly, the focus is often on the ratio of housing costs and the minimum wage (alternatively, the residual income) after the deduction of the cost of housing services (see, for example, Hulchanski 1995, Kutty 2005, and Stone 2006).

11. According to the Central Bureau of Statistics (2010), there were 2.1 million households in Israel in 2009 with an average of 3.36 persons per household. 17.7 percent of the households included one person only while 6.2 percent included seven or more people. 46.2 percent of the households had children younger than 17 and 23.9 percent included people whose age was 65 and over. The size and formation of the households has changed very little during our observed period: In 1989 there were 1.65 million households in Israel with an average of 3.43 persons per household. 17.0 percent of the households included one person and 6.3 percent included seven or more people.

12. See, among many others, Muellbauer and Murphy (1997), Oikarinen (2009), and Hort and Katinka (1998), who include lagged independent variables in the estimation of house price equations.

13. The change in the number of households (HH) is published on an annual basis only. We convert the annual rate of change to quarters by assuming linear growth within the year. Arguably, this linearization might have caused the significant correlation between HH and the other independent variables in equation 24.3.

14. The housing price index in Israel includes two main items: cost of housing services for owner-occupied housing (77 percent of the index) and rent (19.5 percent). Since 1999 the housing services for the owner-occupied housing component is proxied by rents that are quoted in new and renewed rental contracts. A press release by the Bank of Israel from October 4, 2009 states that until 2007, 90 percent of the rental contracts were nominated in USD, but by mid-2009 85 percent of the contracts were nominated in the local currency (NIS). Consequently, the NIS/USD exchange rate transmission for the housing index must have sharply declined in recent years.

15. The average difference between actual and fitted values (in absolute values) of the price-to-wage ratio based on both the 1989–2009 and the 1989–2007 estimates is 2.5 percent.

REFERENCES

Abelson, P., R. Joyeux, G. Milunovich, and D. Chung. 2005. "Explaining House Prices in Australia: 1970–2003." *Economic Record* 81, 96–103.

Arbel, Y., D. Ben-Shahar, S. Gabriel, and Y. Tobol. 2010 "The Local Cost of Terror: Effect of the Second Palestinian Intifada on Jerusalem House Prices." *Regional Science and Urban Economics*, 40: 6, 415–26

Arbel Y., D. Ben-Shahar, and E. Sulganik. 2009. "Mean reversion and Momentum: Another Look at the Price-Volume Correlation in the Real Estate Market." *The Journal of Real Estate Finance and Economics* 39: 3, 316–335.

Bank of Israel. 1990–2009. *Annual Report.* Publications Unit, Bank of Israel, Jerusalem.

Ben-Shahar, D., G. Benchetrit, and E. Sulganik. 2008. "The Israeli Mortgage Market: Mortgage Insurance as a Mechanism for Screening Default Risk." In D. Ben-Shahar, C. Leung, and S. E. Ong, eds., *Mortgage Markets Worldwide.* Blackwell Publishing.

Barnea, A., and J. Djivre. 2004. "Changes in Monetary and Exchange Rate Policies and the Transmission Mechanism in Israel." Bank of Israel Discussion Paper Series, 2004.

Capozza, D. R., C. M. Hendershott, and C. J. Mayer. 2002. "Determinants of Real House Price Dynamics." NBER working paper 9262.

Case, K. E., and J. M. Quigley. 2008. "How Housing Booms Unwind: Income Effects, Wealth Effects, and Feedbacks through Financial Markets." *International Journal of Housing Policy* 8: 2, 161–180.

Case, K. E., and R. J. Shiller. 2003. "Is There a Bubble in the Housing Market?" *Brookings Papers on Economic Activity* 2, 299–362.

Case, K. E., and R. J. Shiller. 1989. "The Efficiency of the Market for Single-Family Homes. *The American Economic Review* 79: 1, 125–137.

Central Bureau of Statistics, 1989–2009. *Employment and Wages Monthly Statistics*. Jerusalem, Israel.

Central Bureau of Statistics, 1989–2010. *Statistical Abstracts of Israel*, Pub. no. 40–61. Jerusalem, Israel.

DiPasquale, D., and W. Wheaton. 1996. *Urban Economics and Real Estate Markets*. Englewood Cliffs, NJ: Prentice-Hall.

Eckstein, Z., and D. Tsiddon. 2004. "Macroeconomic Consequences of Terror: Theory and the Case of Israel." *Journal of Monetary Economics* 51: 1, 971–1002.

Elkayam, D. 2003. "The Long Road from Adjustable Peg to Flexible Exchange Rate Regimes: The Case of Israel." Bank of Israel Monetary Studies Discussion Papers, 2003.

Gan, Q., and R. J. Hill. 2009. "Measuring Housing Affordability: Looking beyond the Median. *Journal of Housing Economics* 18: 2, 115–125.

Hort, K. 1998. "The Determinants of Urban House Price Fluctuations in Sweden 1968–1994." *Journal of Housing Economics* 7, 93–120.

Hulchanski, J. D. 1995. "The Concept of Housing Affordability: Six Contemporary Uses of the Housing Expenditure-to-Income Ratio." *Housing Studies* 10: 4, 471–491.

Jacobsen, D., and B. Naug. 2005. "What Drives House Prices?" Norges Bank Economic Bulletin, No. 05Q1.

Kutty, N. K. 2005. "A New Measure of Housing Affordability: Estimates and Analytical Results." *Housing Policy Debate* 16: 1, 113–142.

Lambertini, L., C. Mendicino, and M. T. Punzi. 2010. "Expectations-Driven Cycles in the Housing Market." MPRA Paper No. 26128.

Lamont, O., and J. Stein. 1999. "Leverage and House Price Dynamics in U.S. Cities." *Rand Journal of Economics* 30, 498–514.

Ling, D. C. 2005. "A Random Walk Down Main Street: Can Experts Predict Returns on Commercial Real Estate?" *Journal of Real Estate Research* 27: 2, 137–154.

Malpezzi, S. 1999. "A Simple Error Correction Model of House Prices." *Journal of Housing Economics* 8, 27–62.

Mei, J., and A. Saunders. 1997. "Have U.S. Financial Institutions' Real Estate Investments Exhibited 'Trend-Chasing' Behavior?" *The Review of Economics and Statistics*, 79: 2, 248–258.

Ministry of Finance. 2010. "The Role of Foreign Citizens in the Local Real Estate Market in 2009." Ministry of Finance, State Revenue Division, Jerusalem.

Muellbauer, J., and A. Murphy. 1997. "Booms and Busts in the UK Housing Market." *The Economic Journal* 107, 1701–1727.

Oikarinen, E. 2009. "The Reaction Speeds of Prices and Transaction Volume in the Finnish Housing Market to Demand Shocks." Aboa Centre for Economics Discussion Paper No. 56.

OECD. 2009. *Economic Survey of Israel, 2009*, OECD Publishing.

OECD. 2010. *OECD Factbook 2010: Economic, Environmental, and Social Statistics*. OECD Publishing.

Ortalo-Magné, F., and S. Rady. 2006. "Housing Market Dynamics: On the Contribution of Income Shocks and Credit Constraints." *Review of Economic Studies* 73, 459–485.

Poterba, J. M. 1984. "Tax Subsidies to Owner-Occupied Housing: An Asset Market Approach." *The Quarterly Journal of Economics* 99: 4, 729–752.

Robinson, M., G. M. Scobie, and B. Hallinan. 2006. "Affordability of Housing: Concepts, Measurement, and Evidence." New Zealand Treasury Working Paper 06/03.

Schnure, C. 2005. "Boom-Bust Cycles in Housing: The Changing Role of Financial Structure." *United States: Selected Issues.* IMF Country Report, No. 05/258.

Soffer, Y. 2006. "Exchange Rate Pass-Through to the Consumer Price Index: A Micro Approach." Bank of Israel Foreign Exchange Discussion Paper Series, 2.06.

Stone, M. 2006. "What Is Housing Affordability? The Case for the Residual Income Approach." *Housing Policy Debate* 17: 1, 151–184.

Strawczynski, M., and J. Zeira. 1999. "Reducing the Relative Size of Government in Israel after 1985." In A. Ben-Bassat, ed., *The Israeli Economy, 1985–1998: From Government Intervention to Market Economics.* Cambridge, MA: MIT Press.

Sutton, G. D. 2002 (September). "Explaining Changes in House Prices." *BIS Quarterly Review,* 46–55.

Terrones, M., and C. Otrok. 2004. "The Global House Price Boom." In *World Economic Outlook,* ch. 2. International Monetary Fund.

Wheaton, W. C., and G. Nechayev. 2008. "The 1998–2005 Housing 'Bubble' and the Current Correction: What's Different This Time?" *Journal of Real Estate Research* 30: 1, 1–26.

Zhou, W. X., and D. Sornette. 2006. "Is There a Real Estate Bubble in the U.S.?" *Physica A: Statistical Mechanics and its Applications* 361: 1, 297–308.

ABOUT THE AUTHORS

DANNY BEN-SHAHAR, is a senior lecturer at the Faculty of Architecture and Town Planning at the Technion–Israel Institute of Technology. His research focuses on theoretical modeling and empirical estimation of agents' behavior in real-estate markets. Among Ben-Shahar's publications are articles in *Economica, Regional Science and Urban Economics, Annals of Regional Science, Contributions to Economic Analysis and Policy, The Journal of Real Estate Finance and Economics, Journal of Real Estate Research,* and the *Journal of Housing Economics.* Ben-Shahar serves on the editorial boards of several academic journals. In addition, he serves as a board member in several corporate entities in Israel and is a member of the board of the Israeli Appraisal Association. Ben-Shahar holds a BA in economics from Tel Aviv University and an MBA and a PhD in real estate finance from the University of California at Berkeley.

JACOB WARSZAWSKI, is a PhD Candidate at the Faculty of Architecture and Town Planning at the Technion–Israel Institute of Technology. His research on housing affordability particularly focuses on socio-economic and demographic aspects. In addition, Warszawski is a managing partner in an international real estate investment group, specializing in development projects mainly in Europe. Warszawski holds a BSc (cum laude) in civil engineering from the Technion–Israel Institute of Technology and an MBA from Tel Aviv University.

Index